STRATEGIC
FINANCIAL
PLANNING
WITH
SIMULATION

STRATEGIC FINANCIAL PLANNING WITH SIMULATION

Dennis E. Grawoig
Georgia State University

Charles L. Hubbard
Georgia State University

PBI
a petrocelli book
new york / princeton

658.15
G-777

Designed by Diane L. Backes
Typesetting by Backes Graphics

Printed in the United States of America.
1 2 3 4 5 6 7 8 9 10

Library of Congress Cataloging in Publication Data

Grawoig, Dennis E.
  Strategic financial planning with simulation.

  Includes bibliographical references and index.
  1. Business enterprises—Finance—Mathematical models. 2. Business enterprises—
Finance—Data processing. 3. Corporations—Finance—Mathematical models. 4.
Corporations—Finance—Data processing. I. Hubbard, Charles L., 1918-
II. Title.
  HG4012.G7   658.1'5   81-15850
  ISBN 0-89433-115-9   AACR2

Contents

14 | Documentation of PAVE Programs 415

Appendix 603

Index 639

Preface

Financial planning is in the process of moving to an extended level. Conventional tools, such as financial budgets, performance ratios, and present value analysis, may be enlarged to incorporate new points of view. Several thrusts provide such opportunities to financial decision makers. One of these is knowledge about human problem solving, particularly the process of reasoning, cognitive styles, and response to uncertainty. Another is advances in the management of information: preparation, storage, transmittal, updating, access, reporting, and display. A third is the microprocessor revolution. The first two add professional power to problem solving under uncertainty; the third provides tools for human-computer modeling.

The more one examines various aspects of the microprocessor revolution, the more apparent becomes an essential unity. No longer, for example, need financial planners and their staffs be isolated from computer facilities. Instead, decision models, information banks, and number-crunching capabilities move right next to managers; now managers interact rather than react. Separate computing functions are also merging. The same intelligent hardware may be used to operate decision models, develop information systems, or prepare and edit printed communications.

This book combines some developments in financial modeling and human decision theory with the power of microprocessors. An effort is made to unify the treatment of these topics; thus an integrated strategic decision system is presented along with one large computer model. The scope is financial planning, policy, and strategic decision making in commercial enterprises. A close relationship between financial management and a total planning process is stressed. If the purpose of a firm is to build economic value, then such value will most often be expressed in financial terms. If plans are formalized, many of them appear as financial budgets. As plans are implemented, financial managers develop strategies for raising capital on the one hand, and distributing income on the other. The book combines three elements for the financial manager—a system of strategic planning, financial-economic measurement of value under uncertainty, and the power of personalized computer modeling systems.

Microprocessor technology has accelerated interest in a new class of decision models called *decision support systems* (DSS). Instead of feeding information into a model to get a "solution," DSS emphasizes an ongoing, interactive relationship between user and model. Scenario building, "what if" exploration, feedback, and sensitivity analysis are features of DSS. A human-computer problem-solving team adds a new dimension for coping with uncertainty and complexity.

The DSS model of this book is named PAVE—planning and valuation of enterprises. It is a model for aggregate financial planning; distributive accounting by product, division, or geographical area must be handled with separate PAVE runs. PAVE inputs a systematic policy decision plan; then outputs information on a firm's market value, budgets, and financial analysis. PAVE is both a descriptive and a prescriptive model. On the one hand, PAVE will prepare budgets and ratio analyses to describe behavior from any set of input policies, whereas, on the other, PAVE makes estimates of economic value as a result of strategic decisions. The PAVE modeling technique is Monte Carlo simulation. This permits explicit treatment of uncertainty and measures outputs in statistical terms. The inputs and outputs are completely interactive with users; thus a knowledge of programming language is not required. The model is written in BASIC to accommodate user interaction with minicomputer video displays and line printers.

Managers are in the midst of an information-processing explosion, which provides new opportunities as well as difficulties. In addition to obtaining decisions with PAVE, the model gives one a chance to examine trade-offs among detail-handling capability, flexibility, and input minilanguages. These are typical design problems of a new generation of complex models for decision. These issues are examined in the development of PAVE.

The books consists of three parts, which meet different user needs. Part I presents a unified financial decision system. Economic-financial valuation of a firm is combined with accounting theory, decision making under uncertainty, simulation techniques, and business policy. The purpose is not to replace conventional theory of the firm, but rather to evolve from standard tools to a new dimension of managerial decision power. This power comes on stream from both advanced theory and personalized computing.

Part II presents the PAVE model and six illustrative business policy cases. There are chapters of instructions about inputs to PAVE and interpretation of outputs. Both explanations and cases are arranged in order of increasing complexity. Sensitivity analysis, evolution of policy making, and comparative analysis are included in case materials. A glossary of all PAVE inputs is furnished in an appendix.

Part III is devoted to explanations of the programming of PAVE. It contains a complete documentation and suggestions for adaptation to various computer and display configurations. End users of PAVE do not need Part III. On the other hand, financial model builders, or those who must adapt PAVE to particular hardware, should find this part quite useful.

This book is intended for both business students and business professionals. Readers should at least have acquired a "principles" level in the following subject areas: economics, accounting, financial management, marketing, and business statistics. Calculus is not required. Computer fundamentals are desirable but not essential. Necessary topics beyond a "principles" level in models of the firm and decision theory are explained and illustrated in chapters 1 through 6. References at the ends of these chapters suggest background, collateral, and expansive reading. An explanatory note accompanies each reference.

Courses in financial planning, strategy, or modeling could use this book as a principal source. The scope of the book is broad enough for general administration; there is sufficient material for business policy courses. With the minicomputer and information-processing revolution, managers of the future may find themselves relating directly to complex models, information bases, and statistical decision tools. The content of the book was specifically chosen to meet this need. Thus the book may be used with courses in M.I.S., strategic planning, quantitative models, decision-making, or computer applications. Theory, applications, and complex modeling are united in a combined decision system for management.

Part I is self-contained. It provides an integrated strategic decision system which does not require access to a computer. If there is a principal interest in computer modeling, on the other hand, focus attention on Part II. In such a case, Part I may be used as a reference for the modeling techniques of Part II. Finally, Part III contains information of most interest to those working with computer applications.

The authors would like to express appreciation to Ralph A. Peterson, Jr., Fred J. Ganoe, and the Department of Quantitative Methods at Georgia State University for permission to use a version of the PAVE simulation in this book. The authors would also like to thank Diane Allis, A. Davant Bullard, John Windsor, and Stephen Winter for developmental work on PAVE. Professors Sandra Beldt and Geoffrey Churchill served as advisors during early stages of the PAVE model development.

The authors appreciate the contribution of Wang Laboratories, Inc., which made available the equipment used to develop the PAVE revisions in this book. Although methods of configuration to various input/output media are considered in chapter 13, the PAVE model of this book is immediately transferrable to twin minidiskette drives of a WANG PCS-II with 32k memory.

Our thanks go to Margaret McDaniel, Jaimie McLaughlin, and Louise Miller for skillful preparation of the manuscript.

Dennis E. Grawoig
Charles L. Hubbard

PART I

Financial Theory
of Strategic Decisions

This book is about financial strategic planning with the aid of a large simulation model —PAVE. Theory and methodology are presented in the first six chapters. Several purposes are served. First, there is a compact presentation of the most important financial theory used for strategic planning. Second, the models that underlie decision processes with PAVE are explained. Third, and perhaps most important, theory and models are molded into a coherent human-computer decision system. The cement is rational thought processes about complex and ill-structured problems in the presence of uncertainty.

Chapter 1 explores a foundation of logical thought for strategic problem solving. How are efficient decision processes developed within the capabilities of human reasoning? What is the significance of models, and how may they cope with uncertainty? How may humans and computers combine as a decision-making team? How does economic-financial measurement relate to the total purposes of a firm?

Chapters 2 through 5 present fundamentals of four modeling systems which contribute to a total strategic plan. Chapter 2 reviews an essential model of economic value under uncertainty, the present value of cash flows. Adjustment processes for risk preferences, certainty equivalence, cost of capital, and risks of leverage are considered in this chapter. Statistical simulation is the general model system employed in PAVE to develop strategic plans. Chapter 3 explains the fundamentals of simulation. Accounting logic is used as a budgeting and planning tool. This logic is considered in Chapter 4. Chapter 5 shifts to an external view of market and opportunity values. Formulas are presented for capitalization of growth, both for cash payouts and for earnings.

Chapter 6 develops a logical decision system for developing strategic plans. How do top planners of a firm relate policies in functional areas such as product, marketing, operations, and organization? This chapter integrates the various models of earlier chapters into a coherent decision system. It suggests how to deal with uncertainty, competing strategies, and alternative measures of value.

The six chapters of Part I furnish a base for applications of PAVE.

1

1 Strategic Decisions and Financial Management

1.1 | Decision Role of a Strategic Planner

Of the many roles a manager has, that of decision maker stands at the top. Power, rewards, and prestige come to those who have demonstrated problem-solving ability, who are willing to accept the consequences of difficult decisions, and who have convinced others to accept those decisions. Knowledge that improves problem-solving performance is well worth pursuing.

A great deal of research has led to some useful insights about the logical processes of both men and machines. The purpose of this chapter is to connect some of these insights to strategic planning processes. Given some understanding about rational behavior in the face of uncertainty—some frame of reference on capabilities and limitations of thought processes—then planning activities gain in sophistication.

A direct emphasis on decision methods becomes important when developing a comprehensive modeling system. As in all types of problem environments, *strategic planning* needs logical method, creativity, and effective information sources. The planner is looking at a large, complex system—the business firm. This planner must conceptualize the entire unit in its environment while at the same time developing functional tasks for each subdivision. The logical structure of all this must be carried out by human reasoning, probably aided by machine logic.

Section 1.2 explores the anatomy of a problem, section 1.3 the nature of a model, section 1.4 the process of reasoning, and section 1.5 the distinction between goals and means. The final two sections look at fundamentals of strategic planning processes in enterprises. What are some useful financial models and how may they be integrated into a decision system? This is examined in section 1.6. The electronic information revolution has opened up new opportunities for the modeling of ill-structured problems. One of these opportunities, *decision support system* (DSS), is introduced in section 1.7. A treatment of uncertainty is postponed until Chapter 2.

3

In the social sciences there is lack of agreement on the precise meanings of technical terms. Not only is there confusion between everyday and specialized usage, but scholars differ among themselves in defining the lingo. Words such as planning, strategic, problem, decision, rationality, uncertainty, system, and goal have broadly understood meanings; but they may become ambiguous in precise discussion. Here, definitions will be presented as the need arises. Choices will be brief, reasonable, and pragmatic rather than exhaustive or academically refined.

In this book, *planning* is defined as the specification of a process that will take place in the future in reaching the goals of an enterprise. The term implies that alternative uses of resources have, in some sense, been considered. A current plan should result from a search for superior performance. The terms *strategic* or *strategy* refer to a problem-solving scope with significant impact on an enterprise as a total system. *Strategy* may be contrasted with narrower terms such as *tactics* or *actions*. It may also be useful to distinguish between *strategic* and *operating* problems. The latter are often concerned with crisis situations such as an expensive breakdown of a manufacturing process. Special methodologies are available for dealing with operating problems (see the references to this chapter).

A *system* is a set of interconnected entities with a recognizable separation from external entities. In other words a system has internal coherence and distinct boundaries. Its internal structure is richer than its links with the external environment. There are also hierarchical relationships among systems. A firm is a system with internal organization and a clear separation from its external environment. It is a component of larger systems such as an industry or an economy. On the other hand, a firm contains *subsystems*—for example, departments, plants, product lines, or functional divisions. In a *systems* approach a decision maker looks upward and outward toward the environment of a problem and seeks to achieve goals by enlarging the field of interacting information. In an *analytical* approach the decision maker looks downward and inward toward anatomical details of structure. If composition is understood, control may be achieved. The two approaches are complementary; they correspond to moving both ways along a chain of logical reasoning (see section 1.5).

1.2 | The Process of Solving Problems

From personal experience everyone knows about problems, but have you ever attempted a precise definition? As a first point, problems occur to systems, specifically to systems interacting with their environments. Furthermore, problem-solving systems are purposeful; they are pursuing goals. Individuals and organizations, including business enterprises, are purposeful systems. There may be many different goals and subgoals, and goals may shift over the passage of time, but there are always efforts toward some set of accomplishments. Figure 1.1 is a block diagram of a business problem. Think of a business firm as one type of purposeful system. Problems occur as it attempts to achieve its goals within its environment. Here, *environment* includes anything significant about a firm; outside its immediate boundaries, however, it could be markets, customers, suppliers, or labor unions. It could be the state of larger systems, such as the condition of an industry or an economy. It could be areas of social control, such as laws, regulations, or cultural demands.

A *problem* exists when a gap develops between desired and actual states of a purposeful system. Deviation from a desired state leads to tension within a system. The system will then employ its resources in an attempt to alleviate the tension. This is an adjustment process within the environment. *Information* may be defined as patterns of data from the environment which a system believes to have predictive value. Systems process information in order to monitor relationships in the environment, and to develop strategies for overcoming problems.

In Figure 1.1 a sharp reduction of sales in market Y leads to a gap between a firm's marketing plans and its actual performance in the environment. This gap develops a tension, a stimulus for action. The environment has imposed a block in the path of the firm's goals. Management directs the processing of information to describe the sales loss and develop strategies to increase sales. It plans to deploy its resources to overcome an undesirable environmental change. A *decision* is made when a strategy has

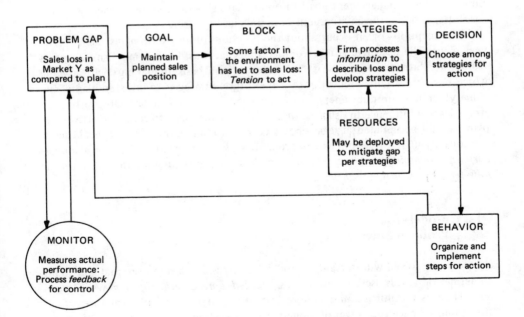

Figure 1.1 Block diagram of a business problem

been committed for action. Then plans must be organized and implemented for positive steps by the firm. Finally, does the chosen strategy solve the problem? Is the sales gap reduced and tension relieved? The control function monitors results and supplies information on progress.

Strategic planning has the same elements as illustrated by the problem blocks of Figure 1.1. A firm has sales and profit goals to achieve, which are discussed in section 1.5. There are environmental constraints which impede achievement, for example, the actions of competitors, limited opportunities in the industry, economic conditions, and social demands on the firm's resources. A firm must develop a strategy for overcoming environmental blocks and achieving reasonable goals. It processes information and develops alternative strategies, using resources at its command. A decision is reached when a particular strategic plan has been selected for action.

Plans alone accomplish little; they must be implemented. Important steps of implementation are organization for action, development of tactics for carrying out plans, and control. Control consists of monitoring actual performance and comparing results with plans. Once a plan has been accepted and completed, all too often it becomes a shelf item. Frequently no systematic comparison is carried out between a preceding plan and what actually happens. Plans and controls should work as a team in an ongoing, dynamic system. Plans should not be cast in concrete for immediate burial in the presence of environmental change; instead performance should be monitored continuously, with management goals in mind. Plans should be systematically adjusted for shifts, either in the environment or in policies of a firm.

Misconceptions often occur about the functions of long-term plans, such as five-year plans. The objective is not to blueprint what must happen in a firm five years from now. Rather, the purpose is to provide a rational basis for making decisions *now*, which have important implications for the future. Strategies to invest in plants, machinery, or new product lines, for example, must be made today. Obviously such strategies will influence the success of a firm for many years to come. Thus five-year plans should be updated at least once a year, or for any important change. Misconceptions about the time dimension probably make terms such as *strategic planning*, *corporate planning*, or *comprehensive business planning* superior to such terms as *long-term plans* or *five-year plans*.

1.3 | Models for Problem Solving

Problems are solved with the aid of models. *Model* is a common word that is difficult to define. Here, it is used to describe a *simplified representation of a real-world problem*. There is too much going on in real situations to develop logic structures of entire systems, hence the power of models. Models abstract from reality those features of interest in particular situations. The degree of abstraction is critical; too much simplification, and a model becomes inaccurate or trivial. Encumber a model with unnecessary detail, on the other hand, and it becomes a burden instead of an aid.

There are many ways of classifying models, such as by form, function, or degree of abstraction. *Pictorial* or *iconic* models retain the physical appearance, and often some functional behavior, of a represented reality. Usually there is a change in scale, and only selected features are assigned to the model. Examples of iconic models on a third-dimensional level are model planes, statues, and wind tunnels. Two-dimensional examples include photographs and pictorial drawings.

Analogue models choose a media whose behavior is similar to that of a represented reality, but whose appearance is different. Colors on a map may be used to represent changes in political subdivisions or types of roads. Movements of colored fluids through glass tubes may simulate hydraulically some principles of invisible electric circuitry. Here, hydraulic behavior is analogous to electrical behavior.

Symbolic models use media whose appearance and physical behavior do not resemble the original reality. Users must learn a symbolic system such as language or mathematics before the model becomes comprehensible. Although symbolic models are often difficult to use, they have a flexibility and economy not shared by the other classes. Symbolic models may be simple—such as a single word or concept—or they may be highly complex. The financial accounting system is a large symbolic model of the economic behavior and value of a firm.

A process of problem solving draws analogies between some model and the real world. A decision maker applies rules of the model to the real problem. Significant relationships are shown in Figure 1.2. A symbolic structure is selected to model the problem. The model is then manipulated in accordance with logical and mathematical rules. Relationships are developed in the model, which, it is hoped, will apply to the real problem. In Figure 1.2, model operations on the right side are applied to a real problem on the left side. In dynamic situations such as planning in a firm, there is a continuing process of adjustment between models and performance. Thus one may "walk the rectangle" in the figure; the cycling emphasizes a dynamic interplay between models and problems.

Various models may be combined to deal with complex decisions. In this book the PAVE model is a Monte Carlo simulation of the future and the value of a firm. The simulation model does not stand alone; it depends on other models. The financial accounting model mentioned above is the basis for flows of a firm's values over time. The present value model is a means of assigning a current worth to cash flows in the future. Both financial accounting and present value models are components of the PAVE decision system. An economic model is used to estimate going concern value; this model develops a logic for valuation under growth and risk. The various models mentioned here are discussed in later chapters of this part. See section 1.6 for a summary of the models used in PAVE and locations in the book where they are examined.

There is no guarantee that a particular model will lead to useful solutions, particularly in new or uncertain situations. The best one can do is to hypothesize a model

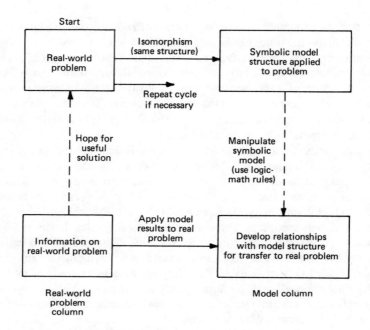

Figure 1.2 The relation between models and problems

which may contain relevant structures for a particular problem. It is important to check results as quickly as possible. Again, a process of analogy is central; one chooses a model that has demonstrated usefulness in past situations which appear similar to the problem at hand. A second key word is *adjustment*. A dynamic process of trial, observation, and correction is appropriate when faced with ill-structured problems.

1.4 | Minds and Problems

Problems are solved by human mental processes, possibly aided by machine logic. A brief consideration of thought processes sheds some light on effective problem-solving methods. If logical structures and formal models are used as a framework for decision making, then the thinking that goes with them should be rational and logical. The term *reflective thinking* will be used here to describe an organized mental process to achieve some goal or, in other words, to solve some problem. In *reflective* thinking, a problem solver employs rational thought, which simply means that each link in a cognitive chain follows logically from its predecessor. In other words, each link infers the thoughts that follow. Stated another way, within a chain of reasoning successive links from an element to its consequence should be relevant and noncontradictory. One does not proceed purposely along a path of contradictions. To do that would be to misinterpret a model structure and disrupt a decision process.

The financial accounting model is an excellent example of chain reasoning. Each entry leads to the next and the next; the entire system is a set of value chains that converge on the "condition" of a firm. Thus a sales entry leads to accounts receivable, receivables to cash, and perhaps cash to payment of an expense. In a parallel chain, sales leads to income, income to net worth, and net worth to condition. Accounting logic is examined again in the next section and in Chapter 4.

Reflective thinking is not the only mental process of problem solving; there is "art" as well as "logic." Intuition, creativity, and a sense of "wholes" figure prominently. Defining a problem or discovering an analogy between a model and a problem cannot be undertaken entirely from detailed, atomistic analysis. There is a perception of *system* that defies breakdown into detailed cause-and-effect thought processes. An attempt to describe problem solving must take into account mental processes that appear to search through and perceive total experience in a problem-solving environment. The cognition of "art" is poorly understood. In contrast, logical reasoning may be efficiently programmed for digital computers.

A physiological basis for distinguishing between two aspects of thought—logical reasoning and systems perception—has been explored in recent split-brain research. The left hemispherical lobe of the cerebral cortex has a major role in linear, sequential, analytical, symbolic, and abstract thought. Words and numbers are its tools and rational chain reasoning its process. A major role of the right lobe, on the other hand, is aggregative, immediate, intuitive, creative, systemic, and multidimensional. The right lobe works with shapes and forms; its capabilities are difficult, if not impossible, to simulate with a computer. Because hemispherical lobes of the brain control motions on opposite sides of the body, one could infer that a right-handed person is dominated by the logical lobe, whereas a left-handed person is dominated by the intuitive and spatial lobe. Speculations in this area have interesting possibilities but are of little practical value to professional problem solvers.

Although some aspects of split-brain theories are controversial, one fact is clear: the two cerebral lobes are richly connected, both to each other and to the lower brain centers. Communication is continuous and almost instantaneous. Instead of erecting a schism between art and logic, split-brain research reinforces an intimate partnership. This is a useful message. Given two dimensions of thought, reflective thinking makes use of the big picture while advancing in linear fashion through specific cause-and-effect relationships.

Strategic-planning tasks emphasize the two dimensions of thought. Decision makers should develop the large picture of a firm. But how will this be worked into plans? Usually one prepares detailed budgets based on chain reasoning models, such as financial accounting. Such an apparent paradox has led to some half-truths such as "models are not much help in solving policy problems." Unless a problem-solver conceptualizes the large system, unless he or she employs intuition and creativity, plans will certainly be inadequate if not outright failures. On the other hand, one must employ models and detailed logic in order to reach specific solutions. There is no other way to think consistently. Combining the two dimensions defines a particular system for solving strategic problems. Such a system is presented in Chapter 6.

1.5 | Means-End
Chains of Thought

A further examination of rational thought helps clarify the problem solving process. Chain reasoning is a lot like riding on a train. You are "on track" to go somewhere, to achieve some destination. Expressions such as "one-track mind," "off your trolly," or "keeping on the track" are based on analogy. A train must achieve each location, in turn, to reach the end of the line; and a person must process related ideas one at a time to reach a decision. Suppose you boarded the Southern Crescent in Atlanta for transportation to Washington, D.C. The train stops in Richmond, Virginia. Is Richmond a *means* or an *end* of your trip? Is it a *goal* or a *strategy*? You could jump to the conclusion that Richmond is merely a means. You do not even plan to get off the train in Richmond. On the other hand, it is important to you that the train does get to Richmond. You will not reach Washington by train unless the subgoal of Richmond is achieved. At this point it is clear that Richmond is both a means and an end. It is a means for all points down the line toward final goals; but it is also an end from all locations before it on the trip.

In a problem-solving chain the dual role of events as means and ends may be extended beyond specific limits such as a trip from Atlanta to Washington. My "real" end is not Washington but the Department of Energy. Again, my "real" end is not the Department of Energy but to keep an appointment with Mr. J. Once more, the final objective is not to converse with Mr. J., but to obtain a government contract. The same type of sequence could be carried on for means prior to reaching the railroad station in Atlanta. The point is that problem-solving chains are open-ended. An appropriate, ultimate goal is not always clear, and it is quite easy to confuse ends with means. Such confusion greatly reduces the efficiency of problem solving. Some suggestions for terminating a problem chain are given later; meanwhile, two consequences about open ends should be noted. First, chain reasoning is, in some sense, hierarchical. Thus, Washington is merely an instrument for interviewing Mr. J. Finally, a decision maker is more interested in the contract and its consequences than in Mr. J. personally. The second consequence is also a function of the hierarchical character of problem chains. Normally, one gets into the middle of a problem, as we did here on the trip to Washington. Although this is not a serious obstacle, it is a confusion frequently unrecognized by problem solvers.

Another example of means-end confusion applies directly to strategic-planning processes. What am I trying to accomplish as a manager of my firm? Perhaps my objective is a particular earnings level, the "bottom line." Is this the real bottom line? Careful thought shows the answer to be no. A given earnings figure is merely one component of a dynamic series of earnings. The series should exhibit a consistent growth pattern to enhance the economic value of a firm. Again, earnings are not a final criterion of value, for one may move up to common stock price. Common stock prices not only reflect earnings, but also stability, debt position, dividends, marketability, and other factors. Even stock price may not reach a high enough goal. Beyond an immediate market price one needs a mix of sound management policies for the long run. Factors such as effective research and development, sufficient capital base, social responsibility, brand-name recognition, and progressive labor relations may not be fully reflected in current market values of firms. An ultimate goal for a well-managed firm might amount to its long-term survival as an organized group of people in society. In the PAVE strategic decision system, economic value of the firm is the numerical goal.

One may think of the operation of a logical model, pursuit of a pattern of thought, or development of a plan, as a means-end decision chain. Examine any such chain as a component of an open-ended hierarchical system. Downward movement through the links presents *instrumental* reasoning from means to ends. It answers the question "how?". It is an analytical approach and is concerned with decomposition of a problem. Upward movement, on the other hand, develops teleological reasoning, is directed toward purpose, and answers the question "why?". This is a systems approach, looks outward toward the environment of a problem, and is concerned with synthesis and enlargement. Figure 1.3 diagrams the principal features of the means-end model of rational thought. A small piece of a marketing problem is shown to illustrate means-end structure. The strategic planning system of this book may also be structured as a means-end process of rational thought (see sections 6.2 and 6.3).

One more dimension is needed to present an adequate model of rationality. Branches occur in chains because alternative strategies are possible. There may be several available plans of action at any given level. Such strategies might be mutually exclusive, or in some cases they may be employed in combination. With the presence of branches our rational model exhibits "width" as well as "length"; thus it acquires the structure of a decision tree. Figure 1.3 shows the added dimension in rudimentary form. The width of a decision tree describes breadth of search, or answers the question "what?".

Overlapping brackets on the right side of Figure 1.3 are labeled *strategies, goals,* and *objectives.* The first label refers to means; the last two to ends. Although each level is both a means and an end, attention tends to shift from strategies toward purpose as one moves upward in a decision tree. Overlapping indicates vague boundaries. Here, an objective is taken as more general than a goal, a distinction which is by no means universal in the literature.

Despite the open-ended character of means-end reasoning, in a practical situation there must be terminations. At one end is a limit of high-level purpose, and at the other a limit of detailed analysis. Given a particular problem, there is considerable latitude in selecting these limits. High levels tend to be broad and vague. Ill-defined concepts need not be excluded, however, especially since they are a normal part of thought about large problems. One should certainly include high-level goals which are

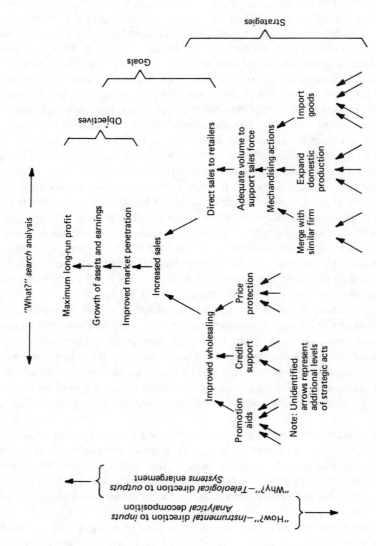

Figure 1.3 Means-end decision tree for a marketing problem

measurable. Measurement is important because a decision maker needs to control a problem situation. This means that one should monitor the consequences of implementation against strategies; otherwise, problem solving becomes only an exercise. In measuring goals of a firm, planners should at least reach a level of economic valuation. This value may be estimated, and is the end point of the PAVE simulation model. It is a counterpart of a market price for owner shares. It was chosen as a high end point because it is a value that may be estimated numerically.

Moving downward in a decision tree, when should one terminate a branch? There are at least three criteria of termination. These criteria are acceptability, risk of failure and feasibility. A given chain should not be pursued into branches that are clearly unacceptable. If a particular branch carries a high risk of failure it is not likely to satisfy the goals of problem solvers. Rationality under uncertainty is discussed in Chapter 2. Paths may appear for which no adequate means of achievement are available with a firm's resources. When blocks occur in the development of means-end logic, and this happens often, it is a signal to move to another branch. Looking at the logical relationships of the decision tree model of Figure 1.3, we can see that it contains the reasoning processes of the problem-solving steps from Figure 1.1.

Important models of strategic planning, as well as science in general, follow means-end logic. Thus the "proof" of a theorem is a series of steps that lead from initial assumptions to a final conclusion. Given a set of initial conditions, the conclusion cannot be contradicted if rules of logical implication are observed. For example, after a plane triangle has been defined as a figure enclosed by three straight lines, the sum of the interior angles must total 180 degrees.

More important for our purposes here is the means-end logic of important models. The financial accounting model is a good example. Starting with entries for revenues and expenditures, the logic proceeds through a series of steps. Journal entries compile original transactions. Ledger accounts are used to assemble and summarize categories of transactions. Account balances are organized into a series of statements. The cost-of-goods-manufactured statement, for example, is a means of obtaining the cost of finished goods. Cost of finished goods statement is an input to cost of goods sold. Cost of goods sold leads to gross profit. The latter—less expenses—provides net income in the income statement. Net income may be processed through capital changes into a final statement of condition (balance sheet). This last statement is the end point for value flows over an accounting period. The statement of condition establishes a figure for owners' equity (an accounting measure for goal achievement in a firm). Thus the financial accounting model is a good example of complex means-end logic. The system of accounting is examined further in Chapter 4.

1.6 | An Assembly of Models for Strategic Planning

In this book the criterion for decision among alternate strategic plans is *value of the going concern*. This value is estimated by using a number of models from microeconomic theory. Section 1.3 mentions that complex decision processes such as the PAVE strategic decision system may combine a battery of models. The most important of these models are identified in this section. Reference is made to other sections, where the models are examined and illustrated.

The value of a firm is not developed in a vacuum but by interaction with an external environment. A starting point for strategic planning is, therefore, the economic and industry environment. This systems approach is discussed in section 2.6. The development of value is measured by cash flows between the system of a firm and other economic systems. Cash flows of planning are distributed over future times, but a strategic decision must be based upon value now. The connecting link between cash "then" and value "now" is the present-value model, a cornerstone of financial-economic theory. The present value model is introduced in section 2.3, then applied to valuation in sections 2.5 and 2.6 and in Chapter 5. Modifications are examined for pricing capital assets—the payback method and return on investment (ROI).

Cash flows of present values are in the future, hence they are uncertain. The most difficult area in applications of present-value models is a logical method for measuring uncertainty. Chapter 2 is devoted to models of uncertainty built around a presen value framework. Risk preferences and certain equivalents are examined in section 2.2. Investors' required rates of return under risk are discussed in sections 2.3 and 2.5. The relation between market value of a firm and intrinsic worth is developed in section 2.5. Specific, present-value models for investment are summarized in Chapter 5. A capitalization of earnings model, introduced in section 5.4, is used in the PAVE system.

Given an underlying economic model structure, focused on present values of cash flows under risk, how does a planner obtain the numbers to operate a model system? Such numbers quantify a strategic plan and fall into two classes. First there is the environment—the behavior of society, the economy and the industry. Second, there are internal policies of a firm. A plan consists of deploying a firm's resources in order to achieve its goals. To a considerable extent the environment is uncontrollable. Thus the scope of decision is to establish policies within constraints of the environment.

To obtain the numbers for planning, access to an information base from financial accounting is almost indispensable. The accounting model, as an example of means-end logic, was introduced in sections 1.4 and 1.5. Not only does accounting data provide historical information, but it may be used to budget the future. Entire sets of projected accounting statements are developed in PAVE for this purpose. Among other things, managers and consultants are accustomed to examining financial statements. Unfortunately, value figures from accounting are usually not identical with net cash flows. Accounting valuation will thus differ from economic valuation. Under certain conditions, however, accounting figures may be used as proxies for cash flows. The theory of accounting information for strategic planners is examined in Chapter 4. Of special interest is section 4.4, which compares accounting income with net cash flows.

Accounting statements are so important that a system of ratio analysis has been developed to summarize information. These summary statistics, often called financial ratios, are of great interest to suppliers of capital and to investment analysts. Ratios are classified and examined in sections 4.5 and 4.6. Selected ratios are developed in the PAVE system to describe the final financial condition of a firm.

What is the means-end logic of the PAVE model for strategic planning? Users input some scenario of forecasted environmental conditions and a strategic plan for deploying resources. These inputs are processed through a financial accounting model with means-end logic. A Monte Carlo simulation is then operated to process a statistical sample of inputs and outputs. A summary of simulation modeling is presented in Chapter 3. Instead of one accounting sequence to convert inputs to outputs, statistical simulation repeats (replicates) the process in order to obtain a range of uncertainty.

The PAVE output contains projected financial statements and ratios, as mentioned above. Cash flows are also derived, and in some cases accounting values are used as proxies for cash flows. Risk is measured and estimates of economic value are developed. These estimates represent the present value of a firm under risk.

1.7 | Decision Support Systems and the Information Revolution

The electronic information revolution may have more impact on the total human condition than did the industrial revolution. The latter substituted machine power for muscle power. Now machine power can take over routine mental operations. The information revolution is much more than the substitution of punched cards and data-processing centers for armies of clerks. It would be easy to stop with such information processing functions as electronic billing, payrolls, automated accounting, and inventory management. Routine processing of large data bases is only the tip of the iceberg. Take, for example, the recent minicomputer revolution. Now inexpensive programmed logic, display, printing, and information storage is available with compact equipment which sits anywhere and goes anywhere. Again, it would be an illusion to believe that this is merely a step improvement in cost reduction and flexibility. The horseless carriage was more than a fast and efficient conveyance from A to B. The conquest of distance permanently altered the structure of society.

What happens when electronic information logic and display machines get sprinkled around offices and shops like typewriters? For one thing, they are no longer the exclusive tools of computer scientists. Inputs and outputs must be available to average business professionals; they must not be limited to specialists on computer languages or systems architecture. Currently, "mini" electronic information technology is way ahead of implementation by business. Surprisingly, many managers and business students choose to ignore the electronic machines and logic models that will certainly figure prominently in their future. At least three applications are converging. The first is decision support systems with interactive computer models. This is examined below. The second is information systems, which may be operated in the local environment of minicomputers and by centralized data processing. The third is word processing, which revolutionizes the preparation, editing, and transfer of documents. The last application may be the quickest to gain acceptance by business. The advantages of electronic processing of documents over electric typewriters are obvious.

All three applications are part of the same technology and the same general system of management information. All depend upon questions and answers between operator and computer. All need a simple language and simple rules to carry out human-computer interactions. All depend on electronic displays for rapid presentation of information. All have auxiliary printers to produce permanent, written records. All have programmed logic capabilities with "wired-in firmware" or user supplied software. All will communicate with magnetic data storage units, such as disks or cassettes. Application areas themselves are closely related. A word processing unit may be used to prepare reports, such as a client's life insurance summary, or a district salesperson's weekly performance record. Suppose a report form may be updated on demand with figures from information files. Then word processing has been combined with information systems. Suppose, furthermore, that some calculations are programmed into the reports. In the case of insurance such calculations might be total cash value or total protection. A performance summary could be programmed into a sales report. Now word processing, information files, and decision-support models have been combined into a total problem-solving system.

Decision support systems (DSS) has been identified as a new technology to aid decision making, a type of information model. What exactly is DSS? It is a flexible information model, often computer-based, which uses the methodology and structures of management science and operations research, but in a different way. DSS provides information quickly from an adaptable structure. The emphasis is on scenario building, sensitivity analysis, and ad hoc modeling. DSS is therefore useful for ill-structured problem solving, the kind of problem that has not responded to conventional management-science techniques. Although DSS may use some methodologies from management science, such as Monte Carlo simulation, it avoids the time delays, rigidities, and optimal solution goals of conventional operations research.

DSS is fundamentally a decision maker's working-partner model. A computer is not essential to DSS; it is the practical tool. It is actually the capabilities of minicomputers that will popularize DSS. This is more than economy, portability, immediate access, and number crunching. Although these features are important, minicomputers actualize a human-machine decision team. Conversational interchanges and video displays promote interaction between decision maker and model. In the past 30 years management science has made some important contributions to decision processes. Statistical quality control now replaces rules of thumb, and methods analysis has revolutionized assembly lines. Management science has not been so successful with strategic problems faced by top executives, particularly ill-structured situations. Handing over such problems to management scientists has been disappointing. Typically, the solution that comes back is untimely, presented in the wrong package for a manager, and rejected for implementation. The manager and scientists do not hear each other. DSS methods attempt to overcome such roadblocks. An expert does not "go away" to solve a problem. Instead, managers become directly involved with the construction of models and with the evolution of input-output processes. This does not mean that a manager must run the computer or learn the rules of a model, although this often does happen. It does mean that DSS, model-building support, and minicomputers become a permanent fixture in a manager's intimate, decision-making environment.

To operate DSS one needs to be "on-line" and "real-time." Minicomputers are inexpensive and compact hardware for this purpose. To gain DSS advantages of flexibility and quick response, decision makers must not divorce themselves from their computers. Since it is inappropriate that decision makers or their support staffs be required to learn computer programming or information processing technology, a special responsibility falls on DSS model designers. DSS programs will be most useful if written in a computer language that is designed for interaction between decision makers and computers with everyday words and numbers. BASIC is such a language, and will probably dominate the DSS-minicomputer field for some time to come. The design of DSS input-output systems is a difficult challenge because the system must be rich and flexible while at the same time avoiding a major learning requirement from users.

The PAVE system is a DSS model for the financial future and valuation of a firm. PAVE supports the strategic planning system which is presented in this book. PAVE software is programmed in BASIC for minicomputers. The arrangement of programs and files is designed for inexpensive machines with moderate capacity. Information may be stored on diskettes or cassette tapes. To facilitate inputs and outputs, full use is made of video displays. Outputs are printed and inputs may be optionally printed. PAVE users do not have to understand BASIC nor any other computer language. Inputs and outputs are completely conversational, an exchange of words and numbers.

Other than interactive computer features, does PAVE meet DSS criteria? A PAVE user can virtually design his or her own specific model system. Any one of three methodologies for modeling uncertainty (see section 2.1) may be chosen with PAVE. Outputs will be obtained with anywhere from a few to several hundred inputs. There are numerous choices in the handling of accounting frameworks and the determination of expense. Environment of the economy and industry may be included or excluded. There are options for the control of cash and supply of capital. There are choices of outputs: valuation, financial budgets, financial statement analysis, or statistical analysis. There are built-in branches for scenario building, sensitivity analysis, and examination of alternative strategies. One may conclude that PAVE is an example of a new generation of DSS models.

In all fairness, everything is not sweetness and light in the DSS model design field. There is a trade-off between power and flexibility in DSS models and the time required to master input-output rules. Many users have a strong preference for simple models. They would like to get useful results with a minimum of initial effort. On the other hand, emerging business support systems from software designers are tending, like PAVE, to require mastery of instruction manuals. Minicomputers have powerful capabilities at small cost. This tempts designers to build models with impressive performance, but users must learn a set of rules to operate such models. One answer is to provide a simplified, basic system of inputs and outputs. Extra power may be added with supplementary input systems. This approach is used in PAVE. Chapters 7 through 10 of Part II present a simplified system. The remaining chapters illustrate extensions. The software of a model may be structured with modules. The simplest feasible system is contained in a basic module. Auxiliary modules may be attached to achieve modifications or additional power. Modular software construction has much to recommend it, but may be difficult to achieve for an integrated system. In the end, users must decide whether a particular DSS model achieves an acceptable balance between output power and input effort. This is certainly true of PAVE.

References and Additional Reading

Modern executive decision making takes place in a human-computer environment. Effective problem-solving processes in such an environment are discussed in nontechnical language by the great psychologist and computer scientist H.A. Simon in *The New Science of Management Decision*, rev. ed., Prentice-Hall, 1977. Much of the modern science of decision stems from John Dewey's work in 1910. His readable, classic work, *How We Think*, rev. ed., Heath, 1933, is well worth reading today. For those who wish to examine a systems approach to problem solving, a penetrating book is J.P. van Gigch, *Applied General Systems Theory*, Harper and Row, 1974.

An excellent, compact discussion of the logic of models and problem-solving processes will be found in .P.H. Rigby, *Models in Business Analyses*, Merrill, 1969. Brief discussions of means-end analysis are contained in A. Easton, *Complex Managerial Decisions Involving Multiple Objectives*, John Wiley, 1973, pp. 61-66; and H.I. Ansoff, *Corporate Strategy*, Mc-Graw Hill, 1965, pp. 24-28.

As mentioned above, modern foundations of problem-solving thought go back to John Dewey. Recent research about brain function, including split-brain theories, is discussed in nontechnical language by M.C. Whittrock et al., *The Human Brain*, Prentice-Hall, 1977. A book of readings on specialization of brain function is S.J. Dimond and J.G. Beaumont,

eds., *Hemisphere Function in the Human Brain*, Halsted, 1974.

Decision support systems (DSS) are starting to develop a literature. As background, read G.J. Burnett and R.L. Nolan, "At Last, Major Roles for Minicomputers," in *Harvard Business Review*, May-June 1975, p. 148. A survey of DSS as a new branch of management science is presented in A. Vazsonyi, "Decision Support Systems: The New Technology of Decision Making?" in *Interfaces*, November 1978, p. 72. A recent book on DSS, which provides a perspective and numerous examples, is P.G.W. Keen and M.S.S. Morton, *Decision Support Systems: An Organizational Perspective*, Addison-Wesley, 1978.

To consider some of the difficulties of implementing management science models in executive decision making, read J.D.C. Little, "Models and Managers, The Concept of a Decision Calculus," *Management Science*, vol. 16, 1970, p. B466; and J.S. Hammond, "Do's and Don'ts of Computer Models for Planning," *Harvard Business Review*, November-December 1967, p. 123.

For readings on computers and thought, consult references at the end of Chapter 3.

Many additional references on strategic planning and executive decision making are listed at the end of Chapter 6.

PROBLEMS TO INVESTIGATE

1-1. Steps in problem solving, as listed by H.A. Simon (*The New Science of Management Decision*, rev. ed., Prentice-Hall, 1975, p. 43) and first described by John Dewey, are:

> What is the problem?
> What are the alternatives?
> Which alternative is best?
> Do these steps agree with the problem-solving model in the chapter? How useful is a knowledge of such steps in the actual process of solving problems?

1-2. Discuss the following statement: "Once a problem has been accurately defined, the solution is readily apparent."

1-3. In solving criminal cases, what were the differences between the methods of the famous detective Sherlock Holmes and the conventional police work of Gregson and Lestrade?

1-4. Outline a system of control for checking actual performance against strategic plans. Why do top managers sometimes ignore formal plans? What should be done to involve managers in planning?

1-5. Give examples of iconic, analogue, and symbolic models. What is the difference in meaning between model, concept, and structure?

1-6. What do you think the most important models used in business are?

1-7. In working with models, discuss processes of feedback and adjustment for ill-structured problem solving.

1-8. In what sense does a computer "think"? Discuss computer capabilities and limitations with respect to left-handed and right-handed mental processes. What is the potential of a human-computer partnership for problem solving?

1-9. Prepare a means-end chart to organize some business problem. Prepare another for a personal problem. Mark paths of recommended strategies.

1-10. Is means-end analysis simply an expression of logical implication? Compare means-end organization with a "proof" in Euclidean geometry, a computer program, an algorithm of operations research (such as simplex method of linear programming), a recipe for baking a cake, and instructions on an income tax form.

1-11. Consider a total decision process. What are the roles of models, environment, strategies, values, and uncertainty? Identify each of these in illustrative simple problems.

1-12. Define a *decision support system* (DSS) in your own words. How does DSS differ from *management information systems* (MIS), operations research models, or conventional financial analysis?

1-13. What types of DSS applications are likely to be accepted first by managers? How may DSS roadblocks be overcome? Describe steps to install a DSS and examine some organizational factors.

1-14. What management science methods may be most useful for DSS design? What methods are unlikely to be used?

1-15. In the last paragraph of the chapter, an important issue was raised. In a DSS model there is a conflict between power and simplicity of operation. In your opinion, is such a conflict inevitable? What steps should be taken in DSS design to alleviate the problem? What steps should be taken to orient users?

2 Measurement of Uncertainty in Decision Models

2.1 | Uncertainty and Model Building

It is unfortunate that many financial models contain no explicit treatment of uncertainty. This is particularly true of computer-budgeting models. Many of these models have a great deal of power and flexibility, but in the end there is only a set of point estimates from financial statements. It is a great temptation to avoid measurement of uncertainty because simple sets of equations become replaced by probability distributions. The number of approximations and compromises tends to multiply in a model as the input-output system is enlarged to accommodate statistical inference.

Measurement of uncertainty is attempted in the PAVE modeling system. Since one objective of PAVE strategic planning is to approximate economic values of going concerns, and not just to produce budgets, it is mandatory to get into statistical measures of risk. Fortunately, the theory of risk is well developed. First, there is the whole methodology of inferential statistics, which rests in turn on the logic of *probability* calculus. This subject matter is not reviewed here. Statistical methods, however, may be applied to decision theory, economic theory, and financial valuation. A review of these topics, as the building blocks of the PAVE model, is summarized in this chapter. Three of the four output divisions of PAVE may print statistical information—usually means, standard deviations, and confidence limits.

Various statistical models are important to develop a structure for financial valuation under risk. Some connections between uncertainty and model building are introduced in the remainder of this section. The subjective utility model and certainty equivalence are reviewed in section 2.2. Models of capital budgeting are summarized in section 2.3. The present value method for net cash flows is rich enough to estimate economic value under risk. Types and sources of risk are examined in sections 2.3 and 2.4. Relationships of risk to market value and "portfolio" theory are considered in section 2.5. An integrated construct of a firm, treated as a problem-solving system in a risky economic environment, is suggested in section 2.6.

21

This chapter introduces some theory of risk modeling. Problems of risk measurement figure prominently in subsequent chapters. Much of Chapter 3 is concerned with simulation of risk by the Monte Carlo method. The present-value models of Chapter 5 apply risk methods discussed in this chapter.

As a part of nature, humanity is able to perceive order and system from observations of nature. People stand erect and, as they perceive the horizon, become aware of the significance of the right angle. If a stone is suspended by a thread of vines, then one establishes a nearly perfect right angle with a level surface, such as a lake or pond. Such relationships are orderly and predictable. It is but a step from a simple right angle to the Pythagorean theorem, a cornerstone of mathematics. As Figure 2.1 demonstrates, one need only play with five cardboard or stone triangles. Thus complex logic-mathematics-modeling systems arise from perceptions of order in the natural environment.

If nature is a means of perceiving order, it is also a source of disorder. There is simply too much going on in most environments; furthermore there is disorder through *change*. A system acquires a problem because its equilibrium with the environment has been disturbed by change. A system must then process information or, in other words, use its perceptions of order to adapt behavior to environmental change. All decision making involves *prediction* about the future; here disorderliness gives rise to *uncertainty*. If an environment is dominated by a single effect, such as the dropping of a large stone in response to the laws of gravity, our uncertainty about what will happen is small. If a number of changes are going on simultaneously, however, and none is dominant, our uncertainty will be high. The latter condition holds for many social environments, such as the behavior of an economy or power struggles within an organization. Words such as *disorder*, *complexity*, and *uncertainty* are closely related; they are all associated with lack of control over environmental change. In management science there are various definitions of the term *uncertainty*. Here, the word is used to describe any indeterminism in predicting an important value. The term *risk* will be applied to situations when decision makers assign probabilities to the occurrence of uncertain events.

In building models to make strategic planning decisions, it is useful to identify three methodologies for coping with uncertainty. In the first method, a single value is used to represent each uncertain prediction. Then a single scenario of the future has been erected under a set of assumptions agreed upon by decision makers. The assumptions are in some sense typical, expected, or most likely. Statistically speaking, the assumptions are point estimates as a basis for decision. Models using this method are deterministic because uncertainty has not been explicitly incorporated in the model. Ordinary budgets fall into this class; one set of figures is approved as the plan for some future periods. Deterministic models have the advantage of simplicity. The system works well as long as deviations from predictions are not critical or are recognized promptly.

The second methodology erects alternative scenarios which combine various possibilities for uncertain events. Suppose you were asked to draw up a plan for a new

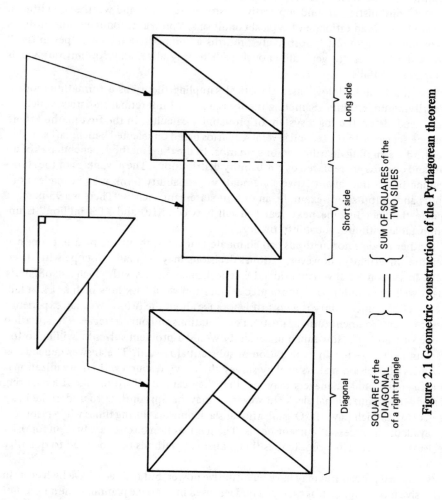

Figure 2.1 Geometric construction of the Pythagorean theorem

ski resort and then make recommendations to an investor group. You might prepare three sets of planning budgets to cover an uncertain range of future revenues. You have no history of consumer demand, nor do you know what kind of winter will occur. The three budgets represent "most likely," "pessimistic," and "optimistic" conditions. "Pessimistic" is built around the lowest revenue you can reasonably foresee and "optimistic" around superlative customer response and weather conditions. "Most likely" is an estimate of typical conditions. You will recommend the business to an investor group if "most likely" returns a competitive income, "pessimistic" allows the business to generate enough cash to stay alive, and "optimistic" yields attractive windfalls.

The third methodology uses statistical sampling theory as a formal method of quantifying uncertainty. Sampling theory is a part of inferential statistics, which, in turn, depends on the logic system of probability calculus. In the first method there was one scenario, in the second several scenarios based on selected benchmarks, and in the third a sampling distribution of scenarios. In the third method, benchmarks of inputs and outputs are replaced by probability distributions. The advantage of the statistical method is that quantitative statements in probability terms may be made about inputs and outputs. For example, an output statement such as "There is a 95-percent chance that net income next year will fall between $1.0 and $1.3 million" is unsupportable without probability theory.

Neither models nor methods can eliminate ignorance about the future. If one can measure uncertainty, however, rational decisions may be made to cope with its effects. In section 1.5 it was mentioned that decision branches with a high risk of failure might well be abandoned. A more precise question would ask how high a risk of failure. In effect, uncertainty is a cost of ignorance about the future. We may experience loss if the environment turns against our expectations and our strategies. The situation is one of trade-off. How much uncertainty would a problem solver be willing to tolerate in exchange for an expectation of substantial reward? The answer depends on attitudes of decision makers as they survey their own resources. If an organization is in a financial bind, managers may feel that they cannot afford to take risks. During periods of organizational slack, however, it may be appropriate to undertake risky projects with high payoffs. Organizational slack appears during times when resources are available in excess of current needs. The next section discusses valuation for risky decisions further. The point here is that statistical methods may be used to quantify such decisions.

Statistical procedures may have quantitative power, but they also have high cost. In extensive modeling, such as financial budgets used in strategic planning, the amount of number crunching increases rapidly as one goes from a single budget to alternative scenario budgets, and finally to repeated budget sampling. Large statistical models, such as PAVE, are impractical without digital computers. The PAVE model may be operated with either benchmarks or probability distributions for its inputs and outputs. Thus all three methodologies for coping with uncertainty may be run on PAVE.

If uncertainty is a cost of planning for the wrong environment, then how should this cost be incorporated into the three methodologies? *Conservative bias* is a subjective adjustment often applied to uncertain decisions. Under the deterministic method, budgets may not contain the most likely figures; instead a safety margin may be incorporated by understating revenues and overstating costs. Under the alternative scenarios method, the decision process may focus on pessimistic scenarios. In the statistical method uncertainty may be treated explicitly using decision methods under risk and probabilities assigned to outcomes.

In all three methods there is a tendency to reduce multiple possibilities to one set of inputs and outputs which becomes the focus of attention. This set is less favorable than the most likely set. The less favorable set is used as a certain equivalent of the uncertain environment. The substitution of a simple certain equivalent for a world of multiple outcomes is important in a logical analysis of uncertainty. In the deterministic and multiple scenario methods, biassing toward a certain equivalent is informal and implicit. In the statistical method, however, a certain equivalent may be explicitly measured as a trade-off for risky events. Such measurements are examined in the next section.

2.2 | Measurement of Risk Preferences

The cost of uncertainty affects both micro and macro levels. At the micro level there is a matter of individual or organizational attitudes toward risk. At the macro level there is a question of price adjustments for risk in capital markets. Both levels interact. If statistical methods are used, strategic planners may explicitly include individual or organizational risk preferences. Those preferences are exercised in an environment of market opportunities and costs. Each level is briefly examined here with particular reference to the development of certain equivalence. Some important issues, which have received a lot of attention in economic-financial theory, are not considered. Rather, the discussion is limited to structures required for strategic planning.

Suppose, at great personal danger, you rescued a billionaire from a possibly horrible death on his South American ranch. You pulled him out of a river infested with carnivorous piranha fish. In return for saving his life, the billionaire offers you a choice between two rewards. The first is a direct payoff of one million dollars tax free. The second is a lottery to be decided by one flip of a fair coin. If the outcome is heads you win two million dollars tax free; but if the outcome is tails, you receive nothing. Which reward would you choose? Most of us, not being millionaires, would probably choose the one million certain. Why? It is clear: starting from almost nothing financially, the first million is worth a lot more to us, in terms of subjective value (utility), than a second million on top of the first. Even though each reward has the same statistical expected value, one million dollars, our utility of money function is not proportional to money values. In other words, our utility of money function is nonlinear.

Consider again just the lottery reward. It is worth less to you than $1,000,000 certain, but obviously more than $0 payoff. Then there must be a single certain payoff of money, called a certain equivalent, between $0 and $1,000,000, which is worth exactly as much to you as the lottery. You are indifferent between receiving this certain reward and receiving the chance to win on the lottery. Your certain equivalent is simply a subjective expression of your personal attitude toward risk. There is no *a priori*, prescribed value; individuals will differ about the figure for a given risk situation. Assume that the certain equivalent for you is $400,000. If less than this certain payoff were offered, you would prefer the lottery, but above $400,000 you will always take the certain payoff, even though it is much less than the expected payoff of the lottery.

The billionaire now realizes that his original choice of rewards was very unequal to you, even though the expected cost to him was the same. Being very generous, he suggests another choice. Suppose you are given an 0.8 probability of winning $2 million and 0.2 probability of receiving nothing. The expected cost and payoff of this new lottery is $1,600,000. The billionaire is very surprised to find that even now you prefer $1 million certain reward. In fact your certain equivalent to the new lottery reward is $960,000.

Figure 2.2 plots your preferences for risky money. Money amounts from $0 to $2 million are scaled on the horizontal axis. An index of value to you, a personal utility, is plotted on the vertical axis. Any index system may be chosen as long as it will lead to the same decisions under payoffs weighted with probabilities, the lotteries in our example. Here, utility was set equal to the probability of winning $2 million in the various lotteries—a convenient but arbitrary choice. The straight diagonal line segment then plots all probabilities of winning $2 million against the expected values of such lotteries.

Your utility of money function is given by the curved graph. The plot of this function is easily found, but first consider *risk-neutral* behavior. The expected value of the billionaire's first gamble was $1 million at E. Suppose you had been indifferent between that gamble and $1 million certain. Then there would be no difference in utility between these choices. Such indifference between expected payoffs of gambles and their certain equivalents throughout some range of lotteries would classify you as a risk-neutral person within that range. The straight-line segment would then represent your risk indifference. On a linear segment, value increments are directly proportional to money increments. Under such conditions the second million would be worth just as much to you as the first million. This would not be true for most people or firms under large risks. It usually is true for small payoff amounts. You are probably indifferent between paying outright and flipping a coin for a cup of coffee.

In the billionaire's reward you were not risk neutral and indifferent to lotteries. You were, in fact, a risk avoider because your certain equivalents were smaller than the expected values of the lotteries. Determination of your certain equivalents for various lotteries makes it easy to plot your personal utility function over some range of payoffs. Return to the first reward with an expected value of $1 million at E. This reward

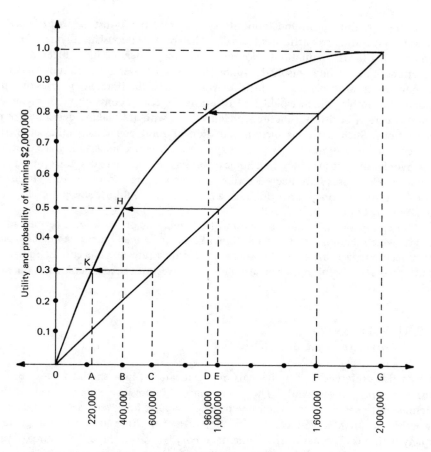

Figure 2.2 Utility values for a risk avoider

offers a 50-50 chance of winning $2 million at G or nothing. You would accept a certain equivalent of $400,000 at B to replace the lottery, or the two choices have the same utility to you. In other words they have the same height on the graph. This permits you to establish a utility value at point H. Your certain equivalent of the lottery is $400,000 at B, and the risk premium is $600,000. On the billionaire's second lottery the probability of winning $2,000,000 is 0.8, and the expected value is $1,600,000 at F. Here your certain equivalent is $960,000 at D, which establishes another point on your utility function at J. By offering various lotteries and determining the corresponding certain equivalents, an entire utility of money function may be plotted. For example, if you are offered only a 0.3 probability of winning the $2,000,000, which has an expectation of $600,000 at C, your certain equivalent drops to $220,000 at A, which plots another utility point at K.

There is nothing profound about utility of money functions; they are merely devices for measuring risk attitudes formally. They provide a consistent system for decision making in risky situations. Not only do different persons have different utility functions, but for one person the function may shift over time, circumstances, or money ranges. Most people are not risk avoiders all of the time. Sometimes they pay money to gamble, which would lead to utility functions convex to the origin. The interest here is in utility functions of individuals who are making decisions for organizations. Such decisions include valuation of going concerns, capital budgeting choices, or opportunities to bid on risky contracts. Since uncertainty is a cost, the risk avoider mode usually applies. Some effort has been made to develop group utility functions. Processes have been described for reconciling executives to a single corporate utility of money function. Such a utility curve could become policy for decision making under risk.

Strategic planners should develop utility functions or work with certain equivalents, which amounts to the same thing. Whether formally measured or not, planners need a logical basis for choosing among risky strategies. The certain equivalent concept is also useful in the valuation of risky investments, as examined in the next section.

2.3 | Valuation of Investments Under Risk

Given risk preferences of individuals or organizations, how should values be established for risky investments? The investments of interest here are commercial firms belonging to shareowners. The same principles apply, however, to any capital asset, whether a capital budgeting project or the worth of an entire going concern. There are many methods of valuation; fundamental theory is reviewed here. The source of value to investors is the net of economic outflows to them over economic inflows from them. This generalization is complicated by time patterns of value flows, the supply and demand for loanable funds, inflation, and whether values are realized or unrealized. In the valuation of commercial enterprises, future economic flows to owners are uncertain, which adds to the problem of valuation. If a share of a business is purchased, then all economic returns to a shareowner are in the future. Last year's dividend might be useful as forecasting information but provides no future payoffs to current owners.

It may be assumed that most businesses will continue indefinitely. This means that expected value flows to investors include components in the distant future. This is a difficult problem because uncertainty overwhelms measurement. Methods of handling this are discussed in Chapter 5.

A business is a system which interacts with many other organizations in various environments. There are economic value exchanges across the boundaries of a firm with owners, creditors, customers, suppliers, employees, government, and other social groups. These economic flows are in cash, near-cash, or valuable commodities, but will be measured in money terms. The total life of a business will consist of value transformations from liquidity (usually cash) to commodities (including services and intangibles), and back to cash again. Thus economic value flows to owners are ultimately cash flows or the equivalent.

A $1,000 *future* cash flow is not worth $1,000 today. There is a price for time delay in paying or receiving money. This price, an interest rate, is determined by the interaction of supply and demand for loanable funds. Thus time patterns of cash flows must be taken into account for investment decision processes. Three methods are payback, return on investment (ROI), and present value. Suppose a new machine costs $100,000 installed. Expected cash savings after taxes from operating this machine are forecasted at $60,000 the first year and $40,000 the second year. If a decision rule is two years minimum payback, then the machine project is barely acceptable. Payback method has advantages of simplicity and emphasis on cash conversion. It omits important economic information, however; for example, the firm's cost of capital and cash flows from the machine after two years are neglected.

Both ROI and present value consider the time pattern of cash inflows and outflows for capital projects. All cash flows are discounted to the present. What rate, the ROI, will equate the sum of present values of all cash inflows or investments into the project with the sum of present values of net cash throwbacks from the project? If the ROI exceeds some "hurdle" rate of return, then the project will be accepted. Apart from decision rules to undertake investments, ROI measures the rate of return projected over the life of a project, a useful measure in its own right.

In present-value method both cash inflows and cash outflows are discounted back to the present at a predetermined "hurdle" rate rather than at ROI. Thus instead of solving for an ROI which equates the present value sum of inflows with outflows, present-value method solves for the present-value sums themselves. The decision rule for accepting investments is still the "hurdle" rate. If the present-value sum of net cash throwbacks exceeds the present value sum of invested inflows, both discounted at the "hurdle" rate, then the project is acceptable. Furthermore, the value of an investment at the "hurdle" rate is the present-value sum of all cash throwbacks. If this value exceeds the present-value sum of costs (inflows from investors), then a positive "windfall" accrues to investors.

The cost-saving machine in the previous example may be used to illustrate both ROI and present-value methods. Assume that the firm expects to use the machine for only two years. At the end of this time the used market value of the machine is projected at $20,000. There is a single cash inflow of $100,000 to purchase and install the machine. This has a present value of $100,000 at time zero (now) at any rate of discount. Neglecting time distributions within years, there is a net cash throwback of $60,000 in year one. In year two, investors receive the sum of $40,000 savings and $20,000 used market value.

Under ROI the problem is to find a rate R that equates the present value of throwbacks with the present value of investment inflows, or in this case with $100,000:

$60,000(1 + R)^{-1} + 60,000(1 + R)^{-2} = 100,000$

$R = .13$ or 13% ROI

Suppose the "hurdle" rate is 10%. Then the present-value sum of net cash throwbacks is given by:

$60,000(1.1)^{-1} + 60,000(1.1)^{-2} = \$104,132$

This is the value of the capital project at a hurdle rate of 10%. Because the above figure exceeds $100,000 present value of investment, the machine should be purchased. If the hurdle rate were 15%, however, then the present value of throwbacks is

$60,000(1.15)^{-1} + 60,000(1.15)^{-2} = \$97,543$

Now the project should be rejected. The same decisions would be reached under the ROI method. At the 10% hurdle the ROI is sufficient for acceptance, but at a 15% hurdle the ROI is inadequate. The establishment of a hurdle rate, which is a difficult problem, is critical to the entire decision process. Given the same hurdle rate, and no unusual patterns of cash flows, either ROI or present-value methods will lead to the same decision. Only the present-value method, however, is rich enough to handle the adjustments required for valuation of strategic plans in the PAVE modeling system. These adjustments are considered here and in the last section of the chapter.

Within a structure of cash flows and discount rates, measurement of value must absorb business risk, inflation, and the time value of money. Business risk occurs because actual earnings fluctuate from planned values. Sources of business risk and financial risk are examined in section 2.4. In the latest theory of capital asset pricing models (CAPMs), projected cash flows could be adjusted for business risk by substitution of certain equivalents under methods outlined in the last section. A time rate would then be chosen which is free of business risk. The long-term government bond meets such a requirement. This does not imply that such securities are risk free. Money received in the future will probably have less purchasing power per dollar (real value) than today. This is inflation risk. There is also risk from changes in the supply and demand for loanable funds. Such changes affect interest rates and hence the prices of outstanding debt instruments. Price uncertainty from interest rate changes is often termed interest rate risk. All the above adjustments may be combined into a CAPM. Figure 2.3 diagrams the processing of cash flows in this model.

As an example of CAPM method, assume an expected value of net cash flow from a business next year will be $100,000. Given the business risks involved, a certain equivalent of $80,000 may be assigned to this cash flow by decision makers. The current government bond rate is 9%. This rate covers inflation and interest rate risks. The adjusted present value for decision purposes is then $80,000 divided by 1.09, or $73,394. This final figure could be combined with other present values, computed under the same method, into a total valuation of a business or capital project.

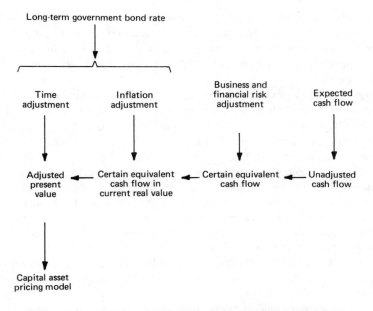

Figure 2.3 Adjustment of cash flows for capital asset pricing

For reasons given in section 2.4, PAVE present values use a simplification of the total CAPM system. Further discussion and illustrations of cash flow adjustments are found in section 5.7.

2.4 | Sources of Business Risk

If there is a significant probability of failing to achieve planned net cash flows, which is usually the case, then business risk is important. The relationship between earnings, or net income after income taxes, and net cash flows from a firm, is examined in section 4.4. A discussion of business risk may be applied to either earnings or net cash flows since both are residuals of business operations. For brevity, the rest of this section will usually refer to earnings. There are two reasons for a closer look at business risk. First, some generalizations are of interest to strategic planners. Second, the pattern of earnings deviations from planned levels is significant in the valuation process of going concerns (section 2.5).

If a business were successfully established in a perfectly stable environment, then only a caretaker management would be required to maintain the status quo. In fact, environments are constantly shifting, often sharply, and much of this shift is beyond the control of individual firms. Problem solving by skilled management teams is vitally concerned with responses to social, technological, and economic change. On the one hand, managers must take advantage of opportunities; on the other hand, they must maintain viability in unfavorable markets. Thus a major source of business risk— changing opportunities for profitable sales dollars—comes from external shifts in the environment.

It is useful to think of environmental change in terms of commodity life cycle theory. Unless a commodity is highly sensitive to fads, fashion, or technological revolution, an intelligent management should be able to recognize growth or decline behavior in various life stages and establish appropriate policy. Commodity life cycle and cash flow are examined in section 4.4. Usually seasonal patterns within a year are quite predictable. Again planning may be used to deploy human and physical capital appropriately. Environmental change, which is difficult to predict, comes from cycles in the economy, social control, and consumer tastes. Of these, the business cycle imposes a systematic risk over the spectrum of commercial enterprises. Some industries, such as food processing, may be cycle-insensitive, whereas others, such as the machine tool industry, are distinctly procyclical. It is difficult to think of business enterprises that are consistently countercyclical, but a possible candidate is automotive replacement parts. Systematic risk in going concerns is an important consideration in the development of a valuation model for a firm.

Since earnings are residual, the severity of an earnings reduction for a given decline in sales revenue will depend on what happens to costs. If costs were totally variable with sales and less than 100% of sales, then earnings would not fluctuate proportionately more than sales, and the risk of negative cash flows would be minimal. If most costs were fixed, however, then almost all of a shift in sales revenue would be passed directly into earnings. Suppose a firm has $100,000 sales, $95,000 costs, and $5000 earnings. During a recession sales revenue drop 10% to $90,000. If costs were totally variable, then costs would drop 10% along with sales to $85,500. Earnings would also drop 10% to $4500. Now suppose the original $95,000 costs were all fixed. Then earnings would have to absorb the entire sales revenue loss of $10,000. The recession earnings would go negative to –$5000. On the other hand, if sales increased by 10% to $10,000, the variable-cost firm would experience an increase in earnings to only $5500. The fixed-cost firm, however, would pass the sales revenue increase into a revised earnings figure of $15,000. Actual firms have some mixture of variable and fixed costs.

As cost structure moves from variable toward fixed, changes in sales revenue leverage into earnings. With fixed costs, or leverage, any increase in sales will produce a proportionately more favorable response in earnings, but a sales decrease may have a disastrous effect on earnings and lead to negative cash flows. Leverage is usually introduced into a firm to reduce its general level of costs. Thus a substitution of capital facilities, a long-term financial commitment, for variable payments to direct labor, purchased materials, rented equipment, or hired services, may increase efficiency at a sacrifice of flexibility. Such capital for direct-cost substitutions are often called *oper-*

ating leverage. In another type of substitution, debt may replace owners' equity in the capital structure of a firm. Now fixed charges for interest and repayment of principal are substituted for discretionary dividends and no obligation to repurchase capital. This is a type of exchange called *financial leverage*. Sometimes financial risk with financial leverage is separated from business risk with operating leverage. Such a separation is not important for the valuation methods here. (For a discussion of the cost of capital under financial leverage, see section 5.4.)

In real estate a counterpart of sales demand is *occupancy*. Most real estate investment depends heavily on financial leverage from purchase money mortgages with fixed payment schedules. To make a profit on real estate, investors usually operate with relatively low interest rates on mortgages secured by the properties. A combination of low occupancy and high financial leverage spells disaster for real estate owners. Real estate investment trusts, apartment complexes, office buildings, shopping malls, and motels are among real properties that depend on high occupancy for survival. Many of these and similar properties suffered severely in the recession of the early seventies. The concept of occupancy may be extended to capital investment in capacity for other types of businesses.

In coping with business risk, planners should first consider the industry sales environment. Particular attention must be given to risks from the business cycle or changes in consumer tastes. Key words for planning are *occupancy* (or *capacity*) and *leverage*. Resources should be deployed to avoid the trap of low occupancy combined with high leverage.

2.5 | Valuation of Going Concerns Under Risk

It is apparent that securities markets discount risky investments. Low-grade bonds require a higher coupon rate than high-grade bonds. Low-quality stocks sell for lower price-earnings multiples than high-quality stocks. *Quality* is simply a nonnumerical term for *risk*. Low-quality securities do not have safety of returns to investors, or, in other words, net cash throwbacks are subject to pronounced uncertainty. If the value —or price—of a security is simply a capitalization of future cash flows, then current price reflects the same uncertainty as future cash flows. The relationship between price and projected cash flows is examined further in section 5.2.

A strategic planning process is concerned with building economic value for a firm. The models in this book estimate economic value from various strategic scenarios. Economic value was defined in section 2.3 as the present value of projected cash outflows from the firm under risk. This system of valuation is often called "intrinsic worth" by investment analysts. A tremendous literature has been generated over a debate about the relation between market price and intrinsic worth. Is a market price simply a concensus at some point in time of intrinsic worth, or does it contain other inputs to valuation? Such other inputs, if they exist, may be lumped under "technical factors," such as the momentum of price movements or investor psychology.

Strategic planners need not take a particular position on the correspondence between market price and intrinsic worth. Some information that has emerged is important, however. If changes in projected performance of a firm become known to the financial community, both market price and intrinsic worth will reflect those changes. As noted above, the market discounts value for risk and will adjust price to reflect perceived changes in risk. All this does not mean that strategic planners will often be able to substitute market price for internal computations of value. In the valuation of alternative strategic scenarios, for example, market prices will be unavailable during planning. At the same time, however, market price is important to strategic planners. Probably nothing will topple an existing management faster than a downward plunge in a firm's stock price, especially when the market as a whole is strong. If a strategic planner builds economic value, then he or she is also bolstering market price. The latter is critically important to successful strategy. Market prices are significant to strategic planners in other ways. Empirical relations may be developed between market prices and risk. Such relations are used in the PAVE model to establish discount rates for cash flows (see section 5.5).

Modern theories of capital asset pricing are an extension of the theory of "efficient portfolios." This theory was developed in the early 1960s. The rate of return on a portfolio—a bundle of marketable securities—is an inverse function of risk. Risk can be measured statistically by fluctuations in projected rates of return. Usually the variance, or standard deviation, of a historical time series is used as an estimate of risk. To avoid artificial weighting, rates are used in place of dollar cash flows. A programming model could be operated to select an "efficient portfolio" from a universe of individual securities, each with its own rate of return and variance. The unit of decision is a portfolio because linear combinations of individual securities might be used to reduce risk without a corresponding sacrifice in the rate of return. To see this, note the division between *systematic* and nonsystematic risks among securities, as mentioned in section 2.4. Nonsystematic or random risk may be directly reduced by diversification; simply include unrelated industries in a portfolio. If risks are random, then some prices will rise while others go down. Under these conditions, portfolio combined value changes may be reduced. Systematic risk, such as a tendency of individual common stock prices to rise and fall together during market cycles, is much harder to eliminate. To reduce procyclical risk, for example, one needs countercyclical performance. Here is an example. If the rate of return (from dividends and price changes) on common stock A is 10% in a growth economy and –5% during recession, then an equal amount of bond B, with rates of return of –5% and 10% under growth and recession, respectively, will eliminate systematic risk. Try to find bond B today! Linear or quadratic programming models for efficient portfolios, however, would discover such opportunities to the extent available.

2.6 | Economic Value of the Firm

Economic value of a firm is measured by the present-value sum of future cash flows under risk. This is the end point of valuation processes by strategic planners and the PAVE model. It is worthwhile to look at this in the environment of an entire economy. An economy has limited human and capital resources; it must allocate these for the benefit of society. A firm is a system within society. It is not valuable for direct consumption; instead, it is an intermediary between resources and final consumption.

What then is the economic justification of a firm? It absorbs capital resources from society, resources which might otherwise be employed immediately toward consumption. A firm is awarded these resources in the hope that value transformations generated by it will enhance society's total consumption. Thus a firm is an input-output system for economic values. It receives valuable economic resources, and is supposed to return to society more value than was put in. The products of a manufacturing company should be more valuable than the sum of purchased materials, labor, and other expenses. Expenses, in turn, are absorbed in processes of development, production, and marketing. What happens to value surpluses? These are allocated to consumers of products, investors who supply capital, and other social units (taxes and contributions). Allocation procedures come from some combination of market mechanisms and social planning.

In considering value surpluses from a firm, it is useful to identify several levels. First, there is an operating level. Here managers are given capital resources, or operating assets, to deploy in the process of generating value transformations in commodities to enhance consumption. The surplus from this level—net cash flow on operations—is available to compensate suppliers of capital. The figure that appears on accounting income statements, net income on operations, is at the same level, but is the net of revenue and expense as defined in financial accounting. The accounting figure is also computed before income taxes. (Consult Table 4.1 for a comparison of accounting figures with the present values of cash flows described here.) At a second level, payments are made to suppliers of capital in the form of fixed obligations. The surplus from this level, net cash flow to owners, differs from net income after income taxes on income statements. The latter uses account values in place of cash flows. At a final level, one could deduct a competitive return to owners under risk. Then a final surplus —net cash flow pure economic profit—becomes a windfall to owners. Of course, surpluses at any level may be positive, negative, or zero.

A highly simplified illustration of the three levels is given below. An indefinite life is assumed, so the present values are capitalizations of perpetual, net-cash flow streams. Competitive rates of return under risk are assumed, which are not developed here explicitly. Expenditures apply to both current operations and perpetual maintenance of a stock of capital assets. Original amounts of owner and creditor capital are assumed to be maintained indefinitely and to receive competitive returns. Remember that each figure except the first two is a present-value sum of periodic cash flows.

Initial investment by creditors		50,000
Initial investment by owners		50,000
		100,000
Present value of sales revenues	400,000	
less present value of expenditures	270,000	
less present value of income taxes	25,000	
PRESENT VALUE NET CASH FLOW ON OPERATIONS	105,000	
less present value of payments to creditors	50,000	50,000
PRESENT VALUE NET CASH FLOW TO OWNERS	55,000	50,000
less present value of competitive return to owners	50,000	50,000
		0
PRESENT VALUE NET CASH PURE ECONOMIC PROFIT— WINDFALL TO OWNERS	5,000	

It is useful for a strategic planner to consider a firm as part of an economic environment. In identifying several levels of subsystems, problems of strategy make use of a systems framework. In terms of ultimate value to owners of firms, strategic plans are looking for positive "windfalls." At operating levels, useful plans develop positive consumption values. To suppliers of capital, plans should generate competitive returns under risk. In order to emphasize the total environment of an economy and an industry, the PAVE model starts with environmental analysis. This is strategic planning imbedded into a total economic system.

References and Additional Reading

A background in business statistics, which is required in this and subsequent chapters, should include summarizing data, probability concepts, and estimation of population parameters. In estimation, the important topics are point estimate of the mean, standard errors for estimating a population or its mean, and interval estimation. Any standard business statistics text discusses these topics. Examples are W.W. Daniel and J.C. Terrell, *Business Statistics*, 2nd ed., Houghton Mifflin, 1979, pp. 7-63, 150-67, and 181-83; and A. Hughes and D. Grawoig, *Statistics: A Foundation for Analysis*, Addison-Wesley, 1971, pp. 1-26 and 136-84.

Topics on risk measurement and the development of utility functions belong to the subject area decision theory and analysis. Excellent sources are available. Two matters of particular interest here are utility functions and probability assessment. For a general understanding of utility functions, see I. Horowitz, *An Introduction to Quantitative Business Analysis*, 2nd ed., McGraw-Hill, 1972, pp. 40-58; or P. Jedamus and R. Frame, *Business Decision Theory*, McGraw-Hill, 1969, pp. 1-51. Professional applications of utility theory in business are examined in C.S. Spetzler, "The Development of a Corporate Risk Policy for Capital Investment Decisions," in *IEEE Transactions on Systems Science and Cybernetics*, vol. SSC-4, no. 3, September 1968; and R.O. Swalm, "Utility Theory—Insights into Risk Taking," *Harvard Business Review*, November-December 1966. An excellent article on probability assessment is A. Tversley and D. Kahneman, "Judgment Under Uncertainty: Heuristics and Biases," in *Science*, vol. 185, September 1974.

Some readers may wish to delve further into *decision theory and analysis* than the topics covered in this book. The previous Horowitz, and Jedamus and Frame references may be used for this purpose. A more extensive work on decision theory is R.L. Winkler, *Introduction to Bayesian Inference and Decision*, Holt Rinehart & Winston, 1972. A compact introduction to decision analyses, with cases, is R.V. Brown, A.S. Kahr, an C. Peterson, *Decision Analysis: Overview*, Holt Rinehart & Winston, 1974.

An excellent survey of capital budgeting models for professionals will be found in H. Bierman, Jr., *Decision Making and Planning for the Corporate Treasurer*, Wiley, 1977; The capital-assets pricing model (CAPM) is discussed on pp. 177-88. Methods of capital budgeting and sources of risks are presented in texts on financial management. A good source is G.C. Philippatos, *Financial Management: Theory and Techniques*, Holden-Day, 1973, pp. 61-161. The economic nature of income and the relation of income to cash flows and risk are succinctly discussed by A.A. Robichek and S.C. Myers, *Optimal Financing Decision*, Prentice-Hall, 1965. An excellent book of readings on financial management is J.F. Weston and D.H. Woods, eds., *Basic Financial Management: Selected Readings*, Wadsworth, 1967.

Readings on portfolio theory and the relationship of market price behavior and intrinsic worth are collected in E.J. Elton and M.J. Gruber, eds., *Security Evaluation and Portfolio Analysis*, Prentice-Hall, 1972. See also the references listed for Chapter 5 of the present book.

PROBLEMS TO INVESTIGATE

2-1. Give examples of phenomena in the natural environment that support perceptions of order. Give other examples that support perceptions of chaos and uncertainty. In what sense is nature the source of both extremes?

2-2. Distinguish among certainty, uncertainty, and risk. Give examples of each.

2-3. What is the relationship between uncertainty and complexity? Between order and certainty? Between pattern and information?

2-4. Relate a point estimate to a single representative value, parallel values, and a sampling distribution of values. Compare a point estimate to a certain equivalent.

2-5. Using the methods of section 2.2 and Figure 2.2, develop several utility-of-money functions for yourself and others. Use a range such as $5,000 loss to $20,000 gain against current wealth. Compare the functions with respect to risk aversion. Develop some simple risk situation. Read the certain equivalents from the utility functions. Do the results seem consistent to people whose utilities have been plotted?

2-6. Is there some money range of lotteries over which you would become a risk seeker? If so, draw a utility function. Describe a simple lottery and locate its certain equivalent. Does the certain equivalent exceed the expected value of the lottery? The difference between the two is called a *risk premium*. Would you be willing to pay this risk premium to participate in the lottery?

2-7. A truck costs $12,000. Expected net cash flows after income taxes are $5000 for the first and second years, and $8000 for the third year. The last figure includes proceeds of selling the truck on the used market. Assign all cash flows to the ends of the years. Would you buy the truck under a payback rule of two years? Compute the return on investment (ROI). Would you buy the truck under ROI or present value methods with a "hurdle" rate of 18%. (ANS. Do not buy under two-year payback of $10,000, which is less than $12,000 cost. The ROI is about 21.3%, which is more than the 18% "hurdle" rate, so *buy*. The present value of cash throwbacks at 18% is $12,697.26. This exceeds the investment of $12,000, so buy.)

2-8. Define the following risks: *business, financial, inflation,* and *interest rate*. Give examples of each type. As an investor or manager, what steps might be taken to reduce or control each one of these types of risk?

2-9. Give industry examples of low, moderate, and high levels of operating leverage and financial leverage. How do these levels compare to the stability of sales demand in each example? Why are the levels appropriate?

2-10. Relate risk to occupancy for facilities investments in schools, churches, cafeterias, fast-food franchises, and parking garages.

2-11. Your stockbroker says you should diversify your portfolio and suggests some trades to increase the number of companies you own. All the shares would remain, however, in the same general class of growth stocks. Discuss the broker's proposal with respect to reduction of systematic and non-systematic risks.

2-12. A *firm* is a system in an environment of customers, suppliers of materials, suppliers of services, suppliers of labor, investors, and taxing authorities. Goods, services, and money pass across the boundaries of a firm to its environment. Identify the direction and type of real economic and money flows associated with sales revenue, payments of expenses, purchases of fixed assets, income taxes, leasehold improvements, payments of interest, retirement of debt, payments of dividends, and an issue of additional common shares.

3 Simulation Modeling

3.1 | Simulation of Decision Processes

A renewed interest in simulation methods has accompanied the introduction of decision support systems (DSS). The reason for this is clear; simulation may be applied to many different kinds of logical processes. Simulation is useful to represent complex chains of events which are beyond the reach of formula models in management science. Accounting transactions, production control, emergency room procedures, traffic flows, and routing of customers through checkouts are a few examples of processes which may be simulated. Simulation is a number-crunching tool, hence a partner of digital computers. An interactive minicomputer, with its flexibility and low cost, makes it feasible to simulate difficult types of problems. As mentioned in section 1.3, the PAVE model is a large simulation that operates on minicomputers. The information in this chapter is not limited to just the PAVE model; rather, an effort has been made to explore a range of simulation capabilities. This will give readers a starting point for the design of DSS models. Section 3.2 examines simulation as a dynamic process in comparison to other management science models. Structures of simulations and related decision techniques are examined in section 3.3. Monte Carlo simulation, which is the fundamental model of PAVE, uses methods of statistical inference; some of these methods are summarized in section 3.4. Simulation design problems are taken up in section 3.5. The validity and relevance of simulation models are discussed in section 3.6.

Although simulations may require a great deal of number crunching, the modeling often follows the same step-by-step processing as a rational manager would use when making a decision. For this reason it may be easier for a manager to accept the structure of a simulation than the logic of mathematical formulas in other types of models. Add to this the capabilities of simulation for risk analysis, and management has a powerful tool for decision. Simulation emphasizes the dynamics of problem areas; it provides models of process change. Since managers are "change agents," they may be able to study more consequences of environmental shifts with simulation than with alternative techniques. Of course there are disadvantages to simulation. These are noted in section 3.2.

The word *simulation* means literally *pretend*, and the process of simulation is like traveling in a time machine. Thus a strategist with pencil and paper, often with the aid of a computer, can cover years of planning in a few hours. Budgets and sets of pro forma accounting statements are in themselves a form of simulation. Simulation is not new—all plans involve simulation—but inexpensive computing makes statistical outputs feasible for the description of large systems.

Three treatments of time may be recognized in model building:

1. Static models use variables that express condition at some point in time. These models are snapshots of status; time does not enter as an explicit variable. Examples are an accounting balance sheet and a present value sum of cash flows.

2. Rate models use variables that describe flows over some specified time interval. Again, time is not an explicit variable in the formulation. Sometimes rate models are classified as comparative statics. Examples are income, cost, and funds-flow statements.

3. Dynamic models describe a process or sequence as a set of transformations of status variables. Such sets are consequences of the passage of time. Thus, time is an active variable in the logical development. Examples are queues, production control, and product life cycles.

Simulation is dynamic because a logic of process is reproduced in the model. A stochastic process is a time series with explicit inclusion of risk by means of probability distributions. Simulations may be either deterministic (no specific components of uncertainty) or probabilistic (stochastic). Stochastic simulation provides a new dimension of power for decisions in complex situations.

Simulation is often an alternative to analytical models. The latter refers to models that organize input-output relationships with a small set of mathematical expressions. Thus sets of equations may be used to summarize the outputs of queueing theory, inventory models, or Markovian processes. If these same processes are simulated, much more information about behavior will be generated. On the other hand, the cost of computations will rise and optimal values must be estimated indirectly. Figure 3.1 suggests some relationships between simulation and other management science models. There are choices between simulation and other methods for the two middle blocks in the right-hand column. Simulation would be required, however, when a real situation failed to meet the simplifying assumptions of analytical models.

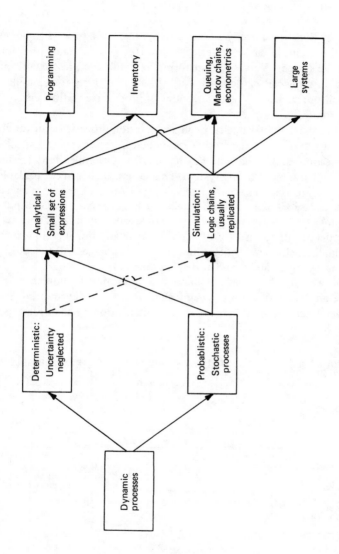

Figure 3.1 Dynamic model building

3.2 | The Dynamics of Simulation

A modeler of simulations must study the underlying logic of a process to be represented. What are the chains of cause and effect? How is each value transformation related to others in the system? Values of transformations will be expressed with either or both numerical and logical relations. In a development of logic for a simulation, model builders will use such tools as descriptions of process steps, flow charts, and computer programming.

Variables are transporters of value through a simulation process. Input variables, outside or exogenous to the system, describe user policies, are under user control, and allocate available resources. Another set of exogenous input variables describes initial conditions and the environment of the system. This set is usually not controllable by users. Status variables are used to keep track of value transformations within a system. They change value as logico-mathematical simulation steps are executed. Output variables are endogenous to the system since they are developed internally. Output variables provide model results for users. Although there are additional complexities in the design of simulators, all contain these three classes of variables. All execute a processing sequence as described above and as diagrammed in Figure 3.2.

The process of preparing financial statements is a deterministic simulation. Here, the economic life and value of a firm is being simulated by the accounting model. Management makes input decisions in the form of capitalization, financing, assets pur-

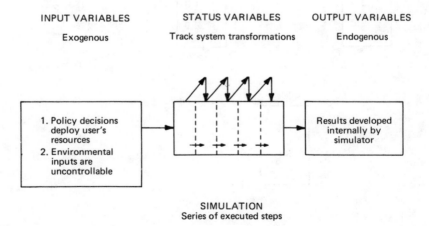

Figure 3.2 Classes of variables in a simulation process

chases, marketing, and operations policies. The firm operates in an economic environment during each period. Status variables keep track of economic entities such as cash, sales, expense, inventories, debt, and owners' equity. Outputs are obtained from financial statements after closing the books at the end of a period. One is interested in the scope and value of a firm, its financial condition, and the levels of profitability.

Some advantages of a simulation as a modeling system are the following:

1. Complex logic and computation may be processed through a simulator, but they may not be managable with formula-type models.
2. Simulations usually provide more behavioral information than do other techniques.
3. Simulations are concerned with process. This facilitates management of change and sensitivity analysis.
4. Simulation is more likely to represent the thinking of managers than other types of modeling. This means that executives can participate actively in formulating and reviewing the model logic. Not only is such participation likely to improve model performance, but it tends to reduce problems of acceptance and implementation.
5. A simulation designer must study a system in detail, reviewing the ramifications of logic before a useful simulation can be constructed. One cannot simply patch on a short-cut model, which is a potential danger with other techniques.
6. The output of simulation often meets behavioral goals, such as satisficing and adaptation, rather than just quantitative goals, such as optimization.

Disadvantages of simulation include the following:

1. Relatively speaking, the amount of computation or number crunching, and the preparation of models, is time-consuming for simulations. Both humans and computers must work harder.
2. A simulation model grows geometrically as detail is added.
3. Simulation models tend to be custom designed for a particular situation, or ad hoc. This difficulty is partly overcome with interactive inputs and flexible logic as used in models such as PAVE.
4. Simulation outputs may lack generalization of systemic behavior, such as optimization of the system. Although these limitations may be partially overcome, this is usually accomplished at considerable cost.
5. Simulation is sometimes used as an inferior surrogate for mathematical models. Simulation may permit levels of abstraction to be reduced and thus avoid formidable mathematics. This kind of substitution can be inefficient if a mathematical model is available for direct solution of the same problem.

3.3 | Structures for Simulations

A large range of management science situations can be simulated. Several technical terms appear in connection with this work. Some important ones are defined in the following paragraphs.

An *algorithm* is a set of specific rules that defines a process leading to a planned output result. Flight instructions from Birmingham to Atlanta constitute an algorithm. In the modeling, field examples are instructions to invert a matrix or to reach an optimal solution in linear programming. Procedures for closing accounts or processing units through a queue are examples of algorithms that would appear in simulation models. Ordinary computer coding is an algorithm for processing some sequence of logic.

Artificial intelligence is the attempted simulation of human thought with machines such as computers. Heuristic methods are often used. Important subareas include pattern recognition, linguistic structure, and robotology. Artificial-intelligence methods are being used to help computers read printed numbers or translate languages.

Econometrics is a set of techniques for building statistical models of the economy, particularly the large-scale macroeconomy. Such models are formulated with sets of equations developed with such techniques as regression and time-series analysis. Because models of the economy lead to stochastic processes, simulation is often useful for the study of behavior under uncertainty over a number of periods. Such simulations project the logic of functional relationships that were previously estimated by statistical methods. Econometric models are used to develop forecasts of the economy.

Gaming is a simulation with periodic human intervention in the process. Human decision is injected at intervals to review results and reset policy variables. In a management game the operations of firms in an industry are simulated over some set of periods. At the end of each period, simulated results are reviewed by human decision makers. Policy changes are fed into the process before simulating the next period. A person or team, as a human decision unit, may be assigned to each of a set of competing firms. The "game" then consists of determining which firm achieves the best performance.

Heuristic methods are used to extend problem-solving power. *Heuristic* is a Greek word meaning "discovery." In management science the term applies to search procedures based on rules that assumed to be analogous to intelligent problem solving. Unlike algorithms, heuristic rules do not guarantee a desired outcome. Heuristics often, but not necessarily, include internal mechanisms for improvement based on experience (artificial intelligence). Heuristics frequently use simulation as a framework for developing outputs. Computers that play games, such as chess, may employ heuristic methods. A computer may be programmed to try out different moves and to "learn" a preference for those that lead to a favorable outcome.

Model sampling is a technique that uses a stochastic process to determine, from multiple trials, values of probability distributions or areas under a curve. Model sampling uses the Monte Carlo method; hence, it is a type of simulation. It is not used in PAVE or other models that are concerned with process.

Monte Carlo techniques utilize a series of pseudo-random numbers to systematically represent uncertainty in a modeling process. The term *pseudo-random numbers* is used here to describe sets of digits generated by a computer to have values uniformly distributed between zero and one. The number of decimal places can be controlled by users. Random numbers can be obtained from printed tables, arithmetic-generating formulas, or system-defined functions in computer languages. Probabilistic simulations use Monte Carlo methods to provide controlled risk. PAVE obtains pseudo-random numbers from system-defined functions.

The statistical properties (probability distributions) of a simulation are seldom represented directly by random numbers between zero and one. Instead, simulators will wish to input uncertainty with some chosen probability distribution and parameters. Here, a *parameter* is a numerical specification for a probability distribution. Thus, times between arrivals into a queue in front of bank-teller windows can be distributed exponentially with a mean of 35 seconds. Process generators convert an input series of ordinary random numbers into an output stream of random values or vectors (sets of values). The output values will conform to a user choice of probability model and parameters.

Simulations may be classified by the method of updating transformations in the system. Each step or cycle of a simulation takes users through a set of value transformations. How should intervals between steps be determined? For event-oriented or discrete-occurrence simulations, the system is updated each time a significant event takes place. In queueing, for example, a new unit arrives or a unit goes into service. Another orientation, often called a *period-oriented* simulation, depends on information flow and efficiency. If there are only a few types of events, and time spans between them are irregular, *event-oriented* processing is usually preferred. Period-oriented simulations, on the other hand, are almost always employed for complex, multidependent systems of events. PAVE is a period-oriented financial simulation.

Event-oriented simulations normally use a variable time-step (asynchronous) plan, since the system is updated when irregularly spaced events occur. If times between events have been divided into small equal intervals, however, event-oriented simulations may use a *fixed-time increment* plan. Period-oriented simulations always use a fixed-time increment plan, usually with equal time periods (synchronous, as PAVE in this book). In both real situations and simulations, for example, accounting transactions are closed into financial reports at regular time intervals. In simulations one goes by the "clock." This is a variable charged with recording elapsed time and controlling when the next round of transformations will take place.

Simulations may be designed as deterministic (no randomized components) or statistical. Statistical simulations use Monte Carlo methods for process generators and statistical sampling. In Monte Carlo, statistical outputs are obtained from planned distributions of risk in the inputs. The Monte Carlo method is a powerful tool because it is often impossible to quantify uncertainty by direct application of statistical formulas. Figure 3.3 is a diagram of various categories of simulations. The directions of arrows show the range of choices available among the blocks.

Here is a checklist of steps in the preparation of a simulation:

1. The problem situation should be carefully specified, with an outline of the information to be obtained.

2. A plan of outputs, options, and limitations should be stated explicitly, with a clear declaration of the goals of the decision model.

3. Is simulation the answer? Examine the cost and feasibility of alternatives. What is the risk of failure to produce useful results? What specific trade off is to be negotiated between complexity of the simulated system and the time and cost of preparing the model? What kind of balance should be achieved among subareas of the model?

4. What data are available for operating the model? In what form? Is model effort compatible with the quality of the data?

5. Develop an abstract of the model:
   (a) define variables: input, output, and status
   (b) make specific decisions on detail levels, precision, and statistical significance
   (c) establish relationships among the variables
   (d) flowchart the logic of the model

6. Prepare the model:
   (a) develop required mathematical-logical routines for establishing relationships among variables
   (b) choose a simulation language or standard language (if computerized)
   (c) code, test run, and pilot run the program

7. Execute simulations:
   (a) collect input data
   (b) estimate or otherwise obtain parameters for runs
   (c) design a set of experiments to meet objectives
   (d) decide which runs are necessary and establish stopping conditions

8. Evaluate and validate the model (see section 3.6):
   (a) perform sensitivity analysis on outputs
   (b) compare results with historical behavior
   (c) analyze predictions of the model
   (d) perform statistical tests of significance when relevant

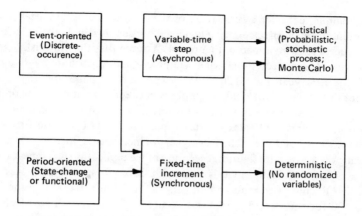

Figure 3.3 Block diagram of simulation structures

3.4 | Monte Carlo Method of Simulation

Monte Carlo method is used in PAVE and most other statistical simulations. The discussion here is divided into three parts: logic processing, statistical analysis of outputs, and the design of process generators. Monte Carlo method always starts with random numbers. Random numbers are used to supply predetermined risk to some inputs. Outputs then belong to sampling distributions whose parameters may be estimated by methods of statistical inference.

The process of a Monte Carlo simulation goes through the following steps:

1. Obtain a random number between zero and one for each risky input.

2. Transform each random number to a variate value from a probability distribution that has been chosen to represent that risky value. There must be a random number, a probability distribution, and a generated variate value for each risky input.

3. Run the complete logic and computations over *all* periods from inputs to outputs. Risky inputs will be supplied variate values from 2. At the end of this step, one sample replication will have been completed.

4. Repeat steps 1 through 3 until a predetermined sample size has been run. Each replication uses a different set of risky inputs because the set of random numbers is different. A given risky input, however, always conforms to the same predetermined probability distribution.

5. Outputs vary because the inputs vary. The outputs belong to a sampling distribution. This distribution may be subjected to the estimation methods of statistical inference.

As an example, consider a simulation of the condition of a firm after two years. Assume ordinary financial accounting logic will be used. A sample size of three is chosen. The process is diagrammed in Figure 3.4. Assume that the only risky inputs are sales each year. It is expected that sales will be *normally* distributed with a mean of $100,000 the first year and $120,000 the second year. The standard deviation is $10,000 for both years. Two random numbers between zero and one are drawn, one for each year's sales. These numbers are transformed into sales figures by a process generator. Assume that sales variates come out $86,000 for the first year and $121,000 for the second year. Then two years of income and financial condition will be run, using the above sales figures. A second sample replication will repeat the whole financial analysis over again but this time with different sales figures. Assume, for example, that the next two random numbers yield sales of $104,000 for the first year and $128,000 for the second year. The second set of outputs will be different from the first because the inputs were different. A third replication will then be run to complete the sample. This draws two more random numbers and develops yet another set of sales figures. Again, the outputs are different. A sample size of three would be too small for most applications, but it does serve to illustrate the whole process.

Statistical estimation theory may be used to make inferences about important output values. The usual population parameter estimates of interest are the mean, standard deviation of the population, standard deviation of the mean, confidence limits for population values, and confidence limits for means. Although estimation procedures and formulas come straight out of elementary business statistics texts, they are repeated below for convenience. The BASIC coding of each estimate is shown beneath conventional formulas.

sum of variates $\qquad = \Sigma X \;= S1$

sum of squares of variates $= \Sigma X^2 = S2$

number of variate values $\; = N \quad =$ sample size

student's t-statistic $\qquad = T$

lower confidence limit $\quad = L$

upper confidence limit $\quad = U$

mean $\overline{X}$ or M

$\quad \overline{X} = \Sigma X/N$ statistical formula

$\quad M = S1/N$ BASIC coding

standard deviation of population

$$\hat{\sigma}_x = \sqrt{\frac{N(\Sigma X^2) - (\Sigma X)^2}{N(N-1)}} = \sqrt{\frac{\Sigma X^2 - N\overline{X}^2}{N-1}} \quad \text{statistical formula}$$

S = SQR((N*S2–S1*S1)/(N*(N–1))) = SQR((S2–N*M*M)/(N–1))   BASIC

standard deviation of the mean

$$\hat{\sigma}_{\overline{x}} = \sqrt{\frac{N(\Sigma X^2) - (\Sigma X)^2}{N^2(N-1)}} \quad \sqrt{\frac{\Sigma X^2 - N\overline{X}^2}{N(N-1)}} \quad \text{statistical formula}$$

SO = SQR((N*S2–S1*S1)/(N*N*(N–1)))
   = SQR((S2–N*M*M)/(N*(N–1)))   BASIC

confidence limits for population values

$$L = \overline{X} - T\hat{\sigma}_x \text{ and } U = \overline{X} + T\hat{\sigma}_x \quad \text{statistical formula}$$
$$L = M - T*S \text{ and } U = M + T*S \quad \text{BASIC}$$

confidence limits for the mean

$$L = \overline{X} - T\hat{\sigma}_{\overline{x}} \text{ and } U = \overline{X} + T\hat{\sigma}_{\overline{x}} \quad \text{statistical formula}$$
$$L = M - T*SO \text{ and } U = M + T*SO \quad \text{BASIC}$$

In the two-year accounting simulation, assume that owners' equity is an important output. To use the formulas above for statistical estimation, one needs only the sum S1 and sum of squares S2 from the sample replications. Such values are easily accumulated as each replication is completed. Accounting and financial simulations are linear combinations of inputs. This means that the central limit theorem of statistics applies to distributions of outputs. If there are more than a few steps between inputs and outputs, outputs will be approximately normally distributed. Thus the Student's t-statistic may be used for small sample inference of confidence limits. Tables of t-statistics may be found in most statistics texts and handbooks. A t-statistic is chosen that matches a desired risk level of estimation with degrees of freedom. In the for-

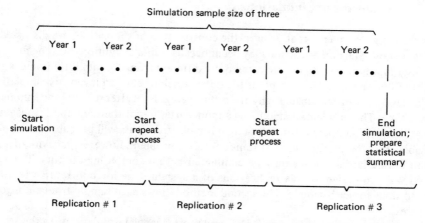

Figure 3.4 Sample replications of a two-year simulation

mulas above, degrees of freedom are always one less than sample size; in the two-year accounting simulation, for example, sample size was three. For a 90% confidence level with two degrees of freedom, the t-statistic is 2.92. Assume that one of the outputs is owners' equity with a mean of $150,000 and a standard deviation of the mean of $12,000. The lower upper confidence limits of mean owners' equity are then $114,960 and $185,040.

The PAVE simulation computes estimates of means, standard deviations of means, and confidence limits for means. In one output division the maximum and minimum sample outputs are also printed. PAVE users need not look up t-statistics in tables. A choice of sample size will lead to representative confidence intervals (Table 8.2).

Routines called process generators convert random numbers into risk-adjusted inputs from a specified probability distribution. One method, which is used in PAVE, is illustrated here. It is an inverse transformation for a symmetric, triangular distribution. For each probability distribution there is a corresponding cumulative distribution. For each value X on the horizontal axis of a cumulative distribution, the probability of obtaining X or less is plotted on the vertical axis. These cumulative probabilities vary between zero and one, which is the same range as uniformly distributed random numbers R. By inverting the formula for cumulative probabilities, one may solve for variate values X. These variates are an inverse function of cumulative probabilities or random numbers R. Figure 3.5 diagrams the triangular probability and cumulative distributions, develops inverse formulas, and illustrates the generation of risk-adjusted inputs. Problems 3-5 to 3-7 at the end of the chapter illustrate a complete, simplified, Monte Carlo simulation by presenting inverse transformations of two discrete probability distributions.

3.5 | Some Design Problems in Simulations

Some design problems that arise in the construction of simulations are discussed in this section. Start-up distortion may occur because initial conditions must be supplied as user inputs. These inputs are often quite different from the equilibrium values generated during runs. An example is the initial stock level of an inventory simulation. This level may differ substantially from the average level after receipts and shipments over time. The problem of stabilizing a model after initial transient conditions is primarily one of sample design. If a sample is large, transients will probably have a negligible effect on performance. If transients are a problem, however, behavior of a system during initial periods may be eliminated before computing outputs. There are two ways to design sample replications of a system. One method returns to initial conditions for each sample. The second method draws each sample from an ongoing process.

The first method is used in PAVE and most financial simulations. In the second method, a stabilization interval is required only once at the beginning of a simulation.

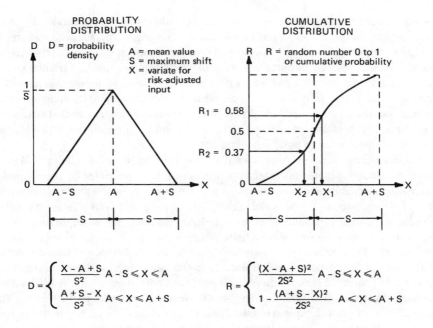

$$D = \begin{cases} \dfrac{X - A + S}{S^2} & A - S \leqslant X \leqslant A \\[2mm] \dfrac{A + S - X}{S^2} & A \leqslant X \leqslant A + S \end{cases}$$

$$R = \begin{cases} \dfrac{(X - A + S)^2}{2S^2} & A - S \leqslant X \leqslant A \\[2mm] 1 - \dfrac{(A + S - X)^2}{2S^2} & A \leqslant X \leqslant A + S \end{cases}$$

Solving the right-hand equations give input variates X from random numbers R:

$$X = \begin{cases} A + S \left(\sqrt{2R} - 1\right) & 0 \leqslant R \leqslant 0.5 \\[2mm] A + S \left(1 - \sqrt{2 - 2R}\right) & 0.5 \leqslant R \leqslant 1 \end{cases}$$

As a numerical example, suppose mean sales are $150,000 per year with maximum shift of 10%. Then A is 150,000 and S is 15,000. Two random numbers are drawn, 0.58 and 0.37. Compute the corresponding input variate values:

If $R_1 = 0.58$, $X_1 = 150000 + 15000(1 - \sqrt{2 - 2(0.58)}) = \$151,252.27$

If $R_2 = 0.37$, $X_2 = 150000 + 15000(\sqrt{2(0.37)} - 1) = \$147,903.49$

When R = 0, then X = $135,000; when R = 1, then X = $165,000

Figure 3.5 Triangular distribution process generator

This is an efficient plan unless variations among simulated periods are substantial. In many simulations such as inventory models, user interest focuses on typical, or average, conditions generated during runs. In such cases initial conditions are a distortion, and terminal conditions carry no particular interest. There are exceptions. In queueing one may be interested in starting with a particular situation such as opening a facility with no one in the system. Concerning queues, there is usually little interest in particular terminal positions. In financial and macroeconomic simulations, however, both initial and terminal states provide important information (this is true of PAVE).

Seed numbers are random numbers which are initially assigned to a simulation. Two series of computer-generated pseudo-random numbers may be kept identical if they are begun with the same seed number. For a single run, the starting seed number may be unimportant. But often one wishes to run several parallel simulations, to compare outputs in response to controlled changes of inputs. If all runs begin with the same seed number, an important source of "between-treatment" variance will be eliminated. Prime numbers—with rejection of numbers ending in even digits, zero, or five—should be chosen for seed numbers. This reduces systematic components in the random number series generated. PAVE programs should be coded so that an internal seed number generates identical sets of random numbers for each run. If this is done, users will seldom need to enter a seed number in the input set.

Variance-reduction techniques can be used to improve efficiency. "Within-treat" variance simulates uncertainty within a run. It is controlled by users through parameter specification of process generators (see section 3.4). As mentioned above, the efficiency of comparison and decision is improved as between-treatment variance is reduced. Several variance-reduction techniques are available. In importance sampling, outcomes of interest are artificially weighted heavier in sample size (number of replications) than those of less interest. Such artificial weights require later correction to remove the "importance bias." In antithetic variance reduction, the second half of a total set of generated random numbers is produced with rules so that it is negatively correlated with the first half. The end result is less total variance in the system. This variance-reduction technique is not used in PAVE because of flexibility in the number of uncertain inputs and in run length. It would be difficult to predict the total quantity of required random numbers in advance.

Values in a time series are often autocorrelated. This means that residual (unexplained) quantities at different points in the series are systematically related to each other in one or more ways. This period's sales, for example, might not only be related to last period's sales but to a series of prior sales. In such a case, the differences among sales of successive periods would be related or correlated. Methods are available for simulating specified proportions of autocorrelation within a sequence of generated random variables. Such adjustment may become important to duplicate the actual behavior of a time series. PAVE builds time series with first-order residuals (differences between successive period values) uncorrelated. There would be some justification for introducing autocorrelation into the coding of dynamic values over periods.

3.6 | Validity and Relevance with Simulation Models

In evaluating the usefulness of models two important areas are relevance and validity. Relevance inquires whether a model has any cost-effective value for the problem at hand, whereas validity questions the level of confidence at which inferences drawn from the model apply to a real system. With respect to relevance, we are concerned first that a model behave as the experimenter intended. Thus part of evaluation is verification that a model is internally consistent. Its design structure must be capable of reproducing important features of the real system. Another aspect of relevance is the ability of a model to permit analysis and interpretation of outputs. How much risk is connected with applying to a real problem the results of operating the model? The precision of a model usually moves in an opposite direction from relevance and validity. A model may be so crude that no one would question its ball-park conclusions. The model may fail, however, in the matter of relevance, because it yields no useful information. Usually there is some point in the refinement of a model, both with respect to the degree of internal complexity and the precision of data manipulation, whichever is most cost effective in application. This point is often difficult to find.

Probably the most important aspect of model evaluation is validity. Seeking agreement between a model and a real system, or correspondence between simulator and reality, might, at first glance, appear simple. But there are several difficulties. Validation is not yes or no, but a matter of degree. Samuel Johnson once said: "Nothing will ever be attempted if all possible objections must be first overcome." The economics of validation require a balance between development cost and the worth of the model to decision makers. Development cost includes effort spent to draw inferences from the real world and adjust model performance. Incremental funds spent on validation usually yield diminishing marginal support for a model. This means that the benefit-cost ratio from model development will probably peak at something less than the most valid possible model.

Apart from questions of how much to spend on validation, there is the intriguing question of how to proceed with a validation. Correspondence between a model and reality seems clear enough, but just what is reality, and what kinds of reality are important? One is plunged into philosophical problems of how to transfer information from observations to organized knowledge of the real world. There are subjectivists who pursue an internal and intuitive development of beliefs; and there are objectivists who insist that all admitted relationships must be supported by observations. In pursuing the truth about reality, problem-solving methodology has achieved a counterpoint between the subjective and the objective. The process of science shifts back and forth between erecting theories and the demand for empirical verification.

A brief review of the philosophical bases for discovering reality suggests three main lines of thought. All start with observations of the real world; the difference among them depends on the way order and system are perceived. A rationalist stresses internal consistency through the use of hypothetical logical-mathematical models. Any construct that does not fly in the face of observed facts is admissible on an *a priori* basis. Such constructs may or may not be open to empirical verification or objective experience. The rationalist is interested in what-if questions.

An empiricist puts primary emphasis on observed data, refusing to entertain relationships that have not been supported independently by experiments with empirical data. A pragmatist is concerned with usefulness, with "truth in application," rather than internal structure or abstractions from knowledge explanations. An exaggerated statement of this point of view might go like this: "If the model works, who cares why?" A pragmatist is not disorderly, but has merely transferred the level of thought to an external system. Pragmatist validation is based on inputs and outputs of a model. Internal relationships are treated as a "black box."

The previous mention of scientific method suggests that all three philosophical bases have merit. One might define a combination as a utilitarian approach to validation. The suggestions below reflect such treatment.

First, examine a face validity on the performance of a model. Does its internal structure give consistent responses? Does it cover the required scope? Does it provide creditable solutions for both ordinary and extreme inputs? Does it come up with results that are intuitively plausible to decision makers? Does the model conform to prior knowledge, past research, and existing theory? Does a change in inputs lead to expected changes in outputs? Face validity is a modified rationalist point of view.

Test the model with available data, using methods of statistical inference and experimental design. Will our hypotheses about relationships, types of functions, choices of probability distributions, and parameters stand up under statistical tests? This is an empirical emphasis.

Can the model predict outputs similar to what really would happen from a given input set? This kind of validation comes from a comparison of input-output transformations. In an *ex ante* validation one uses data from the more distant past to predict behavior in the more recent past. The predicted behavior is then compared directly with actual behavior—both in the recent past. This is a powerful form of validation in application. Of course, success in historical prediction is no guarantee for the future. An ex post validation must await the unfolding of future events. Some models are so critical to life, such as those that describe the reaction of the human body to chemicals, that, regardless of cost, it will take years of testing to gain acceptance. In these extreme cases, nothing short of thorough ex post validation is tenable. The pragmatic validations described here are probably the most powerful for convincing manager-users. They may be technical in nature—such as correlation studies, statistical goodness of fit, or spectral analysis—or they may be human, as in the famous Turing test. Here, a decision model is validated by observing whether a specialist can distinguish the output of the model from that of an informed, human decision maker. Other pragmatic validations are carried out with demonstrations, field tests, case studies, convenience samples, and pilot runs.

Since simulation models are often erected for complex systems, validation may prove extremely difficult. The real situation just does not lend itself to controlled experiments. This problem has hampered the acceptance of simulation, particularly among empiricists. In part, the utilitarian approach demands that model builders relate closely to purposes and expected claims. A scenario-building simulation constructed to explore possibilities and examine ideas should not be discarded for lack of hard evidence. It is clear that all useful simulations must pass reasonable tests of face validity. Beyond this, controlled experiments and *ex ante* replication studies increase validity. The depth of such studies should correspond to the economic and human consequences of decisions reached with the model.

References and Additional Readings

For a comprehensive examination of scientific models available for management problem solving, see M.F. Rubenstein, *Patterns of Problem Solving*, Prentice-Hall, 1975. Another excellent work, which is restricted to conventional management science methods, is the Horowitz book referenced in Chapter 2. Both books avoid heavy mathematics. For a general text on management science methods, which does not exceed a level of ordinary business mathematics, consult A.V. Cabot and D.L. Harnett, *An Introduction to Management Science*, Addison-Wesley, 1977.

Readers may wish to consult additional sources on simulation techniques. The management science references above all have some material that serves as an introduction to simulation. An excellent book that surveys the field with a minimum of mathematical statistics is J.R. Emshoff and R.L. Sisson, *Design and Use of Computer Simulation Models*, Macmillan, 1970. For a reference work to important techniques, consult G.S. Fishman, *Concepts and Methods in Discrete Event Digital Simulation*, Wiley, 1973. Books of readings are H. Guetzkow, P. Kotler, and R.L. Schultz, eds., *Simulation in Social and Administrative Science*, Prentice-Hall, 1972; and A.N. Schrieber, ed., *Corporate Simulation Models*, Office of Publications, Graduate School of Business Administration, University of Washington, 1970.

For an introduction to computers as problem-solving tools, some excellent books are E.M. Awad, *Introduction to Computers in Business*, Prentice-Hall, 1977; and E.A. Tomeski, *Fundamentals of Computers in Business: A Systems Approach*, Holden-Day, 1979. Moving to the area of information processing, some recommended readings are A.F. Cardenas, *Data Base Management Systems*, Allyn and Bacon, 1979; and R.J. Thierauf, *Distributed Processing Systems*, Prentice-Hall, 1978. The use of computers for simulation and model building is the topic of an excellent book—T.G. Lewis and B.J. Smith, *Computer Principles of Modeling and Simulation*, Houghton-Mifflin, 1979. To a considerable extent the information revolution is built on the technology of microprocessing. A somewhat technical book in this area, but one with simple explanations, is A. Veronis, *Microprocessors: Design and Applications*, Reston Publishing, 1978.

The industrial and social implications of computers are discussed in V.Z. Brink, *Computers and Management*, Prentice-Hall, 1971; and S. Rothman and C. Mosmonn, *Computers and Society*, Science Research Associates, 1972.

For readings on the relationship of computers and thought, E. Feigenbaum and J. Feldman, eds., *Computers and Thought*, McGraw-Hill, 1963, is still one of the best sources available. For a nontechnical introduction to artificial intelligence, see H.A. Simon, *The Sciences of the Artificial*, M.I.T. Press, 1969. For further readings in this area, consult E.B. Hunt, *Artificial Intelligence*, Academic Press, 1975; B. Raphael, *The Thinking Computer*, W.H. Freeman, 1976; and readings from M.A. Sass and W.D. Wilkinson, *Computer Augmentation of Human Reasoning*, Macmillan, 1965.

Questions of the validity of science are discussed in broad perspective by T.S. Kuhn in *The Structure of Scientific Revolutions*, 2nd ed., Univ. of Chicago Press, 1970. A comprehensive chapter on the validation of experiments was written by T.D. Cook and D.T. Campbell under the title "The Design and Conduct of Quasi-Experiments and True Experiments in Field Settings," chap. 7 in M. Dunnette, ed., *Handbook of Industrial and Organizational Psychology*, Rand McNally, 1976.

PROBLEMS TO INVESTIGATE

3-1. Describe some business problem situations in which DSS methods would be useful. How many of these situations might employ simulation techniques? What consideration might be given to uncertainty in each situation?

3-2. Which of the three treatments of time—static, rate, and dynamic—may be associated with the following management-science techniques: programming, queueing, inventory control, financial accounting, present value of cash flows, and Markov chains?

3-3. Develop problems to illustrate inventory control, queueing, and Markov chains. For each problem, how much information can be obtained from an analytical formulation? Under what conditions would it be necessary to replace analytic formulas with simulation? Identify input, status, and output variables for each problem.

3-4. Choose an inventory, a queueing, and a financial-accounting situation and design a simulation for each. Describe the operation of the "clock." How are intervals chosen to update each system? How is information collected during each interval?

3-5. Prepare a table of generated inputs under uncertainty for an oversimplified Monte Carlo simulation of earnings during a period. Earnings for one period are to be calculated as the difference between sales revenue and expense over a sample size of three. Uncertainty in sales revenue is to be represented by a discrete probability distribution of four values. The probability of $80,000 sales is 0.3, of $90,000 sales is 0.1, of $100,000 sales is 0.4, and of $110,000 sales is 0.2. A discrete probability distribution will also be used to represent uncertainty of expense. It is represented with three values: $75,000 with a probability of 0.3, $80,000 with 0.4, and $85,000 with 0.3. A series of random numbers from a table is 0.15, 0.47, 0.48, 0.93, 0.40, 0.07, 0.73, and 0.92.

   (ANSWER: cumulative probabilities for the four sales values "or less" are 0.3, 0.4, 0.8, and 1.0, respectively; and for the three expense values "or less" are 0.3, 0.7, and 1.0, respectively. A pair of random numbers for sales revenue and expense will be needed for each of the three sample replications. Using random numbers in the order given, the sales and expense pairs will be $80,000 and $80,000, $100,000 and $85,000, and $100,000 and $75,000. Note that random number 0.00 will be assigned to the lowest values and that a number at a boundary—in this case, 0.40 —will be assigned to the higher adjacent value. These sets of values are examples of inverse transformation method applied to discrete probability distributions.)

3-6. What are the simulated *outputs* from problem 3-5?

(ANSWER: sample earnings outputs are $0, $15,000, and $25,000.)

3-7. Obtain estimates of the value of earnings, using methods of statistical inference.

(ANSWER: a point estimate from the sample mean is $13,333. Estimates of the standard deviation are $12,583 for the population and $7265 for the mean. Confidence limits at 90%, with two degrees of freedom, would require a t-statistic of 2.92. The limits here are –$23,409 to $50,075 for earnings and –$7,881 to $34,547 for mean earnings. The sample size was so small that limits are extremely wide; there is limited value to this information.)

3-8. Consider queueing simulations such as representations of people or machines waiting for service. Decide on start-up conditions and the treatment of atypical performance.

3-9. Describe some situations in which time series of values might be auto-correlated. Suggest a method to introduce autocorrelation into such series.

3-10. Consider some financial simulation. Describe a systematic process for checking face validity. Suggest some methods of empirical verification. Relate various purposes of the simulation to the effort spent on empirical verification.

4 Accounting Information and Valuation

4.1 | **Flows and Position in the Financial Accounting Model**

Financial accounting is an important model system to strategic planners. Not only does it provide a framework for recording a history of value, it may also be used to budget the future. Of particular interest here is the financial accounting model as a component of valuation. First, the theory of accounting is examined as a set of steps to determine net worth to owners. Next, the logic of an accounting process is examined, both double-entry in section 4.2 and means-end hierarchy in section 4.3. Of particular interest to planners is the relationship of valuation in accounting and the economic present value of going concerns. Direct comparisons are drawn between cash flows and income determination in section 4.4. A financial accounting system lends itself to a considerable amount of statistical analysis. Various insights into financial strength and profitability may be drawn from summary statistics (often called financial ratios). Sections 4.5 and 4.6, present financial ratios commonly used in statement analysis.

A process of valuation has two components—value flows and value position. The objective is to establish a value position at some point from a distribution of value flows over time. In the economic value of going concerns (sections 2.3 through 2.6), value position was described as "present value under risk." Net cash flows were the value flows used to establish present value. There are counterpart value flows and positions in financial accounting. The important flows are revenues, expenses, investments, and disinvestments. The last two are capital changes and may be applied to either creditor capital (liabilities) or owner capital (owners' equity). Although a position may be established in financial accounting for any class of resources, the end point of valuation is owners' equity. This is the accounting worth of a firm to owners at some point.

61

In any system of valuation, flows are rates; the figures are incomplete without a stated or implied time duration. Thus a cash flow of $100, interest expense of $1,000, or sales revenue of $4,000 cannot be interpreted unless a time interval is stated or implied. Typical periods are a month, a quarter, or a year. Position values are not rates; they are amounts at some point. Of course, the particular date of a position value is essential information.

Sets of accounting values are organized into statements, each of which describes a subdivision of a firm's activity. Important statements of flows are cost of goods manufactured, cost of goods sold, income, cash receipts and disbursements, flow of funds, retained earnings, and capital changes. The last two are often combined, either together or as schedules in other statements. The important statement-of-position values is the statement of condition, or balance sheet. Statement forms can be used either for a record of historical values or for budgeting the future. Table 4.1 contains a simplified set of statements for a manufacturing concern. Titles of accounts and design of forms were chosen to illustrate the logic system, not to represent the most common practice. The table serves as a basis for numerical illustrations. Its organization of statements is similar to the PAVE model. Statements are related to each other in either the step-by-step or parallel logic of financial accounting methods. This logic is examined in section 4.3. Here, it is important to note that accounting values are processed over successive time periods. Flows are collected for each period and transferred to a statement of condition. Condition is the end point of valuation for that period.

——————— Table 4.1 ———————
SET OF ILLUSTRATIVE FINANCIAL STATEMENTS

Grahub Products, Inc.

Cost of Goods Manufactured
For the year _____

Purchases of direct material		$ 338,190
Add beginning direct material inventory		530,326
Total available		$ 868,516
Less ending direct material inventory		619,797
Cost of direct material used		248,719
Direct Labor		121,226
Manufacturing overhead:		
Indirect labor and superintendence	$27,004	
Depreciation of factory equipment	13,748	
Factory supplies used	2,010	
Light, heat, and power	24,019	
Miscellaneous factory overhead	19,640	86,421

Table 4.1 (continued)

Total cost of goods into process	$ 456,366
Add beginning goods-in-process inventory	1,963,378
Total available	2,419,744
Less ending goods-in-process inventory	2,115,502
Cost of goods manufactured	$ 304,242

Cost of Goods Sold
For the year _____

Cost of goods manufactured	$ 304,242
Add beginning finished goods inventory	25,345
Total available	329,587
Less ending finished goods inventory	26,699
Cost of goods sold	$ 302,888

Income Statement
For the year _____

Net sales		$ 834,598
Less cost of goods sold		302,888
Gross profit on sales		$ 531,710
Operating expenses:		
Selling expense	$125,135	
Office salaries	82,421	
Office and miscellaneous supplies	21,232	
Depreciation on office equipment	2,266	
Amortization of intangibles	10,000	
Uncollectible account expense	10,015	
Miscellaneous operating expense	65,103	316,172
Net income on operations		$ 215,538
Add interest and financial income		3,207
Total		$ 218,745
Less interest expense		105,000
Net income before income taxes		$ 113,745
Less income taxes		51,342
Net income after income taxes		$ 62,403

Table 4.1 (continued)

Retained Earnings and Capital Changes
For the year _____

Paid-in capital (unchanged during year)		$ 600,000
Beginning retained earnings	$428,441	
Add net income after income taxes	62,403	
Total	$490,844	
Less dividends declared and paid	10,000	
Ending retained earnings		480,844
Total owners' equity		$1,080,844

Statement of Condition
December 31, _____

ASSETS

Cash		$ 457,654
Accounts receivable	$ 312,050	
Less allowance for uncollectibles	7,285	304,765
Total cash and net receivables		
(monetary assets)		$ 76,419
Direct material inventory	$ 619,797	
Goods-in-process inventory	2,115,502	
Finished goods inventory	26,699	
Total inventories		2,761,998
Total current assets		$3,524,417
Factory equipment	$ 210,050	
Less reserve for depreciation	85,310	124,740
Office and miscellaneous equipment	$ 25,000	
Less reserve for depreciation	9,890	15,110
Intangibles		60,000
Total assets		$3,724,267

Table 4.1 (continued)

Statement of Condition
December 31, _____

LIABILITIES

Accounts payable	$1,171,215
Short-term notes	435,000
Total current liabilities	1,606,215
Long-term debt due longer than one year	1,037,208
Total liabilities	$2,643,423

OWNERS' EQUITY

Total owners' equity	1,080,844
Total liabilities and owners' equity	$3,724,267

Cash Receipts and Disbursements
For the year _____

Cash receipts from sales		$802,613
Less operating payments		643,591
Net cash flow on operations		$159,022
Add net change in short-term notes	$100,000	
Add net change in long-term debt	85,000	
Add interest income	3,207	188,207
Total		$347,229
Less interest and income tax payments	$156,342	
Less dividends	10,000	166,342
Total net cash flow		$180,887
Add beginning cash balance		276,767
Ending cash balance		$457,654

The accounting model is an alternative to present value of net cash flows, but why is it important? For enterprises of indefinite life, the present-value model in chapters 2 and 5 requires capitalization of net cash flows into the indefinite future. The accounting model, however, comes up with periodic valuation (owners' equity) based on value flows over discrete, short periods. To obtain present values of going concerns over finite steps, opportunity cash flows must enter the process. An opportunity cash flow is the best market value of some resource, a cash flow that may or may not be realized. Assume that 100 shares of General Motors common stock is currently quoted at $61\frac{1}{2}$; then its value now is $6,150, less brokerage fees and other transaction costs. A used car may net $400 after the cost of selling. These are opportunity cash flows—cash that could be generated. The owner may or may not sell the stock or the car; but in both cases, the opportunity value is identical to the cash value on the same date. Opportunity cash flows may be treated as a more general class of values than realized cash flows. Because going concerns do not liquidate all resources at arbitrary times, opportunity cash flows are needed to establish present value if the horizon of valuation is a finite period.

Many assets in going concerns, such as special equipment or in-process inventories, do not have established market values. Thus it may be difficult to estimate opportunity cash values. For this reason, accounting values, which are readily available, are an important proxy for cash values. They fulfill such a role in PAVE.

Strategic planners must present information in useful form. Budgets in accounting-statement form are understood by most business professionals. This is another important reason for using the accounting model. PAVE translates policy inputs into a whole set of budget statements. Such statements may be used to examine the consequences of strategic decisions.

4.2 | The Logic of Double-Entry Bookkeeping

Financial accounting is sometimes described as the oldest management-science method. Its fundamental logic of double-entry bookkeeping dates from the sixteenth century. To understand this logic, start with the "Statement of Condition" in Table 4.1. This is the end point of accounting valuation for a period. One notes immediately that ASSET total is identical to LIABILITIES plus OWNERS' EQUITY total ($3,724,267). The second total, equities, may be interpreted as the end-of-period position of sources of capital. The first total, assets, describes the position of uses of capital. The sum of capital from creditors (liabilities) and from owners (owners' equity) has, at this date, been converted into a bundle of assets—cash, credit extended to customers, material and product inventories, and facilities used to carry on the business. Double entry is a set of rules for maintaining an algebraic balance of values. If appropriate value transfers (closings) are made at any time, end-position values of assets and equities will balance.

A balance is maintained with every ledger account entry. A ledger is a set of individual accounts. The basic mechanism of balance is diagrammed in Figure 4.1. For each entry in the books, the sum of the credits (CR) must balance the 'sum of the debits (DR). The direction of value change from debits and credits is assigned in such a way that the effect on position will maintain balance if total debits equal total credits. Readers may trace these relationships in Figure 4.1 for fundamental transactions. The direction of each type of ledger account change is shown with a plus sign or a minus sign. The "rules" of debits and credits maintain the algebraic balance of position. The same principle of balance applies to transfers or closings among working papers and statements. Again, value exchanges must maintain end-position equality.

Duality of double entry is taken with respect to owners' equity, not to total equity. In double entry, the sources are legal owners' capital position in the firm. The users of owners' capital are the net assets provided by the owners or, in other words, total assets less the claim on assets by creditors (liabilities). The double-entry version of balance appears in Figure 4.1. A balance to owners' equity also ensures a balance of

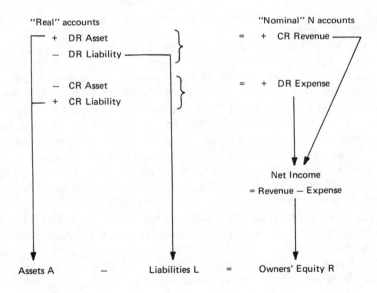

Figure 4.1 Transaction logic of double-entry bookkeeping

total assets and equities (STATEMENT OF CONDITION in Table 4.1). This is true because either balance converts to the other through transposition of an algebraic identity:

$A = E = L + R$

A = total assets

E = total equities

L = total liabilities

R = owners' equity—a residual

If the above equality holds—a balance of assets and equities in a statement of condition—then the following transposition to owners' equity must also hold: $R = A - L$. Accounting transactions that maintain a balance between two sides of a statement of condition will also maintain a balance between owners' equity and assets net of liabilities.

Transactions in double entry may be described as a flow (N) into owners' equity (R), balanced by a change in an asset or a liability account. Accounts used to collect N flows are sometimes called *nominal* because their value effect is indirect. Asset and liability accounts are real because there is a direct impact on a firm's resource position. In recording a sale there is a credit to sales revenue, an N account, and a debit to an asset account, usually *cash* or accounts receivable. There will probably be a second entry, which debits cost of goods sold, an N summary expense account, and credits the asset account finished goods inventory. An entry such as a debit to an N expense account (power and light) is balanced by a credit to a liability account (accounts payable). Not all accounting transactions appear to involve nominal N accounts. There are direct transfers between two assets, between two liabilities, or between an asset and a liability. A customer pays a bill; cash is debited and receivables are credited. Both are asset accounts. An income tax is paid; cash is credited and accrued income taxes—a liability account—is debited. In such cases at least two N account flows also exist, but since they balance out, they usually are not recorded explicitly. When a customer payment debits cash, for example, this is also a credit to owners' equity. This credit is balanced exactly, however, by a debit to owners' equity, which accompanies a credit to accounts receivable.

Against a single-entry system of net cash flows or cash accounting, what are the advantages of double entry, which is a more complex system? First, there is a periodic check on the arithmetical accuracy of the whole system. Second, all transactions are handled under the same general rules of dual balance of debits and credits. Under single entry, on the other hand, transfers among accounts would require different treatment from revenues and expenses. Finally, the ultimate value toward which all transactions are directed, owners' equity, is a legal cushion for the satisfaction of creditor claims against a firm. Historical accounting is very concerned with a firm's financial responsibilities to society as defined by legislation.

4.3 | Accounting Statements as a Means-End System

The financial accounting model is a sophisticated example of means-end logic. (section 1.5). Values of transactions are recorded in books of original entry, often called *journals*. Information from journals is posted to a ledger, which is a complete set of individual accounts. Double-entry rules are observed in the ledger posting (section 4.2 and Figure 4.1). Each ledger account is divided into debit and credit columns. Given double-entry logic, the sum of all debit columns in the ledger must always balance the sum of all credit columns. Sets of financial statements are prepared periodically, such as monthly, quarterly, or annually. Values in statements are derived from net account balances in the ledger. In the past, statements were prepared by hand. Intermediate sets of columns, called *working papers*, were used to assemble net balances from ledger accounts and distribute them among a set of statements. Since financial accounting is a precise logic system, much of the processing of ledger accounts and preparation of statements may be automated by computer. The process just described is a typical "closing of the books" to produce a historical financial record. The same logic applies to the development of strategies for the future, and the same statement forms can be used for budgets and financial forecasts.

Not only is there a means-end logic from transaction to journal to ledger or statement set, but there is an important means-end hierarchy within a set of statements. The principal flows are shown in Figure 4.2. Flow statements are blocked in the left column. Vertical arrows collect the logic of "nominal" revenues and expenses into statements. The latter, in turn, combine into a means-end chain. "Net income after income taxes" is the flow residual of revenues and expenses. Changes over a period in retained earnings position are principally determined by net income and dividend flows. The stated value of paid-in capital may be altered by issue of additional shares or repurchase by a firm of its own shares (treasury stock). In the simple system illustrated here, net flows into retained earnings and paid-in capital combine to establish a final position of owners' equity. In addition to flows that terminate in owners' equity, double entry requires that changes in assets and liabilities also be recorded. Multiple directed arrows on the right side of the figure represent this process. If there are separate products or divisions, flow statements can be added to provide such information. It is easy to separate revenues and expenses which relate directly to a particular activity but difficult to allocate in nonartificial ways general cash flows among activities. PAVE is limited to aggregate planning; divisional separations are not considered.

In the means-end logic of statements, a final set of values is assembled in a statement of condition or balance sheet. This is evident from the connected arrows in Figure 4.2. Since "condition" is a position, it is altered by the flow chain from the set of statements in the left column. Logically, the entire system is an endless chain process. Condition (position) at the beginning of a period is transformed by net flows during that period into condition at the end of the period. The latter is identical with

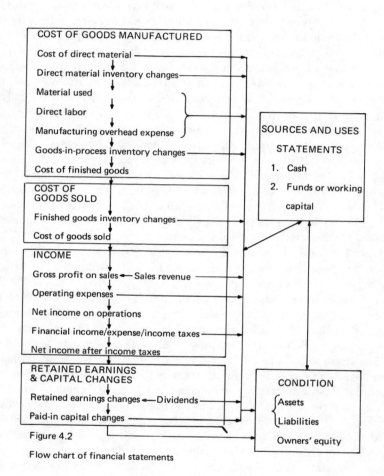

Figure 4.2

Flow chart of financial statements

Figure 4.2 Flow chart of financial statements

condition at the beginning of the next period, which, in turn, is transformed by net flows of this next period, and so forth. The whole accounting system then consists of three levels of means-end value transformations. At the first level, transactions pass from original entries to statements. At the second level is a processing through flow statements into an end-of-period condition. At the third level is an endless chain of values passed along to successive periods. A consistent chain of intermediate values, which facilitates periodic valuation of an entire firm or any of its components, is a major attraction of the financial accounting model. Rules for implementing such a stepped system of valuation—particularly with respect to unrealized market values of assets, inventories, and an entire firm—are, unfortunately, a source of problems. Accounting rules, usually based on formula absorption of historical cost, may not develop an economic value equivalent to opportunity cash flows.

It is convenient to classify commercial firms into "manufacturing," "trade," and "service." Service firms, as classified in the PAVE system, do not maintain inventories of products for sale. Hospitals or law offices offer professional services. Car washes are service firms. On the other hand, trade or merchandising firms maintain product inventories for resale; examples are retailers and wholesalers. In addition, these firms may sell services. Manufacturers not only sell products and provide services, they fabricate and assemble products for sale from materials and subassemblies. In terms of accounting statement logic and PAVE processing, the distinction among classes of firms depends on product inventories. The manufacturing class typically requires inventories of direct materials and subassemblies, plus goods-in-process. A cost-of-finished-goods is computed in a cost-of-goods-manufactured statement. Both manufacturing and trade classes require a finished-goods inventory and an accompanying cost-of-goods-sold statement. Because service firms do not have inventories of products for sale, the two cost-of-goods statements are not required. Of course, all classes of firms may have various inventories of materials and supplies. Given a user input for class of firm, PAVE automatically adjusts required statements and types of inventories.

A "statement of condition" is the termination of mainstream-accounting logic for a period. From section 4.2 this statement is also an expression of sources (equities) and uses of assets. The double-entry system facilitates this classification into two sides of a coin. It was pointed out in section 4.2 that debit and credit logic also leads directly to a balance between owners' equity and net assets. The algebraic transformation of Figure 4.1 could be interpreted as an expression of sources and uses of owners' equity. Since any group of position accounts is algebraically a residual balancer for the rest of the system, any such group may be chosen as a focus of flows during a period. In practice, the groups of most interest are concerned with liquidity, for example, cash or working capital. *Working capital* is defined as current assets net of current liabilities. It is $880,994 for the firm in Table 4.1. Auxiliary sources and uses statements go under various names. For future planning there are cash forecasts or cash budgets. Cash-receipts-and-disbursements statements record flows of cash in and out of cash asset accounts during a period. Sources and uses of working capital are usually assembled in statements labeled "flow of funds."

Sources-and-uses statements provide insight into the dynamics of value changes within a firm. Where does value come from, and where does it go? Both the performance and economic justification of a firm arise from value transformations. Changes in liquidity are particularly important. The conversion of resources into cash is necessary for both short-term and long-term survival. The control of cash has received more attention in recent years than it once did. In one sense, cash is more fundamental than stated income; the accountant is moving in with the economist. Cash plays a central role in the PAVE system. Working capital is less liquid than cash, because it includes short-term credit and inventories. In terms of bill-paying power, working capital is more remote than cash. Flow of funds statements are not prepared in PAVE.

To draw up a sources-and-uses statement for an auxiliary group of assets, one must reassemble flows to describe changes in that group as a residual of the whole system. Such reassembly may be treated as a process parallel to the mainstream flow of financial accounting. This point of view is represented by the block on the right side of Figure 4.2. Illustrative logic for cash receipts and disbursements is presented in the last statement of Table 4.1.

4.4 | Net Income and Cash Flows

To what extent are earnings, or net income after income taxes, as defined by financial accounting rules, similar in behavior to net cash flow from a firm? The question is important, because earnings figures are often more readily available, more stable, and more convenient to use than cash flows. To begin with, both earnings and net cash flow are residuals of profit-making processes. Both are influenced in a similar way by business risk. It remains to be seen whether substitution of earnings for net cash flow will be acceptable in estimating going-concern value.

In financial accounting, flows of cash are recorded in the cash ledger account. Inflows come from collections on sales, investment income, proceeds from issues of new securities, or disposition of assets. Outflows stem from payments of expense, retirement of debt, dividends, or purchases of assets. Ledger transactions may be summarized by sources and uses statements (section 4.3). Like earnings, net cash flow is a residual after all receipts and expenditures. Cash flow parallels income in the sense that collections from customers closely parallel sales and payments on expense closely follow the incurrence of expense. Distortions arise from changes in the level of accounts such as receivables, payables, or various accruals. If externally generated capital changes are separated from internal flows, there remains a question of accounting for fixed asset changes. Cash flow is altered directly by payments or receipts from asset purchase or disposal. For income determination in accounting, however, asset value changes are treated as expense over time with depreciation rules. Cash transactions for fixed assets may be quite irregular, even for large firms. Such firms occasionally go in for massive acquisitions. For this reason, despite the shortcomings of depreciation as an approximation of changes in asset value, earnings may be preferred to cash flow as an estimator of asset value changes over a succession of periods. Discrepancies between earnings and net cash flow are of most concern over the short and the intermediate term. Turning to value accumulation, over the longrun, payments for asset changes and depreciation costs tend to merge.

To illustrate a comparison between net cash flow and earnings, consider again the $100,000 cost-saving machine of section 2.3. After two years of use the plan was to sell the machine for an estimated market value of $20,000. Net cash flow savings after income taxes from the machine were $60,000 for the first year and $40,000 for the second year. With these figures the ROI of the machine was about 13%. If net income after income taxes, computed according to acceptable financial accounting rules, is substituted for net cash flow, how will this affect ROI? Assume straight-line depreciation rules and a marginal income tax rate of 50%. Then the depreciation to be charged against income will be $40,000 each year. Following is a computation of net income for the two years:

	YEAR 1	YEAR 2
net cash savings before depreciation and income taxes	$80,000	$40,000
deduct depreciation	40,000	40,000
net income before income taxes	$40,000	$ 0
income taxes at 50%	20,000	0
net income after income taxes	20,000	0

A net income of $20,000 is returned the first year, and no net income the second year. At the end of the second year, however, the original investment is still intact ($80,000 depreciation withheld from income plus $20,000 used market value). Hence, $100,000 is available for investment elsewhere. This amount is released at the end of the second year. Solving for R as the ROI:

$$20,000(1 + R)^{-1} + 100,000(I + R)^{-2} = 100,000$$

$$R = .105 \text{ or } 10.5\%$$

Compare the income computations here with net cash flow method in section 2.3. Although the pattern of net income is quite different from cash flows, and there is a significant shift in ROI, the capital budgeting decision does not change, given the hurdle rates of the original problem. With both income and net cash flow methods the machine would be purchased with a 10% hurdle rate and rejected with a 15% hurdle rate.

In valuation processes it appears that earnings may be used as estimators for net cash flows as long as investment policies and cash flows are not excessively clustered. One situation with systematic lags is the development of a new product line. There are cash and earnings cycles, as well as a product sales life cycle. The cycles are not in step, particularly during early phases. At first a product project is cash-hungry; negative cash flows support development, introduction, and promotion. During high growth there may be heavy cash outlays for expansion and continued development. When a product line matures it may become a "cash cow" and return large sales dollars for little additional investment. An earnings cycle is likely to fall between product sales and cash cycles (Figure 4.3). A strategic planner may allow for such cash lags, or a firm may be sufficiently diversified to swamp the lag effects.

Net cash flow should not be confused with the term *cash earnings*, which is sometimes used by investment analysts to sum stated earnings and depreciation. In effect, this is net income without a deduction for capital consumption. Such a figure should not be used for valuation because outflows for fixed-asset purchases have been ignored.

Cash control, both short term and long term, is now receiving in financial circles the attention it deserves. It takes cash, not stated earnings, for a firm to stay alive and pay its creditors. There is a strong emphasis on cash in the PAVE modeling system. A cash forecast for all periods appears among the financial planning statements. A probability of technical insolvency, if any occurs, is printed in the valuation output division. Automatic routines borrow short-term funds for seasonal needs. Additional capital, both owner equity and long-term debt, may be supplied by plan and by internal computation. The latter will be determined automatically to meet user policies on liquidity.

4.5 | Ratio Analysis of Profitability from Financial Statements

It is difficult to analyze financial statements because of the great number of figures. Financial ratios taken from statement figures are useful for summarizing the behavior of a firm. Descriptive statistics such as ratios extract important information while eliminating detail. Ratios are especially valuable for comparisons among firms or between periods because they eliminate differences in levels of component values. Like any summary statistics, ratios must be used with caution. Removing levels of values may be dangerous to a rational decision, as illustrated by the following situation.

ROI is a ratio that relates net cash flow returns to initial investment. Suppose a person has exactly $10,000 to invest and does not wish to borrow more. The three available projects each have the same risk. Project A requires an investment of exactly $3,000 and has an ROI of 10%. Project B requires an investment of exactly $8,000, with an ROI of 8%. Any amount up to $10,000 may be invested in Project C, but the

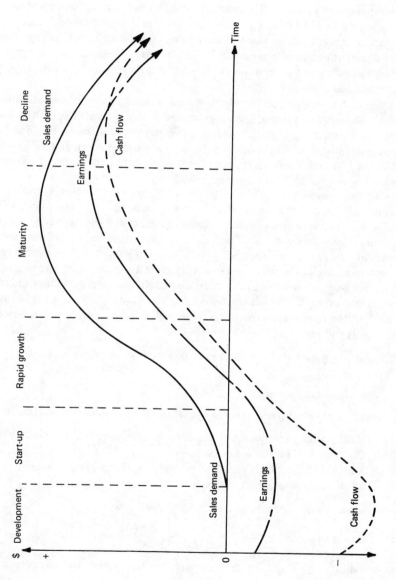

Figure 4.3 Product life cycle with logs of income and net cash flow

ROI is only 5%. A decision based solely on ROI leads to a choice of A. Due to differences in dollars invested, however, the combination of A and C is less profitable than the combination of B and C. The investor would receive only $650 per year from A and C, compared to $740 from B and C. The point here is not to make a decision by ratio comparison alone. One must look at underlying values as well, particularly when they are of different orders of magnitude. Ratio analysis of financial statements is a tool. It should supplement a general analysis, especially with respect to the underlying environment and risk.

Here and in PAVE outputs, ratios from financial statements are divided into three groups. The first, ratios of profitability, is examined in this section. The second and third—ratios of financial strength in continuing operations, and ratios of financial strength in capital structure—are considered in section 4.6. Numerical illustrations of each ratio use the Grahub Products figures from Table 4.1. Illustrative PAVE cases in Part II show how ratios may be interpreted in business environments.

What ratios best measure the profit performance of operating managers? Of financial managers? Of general managers? For the first group, earning power (EP) tells what income was generated from available operating assets. For the last two groups it is appropriate to add the influence of financing and income taxes. EP ratio is an economic measure of production or service from a group of allocated resources. It follows that nonoperating assets, which are currently superfluous to the regular business of a firm, should be excluded from EP computations. Nonoperating revenues and expenses such as interest and income taxes should also be excluded. Look at EP this way: assets were allocated to operating managers. How well did they convert the resources to valuable goods and services?

operating earning power (EP), or total rate of return on operating capital:

$$\frac{\text{EBIT from operation}}{\text{total operating, tangible assets}} = \frac{215,538}{3,664,267} = 5.88\%$$

EBIT = earnings before interest and income taxes, or net income on operations

Intangible assets are often excluded from the denominator, as illustrated here by deducting $60,000 from $3,724,267 total assets. The reason is that operating managers may have no control over the deployment of intangibles. It is also assumed in the example that Grahub has no nonoperating assets.

rate of return to owners, or rate of return on owners' equity:

$$\text{rate of return to owners} = \frac{\text{EAT}}{\text{owners' equity}} = \frac{62,403}{1,080,844} = 5.77\%$$

EAT = earnings after all income and expense, both operating and financial and after income taxes

This is an investor's criterion of performance, because it summarizes all flows from the standpoint of owners. It is easy to compute and is widely used in security analysis of firms. It is also a performance criterion for general management. Financing decisions, such as the use of debt and tax policies, are subsumed in this ratio.

sales margin (SM) or net operating margin:

$$SM = \frac{\text{EBIT from operation}}{\text{net sales}} = \frac{215,538}{834,598} = 25.83\%$$

This is easy to compute, but it needs to be combined with some measure of capital to be of much use for evaluation of performance. Such a combination is given below under "operating efficiency." Ratios of income and expenses to sales provide insights when one is comparing similar firms.

$$\text{gross margin} = \frac{\text{gross profit}}{\text{net sales}} = \frac{531,710}{834,598} = 63.71\%$$

gross profit = net sales – cost of goods sold

This ratio gives the portion of sales dollars tied up in the product itself before sales, general, and administrative expenses. The remarks above, about ratios to sales, also apply here.

operating efficiency (OE) or operating assets turnover:

$$OE = \frac{\text{net sales}}{\text{total operating tangible assets}} = \frac{834,598}{3,664,267} = 0.2278$$

Operating assets are turning over 0.2278 times per year in the form of sales.

The ratio identity—EP = SM times OE; 5.88 = (25.83)(0.2278)—provides useful insights. Profitability is a function of both the margin on sales and the level of assets needed to support sales. Satisfactory profit can be achieved with a low margin if there are large cash sales supported by a relatively small investment. Discount gas stations and supermarkets come to mind. On the other hand, if there is a high investment compared to sales, as in jewelry stores, then a generous margin will be needed to survive.

Profitability ratios from Grahub Products figures (Table 4.1) are suggestive, but beware. There is no background information for a competent analysis. As a starting point, one may note that profitability is low. Low profit is coupled with low asset turnover rather than with low margin. This suggests a top-heavy asset structure. An examination of the asset structure reveals that goods-in-process inventory sticks out like a sore thumb. Now one should dig deeper. Are there problems in operations or in the pricing of inventories? Ratio analysis suggests a critical review of some underlying conditions in a firm and its environment. This is how ratios should be used.

4.6 | Ratio Analysis of Financial Strength

Financial strength depends on reserves available to pay bills as they fall due. Of course, this is a matter of converting resources into cash. In the short run, creditors look to liquid (current) assets to generate cash. Ratios of financial strength in continuing operations measure this strength. In the long run, both creditors and owners must look to future earnings as sources of cash. Ratios of financial strength in capital structure examine long-run values in relation to capital structure. The second group of ratios is discussed in the last half of this section.

There is a hierarchy of liquidity extending down through cash, near-cash, monetary assets and inventories. All of these groups belong to the current-asset class, but as one moves down the hierarchy, turnover time into cash normally lengthens and the risk of discounted value increases. The first three ratios below are general tests, in order of decreasing liquidity.

$$\text{cash ratio} = \frac{\text{cash and near-cash}}{\text{current liabilities}} = \frac{457,654}{1,606,215} = 0.28$$

Near-cash includes time deposits and marketable securities. These have an expectation that almost full value will be realized on demand.

$$\text{quick ratio or acid test} = \frac{\text{current monetary assets}}{\text{current liabilities}} = \frac{762,419}{1,606,215} = 0.47$$

Monetary assets include cash, near-cash, net open accounts receivable, and short-term notes receivable. Accounts-receivable balances should exclude reserves for uncollectible accounts.

$$\text{current ratio} = \frac{\text{net current assets}}{\text{current liabilities}} = \frac{3,524,417}{1,606,215} = 2.19$$

average collection period in days (ACP):

$$\text{ACP} = \frac{\text{net accounts and notes receivable} \times 365}{\text{net sales per year}} = \frac{(304,765)(365)}{834,598} = 133$$

net receivable turns per year is the reciprocal of ACP with the 365 factor excluded: 834,598/304,765 = 2.74.

$$\text{inventory turns per year} = \frac{\text{cost of goods sold}}{\text{mean inventories value}} = \frac{302,888}{2,761,998} = 0.11$$

The figure in the denominator here is end-of-year inventory, since mean inventory level was not available from Table 4.1.

If a firm has difficulty maintaining liquidity, look at one or more of the following areas. Internally generated funds may be insufficient for an expansion of the asset structure required to support high growth. Excessive amounts are perhaps being invested in some class of inventories or facilities. Is the firm being milked? Are owners stripping away funds? Is the firm absorbing resources to overcome operating losses? Although each of these conditions may be justified on occasion, here are some general remedies to consider. High growth, of course, is favorable to value, whereas continuing losses are a disaster. Under growth, the long-term capital base may require expansion from external sources. Acquire additional capital without incurring excessive debt or giving ownership away to outsiders. Liquidate top-heavy inventories, even if it means taking a substantial loss. Rather than excessive investment in facilities, pay rent, lease equipment, or purchase services. Such substitutions use other people's capital in place of your own. Reduce outflows by cutting excessive dividends, owner salaries, or expense accounts. Cannibalizing vital resources to cover operating losses is the deathbed of a firm. Taking an axe to expenses may be the only chance for survival.

Cash ratios tell what fraction of short-term obligations could be paid now. If a quick ratio were maintained at one, then short-term obligations could be paid from assets that normally turn over quickly with minimal loss of value. Current ratios of two or higher provide a cushion for inventory loss in liquidation. It is dangerous to apply rule-of-thumb numbers to liquidity ratios, because one needs to look at the particular environment of a firm. If a sales pattern is seasonal or procyclical, then more liquidity is required than if revenues are stable. The liquidity position of Grahub appears weak but improves markedly in the current ratio, when inventories are included. Turns of receivables and inventories are both slow to very slow. A top-heavy condition of goods-in-process inventories, first noted in the last section, is supported by two more ratios here (current ratio versus quick ratio, and inventory turns).

Since long-term capital must look to future earnings for payment, the profitability ratios of section 4.5 are of great importance. Long-term creditors are especially interested in an income cushion that is available for meeting interest payments. This cushion is summarized by the times interest earned ratio. This ratio, with two others that measure the proportion of debt in capital structure, are given below:

$$\text{times interest earned} = \frac{\text{EBIT from operation}}{\text{interest expense}} = \frac{215,538}{105,000} = 2.05$$

Because income taxes are applied after interest expense, pretax earnings are available to pay interest. Although preferred stock is legally a form of ownership, a financial planner should consider dividends on preferred stock as a fixed obligation. Preferred stock dividends must come from after-tax income (EAT). Thus the times-preferred-stock-dividend-earned ratio is EAT divided by the total preferred stock dividend.

Whereas time interest earned is the dynamic ratio of interest coverage, debt ratios measure the current composition of capital structure. Either of the two ratios below are mutually interdependent, and each reflects the same information as the other.

$$\text{debt to tangible total assets} = \frac{\text{total liabilities}}{\text{tangible net assets}} = \frac{2,643,423}{3,664,267} = 0.72$$

$$\text{debt to tangible owners' equity} = \frac{\text{total liabilities}}{\text{tangible owners' equity}} = \frac{2,643,423}{1,020,844} = 2.59$$

In the event of insolvency, creditors have claims against a firm's assets. Total liabilities are used in place of long-term capital liabilities because short-term creditor claims share equally or have priority over long-term creditor claims. Intangible assets are usually excluded because they are not likely to yield values in liquidation. Tangible owners' equity equals owners' equity less intangible assets. For Grahub, this is $1,080,844 less $60,000, or $1,020,844.

In the case of Grahub, there is a high proportion of debt in capital structure and substantial interest expense. Although interest coverage of two might appear adequate, residuals such as income on operations and net cash flow are highly sensitive to change. First, Grahub creditors face a high risk of loss. Again, such generalizations from ratios should be used to start looking for more information.

References and Additional Readings

To review procedures and interpretations of financial accounting entries and statements, an excellent work is H. Simon, revised by J. Smith and K.F. Skousen, *Intermediate Accounting*, 6th ed., South-Western, 1977. In the field of managerial accounting and controls, some excellent books are: R.N. Anthony, *Management Accounting Principles*, rev. ed., Irwin, 1970; and C.L. Moore and R. K. Jaedicke, *Managerial Accounting*, 4th ed., South-Western, 1976.

A systems approach to accounting theory was formulated by Y. Ijiri in *The Foundations of Accounting Measurement*, Prentice-Hall, 1967. Also consult Chapter 2 of C.L. Hubbard and C.A. Hawkins, *Theory of Valuation*, Intext, 1969.

A series of books explores the relationships of accounting information, economic income, and cash flows. Recommendations for further reading are: N.M. Bedford, *Income Determination Theory: An Accounting Framework*, Addison-Wesley, 1965; R.J. Chambers, *Accounting Evaluation and Economic Behavior*, Prentice-Hall, 1966; E.O. Edwards and P.W.

Bell, *The Theory and Measurement of Business Income*, Univ. of California Press, 1961; and R.K. Jaedicke and R.T. Sprouse, *Accounting Flows: Income, Funds, and Cash*, Prentice-Hall, 1965. A comparison of various types of *goodwills* to value and profit will be found in Edwards and Bell, ibid., pp. 37-69.

A comprehensive work on the analysis of financial statements and the use of financial ratios is R.A. Foulke, *Practical Financial Statement Analysis*, 6th ed., McGraw-Hill, 1968. Compact discussions of financial ratios are found in Richard Sanzo, *Ratios Analysis for Small Business*, Small Business Administration, 1977 and *The Cost of Doing Business Ratios—Corporations*, Dun & Bradstreet, 1977.

Models of product policy in relations to life cycle and cash flow will be found in W.R. King, *Quantitative Analysis for Marketing Management*, McGraw-Hill, 1967. A source with text and cases is Chapter 16 of H.W. Boyd, Jr. and R. Westfall, *Marketing Research*, 3rd ed., Irwin, 1972.

PROBLEMS TO INVESTIGATE

4-1. In a theory of cognitive styles, which stems from psychologist Carl G. Jung, some persons think most effectively in static terms, whereas others think in terms of flows and change. What is your cognitive style? How may cognitive style affect preferences in working with present values, accounting statements, or various classes of models discussed in sections 3.1 and 3.2?

4-2. Compare opportunity value with market value, historical cost, replacement value, depreciated value, and reproduction value. If opportunity value is a fundamental economic measure of worth, why does it seldom appear in financial statements?

4-3. Financial accounting is an important model system whose internal structure is logically consistent. In what ways are its contructs artificial? In what ways is its structure a useful proxy for decision makers? What purposes must financial accounting serve, apart from the needs of business decision makers?

4-4. The main flow of financial accounting is from revenue and cost through income to capital changes and end-of-period condition. The auxiliary logic of sources and uses of various assets may be derived from the main flow. Describe adjustments to main flow in order to assemble sources and uses of cash, working capital, all current assets, book value of fixed assets, and all assets.

4-5. Discuss accounting flows of revenue and expense as proxies for cash flows with respect to accounts receivable, accounts payable, depreciation, prepaid expense, accrued interest and taxes, purchases of fixed assets, and retirement of debt.

4-6. Assume some reasonable accounting flows for problem 2-7. Compute ROI with your accounting flows replacing the original cash flows. Also compute present value at an 18% hurdle rate. Would your decision change, compared to the outcome of problem 2-7?

4-7. State some reasons why product life cycles are important to strategic planners. Explore some implications of crests and ebbs of investment, cash flow, achieved sales, product redevelopment, and earnings. Should managers "ride old horses into the ground"?

4-8. Obtain some financial statements from textbooks, policy cases, annual corporate reports, and financial reporting services. Trace the means-end logic of important flows through the set of statements. Compute the thirteen financial ratios illustrated in this chapter and used in PAVE. Interpret each ratio as a tool for the analysis of performance.

4-9. There are diverse causes for a liquidity squeeze, such as high growth, development of new products, heavy investment in fixed assets, aggressive marketing to improve share of industry, cannibalizing of resources, or expenses in excess of revenues on a continuing basis. Find examples of these. What signals would you expect from ratios for each cause? What might be done to restore liquidity?

4-10. Firm A has shown negative net income each year over the past eight years in its published accounting statements. Despite this, the firm has generated sufficient internal cash flow to continue operations without liquidating fixed assets or raising new capital. Do such situations occur? How would you explain them? If they do occur, what pattern would you expect from ratios?

4-11. Five ratios related to profitability are presented in section 4.5. In what ways do they indicate the economic value of a going concern? In what ways are they artificial? What adjustments might be made to the ratios for an improved indication of economic worth?

4-12. The Small Business Administration explains and illustrates ten important financial ratios (Richard Sanzo, *Ratio Analysis for Small Business*, Small Business Administration, 1977). Compare their set with the set in this chapter. Design a minimal combined set that incorporates the most useful features of each.

5 Present-Value Formulas

5.1 | The Market Value of Investments

Formulas are available for the valuation of enterprises and other investments. Some of these summarize returns from market prices and are presented in this section. Other formulas estimate worth of investments as capitalizations of owner values. Fundamental cash flow capitalizations are examined in section 5.2. The dividend theory of valuation is summarized in section 5.3. The Modigliani and Miller formulation of earnings capitalization is presented in section 5.4. An investors' required rate of return under risk and inflation is estimated in section 5.5. Valuation in liquidation is examined in section 5.6. A final structure for the processing of cash flows is presented in section 5.7.

Before examining specific formulas, readers should review the present-value method of decision making under risk, introduced in section 2.3. The most important discount rate in this chapter, investors' required rate of return under risk and inflation, is discussed in section 2.5 as a means of discounting for risk. Chapter 2 as a whole provides a foundation of valuation, which is applied to the formulas here.

A single set of symbols is used for all the formulas in this chapter. These symbols are assembled alphabetically in Table 5.1.

The only ultimate values to investors are cash flows (or occasionally valuable commodities as substitutes for cash). Cash flows from continuing investments are conveniently divided into two classes: (1) periodic payments D, such as dividends and interest; and (2) market price P of an investment (market price is a capitalization of expected future cash flows). An opportunity cash flow (OCF) is a measure of expected market values of firms or assets, hence potential cash flows to investors. Valuation in OCFs is appropriate for decision making when no actual transaction of

83

───────────────── **Table 5.1** ─────────────────

SYMBOLS USED IN FORMULAS FOR VALUATION

A	expected value of assets
a	factor of asset values realized in liquidation
b	retention rate of earnings for reinvestment
D	expected cash flow to investor during period, such as interest or dividends
E	expected income or earnings during period
g	expected equivalent long-term growth rate
I	expected new investment during period
i	expected risk-free interest rate
j	expected inflation rate
k	investors' required total rate of return
L	total liabilities
m	expected price-earnings multiple
n	specified time horizon
P	market price or worth of an investment
Q	liquidation value to owners
Q^1	liquidation value of assets
q	expected business risk premium rate
r	expected rate of return on incremental assets
t	time as subscript or exponent:
	$t = 0$ for present value
	$t = n$ for specified future horizon at time n
	$t = \infty$ for indefinitely long future time
u	government bond rate
y	current cash yield rate
z	expected total risk premium rate

economic values is expected to take place. Income during a period is the difference in wealth from the beginning to the end of that period, before any consumption expenditures.

income from investment during $t = D_t + P_t - P_{t-1}$ (5.1)

rate of return on investment during $t = \dfrac{D_t + P_t - P_{t-1}}{P_{t-1}}$ (5.2)

Formulas 5.1 and 5.2 can be used for historical income and return or for making decisions about future expectations. Prices, P, may be either realized or OCFs. In decision theory, an opportunity value is worth as much as a realized value. This follows because an opportunity value by definition could be realized in the same amount.

Formulas 5.1 and 5.2 state that an investor, over a given time period, receives a sum of periodic payments plus a difference in price. The most common time period for rates of return is one year. An annual rate is usually implied unless otherwise stated.

> A bond is purchased for $1,010, pays 8% annual interest on a face value of $1,000, and is expected to be worth $1,030 at the end of the year. Compute the income and rate of return.
>
> income = 80 + 1,030 − 1,010 = $100
>
> rate of return = $\dfrac{80 + 1,030 - 1,010}{1,010}$ = 0.099 = 9.9%

$$P_t = mE_t \text{ or } m = P_t/E_t \tag{5.3}$$

Symbols P_t and E_t may describe either the total or the pre-share values of an investment. Note that E_t is a rate, whereas P_t is a spot price. Because of its simplicity, m multiple is a popular valuation ratio in investment circles. The difficulty with valuation methods in formulas 5.1, 5.2, and 5.3 is that some inputs in the formulas are derived rather than being fundamental. Fundamental sources of value are cash flows, earnings, and risk adjustments. The formulas in the remainder of this chapter relate to fundamental sources. Market price P may not be available if one is interested in the influence of alternate strategies on value. Multiple m is not a fundamental source of value; hidden within it are subjective adjustments for risk, cash payouts, inflation, and growth.

> Earnings last year were $1.50 per share, and your broker says this class of stock is worth 25 times annual earnings. What should you be willing to pay for a share?
>
> $P = (25)(1.5) = \$37.50$

> You propose to purchase a firm for cash whose earnings last year were $1,000,000. Your advisor suggests twelve times earnings as a fair valuation multiple. How much should you offer as a purchase price?
>
> $P = (1,000,000)(12) = \$12,000,000$

> Stock in your firm is selling for $16 per share on the market. You offer 100,000 shares of your firm at market price in exchange for all the shares of another firm whose latest expected net income is $90,000 per year. What price-earnings multiple did you assign for valuation of the other firm?
>
> $m = \dfrac{P_t}{E_t} = \dfrac{(100,000)(16)}{90,000} = 17.78$

5.2 | Valuation from the Capitalization of Cash Flows

The worth, P_o, of an investment today is the present-value sum of future, projected cash flows. The discount rate, k, is an investors' required rate of return under risk and inflation. When each term of a sum is related to the next term by a common ratio, one has a geometric progression. Over equal time intervals, simple present-value sums have a common ratio, the present value or discounting factor $1/(1+k)$. If cash flow, D, is a constant for each time interval, or if it grows at a constant rate from term to term, the present-value terms sum to geometric progression. If an investment is a going concern or has no planned maturity, its life is indefinite. This means that the number of present-value terms approaches infinity. If a common ratio between terms holds, the present-value sum becomes an infinite geometric progression (IGP). If convergence also holds—each term over time is numerically smaller than the one before—a simple formula is available for the present-value sum:

$$\text{present value sum of IGP} = \frac{\text{value of first term}}{1 - \text{common ratio between terms}}$$

Extensive use is made of this formula to find present values of investments with indefinite life.

$$P = \frac{D}{1+k} + \frac{D}{(1+k)^2} + \frac{D}{(1+k)^3} + \cdots + \frac{D}{(1+k)^n} + \cdots + \frac{D}{(1+k)^\infty}$$

$$= \sum_{t=1}^{\infty} \frac{D}{(1+k)^t} = D \cdot \sum_{t=1}^{\infty} \frac{1}{(1+k)^t} \tag{5.4}$$

Formula 5.4 gives the present value of an investment with a constant payment per period D, and an indefinite life. It is an infinite geometric progression with a first term, $D/(1+k)$, and a common ratio, $1/(1+k)$. From the IGP formula:

$$P = D \cdot \frac{\frac{1}{1+k}}{1 - \frac{1}{1+k}} = D \cdot \frac{1}{1+k} \cdot \frac{1+k}{1+k-1} = \frac{D}{k} \tag{5.5}$$

Under the specialized conditions above, present value reduces to a simple expression. For this case with a constant cash payout in perpetuity, $m = 1/k$.

> A British consul (bond with no finite maturity) pays $80 per year. What is it worth to you if your required rate of return is 10%? What is its price-earnings multiple?
>
> $$P = \frac{D}{k} = \frac{80}{.10} = \$800 \qquad m = \frac{1}{k} = 10, \quad \text{or } m = \frac{P}{D} = \frac{800}{80} = 10$$

In a more general case of valuation, all cash flows, D_t, in the numerator will be different. For n periods:

$$P_o = \frac{D_1}{1+k} + \frac{D_2}{(1+k)^2} + \frac{D_3}{(1+k)^3} + \cdots + \frac{D_n}{(1+k)^n} \qquad (5.6)$$

Suppose the last cash flow, D_n, is replaced by the sum of a periodic payment, D_n, and the price of the investment, P_n, at time n. In other words, $D_n = D_n + P_n$. The market price, P_n, is an OCF; hence, it may be taken here as a terminal cash flow:

$$P_o = \frac{D_1}{1+k} + \frac{D_2}{(1+k)^2} + \frac{D_3}{(1+k)^3} + \cdots + \frac{D_n}{(1+k)^n} + \frac{1}{(1+k)^n} \cdot P_n \qquad (5.7)$$

But P_n is merely the present value of a future stream of cash flows, which occurs past time horizon n. Combining this information:

$$P_o = \sum_{t=1}^{n} \frac{D_t}{(1+k)^t} + \frac{1}{(1+k)^n} \cdot P_n \qquad \text{restatement of (5.7)}$$

$$P_o = \sum_{t=1}^{n} \frac{D_t}{(1+k)^t} + \frac{1}{(1+k)^n} \cdot \sum_{t=n+1}^{\infty} \frac{D_t}{(1+k)^{t-n}} \qquad \text{restate } P_n \qquad (5.8)$$

$$= \sum_{t=1}^{n} \frac{D_t}{(1+k)^t} + \sum_{t=n+1}^{\infty} \frac{D_t}{(1+k)^t} = \sum_{t=1}^{\infty} \frac{D_t}{(1+k)^t} \qquad (5.9)$$

Formulas 5.8 and 5.9 show that an intermediate price, P_n, may be replaced by a sum of present values of all expected cash flows past it into the future. Expected cash flows are the fundamentals of value. Prices may be used conveniently to collect sets of cash flows.

An investment with a three-year life is expected to yield a net cash flow of $20,000 the first year, $50,000 the second year, and $15,000 the third year. At the end of the third year the investment may be liquidated for $10,000. If your required rate of return is 15%, how much would you be willing to invest now in the project?

$$P_o = \frac{20,000}{1+0.15} + \frac{50,000}{(1+0.15)^2} + \frac{15,000+10,000}{(1+0.15)^3}$$

$$= \frac{20,000}{1.15} + \frac{50,000}{1.3225} + \frac{25,000}{1.520875}$$

$$= 17,391.30 + 37,807.18 + 16,437.90 = \$71,636.38$$

A share of stock is expected to pay dividends of $1, $1.10, and $1.20 over three successive, annual periods. At the end of the third period all shares are to be sold to employees at a price of $30 per share. If you require a 12% return, what would you pay now for a share?

$$P_0 = \frac{1.00}{1 + 0.12} + \frac{1.10}{(1 + 0.12)^2} + \frac{1.20}{(1 + 0.12)^3} + \frac{30}{(1 + 0.12)^3}$$

$$= \frac{1}{1.12} + \frac{1.1}{1.2544} + \frac{1.2 + 30}{1.404928}$$

$$= 0.89286 + 0.87691 + 22.20754 = \$23.98$$

5.3 | Dividend Theory of Common Stock Valuation

The dividend theory of common stock valuation is an application of the present-value sum of cash flows. A stock with assumed perpetual life has no other cash outflows to investors than dividends. The worth of a share of stock is then equal to the present-value sum of a perpetual, future dividend stream. Suppose the dividend stream is growing at some constant rate g, which may be positive, negative, or zero. If D_0 is the base dividend,

$$D_1 = D_0(1 + g)$$
$$D_2 = D_1(1 + g) = D_0(1 + g)^2$$
$$D_n = D_0(1 + g)^n$$

From Formula 5.9,

$$P_0 = \frac{D_0(1 + g)}{1 + k} + \frac{D_0(1 + g)^2}{(1 + k)^2} + \cdots + \frac{D_0(1 + g)^n}{(1 + k)^n} + \cdots + \frac{D_0(1 + g)^\infty}{(1 + k)^\infty}$$

$$= \sum_{t = 1}^{\infty} \frac{D_0(1 + g)^t}{(1 + k)^t} \tag{5.10}$$

Apply the IPG formula in a similar manner to the summation of formula 5.5. The first term is $D_1/(1 + k)$, and the common ratio is $(1 + g)/(1 + k)$:

$$P_0 = D_0 \cdot \sum_{t = 1}^{\infty} \frac{(1 + g)^t}{(1 + k)^t} = D_0 \cdot \frac{\dfrac{1 + g}{1 + k}}{1 - \dfrac{1 + g}{1 + k}} = D_0 \cdot \frac{1 + g}{1 + k} \cdot \frac{1 + k}{1 + k - 1 - g}$$

$$= \frac{D_0(1 + g)}{k - g} = \frac{D_1}{k - g} \tag{5.11}$$

The simple formula 5.11 expresses the value of a stock as next year's dividend divided by the difference between the required rate of return and the growth rate. Formula 5.11 is quite powerful because it takes both risk (incorporated into k) and growth, g, into account. Valuation is developed from a basic outflow, next year's dividend, D.

As g approaches k in value, P approaches infinity. The condition of convergency and finite present-value sum is g smaller than k. The formula shows that very high growth rates of dividends are extremely valuable. It was continued expectations of high growth that accounted for price-earnings multiples of 60 or more for a few growth stocks in past years. It is important to note that g is theoretically a perpetual growth rate. In practice, except at extremely high growth rates, dividends past 30 years contribute little to present values (see problem 5-2). On the other hand, expected high growth for only a few years should not be transferred at full rate to g. For most firms, g will remain close to a general level of economic growth. Also, k will rise with g because unstable valuations at high growth rates are accompanied by high risk.

Several problems arise in the application of formula 5.11. The formula works best with income stocks which have a stable dividend policy and moderate growth. As previously noted, valuation is unstable and explosive at high growth rates. Suppose the expected dividend stream is erratic. Then one must choose an equivalent perpetual growth rate. This kind of choice is difficult for a growth firm which plans to pay little or no dividends for a number of years. One way to refine formula 5.11 is to divide valuation of stocks into several segments.

The expected 1975 per-share dividend for Warner-Lambert is 92¢, and expected earnings are $2.20. The dividend has been growing at 10% for the past five years. The long-run future rate of growth over many years is expected to continue at 10%. The required rate of return is 13%. What should you pay for a share of Warner-Lambert?

$$P_o + \frac{0.92}{0.13 - 0.10} = \frac{0.92}{0.03} = \$30.67$$

The actual September 1975 price was $31^3/_4$ ($31.75), but the total 1975 price range (January-September) was $29^1/_8$ to $33^1/_2$. The earnings information is irrelevant to the solution here.

From formulas 5.11 and 5.8, future prices must grow at the same rate as dividends. In the long run earnings and assets must also grow at the same rate as dividends to support growth of dividends. Transposition of formula 5.11 yields:

$$kP_o - gP_o = D; \quad k = \frac{D}{P_o} + g = y + g \tag{5.12}$$

The total required rate of return k is the sum of current cash (or dividend) yield y, plus the perpetual growth rate, g.

For Warner-Lambert in 1975:

$$k = \frac{0.92}{30.67} + 0.10 = 0.03 + 0.10 = 3\% + 10\% = 13\%$$

To connect formula 5.11 with price-earnings multiples m, note that $D = (1 - b)E$ and $D_1 = (1 - b)E_1$. Factor b is the earnings retention rate. Factor $b = (E - D)/E$. Earnings E_1 equals rA_o where A_o is initial assets and r is the rate of return on assets. Now $g = rb$, since A grows each year at rate g and b is the factor of earnings invested in additional assets. Make the above substitutions in formula 5.11:

$$P_o = \frac{(1 - b)rA_o}{k - rb} \tag{5.13}$$

Solve formula 5.13 again for k, with P and A both at $t = 0$:

$$k = \frac{rA}{P} + \frac{rb(P - A)}{P} = \frac{E}{P} + g \cdot \frac{(P - A)}{P} = \frac{1}{m} + g \cdot \frac{(P - A)}{P} \tag{5.14}$$

If one solves formulas 5.13 and 5.14 for m, a simple expression is obtained for the price-earnings multiple:

$$m = \frac{1 - b}{k - g} \tag{5.15}$$

In formula 5.14 the shareholders' required rate of return k is the reciprocal of the price earnings multiple m, plus a factor that is equal to the perpetual growth rate multiplied by the proportionate difference in price to assets. The components of total return are then current earnings rate, plus the growth rate adjusted downward to eliminate double counting (earnings are sources of both dividends and new investment).

Formula 5.15 shows the factors that determine a price-earnings multiple, m. Multiple m increases with the dividend payout factor $(1 - b)$, decreases as risk increases with an increasing k and increases with growth as g approaches k.

Warner-Lambert sells for a price earnings multiple of 30.67/2.20 or 13.94. Then $1/m = 1/13.94 = .0717$. The assets per share are $12.79. The total rate of return consists of a multiplier reciprocal component and a growth-retention component. From formula 5.14,

$$k = 0.0717 + 0.10 \frac{30.67 - 12.79}{30.67} = 0.717 + 0.0583 = 0.13 = 13\%$$

Alternatively, m for Warner-Lambert may be computed from formula 5.15:

$$\text{Retention rate, } b, \text{ is } \frac{E_1 - D_1}{E_1} = \frac{2.20 - 0.92}{2.20} = 0.581818$$

$$m = \frac{1 - b}{k - g} = \frac{1 - 0.581818}{0.13 - 0.10} = \frac{0.418182}{0.03} = 13.94$$

Formulas 5.12 to 5.15 do nothing to eliminate difficulties with dividend growth analysis; they merely relate growth valuation with price-earnings analysis. Note that if retention factor b is 1 in formula 5.13, then $P_o = 0$. Retention factor of 0 gives $P_o = 0$ in simple formulas. There is no value to investors if there are no expected payouts forever.

The dividend theory formula 5.11 becomes more powerful if expected erratic dividend behavior, including zero dividends, is explicitly included for a few future years. In formula 5.16 dividends from years 1 to n are individually discounted and summed. Years from $n + 1$ to infinity are assumed to follow a perpetual growth rate, g. Then formula 5.11 may be applied to years $n + 1$ and beyond but must be discounted back to the present with factor $(1 + k)^n$:

$$P_o = \sum_{t=1}^{n} \frac{D_t}{(1 + k)^t} + \frac{D_{n+1}}{(1 + k)^n (k - g)} \tag{5.16}$$

A share of stock is projected to pay no dividends for the next two years in the future. Dividends of \$2 are expected during each of the third and fourth years. From the fifth year on, dividends are projected to grow at a rate of 3% per year from a starting level of \$2.20. The investors' required rate of return under risk is 15%. What is the value of a share now?

$$P_o = \frac{0}{1 + 0.15} + \frac{0}{(1 + 0.15)^2} + \frac{2}{(1 + 0.15)^3} + \frac{2}{(1 + 0.15)^4}$$

$$+ \frac{2.20}{(1 + 0.15)^4 (0.15 - 0.03)}$$

$$= 0 + 0 + \frac{2}{1.52} + \frac{2}{1.749} + \frac{2.20}{(1.749)(0.12)}$$

$$P_o = 0 + 0 + 1.315 + 1.144 + 10.482 = \$12.94$$

The terms on the last line provide components of total share value. The first two years contribute nothing, but the third and fourth years sum to \$2.459. Most of the value, \$10.482, comes from the fifth year and beyond. Note that all the components are present values.

5.4 | Earnings Capitalization Formulas for Valuation

Whereas dividend and cash-flow formulas evaluate investments from results to investors, earnings are a source of investor value. Earnings are the property of common shareholders. They may be paid out in dividends or reinvested to enlarge future earnings and dividends. The Modigliani and Miller (MM) formulation investigates value from earnings capitalization. The MM method has the advantage of working with current earnings and total additional investment without regard to sources of funds. Thus, the MM valuation is independent of policy decisions on a mix of retained earnings and external capital. There is no need for specific recognition of a dividend payout (an assertion that is justified below). One can use single or multiple growth rates for incremental investment capital in MM formulas. MM formulas are often more useful than formulas 5.11 or 5.16, because there is no built-in requirement for b smaller than 1, nor the necessity to project a dividend policy.

Valuation is from the point of view of current investors, not the proposed sources of new capital, if any. Value is taken as the sum of capitalized current earnings in perpetuity plus the present values of capitalizations of an indefinite stream of future earnings increments for current investors. These increments come from periodic new investment or disinvestment.

$$P_o = \frac{E}{k} + \sum_{t=1}^{\infty} I_t \cdot \frac{r_t - k}{k} \cdot \frac{1}{(1+k)^t} \tag{5.17}$$

The first term is a perpetual capitalization of the current level of earnings, E, per formula 5.5. The second term is the capitalization of earnings increments (which may be positive, negative, or zero) from the base level, E. Incremental earnings come from new investment (or disinvestment), I_t, during period t. The gross earnings during t are then $I_t r_t$ and the cost of I_t is $I_t k$. Thus the net benefit to current investors is $I_t(r_t - k)$. Each $I_t(r_t - k)$ increment is capitalized perpetually (divide by k), but each must also be discounted back to the present with factor $1/(1+k)^t$.

For a constant rate of return on assets r and a single perpetual growth rate g for I_t, formula 5.17 is transformed into:

$$P_o = \frac{E}{k} + \frac{I_o(r-k)}{k} \cdot \sum_{t=1}^{\infty} \frac{(1+g)^t}{(1+k)^t} \tag{5.18}$$

The IGP summation formula can be applied to the right factor of formula 5.18, whose common ratio is $(1+g)/(1+k)$. The first term is $I_o(1+g)/(1+k)$, and $I_1 = I_o(1+g)$. The substitutions are similar to those in formula 5.11.

$$P_o = \frac{E}{k} + \frac{I_1}{k-g} \cdot \frac{r-k}{k} \tag{5.19}$$

If income taxes and transactions costs are neglected, several interesting conclusions can be drawn from formula 5.19. Investor values are not affected by the source of new investment I. Thus investors are indifferent to the retention factor b and dividend policy D. Assume some mix of retained earnings and new outside capital to achieve I. If dividend yield were insufficient for current expenditures, an investor could sell some shares. If an investor did not need dividends for current expenditures, such dividends could be used to purchase additional shares. Under the simplifying assumptions given, personal action of investors may to any degree offset corporate action with respect to a desired mix of current income and reinvestment. With such free substitution, the market could not support price differences for dividend policy because expensive shares would be sold and inexpensive ones purchased until prices were driven together.

Another MM proposition, again neglecting income taxes and transaction costs, is that the cost of capital to a firm, k, is independent of financial leverage (proportion of debt in capital structure). The reasoning here is that corporate leverage may be substituted for investor leverage. If a firm is financed conservatively (all common stock), investors may introduce leverage by borrowing money to purchase additional shares. On the other hand, if a firm is highly levered, investors may offset this risk by diverting funds from a firm's shares to fixed-income (debt) securities. Again, with perfect substitution, the market would equalize prices.

The substitution principles of the last two paragraphs are sharply modified by income taxes, brokerage fees, and other transaction costs. Dividends, retained earnings, and capital gains are differentially taxed. There are both corporate and personal income taxes whose combined impact depends upon a mix of rates and types of income. Because interest expense is excluded from taxable income, the cost of capital decreases as leverage increases. If personal income taxes are considered, however, there are incentives not to go too far toward corporate debt. Corporate interest payments are usually fully taxable to the owners of debt. Common shareholders, on the other hand, pay reduced personal taxes on retained earnings. They may either defer taxes on such corporate income by holding shares, or pay lower capital gain rates if shares are sold. There probably is an optimal capital mix (leverage) for a firm which leads to a lowest total cost of capital. Figure 5.1 diagrams various behaviors for the cost of capital. Persons in top income tax brackets usually prefer retention of earnings (low dividend payout). Persons on low, fixed income probably prefer high-dividend payouts.

Although different in points of view, formulas 5.11 and 5.19 may be reconciled mathematically (see the references for this chapter).

Warner-Lambert is currently earning $2.20 per share and pays 92¢ in dividends. New investment is then $1.28 per share if all comes from retention. Warner-Lambert expects to earn 17.2% on new investment from retained earnings. The long-run growth rate is 10% and the investors' required rate of return is 13%. What is the worth of a share?

$$P_o = \frac{2.20}{0.13} + \frac{1.28}{0.13 - 0.10} \cdot \frac{0.172 - 0.13}{0.13} = 16.923 + 13.786 = \$30.71$$

The current level of earnings is worth about $16.92. Thus the total value of more than $30 is based on additional growth expectations. These additional expectations are worth about $13.78 if Warner-Lambert is able to earn about 17.2% on its retained earnings.

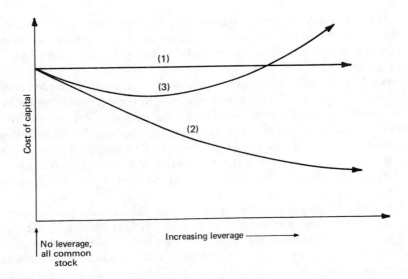

1. The Modigliani and Miller position with no income taxes.
2. The Modigliani and Miller position with the effect of corporate income taxes.
3. The Modigliani and Miller position with possible combined effects of personal and corporate income taxes, a return to the classical economic theory of optimal capital mix.

Figure 5.1 Cost of capital curves

Notice that the $(r-k)/k$ factor of formula 5.19 assigns value to current investors of new investments I from any source. If a firm is able to earn a higher return r than investors' required rate under risk k, then new investments will increase present value to current investors. If r is less than k, which is often the case, and again neglecting income tax effects, current investors are losing if the firm expands with new investments.

Formulas 5.17 and 5.19 are likely to prove more useful for strategic planning valuations than are formulas 5.11 and 5.16. Formulas 5.17 and 5.19 permit flexibility on sources of new capital and dividend policies.

The MM earnings-capitalization formula 5.19 is easily modified to handle various increments of investment over a set of future years followed by a projected steady growth beyond some specified horizon. The development is parallel to the dividend growth formula 5.16.

For the first n years assume a schedule of investments, I_t, and rates of return on assets, r_t. After a horizon, n, there is a single, expected rate of return r_{n+1} on asset increments growing at rate g. These asset increments are based on investment I_{n+1} made during the year $n+1$.

$$P_o = \frac{E}{k} + \sum_{t=1}^{n} \frac{I_t(r_t - k)}{k(1+k)^t} + \frac{I_{n+1}(r_{n+1} - k)}{k(k-g)(1+k)^n} \qquad (5.20)$$

The routines for computing "going-concern" value in PAVE use the logic of formula 5.20.

A share of stock has a current earnings level of $1.50 per share. A dividend of 75¢ will be paid and 50¢ a share will be raised from the sale of new stock. The rate of return on assets purchased next year is expected to be 15%.

Opportunities for the year after next consist only of retained earnings, which are projected at $1 per share. The expected rate of return on assets here is 14%. Looking into the third future year and beyond, the firm expects to invest 25¢ per share, growing at 5% per year and earning 14.5% return on assets.

The investors' required rate of return is 12%.

$$P_o = \frac{1.50}{0.12} + \frac{1.25(0.15 - 0.12)}{0.12(1 + 0.12)} + \frac{1.00(0.14 - 0.12)}{0.12(1 + 0.12)^2}$$

$$+ \frac{0.25(0.145 - 0.12)}{0.145(0.12 - 0.05)(1 + 0.12)^2}$$

$$= \frac{1.50}{0.12} + \frac{0.0375}{0.1344} + \frac{0.02}{0.151} + \frac{0.00625}{0.0127}$$

$$P_o = 12.50 + 0.279 + 0.132 + 0.491 = \$13.40$$

5.5 | Investors' Required Rate of Return under Risk and Inflation

A background discussion for an investors' required rate of return, k, is presented in section 2.5. A method of estimating its value is given in this section. The method examines portfolios in various risk classes and estimates market rates of return. The result is a formula that yields a required rate of return as a function of the variance of rates of return. The variance is used to measure the risk of an expected stream of rates of return. Finally, the required rate of return is adjusted for expected inflation. It is assumed that differences in the long-term government bond rate will reflect expectations about inflation.

Rate k may be approximated by adding the current government bond rate to rates developed in risk-return tables. For example, if risk is measured by the variance of rate of return, an appropriate k may be read from Figure 1-4 of C.L. Hubbard and C.A. Hawkins, *Theory of Valuation* (Intext, 1969). The values of Figure 1-4 are associated with a long-term government bond rate of 3.17. Using the above procedure,

$$k = \text{Expected bond rate} - 3.17 + \text{rate of return from table} \qquad (5.21)$$

If the variance of rate of return is 0.08 and the expected government bond rate, u, is 7.8%,

$$k = 7.8 - 3.17 + 9.1 = 13.73\%$$

The 9.1 value was obtained from Figure 1-4 in the above reference, with an input of 0.08 variance.

A numerical formula 5.25 for investors' required rate of return is given below. The principle here is that k is roughly the sum of components to cover various market conditions and risks,

$$k = u + z \tag{5.22}$$

where u is the government bond rate and z is a rate to cover financial and business risk premiums. Each u and z may be treated as the sum of components:

$$u = i + j; \quad z = f + q$$
$$k = (i + j) + (f + q) = i + j + f + q \tag{5.23}$$

The above four components may be defined as follows:

i is a pure interest rate, or time value of money without risk, plus a return for risk associated with fluctuations in the pure interest rate not connected to inflation. If interest rates vary, then prices of debt instruments will fluctuate, thus injecting market price risk. This is usually called "interest rate risk."

j is a rate required to overcome inflation risk. Inflation destroys the real purchasing power of investments priced in dollars.

f is a rate premium to cover the risk of financial leverage in the capital mix of a firm. It is not usually worthwhile to separate this risk from business risk, (see sections 2.4 and 5.4).

q is a rate premium to cover business risk (see section 2.4). Whereas q is a consequence of fluctuations from operating leverage, f is a consequence of financial leverage.

Assume a pure interest rate of 2%, an expected inflation of 6%, a financial risk premium of 3%, and a business risk premium of 4%. What is the total required rate of return?

$$k = 2 + 6 + 3 + 4 = 15\%$$

If one is aggregating rates, a geometric combination would be preferable to arithmetic addition. Such a geometric accumulation formula would be:

$$(1 + k) = (1 + i)(1 + j)(1 + f)(1 + q)$$
$$k = (1 + i)(1 + j)(1 + f)(1 + q) - 1 \tag{5.24}$$

Redetermine an investors' required rate of return by combining component rates per formula 5.24 in place of 5.23:

$$k = (1 + .02)(1 + .06)(1 + .03)(1 + .04) - 1$$
$$= (1.02)(1.06)(1.03)(1.04) - 1 = 1.158 - 1 = 0.158 = 15.8\%$$

For small values of components, a simple addition of rates does not lead to serious errors; but it does understate a combined rate with positive component rates.

It is well to note that a pure interest rate need not be positive, particularly after taxes. Yields after income taxes are the only relevant measures of value for individual investors. Social equity would suggest that inflation loss be deducted before establishing an income tax base; unfortunately, this is not the case in the United States.

An investors' required rate of return is computed in PAVE from a statistical analysis of market rates of portfolios as described above. The specific formula in PAVE, which could be used for any investment analysis, is:

$$k = \frac{Ln \text{ (variance of annual rates of return)} + 2.7249}{17.74} + j + 0.018 \qquad (5.25)$$

Formula 5.25 is similar to 5.21 but uses a natural log function in place of Figure 1-4 from Hubbard and Hawkins. Formula 5.25 also substitutes inflation rate j for government bond rate u. For PAVE outputs, rate j is taken from inflation factors developed from inputs.

The variance of rates of return is 0.08 and the inflation rate is 6%. What is the investors' required rate of return, k?

$$k = \frac{Ln(0.08) + 2.7249}{17.74} + 0.06 + 0.018$$

$$= \frac{0.52573 + 2.7249}{17.74} + 0.078 = 0.2612 = 26.12\%$$

5.6 | Valuation in Liquidation

An important computation for a firm is the difference between going-concern value and liquidation value. Liquidation value is the market value of assets if a firm is broken up. Then assets should be sold off for their best prices in other uses. Previous valuations in this chapter have been based on projections of earnings or cash flows, a going-concern point of view. It is possible, however, that liquidation value may exceed going-concern value. In such a case, a firm is worth more dead than alive. Rationally, it should be broken up and its assets sold off. As long as a firm has a spark of life, however, liquidation values are seldom computed. As a result many firms continue opera-tions long after they fail to earn a competitive return. The PAVE simulation computes liquidation values for all firms.

With the exception of some types of appreciation, such as land, or occasional in-flation aberrations, realized market price of assets tends to vary inversely with liquid-ity. Typical realizations would be 100% for cash, 80% to 90% for accounts receivable, 50% to 80% for inventories, and scrap value to 50% for fixed assets.

If realization factors are averaged to one figure a, liquidation value of assets will be given by:

$$Q = a \cdot A \tag{5.26}$$

Of more interest to owners is a residual value after assets have been liquidated and all debts (liabilities) have been paid. In many circumstances this value Q^1 is negative:

$$Q^1 = a \cdot A - L = Q - L \tag{5.27}$$

Formulas 5.26 and 5.27 are used in PAVE to estimate liquidation values. Intangible as-sets are unlikely to remain valuable after operations cease. Usually, intangibles should be excluded from total assets, as in PAVE, before a computation of liquidation values.

> A firm has $1.5 million of assets, including $100,000 of intangibles. It is estimated that 40% of the book value of tangible assets would be realized in a liquidation. Liabilities are $1 million and owners' equity is $500,000. What is the liquidation value of the assets? What is the liquidated value of the firm to common stockholders?
>
> $Q = 0.4(1,500,000 - 100,000) = \$560,000$
>
> $Q = 560,000 - 1,000,000 = \$440,000$

For a liquidation under these conditions, creditors would receive slightly more than 50¢ for each $1 of debt, and common shareholders would receive nothing. Such an outcome is quite common.

5.7 | Transformations of Cash Flows

This section summarizes the processing of cash flows as measures of value. It builds on the certainty-equivalent method of sections 2.1 and 2.2, cash-flow-adjustment transformations from section 2.4, and opportunity values introduced in section 4.1. Both going-concern and liquidation values are reducible to cash flows. In fact, cash flows may be used for any economic value comparisons of business decisions. An in-vestors' required rate of return k, used in all preceding computations of this chapter, may be looked upon as a combined market substitute for all discounting, including risk discounting with certain equivalence (see sections 2.1, 2.2, and 2.5). In this section we return to fundamentals of cash flows, including certain equivalents.

Transformations of cash flows as diagrammed in Figure 5.2 (compare Figure 2.3) show an adjustment process to determine equivalent current values for future expected cash flows (AOCFs). Expected realized cash values are treated as a subset of more general opportunity cash flows (OCFs). In any cash flow problem the relevant decision value is an expected, opportunity cash-flow surplus (EOCFS):

$$\text{EOCFS} = \Sigma\text{AOCFs into unit} - \Sigma\text{AOCFs out of unit} \qquad (5.28)$$

A going concern normally has a value based on earning power, which is greater than the net sum of the assets in AOCF terms. This follows because AOCF implies value in best alternative use, or sale to others. The difference between going-concern value and liquidation value of assets to owners may be termed AOCF goodwill. In economic terms, AOCF goodwill is a continuing value (positive, negative, or zero); but it should remain positive to justify a continued commitment of resources in a particular firm.

$$\text{AOCF goodwill} = \text{AOCF going-concern value}$$
$$- \text{AOCF net sum of assets to owners} \qquad (5.29)$$

AOCF net sum of assets to owners is equivalent to the total liquidation value of assets less the monetary value of liabilities. Compare the discussion of a cash flow decision process here with liquidation value formulas 5.26 and 5.27 in section 5.6.

You own two investments—A and B. You expect to sell A as a going entity four years hence for a total cash payoff of $3,000 under risk. You do not expect to liquidate B, but estimate that its market value at the end of four

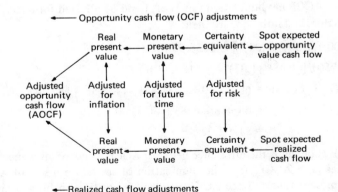

Figure 5.2 Transformation processes for cash flows

years will be $4,000. The expectations for A and B simply summarize a statistical distribution for these values under risk. As a risk averter, you decide that you would be willing to accept $2,500 certain payment for A in place of its risky expectation of $3,000, and a certain equivalent market price of $3,600 for B. The time value of money is taken at 5%. The monetary present values of these certain equivalents are $2,500/(1.05)^4 = \$2,056.76$, and $3,600/(1.05)^4 = \$2,961.73$, respectively. The real, present values, with annual inflation rates of 3%, are $2,056.76/(1.03)^4 = \$1,827.40$ for A, and $2,961.73/(1.03)^4 = \$2,631.46$ for B. Now there is a realized AOCF of $1,827.40 for A, and an unrealized opportunity AOCF of $2,631.46 for B. One would conclude that B is more valuable than A by an AOCF difference of $2,631.46 - 1827.40 = \$804.06$, and that total AOCF wealth is $1,827.40 + 2,631.46 = \$4,458.86$.

Suppose that the original cost (today) of A is $1,200 and of B, $2,800. What is your EOCFS?

EOCFS = $(1,827.40 + 2,631.46) - (1,200 + 2,800) = 4,458.86 - 4,000$
= $458.86

With chosen rates of discount you should purchase A but reject B. Individual EOCFSs are $627.40 for A and –$168.54 for B.

Suppose you could liquidate the assets of A at the end of the fourth year for $1,200 and those of B for $1,000. There would be no payoffs prior to liquidation. At the end of this same fourth year you estimate the liabilities of A at $500, and those of B at $1,200. Thus, net liquidation values to you, from formula 5.27, are $700 and –$200, respectively. These are, of course, uncertain amounts, which you value with certainty equivalents of $600 and –$250, respectively. This means that you would be willing to accept $600 certain for the risky expectation of $700, and would be willing to pay a certain amount $250 to be relieved of the risky expected debt of $200.

The AOCF net liquidation values of A and B, adjusted for uncertainty, present value, and inflation, are then:

$600/[(1.05)^4(1.03)^4] = \$438.58$ for A

$(-250)/[(1.05)^4(1.03)^4] = \$182.74$ for B

AOCF goodwill = $(1827.40 + 2631.46) - (438.58 - 182.74)$

                 = $4458.86 - 255.84$

                 = $4203.02

AOCF goodwill is the difference between AOCF values of investments as going entities, and AOCFs from net liquidation of assets. Both sets of AOCFs are real, present values. Since AOCF goodwill is positive for both A and B, you would not assign current values to expectations of liquidation four years hence.

References and Additional Readings

When it comes to formulas for present values and annuities, almost any textbook or handbook on financial management is useful. An excellent work on financial modeling is J.C.T. Mao, *Quantitative Analysis of Financial Decisions*, Macmillan, 1969; Chapter 6 explains and graphs important formulas. One may also consult Chapter 3 of D. Teichroew, *An Introduction to Management Science: Deterministic Models*, Wiley, 1964. The financial management references of Chapter 2 are another source.

The dividend theory of common stock valuation is developed in M.J. Gordon, *The Investment, Financing and Valuation of the Corporation*, Irwin, 1962; A reconciliation between dividend and earnings capitalizations of value will be found in Chapter 5, pp. 55-77. The reconciliation was mentioned here in section 5.4. For a further reference on dividend theory of valuation, consult B.G. Malkiel, "Equity Yields, Growth, and the Structure of Share Prices," in *The American Economic Review*, December 1963, pp. 1004-31. References on portfolio theory and intrinsic worth in Chapter 2 of this book also apply here. The dividend theory of valuation is discussed in Chapter 4, and an investors' required rate of return in Chapter 1, of C.L. Hubbard and C.A. Hawkins, *Theory of Valuation*, Intext, 1969.

The F. Modigliani and M.H. Miller (MM) propositions on earnings capitalization from section 5.4 are summarized in H. Bierman, *Decision Making and Planning for the Corporate Treasurer*, Wiley, 1977, pp. 108-24. A modern model of cost of capital is explained in Bierman. The original MM articles are "The Cost of Capital, Corporation Finance, and the Theory of Investment," in *American Economic Review*, June 1958, pp. 261-97; "The Cost of Capital, Corporation Finance, and the Theory of Investment: Reply," in *American Economic Review*, September 1959, pp. 655-69; and "Taxes and the Cost of Capital: A Correction," in *American Economic Review*, June 1963, pp. 433-43.

For readings on cash flows, opportunity values, and goodwill, consult the third paragraph of references in Chapter 4.

PROBLEMS TO INVESTIGATE

5-1. Why are price-earnings multiples important in the analysis of market values of investments? What attributes are implied by a high multiple? An intermediate multiple? A low multiple? Are typical multiples different now from those in the sixties? Is the difference more pronounced for growth stocks than for income stocks? Suggest some explanations for changes in multiples. In what ways do multiples fail to provide information for determination of economic value?

5-2. Investment A pays $1,000 per year indefinitely, whereas Investment B pays the same amount but for only 20 years. What are the present values if your required rate of return is 5%? If it is 12%? Compare the various present values.

ANSWER: At 5% the present value of A is $20,000 and of B, $12,462. At 12%, the present value of A is $8,333 and of B, $7,469. A present value of simple annuity formula

$$P = D \cdot k^{-1} \cdot [1 - (1 + k)^{-n}]$$

was used to compute the 20-year values. An increase in required rate k reduces present value. This reduction is most pronounced for the present value of all payments after 20 years.

5-3. A share of stock is expected to pay a $2 dividend for the next four years. At the end of this time, assume a market price of $30. If your required rate of return on this stock is 15%, what perpetual nongrowing dividend must be paid after four years to justify the $30 assumed future price? What should you pay for a share of this stock now?

ANSWER: The perpetual payout after year four must be 30 times 0.15, or $4.50 per share. The present value of this payout is $17.15. The present value of four years at $2 each, using the annuity formula from problem 5-2, is $5.71. The total value per share now is $22.86.

5-4. Two dividend policies appear feasible to directors of firm A. The first is to pay $4 per year indefinitely, starting with the first year. The second is to pay $5 per year indefinitely, but to delay the first payment for four years. Neglecting personal income taxes and inflation, which policy would be more valuable to you at a required rate of 8%? At a rate of 14%? In a real world of taxes and inflation, what influence would these factors have on your decision?

ANSWER: The present values of $4 per year perpetually are $50 at 8% and $28.57 at 14%. The values of $5 per year at the same rates are $62.50 and $35.71. The last two present values are four years hence, however, and must be discounted back to the current year at their respective rates. This gives values now of $45.94 and $21.14 for the second alternative policy. Even at an 8% rate, the second policy develops less total value than the first.

5-5. Companies A and B both currently pay $2 annual dividend per share. Whereas A's dividend is expected to grow over the long term at 5% per year, B's is expected to remain indefinitely at the $2 level. Compare the present worths of the shares. Required rate of return is 10%.

ANSWER: From formula 5.11, A is worth $40, whereas B is worth only $20. Even moderate growth, if continued over a long period, adds substantially to value.

5-6. Use formula 5.19 to compute the present worth of a common share under the following conditions:

(a) current earnings are $2.10 per year
(b) company policy is to retain 60% of earnings for reinvestment and to seek 20% of earnings each year from outside sources for new investments
(c) on the average, earnings are expected to grow at 3% per year indefinitely
(d) new investments on the average are expected to earn 12% net
(e) investors' required rate of return under risk is 10%

ANSWER: $E = 2.10$, and $I_1 = 80\%$ of E, or 1.68. Rates k, g, and r are 0.10, 0.03, and 0.12, respectively. Value $P_o = 21 + 4.80 = \$25.80$.

5-7. Do you have a difficult time relating to the two MM propositions on economic value, which are supported by simplifying assumptions on market substitutions? Can you imagine a world of no income taxes where there are also no differential rates nor other discrimination among classes of borrowers? If the assumptions are so artificial, of what value are the MM propositions to financial planners?

5-8. One really needs a computer to study behavior of economic value with changes of inputs in formulas like 5.20. Use the PAVE program itself. Select some cases, except VALVO, from Chapter 10. Observe changes in GOING CONCERN VALUE in the VALUTION AND SCOPE output division. Change risk inputs (marked with asterisks), sales, expenses, and growth rates. Observe and interpret changes in output values. Note that certain financial parameters may be optionally controlled by users. These are investors required rate of return, k (input ID 96), long-term growth rate, g (input ID 97), and rate of return on incremental assets, r (input ID 98).

5-9. Formulate a cash-flow decision problem similar to the example in section 5.7. Compute AOCFs and EOCFSs. Develop liquidation values at some time horizon and compute AOCF goodwills. What is your optimal decision? Should you operate or liquidate the investments? Why? How does AOCF goodwill compare with the usual meaning of goodwill on financial statements?

6 A Structure for Strategic Planning

6.1 | The Process of Strategic Planning and the Environment

Suppose you are a professional consultant and have been asked to develop a strategic plan for a commercial enterprise. You have been thrown into a new situation and must start from the ground up. What do you look for first? What do you do next? Most planners do not find themselves in this situation; often they have lived with a firm and have a great deal of knowledge about it. Nevertheless, an outsider's objective perspective may help. Possibly you are faced with a new product line, division, plant, or merger prospect. You may even have to plan for a brand new firm. Organized planning for radical change is indeed a scarce skill. Even in routine planning, a systems approach will reach toward long-term goals. Such an approach requires that a strategist be detached from the immediate situation and take a position in the environment of a firm.

The purpose of this chapter is to establish a framework for decision making about strategic plans. This is done from a detached perspective. Strategic planning is treated as problem solving for a commercial enterprise as a social system, a firm interacting with a changing environment. In section 6.2 value transformation is introduced as a basis for structuring decision processes. Objections to formal structures for strategic planning are examined against a process of rational thought about the economic mission of a firm. A specific structure for chain reasoning about strategic problems is suggested in section 6.3. Critical questions of strategy arise in each functional area of a business; section 6.4 summarizes some of these. Ways in which the structure of section 6.3 may be applied to decision models are examined in section 6.5. What kind of planning model outputs will be most useful to decision makers? What are some design factors to obtain these outputs? Such questions, particularly with respect to the PAVE model, are examined in section 6.6.

105

A structure for strategic planning should provide for such questions as "Where does one start, and what happens next?" To build a firm's strategy, planners need to follow a systematic logic. The input sequence of the PAVE model follows a logical structure which is developed in this chapter. Some of the principles that stand behind this structure were developed in preceding chapters; they are repeated here to provide a foundation. A firm is a system that interacts with a social, technological, and economic environment. A firm's existence is justified by its contribution of valuable commodities to ultimate consumption. The term *commodities*, as used here, includes both goods and services. A firm returns valuable commodities to the environment and receives human and physical resources from the environment. It is required to pay competitive prices for resources, including capital, which are allocated to it from the environment. A firm accomplishes its mission by a series of value transformations. Each transformation is intended to increase the value of commodities that a firm will return to the environment. Within a firm—a human-economic system—the goal is either long-term survival or a planned termination with valuable resources to distribute. In either case, an important measurable goal is economic value. Economic value is the present-value sum under risk of net cash flows from a firm. The Modigliani and Miller earnings-capitalization and -growth model is used in PAVE to approximate economic value to owners of a going concern. The financial-accounting model is used to develop period-by-period scenarios of the future behavior of a firm. Accounting flows are sometimes used as proxies for net cash flows. Monte Carlo simulation is used to obtain statistical inferences about risky futures, both in building scenarios and in estimating economic value.

6.2 | Value Transformation as a Basis for Strategic Planning Structures

There is a school of thought that finds it inappropriate to erect formal structures such as flow charts to describe a general decision process of strategic planning. Objections may be divided into two groups. The first has to do with the complexity of a business firm and its environment. If one uses a simple linear flow to describe what is actually a richly interconnected network, important relationships are bound to be overlooked. Decisions from oversimplified models are often suboptimal if not downright dangerous. The second objection is related to the first. A firm is an interacting system, not a series of independent business functions. If one follows a simple flow chart, decisions proceed step by step. Each decision point is a consequence of events at the preceding levels. Actual decisions in a business tend to be mutually dependent on other decisions. Thus a decision about a product line will have a direct impact on marketing strategy, and the latter, in turn, will have an impact on production plans. On the other hand, production constraints may influence both product development and marketing strategy.

In this chapter a series of simple linear flow charts is presented as a framework for general, strategic problem solving. Of course, these charts do not describe an entire system of decision; they merely suggest some fundamental relationships. If models are to be used in strategic planning, there must be logic structures in the models. If the logic of a model is made explicit, one is equipped to judge both its powers and its weaknesses. With such information a model can be used intelligently in a real environment. Apart from models, there are two reasons why a simple structure for strategic planning is presented. The first has to do with the character of human thought; the second is a consequence of value transformations within a firm.

Rational thought is carried out with words and numbers through cause-and-effect chains. Although one part of the brain is devoted to intuition, synthesis, systems, and generalization, there is a second part, which processes means-end logic for specific reasoning. The mind is capable of working through long, complex chains but has limited ability to carry separate sets of ideas in parallel. The "rule of five or seven" states that a limited number of unrelated pieces of information can be consciously retained at one time. Since planning is a process of specification, structure must be required to develop plans. If you deny strategists a formal structure, then some type of implicit structure will be adopted. The simplification of complex environments cannot be avoided, nor should it be; but it can be channeled to keep a decision process useful.

Two concepts were used to develop a simple flow chart of strategic planning. The first is hierarchy and the second is value transformation. Both a systems approach and a means-end organization of problem solving require that structure not only develop upward but move downward through layers of specific detail. At the top are general issues in the process of planning. How does a firm interact with its environment? What are the goals of a firm as a viable system in the environment? As one moves down through a chain of reasoning it becomes a question of implementing the mission established at the top. This is accomplished by developing specific plans for various business functions.

If the firm's mission is to produce valuable commodities, how is this to be accomplished? The process may be described as a series of value transformations. Here are some examples under normal circumstances. An engineering prototype is worth more than just a product idea or a design on paper. A costed, production sample is worth more than an engineering prototype. A finished product is worth more than raw materials or subassemblies. A packaged product is worth more than an unpackaged one. A product on display in a retail store is worth more than the same item in a shipping room at a warehouse.

Figure 6.1 flowcharts both hierarchical levels and value transformations from strategic planning. Horizontal arrows show that the two concepts work together at each level of problem solving. The environment of a firm is first a whole society, then a particular industry or industries within that society. Start by looking for the many types of comparative advantages a firm might enjoy within its environment. A firm might have superior technology or market position. It might enjoy a favorable location or favorable cost factors. It might possess an exceptional management team or unusually good labor relations. It might own surplus resources or have the power to command capital in competitive markets. A careful analysis of comparative advantage should lead to an explicit definition of a firm's competitive niche. Comparative advantage is implemented by establishing a favorable niche among competitors within an industry. Competitive position is a foundation for a firm's specific mission and scope. A special point needs to be made about scope, because many companies seem to have no boundary plans. They are opportunists without coherence. There should be some guidelines about how far to push a product line or service. Some important questions are immediately evident: "How many extensions are planned into product differentiation and related products?" "What is the planned path through channels of distribution and market penetration?" "To what extent will fabrication and assembly be subcontracted?" These questions merely scratch the surface; but they do suggest that scope is an important part of the mission.

After definition of a firm's position in the environment, business functions must be planned. Some of these plans cover development of commodities, marketing of commodities, operations to produce commodities, and the financing of business functions. The levels in Figure 6.1 do not describe the relative importance of various busi-

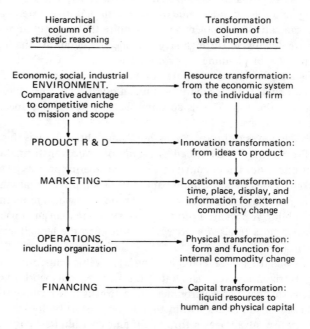

Figure 6.1 Hierarchical logic of value transformations

ness functions; rather, they represent a ranking for the series of value transformations on the right side. This ranking describes a normal sequence of value improvement. Here are some further points on the various levels. There will be no commodity values developed by a firm until resources are transformed from the economy as a whole into assets for the firm. An enterprise must use its assets to transform ideas into marketable commodities. It must develop commodities before it can market and produce them. Until marketing policies are established, a firm would not normally plan production. One needs to know such things as quantity, price, variety, and location before committing to produce a commodity. The operations function physically transforms materials and assemblies into output commodities. The term *operations* is broader than *production*; the latter is usually limited to manufacture of products. Operations may be applied to services such as health delivery or education. In contrast to physical input-output transformations from operations, the *marketing* function adds such values as timing, location, convenience, packaging, display, installation, and customer service. "Organization" was sublisted with "operations" because, at this point, plans are sufficiently developed to structure human requirements. A financing plan cements all business functions together in terms of value. It also determines how much permanent capital must be raised to carry out the rest of a plan. Value transformations from financing are from paid-in sources of capital to human and physical assets. Thus financing implements all other value transformations.

Because a hierarchy of planning for value transformations exists, there is some justification for a linear flow chart of steps in strategic decision. Even though it is not shown on Figure 6.1, dependency among decision levels is an important element in the evolution of strategic plans.

6.3 | A Professional Structure for Strategic Planning

Figure 6.2 presents a set of steps for strategic planning. Figure 6.1 shows how a hierarchical flow of value transformations can be used to develop a structure for planning. Figure 6.2 suggests how this structure can be translated into a set of benchmarks for professional planners. There is much more detail in Figure 6.2 than in Figure 6.1, but the linear flow through important business functions is the same. The sequence of blocks in Figure 6.2 represents social environment, industry environment, product research and development (R&D), marketing, operations, organization, and financing. Important links and value transformations between blocks are enclosed in brackets. Compare the blocks in Figure 6.2 with the left column of Figure 6.1, and the links in Figure 6.2 with the right column of Figure 6.1. The most important benchmarks in Figure 6.2 appear in capital letters.

A strategic planner should execute a total sequence of planning steps from two points of view. These are listed under POINTS OF VIEW in the upper left-hand corner of Figure 6.2. The first point of view is empirical or descriptive. What is a firm doing now

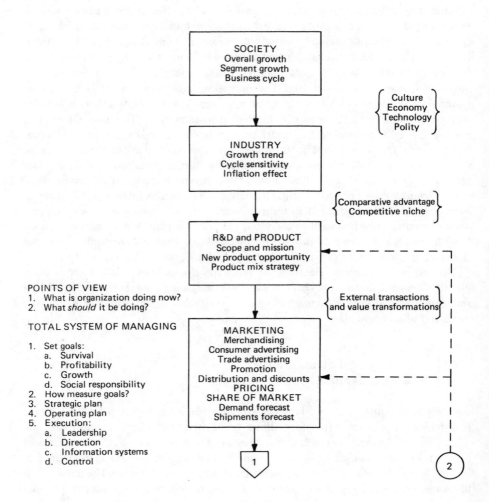

POINTS OF VIEW
1. What is organization doing now?
2. What *should* it be doing?

TOTAL SYSTEM OF MANAGING

1. Set goals:
    a. Survival
    b. Profitability
    c. Growth
    d. Social responsibility
2. How measure goals?
3. Strategic plan
4. Operating plan
5. Execution:
    a. Leadership
    b. Direction
    c. Information systems
    d. Control

Figure 6.2 Flow chart for a professional structure of strategic planning

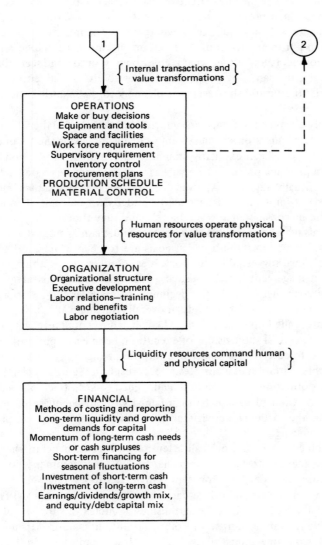

Figure 6.2 (Continued)

and where is it headed if present policies are continued? The second is normative or prescriptive. What would be the most effective plan to reach management's goals? The second point of view incorporates "oughts," or matters of value. Both points of view are essential to planners. You should know where you are at present, before prescribing changes. Given a firm and its complex environment, models and logic structures will be required to understand either what is going on now or to build scenarios of the future. Fortunately, the same logic structure applies to either a descriptive or prescriptive emphasis. It is useful, however, for planners to distinguish between these two activities.

Planning is only one phase of total management. Another inset in the left margin of Figure 6.2 reminds planners of a total system of managing. Plans should not be distributed until goals have been explicitly stated. In fact, a predetermination of goals should overlook a planning process. Otherwise a lot of time may be wasted in building plans that are eventually rejected. An even greater danger is that a plan will be approved that does not implement management's underlying expectations and objectives. Goals should be considered at several levels, and they should be a part of established policy. Goals may be organized into a means-end chain as suggested in section 1.5. It is also important to establish which goals are to be measured and how. The highest measurable goal suggested in this book is economic value of a firm.

Suppose that management has established goals and accepted a strategic plan to implement those goals. This is only the beginning of management's responsibility. There must be detailed plans to carry out an overall strategic plan. Such lower-level plans are sometimes called operating plans. When plans are complete, execution is the next step. There are several subdivisions of execution. People and physical resources must be organized to carry out a plan. One purpose of organization is to establish leadership for implementation of plans. Resources must be directed as a plan is carried out. Finally, an information system should be designed to keep track of results from execution of plans. Control cannot be maintained without adequate information. Strategic planning, the particular activity modeled in this book, is but one phase of a total system of managing.

Items in the blocks of Figure 6.2 call attention to specific benchmarks during a typical planning sequence. Most are self-explanatory, but a few comments may help to clarify the structure. The social environment is divided into several levels. The broadest is overall growth and change, both real and inflationary. Segment growth refers to related groups of industries such as the agribusiness complex or suppliers of energy. The business cycle is an important source of uncertainty in planning. Its impact differs significantly from one industry to another. Resort industries are highly pro-cyclical, chewing gum may be neutral to the cycle, and the demand for automotive repair parts may behave counter-cyclically.

In the translation of social trends to a particular industry, several classes of shifts should be examined. Demographic influences have both cultural and economic impact. The American population is aging. Families are smaller, more urban, more mobile, better educated in certain ways, less stable, and more exposed to mass media. Population and wealth are shifting to the South and the West. There are dictates of fads, fashions, and slower cultural trends—fewer haircuts, hats, and handymen. There are more airplane rides, more pollution-control equipment and digital readouts. Technological change is a major influence in the environment. For example, the electronic information revolution was discussed as a force of change in section 1.7. No business person needs to be reminded that the political environment may make or break him or her. Apart from changes in taxes, inflation, and the money supply, a political shift may create an immediate feast or famine. Two examples are military spending and the construction of low-income housing. Political and social forces combine. There is a massive campaign against smoking; neither it nor hard liquor may be advertised on television. Extending beyond the American scene are international opportunities and risks. These are just a few environmental areas in which planners should do research before developing specific strategies for a firm.

The end point of environmental analysis is a forecast of industry sales. Sales demand available to a firm is the result of some market penetration policy within an industry. Factors to consider in formulating such a policy are suggested in the next section. Returning to industry sales, there is a long-term or secular growth trend, sensitivity to the business cycle, sensitivity to inflation, and a seasonal pattern. Planners should combine these factors into a composite forecast, a process simulated in PAVE. Product life-cycle theory is a useful tool for understanding long-term trends in sales.

An adjustment process for dealing with mutual dependence among business functions is suggested in Figure 6.2. An initial planning scenario can be erected by following a linear sequence from product development to marketing strategy to operations. Organization and financing are next developed to support an initial plan. Most likely, a first pass through the system will not produce an acceptable strategy. Observation of results may suggest changes in policy. Earnings might be improved, for example, if one recycles planning of product features and pricing. A total process of strategic planning, therefore, is a matter of adjustment and feedback. The most common feedback paths are shown by dashed lines. A particular scenario may be constructed with a simple logic chain. A final plan, however, usually requires multiple scenarios. Such a plan should accommodate interactions among business functions. Since adjustment and feedback is a repetitive process, computer models such as PAVE are useful to reduce the burden of computations. PAVE contains an internal feedback loop for sensitivity analysis. One may adjust inputs and note the impact of change on outputs.

6.4 | Some Critical Factors in the Development of Strategy

A strategic plan is a decision about allocating a firm's scarce resources. The survival of a firm depends on how skillfully resources are deployed in functional areas such as product development, marketing, and operations. Of course, planners should team up with functional area specialists, but there is a system level that demands more than specialized expertise. Looking down from this level, the blunt question is, Where should a firm place its chips? One type of decision concerns which projects to enter and which to reject or phase out. The word *project* refers here to major lines of business such as product or service groups. To decide on projects, capital budgeting models under risk may be used, such as those described in section 2.3. The concern here, however, is not on a valuation of cash flows but on factors in the environment that stand behind cash flows. Once a firm has established a project, there is a second type of decision. How should planners support a project with allocation of resources among business functions? From a systems viewpoint certain critical factors must be considered when developing major strategies.

Candidate projects come from a study of the environment and the comparative advantage within an industry. In section 6.3 an introduction to environmental analysis summarizes this point of view. Here, attention shifts to an individual firm's relation to an industry. If a firm has carved out a competitive niche from some comparative advantage, what it really has achieved is market power. With market power, a firm has some degree of control over its product specifications, demand schedule, pricing, marketing policies, and continuity of operations.

Without market power, a firm is merely a victim of environmental conditions. Then markets command firms, and not vice versa. Monopolies and oligopolies (a few sellers share an industry) have a great deal of market power. A telephone company is a monopoly; automobile manufacturers belong to an oligopoly. At the other extreme, family farms and small ranches have almost no market power. Sometimes small operators band together in associations. This is an attempt to acquire some market power. Some individual small businesses, however, may have a great deal of power. Gas stations or fast-food franchises may enjoy a prime location where there is limited room for competitors. Market power is a matter of degree and is almost never complete. "Natural" monopolies such as public utilities are subject to control by rate commissions and government regulations. Why should a firm enter a business where no discernible comparative advantage exists? Such action is hard to justify even though it is often done. With high growth opportunity, is there always room for one more? If you enter, and it is easy for others to enter, the market will soon become flooded, because growth does not continue forever. If you enter, and it is difficult for others to enter, then you have acquired a form of comparative advantage!

How much market power is needed to be successful? For an answer, one must look at the competitive structure of an industry. Most firms compete within a particular niche and with some degree of monopolistic power. The steel-bearings industry is dominated by three or four giant competitors (oligopolists) and eighty or so small firms. This structure is typical of many industries. Unless a firm enjoys some specialized niche, it would not want to end up at the tail of the kite. It boils down to market leadership, especially price leadership. In most industries, if one firm raises its price and others do not follow, the original firm loses much of its market. If a firm lowers its price, however, and it has any force in the market, others will be compelled to respond. Such action might destroy profits for everybody. In mature industries the total market may not expand appreciably when price is lowered. Oligopolists often seek to avoid destructive price wars, preferring, instead, nonprice competition. To maintain market discipline requires a small group of responsible competitors, government intervention, or some sort of professional association. It is not easy to avoid market disorder during periods of low demand. Weak or dying competitors may dump distress merchandise to raise cash. Strong firms may lower prices to drive out competitors.

A firm must have enough power to help maintain an orderly market under cyclical demand. This means it must be a price leader or at least influence price leadership. Such influence is not forthcoming without a substantial share of the industry market. By *substantial*, we mean 10% or more, and certainly not 1% or 2%. Look at firms with small market shares in any major industry; they are the ones that drop out or get swallowed up. Even if such firms appear to prosper for a time, there comes a day of recession or shake out. At best, they struggle along on the fringe of a market. Caution must be exercised when determining market share. It is the immediate competitors that count. You may have 40% of the auto repair business in a small town but only 0.1% in the town's standard metropolitan area. If it is not easy for local people to go elsewhere, it is the 40% that counts. Enter or remain in lines of business where there is an orderly market, and you can achieve a substantial market share. A possible exception is new growth opportunities; but here, the objective is to build a solid market position in the future.

Assuming a reasonable share of market control, a planner must look at pricing structures. We have already mentioned that prices must meet competition. A firm with price leadership can exert considerable pressure to raise prices and protect profit margins. If others follow, the industry gains; if not, the leader will probably retreat. Profits that are not satisfactory at average price levels is a signal for firms to leave the industry. Even in orderly industries profit margins often suffer from prolonged downward pressure—for example, the major American oil companies for several years before the energy crisis. Under such conditions an individual firm is tempted to raise prices and thus suffer a corresponding loss in market share. In the short run this might improve earnings; in the long run it will probably be a disaster. It is extremely expensive, if not impossible, to buy back sizable chunks of market share over short periods. The sounder strategy is usually to promote an orderly market, maintain market share, and meet market prices.

Sophisticated product differentiation and brand-development strategies may improve profitability for a product line, while good margins on deluxe models can offset low margins on loss leaders. Brand recognition may allow a firm to command higher price than "no name" competitors. Price elasticity is a useful ratio for examining market policy. For any schedule of quantity demanded against prices, price elasticity at some point on the schedule is the percentage change in quantity divided by the percentage change in price. Price elasticity is negative because quantity demanded goes down as price rises. Suppose a demand schedule shows that ten million television sets can be sold at an average price of $400 each. In that case, total sales revenue is $4 billion. Assume, at this point, that a 1% drop in sales demand accompanies a 1% increase in price. The elasticity would be -1 (unitary elasticity), and total sales revenue (price times quantity) would remain unchanged at $4 billion. Now assume that sales units drop 2%, for a price increase of 1%. Demand is now elastic at -2, and total revenue drops to about $3.96 million, with a 1% increase in price. If sales units drop only 0.5%, with a price increase of 1%, demand would be inelastic at -0.5% and sales revenue would increase to about $4.02 billion. If prices are raised, profits are likely to improve if demand is inelastic, but profits will usually suffer if demand is elastic. Brand acceptance, market control, and product differentiation tend to make demand more inelastic. One danger is that a company may attach too much importance to its own brand acceptance and assume more inelasticity that it should. Planners should maintain a healthy skepticism and estimate elasticity with controlled experiments.

Position in a product life cycle is significant to planners. Figure 4.3 may be much too smooth for many industries. Products often have periods of growth and decline, long periods of stable maturity, and distinct steps up and down. Think of rapid transit cars or army rifles. Opportunity lies in high-growth periods, but this does not automatically lead to profits. Few manufacturers made money during the rapid growth of consumer television in the 1950s and '60s. The market was disorderly, with many weak competitors. A firm that enjoys a substantial share of a mature-industry market is often in an excellent position. The product may become a "cash cow" especially if management is alert enough to limit additional investments.

Once a product or service policy has been established, how should scarce resources be allocated among business functions? One answer is that funds should accompany comparative advantage. If, for example, a competitive niche depends on engineering and design, this function should be supported internally. If favorable manufacturing cost creates a competitive edge, investments should be made with a view to maintaining and improving this edge. Resources, personnel, and emphasis should reinforce a firm's particular areas of expertise. If resources are scarce a firm might as well contract out activities others can perform as well or better.

The degree of integration of related activities into a firm depends on resource position. Resources are usually scarce during periods of high growth. In such cases it pays to use other people's capital. Rent buildings and facilities instead of owning them. Subcontract for production and services when these are not critical to performance. Let others invest in setting up channels of distribution. On the other hand, firms may accumulate surplus resources. In such cases, a takeover of related functions may become profitable. It is often less risky for a firm to invest in projects closely related to its current business than to venture into unrelated fields where it has no experience. Several types of integration are available. In *vertical* integration a firm invests up and down channels of distribution. A manufacturer, for example, might start to fabricate parts it previously purchased. On the other hand, manufacturer might establish or acquire a chain of retail stores. In *horizontal* integration, a firm ventures into related products or activities at the same levels as its current business. Given profit opportunity and careful planning, integration is more likely to improve value, especially in the short run, than expansion through conglomeration.

6.5 | Structures for Strategic Planning and the Design of Models

Planning is a dynamic process of iterative logic sequences. Adjustment and feedback are connecting links between successive scenarios. Each scenario is a tentative plan from a logical system such as that diagrammed in Figure 6.2. How should models be specified to support strategic planning? Because planning is complex, simple models are not likely to help much at a total system level. Required, instead, are large-scale logic simulators, often operated by number-crunching computers. The financial-accounting model is a large-scale simulator of economic transactions within a firm. As noted in Chapter 4, routine accounting is readily computerized. It follows that accounting simulators may process much of the logic used to quantify strategic plans.

If models are an aid to decision processes, then the mode of partnership between models and humans is important in design. A total decision system becomes a human-model system or a human-computer system; it is a question of how humans and computers interact. A model is an input-output generator; humans intervene between successive cycles of outputs and inputs. If planning models are designed as decision support systems, then human-model interaction should be flexible, conversational, and mutually responsive. Modes of interaction between humans and planning simulators fall into two classes. In the first class are regular simulation models such as PAVE. With PAVE, a user enters policy and environmental inputs; PAVE then processes a scenario of the future over whatever set of periods was commanded. At the end of a scenario, control is returned to users. Users may examine outputs and make adjustments to inputs. The model may be rerun indefinitely on an input-output cycle of human-computer interchange.

The second class is management-simulation gaming. As an example, OPSTAC will be described briefly. Each of one to nine firms designs, manufactures, and sells from one to three of the same type of consumer hard goods. Examples of such goods are home appliances and consumer electronic items. Each period of operation is a quarter of a year, with human intervention in the decision process at the beginning of each quarter. Each firm is managed by a team that analyzes output results from the preceding quarter and makes policy decisions for the next quarter. The OPSTAC computer program provides an economic environment and implements policy decisions one quarter at a time. The cycle of quarterly human-computer decision and output may be repeated indefinitely. Since all firms start with approximately the same environment and resources, and each has the same opportunities for policy decisions, teams may compete for the most successful management performance. The output-reporting system prints financial statements and information on competitive markets. A stock price is estimated; hence, each team faces an economic value in capital markets. A risky environment can be simulated by OPSTAC and many other management games.

The general structure of PAVE and OPSTAC is similar. Both use Monte Carlo simulation methods to incorporate risk and both process accounting logic. Although management-simulation games are usually used as a teaching tool, there are exciting possibilities for research and professional planning. For example, OPSTAC could serve as a focus for experiments on decision-making behavior or methods of efficient problem solving. Either PAVE or OPSTAC may be used for teaching, research, or professional planning. The difference between PAVE and OPSTAC is the timing of human intervention in a dynamic decision process. In PAVE humans interact once at the beginning of each scenario; in OPSTAC humans interact every period during a scenario. Each has a practical application. Strategic plans with only one forward period would seldom be acceptable; hence PAVE is needed for multiple periods. On the other hand, planning should be dynamic. Plans should be adjusted as environmental conditions shift over time. OPSTAC replicates a process of sequential adjustment to change. PAVE also may be used for gaming environments by simulating one period at a time.

What kind of input system should be developed for planning simulators such as PAVE or OPSTAC? How does such a system conform to a logic structure for strategic planning, such as diagrammed in Figure 6.2? To answer such questions the flow charts in figures 6.3 and 6.4 were prepared for the input systems of PAVE and OPSTAC. In Figure 6.3 for PAVE, the first two blocks are not policy inputs. The first block contains general commands which establish scope and statistical specifications for a particular simulation run. Initial conditions (starting balance sheet) of a firm are entered in the second block. The remaining four blocks approximate the strategic logic of figures 6.1 and 6.2. Inputs move through economic environment, industry environment, product policy, marketing strategy, general and administrative expense, and financing. The ENVIRONMENT and MANUFACTURING input sections are optional because their relevance depends on the class of firm and scope of a run. For convenience in a decision process, manufacturing operations are separated from service operations. Policies on service operations are entered under GENERAL EXPENSES. Organizational decisions may thus be divided between manufacturing and general expenses. The whole input system of PAVE is divided into six divisions, which correspond to the blocks of Figure 6.3. In the last four blocks—the policy chain—PAVE will optionally print policy reminder statements (POLREMS). These statements present a checklist of critical decision items for each major business function.

The input structure of OPSTAC also conforms to the logic of business decisions from Figure 6.2. There is a linear system diagrammed in Figure 6.4. Compared to PAVE, OPSTAC has much more detail and much less flexibility. The numbered files which appear in this figure are supplementary decision models. Game participants run these models interactively on minicomputers as aids to decision processes. The inputs under ORGANIZATION are not entered directly in computer runs of OPSTAC. Each

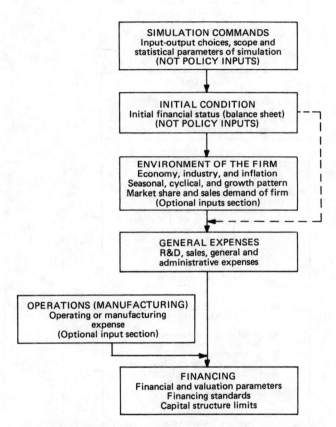

Note: PAVE optionally prints policy reminder statements (POLREMS) at the beginning of each policy input section.

Figure 6.3 Policy planning structure of PAVE input divisions

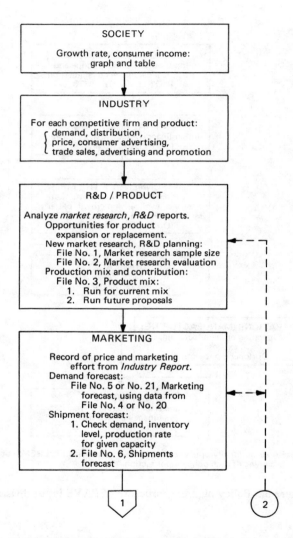

Figure 6.4 Policy planning structure of OPSTAC games

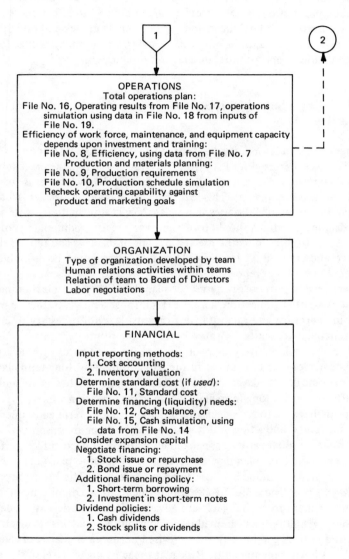

Figure 6.4 (Continued)

team is required to study its own decision-making structure and interpersonal relationships. Professional managers and instructors take on roles as board members to oversee teams. Labor negotiations and collective bargaining are often conducted during a training session with OPSTAC. Provision has been made in the operation of OPSTAC for strikes and other disruptions of normal activity. The input system of PAVE also permits simulation of abrupt shifts in sales and production.

6.6 | Modeling a Set of Outputs for Strategic Plans

Input systems of simulators may be designed to fit a rational structure of strategic decision. This was discussed for PAVE and OPSTAC models in the preceding section. Attention now turns to model outputs. A model is useful only if outputs are perceived as valuable by decision makers. This leads back to planning processes. What kind of plans should be prepared? Who uses these plans? What information do users need? In other words, model outputs should be designed to specific requirements of planners and users. Apart from outputs themselves, designs of displays and reports determine convenience and readability. How should output information be assembled? What formats should be used in reports?

There are several purposes for strategic planning. Every organization needs long-term plans. A written projection should extend for several years. Such a projection may combine narrative and quantitative forecasts. It is not necessary to prepare accounting statement forecasts for several years in the future, but this is often useful. Long-term plans such as five-year plans are not intended to dictate decisions now which will be made some time in the future. Put another way, long-term plans should be revised periodically to take account of changes in opportunities, goals, and environmental shifts. Why make long-term plans if tomorrow's decision is likely to come from a revised plan? Because today's decisions usually have long-term consequences. This is obvious for capital budgeting, but it also applies to other areas, some of which are marketing policy, product strategy, personnel relations, and executive recruitment.

Given some long-term planning, several levels of specific plans may be derived. These are prepared for immediate use in an organization. The lowest level may be termed *budget plans*. These are specific commitments for accomplishment, usually in accounting statement form. Budgets have advantages of task orientation, deterministic programming, and fixing of individual responsibilities. Budgets are often prepared for one future year. A good practice is to revise budgets each quarter of a year, or for any significant environmental shift. Risk plans reach a higher level of decision than budget plans. Flexible budgeting is the simplest approach to risk plans. Multiple levels of budgets may be prepared to meet different conditions. Often this is called *parallel budgeting*. To an extent anticipated by planners, a drop in sales may be matched with reductions in budgeted expenses. In a similar manner budget changes can be planned for other variable conditions. Flexible budgets can be supplemented by statistical analysis. Which changes in the environment are significant and which are trivial? Confidence intervals for estimated future values help to answer such questions. Contingency plans may be prepared to cope with radical change. Strategists are then pre-programming response to turbulence. The impact of a change, such as an outbreak of hostilities or the location of a large plant in a small town, may often be anticipated. But there may be insufficient information to predict whether a particular event will actually take place. There is much to be said for planning responses to crises rather than waiting unprepared for one to descend on you.

In the PAVE model there are four output divisions. Although instructions for using PAVE start with Part II in the next chapter, a preview is given here about how outputs of PAVE relate to various levels of planning. The first output division, VALUATION AND SCOPE, is a summary of economic value under risk. Statistical information is printed—means, standard deviations, and confidence limits. Beginning and ending values of a firm may be compared, specifically, first and final year values over a PAVE simulation. Both total and per share figures are printed. Probabilities of insolvency are estimated, if any occur. Both going-concern and liquidation values are computed. Important parameters of risk and growth are reported.

The second PAVE output division, FINANCIAL SUMMARY, prints the position of a firm at the end of a simulation. Up to thirty-three financial values and ratios describe this final position. Six summary statistics can be printed for each time.

The third output division, FINANCIAL STATEMENTS, projects a complete set of financial information for all periods. In addition to cost, income and condition statements, there are statements of cash flow and some figures on the economic and industry environment. Annual totals are printed, as well as values for each period. In this output division there is no risk analysis; figures are mean values from the simulation.

The fourth PAVE output division, SELECTED ACCOUNTS, provides a statistical analysis for all periods. Up to seventeen accounts are available. Means, standard deviations, and confidence limits may be printed for each account.

Figure 6.5 diagrams how output divisions of PAVE may serve various levels of planning. The four output divisions are labeled VALUATION AND SCOPE, FINANCIAL SUMMARY, FINANCIAL STATEMENTS, and SELECTED ACCOUNTS. Although each output division might contribute something at any level of planning, the most useful paths are shown on the figure. Solid lines relate output divisions to LONG-TERM PLANS. VALUATION AND SCOPE contains long-term measures of value and size. This division focuses on expectations from long-term planning. Because PAVE can be run for many periods into the future, such as twenty quarterly periods over five years, projected financial statements is another useful tool for long-term planning. The same goes for a financial summary at the end of a planning horizon. Budget plans are connected to financial statements with a dashed line. The report form of financial-statements output is in a familiar accounting arrangement. The flexible-budgets level of planning is interconnected with dotted lines. This level may make use of financial-statements outputs. To obtain flexibility, several sets of statements should be prepared. For a statistical analysis of important accounts under risk, flexible budgets may make use of selected-accounts output division. Since financial statements output division is useful for the development of alternate scenarios, it is a tool for preparing contingency budgets. When preparing for contingencies it is usually important to summarize the impact of turbulence on a firm's total position. The financial-summary output division prints this kind of information. Lines with long and short dashes show interconnections at the contingency-budget level.

Budgets can be focused on long-term planning, and long-term planning may be focused, in turn, on the worth of a firm. There are up to four computed of worth in the valuation and scope output division of PAVE. Each is computed at least twice, once at the beginning and again at the end of a simulation. Owner's equity is the financial accounting residual of net worth. A statistical summary of this figure is available for beginning and end of run in VALUATION AND SCOPE. A statistical output of

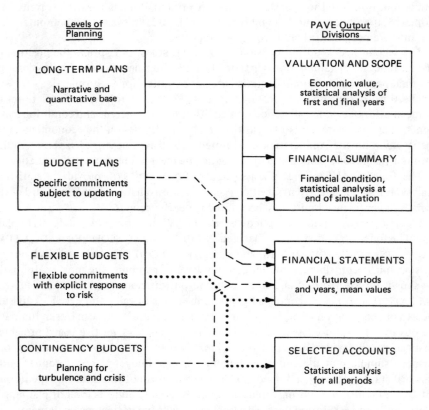

Figure 6.5 Relationship among levels of planning and PAVE outputs

owners' equity for all periods is among the items in the selected-accounts division. Mean values of owners' equity for all periods are printed in the financial statements outputs.

For a sample run of two or more, going-concern values are estimated in VALUATION AND SCOPE. These computations use the Modigliani and Miller earnings capitalization formulas from section 5.4. Important parameters of capitalization are also printed: investors' required rate of return under risk, long-term growth rate, and rate of return on incremental assets. Liquidation values of assets are computed in VALUATION AND SCOPE. Total liabilities are also subtracted from the above values, which leads to liquidation values to owners as a third estimate of worth. If users input nonzero price-earnings multiples, market values will be computed as separate figures for a fourth estimate of value. Otherwise, market values are set equal to the higher of going-concern or liquidation values. In such cases price-earnings multiples are calculated internally. In PAVE, the best estimate of an economic value to owners is the higher of going-concern value or liquidation value.

Whether one is working with flexible budgets, analyses of risk, contingency plans, or merely exploring scenarios, an important purpose is an examination of response to change. The preparation of alternate plans is a basis for rational decision making under uncertainty. In the PAVE model, alternate plans may be developed either by Monte Carlo statistical inference (section 3.4) or by user-controlled reruns. The end result is sensitivity analysis. How large a change occurs in outputs for a given set of changes in inputs? This is at the core of risk management. If outputs are sensitive to some type of unfavorable environmental shift, problem solving should be applied to this area. A program of adjustment, feedback, and sensitivity analysis extracts the most power from models such as PAVE.

References and Additional Readings

One of the best references on strategic planning for financial managers is H. Bierman's *Decision Making and Planning for the Corporate Treasurer*, Wiley, 1977. Another book by Bierman is *Financial Policy Decisions*, Macmillan, 1970. Also consult the references on *capital budgeting* and *financial management* in Chapter 2 of the present book.

Several excellent books are available on long-range planning. Among these are P. Lorange and R.F. Vancil, *Strategic Planning Systems*, Prentice-Hall, 1977; F.T. Paine and W. Naumes, *Strategy and Policy Formulation: An Integrative Approach*, W.B. Saunders, 1974; E. Rhenman, *Organization Theory for Long-Range Planning*, Wiley, 1973; and E.K. Warren, *Long-Range Planning: The Executive Viewpoint*, Prentice-Hall, 1966. How many of the books present structured processes for planning? How do their structures compare with PAVE? Relate these books to problem 6-4.

In the area of management control and information systems, two excellent references are R.N. Anthony, J. Dearden, and R.F. Vancil, *Management Control Systems: Text, Cases, and Readings*, rev. ed., Irwin, 1972; and J.

Dearden, F.W. McFarlan, and W.M. Zani, *Managing Computer-Based Information Systems*, Irwin, 1971.

A number of books were written to improve professional problem solving for practicing executives. Among these are S. Beer, *Decision and Control*, Wiley, 1966; P.F. Drucker, *Managing for Results*, Harper and Row, 1964; P.F. Drucker, *The Effective Executive*, Harper and Row, 1966; and H.A. Simon, *The New Science of Management Decision*, rev. ed., Prentice-Hall, 1977.

The PAVE simulation was originated at Georgia State University in Atlanta. PAVE authors are C.L. Hubbard, R.A. Peterson, Jr., and F.J. Ganoe. Instruction manuals by these authors have been published by the College of Business Administration at Georgia State University.

The OPSTAC decision-oriented management simulation game—Operations Planning, Strategy, and Tactics—is published by the College of Business Administration at Georgia State University.

PROBLEMS TO INVESTIGATE

6-1. Considerable space in Part I is devoted to models and thought processes, especially logic chains in the presence of complexity and uncertainty. At this point indicate your own view of the relation between systematic structures and the development of strategy for a firm.

6-2. Do you agree that some comparative advantage must be recognizable for each going concern? If so, determine such advantages for a group of firms known to you. If not, find examples to support your position. How are such firms able to continue in business?

6-3. For the group of firms known to you from problem 6-2, make a list of major value transformations in each. Are you aware of cases of negative value transformations from action by a firm, which reduced value? Why did these transformations occur?

6-4. Examine several textbooks or professional books on business policy or strategy. How many of these books present a formal structure for solving business problems? Compare similarities and differences among the systems of the other books and this book.

6-5. Discuss market power in relation to comparative advantage, competitive niche, monopoly power, price leadership, nonprice competition, price elasticity of demand, and size of market share. After thinking about market power, would you take a position or continue with a firm which enjoyed a 2% share of its particular market?

6-6. Name some commodities with peculiar life-cycle behavior. What stage are they in now? What stage do you forecast for them ten years from now?

6-7. Do most firm's have one functional area critical for survival, such as marketing, engineering, or production? Should the president of a firm be chosen from the critical function? Look at some firms and check on the above two questions. Would you expect a president from some functional area to favor that area in allocating resources? Might such favoritism be appropriate? Perhaps you favor an external president, for example, a lawyer, a former politician, or a member of the military. If so, support your case.

6-8. Discuss the nature of human-model-computer interactions in various types of problem-solving modes: operations research, outside consulting services, internal task force, product managers imposed as a grid on an organization, DSS, and management-simulation gaming.

6-9. In what sense is long-term planning a misnomer? Compare the assertion, *long-run plans should never be long* with the famous J.M. Keynes, one-liner, *in the long run we are all dead*. Now defend long-term planning.

6-10. Three methods of coping with uncertainty were introduced in section 2.1. Consider each method as a level of modeling. How is each level related to planning activity, formal budgets, management simulation games, and PAVE strategic simulations?

6-11. Why is a process of feedback and adjustment so important when dealing with complex and ill-structured problem solving? Relate this process to sensitivity analysis and the use of models such as PAVE to solve problems. Is this process the essential difference between DSS and conventional operations research activities?

PART II

Simulation of Strategy With PAVE Model

There are two main areas within this part: instructions for operating PAVE simulations, and case examples of PAVE applications. Chapters 7 through 10 contain fundamental information; chapters 11 and 12 present advanced extensions. Chapters 7 through 9 explain the PAVE model itself. Chapter 7 is an overview of PAVE capabilities, logic, input system, output information, and limitations. Chapter 8 is devoted to instructions for inputs and runs of PAVE. A brief glossary of input items appears in the last section of Chapter 8. Chapter 9 contains information on the interpretation of PAVE outputs. Chapters 7 through 9 are intended for users who wish to interact with computers at terminals but do want to become involved in the advanced technology of decision-support-system models. Apart from specific applications of PAVE, there is the general issue of interactive systems between managers and computer models. What are the trade-offs among decision power, flexibility, and minilanguage demands? Chapters 7 through 9 address some of these issues.

The best way to develop expertise in financial modeling is to become directly involved with inputs and outputs for specific firms. Four cases, each progressively more difficult, are presented in Chapter 10. The cases exhibit the four frames available with PAVE: VALVO for environment analysis only, AUTOWASH for a service firm, FLORA-WREATH for merchandising, and ECOFURN for manufacturing. A final section of Chapter 10 exhibits some extended analysis and sensitivity considerations for ECO-FURN. Each case contains a description of the firm's situation, development of PAVE inputs sets, and an interpretation of outputs. It is suggested that users move to the cases in Chapter 10 as soon as possible. Chapters 8 and 9 should be reread as reference material while working on cases.

Chapter 11 provides information on some extended capabilities of the PAVE simulation system. Two advanced cases in Chapter 12, GIFTIQUE and HPG PRODUCTS, illustrate enlarged input systems. There is a further interpretation of outputs and exploration of alternatives.

A glossary of all PAVE inputs is provided in an appendix. The design of PAVE programs is contained in Part III.

129

PART II

Simulation of Strategy With a PAVE Model

7 PAVE–A Decision Support System

7.1 | What Is PAVE and How Do You Start Using It?

PAVE—Planning and Valuation of Enterprises—is a decision support system for aggregate strategic planning of commercial firms. By aggregate is meant an overall economic-financial condition, not individual plants or products.

PAVE interacts with users on minicomputers or time-sharing terminals through video displays and line printing of inputs and outputs.

Inputs are conversational between video displays and keyboard entries. The input system is designed to follow a logical strategic decision plan. Outputs provide the following:

from 1 to 24 consecutive periods, each of any length

statistical confidence limits for risky values

going-concern value of proposed or existing enterprises under risk

capital requirements—equity and debt—short and long term

cash-flow analysis—short and long term

probability of insolvency

value in liquidation

financial analysis—ratios and summary values

budgeted or projected financial statements

social and industrial environment of a firm

influence of inflation on growth, costs, and value

frameworks for manufacturing, trading, and service

contingency, sensitivity, scenario building, and what-if analysis

To apply a large-system model such as PAVE, use a step-by-step arrangement, as adopted here. Chapters 7 through 10 explain and illustrate the basic system; remaining chapters of Part II explore extensions. It is much better to get involved with PAVE in actual planning situations than to read pages of explanations. For this reason, business cases are introduced as early as possible. The cases are presented in order of increasing complexity of inputs. The first two cases, VALVO and AUTOWASH in sections 10.1 and 10.2, require only about twenty input items. The last and most complex case, HPG PRODUCTS in Chapter 12, uses about 200 inputs.

The following steps are suggested for developing proficiency with PAVE:

1. Read a few pages that overview PAVE's scope and limitations. Section 7.2 gives a short introduction to the PAVE system as a software package on your computer. What can PAVE do and what kind of logic does it use in the process? This is examined briefly in section 7.3. PAVE was designed to serve humans in exploring strategic questions. Some of these questions are posed in section 7.4. Section 7.5 summarizes the power and limits of PAVE.

2. Try a personal interaction with PAVE before attempting a complete input set for a simulated firm. What happens when PAVE is called up at the computer? Preliminary exchanges of information are discussed in section 8.1.

3. To extract full power from a model, it is necessary to understand its input rules. This amounts to a minilanguage which is used to inform the model. There are only a few input rules in PAVE, but they are important. PAVE input rules should be surveyed by reading section 8.2 before attempting a full input set at a terminal. Refer to this section while working on cases.

4. Start with the simplest PAVE cases—VALVO and AUTOWASH. These are found in sections 10.1 and 10.2. Along with the cases, read some additional information about the PAVE input system. The structure of PAVE input method is discussed in section 8.3, and user control of input data files in section 8.4. Sections 9.1 to 9.3 describe the information printed by output divisions.

5. Attempt somewhat more complex cases than VALVO and AUTOWASH. Sections 10.3 to 10.5 contain such cases—FLORAWREATH and FURNAIR. Read the additional sections that contain reference information to support the inputs for cases. Of particular interest in section 8.5, which provides a compact glossary of basic input items. The Appendix, an extension of section 8.5, contains a complete glossary of all inputs. Section 9.4 reviews some important choices about simulated conditions during a run. Section 9.5 contains a checklist of errors which frequently destroy useful outputs.

6. For extensions of PAVE capabilities, work with additional instructions in Chapter 10 and the cases of Chapter 12. To meet particular situations, input extensions may be applied selectively.

7.2 | The Organization of a PAVE Run

You are seated at a computer terminal for a PAVE run. Make sure your video display screen has been turned up and your line printer turned on. You will need both of these for each run.

PAVE is not one program but six segments—PAVE1 to PAVE6—which are chained in one after the other. Separate segments keep the work space (RAM) from becoming overloaded with too much coding and data at one time. The two kinds of data files are:

1. Input data files store sets of input items. Each input file stores one input set for one firm. Input data files are named, controlled, and provided with inputs by users in PAVE1, the first program segment. The input process is interactive between keyboard and video display. It is a good idea to furnish new users of PAVE with a complete input data file or two. This introduces them to the PAVE system with a predetermined demonstration of inputs and outputs.

2. Five data transfer files—PAVEFT1 to PAVEFT5—are required to supply information among the six PAVE program segments. The transfer files are separate from input data files.

Here is a summary of the PAVE file system:

Program PAVE1—establishes inputs interactively with users

Program PAVE2—processes values that do not require statistical treatment

Program PAVE3—processes values through a Monte Carlo statistical-simulation sequence

Program PAVE4—determines value of the firm; prints two output divisions, VALUATION AND SCOPE and FINANCIAL SUMMARY FROM FINAL PERIOD

Program PAVE5—Prints first group of FINANCIAL STATEMENTS output division

Program PAVE6—Prints second group of FINANCIAL STATEMENTS output division and SELECTED ACCOUNTS output division

Input data files—as many as required under user names

Transfer data files PAVEFT1 to PAVEFT5—supply information for processing among program segments PAVE1 to PAVE6

PAVE software reproductions in this book access program and data files from dual-floppy minidiskette drives. The drives are labeled *left port* and *right port* in the video displays and operating instructions. Actual installations of PAVE will require adaptations to particular storage media. For example, main and auxiliary cassette tape drives could be substituted for disk drives. For disks or cassettes of sufficient capacity, required drives may be reduced from two to one. The point here is that users must obtain appropriate information about their particular input system. This may lead to minor modifications of the interactive input processing of PAVE1. Such modifications are noted in section 8.1 operating instructions for PAVE1.

Returning to the dual-drive disk storage system, software reproduction here requires that program files PAVE1 through PAVE6 be mounted in the right port drive. All data files, both input and transfer (PAVEFT1 through PAVEFT5), are to be mounted in the left port drive. Again, it is easy to change this. Video displays in PAVE1, however, as described in this book, present the above arrangement.

PAVE is programmed in BASIC computer language because this is the most adaptable to interactive human-machine inputs and report writing of outputs. BASIC is rapidly becoming universal for minicomputers and is also available on most time-sharing systems. Users of PAVE do not need to program in any language. They do need to learn commands to operate their machines according to PAVE input rules. The sequence of steps for a PAVE run is:

1. Turn on computer or terminal; turn up video screen; turn on line printer.
2. LOAD program PAVE1 into work space (RAM).
3. Command RUN for PAVE1.
4. Interact with PAVE1 to establish an input data set for the run and update input data files.
5. When inputs are complete, enter RUN=8 from PAVE1 menu to continue processing.
6. After an output is printed, select another output, return to PAVE1 for input changes, or END the run.

The above sequence shows that after LOAD of PAVE1, users are not involved in the processing of PAVE2 to PAVE6 segments and PAVEFT series transfer files. All this is controlled internally by the PAVE programs. The video display does inform users which program segment is currently in RAM. An incomplete run may abort due to problems in the computer, storage media, or coding. When the problem has been corrected, users may not have to reenter the inputs, but simply rerun the aborted program segment. This will not cause problems if no new values have been introduced at the terminal.

Users may encounter major variations in the time of one run among different machines. There are several reasons for this. Among different computers, speed-of-processing statements may vary by a ratio of 10 to 1 or more. It takes much longer to load programs and data files from cassette tape than from magnetic disks. Disk drives themselves differ on access speeds. After PAVE1 inputs are complete, each RUN requires from three to five additional programs, and from three to five data files. From all sources of variation RUN times may range from less than two minutes to more than half an hour. There is considerable printing for some output choices, and printer speed is another variable.

Fortunately, once PAVE1 has been loaded, variations are moderate in video display response time to keyboard entries. The medium of video displays speeds up interactive inputs. Users with slow machines need not be concerned. Once inputs are complete there is no further human-machine interaction until output is reached. After an output, the system waits for a user's next command.

7.3 | PAVE Capabilities and Logic

Many computer planning and budgeting models are available, which are based on accounting frameworks. Many have elaborate modules for different types of firms and multiple-product cost accounting. When it comes to interactive DSS models for minicomputers, however, available software is limited. Nevertheless, many such systems are under development to match particular computers.

As compared to existing modular business support modules, PAVE has the following special features:

1. Going-concern economic value under risk is estimated.
2. Probability of insolvency is printed.
3. Liquidation values are approximated.
4. Capital requirements may be internally determined from long-term cash-flow processing.
5. Statistical measures of uncertainty may be applied to the final condition of a firm.
6. Statistical measures of uncertainty may be applied to key accounts for all periods.
7. There is a separate computation of sales demand, which may be compared to capacity over periods.
8. Analysis of the economic and industry environment of a firm is available.

The four output divisions of PAVE are:

1. VALUATION AND SCOPE for the first and final years:
   (a) sales, return on owners' equity, owners' equity, total assets, and book value of fixed assets
   (b) probabilities of insolvency
   (c) market, going-concern, and liquidation values
   (d) parameters of going-concern value

2. FINANCIAL SUMMARY from final period
   Scope, ratios of profitability and financial condition, and key financial values

3. FINANCIAL STATEMENTS or budgets projected for all periods
Environment of economy and industry, income, costs of goods, cash flow, capital changes, and condition (balance sheets)
4. SELECTED ACCOUNTS
statistical analyses for one to seventeen key accounts for all periods

For a detailed outline of PAVE outputs, see Table 9.1.

PAVE is a Monte Carlo simulation over a series of periods with user-controlled uncertainty. There is a choice of zero to twelve risky inputs. Statistical summaries are computed for key outputs. The financial accounting model is used for processing values over periods. Analyses of economic value use models of present value of cash flows.

7.4 | Some Strategic Questions for PAVE Processing

Questions of policy for aggregate planning activities are among the areas where PAVE may furnish insights. Some questions are:

1. What are the dynamic cycles of cash flows over a planning horizon?
2. How much cash will be required, and on what time schedule, for a given strategic plan? What are investment requirements, long-term and seasonal, owner equity and debt?
3. What are the generated values and investment requirements of alternate capital budgeting proposals? PAVE can sort out the consequences of major changes within an organization. For example, what is the total effect of completing a new plant two years from now? Compared to existing facilities, a new plant may reduce labor cost but simultaneously increase fixed costs.
4. What is the probability of going technically or legally insolvent, given specified input risks? When will insolvency first occur?
5. What is the comparison between going-concern and liquidation values? What is the value of an enterprise, given business, financial, cyclical, and inflation risks?
6. What are the long- and short-term consequences of various policy alternatives in such areas as pricing, promotion, expansion, and financing?
7. What are the effects of environmental change, either ordinary shifts or extreme turbulence?
8. What is the effect of growth on the performance and value of an enterprise?
9. How sensitive is performance to seasonal or cyclical patterns? How do such patterns affect value, profit, cash flow, and capital needs?

10. How do costs and profit vary with sales volume under various assumptions of capacity?

11. How sensitive are profits to changes in the economy, industry, or market share?

12. What are the influences of various inflation rates on a firm's sales, costs, cash flow, earnings, and market value?

13. How do various assumptions about economic growth change a firm's performance?

14. How do stages of a product life cycle affect a firm's earnings, cash, capital requirements, and value?

15. How should production and inventory planning be related to seasonal or cyclical behavior?

16. What are the relationships among capital investment, depreciation policies, growth, cash flow, earnings, and income taxes?

Central to the PAVE system, both for valuation and capital requirements, is attention to cash flows. Some of the ways in which PAVE manages cash flows are:

1. PAVE determines internally the amount of short-term funds required per input policies on liquidity. Short-term borrowings are adjusted to finance seasonal variations.

2. Capital investment may be internally or externally determined. Under internal control option, PAVE computes required owner and debt permanent capital additions for each period. These additions are incremental to user capital inputs. Under external control option, PAVE determines the adequacy of planned capital by checking and reporting insolvency.

3. The presence of insolvency does not halt a PAVE simulation. Negative income, cash, monetary assets, and owners' equity are permitted.

4. Cash flow analysis for each period determines the operation of automatic cash management policies programmed into PAVE.

5. Cash-flow budgets are available for each period.

7.5 | Scope and Limitations of PAVE

Following is a summary of the range of PAVE capabilities:

1. PAVE adjusts internally to manufacturing, trading, or service choices of handling goods inventories, expense centers, and asset classes.

2. PAVE simulates uncertainty, using Monte Carlo methods. Process generators develop triangular distributions for up to twelve randomized input variables. A deterministic (nonstatistical) mode is also available.

3. Three input modes are available:

   SEQUENTIAL DISPLAYS print the name and a brief description of each input on a video screen as entered. Inputs are entered in sections corresponding to a logical policy-decision process.

   SELECTIVE INTERACTIVE entry facilitates changes and rapid input of small data bases.

   DATA STATEMENTS provide for user input of data program files (not needed for most applications).

4. Since inputs are extensive, PAVE develops files for input data. After an input file is READ, it may be kept unchanged or be updated or replaced.

5. A current set of input values can be optionally printed at a user's terminal.

6. Inputs are arranged in blocks that follow a logical system of strategic planning. Decisions progress from broad policy to specific operations. In SEQUENTIAL DISPLAYS input mode, policy reminder statements (POLREMS) may be optionally printed at the beginning of each strategic decision block.

7. Provision is made for inputs of inflation rate, economic growth, and seasonal-cyclical fluctuations. Thus, PAVE simulates the firm as part of a total industry-economy environment. The importance of market share is stressed.

8. PAVE may be used to develop new enterprises from ground zero or any other initial position prior to full operations. Alternatively, PAVE will simulate the future from any point in the life of ongoing enterprises. Input of starting condition (balance sheet) is optional.

9. Protective features override much incompatible logic from inputs and supply acceptable values of parameters.

10. PAVE determines processing and inventory requirements to meet sales objectives. Inputs are available to smooth production or inventories to seasonal sales fluctuations.

11. PAVE checks plant capacity, with input-controlled efficiency, against sales demand. Scheduling of required overtime labor, outside contractor processing, and reduced sales achievement can be processed internally.

12. PAVE computes going-concern values from an adaptation of the Modigliani and Miller earnings capitalization formula. Risk and inflation are computed as arguments for an investor required rate of return. This required rate, along with a long-term growth rate, incremental assets, and a rate of return on incremental assets, is used to compute going-concern value.

13. PAVE has a set of manufacturing facility costs that are separate from service and general facility costs.

14. Since cash flow logic is simulated throughout PAVE periods, capital needs may be determined internally. PAVE is able to separate long-term capital from short-term credit, and to schedule a combination of equity and debt capital changes.

15. PAVE will determine internally whether technical or legal insolvency has occurred during a simulation. PAVE prints the mean first period of occurrence, and the probability of occurrence over the sample size.

16. A FINANCIAL SUMMARY from the final period prints statistics for up to thirty-three values of firm and industry scope, financial ratios, and key account items. Statistics printed for each item are the mean, standard deviation, upper and lower limits of a statistical confidence interval, and maximum and minimum values encountered during a simulation.

17. Liquidation values are available on total assets and owners' equity.

Some limitations of the PAVE system are:

1. Only financial values are processed in the simulations.

2. Appropriate accounts are not included for financial, investment, or insurance firms.

3. Multiple products must be aggregated or divided into separate simulation units. Product and period costs are separated and identified, but there is no provision for cost allocation among multiple products.

4. Multiple divisions must be aggregated or treated as separate simulation units. There is provision, however, for separate geographical location between production operations and general business functions.

5. It is not possible to interchange inputs and outputs. To perform sensitivity analysis on outputs, it is necessary to use repeated runs with input changes.

8 PAVE Input System

8.1 | Interaction with Input Program PAVE1

Users should try out the first program PAVE1 before entering a complete set of inputs to run a case. Human-computer interaction in PAVE1 may be divided into three functions. All of these functions are conversational between video display and keyboard. First, there are general questions and commands for controlling the input system; these are discussed in this section. Next, sections 8.2 and 8.3 cover a numerical input entry system. Finally, there is input data file control, which is examined in section 8.4. It is suggested that a user start working with cases, such as VALVO and AUTOWASH in sections 10.1 and 10.2, after an initial exposure to PAVE1 and after reading the first four sections of this chapter. Section 8.5 contains information about individual inputs. Chapter 9 discusses interpretation of outputs. The last two chapters may be used for reference while running cases.

Returning to PAVE1, users are asked a series of initial questions. There is an option to print condensed PAVE system instructions. The instructions cover the loading of program and data file diskettes or tape, input rules, the order of reading input files and supplying internal values for selected inputs, principal processing options, and choices of output divisions. If you are at a terminal without notes or are looking for a compact reminder, the instruction printing feature may be useful. If the BASIC interpreter of your system permits, it is useful to bypass the printed instruction option on reruns. This has been done for the software reproduction in this book. Printed instructions may have to be edited to describe the file input system on your equipment.

Another, interactive, question concerns an option to print policy reminder statements (POLREMS) at the beginning of one to four input divisions. POLREMS present a compact checklist of important strategic alternatives that govern input policies. POLREMS follow the structure of strategic planning developed in Chapter 6; the structure itself was flowcharted in figures 6.2 and 6.3. After POLREMS have been displayed, key EXECUTE to continue with inputs. A command, *P*, followed by EXECUTE, will print the set of POLREMS. Command "//", followed by EXECUTE, will return users to the central choice menu.

The third, initial, question permits users to select among input data file options. These options are discussed in section 8.4. Following file options, the next question offers an opportunity to compose a title for each PAVE run. Choices are "D" for PAVE1 to display the currently stored title, if any; "I" for users to enter a new title at the keyboard; and EXECUTE (hereafter abbreviated EXEC) to continue processing. If the current title has been displayed under choice *D*, control branches back to the previous title-processing question. This allows a user to enter a new title after looking at the old one. Under *I*, a user can compose any title of length up to sixty-four characters. Titles may include the name of a firm, the name of an operator, names of data files, and the date and number of a run. Do not insert commas in titles; use other characters as separators. Most BASIC will terminate a title at the first comma. Your title is printed by PAVE in the heading of each output division and each financial statement. Titles are recommended to identify individual runs. They furnish a permanent record of the conditions of a run. Titles are stored in input data files along with numerical inputs. To eliminate a title, enter *I*, followed by EXEC; this will supply a blank in place of a title.

Following preliminary questions the central choice menu of PAVE1 is displayed. Preliminary questions are so arranged under software in this book that an EXEC command for each will make a negative choice and bring users quickly to the menu. Such a rapid sequencing is not available on some BASIC interpreters. Returning to the central menu, a user enters one of ten numbers displayed with descriptions. The first seven numbers select input divisions and modes for numerical values. A user is returned to the menu after completing any of the first seven choices. This means that inputs may be entered in any order and that values may be reentered without limit.

Item PRINT = 10 of the menu lists the descriptions and current values of all inputs. The run title, if any, is also printed. Apart from the option of printing all inputs, users can print individual input displays. From choice 10, control returns to the menu after all inputs have been printed.

Menu items 8 and 9 are the only ones that do not return users to the menu; they terminate an input process. An entry of RUN = 8 is a signal to continue processing through program segments up to outputs. This choice should not be taken until all inputs have been completed. An entry of END = 9 terminates a run at PAVE1 instead of processing inputs into outputs. This should be selected if processing is to be interrupted. If an input data file were selected during preliminary questions, then the current input set may be written to that file before a PAVE1 choice to RUN or END.

After RUN = 8 choice and an internal check of inputs, a pause occurs and a message appears on the video display. This interruption takes place only if an input file were read at the beginning of PAVE1. The interruption gives an opportunity to change data file disks in the left port. The message indicates that a disk with data transfer files PAVEFT1 to PAVEFT5 must be mounted to continue processing. After changing disks, or if a disk with transfer files has already been mounted, EXEC to continue processing. With some types of drive systems this particular interaction may be unnecessary. It is useful for minidiskettes with limited storage capacity. If inappropriate, software may be modified or users may pass on with EXEC.

8.2 | Rules for Input Entries

All PAVE inputs are numeric except run titles. Each numeric input has a unique identification number (ID). IDs run from 1 to 579, with some numbers unused. Think of each input as a pair of numbers, an ID followed by its corresponding value for a run. To see this, key "1" on the menu of PAVE1. A resulting input display is reproduced below:

```
INPUT/OUTPUT SYSTEM CHOICES
   !!  THESE INPUTS CONTROL OTHER DISPLAYS!!

 1   TOTAL NUMBER OF PERIODS (MAX 24) . . . . . . . . . . . . . .          12
 2   NO. OF PERIODS PER YEAR . . . . . . . . . . . . . . . . . . .           4
 3   SAMPLE SIZE--DETERMINISTIC=1/STAT.=2 TO 12 . . . . . . . . .          10
 4   SEED NO.--STANDARD RANDOM SERIES=0 . . . . . . . . . . . .            0
 5   FRAME: SERVICE=0/TRADE=1/MFG=2/ENVRT ONLY         = 3                  2
 6   OUTPUT DIVISION PRINT 1ST FROM LIST BELOW:                            0
        VALUATION 1ST AND FINAL YEARS. SCOPE           = 0
        STATISTICAL SUMMARY FROM FINAL PERIOD          = 1
        FINANCIAL STATEMENTS FOR ALL PERIODS           = 2
        SELECTED ACCOUNTS FOR ALL PERIODS              = 3
```

IDs 1 to 6 appear in the left column. Six corresponding values appear in the right column. Descriptions of each input are printed in the center space. The input pairs in this case are (1,12), (2,4), (3,10), (4,0), (5,2), and (6,0). Every input display has the same general arrangement.

In PAVE, nonentry of any input is equivalent to entering zero. Zeros will appear in displays for IDs unless nonzero entries have been made. There is an exception to this for ten IDs. Nonzero values are assigned to them internally to replace zero values or nonentry.

Some general rules apply to descriptions of inputs. These rules are intended to avoid confusion among dollar values, proportions, and time rates. The basic time unit of simulation is one period. Values are computed and statements are prepared for each period. The length of a period is not built in; it is determined by users. In the above display, twelve periods are simulated per ID 1. There are four periods in a year per ID 2. This means that each period is three months long and that a total of three years will be simulated.

The list of rules for input descriptions is:

1. Dollar input items carry the prefix "$." These items apply to one period, except for IDs 84 and 130, which are clearly marked for a year. It is best to enter integer values for dollar items. Avoid decimals such as dollars and cents.

2. All rate inputs are percentages, not decimals. A percent sign always appears somewhere in the description and is often a prefix.

3. All time rates are percent per year, percent per period.

The two categories of inputs in PAVE are:

1. Single parameters apply to an entire simulation. All the IDs in the preceding display were single parameters. The total range is IDs 1 to 98.

2. Dynamic sets of inputs, grouped into blocks of ten IDs each, describe changing behavior over time. The total range of these IDs is 102 to 579. One or both of the first two digits of such a set are often not used; for example, IDs 100 and 101 are inapplicable. For all dynamic sets, the right-hand units digits fit into a single pattern as follows:

   (0) is a related input parameter, if any. ID 490, for example, gives the depreciation rate that accompanies the dynamic set of general fixed asset class 1 net changes. The base value of the latter is entered under ID 492 (see number 2 below).

   (1) Input uncertainty is expressed as a maximum percent change from mean value, if any (see section 3.4 and Figure 3.5). ID 131, for example, gives *percent max change from mean value of industry growth* for each period. The base value of this input appears in ID 132.

   (2) is a base value of a dynamic input. ID 142, for example, gives *percent base value applied in period 1* of *direct material as percentage of sales*. This percentage of sales will determine the direct material cost in period 1.

   (3) is an *annual* percentage change of a base figure entered in the corresponding number 2 position. This is a dynamic adjustment for changing behavior over time. ID 143, for example, shows the *annual* rate at which the direct labor percentage of sales is to change over the periods. Assume sales in period 1 are $1,000,000. Assume a value of 6 in ID 142 and a value of –10 in ID 143. Then, direct labor cost will be 0.06 times 1,000,000, or $60,000 in period 1. Assume that each period has a duration of three months. For period 5, one year later, direct labor will be 10% lower, or $54,000. Growth rates in the number 3 ID positions may be positive, negative, or zero. Obviously nonentry in number 3 ID positions will merely continue the same base value for the corresponding number 2 IDs over a complete simulation. If the base value is itself a rate, as in the example above, then number 3 is a second-order change, a rate of change of a rate, or an acceleration. There is also a uniform pattern for dynamic set ID digits 4 to 9. These are used to handle discontinuities over periods. Such IDs are only needed occasionally.

Up to twelve dynamic input sets may be selectively assigned uncertainty components (the positive values in number 1 ID positions). Such values are prefixed with an asterisk on both the titles of the dynamic input sets and the uncertainty inputs themselves (number 1 ID positions). A list of these dynamic sets is:

121-129	*NET SALES DEMAND AVAILABLE TO FIRM
131-139	*% ANNUAL INDUSTRY GROWTH COMPARED TO ECONOMY
141-149	*DIRECT PURCHASED MATERIAL OR GOODS AS % OF SALES
181-189	*DIRECT LABOR PAYROLL AS % OF SALES
201-209	*% OPERATING EFFICIENCY OF PROCESSING
251-259	*$ UTILITIES OR ALL INDIRECT COSTS PER PERIOD–MANUFACTURING
391-399	*ACCOUNTS RECEIVABLE LEVEL AS % OF ANNUAL SALES
401-409	*DIRECT SERVICE/OFFICE MATERIALS AS % OF SALES
421-429	*DIRECT SERVICE/OFFICE PAYROLL AS % OF SALES
451-459	*$ UTILITIES OR ALL INDIRECT COSTS PER PERIOD–GENERAL
561-569	*% SHORT-TERM INTEREST RATE ANNUAL
571-579	*% LONG-TERM INTEREST RATE ANNUAL

The following are examples of dynamic input sets. Each is a PRINT from a PAVE run. Assume that twelve periods are simulated (ID 1 = 12), and four periods per year (ID 2 = 4).

| 110 | INFLATE PERIOD COSTS--NO=0/YES=1. . . . . | | 0 |

% ANNUAL AVERAGE INFLATION RATE

| 112 | % | BASE VALUE APPLIED IN PERIOD 1 . . . . | 6 |
| 113 | % | ANNUAL CHANGE TO PERIODS FROM 1ST BASE . . . | 1 |

There is a related parameter ID 110. Its zero value (nonentry) indicates that inflation rates developed over periods in IDs 112 and 113 will not be applied to dollar period costs. In period 1 the inflation rate applied to base industry sales (ID 130) will be at an annual rate of 6% (ID 112). This rate will increase at 1% per year (ID 113). By the fifth period, the annual rate will have increased to 6.06%; by the ninth, to 6.1206%; and by the end of the simulation, to 6.181806%. The quarterly inflation growth will be slightly less than 1.5%; it must compound each quarter to reach an annual rate of 6%.

| 390 | % | UNCOLLECTIBLE ACCOUNTS . . . . | 1.2 |

*ACCOUNTS RECEIVABLE LEVEL AS % OF ANNUAL SALES

| 391 | | *% MAX CHANGE FROM MEAN VALUE. . . . . | 15 |

| 392 | % | BASE VALUE APPLIED IN PERIOD 1 . . . . | 2.5 |
| 393 | % | ANNUAL CHANGE TO PERIODS FROM 1ST BASE . . | 1 |

Here, a parameter ID 390, related to accounts receivable, establishes a rate of uncollectible accounts at 1.2% of total accounts available for collection. The accounts-receivable level is subject to uncertainty. It may vary as much as 15% on either side of the mean value (ID 391). The base value of receivables at the end of period 1 will be established at a mean of 2.5% of annual sales (ID 392). Per ID 391, this base could vary in period 1 between 2.125% and 2.875%. Values near 2.5% will be more likely than the extremes. The growth of accounts receivable percentage level, at 1% per year, will reach a mean of 2.525% by period 5, and a mean of 2.55025% by period 9. The asterisks identify this dynamic set as one of twelve input sets with provisions for input uncertainty (ID 391). Nonentry in ID 391 would remove uncertainty from the inputs of this dynamic set.

```
*$ UTILITIES OR ALL INDIRECT COSTS PER PERIOD--GENERAL
   451      *% MAX CHANGE FROM MEAN VALUE. . . . . . . . .          12.5

   452 $ BASE VALUE APPLIED IN PERIOD1 . . . . . . . . . . . . .    10000
   453 % ANNUAL CHANGE TO PERIODS FROM 1ST BASE  . . . .           16
```

Here, the base level is a mean period cost of $10,000 in period 1 (ID 452). Per ID 451 this level could vary as much as 12.5%, or from $8,750 to $11,250. The $10,000 grows at a mean of 16% per year per ID 453. Thus utility costs will increase to a mean of $11,600 for the fifth period and to a mean of $13,456 for the ninth period. Quarterly values will be computed as compound amounts between the annual values.

A compact description of important input IDs appears in section 8.5 of this chapter. The Appendix contains a glossary of input IDs.

8.3 | Arrangement and Processing of Interactive Inputs

There is a hierarchy of inputs that determines what set of values will be stored or run. If an old input data file has been named by users, its contents will be read into the PAVE1 work space. A check of ten input IDs is performed by PAVE next. An internal value is supplied if any of these ten IDs are nonpositive. Such internally supplied values will appear in displays when users progress to interactive input processing.

The following is a list of internally supplied values to replace nonpositive inputs:

		internal value
ID 1	TOTAL NUMBER OF PERIODS (MAX 24)	1
ID 2	NUMBER OF PERIODS PER YEAR	1
ID 3	SAMPLE SIZE--DETERMINISTIC=1/STATISTICAL $\leq$ 20	1
ID 87	% CASH RATIO MINIMUM, BELOW WHICH CASH DEMANDED	50
ID 88	% CURRENT RATIO MINIMUM FROM SHORT-TERM LOANS	200
ID 89	% COMBINED EFFECTIVE INCOME TAX RATE ($<$100)	50
ID 91	NUMBER OF FIRST PERIOD OWNER EQUITY UNITS (1/SHARE)	1
ID 95	% ASSETS AVERAGE REALIZED IN LIQUIDATION	50
ID 140	INITIAL GOODS INVENTORIES--COST % OF SELLING PRICE	60
ID 202	% OPERATING EFFICIENCY OF PROCESSING	100

After an internal check of ten IDs, PAVE1 is ready for display and keyboard entry of input values. Such keyboard entries will overwrite values, which were read from

an input file or which were supplied internally. For the ten IDs above, do not overwrite internally supplied values with zeros. Such action may lead to aborting a run.
After keyboard entries are complete, there are options to write the final input set to
input data files. Users may continue processing a run (RUN = 8), end the run at this
point (END = 9), or print the complete set of inputs (PRINT = 10).

Keyboard inputs are controlled by a menu of ten choices that are displayed on the
video screen. The first seven are concerned directly with inputs. Numbers one to six
bring up input divisions; each division contains a set of sequential displays. For a complete input set, users may interact with each division and its sequence of displays.
Choice seven brings up SELECTIVE INTERACTIVE ID entry. This processes individual
IDs rather than sequential input displays. Choice "7" is useful for changes and other
short input sets. For any of the first seven choices, users always return eventually to
the menu. This means that an input set may be reworked without limit. The last three
menu choices are RUN = 8, END = 9, and PRINT = 10.

For SEQUENTIAL DISPLAYS input system, each division brings up one or more displays in order. All displays conform to a plan and are commanded by the same set of
rules. Each dynamic input set has a separate display. In addition to the dynamic
system rules described in section 8.2, right-hand units digits numbers 4 to 9 appear
on all dynamic input-set displays. These ID positions may be used occasionally. There
are also many more input IDs available than those described in section 8.5; these inputs are useful under special conditions, but ordinarily they may be ignored. System parameters are grouped into separate displays, which appear at the end of each
input division.

The following is a list of input divisions, with ID range and number of displays
for each:

	dynamic sets		*system parameters*	
	ID nos.	Maximum displays	ID nos.	Maximum displays
1. INPUT/OUTPUT SYSTEM CHOICES			1-6	1
2. INITIAL CONDITIONS (BALANCE SHEET)			9-48	5
3. ENVIRONMENT OF ECONOMY AND INDUSTRY TO SALES DEMAND AVAILABLE TO FIRM	102-139	4	51-74	2
4. MANUFACTURING OR TRADE ITEMS	140-329	19	75-78	1
5. R&D, SALES, AND GENERAL ADMINISTRATION ITEMS	330-529	20	79-84	1
6. FINANCIAL AND VALUATION CONTROL ITEMS	530-579	5	87-98	1

In the various descriptions for manipulating displays, the command EXEC is a symbol to describe a user action of depressing the EXECUTE (sometimes called the CONTROL) key. In the programs of this book, EXEC will either follow another keyboard entry or may be used alone. EXEC cannot be used alone with some BASIC interpreters. In such cases, introduce an entry such as "0" before EXEC.

When an input division has been called, the first display of IDs appears. Each display presents input items as a list of ID numbers, descriptions, and current values. Upon the first call of a display, the top input item is identified in some way. The type of identification depends on user tastes and the capabilities of BASIC interpreters. Instructions in this book are given for "X" markers and flashing cursors. Whatever input has been identified, a space is provided for entering a revised value. After entry of a revised value and the command, EXEC, control moves down to the next input item of the display. The revised value is now displayed for the previous ID. The command EXEC, without a revised entry, will move control to the next input item without changing values. Rotation through a display may be continued indefinitely, since command EXEC at the bottom input line will recycle control back to the top item. Users may step through a display upward instead of downward by entering an asterisk followed by EXEC.

When a user has completed entries or revisions in a particular display, the command /, followed by EXEC, will bring up the next display in sequence in the same input division. If the prior display was the last of that input division, then command / will return control to the menu. A user may return to the menu at any time with the command //, followed by EXEC. When interacting with a particular display, its contents can be printed. Command P, followed by EXEC, prints the set of ID numbers, input descriptions, and current values. Contrast individual control of display printing with the menu command PRINT = 10, which lists the entire input set. After printing a display, control is returned to the user for further commands in that display.

The order of input divisions and displays is important. The input set in division 1, INPUT/OUTPUT SYSTEM CHOICES, should always be current before proceeding to other divisions. There is only one display in this division, but it controls the sequencing of remaining divisions and displays. This is particularly true of ID 5, FRAME: SERVICE = 0/TRADE = 1/MFG = 2/ENVIRONMENT ONLY = 3. Part of division 4 is inapplicable to TRADE, and all of it is inapplicable to SERVICE. Only divisions 1 and 3 are applicable to choice ENVRT ONLY. A user call for an inapplicable division will activate an error message. In such cases, command EXEC will return control to the menu for selecting another choice. Some displays within divisions are eliminated internally if they are inapplicable under certain input choices.

The six input divisions follow a logical strategic decision system. Division 1 is concerned with fundamental control of simulation input and output systems. Division 2 is devoted to the initial condition (or starting balance sheet) of a firm. Nonentry for division 2 is acceptable for a new firm starting at zero. Anything from a skeleton balance sheet to a full set of initial accounts is operational. Assets must balance equities (liabilities plus owners' equity) before a run is permitted to continue past input entries. To assist users with balancing, an extra display appears at the end of division 2. This display is not for entries; it gives totals of assets, liabilities, and owners' equity. If an imbalance occurs, a statement is displayed which shows the amount and direction of imbalance. Imbalance is checked twice, first at the end of division 2 and then after menu choice RUN = 8. A balance display and imbalance statement (if it occurs) may be optionally printed. After a balance display or an imbalance statement, the command EXEC returns control to the menu. Users may recall division 2 or SELECTIVE INTERACTIVE input mode (see menu choice "7" below) to correct imbalances.

Input divisions 3 to 6 contain the main flow of policy and environmental inputs. The plan of these divisions follows the strategic decision system described in section 6.5. Figure 6.3 presents a flow chart of the PAVE input divisions. Policy reminder statements (POLREMS) are optionally displayed at the beginning of the last four input divisions. Compact statements in the POLREMS remind users of critical strategic issues in the decision process for that input division. After a POLREM display, users may command P, followed by EXEC to print the POLREMS, EXEC or /, followed by EXEC, to bring up the first input display of the division, or // followed by EXEC to return to the menu.

Menu choice 7 transfers control to SELECTIVE INTERACTIVE mode of input entries. A video screen message asks for entry of an individual ID number. If an ID entry is invalid—the entered number is not part of the PAVE input set—an error message is displayed after EXEC with a request for another ID number. Such an error message will be displayed repeatedly until a valid ID number is entered. An ID number entry of zero followed by EXEC, or just the command EXEC, are signals to end SELECTIVE INTERACTIVE input mode and return to the menu. Any time during inputs, SELECTIVE INTERACTIVE mode may be called with choice 7 in the menu. By successive choices, the SELECTIVE INTERACTIVE mode may be mingled in any order with the input divisions of SEQUENTIAL DISPLAYS. This causes no problem; the latest input values are always shown on displays.

If a valid ID number has been entered under the SELECTIVE INTERACTIVE input mode, the display with that number is selected automatically and the correct input line marked. A user can now enter a revised value in the display. Once in a display, all the rules previously described under SEQUENTIAL DISPLAYS, with one exception, also apply to SELECTIVE INTERACTIVE mode. In SELECTIVE INTERACTIVE, one may move to other input items in a display, revise any values, and print the display. In SELECTIVE INTERACTIVE, however, the command /, followed by EXEC will not bring up the next sequential display of an input division. Instead, users are returned to a video screen message, which asks for another ID number. Upon receiving the next valid ID number, the corresponding display will again be located for value revision. This process may be repeated until all desired entries have been completed. When, in a display, the command // followed by EXEC will return users to the menu, thus ending the cycle of SELECTIVE INTERACTIVE. The operation of this command is identical to the SEQUENTIAL DISPLAYS mode.

In the SELECTIVE INTERACTIVE mode there is no sorting of divisions or displays to accommodate INPUT/OUTPUT choices such as ID 5 frame (contrast with the SEQUENTIAL DISPLAYS mode). If an ID is valid in general but inapplicable to particular input-output choices, there will be no internal warning or bypassing. As long as users are not misled, unnecessary entries will not cause simulation problems. Inapplicable ID values are simply disregarded during processing. Although there is no limit to the number entries in SELECTIVE INTERACTIVE, this input mode is intended for changes required with reruns.

8.4 | Management of Input Data Files

Users may interact with program PAVE1 to establish and update input data files. Each file stores a run title up to sixty-four characters in length and one complete set of numerical inputs. By operating with input files, repetitive entries of input data at a keyboard are eliminated. Users may maintain a whole set of input data files, one for each run of a firm to be saved. Coding statements for reserving space, writing, and reading are incorporated into PAVE1. Users need merely respond to questions which are displayed on the video screen. Input data files are entirely separate from data transfer files. The latter are used to transfer processing information from one chained PAVE program to another. Data transfer files are not under user control.

A summary of events from input data file choices is listed in Table 8.1. There are four initial choices. The sequence of events under each choice is described in turn. The first choice is NO FILE = 0. Once this choice is made, input files are eliminated from further consideration during a run. In such cases, keyboard inputs while running PAVE1 cannot be saved. NO FILE is usually unwise if there is any intention of rerunning during strategy search, scenario building, or sensitivity analysis. If an unneeded file happens to be set up, it may be overwritten later with inputs or even be given a new name. To be on the safe side, always write a new input set to some file.

——————————————— Table 8.1. ———————————————
SUMMARY OF INPUT DATA FILE CHOICES IN PAVE1.

NO FILE = 0
    Keyboard inputs cannot be saved for another run.

OLD FILE = 1
    Old file data set is read into work space.
        SAME = 0   Contents of *old* file remain unchanged.
        REVISE = 1   Contents of *old* file receive latest input set.

OLD AND NEW FILES = 2
>   *Old* file data set is read into workspace.
>   UNSAVE = 0 Latest input set is written to *old* file
>   space, but under *new* file name.
>   RETAIN = 1 Contents of *old* file remain unchanged.
>   A *new* file is set up.
>   Latest input set is written to *new* file.

NEW FILE = 3
>   A *new* file is set up.
>   Latest input set is written to *new* file.

The second choice is OLD FILE = 1. After this choice, users are asked to enter the name of the old file. To call up an old file from storage, every character and space in the name must be reproduced exactly. Once an old file has been named, it is loaded automatically and its contents are read into the PAVE1 work space. The old file input values will now appear in the input displays. They may all be printed by entering "10" under the PAVE1 control menu. If there are zero values in ten particular input IDs, then they will be overwritten by PAVE1 internal defaults. Also, old-file inputs may be selectively overwritten by users with keyboard entries. After all inputs have been completed (control menu entries 8 or 9), users are given a choice of SAME = 0 or REVISE = 1. Under SAME, the original contents of the old file are not altered. Under REVISE, the latest set of inputs from the PAVE1 work space is written into the old file. This means that the original contents will be overwritten and lost whenever inputs have been changed. A file itself cannot be destroyed through interaction with PAVE1 under the coding given in this book. An old-file name may be revised, however, under the OLD AND NEW FILES choice.

An initial choice NEW FILE = 3 is discussed next. Given this choice, users must enter a name for the new file. Names should not exceed eight characters, including spaces. On most BASICS, characters may be any mixture of letters, numbers, and signs. It is best to suggest the type of run in the name. Different input sets for related runs may be identified with serial numbers as part of the name. It is usually essential that no two files receive the same name. Remember that a run title is available for each file, as well as a name. The processing of new files is simple. Upon completion of inputs in PAVE1, the latest input data set in the work space is automatically written to the new file.

An initial choice of OLD AND NEW FILE = 2 requires users to enter names for both old and new files. Old-file contents are automatically read into the PAVE1 work space in the same manner as under choice OLD FILE = 1. Upon completion of inputs, a user is given the choice UNSAVE = 0 or RETAIN = 1. Under UNSAVE, the latest set of inputs in PAVE1 is written to the old file space. In addition, the old file's name is changed to that entered for the new file. In this case, both the original name and contents of the old file are destroyed. Under choice RETAIN = 1, both the old and new files remain active. The old file retains its original name and contents. In addition, the latest input set in PAVE1 work space is automatically written to the new file. Under any choice which sets up a new file, the latest input set from PAVE1 will always be written to it.

A few suggestions may help with the management of input data files. If NO FILE is chosen, keyboard inputs cannot be saved for another run. If a new set of inputs is to be entered at the keyboard, choose NEW FILE to save the data without disturbing existing files and other input data sets. Suppose there is a file with an obsolete data set. One choice is OLD FILE and REVISE, which writes the new data to the old file name. Another choice is OLD AND NEW FILE and UNSAVE. This writes the new data to the old file space but under a new file name. It is important to note that, under OLD FILE or OLD AND NEW FILE, the old file contents will always be written into the work space. If the old file data is obsolete, it must be completely overwritten with new values or zeros at the keyboard. This may be done systematically by revising each input display in turn.

If existing input data are to be revised, as in repeated runs for strategy development, choose OLD FILE for each repeated run. A second choice of REVISE will update the data in the old file for each run, whereas a choice of SAME will maintain the original inputs. OLD AND NEW FILE, with RETAIN, may be used if it is desirable to save two versions of an input set. In such cases, the original data will remain in the old file, whereas the revised data is written to the new file. OLD AND NEW FILE, with UNSAVE, may be chosen if revised inputs are to be saved, but under a new file name.

8.5 | Description of Basic Input Items

ID numbers appear in order on the left. EOP equals "end of period"; BOP is "beginning of period."

Input-Output System Choices

A correct set of these inputs should be available before proceeding to other input divisions. Choices in this division determine which other input sections will be presented in displays.

1 TOTAL NUMBER OF PERIODS (MAXIMUM 24)
   Enter from 1 to 24. Simulated values are computed for each period. Time intervals are determined by users in ID 2.
2 NUMBER OF PERIODS PER YEAR
   Duration of each period is the reciprocal of ID 2. Any duration works, even multiple years (fractional entry in ID 2). Run quarters (4) or months (12) for seasonal patterns. Run at least 3 years total for meaningful internal valuation under growth.

3 SAMPLE SIZE—DETERMINISTIC = 1/STATISTICAL = 2 TO 20
   To avoid excessive run time on slow machines, do not exceed 12. An input of 1
   eliminates generation of uncertainty for inputs and statistical analysis of outputs.
   If 1 is entered, input uncertainties in any of twelve starred dynamic sets will be
   disregarded. Each sample size greater than 1 offers some combination of risk level
   and confidence interval precision (see Table 8.2).

——————————————————— **Table 8.2.** ———————————————————

RISK LEVELS AND CONFIDENCE INTERVALS FOR SAMPLE SIZE INPUT ID 3.

Confidence intervals for the mean are computed from:

   confidence limit = mean ± (standard deviation of mean X t-statistic)

The smaller the t-statistic, the more precise the confidence interval.

Sample size ID 3	% risk	t-statistic	Sample size ID 3	% risk	t-statistic
2	80	3.1	16	99	3.0
3	90	2.9	17	90	1.7
4	90	2.4	18	95	2.1
5	95	2.8	19	98	2.6
			20	99	2.9
6	90	2.0			
7	95	2.4	21	90	1.6
8	98	2.9	22	95	2.0
9	90	1.9	23	98	2.5
10	95	2.3	24	99	2.8
			25	99	2.8
11	98	2.8			
12	99	3.1	26	99	2.8
13	90	1.8	27	99	2.8
14	95	2.2	28	99	2.8
15	98	2.7	29	99	2.8
			30	99	2.8

For sample size 31 to 40, the confidence level is 99% and the t-statistic is approximately 2.7.

5 FRAME: SERVICE = 0/TRADE = 1/MANUFACTURING = 2/ENVIRONMENT
   ONLY = 3
   PAVE adjusts interactive input displays, internal logic, and output printing statements to the frame of a firm's operations and inventories. See section 9.4 for
   changes in output information under each of these frames. If inputs are entered
   that do not apply to the current ID 5 choice, they are ignored.

6 OUTPUT DIVISION FOR FIRST PRINTING
   VALUATION AND SCOPE for first and final years = 0
   FINANCIAL SUMMARY from final period = 1
   FINANCIAL STATEMENTS projected for all periods = 2
   SELECTED ACCOUNTS for all periods = 3
   An explanation of output divisions is given in sections 9.1 and 9.3. An outline of
   the contents of output divisions is contained in Table 9.1. An initial selection of an
   output division is made with ID 6. After each output has been printed, users may
   select another output division, return to inputs for a rerun, or end.

Initial condition (applies unless ID 5 = 3)

Initial condition is a record of a firm's financial position at the beginning of a
simulation. It may be omitted entirely for a new firm at "ground zero," or a "skeleton" balance sheet may be entered. After inputs have been completed, the balance of
ASSETS and EQUITIES (liabilities plus owners' equity) is checked internally. Unbalance information will be displayed, and processing cannot continue until such unbalance has been corrected.

 9 $ CASH AND MARKETABLE SECURITIES
    This item includes cash, time deposits, certificates of deposit, and all investment
    assets that are marketable in the short term.
10 $ TRADE ACCOUNTS AND NOTES RECEIVABLE
12 $ RESERVE FOR UNCOLLECTIBLE ACCOUNTS
    Include all open account and interest-bearing debt that is a short-term extension
    of credit by the firm in the course of doing business. ID 12 is subtracted from
    ID 10 to compute total assets.
14 $ INTANGIBLES: ORGANIZATION EXPENSE, PATENTS, GOODWILL,
    LEASEHOLD IMPROVEMENTS
    Here are assets without physical substance in liquidation. Included are trade-
    marks, copyrights, franchises, patents, and legal claims. Organization expense
    capitalizes the start-up cost of a firm. Goodwill arises from the difference be-
    tween market and book value of a firm's assets. Leasehold improvements are the
    capitalized expense of modifications to rented property.
15 $ INVENTORY OF GENERAL SUPPLIES, SMALL TOOLS, AND SMALL
    EQUIPMENT
16 INVENTORY OF MANUFACTURED OR TRADE FINISHED GOODS
18 INVENTORY OF MANUFACTURING DIRECT MATERIAL AND SUPPLIES
    These are three essential inventories. ID 18 is used only for manufacturing, ID 16
    for both manufacturing and trade, and ID 15 for manufacturing, trade, or ser-
    vice. Initial inventories in this division correspond to the classes of inventories
    that are processed throughout PAVE. Separate accounts are maintained for
    manufacturing throughout PAVE processing.
20 $ MANUFACTURING FIXED ASSETS AT COST BASIS

25   $ MANUFACTURING FIXED ASSETS RESERVE FOR DEPRECIATION
30   $ GENERAL FIXED ASSETS AT COST BASIS
35   $ GENERAL FIXED-ASSETS RESERVE FOR DEPRECIATION
The book value of fixed assets is cost less reserve for depreciation. Book value is the figure used as a component of total assets.
40   $ TRADE ACCOUNTS AND NOTES PAYABLE
All short-term credit extended to the firm by suppliers should be aggregated into this account.
44   $ SHORT-TERM DEBT AND LOANS PAYABLE
Seasonal financing from bank loans and lines of credit should be entered here. Bonds and other financial obligations with less than a year to maturity should be included in this account.
45   $ LONG-TERM OBLIGATIONS AT FACE OR STATED VALUE
This category includes bonds, purchase-money mortgages, equipment trust certificates, equipment loans, and preferred stock. Any fixed obligation with a maturity of a year or longer should be entered here. Enter the principal amount that must be repaid.
47   $ PAID-IN OWNER EQUITY CAPITAL
48   RETAINED EARNINGS
Consolidate all initial owner equity accounts into IDs 47 and 48.

General system parameters

51   to 62 SEASONAL/CYCLICAL INDICES
Each active index must be greater than 0. The first 0 entry (or nonentry) flags the end of the series. An internal routine repeats positive indices over all periods in the same order as entered. The input set of positive numbers is also normalized internally into indices with a mean of one. Either one or zero positive inputs will omit seasonal effects. See ID set 132 for the application of indices to sales demand.
79   GENERAL SUPPLIES INVENTORY LEVEL AS % OF ANNUAL USAGE
All EOP inventory levels in PAVE are computed as a percentage of annual dollar demand for usage of that inventory class. Demand and inventory levels are computed at cost.
80   ACCOUNTS PAYABLE LEVEL AS % OF ANNUAL ACCOUNT PAYMENTS
Credit EOP extended by suppliers is computed as a percentage of annual purchases from suppliers. Enter 0 if all purchases are for cash. Mean days credit equals ID 80 times 365 divided by 100. Payrolls, interest, income taxes, and dividends are handled as cash payments in PAVE; they are excluded from all accounts-payable computations.
84   $ AMORTIZATION OF INTANGIBLES, YEARLY, NOT PER PERIOD
See ID 14 for a definition and list of intangible assets. ID 84 entry is annual, straight-line dollar amortization. Note, under IDs 280 and 480, that depreciation of tangible fixed assets is declining balance.

91 NUMBER OF FIRST PERIOD OWNER EQUITY UNITS (1/SHARE)

PAVE computes per-share summaries. ID 91 inputs the number of initial owner equity shares that are outstanding at the end of period 1. If additional owner equity capital is raised, the incremental number of issued shares will be computed internally. For a partnership, enter the reciprocal of the fraction of the business owned.

Dynamic sets

The following pattern applies to right-hand units digits:

–0 related input parameter, if any
–1 input uncertainty as maximum percent change from mean value, if any
–2 base value of dynamic input applied in period 1
–3 annual percent change in base value applied to the second and subsequent periods
  * prefix indicates that an input for uncertainty is available

Environment of economy and industry to sales demand available to firm

102, 103   % ANNUAL REAL GROWTH RATE OF ECONOMY

This is the real or deflated growth of national income. Negative values are permitted.

110   INFLATE PERIOD COSTS—NO = 0/YES = 1

If sales demand is computed from an industry analysis, then inflation factors from ID set 112 will be included (see ID set 132). Since variable costs are computed as percentages of sales, they also include the same inflation factors. ID 110 offers the opportunity to extend similar inflation adjustment to fixed costs, asset additions, and sales input not based on industry analysis (see ID 120). For ID 110 = 1 an inflation adjustment occurs; for ID 110 = 0 it is omitted.

112, 113   % ANNUAL AVERAGE INFLATION RATES

Inflation rates developed for each period from these inputs are used throughout the simulation. Negative values will work in the system but would scarcely conform to expected reality.

120   SALES DEMAND—% INDUSTRY SHARE = 0/$ PER PERIOD = 1

Net sales demand available to the firm may be entered in ID set 112 by two different methods. If ID 120 = 0, then a percent market share of industry sales must be entered. For industry sales analysis see ID set 131. If ID 120 = 1, then dollar sales demand of a firm per period must be entered. Thus, firm sales are entered directly if ID 120 = 1.

121, 122, 123   *NET SALES DEMAND AVAILABLE TO FIRM

Enter percent share of industry or dollar sales per period in accordance with ID 120 choice. See further explanation under ID set 131. IDs 121 and 122 must be nonnegative.

130   $ INDUSTRY SALES FOR BASE (PRIOR) YEAR, NOT PERIOD
This is the figure to which growth rates over periods are applied to obtain industry sales each period (see ID set 131). ID 130 is an annual positive figure.

131, 132, 133   *% ANNUAL INDUSTRY GROWTH COMPARED TO
                THE ECONOMY
These are inputs for the growth of the industry compared to the economy. An input of 6 in ID 132, for example, would result in an industry growing 6% per year faster than the economy. ID 131 must be nonnegative.

Total industry sales each period are the compound effect of three growth rates on base industry sales (ID 130). The rates are real growth (ID set 102), inflation (ID set 112), and industry to economy comparison (ID set 131). Any of these growth rates may be positive, negative, or zero. A seasonal pattern is also applied to industry sales period by period per positive indices from IDs 51 to 62. ID 131 is, in effect, an uncertainty input for all growth components, including inflation, and for industry sales.

Market share percent from ID set 121 converts industry sales to demand for a firm if ID 120 = 0. Here, there is another uncertainty input with ID 121. To bypass industry analysis and apply growth rates and seasonal indices directly to a firm's sales demand, enter base sales of a firm in ID 130, 100 in ID 122, and zeros in IDs 120, 121, and 123.

Purchases and goods inventory (applies if ID 5 = 1 for trade or 2 for manufacturing)

141, 142, 143   *DIRECT PURCHASED MATERIAL OR GOODS AS % OF SALES
This is the percent of net sales dollars absorbed into the cost of purchased direct material for manufacturing (ID 5 = 2), or the cost of goods purchased for resale in the case of trade (ID 5 = 1). IDs 141 and 142 must be nonnegative.

152, 153   FINISHED GOODS INVENTORY LEVEL AS % OF ANNUAL COST OF
           GOODS SOLD
There are finished goods inventories for both manufacturing and trade. Throughout PAVE, inventories EOP are some proportion of the annualized rate of demand or activity during the preceding period. The proportion in this case is ID set 152. Finished goods inventories are valued at cost, not selling price. Keep ID 152 nonnegative.

Manufacturing policies and expense (applies only if ID 5 = 2)

172, 173   DIRECT MATERIAL INVENTORY LEVEL AS % OF ANNUAL USAGE
This input follows the same rules as ID set 152 but applies to direct materials inventory EOP instead of to finished goods. All inventories in PAVE are valued at cost. Keep ID 172 nonnegative.

181, 182, 183   *DIRECT LABOR PAYROLL AS % OF SALES

This is percent of net sales dollars which is absorbed in direct labor. IDs 181 and 182 must be nonnegative.

212, 213 $ CAPACITY OF PLANT PER PERIOD AT 100% EFFICIENCY AND SALES VALUE LEVEL

This is the normal capacity of plant production per period in dollar value of goods. The dollar value is set at factory sales level rather than at cost of goods manufactured level. If generated sales demand exceeds this capacity, achieved sales will be reduced to a level that can be supported by inventory and production. A zero entry in ID 212 is acceptable to simulate strikes or other unavailability of production. Entry must be nonnegative.

222, 223 $ INDIRECT SUPPLIES AND SMALL EQUIPMENT USED PER PERIOD

This expense may be optionally combined with ID 251 set; ID 22 must be nonnegative.

232, 233 $ INDIRECT MANUFACTURING PAYROLL PER PERIOD

Labor that varies directly with production should be entered in ID 181 set or ID 191 set. All other labor and supervision may be entered here; ID 332 must be nonnegative.

251, 252, 253   *$ UTILITIES OR ALL INDIRECT COSTS PER PERIOD–MANUFACTURING

Although titled *utilities*, this account may be used to aggregate all period expenses except payroll (see ID set 232); IDs 251 and 252 must be nonnegative.

280   % DEPRECIATION PER YEAR, DECLINING BALANCE ON MANUFACTURING FIXED ASSETS

Use a mean rate over manufacturing tangible fixed assets. The input is an annual rate on declining book value. Double the input figure for double declining balance. Other depreciation systems are not available in PAVE for tangible fixed assets. A negative entry here may cause an endless loop. Entering 0 for no depreciation is acceptable.

282, 283 $ MANUFACTURING FIXED ASSETS NET CHANGES PER PERIOD

Additions of tangible fixed assets are priced at cost net of trade-ins, scrap value, and so on. Include installation and delivery cost. Negative entries may be used to describe net asset shrinkage.

Research and development, sales, and general administrative inputs (applies except for ID 5 = 3)
Manufacturing expenses should be entered in IDs of the preceding section.

330   RESEARCH AND DEVELOPMENT EXPENSES–% SALES = 0/$ PER PERIOD = 1

Per this choice, inputs to ID sets 332 and 342 will change basis between percent of annual sales, and dollar cost per period.

342, 343   RESEARCH AND DEVELOPMENT MATERIAL, CONTRACTS, AND MISCELLANEOUS EXPENSE

Any research, development, or product-engineering expenses may be aggregated into this input set; keep ID 342 nonnegative.

352, 353   SALES SALARIES AND COMMISSIONS PAYROLL AS % OF SALES

This account may be extended to include any selling expenses which are variable with sales. What percent of sales dollars is absorbed in these expenses? Keep ID 352 nonnegative.

382, 383 $ ADVERTISING, PROMOTION, AND MISCELLANEOUS SELLING EXPENSE PER PERIOD

This account may be extended to include all fixed selling cost per period. Note that variable selling cost may be aggregated into ID set 352. Keep ID 382 nonnegative.

390   % UNCOLLECTIBLE ACCOUNTS

This is a planned uncollectible percentage of credit sales. An entry of 0 signals no risk of nonpayment. Uncollectibles are deducted from total available for collection, not directly from sales. Uncollectibles are accumulated in the balance of both accounts receivable and reserve for uncollectibles. ID 390 must be nonnegative.

391, 392, 393   ACCOUNTS RECEIVABLE LEVEL AS % OF ANNUAL SALES

Credit extended to customers EOP is computed as a percentage of annualized net sales. Enter 0 if all sales are for cash. Mean days age of accounts receivable equals ID 390 times 365 divided by 100. IDs 391 and 392 must be nonnegative.

412, 413 $ INDIRECT SERVICE, OFFICE SUPPLIES, AND SMALL EQUIPMENT PER PERIOD

Enter here any supplies or materials which are treated as a fixed expense per period. This must be the counterpart of ID 222 set in manufacturing; ID 412 must be nonnegative.

432, 433 $ GENERAL ADMINISTRATIVE AND INDIRECT SERVICE PAYROLL PER PERIOD

All office, executive, professional, and service labor may be entered here; ID 432 must be nonnegative.

451, 452, 453   *$ UTILITIES OR ALL INDIRECT COSTS PER PERIOD—GENERAL

Although titled *utilities* this account may be used to aggregate all period expenses except payroll (see ID set 432). Compare with ID set 251 for manufacturing. IDs 451 and 452 must be nonnegative.

480   % DEPRECIATION PER YEAR, DECLINING BALANCE ON GENERAL FIXED ASSETS

Use an average rate over general, tangible, fixed assets. This input is an annual rate on declining book value. Double the input figure for double declining balance. Other depreciation systems are not available in PAVE for tangible

fixed assets. Compare with ID 280 for manufacturing. A negative entry here
may cause an endless loop. Entry of 0 for no depreciation is acceptable.

482, 483 $ GENERAL FIXED ASSETS NET CHANGES PER PERIOD
Additions of tangible fixed assets are priced at cost net of trade-ins, scrap value,
and so on. Include installation and delivery cost. Negative entries may be used
to describe net asset shrinkage. Compare with ID set 282 for manufacturing.

Financial and valuation dynamic input sets (applies except for ID 5 = 3)

530   INTERNAL COMPUTATION OF REQUIRED ADDITIONAL INVESTMENT
      —NO = 0/YES = 1
A choice of YES activates an automatic computation of required, additional
long-term capital investment. Such investment, if any, will be incremental to
planned new investment from ID set 532. If ID set 532 inputs are 0, then PAVE
will compute all additional required investment internally. Long-term cash flow
analysis is used to determine the amount needed. ID 540 determines the percent of new required investment that will be placed in long-term obligations.
The balance is placed in owner paid-in capital.

For a choice of NO, capital investment is entirely user-planned through inputs in IDs 47 and 48 and ID set 532. This option should be selected to project
risks of insolvency. Lack of capital does not stop PAVE simulations. Negative
cash, total assets, and owners' equity are permitted.

532, 533 $ OWNER NET CASH INVESTMENT PLANNED CHANGE
           PER PERIOD
These are planned capital changes in contrast to required increases. The latter
are determined internally (see IDs 530 and 540). Negative entries are allowed
in ID set 532 for withdrawals, but owner paid-in capital account is not permitted internally to become negative. Retained earnings and total owners' equity
may become negative (see ID 530).

540   % LONG-TERM OBLIGATIONS IN REQUIRED
      ADDITIONAL INVESTMENT
This gives the proportion of required additional investment in long-term obligations, such as bonds or preferred stock (see ID 530). This input does not apply
to planned capital changes. These are scheduled in ID sets 532 and 542.

542, 543 $ LONG-TERM OBLIGATIONS PLANNED NET CHANGE
           PER PERIOD
This input follows the same rules as ID set 532 but applies to long-term obligations, such as bonds and preferred stock, rather than to owner paid-in common
stock. Negative entries are allowed for reduction of obligations, but the long-
term obligations account is not permitted internally to become negative.

550   DIVIDENDS—% OF EARNINGS = 0/$ PER PERIOD = 1
Per this choice, inputs to ID set 552 will change basis between percent of earnings, and dollar payment per period.

552, 553 DIVIDENDS OR WITHDRAWALS PER PERIOD

This has the same effect on owners' equity as negative inputs to ID set 532; but it is processed through statement accounts for periodic withdrawals. Enter amounts at time of payment, not during periods containing record or declaration dates. Preferred stock dividends may be included here as "after income taxes" or be treated as a component of ID set 572. For the latter option, adjust to the before-tax equivalent. ID 552 must be nonnegative.

561, 562, 563 *% SHORT-TERM INTEREST RATE ANNUAL

Enter a mean annual rate for short-term or seasonal borrowings by a firm. Such borrowings are determined internally to meet a minimum acceptable cash ratio. The source of borrowing is current assets, such as accounts receivable and inventories. Per ID 531 input, a fraction of the short-term interest rate may be earned on a firm's cash and marketable securities account. IDs 561 and 562 must be nonnegative.

571, 572, 573 *% LONG-TERM INTEREST RATE ANNUAL

Enter a mean annual rate for bonds, mortgages, and equipment loans. Interest cost is deducted before computing net income subject to income taxes. The long-term interest rate may be increased to cover preferred stock dividends, but such a dividend must be enlarged to its before-tax effect (see ID set 552). IDs 571 and 572 must be nonnegative.

9 PAVE Output Information

9.1 | The General Control of Outputs

In this chapter we are concerned with the interpretation of PAVE outputs and the relationships of inputs and outputs. This chapter should thus be used for reference; it should not be studied in detail before operating the PAVE system with some of the cases discussed in Chapter 10. After examining the cases, use this chapter as a guide to understanding the outputs.

This section gives some general rules about outputs. A complete guide to output divisions is presented in sections 9.2 and 9.3. The VALUATION and FINANCIAL SUMMARY divisions are described in section 9.2 and the FINANCIAL STATEMENTS and SELECTED ACCOUNTS divisions in section 9.3. The relationship of inputs to outputs is examined in sections 9.4 and 9.5. Some input choices are responsible for major changes in outputs. Input selections critical to the character of output information are described item by item in section 9.4. Experience has shown that PAVE runs are vulnerable to certain errors. The consequences of such errors for processing and outputs are discussed in section 9.5. If a PAVE run produces unsatisfactory results, use section 9.5 as a guide to checking inputs.

An outline of the contents of the four output divisions—VALUATION, FINANCIAL SUMMARY, FINANCIAL STATEMENTS, and SELECTED ACCOUNTS—appears in Table 9.1. Statistical features of inputs and outputs are also covered in section 9.4. Two acronyms used throughout this chapter are BOP for beginning of period, and EOP for end of period.

Outputs are printed as integers or decimals, usually in formated columns. Total dollar values are usually rounded to the nearest dollar. Per share values are rounded to the nearest cent. Industry sales are printed with 000 omitted. Ratios and rates are usually rounded to the nearest hundredth. Rounding may cause an unbalance of account totals up to two digits in the last decimal place.

——————— Table 9.1. ———————
OUTLINE OF PAVE OUTPUT DIVISIONS

1. VALUATION AND SCOPE for first and final years

    (a) statistical summary, total firm and per share, of sales, earnings, rate of return on owners' equity, owners' equity, total assets, and cash and marketable securities
    (b) probabilities of technical and legal insolvency, and mean first periods of occurrence
    (c) for total firm and per share: market value, going-concern value, liquidation value, fixed assets, and tax-loss carryforward
    (d) parameters used to compute going-concern value

2. FINANCIAL SUMMARY from final period

    statistical analysis of:
    (a) scope of firm
    (b) ratio analysis of profitability
    (c) ratio analysis of financial condition
    (d) summary of key financial values for firm and industry

3. FINANCIAL STATEMENTS projected for all periods

    (a) environmental analyses—industry sales, seasonal-cyclical-trend behavior, inflation, real economic growth, and firm's sales demand
    (b) income statements
    (c) cost of goods manufactured schedules, if appropriate
    (d) cost of goods sold schedules, if appropriate
    (e) cash forecasts or flow analyses
    (f) retained earnings and capital changes statements
    (g) condition statements or balance sheets

4. SELECTED ACCOUNTS for all periods

    statistical analysis of up to seventeen key accounts

Since printing space is limited, it is possible to have overflows. Such overflows do not abort the printing; rather, they cause rows of asterisks or pound signs to appear in the print space. The maximum-size printed numbers are: positive integer 9999,999,999; negative integer –999,999,999, positive decimal 19999,999.99; and negative decimal –9999,999.99. Thus the limit of printed sales demand, capital, and expenses of a firm approaches $10 billion and that of an industry, $10 trillion. With a BASIC interpreter of sufficient power, commas may be printed in outputs, as shown above and in this book. Commas should never be inserted into numerical inputs. If an overload occurs, look first for excessive compounding from multiple growth rates. If print space capacity becomes insufficient for a giant firm, simply enter all dollar inputs with "000" omitted. Then all dollar outputs will also be divided by 1,000.

9.2 | VALUATION and
| FINANCIAL SUMMARY Outputs

In VALUATION output division, quantities printed under FIRST YEAR and FINAL YEAR are found by aggregating amounts over the periods that compose those years. If periods are not available to sum to a year, interpolation is used. FIRST and FINAL YEARS will be identical if a simulation is less than one year's duration or if it covers only one period.

The SCOPE OF FIRM section prints important accounting measures of size and value. EARNINGS are identical to NET INCOME AFTER INCOME TAX in INCOME STATEMENTS. OWNERS' EQUITY is the sum of PAID-IN CAPITAL and RETAINED EARNINGS. RETURN ON OWNER'S EQUITY is the quotient of EARNINGS by OWNERS' EQUITY. TOTAL ASSETS include intangible assets.

The number of initial shares EOP 1 is a user input (ID 91) with an internal default of 1. Incremental shares at the end of each period are computed internally from changes in paid-in capital. Such changes are the sum of planned owner net cash investment inputs (ID set 532) and required additions which are computed internally. The value per share at the end of a period is used as a basis for computing changes in the number of shares during the following period. With such a value base, current shareowners are not diluted a priori by incremental investment used to change paid-in capital. Methods of computing the value of a firm are given below. The number of shares outstanding at the end of each period is given in EOP NO. SHARES OUTSTANDING account of RETAINED EARNINGS AND CAPITAL CHANGES statements. Calculations of additional shares do not start until the end of the first period. It is assumed in PAVE that the first period is used to organize capital.

TECHNICAL INSOLVENCY means that a firm is unable to meet current bills as they fall due. In PAVE, this is indicated for a period when EOP cash balance goes negative. LEGAL INSOLVENCY occurs when a firm's total liabilities exceed its total assets. In PAVE, this is indicated for a period when EOP OWNERS' EQUITY goes negative. (For a discussion of cash flow and insolvency, see sections 4.5 and 4.6.) Output printing has the same form and computations for both technical and legal insolvency. In any sample replication the number of the first period of insolvency, if any occurs, is stored. At the end of a simulation the mean of the period numbers of first insolvency occurrences is computed and printed. The inferred probability of insolvency is also printed. This is the ratio of the number of replications when an insolvency occurred to total sample size (ID 3 input). After a first insolvency occurs during a sample replication, additional insolvencies in later periods are not counted. If no insolvencies occur during replications, then the inferred probability of insolvency would be zero. In such case a message is printed ". . . insolvency did not occur." For sample size ID 3 = 1, probabilities of insolvency must be either 1 or 0.

In the "Methods of Valuation" section is a hierarchy of routines for computing the value of a firm. LIQUIDATION VALUES are always computed and printed (for definitions and formulas see section 5.6). GOING-CONCERN ECONOMIC VALUES UNDER RISK are computed and printed for sample size input (ID 3) greater than one. GOING-CONCERN VALUES in PAVE are derived from the earnings capitalization method of Modigliani and Miller. The discount rates are INVESTORS' REQUIRED RATES OF RETURN UNDER RISK AND INFLATION. MARKET VALUES are the products of EARNINGS and PRICE-EARNINGS MULTIPLES. Nonzero price-earnings multiple inputs to IDs 93 or 94 lead to direct computations of market values as products of the multiples with first and final year's earnings. Otherwise, market values are taken as the higher of going-concern values or liquidation values. In such cases multiples are derived internally as the quotients of values and earnings. Thus, nonentry in IDs 93 or 94 signals internal computation of market values and price-earnings multiples. If going-concern is not available (ID 3 = 1) to carry out an internal calculation of multiples, default values of 10 are supplied for nonentry of IDs 93 or 94.

When NET INCOME BEFORE TAXES is negative for a period, a firm will usually carry such loss forward, to offset future taxable income. Such losses are carried forward, period by period in PAVE. Income taxes are computed on positive residuals of net income less accumulated loss carried forward. If a residual taxable income is negative, it is carried forward to the next period. There is provision for an initial entry of LOSS CARRYFORWARD in ID 90. A negative entry in ID 90 would, on the other hand, indicate income on which income taxes were owed. All such taxes are paid in the period due by PAVE. Thus, the final carryforward may only be positive. Note that income is carried forward, not income taxes. Tax loss carrybacks are not processed in PAVE logic. Because the printed outputs of PAVE accounts are means, one may have both income taxes and tax-loss carryforwards for the same period.

The change in number of shares each period will be the quotient of change in paid-in owner capital, divided by the value per incremental share. This quotient is computed directly for nonzero entry in input ID 92. Nonentry in ID 92 substitutes an internal computation of per share value based on market values of the firm. A market value for each period is approximated by interpolating the difference between first and final year market values. If positive, these interpolated market values may be used to compute the value of existing shares. The value per existing share is the quotient of market value by the number of existing shares. This quotient is taken as the price each period of incremental shares to accompany paid-in capital changes. The minimum price of incremental shares is $1 each. This figure is inserted if market values of the firm are insufficiently positive. The minimum number of shares outstanding under any condition is one.

Parameters of going-concern valuation are required for the earnings capitalization formulas (see section 5.4). This output section is omitted if ID 3 = 1. Either one or two values exist for each parameter, because there are two separate computations (first year and final year) of going-concern value. For three of the parameters, users have a choice between external inputs and internal computation (indicator 0 or non-entry). The three parameters are investors' required rate of return (ID 96), long-term firm growth rate with inflation (ID 97), and mean rate of return on incremental assets (ID 98). The second and third apply the same amounts to both first and final year computations of going-concern value. Separate figures for the two years are computed internally for investors' required rate of return; if externally entered, however, one input is applied to both years. See section 5.5 for the internal computation formula.

Long-term growth rate comes from either nonzero entry in ID 97 or the final industry total growth rate (see the environmental analyses statements). Whichever the source, there is further processing. To avoid instability in the capitalization formulas, long-term growth rate is not allowed to exceed 75% of the required rate of return. Since long-term growth rates will be capitalized into the far-distant future, extreme positive values are to be avoided. Thus, if long-term industry growth rate exceeds that of the economy as a whole, the difference between them is reduced by one-half. Since negative, long-term growth rates will not always function consistently in the capitalization formulas, such rates are reset to zero.

The mean rate of return on incremental assets, except for nonzero input in ID 98, is computed internally. It is calculated as the quotient of either incremental earnings during a run by incremental assets, or final earnings by final assets. The latter is substituted for the former if there is only one period, if the total simulation is less than a year, or if changes in assets are less than one-half of final assets. These substitutions avoid unstable values of the rate on incremental assets due to inadequate information. If assets are negative or if the rate on incremental assets is negative, the final value of the rate on incremental assets is reset to zero.

Inflation rates are important components of both the long-term firm growth rate and investors' required rates of return. Both beginning and ending inflation rates are printed for reference. The long-term real growth rate of the economy is a component of the long-term firm growth rate. The final value of long-term real growth rate is printed for reference in both the first and the final columns.

Up to thirty-three key decision values—both quantities and ratios—are printed in four sections of the FINANCIAL SUMMARY output division (see Table 9.1). Discussion and examples of financial ratios are contained in sections 4.5 and 4.6. The same ratios are printed in the financial summary. All outputs in this division are taken from the final period of the simulation. Flow outputs—net sales or revenue, industry sales, cost of sales, gross profit, operating income, net income before income taxes, and net income after income taxes—are extrapolated or interpolated to an annual rate from final period results. Compare the method here with an aggregation of periods into years, which was used for valuation division outputs. Only final period figures are used in the financial summary. Outputs may be severely biased if extreme seasonal adjustments occur during the final period. To avoid this, end the simulation in a period with a neutral seasonal/cyclical index.

Items with all zero values are omitted from the financial summary. Undefined ratios (zero denominator) do not abort the printing. Instead, this condition is indicated with overflow symbols (asterisks or pound signs) in output print fields.

9.3 | Financial Statements and Selected Accounts Outputs

The FINANCIAL STATEMENTS output division contains projected values or budgets for all periods. In general, the form follows conventional accounting practice. Consecutive period outputs are arranged in columns to facilitate comparisons. Fundamentals of financial accounting theory and a logical flow of statements are discussed in sections 4.1 to 4.3. All outputs are a means of individual replication from a simulation sample. Accounts with zero values over all periods are omitted. Statistical information on uncertainty is not printed in this output division.

If the length of a period is a half-year or less, and if more than one period is simulated, then PAVE adds or marks columns of annual figures. The nature of annual information depends on the type of statement and the kind of account. All statements are flows except the last set, which are condition statements or balance sheets. All the flow statements add extra columns at the end of each year for annual figures. The dollar flows in these annual columns are simply the sums of flows in the preceding period columns. Condition accounts are added to some flow statements in order to describe origins of flows. For example, differences of inventory levels—condition accounts—are used to compute cost of goods sold, a flow account in a flow statement. These condition accounts are always labeled BOP, for beginning of period, or EOP, for end of period. The values printed in the corresponding annual columns are beginning of year and end of year. Thus the annual columns of flow statements assemble the same information for a year that is presented for periods in the remaining columns. When outputs are rates instead of dollar amounts, mean values may appear in annual columns in place of totals. In the notes to the statements below, such cases are noted as they arise.

If the end of some period coincides with the end of a year, first-year values will correspond to valuation outputs and financial-statements outputs. Otherwise, the valuation figures are adjusted to a year by interpolation factors, whereas financial-statements annual figures are not interpolated. Annual totals in financial statements always refer to the beginning of a simulation. Final-year outputs in the valuation division, on the other hand, are found by aggregating backward from the final period.

End-of-year outputs in condition statements are handled differently from the annual columns in flow statements. These differences are discussed later, along with other features of condition statements. Returning to flow statements, period column headings list the period number, followed by the year and month. Annual column headings list the year number. A column of asterisks is printed along the right side of annual figures. Standard accounting practice in PAVE statements are not repeated here, but a few comments will be made on particular information available from PAVE.

In a subheading of environmental-analyses-of-firm statements, INDUSTRY BASE SALES for both the year and the period are printed for reference. These outputs are derived from ID 130 input. Inflation rates and real economic growth rates are extended to all periods from input ID sets 112 and 102. The industry total growth percentage is computed thus:

industry growth rate $g = (1 + i)(1 + r)(1 + c) - 1$

i = inflation rate from ID set 112

r = real economic growth rate from ID set 102

c = industry growth rate compared to economy ID set 132

Seasonal/cyclical indices are processed from input IDs 51 to 74. The inputs are normalized and extended to all periods. Industry sales for each period are computed from the following formula:

industry sales = prior industry sales x $(1 + g)$ x current index/preceding index

Industry sales may be further adjusted with an uncertainty factor from ID 131. The firm's industry share percentage is input ID set 122 extended to all periods. Then, FIRM SALES DEMAND AVAILABLE is the product of industry sales and firm's share. This product may be adjusted with an uncertainty input ID 121. If input ID 120 = 1, FIRM SALES DEMAND is obtained directly from input ID set 122. Input ID 121 may still be used for uncertainty adjustment. If ID 120 = 1, INFLATION RATE and REAL ECONOMIC GROWTH are still printed if inputs are nonzero; but the remaining accounts of ENVIRONMENTAL ANALYSES are omitted. Means are printed instead of totals in the annual columns of the five rate accounts.

In income statements and cost-of-goods-manufactured schedules, there is a separation between variable, or direct, costs and fixed, period, or indirect costs. Cost items for each period are extensions of input dynamic sets over the periods. The variable group is entered as percentages of net sales; the fixed group as dollar amounts per period. The account SALES MARGIN OVER DIRECT EXPENSE in the income statements is the difference between net sales and the sum of all variable costs. R&D expense is treated as a variable expense if ID 330 = 0; otherwise, it is excluded from the sales margin. Payrolls, interest expense, income taxes, and dividends are treated as immediate cash payments. All other purchases are processed through accounts payable.

Net operating income is a residual after expenses of operating the business but before financial income and expense. INTEREST AND FINANCE INCOME is computed on the mean of BOP and EOP balances of cash and marketable securities. INTEREST COST, SHORT-TERM applies to short-term loans and notes for a period. The amount shown on CONDITION STATEMENTS is assumed to be borrowed at the beginning of the period and repaid at the beginning of the next period. INTEREST COST, LONG-TERM FIXED is computed on the mean balance of LONG-TERM OBLIGATIONS from BOP to EOP. For the treatment of income taxes and tax loss carryforward, refer to the discussion under valuation outputs.

The following formulas summarize some ordinary accounting logic used in PAVE:

purchases (to accounts payable) = usage (an expense) + inventory EOP – inventory BOP

collections + uncollectibles = net sales + net change in unearned customer advances – accounts receivable EOP + accounts receivable BOP

uncollectibles = uncollectible factor x (collections + uncollectibles)

net accounts receivable EOP = accounts receivable EOP – uncollectibles reserve EOP

cost of finished goods = cost of goods into process + goods-in-process inventory BOP – goods-in-process inventory EOP

cost of goods sold = cost of finished goods + finished goods inventory BOP – finished goods inventory EOP

payments on accounts payable = expenses with vendor credit + net asset additions + net change in prepaid expense + accounts payable BOP – accounts payable EOP

All goods inventories in PAVE statements are priced at cost. Levels of inventories are established from inputs as fractions of annual demand or usage. Manufacturing costs, both variable and fixed, are summed into COST OF GOODS INTO PROCESS. The level of goods inventories at the end of each period is priced from current costs. This means that PAVE uses an absorption-cost method with first-in-first-out (FIFO) valuation. Standard costs, direct costing, LIFO valuation, or average inventory pricing are not available.

If CONTRACT ASSEMBLY USED or OVERTIME PREMIUM PAYROLL accounts appear in COST OF GOODS MANUFACTURED SCHEDULES, then these expenses were activated internally to extend production capacity. OVERTIME PREMIUM is applied to DIRECT LABOR and DIRECT SUPERVISION payrolls. CONTRACT ASSEMBLY, when activated, is applied to all DIRECT MATERIAL USED. If plant capacity is still insufficient after maximum extensions with the above accounts, FIRM NET SALES ACHIEVED on the income statements will be reduced sufficiently below FIRM SALES DEMAND AVAILABLE on the environmental analyses.

Cash effects of sales and expenses are used in cash-forecast statements. Thus, PAYMENTS is subtracted from CASH RECEIPTS. Cash receipts are equivalent to COLLECTIONS ON ACCOUNTS RECEIVABLE, but they will also be identical to NET SALES ACHIEVED for a cash business with no credit to customers. PAYMENTS ON ACCOUNT are processed through credit extended to the firm by vendors in ACCOUNTS PAYABLE. Credit expenses, purchases of materials or goods, and net purchases of assets are trans-

ferred into accounts payable. Accounts available for collection must be further adjusted for net changes in UNEARNED CUSTOMER ADVANCES, and ACCOUNTS PAY-
ABLE for net changes in PREPAID EXPENSE.

NET CHANGE IN SHORT-TERM CREDIT is the EOP difference in SHORT-TERM
LOANS AND NOTES between this period and the preceding one. Planned and internally required changes in long-term obligations are followed by interest and finance
income. The latter is identical to the income-statements figure. Interest cost, both
long-term and short-term, and income taxes, which are separate entries on income
statements, are combined in one account for cash forecasts. Dividends are a cash outflow but not an expense item on income statements. Total net cash flow combines
both operating and financial flows. The EOP cash and securities balance will equal
this flow, plus BOP cash and securities balance, plus net changes in owner capital investment. The latter combines planned and internally required investments.

RETAINED EARNINGS AND CAPITAL CHANGES statements transfer NET INCOME
AFTER INCOME TAXES from income statements, and dividends from cash-flow statements, to changes in retained-earnings accounts. Also, changes in owner net invest-
ment are transferred to revised balances in an OWNER PAID-IN CAPITAL account.
OWNER NET INVESTMENT is the sum of planned and required owner capital invest-
ment accounts, which, if nonzero, will appear at the end of cash-forecast statements.
In the bottom half of retained earnings statements appear the total number of shares
outstanding at the end of each period, as well as three accounts, in dollars per share.
Total shares EOP are used for calculations in the accounts. For NET INCOME PER
SHARE and DIVIDENDS PER SHARE, the annual columns sum the preceding periods.
For EOP owners' equity per share, the annual figure is identical to that of the pre-
ceding period, which must be end-of-year as well as end-of-period.

In condition statements there are no added annual columns. Periods are headed
with the same notation as used for flow statements, the period number followed by
the year and month. Except for the first column, EOP figures are always printed.
EOP figures are identical to BOP figures for the next period. Periods that coincide
with the end of a year are marked with a column of asterisks along the right side.
Condition statements always have an extra column to the left of the first period
labeled *START BOP 1*. This column repeats, for reference, the INITIAL CONDITION
input division. Some of the original entries are consolidated to fit the output arrangement. Consolidations are shown below; where outputs are identical with inputs, they
are not repeated:

ACCOUNTS RECEIVABLE GROSS BOP 1 = ID 10 + ID 17

ACCOUNTS PAYABLE BOP 1 = ID 40 + ID 41 + ID 43

RETAINED EARNINGS BOP 1 = ID 48 – ID 46

Up to five classes of inventories can be combined into the account, TOTAL INVEN-
TORIES. FIXED ASSETS AT BOOK are the total for classes of FIXED ASSETS AT COST,
less the total for classes of FIXED ASSETS DEPRECIATION RESERVES. INTANGIBLE
ASSETS UNAMORTIZED are listed separately; they are not included in book values.

Before any printing of selected-accounts output division, choices are displayed to users. A menu appears, with seventeen key accounts identified by name and number. Users enter the number of the account desired. These are output numbers; they have no relation to input IDs. An entry of 0 prints all seventeen accounts, and an entry of 99 transfers control to the NEXT OUTPUT DIVISION video display. A second entry number is required, which is relevant to first entry account numbers 0 to 17. The absolute value of the second number indicates the type of statistical information to be printed for each account. In addition, if this number is positive, headings will be printed; if negative, headings are omitted. The absolute value of the second entry is irrelevant if input ID 3 = 1, in which case inferential statistics are not available. After any printing of selected accounts, control returns to the menu display. If several accounts are to be printed one after another, it is convenient to eliminate repetition of headings with second number negative entries. The statistical output identification numbers (absolute values of second entry) are:

1 or –1: *mean* only

2 or –2: *standard deviation of the mean* only

3 or –3: *mean* and *standard deviation of the mean*

4 or –4: *mean, standard deviation of the mean*, and *upper* and *lower confidence interval limits of the mean*

The seventeen key accounts contain a mixture of flow and condition items. Flow items occur during a period, and condition items are EOP. Headings are similar to those used previously. The period number is followed by the year and month. The last period of each year is identified with a column of asterisks along the right side. Annual totals are not available. Statistics other than the mean have not been compiled in PAVE for every annual combination of periods. ALL FIXED ASSETS AT BOOK account has no component of uncertainty during the simulation. For this reason only one set of values will always be printed for it. If a particular account is inapplicable or has zero values for all periods, its title is printed along with the message, "all account values are zero."

9.4 | Input-Output Choices for PAVE Simulations

To run a PAVE simulation, several critical input choices are required. The character of output information may be altered significantly by these choices. In this section important choices are recapitulated, together with specific consequences to printed outputs.

The four output divisions are referenced here by the following words in capital letters:

VALUATION and scope for first and final years

FINANCIAL SUMMARY from final period

FINANCIAL STATEMENTS projected for all periods

SELECTED ACCOUNTS for all periods

In the following paragraphs choices are discussed in numerical order of input ID numbers.

DETERMINISTIC (ID 3 = 1) or STATISTICAL INFERENCE (ID 3 > 1)

The deterministic mode develops all outputs from one PAVE replication. Statistical inference uses a Monte Carlo method of repeated sample replications. For ID $3 > 1$, uncertainty may be introduced with triangular probability distributions for up to twelve dynamic input sets. Users input the maximum percentage shift in ID -1 position, which may be 0, for each of these sets. Such inputs are ignored under ID $3 = 1$ deterministic. For statistical ID $3 > 1$, outputs are approximately and normally distributed.

Moving from deterministic to statistical input choice, valuation, financial summary, and selected accounts shift output printing from single values to sets of four summary statistics. These summary statistics are the mean, standard deviation of the mean, and upper and lower confidence interval limits of the mean. Risk levels and precision of confidence intervals accompany sample size (ID 3 value). Combinations used in PAVE are listed in Table 8.2. The last three statistical measures of spread are inferences on the mean of the outputs, not on individual values of outputs. To make inferences on the latter, multiply the standard deviation and the width of the confidence interval by the square root of ID 3 input. In SELECTED ACCOUNTS there is a choice of statistics to be printed. The last account, ALL FIXED ASSETS AT BOOK, has no variability in the simulation.

In VALUATION, probabilities of insolvency for deterministic must be either one or zero ("the insolvency did not occur" message). Going-concern value requires risk analysis. Its amount and accompanying parameters are omitted under *deterministic*. A statistical choice for FINANCIAL SUMMARY prints maximum and minimum values encountered during the simulation, as well as the four summary statistics listed above. FINANCIAL STATEMENTS print only mean values. These are equivalent to single values under *deterministic*.

FRAME (ID 5): SERVICE = 0, TRADE = 1, MANUFACTURING = 2, or ENVIRONMENT ONLY = 3

Logic changes among the first three choices are a matter of goods inventories. Services are intangible; there are no physical accumulations. Only general supplies (IDs 15 and 79) inventories are maintained for service frame. Another inventory, *finished goods* (IDs 16 and set 152) becomes relevant for the trade frame. For *manufacturing*, there are not only three more inventories (five total) but an additional set of inputs for expense accounts and asset classes. The additional manufacturing inventories are direct materials (IDs 18 and set 172), goods-in process, (IDs 17 and set 162), and indirect supplies (IDs 19 and 220). One may use the added set of manufacturing inputs to simulate production at a separate location from general administration. Since inputs are available to set any inventory level to zero, the manufacturing frame could be used for a service business, to gain a richer set of expense and asset inputs. On the other hand, if nonzero entries are made for inventories outside a specified frame, such inputs will be ignored. Carelessness here could create balancing problems in the initial-condition input division.

Continuing with the first three frame choices, valuation outputs do not change form as the frame changes. Under SERVICE FRAME, however, a few items will be omitted from FINANCIAL SUMMARY and SELECTED ACCOUNTS. COST OF SALES and GROSS PROFIT ON SALES apply to products and will be omitted from SERVICE. In financial statements, cost of goods sold schedules are omitted for the service frame, and cost-of-goods-manufactured schedules are printed only in the manufacturing frame. Cost-of-sales and gross-profit-on-sales entries are omitted from income statements under SERVICE FRAME.

The ENVIRONMENT ONLY frame prints a limited output. Processing is restricted to the economic and industry environment; there is no internal analysis of a firm's performance. In other words, processing ends with SALES DEMAND AVAILABLE TO A FIRM. In VALUATION, the only items printed under ENVIRONMENT ONLY are total sales for the first and final years. Pre-share information is not printed. In FINANCIAL SUMMARY, only net sales or revenue per year will be printed if ID 120 = 1. Otherwise, FIRM'S SHARE OF INDUSTRY PERCENTAGE and INDUSTRY SALES PER YEAR will also be printed. In FINANCIAL STATEMENTS, only environmental-analyses-of-the-firm statements are printed. The maximum nonzero accounts under SELECTED ACCOUNTS are industry sales, firm's industry share percentage, and firm net sales achieved.

OUTPUT DIVISION PRINTED FIRST (ID 6): VALUATION = 0, FINANCIAL SUMMARY = 1, FINANCIAL STATEMENTS = 2, and SELECTED ACCOUNTS = 3

After a print of an output division, users are given a choice of branching to any output division, return to PAVE1 for revised inputs and a new run, or END the simulation. Thus the first output division print is only a passing choice. One may mix or match output divisions in any order.

INFLATE DOLLAR PERIOD AMOUNTS (ID 110): NO = 0/YES = 1

This choice works in conjunction with ID set 112 and ID 120. Inflation adjustments over periods are determined by nonzero entries in ID set 112 when ID 110 = 1 or ID 120 = 0. If ID 120 = 0, sales demand of a firm is computed as a share of industry sales. In such cases, inflation adjustments are applied directly to industry sales and indirectly to sales of the firm and all expenses variable with sales. If ID 110 = 1, inflation adjustments will also be applied to period (fixed) costs and asset changes; if ID 110 = 0 they will not. If ID 110 = 0 and ID 120 = 1, inflation adjustments will be applied directly to sales of the firm and to all period (fixed) costs and asset changes. In such cases, inflation adjustments will also be applied indirectly to expenses variable with sales. There is a complete range of inflation options with various combinations of IDs 110 and 120.

SALES DEMAND COMPUTATION (ID 120): % MARKET SHARE OF INDUSTRY = 0/$ SALES PER PERIOD = 1

If ID 120 = 0 industry sales over periods will be computed from base annual industry sales input ID 130 as compounded with three growth rates. The three rates are real economic ID set 102, inflation ID set 112, and industry to economy comparison ID set 132. Inputs ID 131 for uncertainty and IDs 51 to 74 for seasonal-cyclical indices make further adjustments to industry sales. Sales demand available to a firm is computed as a market share of industry with ID set 122. There is a second uncertainty input with ID 121.

If ID 120 = 1, dollar sales demand per period is entered directly in ID set 122. In such cases, industry-sales and percent-of-market-share-of-industry outputs are not available. Consequently, these accounts are omitted from the financial summary, environmental analyses of the firm in financial statements and selected accounts.

Inflation adjustment combinations with ID 120 were discussed under ID 110 above.

RESEARCH AND DEVELOPMENT EXPENSE COMPUTATION (ID 330): PERCENT OF SALES = 0/$ PER PERIOD = 1

This choice determines the basis of inputs in ID sets 332 and 342.

INTERNAL COMPUTATION OF REQUIRED ADDITIONAL CAPITAL INVESTMENT (ID 530): NO = 0/YES = 1

If ID 530 = 1, any required, additional, long-term capital investment is computed internally. A portion of this investment may be placed in long-term obligations if ID 540 is greater than 0. Whatever portion is not in long-term obligations will be assigned to owner-paid-in capital. An internal computation of required investment is always incremental to planned changes in long-term capital. These planned changes are scheduled in ID sets 532 for owner capital and 542 for debt capital. By varying the levels of planned additions, various requirements for incremental capital may be simulated.

Needs for additional capital are computed each period from analysis of cash flows. The cash decision rule is to maintain a minimum acceptable cash ratio (ID 87 with an internal default value of 50%). Short-term borrowing is first initiated up to a limit determined by working capital and inventories (IDs 88 and 95, with internal defaults of 200% and 50%, respectively). Long-term capital is added if short-term borrowing capacity is insufficient. Thus additional long-term capital is incremental to both planned capital changes and the limit of short-term borrowings.

If ID 530 = 0, a firm must depend on planned capital changes and short-term borrowing. If these are insufficient, negative cash, negative retained earnings, and negative owners' equity may occur. Such negative values are permitted and the simulation will not be aborted. To examine risks of insolvency, input ID 530 = 0. If ID 530 = 1, technical insolvency cannot occur and legal insolvency is unlikely.

DIVIDENDS COMPUTATION (ID 550): % OF EARNINGS = 0/$ PER PERIOD = 1

This choice determines the basis of entries in ID set 552.

9.5 | The Output Effects of Some Common Errors in PAVE Inputs

From the authors' experience with PAVE runs, some important sources of input errors are listed below. If run results are unsatisfactory, check your input set against mistakes that occur frequently in the input process.

1. A column of input values may get out of alignment with corresponding IDs and descriptions. Check this problem in each display. The difficulty is particularly prevalent for dynamic input sets. If base values and growth rates are interchanged, the effect on outputs can be weird.

2. In the checking of initial conditions, PAVE will not accept imbalances of more than $1 after truncating inputs to the significant digits available on the computer. This may cause problems with BASIC interpreters of less than nine significant figures. To avoid the problem, make sure that input initial conditions are in balance after rounding to the significant places available.

3. Initial conditions in PAVE may not balance if nonzero inventories or assets are entered for a class of firm different from that specified in the input/output division (ID 5, FRAME). Suppose ID 5 = 0 for SERVICE, but nonzero entries are made in ID 16 for $ INVENTORY OF MANUFACTURED OR TRADE FINISHED GOODS. PAVE will reset the inapplicable accounts to zero, which would unbalance a user's original set of entries.

4. A correct original input may be overwritten by mistake. Since there is a capability for unlimited revision, inadvertent reentry is a risk which should be checked.

5. Be careful to distinguish between "dollar" and "percent" entries. Sometimes the same ID set may be used both ways (ID sets 122, 332, and 552). The wrong selection will completely destroy output results. Check the choice indicator IDs that go with these dynamic input sets. Note the prefixes on video displays, which should always indicate the correct entry.

6. Time rate "percent" entries are always annual rates.

7. Do not enter decimal fractions in place of "percent" entries, or you will divide the effective input by 100.

8. Do not enter choice NO FILE = 0 at the beginning of PAVE1 if there is a possibility of reruns. Under NO FILE, you cannot save anything entered at the keyboard in PAVE1 before starting a run.

9. Be sure that a current set of input/output system choices is available before proceeding to other input divisions. Input/output choices, especially ID 5, FRAME, determine the arrangement and extent of remaining input displays. Input/output choices also affect the values assigned to other inputs during processing.

10. For statistical sampling runs (Monte Carlo method with ID 3 > 1), input uncertainties (up to twelve IDs) may aggregate together to determine output variability. Exaggerated input uncertainties could accumulate confidence limits so wide that imprecision destroys output utility.

11. Sample sizes above 12 are seldom needed. Depending on the hardware, the speed of processing can range from a couple of minutes to more than half an hour. Keep sample sizes small on slow equipment.

12. Inappropriate values for certain input IDs may cause processing to go into an endless loop. Internal protective routines are provided in many places to prevent breakdowns, but there are still possibilities of cycling. Video screen displays inform operators about the progress of processing. They tell which program is currently in the work space. During PAVE3 a count of Monte Carlo sample replications is displayed after each replication has been completed. If indicators of processing fail to advance, and if no error message appears on the screen, the program may have entered an endless loop. In such cases, terminate the run and recheck the input set.

An endless-loop condition has been identified for two cases of incorrect inputs:

(a) negative base values may not be used in certain dynamic input sets. Base values appear in the right-hand digit position −2 (also in −5 and −8 of extended system). In some cases, however, negative base values are not only permitted but necessary. Do not use negative base values unless specifically permitted under descriptions of inputs (see section 8.5 or the Appendix). It is important to note that negative inputs are always permitted in annual growth positions of dynamic sets (right-hand digit position −3, and positions −6 and −9 of the extended system).

(b) negative depreciation rates are not allowed in IDs 280, 290, 300, 310, 320, 480, 490, 500, 510, or 520. Rates of zero are, of course, permitted.

10 Introductory PAVE Cases

10.1 | Industry Environmental Analysis—VALVO

The cases in this chapter are arranged in ascending order of complexity. The input and output features of each case build upon the attributes of the cases which preceded. For this reason it is recommended that cases be examined in the same order as presented.

A section is devoted to each case. The simplest case, VALVO, which is limited to environmental and industry analysis, appears in this section. A complete analysis of a service firm is presented next. This case is AUTOWASH in section 10.2. A retailing firm, FLORAWREATH, is covered in section 10.3. The final case, ECOFURN, is a manufacturing concern. The initial presentation of ECOFURN, appears in section 10.4. Some extensions of ECOFURN problem solving are considered in section 10.5. If some inputs are changed, what is the effect on outputs? Section 10.5 discusses sensitivity and change analysis.

The presentation of each case is divided into four phases:

1. A general description of the firm and its environment. The reader is cast into the role of a consultant who runs PAVE to obtain some insights about a particular problem or a projection of performance.

2. Development and exhibition of PAVE inputs.

3. Discussion and interpretation of PAVE outputs.

4. A summary of conclusions and suggestions for further analysis.

The VALVO case is limited to industry and environmental analysis. There are only a few inputs and outputs because internal planning and budgeting of the firm are not considered. Thus output ends with net sales of VALVO. This is an excellent option (frame choice input ID 5 = 3) for an introduction to PAVE input/output systems.

VALVO manufactures specialized valves for scientific equipment. This is a small industry with sales of about $10 million per year; in fact, last year's sales were $9,792,000. VALVO has about 10% of the market. The problem is to project the next three years of VALVO sales. If the length of simulated periods is a quarter of a year, then a pronounced seasonal peak becomes apparent at the end of each year. The third quarter has average sales, the first quarter slightly below average, and the second quarter the slowest sales. The set of seasonal sales indices in order, starting with the first quarter, is 0.9, 0.8, 1, and 1.3. Uncertainty about future industry sales may be represented with a maximum shift of 25%; uncertainty about VALVO's market share of industry is expected to be only half as great.

The economy is expected to grow at a real rate of 4% during the first year, but this rate will decrease 1% each year thereafter. Inflation is estimated at 6% the first year. This rate is expected to increase by 0.5% per year. The specialized valve industry is expected to grow 2% faster than the economy during the first year. This comparison rate will grow at 2% a year.

VALVO is interested in studying available sales demands under the above conditions. You decide to run two simulations, one deterministic and one Monte Carlo. The risk inputs will not be operational during the first simulation. A sample size of 5 will be used for risk analysis during the second simulation. This will print a 95% confidence interval for output means.

The complete set of PAVE inputs for a deterministic simulation is reproduced in Table 10.1. Outputs for this simulation are exhibited in Table 10.2. The only change of inputs required for a Monte Carlo simulation is reentry of ID 3 at 5 in place of 1. The Monte Carlo statistical outputs are presented in Table 10.3.

In comparing the mean outputs between tables 10.2 and 10.3, figures in Table 10.2 are precise functions of the inputs, whereas Table 10.3 figures are sample means. Risk inference, however, is available only from Table 10.3. *Net Sales* is the only account available in VALUATION AND SCOPE output division under *environment only* frame (ID 5 = 3). Such a limited output is scarcely worth printing, but was included here for illustrative purposes.

Statistical outputs in FINANCIAL SUMMARY output division will be discussed briefly. The simulated mean of firm's share of industry is 10.24% as compared to a base input value of 10%. Confidence limits of the mean are rather narrow with a small standard deviation of 0.15%. Over a sample size of 5 the lowest share reached was 9.78%, and the highest share was 10.58%. Confidence limits of the mean are more significant for risk statements than the lowest (min) and highest (max) values, but the latter measure may appeal to some users. The interpretation of statistics for the other FINANCIAL SUMMARY items is similar to a firm's share of industry. Notice that mean industry sales, annualized from the final simulated quarter, are over 1.7 times the initial base value of about $10 million. This is the result of about 12.5% compounded growth per year over three years, and the fourth quarter seasonal index, which reaches a peak of 1.3. The compounded growth comes from a combination of about 4% real, 6% inflation, and 2% industry premium over the economy. Since FINANCIAL SUMMARY statistics are an annual extrapolation of final quarter re-

— Table 10.1. —
INPUT SET FOR VALVO

VALVO

130 $ INDUSTRY SALES FOR BASE (PRIOR) YEAR . 9792000

*% ANNUAL INDUSTRY GROWTH COMPARED TO ECONOMY
131   *% MAX CHANGE FROM MEAN VALUE . . 25

132 % BASE VALUE APPLIED IN PERIOD 1 . . 2
133 % ANNUAL CHANGE TO PERIODS FROM 1ST BASE 2

SEASONAL/CYCLICAL INDICES--1ST SET STOPS AT 1ST ZERO
51 INDEX 1 9
52 INDEX 2 8
53 INDEX 3 1
54 INDEX 4 . . . . 1.3
55 INDEX 5 0
56 INDEX 6 0
57 INDEX 7 0
58 INDEX 8 0
59 INDEX 9 0
60 INDEX 10 0
61 INDEX 11 0
62 INDEX 12 0

INPUT/OUTPUT SYSTEM CHOICES
!! THESE INPUTS CONTROL OTHER DISPLAYS!!

1 TOTAL NUMBER OF PERIODS (MAX 24) . . 12
2 NO. OF PERIODS PER YEAR . . 4
3 SAMPLE SIZE--DETERMINISTIC=1/STAT.=2 TO 12. 1
4 SEED NO.--STANDARD RANDOM SERIES=0 . 0
5 FRAME: SERVICE=0/TRADE=1/MFG=2/ENVRT ONLY=3 3
6 OUTPUT DIVISION PRINT 1ST FROM LIST BELOW: 0
   VALUATION 1ST AND FINAL YEARS, SCOPE =0
   STATISTICAL SUMMARY FROM FINAL PERIOD =1
   FINANCIAL STATEMENTS FOR ALL PERIODS =2
   SELECTED ACCOUNTS FOR ALL PERIODS =3

% ANNUAL REAL GROWTH RATE OF ECONOMY

102 % BASE VALUE APPLIED IN PERIOD 1 . 4
103 % ANNUAL CHANGE TO PERIODS FROM 1ST BASE -1

110 INFLATE PERIOD COSTS--NO=0/YES=1 . 0

% ANNUAL AVERAGE INFLATION RATE

112 % BASE VALUE APPLIED IN PERIOD 1 . 6
113 % ANNUAL CHANGE TO PERIODS FROM 1ST BASE .5

120 SALES--% INDUSTRY SHARE=0/$ PER PERIOD=1. 0

* NET SALES DEMAND AVAILABLE TO FIRM
121   *% MAX CHANGE FROM MEAN VALUE . 12.5

122 % BASE VALUE APPLIED IN PERIOD 1 . 10
123 % ANNUAL CHANGE TO PERIODS FROM 1ST BASE 0

Table 10.2.

DETERMINISTIC OUTPUTS FOR VALVO

```
           ********************
            VALUATION AND SCOPE
           ********************

VALVO--DETERMINISTIC SIMULATION

   12 PERIODS OVER  3.00 YEARS;  4.00 PERIODS PER YEAR, EACH  0.25 YEARS

******  SCOPE OF FIRM -- INITIAL SHARES 1 -- FINAL SHARES 1 -- EOP = END OF PERIOD  ******

SALES            TOTAL       FIRST YEAR      1,059,756
                             FINAL YEAR      1,341,169


           ************************************
            FINANCIAL SUMMARY FROM FINAL PERIOD
           ************************************

VALVO--DETERMINISTIC SIMULATION

   12 PERIODS OVER  3.00 YEARS;  4.00 PERIODS PER YEAR, EACH  0.25 YEARS
   UNDEFINED RATIOS APPEAR '####--'; YEARLY VALUES ARE EXTRAPOLATED FROM THE FINAL PERIOD; 0 VALUES OMITTED

******  SCOPE OF FIRM  ******

FIRM'S SHARE OF INDUSTRY %          10.00
NET SALES OR REVENUE PER YEAR    1,812,022

******  SELECTED FINANCIAL SUMMARY VALUES  ******

INDUSTRY SALES PER YR--000 OMIT    18,120
```

Table 10.2 (continued)

```
**********************************
  FINANCIAL STATEMENTS PROJECTED FOR ALL PERIODS
**********************************
```

ADMIN	ADMINISTRATIVE	DEPRC	DEPRECIATION	GEN	GENERAL
AMORT	AMORTIZATION	EOP	END OF PERIOD	INVY	INVENTORY
BOP	BEGINNING OF PERIOD	GEN	GENERAL	MFG	MANUFACTURING
MISC	MISCELLANEOUS	PURCH	PURCHASES OF	R&D	RESEARCH AND DEVELOPMENT

12 PERIODS OVER 3.00 YEARS; 4.00 PERIODS PER YEAR, EACH 0.25 YEARS

VALUES ARE ACCOUNT MEANS; ACCOUNT OMITTED WHEN ALL VALUES 0
HEADINGS ARE: PERIOD NO. AND YEAR/MONTH; OR CUMULATIVE *FOR YEAR NO.*

VALVO--DETERMINISTIC SIMULATION

```
**********************************
ENVIRONMENTAL ANALYSES OF FIRM
**********************************
```

INDUSTRY BASE SALES--000S OMITTED; YEAR= 9792 -- PERIOD= 2448

	1 0/3	2 0/6	3 0/9	4 1/0	*FOR YEAR 1*	5 1/3
INFLATION RATE ANNUAL %	6.00	6.01	6.01	6.02	6.01*	6.03
REAL ECONOMY GROWTH ANNUAL %	4.00	3.99	3.98	3.97	3.99*	3.96
INDUSTRY TOTAL GROWTH %	12.44	12.45	12.46	12.47	12.46*	12.48
SEASONAL/CYCLICAL INDICES	0.90	0.80	1.00	1.30	1.00*	0.90
INDUSTRY SALES--000S OMITTED	2,269	2,077	2,673	3,579	10,598*	2,552
FIRM'S INDUSTRY SHARE %	10.00	10.00	10.00	10.00	10.00*	10.00
FIRM SALES DEMAND AVAILABLE	226,876	207,672	267,325	357,883	1,059,756*	255,156

```
ENVIRONMENTAL ANALYSES OF FIRM
**********************************
                               (CONTINUED)
```

	6 1/6	7 1/9	8 2/0	*FOR YEAR 2*	9 2/3	10 2/6
INFLATION RATE ANNUAL %	6.04	6.04	6.05	6.04*	6.06	6.07
REAL ECONOMY GROWTH ANNUAL %	3.95	3.94	3.93	3.95*	3.92	3.91
INDUSTRY TOTAL GROWTH %	12.49	12.49	12.50	12.49*	12.51	12.52
SEASONAL/CYCLICAL INDICES	0.80	1.00	1.30	1.00*	0.90	0.80
INDUSTRY SALES--000S OMITTED	2,336	3,007	4,026	11,921*	2,870	2,628
FIRM'S INDUSTRY SHARE %	10.00	10.00	10.00	10.00*	10.00	10.00
FIRM SALES DEMAND AVAILABLE	233,576	300,691	402,583	1,192,006*	287,048	262,790

Table 10.2 (continued)

ENVIRONMENTAL ANALYSES OF FIRM (CONTINUED)
****

	11 2/9	12 3/0	*FOR YEAR 3*
INFLATION RATE ANNUAL %	6.08	6.08	6.07*
REAL ECONOMY GROWTH ANNUAL %	3.90	3.89	3.91*
INDUSTRY TOTAL GROWTH %	12.53	12.54	12.53*
SEASONAL/CYCLICAL INDICES	1.00	1.30	1.00*
INDUSTRY SALES--000S OMITTED	3,383	4,530	13,411*
FIRM'S INDUSTRY SHARE %	10.00	10.00	10.00*
FIRM SALES DEMAND AVAILABLE	338,326	453,006	1,341,170*

VALVO--DETERMINISTIC SIMULATION
****
　SELECTED ACCOUNTS FOR ALL PERIODS
****

CONDITION ITEMS ARE END-OF-PERIOD

	1 0/3	2 0/6	3 0/9	4 1/0*	5 1/3	6 1/6
INDUSTRY SALES--000 OMIT	2,269	2,077	2,673	3,579*	2,552	2,336
FIRM'S INDUSTRY SHARE %	10.00	10.00	10.00	10.00*	10.00	10.00
FIRM NET SALES ACHIEVED	226,876	207,672	267,325	357,883*	255,156	233,576

	7 1/9	8 2/0*	9 2/3	10 2/6	11 2/9	12 3/0*
INDUSTRY SALES--000 OMIT	3,007	4,025*	2,870	2,628	3,383	4,530*
FIRM'S INDUSTRY SHARE %	10.00	10.00*	10.00	10.00	10.00	10.00*
FIRM NET SALES ACHIEVED	300,691	402,583*	287,048	262,790	338,326	453,006*

Table 10.3.
STATISTICAL OUTPUTS FOR VALVO

```
*******************
  VALUATION AND SCOPE
*******************

VALVO--STATISTICAL SIMULATION

12 PERIODS OVER  3.00 YEARS;  4.00 PERIODS PER YEAR, EACH  0.25 YEARS

******  SCOPE OF FIRM -- INITIAL SHARES 1 -- FINAL SHARES 1 -- EOP = END OF PERIOD  ******

     95 % CONFIDENCE LIMITS FOR MEANS WITH SAMPLE SIZE 5
```

		MEAN	STANDARD DEVIATION	95 % LOWER CONFIDENCE	95 % UPPER CONFIDENCE
SALES	TOTAL				
	FIRST YEAR	1,067,634	18,464	1,015,935	1,119,333
	FINAL YEAR	1,311,016	12,912	1,274,863	1,347,169

```
*********************************
  FINANCIAL SUMMARY FROM FINAL PERIOD
*********************************

VALVO--STATISTICAL SIMULATION

12 PERIODS OVER  3.00 YEARS;  4.00 PERIODS PER YEAR, EACH  0.25 YEARS
UNDEFINED RATIOS APPEAR '####--'; YEARLY VALUES ARE EXTRAPOLATED FROM THE FINAL PERIOD; 0 VALUES OMITTED

     95 % CONFIDENCE LIMITS FOR MEANS WITH SAMPLE SIZE 5
```

	MEAN	STANDARD DEVIATION	95 % LOWER CONFIDENCE	95 % UPPER CONFIDENCE	MINIMUM	MAXIMUM
****** SCOPE OF FIRM ******						
FIRM'S SHARE OF INDUSTRY %	10.24	0.15	9.82	10.66	9.78	10.58
NET SALES OR REVENUE PER YEAR	1,762,137	102,974	1,473,809	2,050,464	1,508,151	2,093,024
****** SELECTED FINANCIAL SUMMARY VALUES ******						
INDUSTRY SALES PER YR--000 OMIT	17,170	796	14,941	19,398	15,111	19,783

Table 10.3 (continued)

```
************************************
   FINANCIAL STATEMENTS PROJECTED FOR ALL PERIODS
************************************

ADMIN   ADMINISTRATIVE         DEPRC   DEPRECIATION      GEN    GENERAL
AMORT   AMORTIZATION           EOP     END OF PERIOD     INVY   INVENTORY
BOP     BEGINNING OF PERIOD    GEN     GENERAL           MFG    MANUFACTURING
MISC    MISCELLANEOUS          PURCH   PURCHASES OF      R&D    RESEARCH AND DEVELOPMENT

12 PERIODS OVER 3.00 YEARS;  4.00 PERIODS PER YEAR, EACH 0.25 YEARS

VALUES ARE ACCOUNT MEANS; ACCOUNT OMITTED WHEN ALL VALUES 0
HEADINGS ARE: PERIOD NO. AND YEAR/MONTH; OR CUMULATIVE *FOR YEAR NO.*

VALVO--STATISTICAL SIMULATION

************************************
ENVIRONMENTAL ANALYSES OF FIRM
************************************
```

INDUSTRY BASE SALES--000S OMITTED; YEAR= 9792 -- PERIOD= 2448

	1 0/3	2 0/6	3 0/9	4 1/0	1/ 0 *FOR YEAR 1*	5 1/3
INFLATION RATE ANNUAL %	6.00	6.01	6.01	6.02	6.01*	6.03
REAL ECONOMY GROWTH ANNUAL %	4.00	3.99	3.98	3.97	3.99*	3.96
INDUSTRY TOTAL GROWTH %	12.44	12.45	12.46	12.47	12.46*	12.48
SEASONAL/CYCLICAL INDICES	0.90	0.80	1.00	1.30	1.00*	0.90
INDUSTRY SALES--000S OMITTED	2,366	2,007	2,847	3,511	10,731*	2,526
FIRM'S INDUSTRY SHARE %	9.81	10.43	10.12	9.64	10.00*	10.27
FIRM SALES DEMAND AVAILABLE	232,890	209,120	287,977	337,647	1,067,634*	259,357

ENVIRONMENTAL ANALYSES OF FIRM
```
************************************
```
(CONTINUED)

	6 1/6	7 1/9	8 2/0	2/ 0 *FOR YEAR 2*	9 2/3	10 2/6
INFLATION RATE ANNUAL %	6.04	6.05	6.05	6.04*	6.06	6.07
REAL ECONOMY GROWTH ANNUAL %	3.95	3.94	3.93	3.95*	3.92	3.91
INDUSTRY TOTAL GROWTH %	12.49	12.49	12.50	12.49*	12.51	12.52
SEASONAL/CYCLICAL INDICES	0.80	1.00	1.30	1.00*	0.90	0.80
INDUSTRY SALES--000S OMITTED	2,376	3,169	3,965	12,036*	2,813	2,739
FIRM'S INDUSTRY SHARE %	10.05	9.88	10.11	10.08*	10.00	9.76
FIRM SALES DEMAND AVAILABLE	238,722	313,917	401,968	1,213,964*	282,593	267,625

Table 10.3 (continued)

ENVIRONMENTAL ANALYSES OF FIRM (CONTINUED)
****

	11 2/ 9	12 3/ 0	*FOR YEAR 3*
INFLATION RATE ANNUAL %	6.08	6.08	6.07*
REAL ECONOMY GROWTH ANNUAL %	3.90	3.89	3.91*
INDUSTRY TOTAL GROWTH %	12.53	12.54	12.53*
SEASONAL/CYCLICAL INDICES	1.00	1.30	1.00*
INDUSTRY SALES--000S OMITTED	3,323	4,292	13,167*
FIRM'S INDUSTRY SHARE %	9.65	10.24	9.91*
FIRM SALES DEMAND AVAILABLE	320,264	440,534	1,311,016*

VALVO--STATISTICAL SIMULATION

****
SELECTED ACCOUNTS FOR ALL PERIODS
****

CONDITION ITEMS ARE END-OF-PERIOD; 95 % CONFIDENCE LIMITS FOR MEANS WITH SAMPLE SIZE 5

	1 0/ 3	2 0/ 6	3 0/ 9	4 1/ 0*	5 1/ 3	6 1/ 6
INDUSTRY SALES--000 OMIT						
MEANS	2,366	2,007	2,847	3,511*	2,526	2,376
STANDARD DEVIATIONS	136	112	81	114*	69	70
LOWER CONFIDENCE LIMITS	1,986	1,694	2,621	3,191*	2,333	2,180
UPPER CONFIDENCE LIMITS	2,746	2,321	3,074	3,830*	2,720	2,572
FIRM'S INDUSTRY SHARE %						
MEANS	9.81	10.43	10.12	9.64*	10.27	10.05
STANDARD DEVIATIONS	0.19	0.27	0.21	0.17*	0.28	0.20
LOWER CONFIDENCE LIMITS	9.28	9.66	9.54	9.16*	9.48	9.50
UPPER CONFIDENCE LIMITS	10.34	11.19	10.70	10.12*	11.06	10.60
FIRM NET SALES ACHIEVED						
MEANS	232,890	209,120	287,977	337,647*	259,357	238,722
STANDARD DEVIATIONS	16,666	12,642	7,912	6,464*	9,459	7,799
LOWER CONFIDENCE LIMITS	186,225	173,722	265,824	319,547*	232,871	216,885
UPPER CONFIDENCE LIMITS	279,555	244,519	310,129	355,747*	285,843	260,559

Table 10.3 (continued)

	7 1/9	8 2/0*	9 2/3	10 2/6	11 2/9	12 3/0*
INDUSTRY SALES--000 OMIT						
MEANS	3,169	3,965*	2,813	2,739	3,323	4,292*
STANDARD DEVIATIONS	131	230*	177	85	133	199*
LOWER CONFIDENCE LIMITS	2,801	3,320*	2,318	2,500	2,951	3,736*
UPPER CONFIDENCE LIMITS	3,537	4,610*	3,309	2,978	3,695	4,849*
FIRM'S INDUSTRY SHARE %						
MEANS	9.88	10.11*	10.00	9.76	9.65	10.24*
STANDARD DEVIATIONS	0.24	0.26*	0.19	0.27	0.20	0.15*
LOWER CONFIDENCE LIMITS	9.20	9.39*	9.47	9.02	9.09	9.81*
UPPER CONFIDENCE LIMITS	10.55	10.83*	10.53	10.50	10.22	10.67*
FIRM NET SALES ACHIEVED						
MEANS	313,917	401,968*	282,593	267,625	320,264	440,534*
STANDARD DEVIATIONS	19,580	29,348*	23,141	12,720	11,208	25,744*
LOWER CONFIDENCE LIMITS	259,095	319,794*	217,798	232,010	288,882	368,452*
UPPER CONFIDENCE LIMITS	368,740	484,143*	347,387	303,240	351,645	512,616*

sults, seasonal effects are exaggerated. This distortion could have been overcome by ending the simulation at a neutral quarter, here the third. To note the distortion, compare net sales for the final year between VALUATION and FINANCIAL SUMMARY output divisions.

Net sales demand of the firm is approximately 10% of industry sales throughout the VALVO simulation. Net sales is subject to uncertainty from randomization of both industry sales and firms's share of industry. This is regulated by maximum shift inputs in IDs 121 and 131.

In FINANCIAL STATEMENTS output division seven accounts in ENVIRON-MENTAL ANALYSES OF FIRM are available for printing. Remaining statements are not printed because they deal with internal planning of a firm. The mean simulated value is printed for every period in each account. Period numbers increase across rows, as shown by the first item in headings. The second item of headings shows elapsed years and months. At the end of the fourth period (quarter), one year has elapsed, and at the end of the simulation exactly three years. Annual figures are also printed. In FINANCIAL STATEMENTS, dollar flow amounts apply to a particular period. In FINANCIAL SUMMARY, on the other hand, final period results are extrapolated to a year (in this case multiplied by four). Except for rounding, note that Period 12 industry sales and net sales demand available to the firm, if multiplied by four, will equal the corresponding accounts of the FINANCIAL SUMMARY.

The input seasonal indices (IDs 51 to 54) for quarters are repeated in the output account, but have been internally cycled over all periods. They would also have been normalized (converted to a mean of one) in the output account if such processing had been required. The mean of firm's industry share differs from period to period around a central value of 10%. Differences are due to randomization. Annual figures for industry sales and firm sales demand are the sums of quarterly figures. All other annual figures are the means of quarterly ratios.

In SELECTED ACCOUNTS output division, only the first three accounts out of a total of 17 are applicable to the *environment only* frame (ID $5 = 3$). These are the accounts shown in tables 10.2 and 10.3. If a user asks to have all accounts printed, remaining titles in VALVO will appear followed by the message ALL ACCOUNT VALUES ARE ZERO OR INAPPLICABLE.

In the VALVO case PAVE has presented a statistical summary of the derivation of sales demand of a firm by environmental analysis from economy and industry data. This is a conventional sales analysis using trends and a seasonal pattern. The seasonal indices may also be chosen to include business cycle expectations. Here a neutral cycle was projected.

10.2 | A Service Firm—AUTOWASH

You have just been offered all the physical facilities of AUTOWASH, a self-service washing shed for motor vehicles. You may acquire the land, building, and equipment for $100,000. You would also acquire the right to continue services to the public under the AUTOWASH name used by former owners. No interruption of service need take place if you start your business with existing facilities.

To help decide if the asking price is reasonable you decide to run PAVE simulations. These will project the future of your business over the next 10 years.

Sales the previous year were $120,000.

The following annual expenses occurred in the most recent year:

Payrolls, including your own salary as manager	$38,000
Supplies	4,000
Period expenses, including utilities, property taxes, licenses, legal fees, and maintenance	$50,000

All sales are for cash. Both sales and expenses are expected to grow over the next few years at a rate equal to annual inflation, which is projected at 7%. Your average credit period from suppliers is 10 days (2.8% of annual accounts payable expense). The fixed assets (building and equipment) are approximately worth current book value of $40,000. They will be depreciated at an average rate of 15% on declining balance. Replacement of equipment and modernization is expected to run about $5,000 every year.

Purchase terms of AUTOWASH are $40,000 in cash and a term loan for the balance of $60,000. The principal of this loan must be reduced by $7,500 each year, and interest on the unpaid balance is estimated at 10% per annum. Interest on short-term loans, if any are required, is also projected at 10% per annum.

Since you would have to pay $100,000 for assets with a book value of $40,000, $60,000 will be set up as intangible assets during the first year. These intangible assets will be written off at $8000 per year. Because income will be understated by this amount for tax purposes, an effective income tax rate of 50% will be used.

You plan to deposit $10,000 cash in the business as initial working capital. Your total beginning cash investment is then $50,000. No cash withdrawals from earnings will be scheduled in the simulation.

There are two questions to be answered. Is your $50,000 initial investment sufficient to run the business with small risk of insolvency? Is the business worth the asking price?

Two 10-year simulations will be run. The first will be deterministic. Price-earnings multiples of 7 will be used to estimate market value. The second simulation will include risk. A sample size of 7 will be chosen which will produce 95% confidence limits for outputs. The following are maximum deviations from expected input values: Sales −35%, Period expense−20%. For the second simulation, financial valuation parameters will be determined internally.

A PAVE print of all inputs for the first simulation is condensed into Table 10.4. Ten periods are simulated (ID 1), each one year in duration (ID 2). The first simulation is deterministic (ID 3 = 1). AUTOWASH is a service concern without product inventories, hence ID 5 = 0. Input Division 2 for INITIAL CONDITION will not be used.

Starting assets and equities are entered as first-period additions, instead. Thus $45,000 *fixed asset net changes* EOP 1 (ID 482) covers $40,000 initial value plus $5000 replacement. This schedule ends in Period 1 (ID 484). An amount of $5000 is added during all periods after the first (ID 485). Owner net cash investment is $50,000 during Period 1 (ID 532). This is the sum of $40,000 purchase price and $10,000 initial working capital. Again this cash addition takes place only in Period 1 (ID 534).

The remaining $60,000 of the purchase price is financed with a term loan, and $7500 is to be repaid the first year. Thus there is a net addition to long-term debt of $52,500 EOP 1 (ID 542), which again ends at Period 1 (ID 545).

Goodwill of $60,000 is incurred during Period 1 at the time of purchase (ID 83), and is to be amortized at $8000 per year or period (ID 84).

Industry analysis is not used for this case. Thus per ID 120 = 1, base sales of the firm are entered directly in ID 122. Sales and expense grow at the rate of inflation (ID 112) per ID 110 = 1 and ID 123 = 0.

Risk inputs are 35 in ID 121 for sales and 20 in ID 451 for period expense. These inputs will be disregarded during the first run when ID 3 = 1 for deterministic. Since ID 530 = 0, required additional investment is not computed internally. This facilitates checks on the adequacy of initial cash and probabilities of insolvency.

Remaining inputs repeat the case information directly. The only user inputs required under FINANCIAL AND VALUATION SYSTEM PARAMETERS are amounts of 7 in IDs 93 and 94. These are reset to 0 for the statistical run (see below).

All four output divisions for a deterministic simulation are reproduced in Table 10.5. In VALUATION AND SCOPE division, first year sales equal a $120,000 base plus 7% inflation growth. This 7% is applied as a compound rate each year. Per share values for AUTOWASH are the same as total values. The internal default of one share (ID 91) was not overwritten, and no additional owner capital was invested. For Table 10.5 outputs there was no insolvency and cash balance was sufficient, but compare this result with Table 10.6 under risk. Market value is simply the product of earnings each year and the user parameter of 7 in IDs 93 and 94. According to this analysis AUTOWASH is overpriced at $100,000. It is worth slightly more than half that now, and about $165,000 ten years from now.

Remember that FINANCIAL SUMMARY describes AUTOWASH finances ten years hence. There are no stated inventories, hence the undefined inventory turns. *Earning power* and *return on owners' equity* appear adequate, although not outstanding. *Current condition* ratios show high values because all sales are for cash and there is only a small amount of accounts payable in current liabilities. The initial $60,000 long-term debt is fully repaid by EOP 8, hence debt ratios EOP 10 are negligible. There is actually no interest cost in Period 10, but internal rounding puts a very high figure on *times interest earned ratio* instead of an undefined overflow.

FINANCIAL STATEMENTS output division is straightforward and requires only a few explanatory comments. Since there was no industry analysis, only inflation rate and net sales appear in ENVIRONMENTAL ANALYSES. Note the inflation adjustments to sales and expenses in INCOME STATEMENTS. There is sufficient cash so that short-term funds are not borrowed during this simulation. There are no negative

Table 10.4.
INPUT SET FOR AUTOWASH

AUTOWASH--DETERMINISTIC

INPUT/OUTPUT SYSTEM CHOICES
!! THESE INPUTS CONTROL OTHER DISPLAYS!!

```
  1 TOTAL NUMBER OF PERIODS (MAX 24) . . .          10
  2 NO. OF PERIODS PER YEAR . . .                    1
  3 SAMPLE SIZE--DETERMINISTIC=1/STAT.=2 TO 12.       1
  4 SEED NO.--STANDARD RANDOM SERIES=0                0
  5 FRAME: SERVICE=0/TRADE=1/MFG=2/ENVRT ONLY=3       0
  6 OUTPUT DIVISION PRINT 1ST FROM LIST BELOW:        0
      VALUATION 1ST AND FINAL YEARS, SCOPE  =0
      STATISTICAL SUMMARY FROM FINAL PERIOD  =1
      FINANCIAL STATEMENTS FOR ALL PERIODS   =2
      SELECTED ACCOUNTS FOR ALL PERIODS      =3

110   INFLATE PERIOD COSTS--NO=0/YES=1 .  .  .        1

% ANNUAL AVERAGE INFLATION RATE

112 % BASE VALUE APPLIED IN PERIOD 1 .  .  .          7
113 % ANNUAL CHANGE TO PERIODS FROM 1ST BASE .        0

120 SALES--% INDUSTRY SHARE=0/$ PER PERIOD=1.         1

* NET SALES DEMAND AVAILABLE TO FIRM
121   *% MAX CHANGE FROM MEAN VALUE .  .  .          35

122 $ BASE VALUE APPLIED IN PERIOD 1 .  .  .     120000
123 % ANNUAL CHANGE TO PERIODS FROM 1ST BASE         0

$ INDIRECT SERVICE/OFFICE SUPPLIES/SMALL EQPT PERIOD

412 $ BASE VALUE APPLIED IN PERIOD 1 .  .          4000
413 % ANNUAL CHANGE TO PERIODS FROM 1ST BASE         0

$ GENERAL ADMINISTRATIVE/INDIRECT SERV. PAYROLL PERIOD

432 $ BASE VALUE APPLIED IN PERIOD 1 .  .  .      38000
433 % ANNUAL CHANGE TO PERIODS FROM 1ST BASE         0
```

```
**$ UTILITIES OR ALL INDIRECT COSTS PER PERIOD--GENERAL
451   *% MAX CHANGE FROM MEAN VALUE .  .  .          20

452 $ BASE VALUE APPLIED IN PERIOD 1 .  .         50000
453 % ANNUAL CHANGE TO PERIODS FROM 1ST BASE .        0

480 % DEPREC'N YRLY DECLINE BAL GENERAL CLASS 1      15

$ GENERAL FIXED ASSETS CLASS 1 NET CHANGES PER PERIOD

482 $ BASE VALUE APPLIED IN PERIOD 1 .  .         45000
483 % ANNUAL CHANGE TO PERIODS FROM 1ST BASE          0
484   LAST PERIOD NO., 1ST SCHEDULE (ALL=0).          1
485 $ 2ND BASE VALUE NEXT PERIOD (CONTINUE=-1).    5000
486 % ANNUAL CHANGE TO PERIODS FROM 2ND BASE          0
487   LAST PERIOD NO., 2ND SCHEDULE (ALL=0).          0
488 $ 3RD BASE VALUE NEXT PERIOD (CONTINUE=-1).       0
489 % ANNUAL CHANGE TO PERIODS FROM 3RD BASE          0

GENERAL ADMINISTRATIVE SYSTEM PARAMETERS

 79 GENL SUPPLIES INV'Y LEVEL AS % ANNUAL USAGE       0
 80 ACCTS PAYABLE LEVEL AS % OF ANNUAL ACCT PAY'     2.8
 81 PREPAID EXPENSE LEVEL AS % OF ANNUAL PAY'TS       0
 82 ADVANCES BY CUSTOMERS AS % OF ANNUAL SALES        0
 83 $ ORGAN EXP./GOODWILL INCURRED IN PERIOD 1.   60000
 84 $ AMORTIZ/N OF INTANGIBLES YRLY, NOT PERIOD    8000

530 INTERNAL COMPUTE REQD INVEST--NO=0/YES=1.         0

$ OWNER NET CASH INVESTMENT PLANNED CHANGE PER PERIOD
531   EARN ON NEAR CASH AS % SHORT-TERM INT RATE      0

532 $ BASE VALUE APPLIED IN PERIOD 1 .  .         50000
533 % ANNUAL CHANGE TO PERIODS FROM 1ST BASE          0
534   LAST PERIOD NO., 1ST SCHEDULE (ALL=0).          1
535 $ 2ND BASE VALUE NEXT PERIOD (CONTINUE=-1).       0
536 % ANNUAL CHANGE TO PERIODS FROM 2ND BASE          0
537   LAST PERIOD NO., 2ND SCHEDULE (ALL=0).          0
538 $ 3RD BASE VALUE NEXT PERIOD (CONTINUE=-1).       0
539 % ANNUAL CHANGE TO PERIODS FROM 3RD BASE          0
```

Table 10.4 (continued)

```
    540 % LONG-TERM OBLIGA'S IN REQD ADDED INVEST        0

$ LONG-TERM OBLIGATIONS PLANNED NET CHANGE PER PERIOD

    542 $ BASE VALUE APPLIED IN PERIOD 1 .   .   .   .    52500
    543 % ANNUAL CHANGE TO PERIODS FROM 1ST BASE  .      0
    544   LAST PERIOD NO., 1ST SCHEDULE (ALL=O).  .     1
    545 $ 2ND BASE VALUE NEXT PERIOD (CONTINUE=-1).      -7500
    546 % ANNUAL CHANGE TO PERIODS FROM 2ND BASE  .      0
    547   LAST PERIOD NO., 2ND SCHEDULE (ALL=O).  .     0
    548 $ 3RD BASE VALUE NEXT PERIOD (CONTINUE=-1).      0
    549 % ANNUAL CHANGE TO PERIODS FROM 3RD BASE  .      0


*% SHORT-TERM INTEREST RATE ANNUAL
    561      *% MAX CHANGE FROM MEAN VALUE .   .   .      0

    562 % BASE VALUE APPLIED IN PERIOD 1 .   .   .   .    10
    563 % ANNUAL CHANGE TO PERIODS FROM 1ST BASE  .      0


*% LONG-TERM INTEREST RATE ANNUAL
    571      *% MAX CHANGE FROM MEAN VALUE .   .   .      0

    572 % BASE VALUE APPLIED IN PERIOD 1 .   .   .   .    10
    573 % ANNUAL CHANGE TO PERIODS FROM 1ST BASE  .      0

FINANCIAL AND VALUATION SYSTEM PARAMETERS
    87 % CASH RATIO MIN, BELOW WHICH CASH DEMANDED       50
    88 % CURRENT RATIO MIN FROM SHORT-TERM LOANS .       200
    89 % COMBINED EFFECTIVE INCOME TAX RATE (<100)       50
    90 $ INITIAL TAX LOSS CREDIT FOR CARRY FORWARD       0
    91 NO. 1ST PERIOD OWNER EQUITY UNITS (1/SHARE)       1
    92 $ ADDED SHARE COST--INTERNAL COMPUTATION=O.       0
    93 PRICE-EARNINGS MULTIPLE YR 1--INTER'L COMP=O      7
    94 PRICE-EARN MULTIPLE FINAL YR--INTER'L COMP=O      7
    95 % ASSETS AVERAGE REALIZED IN LIQUIDATION  .       50
    96 % INVESTOR REQD RATE RETURN YR--INTL COMP=O       0
    97 % LONG-TERM AVG GROWTH RATE YR--INTL COMP=O       0
    98 % RETURN ON INCREM'L ASSETS YR--INTL COMP=O       0
```

Table 10.5.

DETERMINISTIC OUTPUTS FOR AUTOWASH

```
*************************
  VALUATION AND SCOPE
*************************

AUTOWASH--DETERMINISTIC

  10 PERIODS OVER 10.00 YEARS;  1.00 PERIODS PER YEAR, EACH 1.00 YEARS

******  SCOPE OF FIRM -- INITIAL SHARES 1 -- FINAL SHARES 1 --- EOP = END OF PERIOD  ******

SALES                          TOTAL        FIRST YEAR        128,400
                                            FINAL YEAR        236,058

                               PER SHARE    FIRST YEAR        128,400.00
                                            FINAL YEAR        236,058.16

EARNINGS                       TOTAL        FIRST YEAR        7,862
                                            FINAL YEAR        23,651

                               PER SHARE    FIRST YEAR        7,861.83
                                            FINAL YEAR        23,651.27

RETURN ON OWNERS' EQUITY %     TOTAL        FIRST YEAR        13.59
                                            FINAL YEAR        12.95

OWNERS' EQUITY                 TOTAL        AT EOP 1          57,862
                                            END OF RUN        182,606

                               PER SHARE    AT EOP 1          57,861.83
                                            END OF RUN        182,606.34

TOTAL ASSETS                   TOTAL        AT EOP 1          115,008
                                            END OF RUN        185,856

                               PER SHARE    AT EOP 1          115,007.87
                                            END OF RUN        185,856.07

CASH AND MARKETABLE SECURITIES TOTAL        AT EOP 1          18,469
                                            END OF RUN        136,865

                               PER SHARE    AT EOP 1          18,469.12
                                            END OF RUN        136,865.18

TECHNICAL INSOLVENCY DID NOT OCCUR
LEGAL INSOLVENCY DID NOT OCCUR
```

Table 10.5 (continued)

****** METHODS OF VALUATION ******

	FIRST YEAR OR EOP 1	FINAL YEAR OR END	FIRST YEAR PER SHARE	FINAL YEAR PER SHARE
MARKET VALUE WITH PRICE-EARNINGS MULTIPLES	55,033	165,559	55,032.77	165,558.92
PRICE-EARNINGS MULTIPLES	7	7		
LIQUIDATION VALUE TO OWNERS	-25,642	89,678	-25,642.11	89,678.30
LIQUIDATION VALUE OF TANGIBLE ASSETS	31,504	92,928	31,503.93	92,928.04
FIXED ASSETS AT BOOK VALUE WITH INTANGIBLES	96,539	48,991	96,538.75	48,990.89
TAX LOSS CARRYFORWARD--INITIAL & END OF RUN	0	0		

Table 10.5 (continued)

```
****************************************
   FINANCIAL SUMMARY FROM FINAL PERIOD
****************************************

AUTOWASH--DETERMINISTIC

   10 PERIODS OVER 10.00 YEARS;  1.00 PERIODS PER YEAR, EACH 1.00 YEARS
   UNDEFINED RATIOS APPEAR '####--'; YEARLY VALUES ARE EXTRAPOLATED FROM THE FINAL PERIOD; 0 VALUES OMITTED

******  SCOPE OF FIRM ******

NET SALES OR REVENUE PER YEAR            236,058

CASH AND MARKETABLE SECURITIES          136,865
TOTAL ASSETS                            185,856
TOTAL OWNERS' EQUITY                     182,606

******  RATIO ANALYSIS OF PROFITABILITY ******

NET OPERATING MARGIN ON SALES %           20.04
OPERATING EARNING POWER %                 25.45
OPERAT'G EFFIC'Y OR CAP'L TURNS            1.27
RETURN ON OWNERS' EQUITY %                12.95

******  RATIO ANALYSIS OF FINANCIAL CONDITION ******

CASH RATIO %                           4,211.58
ACID TEST OR QUICK RATIO %             4,211.58
CURRENT RATIO %                        4,211.58

DEBT TO TANGIBLE ASSETS %                  1.75
DEBT TO TANGIBLE OWNER EQUITY %            1.78
TIMES INTEREST EARNED RATIO          473,026.48

INVENTORY TURNS PER YEAR            #####,###.##

******  SELECTED FINANCIAL SUMMARY VALUES ******

OPERATING INCOME PER YEAR                47,303
NET INCOME BEFORE TAX PER YEAR           47,303
NET INCOME AFTER TAX PER YEAR            23,651

CASH+MKT SECURITIES+ACCTS RECV          136,865
TOTAL CURRENT ASSETS                    136,865
NET TANGIBLE FIXED ASSETS                48,991

ACCOUNTS PAYABLE                          3,250

TOTAL LIABILITIES                         3,250
TOTAL PAID-IN OWNERS' EQUITY             50,000
```

Table 10.5 (continued)

```
**********************************
  FINANCIAL STATEMENTS PROJECTED FOR ALL PERIODS
**********************************
```

ADMIN	ADMINISTRATIVE	DEPRC	DEPRECIATION	GEN	GENERAL
AMORT	AMORTIZATION	EOP	END OF PERIOD	INVY	INVENTORY
BOP	BEGINNING OF PERIOD	GEN	GENERAL	MFG	MANUFACTURING
MISC	MISCELLANEOUS	PURCH	PURCHASES OF	R&D	RESEARCH AND DEVELOPMENT

10 PERIODS OVER 10.00 YEARS; 1.00 PERIODS PER YEAR, EACH 1.00 YEARS

VALUES ARE ACCOUNT MEANS; ACCOUNT OMITTED WHEN ALL VALUES 0
HEADINGS ARE: PERIOD NO. AND YEAR/MONTH; OR CUMULATIVE *FOR YEAR NO.*

AUTOWASH--DETERMINISTIC

```
**********************************
ENVIRONMENTAL ANALYSES OF FIRM
**********************************
```

	1 1/ 0	2 2/ 0	3 3/ 0	4 4/ 0	5 5/ 0	6 6/ 0
INFLATION RATE ANNUAL %	7.00	7.00	7.00	7.00	7.00	7.00
FIRM SALES DEMAND AVAILABLE	128,400	137,388	147,005	157,296	168,306	180,088

```
**********************************
ENVIRONMENTAL ANALYSES OF FIRM   (CONTINUED)
**********************************
```

	7 7/ 0	8 8/ 0	9 9/ 0	10 10/ 0
INFLATION RATE ANNUAL %	7.00	7.00	7.00	7.00
FIRM SALES DEMAND AVAILABLE	192,694	206,182	220,615	236,058

Table 10.5 (continued)

AUTOWASH--DETERMINISTIC

```
********************
INCOME STATEMENTS
********************
```

	1 1/ 0	2 2/ 0	3 3/ 0	4 4/ 0	5 5/ 0	6 6/ 0
FIRM NET SALES ACHIEVED	128,400	137,388	147,005	157,296	168,306	180,088
PERIOD GEN ADMIN PAYROLL	40,660	43,506	46,552	49,810	53,297	57,028
PURCH GEN SUPPLIES	4,280	4,580	4,900	5,243	5,610	6,003
PERIOD GEN SUPPLIES USED	4,280	4,580	4,900	5,243	5,610	6,003
UTILITIES--GEN	53,500	57,245	61,252	65,540	70,128	75,037
DEPRC ON FIXED ASSETS--GEN	3,611	7,110	6,932	6,843	6,834	6,898
AMORT OF INTANGIBLES	8,000	8,000	8,000	8,000	8,000	8,000
TOTAL GEN AND ADMIN EXP	110,051	120,441	127,636	135,437	143,869	152,965
TOTAL OPERATING EXPENSE	110,051	120,441	127,636	135,437	143,869	152,965
SALES MARGIN OVER DIRECT EXP	128,400	137,388	147,005	157,296	168,306	180,088
NET OPERATING INCOME	18,349	16,947	19,369	21,859	24,437	27,122
-INTEREST COST, SHORT-TERM	0	0	0	0	0	0
-INTEREST, LONG-TERM FIXED	2,625	4,875	4,125	3,375	2,625	1,875
NET INCOME BEFORE INCOME TAX	15,724	12,072	15,244	18,484	21,812	25,247
-INCOME TAXES	7,862	6,036	7,622	9,242	10,906	12,624
NET INCOME AFTER INCOME TAX	7,862	6,036	7,622	9,242	10,906	12,624

Table 10.5 (continued)

INCOME STATEMENTS (CONTINUED)
****

	7 7/ 0	8 8/ 0	9 9/ 0	10 10/ 0
FIRM NET SALES ACHIEVED	192,694	206,182	220,615	236,058
PERIOD GEN ADMIN PAYROLL	61,020	65,291	69,861	74,752
PURCH GEN SUPPLIES	6,423	6,873	7,354	7,869
PERIOD GEN SUPPLIES USED	6,423	6,873	7,354	7,869
UTILITIES--GEN	80,289	85,909	91,923	98,358
DEPRC ON FIXED ASSETS--GEN	7,028	7,220	7,471	7,778
AMORT OF INTANGIBLES	8,000	4,000	0	0
TOTAL GEN AND ADMIN EXP	162,760	169,294	176,609	188,756
TOTAL OPERATING EXPENSE	162,760	169,294	176,609	188,756
SALES MARGIN OVER DIRECT EXP	192,694	206,182	220,615	236,058
NET OPERATING INCOME	29,934	36,889	44,006	47,303
-INTEREST COST, SHORT-TERM	0	0	0	0
-INTEREST, LONG-TERM FIXED	1,125	375	0	0
NET INCOME BEFORE INCOME TAX	28,809	36,514	44,006	47,303
-INCOME TAXES	14,404	18,257	22,003	23,651
NET INCOME AFTER INCOME TAX	14,404	18,257	22,003	23,651

Table 10.5 (continued)

AUTOWASH--DETERMINISTIC
****
CASH FORECASTS AND FLOW ANALYSES
****

	1 1/0	2 2/0	3 3/0	4 4/0	5 5/0	6 6/0
CASH RECEIPTS FROM SALES	128,400	137,388	147,005	157,296	168,306	180,088
PAYMENTS ON ACCOUNT	161,284	70,304	72,145	77,195	82,599	88,381
PAYMENTS ON PAYROLLS	40,660	43,506	46,552	49,810	53,297	57,028
TOTAL OPERATING PAYMENTS	201,944	113,810	118,697	127,006	135,896	145,409
NET CASH FLOW ON OPERATIONS	-73,544	23,578	28,308	30,290	32,410	34,679
PLAN CHANGE LONG OBLIGATIONS	52,500	-7,500	-7,500	-7,500	-7,500	-7,500
-INTEREST, INCOME TAX COST	10,487	10,911	11,747	12,617	13,531	14,499
TOTAL NET CASH FLOW	-31,531	5,167	9,061	10,173	11,379	12,680
PLAN CHANGE OWNERS' EQUITY	50,000	0	0	0	0	0
+BOP CASH AND SECURITIES	0	18,469	23,636	32,697	42,870	54,250
CASH AND SECURITIES EOP	18,469	23,636	32,697	42,870	54,250	66,930

CASH FORECASTS AND FLOW ANALYSES (CONTINUED)
****

	7 7/0	8 8/0	9 9/0	10 10/0
CASH RECEIPTS FROM SALES	192,694	206,182	220,615	236,058
PAYMENTS ON ACCOUNT	94,568	101,187	108,270	115,849
PAYMENTS ON PAYROLLS	61,020	65,291	69,861	74,752
TOTAL OPERATING PAYMENTS	155,587	166,478	178,132	190,601
NET CASH FLOW ON OPERATIONS	37,107	39,704	42,483	45,457
PLAN CHANGE LONG OBLIGATIONS	-7,500	-7,500	0	0
-INTEREST, INCOME TAX COST	15,529	18,632	22,003	23,651
TOTAL NET CASH FLOW	14,077	13,572	20,480	21,806
PLAN CHANGE OWNERS' EQUITY	0	0	0	0
+BOP CASH AND SECURITIES	66,930	81,007	94,579	115,059
CASH AND SECURITIES EOP	81,007	94,579	115,059	136,865

Table 10.5 (continued)

```
AUTOWASH--DETERMINISTIC

*************************************
RETAINED EARNINGS AND CAPITAL CHANGES
*************************************
```

	1 1/ 0	2 2/ 0	3 3/ 0	4 4/ 0	5 5/ 0	6 6/ 0
BOP OWNER PAID-IN CAPITAL	0	50,000	50,000	50,000	50,000	50,000
+OWNER NET INVESTMENT	50,000	0	0	0	0	0
EOP OWNER PAID-IN CAPITAL	50,000	50,000	50,000	50,000	50,000	50,000
BOP RETAINED EARNINGS	0	7,862	13,898	21,520	30,762	41,668
+NET INCOME	7,862	6,036	7,622	9,242	10,906	12,624
EOP RETAINED EARNINGS	7,862	13,898	21,520	30,762	41,668	54,291
EOP TOTAL OWNERS' EQUITY	57,862	63,898	71,520	80,762	91,668	104,291
EOP NO. SHARES OUTSTANDING	1	1	1	1	1	1
NET INCOME PER SHARE	7,861.83	6,035.98	7,621.87	9,241.87	10,905.96	12,623.68
EOP OWNERS' EQUITY PER SHARE	57,861.83	63,897.80	71,519.67	80,761.55	91,667.51	104,291.18

```
RETAINED EARNINGS AND CAPITAL CHANGES (CONTINUED)
*************************************
```

	7 7/ 0	8 8/ 0	9 9/ 0	10 10/ 0
BOP OWNER PAID-IN CAPITAL	50,000	50,000	50,000	50,000
+OWNER NET INVESTMENT	0	0	0	0
EOP OWNER PAID-IN CAPITAL	50,000	50,000	50,000	50,000
BOP RETAINED EARNINGS	54,291	68,695	86,952	108,955
+NET INCOME	14,404	18,257	22,003	23,651
EOP RETAINED EARNINGS	68,695	86,952	108,955	132,606
EOP TOTAL OWNERS' EQUITY	118,695	136,952	158,955	182,606
EOP NO. SHARES OUTSTANDING	1	1	1	1
NET INCOME PER SHARE	14,404.27	18,256.81	22,002.80	23,651.27
EOP OWNERS' EQUITY PER SHARE	118,695.45	136,952.26	158,955.06	182,606.34

Table 10.5 (continued)

```
AUTOWASH--DETERMINISTIC
*******************************************
CONDITION STATEMENTS (BALANCE SHEETS)
*******************************************
```

EOP ALL COLUMNS EXCEPT FIRST

	START BOP 1	1 1/0	2 2/0	3 3/0	4 4/0	5 5/0
****** ASSETS ******						
CASH AND MARKET SECURITIES	0	18,469	23,636	32,697	42,870	54,250
CASH+SECURITIES+ACCT RECV	0	18,469	23,636	32,697	42,870	54,250
TOTAL CURRENT ASSETS	0	18,469	23,636	32,697	42,870	54,250
GEN FIXED ASSETS AT COST: CLASS 1	0	48,150	53,875	60,000	66,554	73,566
GEN FIXED ASSETS DEPRC RESERVES: CLASS 1	0	3,611	10,721	17,654	24,497	31,332
GEN FIXED ASSETS AT BOOK	0	44,539	43,153	42,346	42,056	42,235
UNAMORTIZED INTANGIBLES	0	52,000	44,000	36,000	28,000	20,000
TOTAL ASSETS	0	115,008	110,789	111,043	112,927	116,485

CONDITION STATEMENTS (BALANCE SHEETS) (CONTINUED)

START BOP 1 ******

****** LIABILITIES AND OWNERS' EQUITY ******

	START BOP 1	1 1/0	2 2/0	3 3/0	4 4/0	5 5/0
ACCOUNTS PAYABLE	0	4,646	1,891	2,024	2,165	2,317
TOTAL CURRENT LIABILITIES	0	4,646	1,891	2,024	2,165	2,317
LONG-TERM OBLIGATIONS	0	52,500	45,000	37,500	30,000	22,500
TOTAL LIABILITIES	0	57,146	46,891	39,524	32,165	24,817
TOTAL OWNERS' EQUITY	0	57,862	63,898	71,520	80,762	91,668
LIABILITIES & OWNER EQUITY	0	115,008	110,789	111,043	112,927	116,485

Table 10.5 (continued)

CONDITION STATEMENTS (BALANCE SHEETS) (CONTINUED)
****

	6 6/ 0	7 7/ 0	8 8/ 0	9 9/ 0	10 10/ 0
****** ASSETS ******					
CASH AND MARKET SECURITIES	66,930	81,007	94,579	115,059	136,865
CASH+SECURITIES+ACCT RECV	66,930	81,007	94,579	115,059	136,865
TOTAL CURRENT ASSETS	66,930	81,007	94,579	115,059	136,865
GEN FIXED ASSETS AT COST: CLASS 1	81,070	89,099	97,690	106,882	116,718
GEN FIXED ASSETS DEPRC RESERVES: CLASS 1	38,230	45,258	52,478	59,950	67,727
GEN FIXED ASSETS AT BOOK	42,840	43,841	45,212	46,933	48,991
UNAMORTIZED INTANGIBLES	12,000	4,000	0	0	0
TOTAL ASSETS	121,770	128,848	139,791	161,992	185,856

CONDITION STATEMENTS (BALANCE SHEETS) (CONTINUED)

	6 6/ 0	7 7/ 0	8 8/ 0	9 9/ 0	10 10/ 0
****** LIABILITIES AND OWNERS' EQUITY ******					
ACCOUNTS PAYABLE	2,479	2,653	2,838	3,037	3,250
TOTAL CURRENT LIABILITIES	2,479	2,653	2,838	3,037	3,250
LONG-TERM OBLIGATIONS	15,000	7,500	0	0	0
TOTAL LIABILITIES	17,479	10,153	2,838	3,037	3,250
TOTAL OWNERS' EQUITY	104,291	118,695	136,952	158,955	182,606
LIABILITIES & OWNER EQUITY	121,770	128,848	139,791	161,992	185,856

Table 10.5 (continued)

```
AUTOWASH--DETERMINISTIC

    ***********************************
        SELECTED ACCOUNTS FOR ALL PERIODS
    ***********************************

CONDITION ITEMS ARE END-OF-PERIOD
```

	1 1/0	2 2/0	3 3/0	4 4/0	5 5/0	6 6/0
INDUSTRY SALES--000 OMIT						
ALL ACCOUNT VALUES ARE ZERO OR INAPPLICABLE						
FIRM'S INDUSTRY SHARE %						
ALL ACCOUNT VALUES ARE ZERO OR INAPPLICABLE						
FIRM NET SALES ACHIEVED	128,400	137,388	147,005	157,296	168,306	180,088
COST OF SALES						
ALL ACCOUNT VALUES ARE ZERO OR INAPPLICABLE						
GROSS PROFIT ON SALES						
ALL ACCOUNT VALUES ARE ZERO OR INAPPLICABLE						
TOTAL OPERATING EXPENSE	110,051	120,441	127,636	135,437	143,869	152,965
NET OPERATING INCOME	18,349	16,947	19,369	21,859	24,437	27,122
NET INCOME AFTER TAX	7,862	6,036	7,622	9,242	10,906	12,624
CASH AND MARKET SECURITIES	18,469	23,636	32,697	42,870	54,250	66,930
CASH+SECURITIES+ACCT RECV	18,469	23,636	32,697	42,870	54,250	66,930

Table 10.5 (continued)

TOTAL INVENTORIES
ALL ACCOUNT VALUES ARE ZERO OR INAPPLICABLE

TOTAL CURRENT ASSETS	18,469	23,636	32,697	42,870	54,250	66,930
TOTAL ASSETS	115,008	110,789	111,043	112,927	116,485	121,770
TOTAL CURRENT LIABILITIES	4,646	1,891	2,024	2,165	2,317	2,479
TOTAL LIABILITIES	57,146	46,891	39,524	32,165	24,817	17,479
TOTAL OWNERS' EQUITY	57,862	63,898	71,520	80,762	91,668	104,291
ALL FIXED ASSETS AT BOOK	96,539	87,153	78,346	70,056	62,235	54,840

Table 10.5 (continued)

	7	7/ 0	8	8/ 0	9	9/ 0	10	10/ 0
INDUSTRY SALES---000 OMIT ALL ACCOUNT VALUES ARE ZERO OR INAPPLICABLE
FIRM'S INDUSTRY SHARE % ALL ACCOUNT VALUES ARE ZERO OR INAPPLICABLE
FIRM NET SALES ACHIEVED		192,694		206,182		220,615		236,058
COST OF SALES ALL ACCOUNT VALUES ARE ZERO OR INAPPLICABLE
GROSS PROFIT ON SALES ALL ACCOUNT VALUES ARE ZERO OR INAPPLICABLE
TOTAL OPERATING EXPENSE		162,760		169,294		176,609		188,756
NET OPERATING INCOME		29,934		36,889		44,006		47,303
NET INCOME AFTER TAX		14,404		18,257		22,003		23,651
CASH AND MARKET SECURITIES		81,007		94,579		115,059		136,865
CASH+SECURITIES+ACCT RECV		81,007		94,579		115,059		136,865
TOTAL INVENTORIES ALL ACCOUNT VALUES ARE ZERO OR INAPPLICABLE
TOTAL CURRENT ASSETS		81,007		94,579		115,059		136,865
TOTAL ASSETS		128,848		139,791		161,992		185,856
TOTAL CURRENT LIABILITIES		2,653		2,838		3,037		3,250
TOTAL LIABILITIES		10,153		2,838		3,037		3,250
TOTAL OWNERS' EQUITY		118,695		136,952		158,955		182,606
ALL FIXED ASSETS AT BOOK		47,841		45,212		46,933		48,991

cash and securities EOP, hence no technical insolvency. Although inputs apply to all periods for long-term obligations net change (–7500 in ID 545), and for amortization of intangibles (8000 in ID 84), reductions cease automatically when the respective accounts reach zero (see Periods 7 and 8 in CONDITION STATEMENTS). The first column of CONDITION STATEMENTS has all zeros because initial condition was taken as zero.

Only one value may be printed for each SELECTED ACCOUNT each period in this deterministic run. These values correspond to items in FINANCIAL STATEMENTS. If a user elects to print out all 17 accounts, as shown in Table 10.5, then 5 of these accounts do not apply to AUTOWASH. The titles of all 5 are given, followed by the message ALL ACCOUNT VALUES ARE ZERO OR INAPPLICABLE.

To run a *statistical simulation* with input decisions stated earlier, the following alterations to the input set of Table 10.4 will be required: ID 3 = 7, ID 93 = 0, ID 94 = 0. The sample size is increased from 1 to 7; internally computed parameters are substituted for the original price-earnings multiple inputs of value 7. Output results are condensed into Table 10.6. Compare these results with corresponding values in Table 10.5. Risk inputs were included in Table 10.4, but were not operational under ID 3 = 1 (see above).

In VALUATION AND SCOPE division there is now a statistical analysis of important values. Mean earnings may go negative during year one. Cash balance EOP 1 may also go negative, but not mean cash. To see this, multiply the standard deviation and confidence interval by $\sqrt{7}$ or 2.646. There is about a 30% chance of running out of cash (technical insolvency) during the first few years. There is an insignificant probability of negative owners' equity (legal insolvency).

Price-earnings multiples are computed internally from going-concern value under risk. Internal multiples of 4 and 9 for first and final years compare to user inputs of 7 in the previous run (Table 10.5). Here the final year value is higher because negative earnings do not occur after early years.

Investors' required rates of return are computed internally. The rates decrease from 27.36% to 16.38% over the simulation. This reduction reflects reduced risk of rate of return and negative income as time passes.

Negative earnings are eliminated after early years. At the end of the simulation, rate of return on incremental assets at 24.23% is well in excess of investors required return at 16.38%. This is a substantial contributing factor to going-concern value. The whole section on PARAMETERS OF GOING-CONCERN VALUATION appears only with statistical runs (it is omitted in Table 10.5). This occurs because risk analysis is used to establish this set of parameters.

Analysis of FINANCIAL SUMMARY does not differ substantially from Table 10.5. Now, however, six statistics for each item replace single values. To save space, FINANCIAL STATEMENTS output division was omitted from Table 10.6. The arrangement is exactly the same as Table 10.5. Values differ slightly from Table 10.5 because sample means are printed for statistical runs. The SELECTED ACCOUNTS

Table 10.6.
STATISTICAL OUTPUT FOR AUTOWASH

```
**********************
 VALUATION AND SCOPE
**********************
```

AUTOWASH--STATISTICAL

****** 10 PERIODS OVER 10.00 YEARS; 1.00 PERIODS PER YEAR, EACH 1.00 YEARS

****** SCOPE OF FIRM -- INITIAL SHARES 1 -- FINAL SHARES 1 -- EOP = END OF PERIOD ******

95 % CONFIDENCE LIMITS FOR MEANS WITH SAMPLE SIZE 7

		MEAN	STANDARD DEVIATION	95 % LOWER CONFIDENCE	95 % UPPER CONFIDENCE
SALES	TOTAL				
	FIRST YEAR	131,476	9,539	108,582	154,370
	FINAL YEAR	247,125	11,096	220,494	273,756
	PER SHARE				
	FIRST YEAR	131,475.74	9,539.20	108,581.66	154,369.81
	FINAL YEAR	247,124.87	11,096.17	220,494.07	273,755.67
EARNINGS	TOTAL				
	FIRST YEAR	7,976	5,371	-4,913	20,866
	FINAL YEAR	30,004	6,935	13,359	46,648
	PER SHARE				
	FIRST YEAR	7,976.07	5,370.60	-4,913.36	20,865.51
	FINAL YEAR	30,003.58	6,935.33	13,358.80	46,648.37
RETURN ON OWNERS' EQUITY %	TOTAL				
	FIRST YEAR	9.07	8.66	-11.72	29.85
	FINAL YEAR	14.67	3.24	6.90	22.43
OWNERS' EQUITY	TOTAL				
	AT EOP 1	57,976	5,371	45,087	70,866
	END OF RUN	202,791	9,756	179,377	226,206
	PER SHARE				
	AT EOP 1	57,976.07	5,370.60	45,086.64	70,865.51
	END OF RUN	202,791.43	9,756.01	179,377.00	226,205.86
TOTAL ASSETS	TOTAL				
	AT EOP 1	115,147	5,366	102,269	128,025
	END OF RUN	206,069	9,762	182,640	229,498
	PER SHARE				
	AT EOP 1	115,147.19	5,365.81	102,269.25	128,025.13
	END OF RUN	206,068.96	9,761.99	182,640.19	229,497.74
CASH AND MARKETABLE SECURITIES	TOTAL				
	AT EOP 1	18,608	5,366	5,731	31,486
	END OF RUN	157,078	9,762	133,649	180,507
	PER SHARE				
	AT EOP 1	18,608.44	5,365.81	5,730.50	31,486.38
	END OF RUN	157,078.08	9,761.99	133,649.30	180,506.85

TECHNICAL INSOLVENCY OCCURRED WITH PROBABILITY .29 -- ON AVERAGE BEGAN DURING PERIOD 1.5
LEGAL INSOLVENCY DID NOT OCCUR

Table 10.6 (continued)

****** METHODS OF VALUATION ******

	FIRST YEAR OR EOP 1	FINAL YEAR OR END	FIRST YEAR PER SHARE	FINAL YEAR PER SHARE
MARKET VALUE WITH PRICE-EARNINGS MULTIPLES	33,996	256,882	33,995.99	256,882.35
PRICE-EARNINGS MULTIPLES	4	9		
GOING CONCERN ECONOMIC VALUE UNDER RISK	33,996	256,882	33,995.99	256,882.35
LIQUIDATION VALUE TO OWNERS	-25,598	99,757	-25,597.52	99,756.94
LIQUIDATION VALUE OF TANGIBLE ASSETS	31,574	103,034	31,573.59	103,034.48
FIXED ASSETS AT BOOK VALUE WITH INTANGIBLES	96,539	48,991	96,538.75	48,990.89
TAX LOSS CARRYFORWARD--INITIAL & END OF RUN	0	0		

****** PARAMETERS OF GOING-CONCERN VALUATION ******

	APPLIED EOP 1	APPLIED END OF RUN
INVESTORS' REQUIRED RATE OF RETURN %	27.36	16.38
INFLATION RATE %	7.00	7.00
LONG-TERM FIRM GROWTH RATE WITH INFLATION %	7.00	7.00
LONG-TERM REAL GROWTH RATE OF THE ECONOMY %	0.00	0.00
MEAN RATE OF RETURN ON INCREMENTAL ASSETS %	24.23	24.23

Table 10.6 (continued)

```
*********************************
FINANCIAL SUMMARY FROM FINAL PERIOD
*********************************

AUTOWASH--STATISTICAL

10 PERIODS OVER 10.00 YEARS; 1.00 PERIODS PER YEAR, EACH 1.00 YEARS
UNDEFINED RATIOS APPEAR '####--'; YEARLY VALUES ARE EXTRAPOLATED FROM THE FINAL PERIOD; 0 VALUES OMITTED

      95 % CONFIDENCE LIMITS FOR MEANS WITH SAMPLE SIZE 7
```

	MEAN	STANDARD DEVIATION	95 % LOWER CONFIDENCE	95 % UPPER CONFIDENCE	MINIMUM	MAXIMUM
****** SCOPE OF FIRM ******						
NET SALES OR REVENUE PER YEAR	247,125	11,096	220,494	273,755	199,547	295,193
CASH AND MARKETABLE SECURITIES	157,078	9,762	133,649	180,506	129,989	191,169
TOTAL ASSETS	206,069	9,762	182,640	229,497	178,979	240,160
TOTAL OWNERS' EQUITY	202,791	9,756	179,376	226,205	175,785	236,781
****** RATIO ANALYSIS OF PROFITABILITY ******						
NET OPERATING MARGIN ON SALES %	22.09	4.25	11.89	32.29	6.40	40.20
OPERATING EARNING POWER %	27.52	5.85	13.48	41.56	7.13	51.61
OPERAT'G EFFIC'Y OR CAP'L TURNS	1.21	0.06	1.06	1.35	0.99	1.35
RETURN ON OWNERS' EQUITY %	14.67	3.24	6.89	22.44	3.63	26.13

Table 10.6 (continued)

****** RATIO ANALYSIS OF FINANCIAL CONDITION ******

CASH RATIO %	4,813.06	327.78	4,026.38	5,599.73	3,847.61	6,224.67
ACID TEST OR QUICK RATIO %	4,813.06	327.78	4,026.38	5,599.73	3,847.61	6,224.67
CURRENT RATIO %	4,813.06	327.78	4,026.38	5,599.73	3,847.61	6,224.67
DEBT TO TANGIBLE ASSETS %	1.61	0.08	1.41	1.80	1.26	1.91
DEBT TO TANGIBLE OWNER EQUITY %	1.64	0.09	1.42	1.85	1.28	1.94
TIMES INTEREST EARNED RATIO	573,763.72	131,040.98	259,265.36	888,262.07	127,613.63	1186,721.20
INVENTORY TURNS PER YEAR	#####,###.##	#####,###.##	#####,###.##	#####,###.##	#####,###.##	#####,###.##

****** SELECTED FINANCIAL SUMMARY VALUES ******

OPERATING INCOME PER YEAR	57,376	13,104	25,926	88,825	12,761	118,672
NET INCOME BEFORE TAX PER YEAR	57,376	13,104	25,926	88,825	12,761	118,672
NET INCOME AFTER TAX PER YEAR	30,004	6,935	13,360	46,648	6,381	59,336
CASH+MKT SECURITIES+ACCTS RECV	157,078	9,762	133,649	180,506	129,989	191,169
TOTAL CURRENT ASSETS	157,078	9,762	133,649	180,506	129,989	191,169
NET TANGIBLE FIXED ASSETS	48,991	0	48,991	48,991	48,991	48,991
ACCOUNTS PAYABLE	3,278	90	3,062	3,494	2,907	3,610
TOTAL LIABILITIES	3,278	90	3,062	3,494	2,907	3,610
TOTAL PAID-IN OWNERS' EQUITY	50,000	50,000	50,000	50,000	50,000	50,000

Table 10.6 (continued)

```
AUTOWASH--STATISTICAL

    ***********************************
        SELECTED ACCOUNTS FOR ALL PERIODS
    ***********************************

CONDITION ITEMS ARE END-OF-PERIOD; 95 % CONFIDENCE LIMITS FOR MEANS WITH SAMPLE SIZE 7
```

	1 1/0	2 2/0	3 3/0	4 4/0	5 5/0	6 6/0
INDUSTRY SALES--000 OMIT						
ALL ACCOUNT VALUES ARE ZERO OR INAPPLICABLE						
FIRM'S INDUSTRY SHARE %						
ALL ACCOUNT VALUES ARE ZERO OR INAPPLICABLE						
FIRM NET SALES ACHIEVED						
MEANS	131,476	131,897	154,540	153,205	152,837	198,728
STANDARD DEVIATIONS	9,539	7,732	4,297	9,844	10,010	6,761
LOWER CONFIDENCE LIMITS	108,582	113,340	144,227	129,580	128,812	182,502
UPPER CONFIDENCE LIMITS	154,370	150,453	164,852	176,830	176,862	214,954
COST OF SALES						
ALL ACCOUNT VALUES ARE ZERO OR INAPPLICABLE						
GROSS PROFIT ON SALES						
ALL ACCOUNT VALUES ARE ZERO OR INAPPLICABLE						
TOTAL OPERATING EXPENSE						
MEANS	110,947	118,263	130,948	136,930	142,902	155,940
STANDARD DEVIATIONS	1,398	1,809	2,233	2,625	1,159	1,844
LOWER CONFIDENCE LIMITS	107,591	113,922	125,590	130,630	140,121	151,514
UPPER CONFIDENCE LIMITS	114,302	122,603	136,307	143,230	145,684	160,365
NET OPERATING INCOME						
MEANS	20,529	13,634	23,591	16,275	9,934	42,788
STANDARD DEVIATIONS	9,718	7,213	5,127	9,932	9,711	7,053
LOWER CONFIDENCE LIMITS	-2,794	-3,677	11,287	-7,562	-13,372	25,862
UPPER CONFIDENCE LIMITS	43,852	30,944	35,895	40,111	33,241	59,715
NET INCOME AFTER TAX						
MEANS	7,976	3,301	11,582	3,741	2,188	24,752
STANDARD DEVIATIONS	5,371	4,052	3,020	6,758	7,223	4,831
LOWER CONFIDENCE LIMITS	-4,913	-6,425	4,334	-12,479	-15,148	13,156
UPPER CONFIDENCE LIMITS	20,866	13,027	18,830	19,961	19,524	36,347

Table 10.6 (continued)

CASH AND MARKET SECURITIES						
MEANS	18,608	20,954	34,130	40,470	41,343	66,262
STANDARD DEVIATIONS	5,366	7,143	5,829	7,777	7,609	3,432
LOWER CONFIDENCE LIMITS	5,731	3,810	20,140	21,804	23,082	58,025
UPPER CONFIDENCE LIMITS	31,486	38,098	48,119	59,135	59,604	74,498
CASH+SECURITIES+ACCT RECV						
MEANS	18,608	20,954	34,130	40,470	41,343	66,262
STANDARD DEVIATIONS	5,366	7,143	5,829	7,777	7,609	3,432
LOWER CONFIDENCE LIMITS	5,731	3,810	20,140	21,804	23,082	58,025
UPPER CONFIDENCE LIMITS	31,486	38,098	48,119	59,135	59,604	74,498
TOTAL INVENTORIES						
ALL ACCOUNT VALUES ARE ZERO OR INAPPLICABLE						
TOTAL CURRENT ASSETS						
MEANS	18,608	20,954	34,130	40,470	41,343	66,262
STANDARD DEVIATIONS	5,366	7,143	5,829	7,777	7,609	3,432
LOWER CONFIDENCE LIMITS	5,731	3,810	20,140	21,804	23,082	58,025
UPPER CONFIDENCE LIMITS	31,486	38,098	48,119	59,135	59,604	74,498
TOTAL ASSETS						
MEANS	115,147	108,107	112,476	110,526	103,578	121,102
STANDARD DEVIATIONS	5,366	7,143	5,829	7,777	7,609	3,432
LOWER CONFIDENCE LIMITS	102,269	90,963	98,486	91,861	85,317	112,865
UPPER CONFIDENCE LIMITS	128,025	125,251	126,465	129,191	121,838	129,339
TOTAL CURRENT LIABILITIES						
MEANS	4,671	1,830	2,117	3,926	2,290	2,562
STANDARD DEVIATIONS	39	51	63	1,725	32	52
LOWER CONFIDENCE LIMITS	4,577	1,709	1,966	-214	2,212	2,439
UPPER CONFIDENCE LIMITS	4,765	1,952	2,267	8,066	2,368	2,686
TOTAL LIABILITIES						
MEANS	57,171	46,830	39,617	33,926	24,790	17,562
STANDARD DEVIATIONS	39	51	63	1,725	32	52
LOWER CONFIDENCE LIMITS	57,077	46,709	39,466	29,786	24,712	17,439
UPPER CONFIDENCE LIMITS	57,265	46,952	39,767	38,066	24,868	17,686
TOTAL OWNERS' EQUITY						
MEANS	57,976	61,277	72,859	76,600	78,788	103,540
STANDARD DEVIATIONS	5,371	7,140	5,856	9,174	7,634	3,440
LOWER CONFIDENCE LIMITS	45,087	44,141	58,804	54,583	60,466	95,284
UPPER CONFIDENCE LIMITS	70,866	78,413	86,914	98,617	97,109	111,795
ALL FIXED ASSETS AT BOOK	96,539	87,153	78,346	70,056	62,235	54,840

Table 10.6 (continued)

	7	7/ 0	8	8/ 0	9	9/ 0	10	10/ 0
INDUSTRY SALES--OOO OMIT   ALL ACCOUNT VALUES ARE ZERO OR INAPPLICABLE

FIRM'S INDUSTRY SHARE %
  ALL ACCOUNT VALUES ARE ZERO OR INAPPLICABLE

FIRM NET SALES ACHIEVED

MEANS	203,045	228,244	217,193	247,125
STANDARD DEVIATIONS	12,488	4,966	15,058	11,096
LOWER CONFIDENCE LIMITS	173,074	216,326	181,054	220,494
UPPER CONFIDENCE LIMITS	233,017	240,161	253,331	273,756

COST OF SALES
  ALL ACCOUNT VALUES ARE ZERO OR INAPPLICABLE

GROSS PROFIT ON SALES
  ALL ACCOUNT VALUES ARE ZERO OR INAPPLICABLE

TOTAL OPERATING EXPENSE

MEANS	157,964	168,249	179,642	189,748
STANDARD DEVIATIONS	2,550	3,085	2,283	3,222
LOWER CONFIDENCE LIMITS	151,845	160,845	174,162	182,016
UPPER CONFIDENCE LIMITS	164,083	175,652	185,122	197,481

NET OPERATING INCOME

MEANS	45,082	59,995	37,551	57,376
STANDARD DEVIATIONS	11,209	7,628	14,739	13,104
LOWER CONFIDENCE LIMITS	18,180	41,688	2,178	25,927
UPPER CONFIDENCE LIMITS	71,983	78,303	72,924	88,826

NET INCOME AFTER TAX

MEANS	21,606	30,182	17,460	30,004
STANDARD DEVIATIONS	5,882	3,787	8,265	6,935
LOWER CONFIDENCE LIMITS	7,490	21,093	-2,376	13,359
UPPER CONFIDENCE LIMITS	35,723	39,271	37,296	46,648

Table 10.6 (continued)

```
CASH AND MARKET SECURITIES
  MEANS                         87,323      112,925     128,977     157,078
  STANDARD DEVIATIONS            6,822        8,396      10,081       9,762
  LOWER CONFIDENCE LIMITS       70,950       92,775     104,783     133,649
  UPPER CONFIDENCE LIMITS      103,696      133,076     153,172     180,507

CASH+SECURITIES+ACCT RECV
  MEANS                         87,323      112,925     128,977     157,078
  STANDARD DEVIATIONS            6,822        8,396      10,081       9,762
  LOWER CONFIDENCE LIMITS       70,950       92,775     104,783     133,649
  UPPER CONFIDENCE LIMITS      103,696      133,076     153,172     180,507

TOTAL INVENTORIES
  ALL ACCOUNT VALUES ARE ZERO OR INAPPLICABLE

TOTAL CURRENT ASSETS
  MEANS                         87,323      112,925     128,977     157,078
  STANDARD DEVIATIONS            6,822        8,396      10,081       9,762
  LOWER CONFIDENCE LIMITS       70,950       92,775     104,783     133,649
  UPPER CONFIDENCE LIMITS      103,696      133,076     153,172     180,507

TOTAL ASSETS
  MEANS                        135,164      158,137     175,910     206,069
  STANDARD DEVIATIONS            6,822        8,396      10,081       9,762
  LOWER CONFIDENCE LIMITS      118,792      137,986     151,715     182,640
  UPPER CONFIDENCE LIMITS      151,537      178,288     200,104     229,498

TOTAL CURRENT LIABILITIES
  MEANS                          2,518        2,809       3,122       3,278
  STANDARD DEVIATIONS               71           86          64          90
  LOWER CONFIDENCE LIMITS        2,347        2,602       2,969       3,061
  UPPER CONFIDENCE LIMITS        2,690        3,016       3,275       3,494

TOTAL LIABILITIES
  MEANS                         10,018        2,809       3,122       3,278
  STANDARD DEVIATIONS               71           86          64          90
  LOWER CONFIDENCE LIMITS        9,847        2,602       2,969       3,061
  UPPER CONFIDENCE LIMITS       10,190        3,016       3,275       3,494

TOTAL OWNERS' EQUITY
  MEANS                        125,146      155,328     172,788     202,791
  STANDARD DEVIATIONS            6,797        8,454      10,059       9,756
  LOWER CONFIDENCE LIMITS      108,833      135,037     148,645     179,377
  UPPER CONFIDENCE LIMITS      141,459      175,618     196,930     226,206

ALL FIXED ASSETS AT BOOK
                                47,841       45,212      46,933      48,991
```

output division was included in Table 10.6. Now four statistics are available for each account each period, except for all fixed assets at book. There is no probability applied to this account in the simulation. As in Table 10.5, all 17 accounts are printed, but 5 are not applicable.

It would be wise to run additional simulations to study cash needs in relation to risky sales and expense. Based on the information from tables 10.5 and 10.6, one would offer somewhat less than $100,000 for AUTOWASH. Cash saved from a reduced purchase price should be used to bolster the proposed $10,000 initial working capital.

10.3 | Retailer Simulation— FLORAWREATH

Do not undertake the FLORAWREATH case until you have examined VALVO and AUTOWASH in the previous two sections. Each case builds on input information from previous cases. Explanations of input rules from earlier cases are not repeated.

FLORAWREATH is an independent retail florist located in a small shopping center. It is organized as a partnership, and has the following current statement of condition:

Current assets:		
Cash	$28,500	
Accounts receivable net	30,100	
Inventory of plants and accessories	65,400	
		$124,000
Store equipment and fixtures	$63,900	
Less accumulated depreciation	42,000	21,900
Total assets		$145,900
Current Liabilities:		
Accounts payable		$8,500
Owners' Equity		
Paid-in capital	$50,000	
Retained earnings	87,400	
Total owners' equity		$137,400
Total liabilities and owners' equity		$145,900

FLORAWREATH management has employed you to project the 4-year future of the firm. You decide to simulate 4 periods per year on PAVE—16 periods total—since there is a pronounced seasonal pattern. To make statistical inferences about outputs, you choose a sample size of 6. This will develop 90% confidence limits for outputs means.

You examine the sales demand available to the firm. You agree with management to use 6% inflation and 1% real growth to forecast economic behavior over the 4-year study. Management's uncertainty about sales demand suggests the possibility of large shifts during any particular period from forecasted mean values. Growth of sales demand will be projected from a base of $185,000, which was FLORAWREATH sales last year. Easter, Mother's Day, graduations, and weddings lead to maximum demand during the second quarter. Demand is considerably less in the first and fourth quarters, but lowest in the third quarter of late summer and early fall. The seasonal pattern will be simulated with input indices 10, 17, 7 and 12.

Inflation adjustments will be applied by PAVE to projected period costs. Thus inputs to such costs will be at current price levels. Growth rates in the rest of this paragraph are estimated as incremental to inflation adjustments. On the average, purchased goods cost 50% of selling price. Uncertainty about this does not exceed 20%. Inventory levels are normally maintained at 65% of annual cost of goods sold. Accounts receivable balance is about 10% of annual sales and accounts payable balance about 5% of annual credit payments. Uncollectible accounts are estimated at 2% of credit sales. Supplies average $750 per month ($2250 per quarter), and are expected to grow at 3% per year. Payrolls are expected to average $6000 per quarter, and all other expenses $7000 per quarter. Cost of both these items is expected to grow 2% per year. Uncertainty about fixed expenses does not exceed 25% of mean input value. Depreciation on store equipment and fixtures is 15% declining balance. Additions of new equipment are estimated at $8000 per year ($2000 per quarter).

One of the objects of the simulation is to determine if additional owner capital will be required. Short-term bank credit may be used at an estimated 10% annual interest cost. Long-term debt will not be used. Owner drawings are projected at 20% of net income after taxes. Per share computations are of no interest to management in this case.

The inputs of FLORAWREATH differ from those of AUTOWASH in the following general ways:

1. FLORAWREATH is a merchandising firm with finished goods inventory. Thus the frame choice is ID 5 = 1.

2. FLORAWREATH simulation starts with a nonzero initial condition. Inputs in IDs 9 to 48 reproduce the preceding statement of condition.

3. FLORAWREATH simulation has more than one period per year (quarters per ID 2), and uses seasonal indices (IDs 51 to 54). The growth of the firm has two components, *real* at 1% in ID 102, and *inflation* at 6% in ID 112. Like AUTOWASH, inflation adjustments are applied to revenues and costs (ID 110 = 1).

4. FLORAWREATH inputs use a system of applying a firm's base sales to ID 130, with 100 entered in ID 122. This system was described under ID set 131 in the glossary of section 8.5. Under this method, growth rates and seasonal pattern are applied directly to sales of a firm.

5. There is a high uncertainty about FLORAWREATH sales during any one period (3-month interval). This is represented with a maximum shift of 75% in ID 131. Since the 100% input to ID 122 is a means of applying FLORAWREATH sales directly to base sales in ID 130, no uncertainty is applied to ID 122 from an input in ID 121.

6. Unlike AUTOWASH, internal routines to add required owner capital are activated in FLORAWREATH (ID 530 = 1). This means that PAVE will determine the total capital required rather than test for insolvency given some planned schedule of investment. There is in fact no external plan for new capital (ID 532 = 0).

7. Owner drawings for FLORAWREATH are taken as 20% of positive earnings (ID 532).

8. Like the statistical run of AUTOWASH, all FINANCIAL AND VALUATION SYSTEM PARAMETERS are to be computed internally.

A list of inputs for FLORAWREATH, as printed by PAVE, is reproduced in Table 10.7.

Four output divisions for FLORAWREATH are exhibited in Table 10.8. VALUATION AND SCOPE division summarizes investment information. Sales, earnings, owners' equity, and rate of return on owners' equity all increase from the first to the final year. There is moderate long-term growth of 7.03%. The probability of negative earnings decreases over the years (see below). Going-concern value does not increase as fast as earnings because risk also increases. Thus the standard deviation of the mean return on owners' equity rises from 2.72% the first year to 3.09% the final year. This accounts for an increase of internally computed investors' required rate of return from 12.6% to 14%. This increase in turn is a factor in the decrease of internally computed price-earnings multiples from 13 down to 10.

As an investment FLORAWREATH is a reasonable but not spectacular performer. The final mean rate of return on owners' equity is only a modest 11.85%. The long-term value of the firm is supported by two factors. There is reasonable growth and the mean rate of return on incremental assets at 18.95% exceeds the final investors' required return at 14% by a fair increment.

The high risk assigned to period sales coupled with a small sample size influences the interpretation of FLORAWREATH outputs. Thus incomes near zero were sampled even during the final period when the mean income was $6950. To see this, note $1355 after extrapolation to a year in the fifth column of FINANCIAL SUMMARY. Such swings explain how mean values of positive net income (earnings), income tax payments, and final tax loss carryforward may all occur in runs during the final period.

In FINANCIAL SUMMARY the outputs vary somewhat from input specifications because all outputs are sample means. Firm's share of industry does not deviate from

Table 10.7.
INPUT SET FOR FLORAWREATH

FLORAWREATH

INPUT/OUTPUT SYSTEM CHOICES
!! THESE INPUTS CONTROL OTHER DISPLAYS!!

```
1 TOTAL NUMBER OF PERIODS (MAX 24) . . .        16
2 NO. OF PERIODS PER YEAR . . . . . . .          4
3 SAMPLE SIZE--DETERMINISTIC=1/STAT.=2 TO 12.    6
4 SEED NO.--STANDARD RANDOM SERIES=0             1
5 FRAME: SERVICE=0/TRADE=1/MFG=2/ENVRT ONLY=3    0
6 OUTPUT DIVISION PRINT 1ST FROM LIST BELOW:
    VALUATION 1ST AND FINAL YEARS, SCOPE    =0
    STATISTICAL SUMMARY FROM FINAL PERIOD   =1
    FINANCIAL STATEMENTS FOR ALL PERIODS    =2
    SELECTED ACCOUNTS FOR ALL PERIODS       =3
```

INITIAL CONDITION--CURRENT AND INTANGIBLE ASSETS
(START BAL SHEET: NEW FIRM--DMIT/SKELETON)

```
 9 $ CASH AND MARKETABLE SECURITIES. . .       28500
10 $ TRADE ACCOUNTS AND NOTES RECEIVABLE .     30100
11 $ NONTRADE ADVANCES AND ACCRUED RECEIVABLES     0
12 $ RESERVE FOR UNCOLLECTIBLE ACCOUNTS .          0
13 $ PREPAID EXPENSE AND DEFERRED CHARGES .        0
14 $ INTANGIBLES: ORGAN EXP., PATENT, GOODWILL     0
15 $ INVENTORY OF GENERAL SUPPLIES/SMALL EQPT.     0
16 $ INVENTORY OF MFG OR TRADE FINISHED GOODS. 65400
```

INITIAL CONDITION--GENERAL FIXED ASSETS

```
30 $ CLASS 1 AT COST BASIS . . . . . .        63900
31 $ CLASS 2 AT COST BASIS . . . . . .            0
32 $ CLASS 3 AT COST BASIS . . . . . .            0
33 $ CLASS 4 AT COST BASIS . . . . . .            0
34 $ CLASS 5 AT COST BASIS . . . . . .        42000
35 $ CLASS 1 RESERVE FOR DEPRECIATION             0
36 $ CLASS 2 RESERVE FOR DEPRECIATION             0
37 $ CLASS 3 RESERVE FOR DEPRECIATION             0
38 $ CLASS 4 RESERVE FOR DEPRECIATION             0
39 $ CLASS 5 RESERVE FOR DEPRECIATION             0
```

INITIAL CONDITION--LIABILITIES AND OWNERS' EQUITY
(TOTAL ASSETS, EQUITIES, AND BALANCE
CHECK IN NEXT DISPLAY)

```
40 $ TRADE ACCOUNTS AND NOTES PAYABLE .         8500
41 $ NONTRADE ACCTS, DIVIDENDS, TAXES PAYABLE.     0
42 $ UNEARNED ADVANCES FROM CUSTOMERS              0
43 $ ACCRUED EXPENSE AND LIABILITIES.              0
44 $ SHORT-TERM DEBT AND LOANS PAYABLE .           0
45 $ LONG-TERM OBLIGATIONS AT FACE OR STATED       0
46 $ BOND (PREFERRED STOCK) PREMIUM (DISCOUNT)     0
47 $ PAID-IN OWNER EQUITY CAPITAL.             50000
48 $ RETAINED EARNINGS                         87400
```

INITIAL CONDITION (STARTING BALANCE SHEET) TOTALS

```
TOTAL ASSETS.  .  .  .  .  .  .  $ 145900
TOTAL LIABILITIES .  .  .  .  .  $   8500
TOTAL OWNERS' EQUITY .  .  .  .  $ 137400
```

% ANNUAL REAL GROWTH RATE OF ECONOMY

```
102 % BASE VALUE APPLIED IN PERIOD 1 .  .  .      1
103 % ANNUAL CHANGE TO PERIODS FROM 1ST BASE  .   0

110   INFLATE PERIOD COSTS--NO=0/YES=1 .  .  .    1
```

% ANNUAL AVERAGE INFLATION RATE

```
112 % BASE VALUE APPLIED IN PERIOD 1 .  .  .      6
113 % ANNUAL CHANGE TO PERIODS FROM 1ST BASE  .   0

120   SALES--% INDUSTRY SHARE=0/$ PER PERIOD=1.   0
```

* NET SALES DEMAND AVAILABLE TO FIRM
```
121       *% MAX CHANGE FROM MEAN VALUE            0

122 % BASE VALUE APPLIED IN PERIOD 1 .  .        100
123 % ANNUAL CHANGE TO PERIODS FROM 1ST BASE  .    0
```

Table 10.7 (continued)

130 $ INDUSTRY SALES FOR BASE (PRIOR) YEAR .   185000
*% ANNUAL INDUSTRY GROWTH COMPARED TO ECONOMY
131   *% MAX CHANGE FROM MEAN VALUE .   75
132 % BASE VALUE APPLIED IN PERIOD 1 .   0
133 % ANNUAL CHANGE TO PERIODS FROM 1ST BASE   0

SEASONAL/CYCLICAL INDICES--1ST SET STOPS AT 1ST ZERO
51 INDEX 1   10
52 INDEX 2   17
53 INDEX 3   7
54 INDEX 4   12
55 INDEX 5   0
56 INDEX 6   0
57 INDEX 7   0
58 INDEX 8   0
59 INDEX 9   0
60 INDEX 10   0
61 INDEX 11   0
62 INDEX 12   0

140 INITIAL GOODS INV'S--COST % OF SELL PRICE   50

*DIRECT PURCHASED MATERIAL OR GOODS AS % OF SALES
141   *% MAX CHANGE FROM MEAN VALUE .   20
142 % BASE VALUE APPLIED IN PERIOD 1 .   50
143 % ANNUAL CHANGE TO PERIODS FROM 1ST BASE   0

150 % DESEASONALIZE GOODS PRODUCTION/PURCHASE   0

FINISHED GOODS INVENTORY LEVEL AS % ANNUAL COST GOODS
152 % BASE VALUE APPLIED IN PERIOD 1 .   65
153 % ANNUAL CHANGE TO PERIODS FROM 1ST BASE   0

390 % UNCOLLECTIBLE ACCOUNTS .   .   .   2

*ACCOUNTS RECEIVABLE LEVEL AS % OF ANNUAL SALES
391   *% MAX CHANGE FROM MEAN VALUE .   0
392 % BASE VALUE APPLIED IN PERIOD 1 .   10
393 % ANNUAL CHANGE TO PERIODS FROM 1ST BASE   0

$ INDIRECT SERVICE/OFFICE SUPPLIES/SMALL EQPT PERIOD
412 $ BASE VALUE APPLIED IN PERIOD 1 .   2250
413 % ANNUAL CHANGE TO PERIODS FROM 1ST BASE   3

130 $ GENERAL ADMINISTRATIVE/INDIRECT SERV. PAYROLL PERIOD
432 $ BASE VALUE APPLIED IN PERIOD 1 .   6000
433 % ANNUAL CHANGE TO PERIODS FROM 1ST BASE .   2

*$ UTILITIES OR ALL INDIRECT COSTS PER PERIOD--GENERAL
451   *% MAX CHANGE FROM MEAN VALUE .   25

452 $ BASE VALUE APPLIED IN PERIOD 1 .   7000
453 % ANNUAL CHANGE TO PERIODS FROM 1ST BASE .   2

480 % DEPREC'N YRLY DECLINE BAL GENERAL CLASS 1   15

$ GENERAL FIXED ASSETS CLASS 1 NET CHANGES PER PERIOD
482 $ BASE VALUE APPLIED IN PERIOD 1 .   2000
483 % ANNUAL CHANGE TO PERIODS FROM 1ST BASE .   0

GENERAL ADMINISTRATIVE SYSTEM PARAMETERS

79 GENL SUPPLIES INV'Y LEVEL AS % ANNUAL USAGE   0
80 ACCTS PAYABLE LEVEL AS % OF ANNUAL ACCT PAY'   5
81 PREPAID EXPENSE LEVEL AS % OF ANNUAL PAY'TS   0
82 ADVANCES BY CUSTOMERS AS % OF ANNUAL SALES   0
83 $ ORGAN EXP./GOODWILL INCURRED IN PERIOD 1.   0
84 $ AMORTIZ'N OF INTANGIBLES YRLY, NOT PERIOD   0

530 INTERNAL COMPUTE REQD INVEST--NO=0/YES=1.   1

$ OWNER NET CASH INVESTMENT PLANNED CHANGE PER PERIOD
531   EARN ON NEAR CASH AS % SHORT-TERM INT RATE 0
532 $ BASE VALUE APPLIED IN PERIOD 1 .   0
533 % ANNUAL CHANGE TO PERIODS FROM 1ST BASE .   0

550 DIVIDENDS--% EARNINGS=0/$ PER PERIOD=1 .   0

DIVIDENDS OR WITHDRAWLS PER PERIOD
552 % BASE VALUE APPLIED IN PERIOD 1 .   20
553 % ANNUAL CHANGE TO PERIODS FROM 1ST BASE .   0

Table 10.7 (continued)

```
*% SHORT-TERM INTEREST RATE ANNUAL
   561      *% MAX CHANGE FROM MEAN VALUE .  .  .      0

   562 % BASE VALUE APPLIED IN PERIOD 1 .  .  .  .    10
   563 % ANNUAL CHANGE TO PERIODS FROM 1ST BASE  .     0


FINANCIAL AND VALUATION SYSTEM PARAMETERS
   87 % CASH RATIO MIN, BELOW WHICH CASH DEMANDED     50
   88 % CURRENT RATIO MIN FROM SHORT-TERM LOANS .    200
   89 % COMBINED EFFECTIVE INCOME TAX RATE (<100)     50
   90 $ INITIAL TAX LOSS CREDIT FOR   RRY FORWARD      0
   91 NO. 1ST PERIOD OWNER EQUITY UNITS (1/SHARE)      1
   92 $ ADDED SHARE COST--INTERNAL COMPUTATION=0.      0
   93 PRICE-EARNINGS MULTIPLE YR 1--INTER'L COMP=0     0
   94 PRICE-EARN MULTIPLE FINAL YR--INTER'L COMP=0     0
   95 % ASSETS AVERAGE REALIZED IN LIQUIDATION  .     50
   96 % INVESTOR REQD RATE RETURN YR--INTL COMP=0      0
   97 % LONG-TERM AVG GROWTH RATE YR--INTL COMP=0      0
   98 % RETURN ON INCREM'L ASSETS YR--INTL COMP=0      0
```

Table 10.8.
OUTPUT FOR FLORAWREATH

```
*********************
  VALUATION AND SCOPE
*********************
```

FLORAWREATH

16 PERIODS OVER 4.00 YEARS; 4.00 PERIODS PER YEAR, EACH 0.25 YEARS

****** SCOPE OF FIRM -- INITIAL SHARES 1 -- FINAL SHARES 1 -- EOP = END OF PERIOD ******

90 % CONFIDENCE LIMITS FOR MEANS WITH SAMPLE SIZE 6

			MEAN	STANDARD DEVIATION	90 % LOWER CONFIDENCE	90 % UPPER CONFIDENCE
SALES	TOTAL	FIRST YEAR	208,471	12,486	183,500	233,443
		FINAL YEAR	260,491	14,617	231,257	289,725
	PER SHARE	FIRST YEAR	208,471.39	12,485.83	183,499.72	233,443.05
		FINAL YEAR	260,490.89	14,616.83	231,257.23	289,724.55
EARNINGS	TOTAL	FIRST YEAR	13,311	4,015	5,280	21,341
		FINAL YEAR	20,587	5,006	10,575	30,600
	PER SHARE	FIRST YEAR	13,310.63	4,015.28	5,280.07	21,341.19
		FINAL YEAR	20,587.46	5,006.09	10,575.28	30,599.64
RETURN ON OWNERS' EQUITY %		FIRST YEAR	8.76	2.72	3.31	14.21
		FINAL YEAR	11.85	3.09	5.67	18.03
OWNERS' EQUITY	TOTAL	AT EOP 1	140,512	721	139,070	141,954
		END OF RUN	172,819	8,087	156,645	188,992
	PER SHARE	AT EOP 1	140,511.99	721.04	139,069.92	141,954.07
		END OF RUN	172,818.65	8,086.78	156,645.08	188,992.22
TOTAL ASSETS	TOTAL	AT EOP 1	149,398	2,046	145,306	153,490
		END OF RUN	187,791	7,770	172,250	203,332
	PER SHARE	AT EOP 1	149,398.22	2,045.94	145,306.34	153,490.10
		END OF RUN	187,791.44	7,770.47	172,250.50	203,332.39
CASH AND MARKETABLE SECURITIES	TOTAL	AT EOP 1	32,370	5,052	22,266	42,474
		END OF RUN	25,296	9,001	7,293	43,298
	PER SHARE	AT EOP 1	32,370.09	5,051.97	22,266.15	42,474.03
		END OF RUN	25,295.70	9,001.31	7,293.07	43,298.32

TECHNICAL INSOLVENCY DID NOT OCCUR
LEGAL INSOLVENCY DID NOT OCCUR

Table 10.8 (continued)

****** METHODS OF VALUATION ******

	FIRST YEAR OR EOP 1	FINAL YEAR OR END	FIRST YEAR PER SHARE	FINAL YEAR PER SHARE
MARKET VALUE WITH PRICE-EARNINGS MULTIPLES	168,834	214,115	168,833.91	214,115.24
PRICE-EARNINGS MULTIPLES	13	10		
GOING CONCERN ECONOMIC VALUE UNDER RISK	168,834	214,115	168,833.91	214,115.24
LIQUIDATION VALUE TO OWNERS	65,813	78,923	65,812.88	78,922.93
LIQUIDATION VALUE OF TANGIBLE ASSETS	74,699	93,896	74,699.11	93,895.72
FIXED ASSETS AT BOOK VALUE WITH INTANGIBLES	23,070	39,360	23,070.04	39,359.57
TAX LOSS CARRYFORWARD--INITIAL & END OF RUN	0	1,614		

****** PARAMETERS OF GOING-CONCERN VALUATION ******

	APPLIED EOP 1	APPLIED END OF RUN
INVESTORS' REQUIRED RATE OF RETURN %	12.60	14.00
INFLATION RATE %	6.00	6.00
LONG-TERM FIRM GROWTH RATE WITH INFLATION %	7.03	7.03
LONG-TERM REAL GROWTH RATE OF THE ECONOMY %	1.00	1.00
MEAN RATE OF RETURN ON INCREMENTAL ASSETS %	18.95	18.95

Table 10.8 (continued)

```
*************************************
  FINANCIAL SUMMARY FROM FINAL PERIOD
*************************************
```

FLORAWREATH

16 PERIODS OVER 4.00 YEARS; 4.00 PERIODS PER YEAR, EACH 0.25 YEARS
UNDEFINED RATIOS APPEAR '#####--'; YEARLY VALUES ARE EXTRAPOLATED FROM THE FINAL PERIOD; 0 VALUES OMITTED

90 % CONFIDENCE LIMITS FOR MEANS WITH SAMPLE SIZE 6

	MEAN	STANDARD DEVIATION	90 % LOWER CONFIDENCE	90 % UPPER CONFIDENCE	MINIMUM	MAXIMUM
****** SCOPE OF FIRM ******						
FIRM'S SHARE OF INDUSTRY %	100.00	0.00	100.00	100.00	100.00	100.00
NET SALES OR REVENUE PER YEAR	287,693	22,945	241,803	333,583	215,751	340,651
CASH AND MARKETABLE SECURITIES	25,296	9,001	7,294	43,298	7,250	68,599
TOTAL ASSETS	187,791	7,770	172,251	203,331	153,845	206,188
TOTAL OWNERS' EQUITY	172,819	8,087	156,645	188,993	146,811	200,581
****** RATIO ANALYSIS OF PROFITABILITY ******						
GROSS MARGIN ON SALES %	47.04	1.05	44.94	49.14	42.87	49.90
NET OPERATING MARGIN ON SALES %	13.42	3.42	6.58	20.26	0.63	22.14
OPERATING EARNING POWER %	22.23	5.93	10.37	34.09	0.66	37.18
OPERAT'G EFFIC'Y OR CAP'L TURNS	1.53	0.11	1.31	1.75	1.05	1.70
RETURN ON OWNERS' EQUITY %	16.15	4.53	7.09	25.21	0.68	30.90
****** RATIO ANALYSIS OF FINANCIAL CONDITION ******						
CASH RATIO %	314.51	186.71	-58.91	687.93	49.82	1,223.40
ACID TEST OR QUICK RATIO %	551.28	221.80	107.68	994.88	156.41	1,608.17
CURRENT RATIO %	1,337.76	359.98	617.80	2,057.72	500.91	2,975.22
DEBT TO TANGIBLE ASSETS %	7.96	1.84	4.28	11.64	2.72	15.76
DEBT TO TANGIBLE OWNER EQUITY %	8.88	2.26	4.36	13.40	2.80	18.70
TIMES INTEREST EARNED RATIO	#####,###.##	###.##	####,###.##	#####,###.##	40.54	#####,###.##
AVG COLLECTION PERIOD IN DAYS	36.50	0.00	36.50	36.50	36.50	36.50
INVENTORY TURNS PER YEAR	1.61	0.00	1.61	1.61	1.61	1.61

Table 10.8 (continued)

****** SELECTED FINANCIAL SUMMARY VALUES ******

INDUSTRY SALES PER YR--000 OMIT	288	23	242	334	216	341
COST OF SALES PER YEAR	151,746	10,966	129,814	173,678	112,051	173,360
GROSS PROFIT PER YEAR	135,947	12,469	111,009	160,885	92,488	169,971
OPERATING INCOME PER YEAR	42,301	12,054	18,193	66,409	1,355	75,433
NET INCOME BEFORE TAX PER YEAR	41,971	12,012	17,947	65,995	1,355	75,433
NET INCOME AFTER TAX PER YEAR	27,798	8,407	10,984	44,612	1,355	54,732
CASH+MKT SECURITIES+ACCTS RECV	54,065	7,664	38,737	69,393	37,915	90,174
TOTAL INVENTORIES	94,367	6,820	80,727	108,007	69,682	107,809
TOTAL CURRENT ASSETS	148,432	7,770	132,892	163,972	114,485	166,828
NET TANGIBLE FIXED ASSETS	39,360	0	39,360	39,360	39,360	39,360
ACCOUNTS PAYABLE	11,682	2,135	7,412	15,952	5,607	18,148
SHORT-TERM LOANS AND NOTES	3,291	2,317	-1,343	7,925	0	13,812
TOTAL LIABILITIES	14,973	3,510	7,953	21,993	5,607	29,417
TOTAL PAID-IN OWNERS' EQUITY	50,000	0	50,000	50,000	50,000	50,000

Table 10.8 (continued)

```
*****************************************
     FINANCIAL STATEMENTS PROJECTED FOR ALL PERIODS
*****************************************
```

ADMIN	ADMINISTRATIVE	DEPRC	DEPRECIATION	GEN	GENERAL
AMORT	AMORTIZATION	EOP	END OF PERIOD	INVY	INVENTORY
BOP	BEGINNING OF PERIOD	GEN	GENERAL	MFG	MANUFACTURING
MISC	MISCELLANEOUS	PURCH	PURCHASES OF	R&D	RESEARCH AND DEVELOPMENT

16 PERIODS OVER 4.00 YEARS; 4.00 PERIODS PER YEAR, EACH 0.25 YEARS

VALUES ARE ACCOUNT MEANS; ACCOUNT OMITTED WHEN ALL VALUES 0
HEADINGS ARE: PERIOD NO. AND YEAR/MONTH; OR CUMULATIVE *FOR YEAR NO.*

FLORAWREATH

```
*****************************************
ENVIRONMENTAL ANALYSES OF FIRM
*****************************************
```

INDUSTRY BASE SALES--000S OMITTED; YEAR= 185; --- PERIOD= 46

	1 0/3	2 0/6	3 0/9	4 1/0 *FOR YEAR 1*	5 1/3
INFLATION RATE ANNUAL %	6.00	6.00	6.00	6.00*	6.00
REAL ECONOMY GROWTH ANNUAL %	1.00	1.00	1.00	1.00*	1.00
INDUSTRY TOTAL GROWTH %	7.06	7.06	7.06	7.06*	7.06
SEASONAL/CYCLICAL INDICES	0.87	1.48	0.61	1.00*	0.87
INDUSTRY SALES--000S OMITTED	50	83	31	209*	42
FIRM'S INDUSTRY SHARE %	100.00	100.00	100.00	100.00*	100.00
FIRM SALES DEMAND AVAILABLE	49,614	83,022	31,016	208,471*	41,845

```
*****************************************
ENVIRONMENTAL ANALYSES OF FIRM
*****************************************
(CONTINUED)
```

	6 1/6	7 1/9	8 2/0 *FOR YEAR 2*	9 2/3	10 2/6
INFLATION RATE ANNUAL %	6.00	6.00	6.00*	6.00	6.00
REAL ECONOMY GROWTH ANNUAL %	1.00	1.00	1.00*	1.00	1.00
INDUSTRY TOTAL GROWTH %	7.06	7.06	7.06*	7.06	7.06
SEASONAL/CYCLICAL INDICES	1.48	0.61	1.00*	0.87	1.48
INDUSTRY SALES--000S OMITTED	77	25	210*	43	73
FIRM'S INDUSTRY SHARE %	100.00	100.00	100.00*	100.00	100.00
FIRM SALES DEMAND AVAILABLE	77,377	24,838	209,731*	42,634	73,135

Table 10.8 (continued)

ENVIRONMENTAL ANALYSES OF FIRM (CONTINUED)
****

	11 2/ 9	12 3/ 0	*FOR YEAR 3*	13 3/ 3	14 3/ 6	15 3/ 9
INFLATION RATE ANNUAL %	6.00	6.00	6.00*	6.00	6.00	6.00
REAL ECONOMY GROWTH ANNUAL %	1.00	1.00	1.00*	1.00	1.00	1.00
INDUSTRY TOTAL GROWTH %	7.06	7.06	7.06*	7.06	7.06	7.06
SEASONAL/CYCLICAL INDICES	0.61	1.04	1.00*	0.87	1.48	0.61
INDUSTRY SALES--000S OMITTED	41	32	189*	58	92	39
FIRM'S INDUSTRY SHARE %	100.00	100.00	100.00*	100.00	100.00	100.00
FIRM SALES DEMAND AVAILABLE	41,335	32,098	189,202*	58,381	91,522	38,665

ENVIRONMENTAL ANALYSES OF FIRM (CONTINUED)
****

	16 4/ 0 *FOR YEAR 4*
INFLATION RATE ANNUAL %	6.00*
REAL ECONOMY GROWTH ANNUAL %	1.00*
INDUSTRY TOTAL GROWTH %	7.06*
SEASONAL/CYCLICAL INDICES	1.04*
INDUSTRY SALES--000S OMITTED	261*
FIRM'S INDUSTRY SHARE %	100.00*
FIRM SALES DEMAND AVAILABLE	260,491*

Table 10.8 (continued)

FLORAWREATH

```
*********************
INCOME STATEMENTS
*********************
```

	1 0/3	2 0/6	3 0/9	4 1/0	*FOR YEAR 1*	5 1/3
FIRM NET SALES ACHIEVED	49,614	83,022	31,016	44,819	208,471*	41,845
-COST OF SALES	24,663	42,786	15,768	22,471	105,688*	22,275
GROSS PROFIT ON SALES	24,951	40,236	15,248	22,348	102,783*	19,570
PERIOD GEN ADMIN PAYROLL	6,088	6,208	6,330	6,455	25,081*	6,582
PURCH GEN SUPPLIES	2,283	2,334	2,386	2,438	9,441*	2,493
PERIOD GEN SUPPLIES USED	2,283	2,334	2,386	2,438	9,441*	2,493
UTILITIES--GEN	6,743	7,538	7,373	7,379	29,033*	7,574
DEPRC ON FIXED ASSETS--GEN	859	904	948	991	3,702*	1,034
UNCOLLECTIBLE ACCOUNTS	1,197	1,393	1,036	786	4,412*	861
TOTAL GEN AND ADMIN EXP	17,171	18,376	18,073	18,049	71,669*	18,543
TOTAL OPERATING EXPENSE	17,171	18,376	18,073	18,049	71,669*	18,543
SALES MARGIN OVER DIRECT EXP	24,092	39,332	14,300	21,357	99,081*	18,536
NET OPERATING INCOME	7,780	21,859	-2,825	4,299	31,113*	1,026
-INTEREST COST, SHORT-TERM	0	0	0	0	0*	53
NET INCOME BEFORE INCOME TAX	7,780	21,859	-2,825	4,299	31,113*	973
-INCOME TAXES	3,890	10,930	259	2,724	17,803*	1,516
NET INCOME AFTER INCOME TAX	3,890	10,930	-3,084	1,575	13,311*	-543

Table 10.8 (continued)

INCOME STATEMENTS (CONTINUED)
****

	6 1/6	7 1/9	8 2/0	*FOR YEAR 2*	9 2/3	10 2/6
FIRM NET SALES ACHIEVED	77,377	24,838	65,671	209,731*	42,634	73,135
-COST OF SALES	36,894	12,566	31,671	103,406*	22,487	36,028
GROSS PROFIT ON SALES	40,483	12,273	34,000	106,326*	20,148	37,107
PERIOD GEN ADMIN PAYROLL	6,712	6,844	6,979	27,117*	7,117	7,257
PURCH GEN SUPPLIES	2,548	2,604	2,662	10,307*	2,721	2,782
PERIOD GEN SUPPLIES USED	2,548	2,604	2,662	10,307*	2,721	2,782
UTILITIES--GEN	7,371	7,493	8,442	30,880*	8,468	7,921
DEPRC ON FIXED ASSETS--GEN	1,076	1,119	1,160	4,389*	1,202	1,243
UNCOLLECTIBLE ACCOUNTS	1,263	917	987	4,028*	1,037	1,219
TOTAL GEN AND ADMIN EXP	18,970	18,977	20,231	76,721*	20,545	20,421
TOTAL OPERATING EXPENSE	18,970	18,977	20,231	76,721*	20,545	20,421
SALES MARGIN OVER DIRECT EXP	39,406	11,154	32,840	101,936*	18,946	35,864
NET OPERATING INCOME	21,512	-6,704	13,769	29,603*	-398	16,686
-INTEREST COST, SHORT-TERM	0	0	156	209*	0	0
NET INCOME BEFORE INCOME TAX	21,512	-6,704	13,613	29,394*	-398	16,686
-INCOME TAXES	7,481	0	4,087	13,084*	934	7,490
NET INCOME AFTER INCOME TAX	14,032	-6,704	9,525	16,310*	-1,332	9,196

Table 10.8 (continued)

INCOME STATEMENTS   (CONTINUED)
****

	11 2/9	12 3/0	*FOR YEAR 3*	13 3/3	14 3/6	15 3/9
FIRM NET SALES ACHIEVED	41,335	32,098	189,202*	58,381	91,522	38,665
-COST OF SALES	20,800	15,273	94,588*	31,036	46,036	18,955
GROSS PROFIT ON SALES	20,535	16,825	94,615*	27,344	45,485	19,710
PERIOD GEN ADMIN PAYROLL	7,400	7,546	29,320*	7,695	7,846	8,001
PURCH GEN SUPPLIES	2,844	2,907	11,254*	2,971	3,037	3,105
PERIOD GEN SUPPLIES USED	2,844	2,907	11,254*	2,971	3,037	3,105
UTILITIES--GEN	9,316	8,850	34,555*	9,029	9,019	9,790
DEPRC ON FIXED ASSETS--GEN	1,283	1,324	5,052*	1,364	1,404	1,444
UNCOLLECTIBLE ACCOUNTS	1,081	716	4,053*	957	1,565	1,196
TOTAL GEN AND ADMIN EXP	21,924	21,342	84,232*	22,017	22,873	23,537
TOTAL OPERATING EXPENSE	21,924	21,342	84,232*	22,017	22,873	23,537
SALES MARGIN OVER DIRECT EXP	19,251	15,501	89,562*	25,980	44,081	18,266
NET OPERATING INCOME	-1,389	-4,517	10,382*	5,328	22,613	-3,826
-INTEREST COST, SHORT-TERM	0	0	0*	270	0	74
NET INCOME BEFORE INCOME TAX	-1,389	-4,517	10,382*	5,058	22,613	-3,900
-INCOME TAXES	284	112	8,820*	1,646	8,224	262
NET INCOME AFTER INCOME TAX	-1,673	-4,629	1,562*	3,412	14,388	-4,162

Table 10.8 (continued)

```
INCOME STATEMENTS   (CONTINUED)
*******************

                                16   4/ 0 *FOR YEAR  4*

FIRM NET SALES ACHIEVED         71,923    260,491*
  -COST OF SALES                37,936    133,963*
GROSS PROFIT ON SALES           33,987    126,526*


PERIOD GEN ADMIN PAYROLL         8,159     31,701*

PURCH GEN SUPPLIES               3,174     12,287*
PERIOD GEN SUPPLIES USED         3,174     12,287*

UTILITIES--GEN                   9,423     37,261*

DEPRC ON FIXED ASSETS--GEN       1,484      5,696*
UNCOLLECTIBLE ACCOUNTS           1,172      4,890*
   TOTAL GEN AND ADMIN EXP      23,412     91,839*

TOTAL OPERATING EXPENSE         23,412     91,839*
SALES MARGIN OVER DIRECT EXP    32,503    120,830*

NET OPERATING INCOME            10,575     34,690*
  -INTEREST COST, SHORT-TERM        82        426*
NET INCOME BEFORE INCOME TAX    10,493     34,264*

  -INCOME TAXES                  3,543     13,675*
NET INCOME AFTER INCOME TAX      6,950     20,588*
```

Table 10.8 (continued)

FLORAWREATH

```
*******************************
COST OF GOODS SOLD SCHEDULES
*******************************
```

	1 0/3	2 0/6	3 0/9	4 1/0	*FOR YEAR 1*	5 1/3
COST OF FINISHED GOODS	33,376	42,544	16,785	14,563	107,268*	28,660
+BOP FINISHED GOODS INVY	65,400	74,112	73,870	74,886	65,400*	66,979
-EOP FINISHED GOODS INVY	74,112	73,870	74,886	66,979	66,979*	73,364
COST OF GOODS SOLD	24,663	42,786	15,768	22,471	105,688*	22,275

```
COST OF GOODS SOLD SCHEDULES (CONTINUED)
*******************************
```

	6 1/6	7 1/9	8 2/0	*FOR YEAR 2*	9 2/3	10 2/6
COST OF FINISHED GOODS	36,719	2,571	47,259	115,209*	22,263	23,683
+BOP FINISHED GOODS INVY	73,364	73,189	63,194	66,979*	78,782	78,558
-EOP FINISHED GOODS INVY	73,189	63,194	78,782	78,782*	78,558	66,213
COST OF GOODS SOLD	36,894	12,566	31,671	103,406*	22,487	36,028

```
COST OF GOODS SOLD SCHEDULES (CONTINUED)
*******************************
```

	11 2/9	12 3/0	*FOR YEAR 3*	13 3/3	14 3/6	15 3/9
COST OF FINISHED GOODS	44,769	3,286	94,001*	46,105	40,529	20,211
+BOP FINISHED GOODS INVY	66,213	90,182	78,782*	78,196	93,265	87,758
-EOP FINISHED GOODS INVY	90,182	78,196	78,196*	93,265	87,758	89,014
COST OF GOODS SOLD	20,800	15,273	94,588*	31,036	46,036	18,955

```
COST OF GOODS SOLD SCHEDULES (CONTINUED)
*******************************
```

	16 4/0	*FOR YEAR 4*
COST OF FINISHED GOODS	43,289	150,134*
+BOP FINISHED GOODS INVY	89,014	78,196*
-EOP FINISHED GOODS INVY	94,367	94,367*
COST OF GOODS SOLD	37,936	133,963*

Table 10.8 (continued)

FLORAWREATH
****
CASH FORECASTS AND FLOW ANALYSES
****

	1 0/ 3	2 0/ 6	3 0/ 9	4 1/ 0 *FOR YEAR 1*	5 1/ 3
CASH RECEIPTS FROM SALES	58,671	68,266	50,782	216,231*	42,174
PAYMENTS ON ACCOUNT	44,045	52,466	33,801	157,239*	38,002
PAYMENTS ON PAYROLLS	6,088	6,208	6,330	25,081*	6,582
TOTAL OPERATING PAYMENTS	50,133	58,674	40,131	182,320*	44,585
NET CASH FLOW ON OPERATIONS	8,538	9,592	10,651	33,911*	-2,411
NET CHANGE SHORT-TERM CREDIT	0	0	0	0*	2,118
-INTEREST, INCOME TAX COST	3,890	10,930	259	17,803*	1,569
-DIVIDENDS, OWNER DRAWINGS	778	2,186	52	3,693*	384
TOTAL NET CASH FLOW	3,870	-3,523	10,340	12,416*	-2,246
+BOP CASH AND SECURITIES	28,500	32,370	28,847	28,500*	40,916
CASH AND SECURITIES EOP	32,370	28,847	39,186	40,916*	38,670

CASH FORECASTS AND FLOW ANALYSES (CONTINUED)
****

	6 1/ 6	7 1/ 9	8 2/ 0 *FOR YEAR 2*	9 2/ 3	10 2/ 6
CASH RECEIPTS FROM SALES	61,901	44,937	197,363*	50,812	59,716
PAYMENTS ON ACCOUNT	47,232	21,670	158,369*	40,708	36,506
PAYMENTS ON PAYROLLS	6,712	6,844	27,117*	7,117	7,257
TOTAL OPERATING PAYMENTS	53,944	28,515	185,489*	47,825	43,763
NET CASH FLOW ON OPERATIONS	7,957	16,422	11,875*	2,987	15,953
NET CHANGE SHORT-TERM CREDIT	-2,118	0	6,244*	-6,244	0
-INTEREST, INCOME TAX COST	7,481	0	13,294*	934	7,490
-DIVIDENDS, OWNER DRAWINGS	2,806	0	5,095*	197	1,839
TOTAL NET CASH FLOW	-4,448	16,422	-270*	-4,388	6,624
+BOP CASH AND SECURITIES	38,670	34,222	40,916*	40,646	36,257
CASH AND SECURITIES EOP	34,222	50,644	40,646*	36,257	42,881

Table 10.8 (continued)

CASH FORECASTS AND FLOW ANALYSES (CONTINUED)
****

	11 2/9	12 3/0	*FOR YEAR 3*	13 3/3	14 3/6	15 3/9
CASH RECEIPTS FROM SALES	52,974	35,077	198,579*	46,910	76,700	58,612
PAYMENTS ON ACCOUNT	54,761	25,795	157,770*	51,903	56,135	39,483
PAYMENTS ON PAYROLLS	7,400	7,546	29,320*	7,695	7,846	8,001
TOTAL OPERATING PAYMENTS	62,161	33,341	187,090*	59,598	63,982	47,484
NET CASH FLOW ON OPERATIONS	-9,187	1,736	11,489*	-12,687	12,719	11,127
NET CHANGE SHORT-TERM CREDIT	0	0	-6,244*	10,803	-10,803	2,972
-INTEREST, INCOME TAX COST	284	112	8,820*	1,916	8,224	336
-DIVIDENDS, OWNER DRAWINGS	57	161	2,254*	870	2,997	52
TOTAL NET CASH FLOW	-9,528	1,463	-5,829*	-4,671	-9,306	13,711
+BOP CASH AND SECURITIES	42,881	33,353	40,646*	34,816	30,146	20,840
CASH AND SECURITIES EOP	33,353	34,816	34,816*	30,146	20,840	34,551

CASH FORECASTS AND FLOW ANALYSES (CONTINUED)
****

	16 4/0	*FOR YEAR 4*
CASH RECEIPTS FROM SALES	57,448	239,670*
PAYMENTS ON ACCOUNT	53,847	201,368*
PAYMENTS ON PAYROLLS	8,159	31,701*
TOTAL OPERATING PAYMENTS	62,006	233,070*
NET CASH FLOW ON OPERATIONS	-4,558	6,601*
NET CHANGE SHORT-TERM CREDIT	319	3,291*
-INTEREST, INCOME TAX COST	3,626	14,102*
-DIVIDENDS, OWNER DRAWINGS	1,390	5,309*
TOTAL NET CASH FLOW	-9,255	-9,521*
+BOP CASH AND SECURITIES	34,551	34,816*
CASH AND SECURITIES EOP	25,296	25,296*

Table 10.8 (continued)

FLORAWREATH

```
*********************************
RETAINED EARNINGS AND CAPITAL CHANGES
*********************************
```

	1 0/3	2 0/6	3 0/9	4 1/0	*FOR YEAR 1*	5 1/3
BOP OWNER PAID-IN CAPITAL	50,000	50,000	50,000	50,000	50,000*	50,000
EOP OWNER PAID-IN CAPITAL	50,000	50,000	50,000	50,000	50,000*	50,000
BOP RETAINED EARNINGS	87,400	90,512	99,256	96,120	87,400*	97,018
+NET INCOME	3,890	10,930	-3,084	1,575	13,311*	-543
-DIVIDENDS PAID	778	2,186	52	677	3,693*	384
EOP RETAINED EARNINGS	90,512	99,256	96,120	97,018	97,018*	96,091
EOP TOTAL OWNERS' EQUITY	140,512	149,256	146,120	147,018	147,018*	146,091
EOP NO. SHARES OUTSTANDING	1	1	1	1	1*	1
NET INCOME PER SHARE	3,889.99	10,929.74	-3,084.19	1,575.09	13,310.63*	-542.93
DIVIDENDS PER SHARE	778.00	2,185.95	51.82	676.73	3,692.50*	383.76
EOP OWNERS' EQUITY PER SHARE	140,511.99	149,255.78	146,119.77	147,018.14	147,018.14*	146,091.45

```
*********************************
RETAINED EARNINGS AND CAPITAL CHANGES (CONTINUED)
*********************************
```

	6 1/6	7 1/9	8 2/0	*FOR YEAR 2*	9 2/3	10 2/6
BOP OWNER PAID-IN CAPITAL	50,000	50,000	50,000	50,000*	50,000	50,000
EOP OWNER PAID-IN CAPITAL	50,000	50,000	50,000	50,000*	50,000	50,000
BOP RETAINED EARNINGS	96,091	107,317	100,612	97,018*	108,233	106,704
+NET INCOME	14,032	-6,704	9,525	16,310*	-1,332	9,196
-DIVIDENDS PAID	2,806	0	1,905	5,095*	197	1,839
EOP RETAINED EARNINGS	107,317	100,612	108,233	108,233*	106,704	114,060
EOP TOTAL OWNERS' EQUITY	157,317	150,612	158,233	158,233*	156,704	164,060
EOP NO. SHARES OUTSTANDING	1	1	1	1*	1	1
NET INCOME PER SHARE	14,031.79	-6,704.39	9,525.32	16,309.79*	-1,331.95	9,195.55
DIVIDENDS PER SHARE	2,806.36	0.00	1,905.06	5,095.18*	196.89	1,839.11
EOP OWNERS' EQUITY PER SHARE	157,316.88	150,612.49	158,232.75	158,232.75*	156,703.90	164,060.34

Table 10.8 (continued)

RETAINED EARNINGS AND CAPITAL CHANGES (CONTINUED)
****

	11 2/ 9	12 3/ 0	*FOR YEAR 3*	13 3/ 3	14 3/ 6	15 3/ 9
BOP OWNER PAID-IN CAPITAL	50,000	50,000	50,000*	50,000	50,000	50,000
EOP OWNER PAID-IN CAPITAL	50,000	50,000	50,000*	50,000	50,000	50,000
BOP RETAINED EARNINGS	114,060	112,330	108,233*	107,541	110,082	121,474
+NET INCOME	-1,673	-4,629	1,562*	3,412	14,388	-4,162
-DIVIDENDS PAID	57	161	2,254*	870	2,997	52
EOP RETAINED EARNINGS	112,330	107,541	107,541*	110,082	121,474	117,259
EOP TOTAL OWNERS' EQUITY	162,330	157,541	157,541*	160,082	171,474	167,259
EOP NO. SHARES OUTSTANDING	1	1	1*	1	1	1
NET INCOME PER SHARE	-1,673.08	-4,629.05	1,561.47*	3,411.76	14,388.31	-4,162.20
DIVIDENDS PER SHARE	56.77	160.82	2,253.59*	870.28	2,996.87	52.36
EOP OWNERS' EQUITY PER SHARE	162,330.48	157,540.62	157,540.62*	160,082.10	171,473.54	167,258.98

RETAINED EARNINGS AND CAPITAL CHANGES (CONTINUED)
****

	16 4/ 0	*FOR YEAR 4*
BOP OWNER PAID-IN CAPITAL	50,000	50,000*
EOP OWNER PAID-IN CAPITAL	50,000	50,000*
BOP RETAINED EARNINGS	117,259	107,541*
+NET INCOME	6,950	20,588*
-DIVIDENDS PAID	1,390	5,309*
EOP RETAINED EARNINGS	122,819	122,819*
EOP TOTAL OWNERS' EQUITY	172,819	172,819*
EOP NO. SHARES OUTSTANDING	1	1*
NET INCOME PER SHARE	6,949.59	20,587.46*
DIVIDENDS PER SHARE	1,389.92	5,309.43*
EOP OWNERS' EQUITY PER SHARE	172,818.65	172,818.65*

Table 10.8 (continued)

FLORAWREATH

```
*****************************
CONDITION STATEMENTS (BALANCE SHEETS)
*****************************
```

****** ASSETS ******

EOP ALL COLUMNS EXCEPT FIRST

	START BOP 1	1 0/3	2 0/6	3 0/9	4 1/0*	5 1/3
CASH AND MARKET SECURITIES	28,500*	32,370	28,847	39,186	40,916*	38,670
+ACCOUNTS RECEIVABLE GROSS	30,100*	21,043	35,800	16,033	22,341*	22,011
-UNCOLLECTIBLES RESERVE	0*	1,197	2,591	3,627	4,413*	5,274
CASH+SECURITIES+ACCT RECV	58,600*	52,216	62,056	51,593	58,844*	55,407
FINISHED GOODS INVENTORY	65,400*	74,112	73,870	74,886	66,979*	73,364
TOTAL INVENTORIES	65,400*	74,112	73,870	74,886	66,979*	73,364
TOTAL CURRENT ASSETS	124,000*	126,328	135,925	126,479	125,822*	128,771
GEN FIXED ASSETS AT COST: CLASS 1	63,900*	65,929	67,988	70,078	72,198*	74,349
GEN FIXED ASSETS DEPRC RESERVES: CLASS 1	42,000*	42,859	43,763	44,711	45,702*	46,736
GEN FIXED ASSETS AT BOOK	21,900*	23,070	24,225	25,367	26,496*	27,613
TOTAL ASSETS	145,900*	149,398	160,151	151,846	152,318*	156,385

CONDITION STATEMENTS (BALANCE SHEETS) (CONTINUED)

****** LIABILITIES AND OWNERS' EQUITY ******

	START BOP 1	1 0/3	2 0/6	3 0/9	4 1/0*	5 1/3
ACCOUNTS PAYABLE	8,500*	8,886	10,895	5,727	5,300*	8,176
SHORT-TERM LOANS AND NOTES	0*	0	0	0	0*	2,118
TOTAL CURRENT LIABILITIES	8,500*	8,886	10,895	5,727	5,300*	10,293
TOTAL LIABILITIES	8,500*	8,886	10,895	5,727	5,300*	10,293
TOTAL OWNERS' EQUITY	137,400*	140,512	149,256	146,120	147,018*	146,091
LIABILITIES & OWNER EQUITY	145,900*	149,398	160,151	151,846	152,318*	156,385

Table 10.8 (continued)

CONDITION STATEMENTS (BALANCE SHEETS) (CONTINUED)
****

****** ASSETS ******

	6 1/6	7 1/9	8 2/0*	9 2/3	10 2/6	11 2/9
CASH AND MARKET SECURITIES	34,222	50,644	40,646*	36,257	42,881	33,353
+ACCOUNTS RECEIVABLE GROSS	37,488	17,389	34,709*	26,531	39,950	28,311
-UNCOLLECTIBLES RESERVE	6,537	7,454	8,441*	9,478	10,696	11,777
CASH+SECURITIES+ACCT RECV	65,173	60,579	66,914*	53,311	72,135	49,887
FINISHED GOODS INVENTORY	73,189	63,194	78,782*	78,558	66,213	90,182
TOTAL INVENTORIES	73,189	63,194	78,782*	78,558	66,213	90,182
TOTAL CURRENT ASSETS	138,361	123,773	145,696*	131,869	138,348	140,069
GEN FIXED ASSETS AT COST: CLASS 1	76,532	78,746	80,993*	83,274	85,587	87,935
GEN FIXED ASSETS DEPRC RESERVES: CLASS 1	47,812	48,931	50,091*	51,292	52,535	53,819
GEN FIXED ASSETS AT BOOK	28,720	29,816	30,903*	31,981	33,052	34,116
TOTAL ASSETS	167,081	153,589	176,599*	163,850	171,400	174,186

CONDITION STATEMENTS (BALANCE SHEETS) (CONTINUED)

****** LIABILITIES AND OWNERS' EQUITY ******

	6 1/6	7 1/9	8 2/0*	9 2/3	10 2/6	11 2/9
ACCOUNTS PAYABLE	9,764	2,977	12,122*	7,147	7,340	11,855
SHORT-TERM LOANS AND NOTES	0	0	6,244*	0	0	0
TOTAL CURRENT LIABILITIES	9,764	2,977	18,366*	7,147	7,340	11,855
TOTAL LIABILITIES	9,764	2,977	18,366*	7,147	7,340	11,855
TOTAL OWNERS' EQUITY	157,317	150,612	158,233*	156,704	164,060	162,330
LIABILITIES & OWNER EQUITY	167,081	153,589	176,599*	163,850	171,400	174,186

Table 10.8 (continued)

CONDITION STATEMENTS (BALANCE SHEETS) (CONTINUED)
****

****** ASSETS ******

	12 3/ 0*	13 3/ 3	14 3/ 6	15 3/ 9	16 4/ 0*
CASH AND MARKET SECURITIES	34,816*	30,146	20,840	34,551	25,296*
+ACCOUNTS RECEIVABLE GROSS	25,333*	36,803	51,625	31,678	46,154*
-UNCOLLECTIBLES RESERVE	12,493*	13,451	15,016	16,212	17,385*
CASH+SECURITIES+ACCT RECV	47,655*	53,498	57,449	50,017	54,065*
FINISHED GOODS INVENTORY	78,196*	93,265	87,758	89,014	94,367*
TOTAL INVENTORIES	78,196*	93,265	87,758	89,014	94,367*
TOTAL CURRENT ASSETS	125,851*	146,763	145,206	139,031	148,432*
GEN FIXED ASSETS AT COST: CLASS 1	90,317*	92,734	95,186	97,675	100,200*
GEN FIXED ASSETS DEPRC RESERVES: CLASS 1	55,143*	56,507	57,911	59,356	60,840*
GEN FIXED ASSETS AT BOOK	35,174*	36,227	37,275	38,319	39,360*
TOTAL ASSETS	161,026*	182,990	182,481	177,350	187,791*

CONDITION STATEMENTS (BALANCE SHEETS) (CONTINUED)

****** LIABILITIES AND OWNERS' EQUITY ******

	12 3/ 0*	13 3/ 3	14 3/ 6	15 3/ 9	16 4/ 0*
ACCOUNTS PAYABLE	3,485*	12,104	11,008	7,119	11,682*
SHORT-TERM LOANS AND NOTES	0*	10,803	0	2,972	3,291*
TOTAL CURRENT LIABILITIES	3,485*	22,907	11,008	10,091	14,973*
TOTAL LIABILITIES	3,485*	22,907	11,008	10,091	14,973*
TOTAL OWNERS' EQUITY	157,541*	160,082	171,474	167,259	172,819*
LIABILITIES & OWNER EQUITY	161,026*	182,990	182,481	177,350	187,791*

Table 10.8 (continued)

FLORAWREATH
****
SELECTED ACCOUNTS FOR ALL PERIODS
****
CONDITION ITEMS ARE END-OF-PERIOD; 90 % CONFIDENCE LIMITS FOR MEANS WITH SAMPLE SIZE 6

	1 0/3	2 0/6	3 0/9	4 1/0*	5 1/3	6 1/6
INDUSTRY SALES--OOO OMIT						
MEANS	50	83	31	45*	42	77
STANDARD DEVIATIONS	3	5	4	9*	8	8
LOWER CONFIDENCE LIMITS	43	74	24	26*	26	62
UPPER CONFIDENCE LIMITS	56	92	38	63*	57	93
FIRM'S INDUSTRY SHARE %						
MEANS	100.00	100.00	100.00	100.00*	100.00	100.00
STANDARD DEVIATIONS	0.00	0.00	0.00	0.00*	0.00	0.00
LOWER CONFIDENCE LIMITS	100.00	100.00	100.00	100.00*	100.00	100.00
UPPER CONFIDENCE LIMITS	100.00	100.00	100.00	100.00*	100.00	100.00
FIRM NET SALES ACHIEVED						
MEANS	49,614	83,022	31,016	44,819*	41,845	77,377
STANDARD DEVIATIONS	3,174	4,560	3,506	9,178*	7,717	7,865
LOWER CONFIDENCE LIMITS	43,266	73,903	24,004	26,463*	26,410	61,648
UPPER CONFIDENCE LIMITS	55,962	92,142	38,027	63,176*	57,279	93,107
COST OF SALES						
MEANS	24,663	42,786	15,768	22,471*	22,275	36,894
STANDARD DEVIATIONS	1,952	2,651	2,066	4,667*	4,275	3,871
LOWER CONFIDENCE LIMITS	20,759	37,485	11,635	13,138*	13,724	29,152
UPPER CONFIDENCE LIMITS	28,567	48,088	19,901	31,804*	30,826	44,637
GROSS PROFIT ON SALES						
MEANS	24,951	40,236	15,248	22,348*	19,570	40,483
STANDARD DEVIATIONS	1,598	2,449	1,593	4,561*	3,508	4,450
LOWER CONFIDENCE LIMITS	21,755	35,338	12,061	13,226*	12,554	31,583
UPPER CONFIDENCE LIMITS	28,147	45,134	18,435	31,470*	26,585	49,382
TOTAL OPERATING EXPENSE						
MEANS	17,171	18,376	18,073	18,049*	18,543	18,970
STANDARD DEVIATIONS	224	174	407	335*	287	405
LOWER CONFIDENCE LIMITS	16,722	18,029	17,258	17,379*	17,969	18,160
UPPER CONFIDENCE LIMITS	17,619	18,724	18,888	18,720*	19,118	19,780
NET OPERATING INCOME						
MEANS	7,780	21,859	-2,825	4,299*	1,026	21,512
STANDARD DEVIATIONS	1,803	2,499	1,775	4,324*	3,344	4,337
LOWER CONFIDENCE LIMITS	4,175	16,862	-6,376	-4,349*	-5,662	12,838
UPPER CONFIDENCE LIMITS	11,385	26,857	726	12,946*	7,715	30,187
NET INCOME AFTER TAX						
MEANS	3,890	10,930	-3,084	1,575*	-543	14,032
STANDARD DEVIATIONS	901	1,249	1,650	2,679*	2,167	2,756
LOWER CONFIDENCE LIMITS	2,087	8,431	-6,385	-3,783*	-4,877	8,519
UPPER CONFIDENCE LIMITS	5,693	13,428	217	6,934*	3,791	19,545

Table 10.8 (continued)

	Col 1	Col 2	Col 3	Col 4	Col 5	Col 6
CASH AND MARKET SECURITIES						
MEANS	32,370	28,847	39,186	40,916*	38,670	34,222
STANDARD DEVIATIONS	5,052	3,922	6,245	6,873*	8,233	5,232
LOWER CONFIDENCE LIMITS	22,266	21,002	26,696	27,169*	22,203	23,758
UPPER CONFIDENCE LIMITS	42,474	36,691	51,677	54,662*	55,136	44,685
CASH+SECURITIES+ACCT RECV						
MEANS	52,216	62,056	51,593	58,844*	55,407	65,173
STANDARD DEVIATIONS	3,927	2,301	5,534	4,447*	5,890	6,652
LOWER CONFIDENCE LIMITS	44,361	57,453	40,525	49,950*	43,628	51,868
UPPER CONFIDENCE LIMITS	60,070	66,658	62,661	67,737*	67,187	78,478
TOTAL INVENTORIES						
MEANS	74,112	73,870	74,886	66,979*	73,364	73,189
STANDARD DEVIATIONS	5,866	4,576	7,221	8,076*	12,103	5,646
LOWER CONFIDENCE LIMITS	62,380	64,717	60,444	50,826*	49,158	61,898
UPPER CONFIDENCE LIMITS	85,845	83,022	89,329	83,131*	97,570	84,480
TOTAL CURRENT ASSETS						
MEANS	126,328	135,925	126,479	125,822*	128,771	138,361
STANDARD DEVIATIONS	2,046	2,497	3,089	5,222*	7,602	3,165
LOWER CONFIDENCE LIMITS	122,236	130,932	120,301	115,378*	113,567	132,032
UPPER CONFIDENCE LIMITS	130,420	140,918	132,658	136,266*	143,976	144,691
TOTAL ASSETS						
MEANS	149,398	160,151	151,846	152,318*	156,385	167,081
STANDARD DEVIATIONS	2,046	2,497	3,089	5,222*	7,602	3,165
LOWER CONFIDENCE LIMITS	145,306	155,157	145,668	141,874*	141,180	160,752
UPPER CONFIDENCE LIMITS	153,490	165,144	158,025	162,762*	171,589	173,410
TOTAL CURRENT LIABILITIES						
MEANS	8,886	10,895	5,727	5,300*	10,293	9,764
STANDARD DEVIATIONS	1,518	2,237	1,377	2,302*	4,780	2,070
LOWER CONFIDENCE LIMITS	5,849	6,421	2,973	697*	733	5,625
UPPER CONFIDENCE LIMITS	11,923	15,369	8,480	9,903*	19,853	13,904
TOTAL LIABILITIES						
MEANS	8,886	10,895	5,727	5,300*	10,293	9,764
STANDARD DEVIATIONS	1,518	2,237	1,377	2,302*	4,780	2,070
LOWER CONFIDENCE LIMITS	5,849	6,421	2,973	697*	733	5,625
UPPER CONFIDENCE LIMITS	11,923	15,369	8,480	9,903*	19,853	13,904
TOTAL OWNERS' EQUITY						
MEANS	140,512	149,256	146,120	147,018*	146,091	157,317
STANDARD DEVIATIONS	721	726	2,089	3,574*	3,969	2,994
LOWER CONFIDENCE LIMITS	139,070	147,803	141,942	139,871*	138,153	151,328
UPPER CONFIDENCE LIMITS	141,954	150,709	150,297	154,166*	154,030	163,305
ALL FIXED ASSETS AT BOOK	23,070	24,225	25,367	26,496*	27,613	28,720

Table 10.8 (continued)

	7 1/9	8 2/0*	9 2/3	10 2/6	11 2/9	12 3/0*
INDUSTRY SALES--000 OMIT						
MEANS	25	66*	43	73	41	32*
STANDARD DEVIATIONS	3	6*	5	8	3	5*
LOWER CONFIDENCE LIMITS	19	54*	33	57	36	22*
UPPER CONFIDENCE LIMITS	31	78*	52	90	47	42*
FIRM'S INDUSTRY SHARE %						
MEANS	100.00	100.00*	100.00	100.00	100.00	100.00*
STANDARD DEVIATIONS	0.00	0.00*	0.00	0.00	0.00	0.00*
LOWER CONFIDENCE LIMITS	100.00	100.00*	100.00	100.00	100.00	100.00*
UPPER CONFIDENCE LIMITS	100.00	100.00*	100.00	100.00	100.00	100.00*
FIRM NET SALES ACHIEVED						
MEANS	24,838	65,671*	42,634	73,135	41,335	32,098*
STANDARD DEVIATIONS	2,842	6,049*	4,847	8,236	2,713	5,135*
LOWER CONFIDENCE LIMITS	19,154	53,574*	32,940	56,663	35,908	21,828*
UPPER CONFIDENCE LIMITS	30,523	77,768*	52,329	89,606	46,761	42,369*
COST OF SALES						
MEANS	12,566	31,671*	22,487	36,028	20,800	15,273*
STANDARD DEVIATIONS	1,167	3,943*	2,751	3,519	1,700	2,668*
LOWER CONFIDENCE LIMITS	10,231	23,785*	16,985	28,990	17,400	9,937*
UPPER CONFIDENCE LIMITS	14,900	39,558*	27,988	43,065	24,200	20,609*
GROSS PROFIT ON SALES						
MEANS	12,273	34,000*	20,148	37,107	20,535	16,825*
STANDARD DEVIATIONS	1,797	2,575*	2,573	4,940	1,107	2,573*
LOWER CONFIDENCE LIMITS	8,678	28,850*	15,002	27,227	18,322	11,679*
UPPER CONFIDENCE LIMITS	15,867	39,150*	25,293	46,987	22,748	21,972*
TOTAL OPERATING EXPENSE						
MEANS	18,977	20,231*	20,545	20,421	21,924	21,342*
STANDARD DEVIATIONS	363	247*	266	431	220	303*
LOWER CONFIDENCE LIMITS	18,251	19,737*	20,014	19,558	21,484	20,737*
UPPER CONFIDENCE LIMITS	19,704	20,724*	21,077	21,284	22,364	21,948*
NET OPERATING INCOME						
MEANS	-6,704	13,769*	-398	16,686	-1,389	-4,517*
STANDARD DEVIATIONS	1,783	2,525*	2,544	4,922	1,147	2,599*
LOWER CONFIDENCE LIMITS	-10,269	8,720*	-5,486	6,842	-3,683	-9,714*
UPPER CONFIDENCE LIMITS	-3,139	18,818*	4,691	26,530	905	680*
NET INCOME AFTER TAX						
MEANS	-6,704	9,525*	-1,332	9,196	-1,673	-4,629*
STANDARD DEVIATIONS	1,783	1,826*	2,154	2,206	923	2,513*
LOWER CONFIDENCE LIMITS	-10,269	5,873*	-5,640	4,783	-3,519	-9,656*
UPPER CONFIDENCE LIMITS	-3,139	13,178*	2,976	13,608	173	398*

Table 10.8 (continued)

CASH AND MARKET SECURITIES						
MEANS	50,644	40,646*	36,257	42,881	33,353	34,816*
STANDARD DEVIATIONS	4,878	7,171*	7,674	4,736	3,951	4,777*
LOWER CONFIDENCE LIMITS	40,888	26,305*	20,910	33,410	25,451	25,262*
UPPER CONFIDENCE LIMITS	60,400	54,987*	51,605	52,352	41,255	44,370*
CASH+SECURITIES+ACCT RECV						
MEANS	60,579	66,914*	53,311	72,135	49,887	47,655*
STANDARD DEVIATIONS	5,141	5,760*	8,024	5,673	3,518	6,410*
LOWER CONFIDENCE LIMITS	50,297	55,395*	37,263	60,789	42,850	34,835*
UPPER CONFIDENCE LIMITS	70,861	78,433*	69,359	83,481	56,924	60,475*
TOTAL INVENTORIES						
MEANS	63,194	78,782*	78,558	66,213	90,182	78,196*
STANDARD DEVIATIONS	4,288	9,809*	5,653	3,250	7,370	6,834*
LOWER CONFIDENCE LIMITS	54,618	59,165*	67,252	59,714	75,442	64,528*
UPPER CONFIDENCE LIMITS	71,770	98,399*	89,864	72,712	104,923	91,864*
TOTAL CURRENT ASSETS						
MEANS	123,773	145,696*	131,869	138,348	140,069	125,851*
STANDARD DEVIATIONS	4,851	8,434*	5,706	7,187	7,589	7,988*
LOWER CONFIDENCE LIMITS	114,070	128,828*	120,458	123,973	124,891	109,876*
UPPER CONFIDENCE LIMITS	133,476	162,565*	143,281	152,723	155,248	141,826*
TOTAL ASSETS						
MEANS	153,589	176,599*	163,850	171,400	174,186	161,026*
STANDARD DEVIATIONS	4,851	8,434*	5,706	7,187	7,589	7,988*
LOWER CONFIDENCE LIMITS	143,886	159,730*	152,439	157,025	159,007	145,050*
UPPER CONFIDENCE LIMITS	163,292	193,467*	175,262	185,775	189,365	177,001*
TOTAL CURRENT LIABILITIES						
MEANS	2,977	18,366*	7,147	7,340	11,855	3,485*
STANDARD DEVIATIONS	418	8,442*	2,178	1,269	1,956	632*
LOWER CONFIDENCE LIMITS	2,140	1,482*	2,790	4,803	7,943	2,221*
UPPER CONFIDENCE LIMITS	3,813	35,250*	11,503	9,877	15,767	4,748*
TOTAL LIABILITIES						
MEANS	2,977	18,366*	7,147	7,340	11,855	3,485*
STANDARD DEVIATIONS	418	8,442*	2,178	1,269	1,956	632*
LOWER CONFIDENCE LIMITS	2,140	1,482*	2,790	4,803	7,943	2,221*
UPPER CONFIDENCE LIMITS	3,813	35,250*	11,503	9,877	15,767	4,748*
TOTAL OWNERS' EQUITY						
MEANS	150,612	158,233*	156,704	164,060	162,330	157,541*
STANDARD DEVIATIONS	4,625	4,070*	4,872	6,206	6,376	7,806*
LOWER CONFIDENCE LIMITS	141,362	150,093*	146,961	151,649	149,579	141,928*
UPPER CONFIDENCE LIMITS	159,863	166,373*	166,447	176,472	175,082	173,153*
ALL FIXED ASSETS AT BOOK	29,816	30,903*	31,981	33,052	34,116	35,174*

Table 10.8 (continued)

	13	3/ 3	14	3/ 6	15	3/ 9	16	4/ 0*
INDUSTRY SALES--000 OMIT								
MEANS		58		92		39		72*
STANDARD DEVIATIONS		7		11		4		6*
LOWER CONFIDENCE LIMITS		45		70		30		60*
UPPER CONFIDENCE LIMITS		72		113		47		83*
FIRM'S INDUSTRY SHARE %								
MEANS		100.00		100.00		100.00		100.00*
STANDARD DEVIATIONS		0.00		0.00		0.00		0.00*
LOWER CONFIDENCE LIMITS		100.00		100.00		100.00		100.00*
UPPER CONFIDENCE LIMITS		100.00		100.00		100.00		100.00*
FIRM NET SALES ACHIEVED								
MEANS		58,381		91,522		38,665		71,923*
STANDARD DEVIATIONS		6,918		10,968		4,223		5,736*
LOWER CONFIDENCE LIMITS		44,544		69,585		30,219		60,451*
UPPER CONFIDENCE LIMITS		72,217		113,458		47,111		83,396*
COST OF SALES								
MEANS		31,036		46,036		18,955		37,936*
STANDARD DEVIATIONS		3,821		4,760		2,356		2,742*
LOWER CONFIDENCE LIMITS		23,395		36,515		14,242		32,453*
UPPER CONFIDENCE LIMITS		38,678		55,557		23,667		43,420*
GROSS PROFIT ON SALES								
MEANS		27,344		45,485		19,710		33,987*
STANDARD DEVIATIONS		3,177		6,359		1,976		3,117*
LOWER CONFIDENCE LIMITS		20,990		32,768		15,758		27,752*
UPPER CONFIDENCE LIMITS		33,698		58,203		23,663		40,221*
TOTAL OPERATING EXPENSE								
MEANS		22,017		22,873		23,537		23,412*
STANDARD DEVIATIONS		405		348		401		427*
LOWER CONFIDENCE LIMITS		21,207		22,176		22,734		22,557*
UPPER CONFIDENCE LIMITS		22,826		23,569		24,339		24,266*
NET OPERATING INCOME								
MEANS		5,328		22,613		-3,826		10,575*
STANDARD DEVIATIONS		3,391		6,412		2,197		3,013*
LOWER CONFIDENCE LIMITS		-1,454		9,789		-8,220		4,548*
UPPER CONFIDENCE LIMITS		12,110		35,436		568		16,602*
NET INCOME AFTER TAX								
MEANS		3,412		14,388		-4,162		6,950*
STANDARD DEVIATIONS		2,570		4,495		1,986		2,102*
LOWER CONFIDENCE LIMITS		-1,729		5,398		-8,134		2,746*
UPPER CONFIDENCE LIMITS		8,552		23,378		-191		11,153*

Table 10.8 (continued)

```
CASH AND MARKET SECURITIES
   MEANS                        30,146      20,840      34,551      25,296*
   STANDARD DEVIATIONS           6,421       6,488       6,978       9,001*
   LOWER CONFIDENCE LIMITS      17,304       7,864      20,594       7,293*
   UPPER CONFIDENCE LIMITS      42,987      33,816      48,507      43,298*

CASH+SECURITIES+ACCT RECV
   MEANS                        53,498      57,449      50,017      54,065*
   STANDARD DEVIATIONS           5,010       8,466       6,865       7,664*
   LOWER CONFIDENCE LIMITS      43,478      40,517      36,288      38,736*
   UPPER CONFIDENCE LIMITS      63,518      74,380      63,746      69,394*

TOTAL INVENTORIES
   MEANS                        93,265      87,758      89,014      94,367*
   STANDARD DEVIATIONS          11,481       3,099       6,958       6,820*
   LOWER CONFIDENCE LIMITS      70,303      81,560      75,098      80,728*
   UPPER CONFIDENCE LIMITS     116,226      93,956     102,930     108,006*

TOTAL CURRENT ASSETS
   MEANS                       146,763     145,206     139,031     148,432*
   STANDARD DEVIATIONS          11,004       8,723       9,695       7,770*
   LOWER CONFIDENCE LIMITS     124,754     127,760     119,642     132,891*
   UPPER CONFIDENCE LIMITS     168,771     162,652     158,420     163,973*

TOTAL ASSETS
   MEANS                       182,990     182,481     177,350     187,791*
   STANDARD DEVIATIONS          11,004       8,723       9,695       7,770*
   LOWER CONFIDENCE LIMITS     160,981     165,035     157,961     172,250*
   UPPER CONFIDENCE LIMITS     204,998     199,927     196,739     203,332*

TOTAL CURRENT LIABILITIES
   MEANS                        22,907      11,008      10,091      14,973*
   STANDARD DEVIATIONS           8,827       2,925       4,690       3,510*
   LOWER CONFIDENCE LIMITS       5,253       5,157         710       7,952*
   UPPER CONFIDENCE LIMITS      40,562      16,858      19,471      21,993*

TOTAL LIABILITIES
   MEANS                        22,907      11,008      10,091      14,973*
   STANDARD DEVIATIONS           8,827       2,925       4,690       3,510*
   LOWER CONFIDENCE LIMITS       5,253       5,157         710       7,952*
   UPPER CONFIDENCE LIMITS      40,562      16,858      19,471      21,993*

TOTAL OWNERS' EQUITY
   MEANS                       160,082     171,474     167,259     172,819*
   STANDARD DEVIATIONS           7,743       8,022       8,198       8,087*
   LOWER CONFIDENCE LIMITS     144,597     155,430     150,863     156,645*
   UPPER CONFIDENCE LIMITS     175,568     187,518     183,655     188,992*

ALL FIXED ASSETS AT BOOK
                                36,227      37,275      38,319      39,360*
```

100% because no uncertainty was associated with this figure. The same remark applies to total paid-in owners' equity, fixed assets, inventories, and accounts receivable. Means of net income, operating earning power, and return on owners' equity are much more optimistic in FINANCIAL SUMMARY than in VALUATION AND SCOPE. The reason is that FINANCIAL SUMMARY is an extrapolation of final period results, and the last period has the second highest seasonal index. The pronounced seasonal pattern of FLORAWREATH affects operating results significantly. For investment decisions and economic valuation, figures in VALUATION AND SCOPE are superior to extrapolations in FINANCIAL SUMMARY. Again, with intense seasonal effects, short-term loans are generated in FLORAWREATH to supply cash for inventory build-ups. In the fifth column of FINANCIAL SUMMARY, minimum cash ratio is held close to 50% (49.82%), but only a part of borrowing capacity is used (minimum 500.91% against a limit of 200%). These benchmarks are established by internal inputs in IDs 87 and 88, which were not overwritten in this case.

In ENVIRONMENTAL ANALYSES of FINANCIAL STATEMENTS output division, base sales of FLORAWREATH, at \$185,000, appear under an industry heading. Again, firm's industry share remains constant at 100%. The set of seasonal inputs in IDs 51 to 54 has been normalized to a mean of one and applied to all periods. The total growth of the firm is a compound factor at 7.06% of 6% inflation and 1% real economic growth.

Examine the CASH FORECASTS among the FINANCIAL STATEMENTS to determine if additional capital will be required over the simulation. Varying amounts of short-term credit are required, starting with the fifth period. As previously noted, short-term borrowing capacity is never reached. Thus there is no demand in this case for additional permanent capital.

In conclusion, FLORAWREATH should achieve a modest investment value increase over the next four years. Its value is somewhat depressed by possible low or negative projected earnings in early years. Increases in earnings during the final year lead to a restricted increase in going-concern value because risk also increases (standard deviation of return on owners' equity rises from 2.72% to 3.09%). Nevertheless, FLORAWREATH going-concern values are well in excess of liquidation values, or even the stated value of total assets. FLORAWREATH has been simulated as a high risk firm in respect to sales demand. Despite this risk, the firm is not likely to experience problems of cash shortages.

10.4 | Manufacturing firm— ECOFURN

A group of engineers has completed operating prototypes and performance studies of a new heating plant accessory trade-named ECOFURN. When attached to gas furnaces this electromechanical device will pay for itself in fuel savings in two years on new equipment and in three to four years on retrofits. ECOFURN is protected by patents, has a long life, and is relatively free of maintenance. No direct competition is expected over the next few years.

The engineer group decides to start a small corporation to manufacture and market ECOFURN. They believe $200,000 initial cash may be raised from some private investors. The firm will be capitalized initially with 20,000 shares, 40% of which will be issued to the originating engineers. These engineers will contribute all the development of the ECOFURN accessory, which is now ready to manufacture and sell. The engineers' contribution includes their own time, skill, and out of pocket costs to date. The engineer group will also pay expenses to organize the new corporation. The value of the engineers' contribution and initial intangibles will not be capitalized in the beginning condition statement of the new firm. The new firm will be named ECOFURN.

The engineer group needs to project the future of ECOFURN as information to prospective investors. You prepare a PAVE simulation for this purpose. Annual projections for the next five years will be assembled. It is very important to include risk analysis. A sample size of 15 has been chosen for 98% confidence intervals on mean values. This rather large sample size was selected to overcome some of the instability of simulating a high-growth situation.

A skeleton initial condition statement will show only $200,000 initial cash assets balanced by $200,000 paid-in capital.

A detailed analysis was made of ECOFURN market prospects. New gas furnace sales during the year prior to launching ECOFURN were about 2,000,000 units. If each of these were equipped with an ECOFURN accessory at an estimated factory selling price of $20 each, then the total market for ECOFURN would be $40,000,000. ECOFURN expects to get only 1.25% of this market the first year, but growth should be rapid. In fact, a 30% increase in market penetration is expected each year over the next five years. Meanwhile, the new furnace market itself is expected to grow 3% faster than the economy. General economic growth is estimated at 2% real and 4% inflationary. Uncertainty about industry growth is 20% maximum shift, but uncertainty about ECOFURN market penetration is even higher. A maximum shift of 25% from forecast is not considered excessive. Inflation adjustments will be applied to all future projected costs. The ECOFURN retrofit market is less favorable economically than new installations, is difficult to forecast, and would require a separate distributing organization. For this reason it is excluded from initial projections. Although new furnace sales do exhibit some seasonal pattern, this was omitted to simplify initial outputs.

ECOFURN furnace units will be manufactured by the new firm. Direct purchased material is estimated at 24%, and direct labor at 13%, of factory selling price. Maximum shifts of 5% due to uncertainty are estimated for each of these. During the first year indirect manufacturing payroll is projected at $40,000, indirect manufacturing supplies at $3000, and all other utilities and period costs at $65,000. All three of these expense groups will grow at about 30% per year in addition to inflation adjustments.

An uncertainty component of 10% maximum shift will be applied to the $65,000 in utilities and other manufacturing expenses. Factory equipment is expected to increase by $25,000 each year. The depreciation rate on this equipment is 10% declining balance. The capacity of the plant will keep pace with increases in equipment. Starting at $600,000 factory sales level by the end of the first year, capacity will increase by 50% each year. Inventory levels are planned as 20% of annual cost for direct materials and 10% for finished goods. Goods-in-process inventories are assumed negligible, and factory supplies are all expensed.

General and administrative expenses are separated from the manufacturing expenses above. Research and engineering expenses are taken at 2.5% of sales. Variable marketing expense is estimated at 8% of sales. Fixed marketing expense is projected at $40,000 the first year with a 40% annual growth rate. Accounts receivable are forecasted at 5% of annual sales with uncollectibles at 0.5%. Accounts payable will average 4% of annual credit from suppliers. Office supplies and small equipment are taken at $4000 the first year with a 45% growth rate each year thereafter. Such supplies will be expensed when purchased. Administrative and office payroll is $55,000 the first year with an estimated 30% annual growth. All other general expenses are projected at $50,000 the first year with a 35% annual growth rate. Uncertainty about general expense will be taken at 8% maximum shift. Office and engineering equipment will increase by $12,000 each year. The depreciation rate is 15% declining balance.

There are two main purposes of the simulation. Are the prospects for growth in value of ECOFURN sufficient to interest high-risk investors? Is the original $200,000 sufficient to support projected growth? To shed light on these questions there will be no planned additional investments during the first five years. Short-term financing will be permitted at an estimated interest cost of 12%. No long-term debt will be used, and no payments of dividends will be projected.

Inputs to PAVE follow directly from the demands and conditions of ECOFURN projections. The complete set is reproduced from PAVE in Table 10.9. Five periods are simulated (ID 1) with one period per year (ID 2). The sample size is 15 (ID 3) and a manufacturing frame is required (ID 5 = 2). There are two reasons for using a manufacturing frame. There is a direct materials inventory (ID 172), and manufacturing expenses are to be compiled separately from general expenses.

There is a skeleton initial condition with the only entries in IDs 9 and 47 ($200,000 each).

There are potential starting industry sales of $40,000,000 (ID 130), but ECO-FURN begins with only 1.25% market penetration (ID 122). This penetration is expected to grow rapidly at 30% per year in ID 123. Since ECOFURN uses industry analysis to determine available demand rather than direct inputs of firm sales, ID 120 is 0. Components of economic growth are 2% real (ID 102) and 4% inflation (ID 112). Furnace sales are expected to grow 2% faster than the economy as a whole (ID 132). Thus a total of three growth components are used to determine industry sales (IDs 102, 112, and 132). ECOFURN sales are derived from this industry growth with a

Table 10.9.
INPUT SET FOR ECOFURN

ECOFURN

INPUT/OUTPUT SYSTEM CHOICES
!! THESE INPUTS CONTROL OTHER DISPLAYS!!

```
1 TOTAL NUMBER OF PERIODS (MAX 24) . . .          5
2 NO. OF PERIODS PER YEAR . . . . .                1
3 SAMPLE SIZE--DETERMINISTIC=1/STAT.=2 TO 12.     15
4 SEED NO.--STANDARD RANDOM SERIES=0 .             0
5 FRAME: SERVICE=0/TRADE=1/MFG=2/ENVRT ONLY=3      2
6 OUTPUT DIVISION PRINT 1ST FROM LIST BELOW:       0
  VALUATION 1ST AND FINAL YEARS, SCOPE    =0
  STATISTICAL SUMMARY FROM FINAL PERIOD   =1
  FINANCIAL STATEMENTS FOR ALL PERIODS    =2
  SELECTED ACCOUNTS FOR ALL PERIODS       =3
```

INITIAL CONDITION--CURRENT AND INTANGIBLE ASSETS
(START BAL SHEET: NEW FIRM--OMIT/SKELETON)

```
 9 $ CASH AND MARKETABLE SECURITIES . . .        200000
10 $ TRADE ACCOUNTS AND NOTES RECEIVABLE .             0
11 $ NONTRADE ADVANCES AND ACCRUED RECEIVABLES        0
12 $ RESERVE FOR UNCOLLECTIBLE ACCOUNTS .             0
13 $ PREPAID EXPENSE AND DEFERRED CHARGES .           0
14 $ INTANGIBLES: ORGAN EXP., PATENT, GOODWILL        0
15 $ INVENTORY OF GENERAL SUPPLIES/SMALL EQPT.        0
16 $ INVENTORY OF MFG OR TRADE FINISHED GOODS.        0
17 $ INVENTORY OF MFG GOODS-IN-PROCESS .              0
18 $ INVENTORY OF MFG DIRECT MAT'L & SUPPLIES.        0
19 $ INVENTORY OF MFG PERIOD SUPPLIES & EQPT.         0
```

INITIAL CONDITION--LIABILITIES AND OWNERS' EQUITY
(TOTAL ASSETS, EQUITIES, AND BALANCE
CHECK IN NEXT DISPLAY)

```
40 $ TRADE ACCOUNTS AND NOTES PAYABLE .               0
41 $ NONTRADE ACCTS, DIVIDENDS, TAXES PAYABLE.        0
42 $ UNEARNED ADVANCES FROM CUSTOMERS .               0
43 $ ACCRUED EXPENSE AND LIABILITIES. .               0
44 $ SHORT-TERM DEBT AND LOANS PAYABLE .              0
45 $ LONG-TERM OBLIGATIONS AT FACE OR STATED .        0
46 $ BOND (PREFERRED STOCK) PREMIUM (DISCOUNT)        0
47 $ PAID-IN OWNER EQUITY CAPITAL. . . .         200000
48 $ RETAINED EARNINGS:                               0
```

INITIAL CONDITION (STARTING BALANCE SHEET) TOTALS

```
TOTAL ASSETS. . . . .        $ 200000
TOTAL LIABILITIES . . .      $      0
TOTAL OWNERS' EQUITY . . .   $ 200000
```

% ANNUAL REAL GROWTH RATE OF ECONOMY

```
102 % BASE VALUE APPLIED IN PERIOD 1 . .            2
103 % ANNUAL CHANGE TO PERIODS FROM 1ST BASE        0

110   INFLATE PERIOD COSTS--NO=0/YES=1 . .          1
```

% ANNUAL AVERAGE INFLATION RATE

```
112 % BASE VALUE APPLIED IN PERIOD 1 . .            4
113 % ANNUAL CHANGE TO PERIODS FROM 1ST BASE        0

120   SALES--% INDUSTRY SHARE=0/$ PER PERIOD=1.     0
```

* NET SALES DEMAND AVAILABLE TO FIRM

```
121     *% MAX CHANGE FROM MEAN VALUE .            25

122 % BASE VALUE APPLIED IN PERIOD 1 . .         1.25
123 % ANNUAL CHANGE TO PERIODS FROM 1ST BASE       30

130 $ INDUSTRY SALES FOR BASE (PRIOR) YEAR    40000000
```

*% ANNUAL INDUSTRY GROWTH COMPARED TO ECONOMY

```
131     *% MAX CHANGE FROM MEAN VALUE .            20

132 % BASE VALUE APPLIED IN PERIOD 1 . .            3
133 % ANNUAL CHANGE TO PERIODS FROM 1ST BASE        0
```

Table 10.9 (continued)

```
140 INITIAL GOODS INVY'S--COST % OF SELL PRICE          60

*DIRECT PURCHASED MATERIAL OR GOODS AS % OF SALES
 141    *% MAX CHANGE FROM MEAN VALUE .  .  .            5
 142    % BASE VALUE APPLIED IN PERIOD 1 .  .           24
 143    % ANNUAL CHANGE TO PERIODS FROM 1ST BASE .       0

150 % DESEASONALIZE GOODS PRODUCTION/PURCHASE            0

$ FINISHED GOODS INVENTORY LEVEL AS % ANNUAL COST GOODS
 152    $ BASE VALUE APPLIED IN PERIOD 1 .  .           10
 153    % ANNUAL CHANGE TO PERIODS FROM 1ST BASE .       0

DIRECT MATERIAL INVENTORY LEVEL AS % ANNUAL USAGE
 172    % BASE VALUE APPLIED IN PERIOD 1 .  .           20
 173    % ANNUAL CHANGE TO PERIODS FROM 1ST BASE .       0

*DIRECT LABOR PAYROLL AS % OF SALES
 181    *% MAX CHANGE FROM MEAN VALUE .  .  .            5
 182    % BASE VALUE APPLIED IN PERIOD 1 .  .           13
 183    % ANNUAL CHANGE TO PERIODS FROM 1ST BASE .       0

*% OPERATING EFFICIENCY OF PROCESSING
 201    *% MAX CHANGE FROM MEAN VALUE .  .  .            0
 202    % BASE VALUE APPLIED IN PERIOD 1 .  .          100
 203    % ANNUAL CHANGE TO PERIODS FROM 1ST BASE .       0

$ CAPACITY OF PLANT PER PERIOD, 100% EFFIC'Y, SALES $
 212    $ BASE VALUE APPLIED IN PERIOD 1 .  .       600000
 213    % ANNUAL CHANGE TO PERIODS FROM 1ST BASE .      50

220 MFG SUPPLIES INV'Y LEVEL AS % ANNUAL USAGE          0

$ INDIRECT SUPPLIES/SMALL EQPT USED PER PERIOD
 222    $ BASE VALUE APPLIED IN PERIOD 1 .  .         3000
 223    % ANNUAL CHANGE TO PERIODS FROM 1ST BASE .      30

$ INDIRECT MFG PAYROLL PER PERIOD
 232    $ BASE VALUE APPLIED IN PERIOD 1 .  .        40000
 233    % ANNUAL CHANGE TO PERIODS FROM 1ST BASE .      30


*$ UTILITIES OR ALL INDIRECT COSTS PER PERIOD--MFG
 251    *% MAX CHANGE FROM MEAN VALUE .  .  .           10
 252    $ BASE VALUE APPLIED IN PERIOD 1 .  .        65000
 253    % ANNUAL CHANGE TO PERIODS FROM 1ST BASE .      30

280 DEPREC'N PER YR DECLINING BAL MFG CLASS 1           10

$ MFG FIXED ASSETS CLASS 1 NET CHANGES PER PERIOD
 282    $ BASE VALUE APPLIED IN PERIOD 1 .  .        25000
 283    % ANNUAL CHANGE TO PERIODS FROM 1ST BASE .       0

330 R&D EXPENSES--% SALES=0/$ PER PERIOD=1 .            0

RESEARCH AND DEVELOPMENT PAYROLL
 332    % BASE VALUE APPLIED IN PERIOD 1 .  .            0
 333    % ANNUAL CHANGE TO PERIODS FROM 1ST BASE .       0

RES & DVLPT MATERIAL/CONTRACTS/MISC EXPENSE PER PERIOD
 342    % BASE VALUE APPLIED IN PERIOD 1 .  .          2.5
 343    % ANNUAL CHANGE TO PERIODS FROM 1ST BASE .       0

SALES SALARIES/COMMISSIONS PAYROLL AS % OF SALES
 352    % BASE VALUE APPLIED IN PERIOD 1 .  .            8
 353    % ANNUAL CHANGE TO PERIODS FROM 1ST BASE .       0

$ ADVERTISE/PROMOTE/MISC SALES EXPENSE PER PERIOD
 382    $ BASE VALUE APPLIED IN PERIOD 1 .  .        40000
 383    % ANNUAL CHANGE TO PERIODS FROM 1ST BASE .      40

390 % UNCOLLECTIBLE ACCOUNTS .  .  .  .  .             .5

*ACCOUNTS RECEIVABLE LEVEL AS % OF ANNUAL SALES
 391    *% MAX CHANGE FROM MEAN VALUE .  .  .            0
 392    % BASE VALUE APPLIED IN PERIOD 1 .  .            5
 393    % ANNUAL CHANGE TO PERIODS FROM 1ST BASE .       0

$ INDIRECT SERVICE/OFFICE SUPPLIES/SMALL EQPT PERIOD
 412    $ BASE VALUE APPLIED IN PERIOD 1 .  .         4000
 413    % ANNUAL CHANGE TO PERIODS FROM 1ST BASE .      45
```

Table 10.9 (continued)

```
$ GENERAL ADMINISTRATIVE/INDIRECT SERV. PAYROLL PERIOD

   432 $ BASE VALUE APPLIED IN PERIOD 1 . . . .    55000
   433 % ANNUAL CHANGE TO PERIODS FROM 1ST BASE .    30


*$ UTILITIES OR ALL INDIRECT COSTS PER PERIOD--GENERAL
   451      *% MAX CHANGE FROM MEAN VALUE . . .      8

   452 $ BASE VALUE APPLIED IN PERIOD 1 . . . .    50000
   453 % ANNUAL CHANGE TO PERIODS FROM 1ST BASE .    35


   480 % DEPREC'N YRLY DECLINE BAL GENERAL CLASS 1   15

$ GENERAL FIXED ASSETS CLASS 1 NET CHANGES PER PERIOD

   482 $ BASE VALUE APPLIED IN PERIOD 1 . . . .    12000
   483 % ANNUAL CHANGE TO PERIODS FROM 1ST BASE .     0


GENERAL ADMINISTRATIVE SYSTEM PARAMETERS


   79 GENL SUPPLIES INV'Y LEVEL AS % ANNUAL USAGE    0
   80 ACCTS PAYABLE LEVEL AS % OF ANNUAL ACCT PAY'   4
   81 PREPAID EXPENSE LEVEL AS % OF ANNUAL PAY'TS    0
   82 ADVANCES BY CUSTOMERS AS % OF ANNUAL SALES     0
   83 $ ORGAN EXP./GOODWILL INCURRED IN PERIOD 1.    0
   84 $ AMORTIZ/N OF INTANGIBLES YRLY, NOT PERIOD    0


*% SHORT-TERM INTEREST RATE ANNUAL
   561      *% MAX CHANGE FROM MEAN VALUE . . .      0

   562 % BASE VALUE APPLIED IN PERIOD 1 . . . .     12
   563 % ANNUAL CHANGE TO PERIODS FROM 1ST BASE .     0


FINANCIAL AND VALUATION SYSTEM PARAMETERS
   87 % CASH RATIO MIN, BELOW WHICH CASH DEMANDED    50
   88 % CURRENT RATIO MIN FROM SHORT-TERM LOANS .   200
   89 % COMBINED EFFECTIVE INCOME TAX RATE (<100)    50
   90 $ INITIAL TAX LOSS CREDIT FOR CARRY FORWARD     0
   91 NO. 1ST PERIOD OWNER EQUITY UNITS (1/SHARE) 20000
   92 $ ADDED SHARE COST--INTERNAL COMPUTATION=0.     0
   93 PRICE-EARNINGS MULTIPLE YR 1--INTER'L COMP=0    0
   94 PRICE-EARN MULTIPLE FINAL YR--INTER'L COMP=0    0
   95 % ASSETS AVERAGE REALIZED IN LIQUIDATION  .    50
   96 % INVESTOR REQD RATE RETURN YR--INTL COMP=0     0
   97 % LONG-TERM AVG GROWTH RATE YR--INTL COMP=0     0
   98 % RETURN ON INCREM'L ASSETS YR--INTL COMP=0     0
```

further 30% growth of its market share (ID 123). Seasonal-cyclical indices are not applied to sales demand, hence there are no inputs in IDs 51 to 64. Inflation adjustments will be applied to period costs and asset additions (ID 110 = 1).

Two sources of uncertainty are applied to sales demand. These are a 20% maximum shift of industry sales (ID 131) and a 25% maximum shift in ECOFURN's market share (ID 121).

Expense inputs follow exactly from the description of the case. Uncertainties in manufacturing direct labor payroll and direct purchased material are entered in IDs 141 and 181. Additional uncertainty is not introduced into operating efficiency. This parameter remains at its internal default of 100% (ID 202). Uncertainty of indirect or period costs of manufacturing is represented by the 10% entry in ID 251.

There are two inventories established at the manufacturing level. These are finished goods as a percent of annual cost of goods sold (ID 152), and direct material inventory as a percent of the cost of direct material used (ID 172). The 25000 input in ID 282 indicates that $25,000 worth of net new fixed manufacturing assets will be added to the plant each period (year). No other method of expanding capacity was programmed (IDs 75 to 78 equal 0). Manufacturing fixed assets will be depreciated at a mean rate of 10% per year on declining balance method. Fixed cost inputs (both manufacturing and general) are all stated at current price levels. Note the application of inflation adjustments in the outputs at 4% per year (from ID 110 = 1 and ID 112 = 4). In ECOFURN inflation adjustments are applied directly to ID sets 212, 222, 232, 251, 282, 382, 412, 432, 452, and 482. These adjustments are in addition to growth rate inputs in IDs 213, 223, 233, 253, 383, 413, 433, and 453. Other expenses are variable with sales and hence receive the 4% inflation component of sales growth.

Sales and general administrative inputs follow the same plan as manufacturing inputs. Development and engineering expenses are to be simulated at 2.5% of sales (ID 342 with indicator ID 330 = 0). Variable sales expense is collected into ID 352, and fixed sales expense into ID set 382. Inventories are not maintained outside of manufacturing (ID 79 = 0). Office supplies are expensed each period per ID set 412. All general administrative expense is considered indirect per ID sets 412, 432, and 451. The only input uncertainty for general expense is the 8% maximum shift applied to ID 451. General assets of $12,000 net are to be added each period (year) per ID 482. The mean depreciation rate on these assets is 15% declining balance (ID 480). The mean level of accounts receivable to credit sales is 5% (ID 392) with uncollectible accounts at 0.5% (ID 390). The mean level of accounts payable is 4% of generated payables (ID 80). Organization expense and intangibles were written off before the start of the case (IDs 83 and 84 equal 0).

The only entry in financial ID sets is 12% short-term interest rate in ID 562. Per ID 530 equal to 0, additional owner required capital will not be applied to PAVE runs. This decision will test the adequacy of the initial $200,000 investment (ID 47), and compute probability estimates of insolvency. The decision also means that 20,000 initial common shares (ID 91) will remain fixed over the five years. All other financial and valuation system parameters are to be determined internally.

Roughly speaking, PAVE outputs present an ECOFURN scenario of high growth coupled with only break-even performance. The complete set of PAVE outputs is exhibited in Table 10.10. Note the mean close to zero of return on owners' equity in VALUATION AND SCOPE output division. This ratio actually deteriorates over time from 0.56% to -1.38%. Despite the negative figure in the final mean of this ratio, sales, earnings, and owners' equity all grow rapidly over the simulation, and all maintain mean positive values.

Assets must expand to support high growth, but in ECOFURN there is neither earnings nor additional outside investment to finance such expansion. The result is to use up the initial $200,000 cash investment and develop a mean cash deficit of -$11,375 EOP Year 5. On the average, technical insolvency occurs shortly after EOP 4. There is a 40% probability of running out of cash. This probability and the small cash deficit do not appear too frightening, but remember that these are mean figures. In the worst replication there was a cash deficit of -$271,084 (see fifth column of FINANCIAL SUMMARY). It is encouraging that negative owners' equity (legal insolvency) was not encountered during the simulation.

Valuation information provides some useful clues to projected performance. Not only does the mean return on owners' equity deteriorate over the five years, but also risk. Note the increase in standard deviation from 2.64% to 24.03%. This increase accounts for the internal doubling of investor's required rate of return from 15.34% the first year to a final 30.8%. The first rate is moderate, the second reflects high risk. Now compare the required rates of return with the mean rate of return on incremental assets. The latter rate is quite high at 28.57%, which is probably the only component which props up going-concern value. The 28.58% rate compares favorably for valuation with the initial required rate of return of 15.34%, but somewhat unfavorably with the final rate of 30.8%.

All determinants of value come together in the computations of going-concern economic values. Due to low and deteriorating mean return on owners' equity, and the other rate interactions noted above, going-concern value over five years increases by a factor of only 1.3 while mean sales increase by 4.3 and mean earnings by 28. The internally computed price-earnings multiple of 3 does seem appropriate for ECOFURN's low return under high risk. The high multiple of 65 for the first year is a mechanical result of very low first-year mean earnings of $2858. If second-year mean earnings of $10,475 had been used, the first-year multiple would drop immediately to less than 18. An encouraging note for ECOFURN is that going-concern values at least exceed estimates of the liquidation value of assets.

The long-term growth rate of 7.63%, which is applied to going-concern value formulas, is a mean between final growth rate of the industry at 9.26% (see ENVIRONMENTAL ANALYSES OF FIRM statements) and the long-term growth rate of the economy with inflation at 6%.

There are a few remaining points to be noted in the outputs. Short-term credit is used to ease cash shortages in all periods past the first. This credit builds to a mean of $65,504 EOP 5 (CONDITION STATEMENTS). The credit is limited by internal ef-

Table 10.10.

OUTPUT FOR ECOFURN FIRST RUN

```
****************
VALUATION AND SCOPE
****************
ECOFURN

 5 PERIODS OVER  5.00 YEARS;  1.00 PERIODS PER YEAR, EACH  1.00 YEARS
******  SCOPE OF FIRM -- INITIAL SHARES 20000 -- FINAL SHARES 20000 -- EOP = END OF PERIOD ******

        98 % CONFIDENCE LIMITS FOR MEANS WITH SAMPLE SIZE 15
```

			MEAN	STANDARD DEVIATION	98 % LOWER CONFIDENCE	98 % UPPER CONFIDENCE
SALES	TOTAL	FIRST YEAR	522,630	11,666	491,130	554,129
		FINAL YEAR	2,229,594	84,120	2,002,470	2,456,718
	PER SHARE	FIRST YEAR	26.13	0.58	24.56	27.71
		FINAL YEAR	111.48	4.21	100.12	122.84
EARNINGS	TOTAL	FIRST YEAR	2,858	4,710	-9,860	15,576
		FINAL YEAR	79,887	24,487	13,771	146,003
	PER SHARE	FIRST YEAR	0.14	0.24	-0.49	0.78
		FINAL YEAR	3.99	1.22	0.69	7.30
RETURN ON OWNERS' EQUITY %	TOTAL	FIRST YEAR	0.56	2.64	-6.56	7.67
		FINAL YEAR	-1.38	24.03	-66.26	63.50
OWNERS' EQUITY	TOTAL	AT EOP 1	202,858	4,710	190,140	215,576
		END OF RUN	369,280	39,297	263,178	475,383
	PER SHARE	AT EOP 1	10.14	0.24	9.51	10.78
		END OF RUN	18.46	1.96	13.16	23.77
TOTAL ASSETS	TOTAL	AT EOP 1	218,329	4,844	205,249	231,409
		END OF RUN	487,903	40,732	377,928	597,878
	PER SHARE	AT EOP 1	10.92	0.24	10.26	11.57
		END OF RUN	24.40	2.04	18.90	29.89
CASH AND MARKETABLE SECURITIES	TOTAL	AT EOP 1	98,457	3,385	89,317	107,597
		END OF RUN	-11,375	31,357	-96,038	73,288
	PER SHARE	AT EOP 1	4.92	0.17	4.47	5.38
		END OF RUN	-0.57	1.57	-4.80	3.66

```
TECHNICAL INSOLVENCY OCCURRED WITH PROBABILITY .4 -- ON AVERAGE BEGAN DURING PERIOD 4.2
LEGAL INSOLVENCY DID NOT OCCUR
```

Table 10.10 (continued)

****** METHODS OF VALUATION ******

	FIRST YEAR OR EOP 1	FINAL YEAR OR END	FIRST YEAR PER SHARE	FINAL YEAR PER SHARE
MARKET VALUE WITH PRICE-EARNINGS MULTIPLES	186,812	247,760	9.34	12.39
PRICE-EARNINGS MULTIPLES	65	3		12.39
GOING CONCERN ECONOMIC VALUE UNDER RISK	186,812	247,760	9.34	12.39
LIQUIDATION VALUE TO OWNERS	93,694	125,329	4.68	6.27
LIQUIDATION VALUE OF TANGIBLE ASSETS	109,164	243,952	5.45	12.20
FIXED ASSETS AT BOOK VALUE WITH INTANGIBLES	36,244	157,436	1.81	7.87
TAX LOSS CARRYFORWARD--INITIAL & END OF RUN	0	14,962		

****** PARAMETERS OF GOING-CONCERN VALUATION ******

	APPLIED EOP 1	APPLIED END OF RUN
INVESTORS' REQUIRED RATE OF RETURN %	15.34	30.80
INFLATION RATE %	4.00	4.00
LONG-TERM FIRM GROWTH RATE WITH INFLATION %	7.63	7.63
LONG-TERM REAL GROWTH RATE OF THE ECONOMY %	2.00	2.00
MEAN RATE OF RETURN ON INCREMENTAL ASSETS %	28.57	28.57

Table 10.10 (continued)

```
*************************************
       FINANCIAL SUMMARY FROM FINAL PERIOD
*************************************

ECOFURN

  5 PERIODS OVER 5.00 YEARS;  1.00 PERIODS PER YEAR, EACH 1.00 YEARS
UNDEFINED RATIOS APPEAR '####--'; YEARLY VALUES ARE EXTRAPOLATED FROM THE FINAL PERIOD; 0 VALUES OMITTED

       98 % CONFIDENCE LIMITS FOR MEANS WITH SAMPLE SIZE 15
```

	MEAN	STANDARD DEVIATION	98 % LOWER CONFIDENCE	98 % UPPER CONFIDENCE	MINIMUM	MAXIMUM
****** SCOPE OF FIRM ******						
FIRM'S SHARE OF INDUSTRY %	3.54	0.10	3.27	3.81	2.90	4.24
NET SALES OR REVENUE PER YEAR	2,229,594	84,120	2,002,470	2,456,718	1,562,400	2,671,352
CASH AND MARKETABLE SECURITIES	-11,375	31,357	-96,038	73,288	-271,084	140,008
TOTAL ASSETS	487,903	40,732	377,926	597,879	135,200	700,322
TOTAL OWNERS' EQUITY	369,280	39,297	263,178	475,381	47,733	640,793
****** RATIO ANALYSIS OF PROFITABILITY ******						
GROSS MARGIN ON SALES %	45.79	0.68	43.95	47.62	39.50	48.82
NET OPERATING MARGIN ON SALES %	6.96	1.80	2.10	11.82	-9.88	14.60
OPERATING EARNING POWER %	25.69	11.39	-5.06	56.44	-114.15	63.55
OPERAT'G EFFIC'Y OR CAP'L TURNS	5.15	0.55	3.66	6.63	3.58	11.56
RETURN ON OWNERS' EQUITY %	-1.38	24.03	-66.26	63.50	-334.33	37.83
****** RATIO ANALYSIS OF FINANCIAL CONDITION ******						
CASH RATIO %	-26.19	44.26	-145.69	93.31	-460.06	235.19
ACID TEST OR QUICK RATIO %	91.16	48.46	-39.68	222.00	-262.22	459.57
CURRENT RATIO %	333.00	68.54	147.94	518.05	-25.42	911.97
DEBT TO TANGIBLE ASSETS %	27.03	3.62	17.25	36.80	8.50	64.69
DEBT TO TANGIBLE OWNER EQUITY %	44.07	10.75	15.04	73.09	9.29	183.24
TIMES INTEREST EARNED RATIO	#####,###.##	#####,###.##	-#####,###.##	#####,###.##	-29.37	#####,###.##
AVG COLLECTION PERIOD IN DAYS	18.25	0.00	18.25	18.25	18.25	18.25
INVENTORY TURNS PER YEAR	5.23	0.03	5.14	5.31	5.08	5.54

Table 10.10 (continued)

****** SELECTED FINANCIAL SUMMARY VALUES: ******

INDUSTRY SALES PER YR--000 OMIT	62,920	1,567	58,689	67,150	52,409	70,231

COST OF SALES PER YEAR	1,200,832	32,211	1,113,862	1,287,801	945,200	1,373,400
GROSS PROFIT PER YEAR	1,028,762	52,144	887,973	1,169,550	617,200	1,304,231
OPERATING INCOME PER YEAR	176,134	42,263	62,023	290,244	-154,331	389,101
NET INCOME BEFORE TAX PER YEAR	168,274	42,530	53,443	283,105	-159,586	389,101
NET INCOME AFTER TAX PER YEAR	79,887	24,487	13,772	146,001	-159,586	194,551
CASH+MKT SECURITIES+ACCTS RECV	100,105	34,625	6,617	193,592	-192,964	273,575
TOTAL INVENTORIES	230,362	7,402	210,376	250,347	170,729	269,311
TOTAL CURRENT ASSETS	330,467	40,732	220,490	440,443	-22,236	542,886
NET TANGIBLE FIXED ASSETS	157,436	0	157,436	157,436	157,436	157,436
ACCOUNTS PAYABLE	53,119	1,126	50,078	56,159	43,675	59,529
SHORT-TERM LOANS AND NOTES	65,504	13,384	29,367	101,640	0	144,212
TOTAL LIABILITIES	118,623	13,374	82,513	154,732	48,685	194,463
TOTAL PAID-IN OWNERS' EQUITY	200,000	0	200,000	200,000	200,000	200,000

****
FINANCIAL STATEMENTS PROJECTED FOR ALL PERIODS
****

ADMIN	ADMINISTRATIVE	DEPRC	DEPRECIATION	GEN	GENERAL
AMORT	AMORTIZATION	EDP	END OF PERIOD	INVY	INVENTORY
BOP	BEGINNING OF PERIOD	GEN	GENERAL	MFG	MANUFACTURING
MISC	MISCELLANEOUS	PURCH	PURCHASES OF	R&D	RESEARCH AND DEVELOPMENT

5 PERIODS OVER 5.00 YEARS; 1.00 PERIODS PER YEAR, EACH 1.00 YEARS

VALUES ARE ACCOUNT MEANS; ACCOUNT OMITTED WHEN ALL VALUES 0
HEADINGS ARE: PERIOD NO. AND YEAR/MONTH; OR CUMULATIVE *FOR YEAR NO.*

ECOFIRN

****
ENVIRONMENTAL ANALYSES OF FIRM
****

INDUSTRY BASE SALES--000S OMITTED; YEAR= 40000 -- PERIOD= 40000

	1	1/0	2	2/0	3	3/0	4	4/0	5	5/0
INFLATION RATE ANNUAL %		4.00		4.00		4.00		4.00		4.00
REAL ECONOMY GROWTH ANNUAL %		2.00		2.00		2.00		2.00		2.00
INDUSTRY TOTAL GROWTH %		9.26		9.26		9.26		9.26		9.26
SEASONAL/CYCLICAL INDICES		1.00		1.00		1.00		1.00		1.00
INDUSTRY SALES--000S OMITTED		43,713		48,089		53,572		58,318		62,920
FIRM'S INDUSTRY SHARE %		1.24		1.60		1.98		2.75		3.54
FIRM SALES DEMAND AVAILABLE		541,300		771,607		1,066,093		1,597,421		2,229,594

Table 10.10 (continued)

ECOFURN

```
*******************
INCOME STATEMENTS
*******************
```

	1 1/0	2 2/0	3 3/0	4 4/0	5 5/0
FIRM NET SALES ACHIEVED	522,630	768,762	1,066,093	1,597,421	2,229,594
-COST OF SALES	298,157	436,452	596,911	871,327	1,200,832
GROSS PROFIT ON SALES	224,473	332,310	469,182	726,093	1,028,762
R&D MATERIAL AND MISC EXP	13,066	19,219	26,652	39,936	55,740
TOTAL R&D EXPENSE	13,066	19,219	26,652	39,936	55,740
DIRECT SALES PAYROLL	41,810	61,501	85,287	127,794	178,358
PERIOD ADVERTISE, MISC SALES	41,600	60,570	88,189	128,404	186,956
TOTAL SALES EXPENSE	83,410	122,071	173,477	256,197	365,323
PERIOD GEN ADMIN PAYROLL	57,200	77,334	104,556	141,360	191,119
PURCH GEN SUPPLIES	4,160	6,273	9,460	14,266	21,513
PERIOD GEN SUPPLIES USED	4,160	6,273	9,460	14,266	21,513
UTILITIES--GEN	51,731	73,955	101,281	145,292	200,944
DEPRC ON FIXED ASSETS--GEN	936	2,705	4,285	5,708	6,999
UNCOLLECTIBLE ACCOUNTS	2,482	3,782	5,256	7,854	10,990
TOTAL GEN AND ADMIN EXP	116,510	164,050	224,839	314,480	431,564
TOTAL OPERATING EXPENSE	212,986	305,340	424,968	610,613	852,628
SALES MARGIN OVER DIRECT EXP	169,597	251,590	357,243	558,364	794,655
NET OPERATING INCOME	11,487	26,970	44,215	115,481	176,134
-INTEREST COST, SHORT-TERM	0	96	6,310	6,498	7,860
NET INCOME BEFORE INCOME TAX	11,487	26,874	37,905	108,983	168,274
-INCOME TAXES	8,629	16,399	25,860	44,967	88,387
NET INCOME AFTER INCOME TAX	2,858	10,475	12,044	64,016	79,887

Table 10.10 (continued)

ECOFURN

```
*****************************************
COST OF GOODS MANUFACTURED SCHEDULES
*****************************************
```

	1 1/0	2 2/0	3 3/0	4 4/0	5 5/0
PURCH DIRECT MFG MATERIAL	166,084	200,051	276,417	423,723	582,685
+BOP DIRECT MATERIAL INVY	0	27,681	37,955	52,395	79,353
-EOP DIRECT MATERIAL INVY	27,681	37,955	52,395	79,353	110,340
DIRECT REGULAR MATERIAL USED	138,403	189,776	261,977	396,766	551,698
PURCH PERIOD SUPPLIES	3,120	4,218	5,703	7,711	10,425
PERIOD SUPPLIES USED	3,120	4,218	5,703	7,711	10,425
DIRECT LABOR PAYROLL	75,018	104,037	142,535	213,243	297,477
PERIOD MFG ADMIN PAYROLL	41,600	56,243	76,041	102,807	138,995
UTILITIES--MFG	68,532	92,194	120,457	169,687	224,689
DEPRC ON FIXED ASSETS--MFG	1,300	3,822	6,198	8,446	10,585
COST OF GOODS INTO PROCESS	327,973	450,291	612,911	898,659	1,233,868
COST OF FINISHED GOODS	327,973	450,291	612,911	898,659	1,233,868

ECOFURN

```
*****************************************
COST OF GOODS SOLD SCHEDULES
*****************************************
```

	1 1/0	2 2/0	3 3/0	4 4/0	5 5/0
COST OF FINISHED GOODS	327,973	450,291	612,911	898,659	1,233,868
+BOP FINISHED GOODS INVY	0	29,816	43,655	59,654	86,987
-EOP FINISHED GOODS INVY	29,816	43,655	59,654	86,987	120,023
COST OF GOODS SOLD	298,157	436,452	596,911	871,327	1,200,832

Table 10.10 (continued)

ECOFURN
****
CASH FORECASTS AND FLOW ANALYSES
****

	1 1/0	2 2/0	3 3/0	4 4/0	5 5/0
CASH RECEIPTS FROM SALES	494,016	752,673	1,045,971	1,563,000	2,188,936
PAYMENTS ON ACCOUNT	371,302	492,111	662,848	960,202	1,313,740
PAYMENTS ON PAYROLLS	215,628	299,116	408,420	585,203	805,958
TOTAL OPERATING PAYMENTS	586,930	791,226	1,071,268	1,545,405	2,119,698
NET CASH FLOW ON OPERATIONS	-92,914	-38,553	-25,298	17,594	67,298
NET CHANGE SHORT-TERM CREDIT	0	797	51,787	1,564	11,356
-INTEREST, INCOME TAX COST	8,629	16,495	32,170	51,464	96,248
TOTAL NET CASH FLOW	-101,543	-54,251	-5,681	-32,306	-17,594
+BOP CASH AND SECURITIES	200,000	98,457	44,206	38,525	6,220
CASH AND SECURITIES EOP	98,457	44,206	38,525	6,220	-11,375

ECOFURN
****
RETAINED EARNINGS AND CAPITAL CHANGES
****

	1 1/0	2 2/0	3 3/0	4 4/0	5 5/0
BOP OWNER PAID-IN CAPITAL	200,000	200,000	200,000	200,000	200,000
EOP OWNER PAID-IN CAPITAL	200,000	200,000	200,000	200,000	200,000
BOP RETAINED EARNINGS	0	2,858	13,333	25,378	89,394
+NET INCOME	2,858	10,475	12,044	64,016	79,887
EOP RETAINED EARNINGS	2,858	13,333	25,378	89,394	169,280
EOP TOTAL OWNERS' EQUITY	202,858	213,333	225,378	289,394	369,280
EOP NO. SHARES OUTSTANDING	20,000	20,000	20,000	20,000	20,000
NET INCOME PER SHARE	0.14	0.52	0.60	3.20	3.99
EOP OWNERS' EQUITY PER SHARE	10.14	10.67	11.27	14.47	18.46

Table 10.10 (continued)

ECOFURN

```
*********************************
CONDITION STATEMENTS (BALANCE SHEETS)        EOP ALL COLUMNS EXCEPT FIRST
*********************************
```

****** ASSETS ******

	START EOP 1	1 1/0	2 2/0	3 3/0	4 4/0	5 5/0
CASH AND MARKET SECURITIES	200,000	98,457	44,206	38,525	6,220	-11,375
+ACCOUNTS RECEIVABLE GROSS	0	28,614	44,703	64,826	99,246	141,845
-UNCOLLECTIBLES RESERVE	0	2,482	6,265	11,521	19,375	30,365
CASH+SECURITIES+ACCT RECV	200,000	124,589	82,644	91,830	86,091	100,105
DIRECT MATERIAL INVY--MFG	0	27,681	37,955	52,395	79,353	110,340
FINISHED GOODS INVENTORY	0	29,816	43,655	59,654	86,987	120,023
TOTAL INVENTORIES	0	57,496	81,610	112,050	166,340	230,362
TOTAL CURRENT ASSETS	200,000	182,085	164,254	203,880	252,430	330,467
MFG FIXED ASSETS AT COST:						
CLASS 1	0	26,000	53,040	81,162	110,408	140,824
MFG FIXED ASSETS DEPRC RESERVES:						
CLASS 1	0	1,300	5,122	11,320	19,766	30,351
MFG FIXED ASSETS AT BOOK	0	24,700	47,918	69,842	90,642	110,473
GEN FIXED ASSETS AT COST:						
CLASS 1	0	12,480	25,459	38,958	52,996	67,596
GEN FIXED ASSETS DEPRC RESERVES:						
CLASS 1	0	936	3,641	7,926	13,634	20,633
GEN FIXED ASSETS AT BOOK	0	11,544	21,818	31,031	39,362	46,963
TOTAL ASSETS	200,000	218,329	233,991	304,753	382,434	487,903

Table 10.10 (continued)

CONDITION STATEMENTS (BALANCE SHEETS) (CONTINUED)

	START BOP 1	1 1/ 0	2 2/ 0	3 3/ 0	4 4/ 0	5 5/ 0
****** LIABILITIES AND OWNERS' EQUITY ******						
ACCOUNTS PAYABLE	0	15,471	19,860	26,791	38,892	53,119
SHORT-TERM LOANS AND NOTES	0	0	797	52,584	54,148	65,504
TOTAL CURRENT LIABILITIES	0	15,471	20,657	79,375	93,041	118,623
TOTAL LIABILITIES	0	15,471	20,657	79,375	93,041	118,623
TOTAL OWNERS' EQUITY	200,000	202,858	213,333	225,378	289,394	369,280
LIABILITIES & OWNER EQUITY	200,000	218,329	233,991	304,753	382,434	487,903

Table 10.10 (continued)

ECOFURN

```
*******************************
  SELECTED ACCOUNTS FOR ALL PERIODS
*******************************
```

CONDITION ITEMS ARE END-OF-PERIOD; 98 % CONFIDENCE LIMITS FOR MEANS WITH SAMPLE SIZE 15

	1 1/0	2 2/0	3 3/0	4 4/0	5 5/0
INDUSTRY SALES--000 OMIT					
MEANS	43,713	48,089	53,572	58,318	62,920
STANDARD DEVIATIONS	794	1,096	1,148	1,299	1,567
LOWER CONFIDENCE LIMITS	41,570	45,130	50,472	54,810	58,688
UPPER CONFIDENCE LIMITS	45,856	51,048	56,671	61,826	67,151
FIRM'S INDUSTRY SHARE %					
MEANS	1.24	1.60	1.98	2.75	3.54
STANDARD DEVIATIONS	0.03	0.04	0.06	0.06	0.10
LOWER CONFIDENCE LIMITS	1.15	1.50	1.82	2.59	3.26
UPPER CONFIDENCE LIMITS	1.33	1.70	2.15	2.91	3.82
FIRM NET SALES ACHIEVED					
MEANS	522,630	768,762	1,066,093	1,597,421	2,229,594
STANDARD DEVIATIONS	11,666	26,859	46,248	32,998	84,120
LOWER CONFIDENCE LIMITS	491,130	696,243	941,223	1,508,327	2,002,470
UPPER CONFIDENCE LIMITS	554,129	841,281	1,190,964	1,686,514	2,456,718
COST OF SALES					
MEANS	298,157	436,452	596,911	871,327	1,200,832
STANDARD DEVIATIONS	4,164	10,194	16,465	12,948	32,211
LOWER CONFIDENCE LIMITS	286,914	408,927	552,454	836,368	1,113,862
UPPER CONFIDENCE LIMITS	309,400	463,977	641,367	906,286	1,287,803
GROSS PROFIT ON SALES					
MEANS	224,473	332,310	469,182	726,093	1,028,762
STANDARD DEVIATIONS	7,737	16,764	29,970	20,419	52,144
LOWER CONFIDENCE LIMITS	203,582	287,048	388,263	670,963	887,974
UPPER CONFIDENCE LIMITS	245,363	377,572	550,102	781,224	1,169,551
TOTAL OPERATING EXPENSE					
MEANS	212,986	305,340	424,968	610,613	852,628
STANDARD DEVIATIONS	1,245	3,024	5,177	3,986	10,107
LOWER CONFIDENCE LIMITS	209,623	297,175	410,990	599,851	825,339
UPPER CONFIDENCE LIMITS	216,348	313,505	438,946	621,374	879,916
NET OPERATING INCOME					
MEANS	11,487	26,970	44,215	115,481	176,134
STANDARD DEVIATIONS	6,604	13,864	24,873	16,594	42,263
LOWER CONFIDENCE LIMITS	-6,343	-10,464	-22,941	70,676	62,025
UPPER CONFIDENCE LIMITS	29,317	64,404	111,370	160,285	290,243
NET INCOME AFTER TAX					
MEANS	2,858	10,475	12,044	64,016	79,887
STANDARD DEVIATIONS	4,710	8,794	17,553	9,963	24,487
LOWER CONFIDENCE LIMITS	-9,860	-13,268	-35,347	37,116	13,771
UPPER CONFIDENCE LIMITS	15,576	34,218	59,436	90,917	146,003

Table 10.10 (continued)

CASH AND MARKET SECURITIES					
MEANS	98,457	44,206	38,525	6,220	-11,375
STANDARD DEVIATIONS	3,385	5,007	8,513	20,288	31,357
LOWER CONFIDENCE LIMITS	89,317	30,687	15,540	-48,558	-96,038
UPPER CONFIDENCE LIMITS	107,597	57,726	61,511	60,997	73,288
CASH+SECURITIES+ACCT RECV					
MEANS	124,589	82,644	91,830	86,091	100,105
STANDARD DEVIATIONS	3,942	6,175	10,085	20,710	34,625
LOWER CONFIDENCE LIMITS	113,944	65,973	64,601	30,174	6,618
UPPER CONFIDENCE LIMITS	135,233	99,316	119,059	142,007	193,592
TOTAL INVENTORIES					
MEANS	57,496	81,610	112,050	166,340	230,362
STANDARD DEVIATIONS	975	2,444	3,900	3,057	7,402
LOWER CONFIDENCE LIMITS	54,865	75,011	101,519	158,086	210,376
UPPER CONFIDENCE LIMITS	60,128	88,209	122,581	174,594	250,349
TOTAL CURRENT ASSETS					
MEANS	182,085	164,254	203,880	252,430	330,467
STANDARD DEVIATIONS	4,844	8,411	13,221	21,654	40,732
LOWER CONFIDENCE LIMITS	169,005	141,544	168,182	193,965	220,492
UPPER CONFIDENCE LIMITS	195,165	186,965	239,577	310,896	440,443
TOTAL ASSETS					
MEANS	218,329	233,991	304,753	382,434	487,903
STANDARD DEVIATIONS	4,844	8,411	13,221	21,654	40,732
LOWER CONFIDENCE LIMITS	205,249	211,280	269,055	323,968	377,928
UPPER CONFIDENCE LIMITS	231,409	256,701	340,450	440,900	597,878
TOTAL CURRENT LIABILITIES					
MEANS	15,471	20,657	79,375	93,041	118,623
STANDARD DEVIATIONS	151	855	11,982	11,604	13,374
LOWER CONFIDENCE LIMITS	15,064	18,350	47,024	61,710	82,513
UPPER CONFIDENCE LIMITS	15,877	22,965	111,727	124,371	154,732
TOTAL LIABILITIES					
MEANS	15,471	20,657	79,375	93,041	118,623
STANDARD DEVIATIONS	151	855	11,982	11,604	13,374
LOWER CONFIDENCE LIMITS	15,064	18,350	47,024	61,710	82,513
UPPER CONFIDENCE LIMITS	15,877	22,965	111,727	124,371	154,732
TOTAL OWNERS' EQUITY					
MEANS	202,858	213,333	225,378	289,394	369,280
STANDARD DEVIATIONS	4,710	8,339	21,806	20,957	39,297
LOWER CONFIDENCE LIMITS	190,140	190,817	166,502	232,811	263,178
UPPER CONFIDENCE LIMITS	215,576	235,849	284,253	345,977	475,383
ALL FIXED ASSETS AT BOOK	11,544	21,818	31,031	39,362	46,963

forts to maintain either a 2 to 1 current ratio (ID 88) or 50% of the value of inventories (ID 95). Although mean interest expense (on short-term credit) occurs for Periods 2 to 5, final times interest earned ratio is usually undefined (FINANCIAL SUMMARY). This will occur if there is even one replication of the 15-run sample with no short-term credit (zero interest cost denominator of ratio).

Compare firm sales demand available from ENVIRONMENTAL ANALYSES statements with firm net sales achieved from INCOME statements. Sales achieved is slightly smaller for the first two years. On some sample replications, sales demand exceeded the input plant capacity of $600,000 in ID 212, but the capacity growth of 50% per year in ID 213 was able to absorb all extremes of demand after Period 2. No capacity extensions were programmed in IDs 75 to 78 (see discussion of inputs above). Capacity reductions of achieved sales are insignificant here.

In COST OF GOODS MANUFACTURED SCHEDULES, cost of goods into process is always equal to cost of finished goods. This occurs because goods-in-process inventories were assumed negligible for ECOFURN.

In CASH FORECASTS, note that mean net cash flow for every year is negative, even though there is some tendency for the deficit to decrease over the simulation.

In CONDITION STATEMENTS there are only two items, other than totals, in the first column. These are inputs from IDs 9 and 47.

Given the ECOFURN simulation discussed so far, the originating group of engineers finds such a scenario unsalable to investors. The high growth does not earn enough for high value. Estimates of going-concern present value at $186,812 are less than the planned $200,000 initial investment. This projects an expected loss under risk to the new investor group, especially since they will own only 60% of ECOFURN, or $112,087 of estimated going-concern value. Possibilities of large cash deficits compound the problem. As noted earlier, such deficits could reach toward an extreme of $300,000 over the five years, although not serious on average. If attempts were made to raise more cash either initially or at a later date, then this would only reduce the value of ECOFURN to founding owners. In such cases there would be more investors to share the same going-concern values. On average, ECOFURN does not have to plow in cash to cover operating losses. On the other hand, ECOFURN fails to develop surplus values for investors. This surplus could be used to finance growth, but there is not enough of it.

The decision of the ECOFURN originating group was to study projected performance more carefully. Some of this further study is discussed in the next section.

10.5 | Sensitivity Analysis with ECOFURN

Some additional studies of ECOFURN are discussed in this section. All inputs and outputs are adjustments to the first simulation of ECOFURN, which was examined in detail in section 10.4. All the information about ECOFURN from that section is necessary to the further development here.

The initial simulation of ECOFURN did not develop enough going-concern economic value to interest a new investor group. Furthermore, there was a substantial risk that a projected $200,000 initial cash investment would be inadequate. The situation was not hopeless; there was substantial growth and a positive mean income.

ECOFURN originators decided to review again the projections behind the simulation. One of the first things that stands out in Table 10.10 is wide swings of certain outputs. Thus Year 5 rate of return on owners's equity ranged from -334.3% to 37.83%, net income from -$159,586 to $194,551, and EOP cash balance from -$271,084 to $140,008 (see 5th and 6th columns of FINANCIAL SUMMARY in Table 10.10). What would happen if input risks were reduced somewhat? How *sensitive* is the simulation to shifts in projected *sales demand*? To study these questions, a simulation was run with sales demand risks cut in half, but no other changes. Outputs for VALUATION AND SCOPE and FINANCIAL SUMMARY divisions are reproduced in Table 10.11.

Specific changes of inputs were as follows:

ID 121 % maximum change in sales demand available to firm—in this case market share—to 12.5% from 25%

ID 131 % maximum change in industry sales to 10% from 20%

Several differences stand out in a comparison between outputs in Table 10.11 and the first two divisions of Table 10.10. The mean *return on owners' equity* has improved, in the case of final year from a negative figure to a respectable 20.36% (VALUATION AND SCOPE). Such an improvement will have a substantial impact on valuation (see below). The major reason for this improvement is a reduction in sampling variance of the mean. Compare the final year mean return on equity confidence limits of 16.56% to 21.42% in Table 10.11 with -66.26% to 62.5% in Table 10.10.

Maximum swings in period 5 for cash and net income have been substantially reduced (compare the last two columns in FINANCIAL SUMMARY between tables 10.11 and 10.10). Minimum EOP 5 cash is now -$69,445 instead of -271,084. Mean final cash is $32,257 in place of -$11,375. Investors could probably live with the new cash projection, or at most try to raise a small amount of additional capital. The probability of a cash deficit has been reduced to 27%, and its mean occurrence time is close to the end of the simulation. Returning to a comparison on methods of valuation under VALUATION AND SCOPE, going-concern value has improved to a satisfactory level in excess of $1 million. Risk has been reduced to the point where first-year investors' required rate of return has reached a rate free of business risk (5.8% equal to 4% inflation rate plus 1.8% basic money rate). Risk at the end of the run (EOP 5) assumes a normal level with an investors' required rate of 13.38%. Current going-concern value now exceeds EOP 5 value because risk is simulated at lower levels in early years. As compared to Table 10.10 results, there are three reasons for a dramatic improvement in going-concern value. Mean rates of return on equity have advanced, particularly for Year 5. Investor required rates have been reduced sharply

Table 10.11.

OUTPUT FOR ECOFURN WITH REDUCED RISK OF SALES DEMAND

```
*********************
 VALUATION AND SCOPE
*********************
ECOFURN--RERUN WITH REDUCED RISK OF SALES DEMAND

   5 PERIODS OVER  5.00 YEARS;  1.00 PERIODS PER YEAR, EACH  1.00 YEARS
****** SCOPE OF FIRM -- INITIAL SHARES 20000 -- FINAL SHARES 20000 -- EOP = END OF PERIOD ******
```

98 % CONFIDENCE LIMITS FOR MEANS WITH SAMPLE SIZE 15

			MEAN	STANDARD DEVIATION	98 % LOWER CONFIDENCE	98 % UPPER CONFIDENCE
SALES	TOTAL	FIRST YEAR	536,750	6,634	518,839	554,661
		FINAL YEAR	2,226,662	42,515	2,111,873	2,341,452
	PER SHARE	FIRST YEAR	26.84	0.33	25.94	27.73
		FINAL YEAR	111.33	2.13	105.59	117.07
EARNINGS	TOTAL	FIRST YEAR	8,924	2,324	2,649	15,198
		FINAL YEAR	81,411	10,571	52,871	109,952
	PER SHARE	FIRST YEAR	0.45	0.12	0.13	0.76
		FINAL YEAR	4.07	0.53	2.64	5.50
RETURN ON OWNERS' EQUITY %	TOTAL	FIRST YEAR	4.10	1.10	1.14	7.06
		FINAL YEAR	20.36	2.21	14.39	26.33
OWNERS' EQUITY	TOTAL	AT EOP 1	208,924	2,324	202,649	215,198
		END OF RUN	379,720	18,001	331,118	428,323
	PER SHARE	AT EOP 1	10.45	0.12	10.13	10.76
		END OF RUN	18.99	0.90	16.56	21.42
TOTAL ASSETS	TOTAL	AT EOP 1	224,591	2,380	218,165	231,016
		END OF RUN	531,170	16,992	485,291	577,049
	PER SHARE	AT EOP 1	11.23	0.12	10.91	11.55
		END OF RUN	26.56	0.85	24.26	28.85
CASH AND MARKETABLE SECURITIES	TOTAL	AT EOP 1	102,725	1,666	98,227	107,223
		END OF RUN	32,257	12,765	-2,208	66,721
	PER SHARE	AT EOP 1	5.14	0.08	4.91	5.36
		END OF RUN	1.61	0.64	-0.11	3.34

TECHNICAL INSOLVENCY OCCURRED WITH PROBABILITY .27 -- ON AVERAGE BEGAN DURING PERIOD 4.8
LEGAL INSOLVENCY DID NOT OCCUR

Table 10.11 (continued)

****** METHODS OF VALUATION ******

	FIRST YEAR OR EOP 1	FINAL YEAR OR END	FIRST YEAR PER SHARE	FINAL YEAR PER SHARE
MARKET VALUE WITH PRICE-EARNINGS MULTIPLES	1,427,218	1,149,065	71.36	57.45
PRICE-EARNINGS MULTIPLES	160	14		
GOING CONCERN ECONOMIC VALUE UNDER RISK	1,427,218	1,149,065	71.36	57.45
LIQUIDATION VALUE TO OWNERS	96,628	114,135	4.83	5.71
LIQUIDATION VALUE OF TANGIBLE ASSETS	112,295	265,585	5.61	13.28
FIXED ASSETS AT BOOK VALUE WITH INTANGIBLES	36,244	157,436	1.81	7.87
TAX LOSS CARRYFORWARD--INITIAL & END OF RUN	0	0		

****** PARAMETERS OF GOING-CONCERN VALUATION ******

	APPLIED EOP 1	APPLIED END OF RUN
INVESTORS' REQUIRED RATE OF RETURN %	5.80	13.38
INFLATION RATE %	4.00	4.00
LONG-TERM FIRM GROWTH RATE WITH INFLATION %	7.63	7.63
LONG-TERM REAL GROWTH RATE OF THE ECONOMY %	2.00	2.00
MEAN RATE OF RETURN ON INCREMENTAL ASSETS %	23.64	23.64

Table 10.11 (continued)

```
**********************************
   FINANCIAL SUMMARY FROM FINAL PERIOD
**********************************
```

ECOFURN--RERUN WITH REDUCED RISK OF SALES DEMAND

5 PERIODS OVER 5.00 YEARS; 1.00 PERIODS PER YEAR, EACH 1.00 YEARS
UNDEFINED RATIOS APPEAR '####--'; YEARLY VALUES ARE EXTRAPOLATED FROM THE FINAL PERIOD; 0 VALUES OMITTED

98 % CONFIDENCE LIMITS FOR MEANS WITH SAMPLE SIZE 15

	MEAN	STANDARD DEVIATION	98 % LOWER CONFIDENCE	98 % UPPER CONFIDENCE	MINIMUM	MAXIMUM
****** SCOPE OF FIRM ******						
FIRM'S SHARE OF INDUSTRY %	3.56	0.05	3.42	3.69	3.23	3.91
NET SALES OR REVENUE PER YEAR	2,226,662	42,515	2,111,871	2,341,452	1,878,556	2,443,651
CASH AND MARKETABLE SECURITIES	32,257	12,765	-2,208	66,722	-69,445	90,521
TOTAL ASSETS	531,170	16,992	485,291	577,048	380,327	604,449
TOTAL OWNERS' EQUITY	379,720	18,001	331,117	428,322	248,178	508,584
****** RATIO ANALYSIS OF PROFITABILITY ******						
GROSS MARGIN ON SALES %	46.04	0.32	45.17	46.90	43.47	48.00
NET OPERATING MARGIN ON SALES %	7.63	0.82	5.41	9.84	0.56	11.25
OPERATING EARNING POWER %	31.83	3.38	22.70	40.95	2.74	47.97
OPERAT'G EFFIC'Y OR CAP'L TURNS	4.23	0.09	3.98	4.47	3.64	4.94
RETURN ON OWNERS' EQUITY %	20.36	2.21	14.39	26.32	0.06	29.29
****** RATIO ANALYSIS OF FINANCIAL CONDITION ******						
CASH RATIO %	21.59	9.10	-2.98	46.16	-52.55	64.14
ACID TEST OR QUICK RATIO %	103.94	16.14	60.36	147.51	18.53	280.08
CURRENT RATIO %	273.80	36.01	176.57	371.02	168.67	720.62
DEBT TO TANGIBLE ASSETS %	28.80	1.89	23.69	33.90	10.01	35.83
DEBT TO TANGIBLE OWNER EQUITY %	41.67	3.32	32.70	50.63	11.13	55.83
TIMES INTEREST EARNED RATIO	#####,###.##	#####,###.##	#####,###.##	#####,###.##	1.03	#####,###.##
AVG COLLECTION PERIOD IN DAYS	18.25	0.00	18.25	18.25	18.25	18.25
INVENTORY TURNS PER YEAR	5.22	0.02	5.16	5.27	5.12	5.35

Table 10.11 (continued)

****** SELECTED FINANCIAL SUMMARY VALUES ******

INDUSTRY SALES PER YR--000 OMIT	62,605	784	60,488	64,721	57,349	66,260
COST OF SALES PER YEAR	1,199,740	16,962	1,153,942	1,245,537	1,061,894	1,292,579
GROSS PROFIT PER YEAR	1,026,922	26,010	956,695	1,097,149	816,662	1,161,220
OPERATING INCOME PER YEAR	174,620	20,751	118,592	230,647	10,426	273,743
NET INCOME BEFORE TAX PER YEAR	162,823	21,141	105,742	219,903	322	271,096
NET INCOME AFTER TAX PER YEAR	81,411	10,571	52,869	109,952	161	135,548
CASH+MKT SECURITIES+ACCTS RECV	143,590	14,190	105,277	181,903	24,483	197,655
TOTAL INVENTORIES	230,144	3,804	219,873	240,414	198,409	249,359
TOTAL CURRENT ASSETS	373,734	16,992	327,855	419,612	222,892	447,014
NET TANGIBLE FIXED ASSETS	157,436	0	157,436	157,436	157,436	157,436
ACCOUNTS PAYABLE	53,138	606	51,501	54,774	47,947	56,580
SHORT-TERM LOANS AND NOTES	98,312	10,177	70,834	125,789	0	145,216
TOTAL LIABILITIES	151,450	10,090	124,207	178,693	56,580	196,885
TOTAL PAID-IN OWNERS' EQUITY	200,000	0	200,000	200,000	200,000	200,000

as a consequence of reduced input risk. Investors' required rates are now substantially below the mean rate of return on incremental assets.

One thing which shows up clearly in comparisons of Table 10.11 with Table 10.10 is the importance to value and precision of the confidence interval for the mean rate of return on owners' equity. Since this return is a residual of all revenue and cost combinations over time, it is likely to become unstable, particularly under high growth and risk. The range of this rate of return in Table 10.10 is just too wide for precise conclusions. By experimenting with various sample sizes and risk levels, one could obtain an acceptable precision at appropriate risk levels. There is no built-in limit to sample size in PAVE; the practical limit is determined by processing time.

ECOFURN originators decided not to pursue further combinations of risk and sample size. What discouraged them was a reexamination of the original risk estimates. It certainly was reasonable for industry sales to vary 25% from forecast (ID 131), and to overestimate ECOFURN's market share by as much as 25% (ID 121). Original risk figures would probably be acceptable to an investor group; smaller risks would require supporting evidence not available. For these reasons the original risk IDs in Table 10.9 were restored (ID 121 = 25, ID 131 = 20).

ECOFURN originators returned again to examine figures in the strategic plan. The basis of each figure was studied in detail. Certain period costs were projected in the original inputs to grow at high rates. In many cases these rates exceeded sales growth. Recall again that inflation growth is added to input growth rates. Under normal cost behavior, on the other hand, period costs often grow more slowly than variable costs. Careful cost analysis revealed that growth rates of some period costs had been overestimated. The revised growth estimates of these costs are as follows:

ID 233   Growth of indirect manufacturing payroll, to 25% from 30%

ID 383   Growth of period selling expense, to 25% from 40%

ID 433   Growth of general administrative payroll, to 25% from 30%

ID 453   Growth of general utilities and period costs, to 25% from 35%

Table 10.12 shows three divisions of outputs from the above changes.

Referring to VALUATION AND SCOPE outputs in Table 10.12, earnings and rate of return on owners' equity do not improve over Table 10.10 for the first year because costs for that year have not been reduced. For the final year, however, both accounts are now at healthy levels. The confidence limits for mean return on owners' equity for the fifth year are reasonable (unlike Table 10.10 figures). It is now possible to estimate value with reasonable precision. The present and future going-concern values have reached sufficient levels to hold out windfalls to prospective investors. An ECOFURN investor group, for example, would be looking at an expected present value of about $600,000, which is 60% of $1,000,000. This compares favorably with an initial cash outlay of $200,000. Return on incremental asset improves to 42.39%, and this rate is well above investors' required rates of return in the 15% to 16% range.

Table 10.12.

OUTPUT FOR ECOFURN WITH REDUCED GROWTH OF SELECTED COSTS

```
****************************
   VALUATION AND SCOPE
****************************
```

ECOFURN--RERUN WITH REDUCED GROWTH OF SELECTED COSTS

5 PERIODS OVER 5.00 YEARS; 1.00 PERIODS PER YEAR, EACH 1.00 YEARS

****** SCOPE OF FIRM -- INITIAL SHARES 20000 -- FINAL SHARES 20000 -- EOP = END OF PERIOD ******

98 % CONFIDENCE LIMITS FOR MEANS WITH SAMPLE SIZE 15

			MEAN	STANDARD DEVIATION	98 % LOWER CONFIDENCE	98 % UPPER CONFIDENCE
SALES	TOTAL	FIRST YEAR	522,630	11,666	491,130	554,129
		FINAL YEAR	2,229,594	84,120	2,002,470	2,456,718
	PER SHARE	FIRST YEAR	26.13	0.58	24.56	27.71
		FINAL YEAR	111.48	4.21	100.12	122.84
EARNINGS	TOTAL	FIRST YEAR	2,858	4,710	-9,860	15,576
		FINAL YEAR	170,938	21,761	112,184	229,693
	PER SHARE	FIRST YEAR	0.14	0.24	-0.49	0.78
		FINAL YEAR	8.55	1.09	5.61	11.48
RETURN ON OWNERS' EQUITY %		FIRST YEAR	0.56	2.64	-6.56	7.67
		FINAL YEAR	29.45	2.96	21.47	37.42
OWNERS' EQUITY	TOTAL	AT EOP 1	202,858	4,710	190,140	215,576
		END OF RUN	545,833	36,483	447,330	644,336
	PER SHARE	AT EOP 1	10.14	0.24	9.51	10.78
		END OF RUN	27.29	1.82	22.37	32.22
TOTAL ASSETS	TOTAL	AT EOP 1	218,329	4,844	205,249	231,409
		END OF RUN	614,864	29,665	534,768	694,961
	PER SHARE	AT EOP 1	10.92	0.24	10.26	11.57
		END OF RUN	30.74	1.48	26.74	34.75
CASH AND MARKETABLE SECURITIES	TOTAL	AT EOP 1	98,457	3,385	89,317	107,597
		END OF RUN	117,551	20,815	61,350	173,752
	PER SHARE	AT EOP 1	4.92	0.17	4.47	5.38
		END OF RUN	5.88	1.04	3.07	8.69

TECHNICAL INSOLVENCY OCCURRED WITH PROBABILITY .07 -- ON AVERAGE BEGAN DURING PERIOD 4
LEGAL INSOLVENCY DID NOT OCCUR

Table 10.12 (continued)

****** METHODS OF VALUATION ******

	FIRST YEAR OR EOP 1	FINAL YEAR OR END	FIRST YEAR PER SHARE	FINAL YEAR PER SHARE
MARKET VALUE WITH PRICE-EARNINGS MULTIPLES	1,001,277	1,837,858	50.06	91.89
PRICE-EARNINGS MULTIPLES	350	11		
GOING CONCERN ECONOMIC VALUE UNDER RISK	1,001,277	1,837,858	50.06	91.89
LIQUIDATION VALUE TO OWNERS	93,694	238,401	4.68	11.92
LIQUIDATION VALUE OF TANGIBLE ASSETS	109,164	307,432	5.45	15.37
FIXED ASSETS AT BOOK VALUE WITH INTANGIBLES	36,244	157,436	1.81	7.87
TAX LOSS CARRYFORWARD--INITIAL & END OF RUN	0	224		

****** PARAMETERS OF GOING-CONCERN VALUATION ******

	APPLIED EOP 1	APPLIED END OF RUN
INVESTORS' REQUIRED RATE OF RETURN %	15.34	16.62
INFLATION RATE %	4.00	4.00
LONG-TERM FIRM GROWTH RATE WITH INFLATION %	7.63	7.63
LONG-TERM REAL GROWTH RATE OF THE ECONOMY %	2.00	2.00
MEAN RATE OF RETURN ON INCREMENTAL ASSETS %	42.39	42.39

Table 10.12 (continued)

```
*********************************
FINANCIAL SUMMARY FROM FINAL PERIOD
*********************************
```

ECOFURN--RERUN WITH REDUCED GROWTH OF SELECTED COSTS

5 PERIODS OVER 5.00 YEARS; 1.00 PERIODS PER YEAR, EACH 1.00 YEARS
UNDEFINED RATIOS APPEAR '####--'; YEARLY VALUES ARE EXTRAPOLATED FROM THE FINAL PERIOD; 0 VALUES OMITTED

98 % CONFIDENCE LIMITS FOR MEANS WITH SAMPLE SIZE 15

	MEAN	STANDARD DEVIATION	98 % LOWER CONFIDENCE	98 % UPPER CONFIDENCE	MINIMUM	MAXIMUM
****** SCOPE OF FIRM ******						
FIRM'S SHARE OF INDUSTRY %	3.54	0.10	3.27	3.81	2.90	4.24
NET SALES OR REVENUE PER YEAR	2,229,594	84,120	2,002,470	2,456,718	1,562,400	2,671,352
CASH AND MARKETABLE SECURITIES	117,551	20,815	61,350	173,751	27,374	301,750
TOTAL ASSETS	614,864	29,665	534,768	694,959	449,764	860,118
TOTAL OWNERS' EQUITY	545,833	36,483	447,328	644,337	282,974	805,593
****** RATIO ANALYSIS OF PROFITABILITY ******						
GROSS MARGIN ON SALES %	46.68	0.65	44.92	48.43	40.74	49.55
NET OPERATING MARGIN ON SALES %	14.68	1.49	10.65	18.70	0.77	21.01
OPERATING EARNING POWER %	53.65	5.37	39.15	68.14	2.67	75.73
OPERAT'G EFFIC'Y OR CAP'L TURNS	3.66	0.09	3.41	3.90	3.11	4.26
RETURN ON OWNERS' EQUITY %	29.45	2.96	21.45	37.44	-1.19	40.86
****** RATIO ANALYSIS OF FINANCIAL CONDITION ******						
CASH RATIO %	220.15	42.98	104.10	336.19	27.28	553.41
ACID TEST OR QUICK RATIO %	420.37	56.72	267.22	573.51	74.11	798.38
CURRENT RATIO %	829.41	89.10	588.84	1,069.98	175.27	1,288.73
DEBT TO TANGIBLE ASSETS %	12.32	2.49	5.59	19.04	6.34	37.08
DEBT TO TANGIBLE OWNER EQUITY %	15.65	4.04	4.74	26.55	6.77	58.94
TIMES INTEREST EARNED RATIO	#####,###.##	#####,###.##	#####,###.##	#####,###.##	#####,###.##	###.##
AVG COLLECTION PERIOD IN DAYS	18.25	0.00	18.25	18.25	18.25	18.25
INVENTORY TURNS PER YEAR	5.19	0.03	5.10	5.27	5.04	5.49

Table 10.12 (continued)

```
******  SELECTED FINANCIAL SUMMARY VALUES  ******
```

INDUSTRY SALES PER YR--000 DMIT	62,920	1,567	58,689	67,150	52,409	70,231
COST OF SALES PER YEAR	1,181,510	32,208	1,094,548	1,268,471	925,934	1,354,086
GROSS PROFIT PER YEAR	1,048,084	52,147	907,287	1,188,880	636,466	1,323,591
OPERATING INCOME PER YEAR	344,592	42,434	230,020	459,163	11,989	561,305
NET INCOME BEFORE TAX PER YEAR	342,100	43,394	224,936	459,263	-3,357	561,305
NET INCOME AFTER TAX PER YEAR	170,938	21,761	112,183	229,692	-3,357	280,653
CASH+MKT SECURITIES+ACCTS RECV	229,031	23,847	164,644	293,417	123,614	435,318
TOTAL INVENTORIES	228,398	7,406	208,401	248,394	168,715	267,364
TOTAL CURRENT ASSETS	457,429	29,665	377,333	537,524	292,328	702,682
NET TANGIBLE FIXED ASSETS	157,436	0	157,436	157,436	157,436	157,436
ACCOUNTS PAYABLE	48,263	1,117	45,247	51,278	38,903	54,525
SHORT-TERM LOANS AND NOTES	20,768	11,295	-9,728	51,264	0	127,887
TOTAL LIABILITIES	69,031	10,503	40,672	97,389	44,150	166,790
TOTAL PAID-IN OWNERS' EQUITY	200,000	0	200,000	200,000	200,000	200,000

```
*****************************************************
      FINANCIAL STATEMENTS PROJECTED FOR ALL PERIODS
*****************************************************
```

ADMIN	ADMINISTRATIVE	DEPRC	DEPRECIATION	GEN	GENERAL
AMORT	AMORTIZATION	EOP	END OF PERIOD	INVY	INVENTORY
BOP	BEGINNING OF PERIOD	GEN	GENERAL	MFG	MANUFACTURING
MISC	MISCELLANEOUS	PURCH	PURCHASES OF	R&D	RESEARCH AND DEVELOPMENT

5 PERIODS OVER 5.00 YEARS; 1.00 PERIODS PER YEAR, EACH 1.00 YEARS

VALUES ARE ACCOUNT MEANS; ACCOUNT OMITTED WHEN ALL VALUES 0
HEADINGS ARE: PERIOD NO. AND YEAR/MONTH; OR CUMULATIVE *FOR YEAR NO.*

Table 10.12 (continued)

ECOFIRM--RERUN WITH REDUCED GROWTH OF SELECTED COSTS

```
*************************************
ENVIRONMENTAL ANALYSES OF FIRM
*************************************
```

INDUSTRY BASE SALES--000S OMITTED; YEAR= 40000 -- PERIOD= 40000

	1 1/.0	2 2/.0	3 3/.0	4 4/.0	5 5/.0
INFLATION RATE ANNUAL %	4.00	4.00	4.00	4.00	4.00
REAL ECONOMY GROWTH ANNUAL %	2.00	2.00	2.00	2.00	2.00
INDUSTRY TOTAL GROWTH %	9.26	9.26	9.26	9.26	9.26
SEASONAL/CYCLICAL INDICES	1.00	1.00	1.00	1.00	1.00
INDUSTRY SALES--000S OMITTED	43,713	48,089	53,572	58,318	62,920
FIRM'S INDUSTRY SHARE %	1.24	1.60	1.98	2.75	3.54
FIRM SALES DEMAND AVAILABLE	541,300	771,607	1,066,093	1,597,421	2,229,594

Table 10.12 (continued)

ECOFURN--RERUN WITH REDUCED GROWTH OF SELECTED COSTS

```
*************
INCOME STATEMENTS
*************
```

	1 1/0	2 2/0	3 3/0	4 4/0	5 5/0
FIRM NET SALES ACHIEVED	522,630	768,762	1,066,093	1,597,421	2,229,594
-COST OF SALES	298,157	434,499	591,523	860,461	1,181,510
GROSS PROFIT ON SALES	224,473	334,263	474,570	736,959	1,048,084
R&D MATERIAL AND MISC EXP	13,066	19,219	26,652	39,936	55,740
TOTAL R&D EXPENSE	13,066	19,219	26,652	39,936	55,740
DIRECT SALES PAYROLL	41,810	61,501	85,287	127,794	178,368
PERIOD ADVERTISE, MISC SALES	41,600	54,080	70,304	91,395	118,814
TOTAL SALES EXPENSE	83,410	115,581	155,591	219,189	297,181
PERIOD GEN ADMIN PAYROLL	57,200	74,360	96,668	125,668	163,369
PURCH GEN SUPPLIES	4,160	6,273	9,460	14,266	21,513
PERIOD GEN SUPPLIES USED	4,160	6,273	9,460	14,266	21,513
UTILITIES--GEN	51,751	68,477	86,832	115,338	147,700
DEPRC ON FIXED ASSETS--GEN	936	2,705	4,285	5,708	6,999
UNCOLLECTIBLE ACCOUNTS	2,482	3,782	5,256	7,854	10,990
TOTAL GEN AND ADMIN EXP	116,510	155,598	202,502	268,834	350,571
TOTAL OPERATING EXPENSE	212,986	290,398	384,745	527,958	703,492
SALES MARGIN OVER DIRECT EXP	169,597	253,543	362,631	569,230	813,977
NET OPERATING INCOME	11,487	43,866	89,825	209,001	344,592
-INTEREST COST, SHORT-TERM	0	0	2,360	2,029	2,492
NET INCOME BEFORE INCOME TAX	11,487	43,866	87,465	206,972	342,100
-INCOME TAXES	8,629	22,071	45,575	98,620	171,162
NET INCOME AFTER INCOME TAX	2,858	21,794	41,890	108,353	170,938

Table 10.12 (continued)

ECOFURN--RERUN WITH REDUCED GROWTH OF SELECTED COSTS
```
********************************
COST OF GOODS MANUFACTURED SCHEDULES
********************************
```

	1 1/ 0	2 2/ 0	3 3/ 0	4 4/ 0	5 5/ 0
PURCH DIRECT MFG MATERIAL	166,084	200,051	276,417	423,723	582,685
+BOP DIRECT MATERIAL INVY	0	27,681	37,955	52,395	79,353
-EOP DIRECT MATERIAL INVY	27,681	37,955	52,395	79,353	110,340
DIRECT REGULAR MATERIAL USED	138,403	189,776	261,977	396,766	551,698
PURCH PERIOD SUPPLIES	3,120	4,218	5,703	7,711	10,425
PERIOD SUPPLIES USED	3,120	4,218	5,703	7,711	10,425
DIRECT LABOR PAYROLL	75,018	104,037	142,535	213,243	297,477
PERIOD MFG ADMIN PAYROLL	41,600	54,080	70,304	91,395	118,814
UTILITIES-MFG	68,532	92,194	120,457	169,687	224,689
DEPRC ON FIXED ASSETS--MFG	1,300	3,822	6,198	8,446	10,585
COST OF GOODS INTO PROCESS	327,973	448,128	607,174	887,247	1,213,687
COST OF FINISHED GOODS	327,973	448,128	607,174	887,247	1,213,687

ECOFURN--RERUN WITH REDUCED GROWTH OF SELECTED COSTS
```
********************************
COST OF GOODS SOLD SCHEDULES
********************************
```

	1 1/ 0	2 2/ 0	3 3/ 0	4 4/ 0	5 5/ 0
COST OF FINISHED GOODS	327,973	448,128	607,174	887,247	1,213,687
+BOP FINISHED GOODS INVY	0	29,816	43,445	59,096	85,882
-EOP FINISHED GOODS INVY	29,816	43,445	59,096	85,882	118,058
COST OF GOODS SOLD	298,157	434,499	591,523	860,461	1,181,510

Table 10.12 (continued)

ECOFURN--RERUN WITH REDUCED GROWTH OF SELECTED COSTS

```
***********************************
CASH FORECASTS AND FLOW ANALYSES
***********************************
```

	1 1/ 0	2 2/ 0	3 3/ 0	4 4/ 0	5 5/ 0
CASH RECEIPTS FROM SALES	494,016	752,673	1,045,971	1,563,000	2,186,996
PAYMENTS ON ACCOUNT	371,302	480,622	631,329	894,624	1,194,531
PAYMENTS ON PAYROLLS	215,628	293,978	394,795	558,100	758,027
TOTAL OPERATING PAYMENTS	586,930	774,600	1,026,124	1,452,724	1,952,557
NET CASH FLOW ON OPERATIONS	-92,914	-21,926	19,847	110,276	234,438
NET CHANGE SHORT-TERM CREDIT	0	0	19,663	-2,758	3,863
-INTEREST, INCOME TAX COST	8,629	22,071	47,935	100,648	173,654
TOTAL NET CASH FLOW	-101,543	-43,998	-8,425	6,869	64,647
+BOP CASH AND SECURITIES	200,000	98,457	54,459	46,034	52,904
CASH AND SECURITIES EOP	98,457	54,459	46,034	52,904	117,551

ECOFURN--RERUN WITH REDUCED GROWTH OF SELECTED COSTS

```
***********************************
RETAINED EARNINGS AND CAPITAL CHANGES
***********************************
```

	1 1/ 0	2 2/ 0	3 3/ 0	4 4/ 0	5 5/ 0
BOP OWNER PAID-IN CAPITAL	200,000	200,000	200,000	200,000	200,000
EOP OWNER PAID-IN CAPITAL	200,000	200,000	200,000	200,000	200,000
BOP RETAINED EARNINGS	0	2,858	24,652	66,542	174,895
+NET INCOME	2,858	21,794	41,890	108,353	170,938
EOP RETAINED EARNINGS	2,858	24,652	66,542	174,895	345,833
EOP TOTAL OWNERS' EQUITY	202,858	224,652	266,542	374,895	545,833
EOP NO. SHARES OUTSTANDING	20,000	20,000	20,000	20,000	20,000
NET INCOME PER SHARE	0.14	1.09	2.09	5.42	8.55
EOP OWNERS' EQUITY PER SHARE	10.14	11.23	13.33	18.74	27.29

Table 10.12 (continued)

```
ECOFURN--RERUN WITH REDUCED GROWTH OF SELECTED COSTS
***********************************
CONDITION STATEMENTS (BALANCE SHEETS)          EOP ALL COLUMNS EXCEPT FIRST
***********************************
```

	START BOP 1	1 1/0	2 2/0	3 3/0	4 4/0	5 5/0
****** ASSETS ******						
CASH AND MARKET SECURITIES	200,000	98,457	54,459	46,034	52,904	117,551
+ACCOUNTS RECEIVABLE GROSS	0	28,614	44,703	64,826	99,246	141,845
-UNCOLLECTIBLES RESERVE	0	2,482	6,265	11,521	19,375	30,365
CASH+SECURITIES+ACCT RECV	200,000	124,589	92,897	99,339	132,775	229,031
DIRECT MATERIAL INVY--MFG	0	27,681	37,955	52,395	79,353	110,340
FINISHED GOODS INVENTORY	0	29,816	43,445	59,096	85,882	118,058
TOTAL INVENTORIES	0	57,496	81,400	111,491	165,235	228,398
TOTAL CURRENT ASSETS	200,000	182,085	174,297	210,830	298,010	457,429
MFG FIXED ASSETS AT COST: CLASS 1	0	26,000	53,040	81,162	110,408	140,824
MFG FIXED ASSETS DEPRC RESERVES: CLASS 1	0	1,300	5,122	11,320	19,766	30,351
MFG FIXED ASSETS AT BOOK	0	24,700	47,918	69,842	90,642	110,473
GEN FIXED ASSETS AT COST: CLASS 1	0	12,480	25,459	38,958	52,996	67,596
GEN FIXED ASSETS DEPRC RESERVES: CLASS 1	0	936	3,641	7,926	13,634	20,633
GEN FIXED ASSETS AT BOOK	0	11,544	21,818	31,031	39,362	46,963
TOTAL ASSETS	200,000	218,329	244,033	311,703	428,014	614,864

Table 10.12 (continued)

CONDITION STATEMENTS (BALANCE SHEETS) (CONTINUED)

	START BOP 1	1 1/0	2 2/0	3 3/0	4 4/0	5 5/0
****** LIABILITIES AND OWNERS' EQUITY ******						
ACCOUNTS PAYABLE	0	15,471	19,381	25,498	36,214	48,263
SHORT-TERM LOANS AND NOTES	0	0	0	19,663	16,905	20,768
TOTAL CURRENT LIABILITIES	0	15,471	19,381	45,161	53,118	69,031
TOTAL LIABILITIES	0	15,471	19,381	45,161	53,118	69,031
TOTAL OWNERS' EQUITY	200,000	202,858	224,652	266,542	374,895	545,833
LIABILITIES & OWNER EQUITY	200,000	218,329	244,033	311,703	428,014	614,864

Final capitalization of earnings reaches a reasonable multiple of 11. The initial multiple of 350 simply reflects an extremely low starting level of $2558 mean earnings. With some relief in the growth of costs, earnings grow much more rapidly in Table 10.12 than in either of the two preceding simulations (tables 10.10 and 10.11).

Looking at the last two columns of FINANCIAL SUMMARY in Table 10.12, negative cash balance EOP 5 is not encountered. There is a small probability of 0.07 that ECOFURN will run out of cash around EOP 4. Under this projection most investors would conclude that initial cash is adequate.

ECOFURN originators decided that the strategic plan and valuation from Table 10.12 were adequate to interest high-risk investors. The outputs were also considered a fair representation of ECOFURN's prospects. In situations of high growth, costs and values are very sensitive to small changes in policy.

11 Extended System of PAVE Inputs

11.1 | Dynamic Input Sets with Discontinuities

Input features are available to extend the power of PAVE beyond the basic system described in chapter 8. These features may be used selectively to meet particular situations. They are divided into five groups in this chapter. Use the chapter for reference while working with the extended cases of chapter 12. Additional inputs are available to simulate discontinuities in dynamic behavior over time. These are described and illustrated in the remaining paragraphs of this section. A DATA STATEMENT input mode is available for PAVE; this is discussed in section 11.2. Section 11.3 is a general summary of the management of PAVE files. More inputs are available to describe operating behavior than defined in section 8.5; these inputs are examined in section 11.4. The PAVE system of economic valuation, as described in section 9.2, pointed out that it was unnecessary to input parameters for valuation; most parameters could be determined internally. There are occasions, however, when it is desirable to impose external financial and valuation parameters on the system. Section 11.5 gives some rules for user control of such parameters.

Dynamic input sets of IDs are provided in PAVE to describe policy and behavior over simulated periods. (Refer to Section 8.2, which lists the fundamental rules.) For each dynamic input set, the right-hand or units digits are assigned in a uniform pattern. ID position −0 is used for an *input parameter*, if any, which is *related* to a corresponding dynamic input set. ID position −1 is used to specify input uncertainty of a dynamic input set. It is available for up to 12 input sets only. A dynamic input set itself starts with ID position −2. A *base* value is entered in ID position −2. An annual growth rate of the base value, which is applied to periods beyond the first, is entered in ID position −3. This reviews the fundamental system which was described and illustrated in section 8.2. The fundamental system may be extended to simulate discontinuities and changes in growth rates. This is accomplished through nonzero entries in the remaining ID positions −4 through −9. Like the system of ID position

283

–0 to –3, the input rules for IDs –4 to –9 apply to all dynamic input sets. The complete set of rules is summarized in Table 11.1. The rules combine into a minilanguage which describes dynamic behavior over simulated periods.

————————Table 11.1————————

RULES FOR THE SYSTEM OF DYNAMIC INPUT SETS

ID position	Behavior rules for dynamic input sets
–0	Input parameter, if any, related to dynamic input set.
–1	Input uncertainty, if any available, for dynamic input set.
–2	*Base* value of dynamic input for Period 1; may be zero, positive, or negative (if allowed under particular input set).
–3	*Annual* percentage change in *base* value for dynamic behavior over periods; applies to Period 2 and up. *Positive* entry will increase *base* value, *negative* entry will decrease it. Zero or nonentry will apply *base* value over following periods unchanged.
–4	Last period *number* of dynamic schedule from –2 and –3 allows for a discontinuity after the period number of –3. By special rule, any entry other than a valid period number will continue the –2 and –3 schedule over the remainder of the simulation. In such cases nonzero entries in ID positions –5 to –9 will be disregarded. Then zero or nonentry here will merely extend –2 and –3 schedule over the whole simulation.
–5	A second *base* value will be applied to the *next* period above the number in –4, except for entry of (-1). The latter signals a continuation of the value series from –2 and –3 schedule, but at a new growth rate entered in –6. The input value generated for the period number of –4 starts to grow at the rate of –6 in the next period number to –4, and beyond.
–6	A second *annual* growth rate which has the same effect on the second base value in –5 as –3 rate had on the first base in –2.
–7	Last period *number* of dynamic schedule from –5 and –6 provides for a second discontinuity and growth rate. This ID position follows the same rules as –4. A valid period number here must be at least one higher than –4 entry.
–8	A third *base* value follows identical rules to –5, including the (-1) signal.
–9	A third *annual* growth rate follows the same rules as –6. A third dynamic schedule from –8 and –9 will continue to the end of the simulation.

The best way to understand dynamic input sets is through illustrations. For eleven cases in Table 11.2 assume that eight periods are being simulated over a total span of two years (each period is one-quarter year). Various levels of complexity are exemplified. Inputs are confined to ID positions −2 through −9 because that group determines value dynamics over periods. If a nonzero uncertainty input were entered in an ID position −1, then values over periods become the *means* of probability distributions. Growth value series are computed as compound amounts with fractional exponents. Your figures may deviate slightly from these because numerical approximations of exponential functions differ among computers and calculators. The figures shown here are rounded to the fourth decimal place. Calculations for each case are summarized in Table 11.2.

One column of Table 11.2 is assigned to each case. The first eight items in each column are user inputs under ID positions −2 to −9. In PAVE2 user inputs are processed into values which will be applied to each period. The last eight items per column show processed means which will be applied to the simulation for each period.

————————Table 11.2————————
ILLUSTRATIONS OF DYNAMIC INPUT SETS

			INPUT ID POSITIONS			
Case	1	2	3	4	5	6
−2	0	50000	5	5	5	10000
−3	0	0	10	10	10	−4
−4	0	0	0	8	4	5
−5	0	0	0	6	0	5000
−6	0	0	0	7	0	0
−7	0	0	0	3	0	0
−8	0	0	0	0	0	0
−9	0	0	0	0	0	0

PROCESSED INPUT MEANS FOR EACH PERIOD

1	0	50,000	5	5	5	10,000
2	0	50,000	5.1206	5.1206	5.1206	9,898.46
3	0	50,000	5.2440	5.2440	5.2440	9,797.96
4	0	50,000	5.3705	5.3705	5.3705	9,698.47
5	0	50,000	5.5	5.5	0	9,600
6	0	50,000	5.6326	5.6326	0	5,000
7	0	50,000	5.7684	5.7684	0	5,000
8	0	50,000	5.9075	5.9075	0	5,000

Table 11.2 (continued)

INPUT ID POSITIONS (continued)

Cases	7	8	9	10	11
−2	10000	10000	10000	7	7
−3	−4	8	8	10	10
−4	5	3	3	3	3
−5	−1	−2000	−1	9	−1
−6	0	−5	−5	0	0
−7	0	0	0	6	6
−8	0	0	0	10	−1
−9	0	0	0	−6	−6

PROCESSED INPUT MEANS FOR EACH PERIOD (continued)

1	10,000	10,000	10,000	7	7
2	9,898.46	10,194.26	10,194.26	7.1688	7.1688
3	9,797.96	10,392.30	10,392.30	7.3417	7.3417
4	9,698.47	−2,000	10,259.89	9	7.3417
5	9,600	−1,974.52	10,129.17	9	7.3417
6	9,600	−1,949.36	10,000.11	9	7.3417
7	9,600	−1,924.52	9,872.69	10	7.2290
8	9,600	−1,900.00	9,746.90	9.8469	7.1180

Case 1 is a set of inputs in IDs 102 to 109, % ANNUAL REAL GROWTH RATE OF ECONOMY. Since all the ID positions are zero or nonentry, zero real growth will be applied to all periods. Case 2 is a set of entries in IDs 212 to 219 for $ CAPACITY OF PLANT PER PERIOD. The base amount per ID 212 for Period 1 is $50,000; the growth rate per ID 213 is zero. In this case the base value will be extended to all periods, since a valid period number does not appear under ID 214. Zero or nonentry in ID 214 is a signal to extend the first schedule over all periods. To apply a constant value over all periods, make just one entry in ID position −2.

Cases 3 to 5 show several input patterns in IDs 112 to 119, % ANNUAL AVERAGE INFLATION RATE. In all these cases the Period 1 base amount is 5% (ID 112), which grows at an annual rate of 10% (ID 113). Since growth starts at the second period, inflation should be 10% higher by a year later. This conclusion is confirmed by the 5.5% rate in the fifth period for cases 3 and 4. Increases for each quarter year are compounded by fractional exponents in compound amount factors. This system insures that annual input rates will be reached independently of the number of periods per year. Case 3 has a zero entry in ID 114, which signals a continuation of the original schedule over all periods. Since the last period number was entered in ID 114 of Case 4, there is no difference in values between cases 3 and 4. An entry of zero in ID 114 of Case 4, or some number greater than eight, would have had exactly the same effect. Note that if the last period number is entered in ID 114, entries in IDs 115 to 119 will be disregarded. In Case 5 the entry in ID 114 terminates the original base and growth schedule at Period 4. Since the next base value is zero in ID 115, values are zeros for all remaining periods. Because all time rate inputs in PAVE are annual, rates developed for each period are also annual. In this example there are four periods per year, so about one-quarter of annual rates will be applied as factors for each period. Thus inflation rates from ID set 112 actually applied to periods will be about 1.0241, which compounds over four periods to 1.1. The foregoing remarks about annual and period rates apply to all dynamic input sets of time rates.

Cases 6 to 9 illustrate sets of inputs for IDs 482 to 489, $ GENERAL FIXED ASSETS CLASS 1 NET CHANGES PER PERIOD. For cases 6 and 7 the first schedule continues to Period 5. Starting with a Period 1 $10,000 base, in ID 482, amounts decrease at an annual rate of 4% per ID 483. Note that in the fifth period assets increment by $9600, which is 96% of the value of $10,000 one year before. For Case 6 a new base of $5000, which starts during Period 6, is established by ID 485 input. Zero entries in IDs 486 to 489 extend $5000 unchanged over remaining periods. Case 7 is the same as Case 6 except that (-1) was entered in place of 5000 in ID 485. This is an indicator to stay with the amount generated in Period 5, but to change the annual growth rate per ID 486 entry. Since both IDs 486 and 487 are zero or nonentry, the Period 5 value is merely extended over all remaining periods.

Case 8 is similar to Case 6 except that now the second base entry in ID 485 will decline at 5% per year (ID 486) instead of remaining constant. The first growth schedule in Case 8 uses different figures from Case 6. The $10,000 in Period 1 grows at 8% annually through the third period (ID 484). Notice that the second base value itself is negative in Case 8 (-$2000 in ID 485). In PAVE only a few negative base values (ID positions −2, −5, and −8) are permitted (see section 8.5 or the Appendix). Negative annual growth rates (ID positions −3, −6, and −9), however, are always operational. Returning to Case 8, the original -$2000 in Period 4 has decreased in magnitude to -$1900 a year later during Period 8 (per -5 entry in ID 486). In Case 9 the -2000 entry in ID 485 has been replaced by the (-1) indicator. This means that the $10,392.30 growth of assets reached during Period 3 will be subjected to a new growth rate starting with Period 4. This new rate is -5% annually per ID 486. The zero in ID 487 extends the second negative growth schedule to the end of the simulation. Case 9 starts with $10,000 during Period 1. This amount grows at 8% per year until Period 3, at which time it has reached $10,392.30. Starting with Period 4, values now decline from Period 3 figure at a 5% annual rate.

Cases 10 and 11 are examples of input set IDs 572 to 579, % LONG-TERM INTEREST RATE ANNUAL. The base value is 7%, which grows 10% per year (ID 573) through Period 3 (ID 574). Referring to Case 10, there is a new base value of 9% (ID

575) in Period 4. This does not grow (zero input in ID 576), but its schedule is terminated in Period 6 per ID 577. A third base value of 10% (ID 578) is started at the next period (Period 7), and this value declines 6% annually per ID 579. The third schedule continues automatically to the end of the simulation. Case 10 illustrates two discontinuities in simulated behavior over the period. Three separate growth schedules with two discontinuities is the maximum variety available from dynamic input sets. Case 11 is the same as Case 10 except that (–1) signals have been substituted for new base values in Periods 4 and 7 (IDs 575 and 578). This means that the Period 3 value will grow at a new annual rate per ID 576, and that the Period 6 value will decline at a second new annual rate per ID 579. These rates are zero (ID 576) applied to Period 3 value for periods 4 to 6, and –6% annual (ID 579) applied to Period 6 value for periods 7 and 8.

11.2 | DATA STATEMENTS
| Input Mode

PAVE has the capability of reading inputs from *data statements*. The following rules apply to the preparation of *data statements*:

1. Confine data statement line numbers between 1 and 2000.

2. Enter each input item as a pair of numbers—an ID number followed by its corresponding value.

3. Up to a limit of the number of characters per statement line on your computer, any quantity of input pairs may be entered on a statement line.

4. Use commas to separate each numerical entry within a line. Commas must be used both within and between item pairs. Place no commas at the end of a statement line. Do not split input item pairs between statement lines.

5. It is suggested, but not required, that an extra space be inserted between each input item pair. The space will not be read by a computer, but will help to define pairs visually. In trying to deal with a long string of numbers separated only by commas, there is a risk of transposing ID numbers and values.

6. Input item pairs may be entered in any order. If the same ID number appears in several places, only the last entry will be used for an input.

7. The data pair 0,0 is a flag signal which ends the reading of inputs. If this pair is encountered, no input item pairs beyond it will be read. The use of this pair, or an END statement, will usually have no effect on processing if placed after the last input item pair to be read. Note that 0 is not an ID number used for input items.

8. PAVE does not read a title, run description, or any other verbal information from data statements.

One may enter data statements at a keyboard just prior to a PAVE run. Data statement programs may also be entered at a keyboard, stored on disk or tape, and LOADED into the work space with PAVE1 for a run. Data statements at a keyboard would usually be used for changes; data statement programs are appropriate for complete input sets. A data statement program is exhibited in Figure 11.1 for inputs to the VALVO case (section 10.1). *Data statements*, whether entered singly or collected into programs, follow the same syntax. A typical keyboard entry for changes is shown below:

```
100 DATA 1,3, 103,-1, 130,1000000

100 REM ** PAVED1, DATA STATEMENTS INPUT FOR VALVO
110 REM ** 3 YRS BY QTRS, ENYRT ANALYSIS, J. MCLAUGHLIN
120 REM *  INPUT-OUTPUT CHOICES
130 DATA 1, 12, 2,4, 3,1, 5,3
140 REM *  SEASONAL INDICES
150 DATA 51,0.9, 52,0.8, 53,1, 54,1.3
160 REM *  ENVIRONMENT DYNAMIC SETS
170 DATA 102,4, 103,-1, 112,6, 113,0.5, 121,12.5, 122,10
180 DATA 130,9792000, 131,25, 132,2, 133,2
190 REM *  END OF INPUT DATA SET
```

Figure 11.1.
DATA STATEMENTS INPUT PROGRAM FOR VALVO CASE

When this statement is read, a total of 3 periods will be simulated under ID 1, the rate of change of % ANNUAL REAL GROWTH RATE OF ECONOMY will be established at -1% under ID 103, and $ INDUSTRY SALES FOR BASE YEAR will be set at $1,000,000 in ID 130. Note that commas cannot be used within numerical entries, which is true of all BASIC language inputs. It is convenient, but not necessary, to keep ID numbers in order. After entering or loading data statements, reading is automatic when a PAVE command RUN is being executed.

Data statements may be combined in the same run with other input modes. Other modes are SEQUENTIAL DISPLAYS or SELECTIVE INTERACTIVE (see section 8.3). The hierarchy of reading inputs is as follows:

a. Read *input data file* if OLD FILE is chosen.

b. Read *data statements* if any are present.

c. Apply internal values for up to 10 nonpositive inputs.

d. Enter inputs at keyboard; SEQUENTIAL DISPLAYS or

e. SELECTIVE INTERACTIVE modes.

f. Check balance of *initial condition*.

g. Write to *input data files* if NEW FILE is chosen.

h. If processing is continued, write inputs to *data transfer file* PAVEFT1 and chain in next program PAVE2.

Data statements are read *after* an optional OLD FILE so that users may enter data statements at the keyboard to change inputs stored in files. Note that input information from data statements, whether programs or keyboard lines, may be merged into input data files. If data statements are read into the work space at the start of a PAVE run, then they may be written to an input data file under NEW FILE choices. (For the management of input data file options, see section 8.4.) Is the DATA STATEMENTS input mode worthwhile for most users? The answer to this is probably *no*. In general, a process of entering data statements will be neither faster nor provide more information than SEQUENTIAL DISPLAYS mode. Compare data statements with input data files. The first are programs, or pieces of programs, even though they contain only input values. BASIC language programs must be prepared, debugged, and modified directly by humans. Input data files, on the other hand, are not programs. They are not written directly by users, but indirectly through other programs such as PAVE1. To initiate a new input set, one could prepare a DATA STATEMENTS mode program in place of interacting with SEQUENTIAL DISPLAYS. With reasonable speed on a video screen, the former is not likely to be faster. ID numbers do not have to be entered under SEQUENTIAL DISPLAYS mode. With DATA STATEMENTS mode the risk of input mistakes is substantial. Under SEQUENTIAL DISPLAYS, on the other hand, both ID numbers and item descriptions are supplied during entry. Each input may be examined in direct relation to accompanying inputs. Furthermore, the whole input system is presented in a logical order.

Returning to DATA STATEMENTS mode programs, there are some minor advantages. Data statements may be laid out or entered when a PAVE1 program is not available. Explanatory remarks (REM statements) may be liberally supplied within data statements programs. REM statements will be ignored when inputs are read. On the other hand, there is provision for a stored title with PAVE input data files. If data statements are used for inputs, each run title must be supplied at the keyboard. Both data statements and input data files may be used to store input sets. Any changes in the former must be handled with a manual program update; the latter may be revised during a RUN of PAVE1.

When it comes to changes of input sets, a data statement line entry may be slightly faster than SELECTIVE INTERACTIVE mode. Both methods require input of an ID number followed by a corresponding value. SELECTIVE INTERACTIVE, however, provides useful checking features on video displays. The only penalty of SELECTIVE INTERACTIVE is the time required to project new displays. When it comes to storing an input change, users may prefer the input data file system. A data statement at the beginning of a PAVE run will be lost unless it is stored as part of an input data file, or unless it is saved under some name as a separate program.

There are automatic checks and error messages for invalid ID numbers under SEQUENTIAL DISPLAYS and SELECTIVE INTERACTIVE modes. No corresponding checks are available when reading or writing data statements. Under this mode values entered for invalid ID numbers within the range of 1 to 579 are simply ignored.

A data statement entry of ID numbers beyond the range of integers 0 to 579 will abort a RUN. DATA STATEMENTS input mode is not recommended for users until they have acquired considerable experience with the PAVE system.

11.3 | Servicing of PAVE Files

This section reviews classes of PAVE files. Instructions are given for the operation of auxiliary programs which are available for servicing of files. Consider the information here as an extension to sections 7.2 and 8.4. The categories of PAVE program and data files are:

1. PAVE *input data files*—each named by users
2. PAVE *input data statement programs*—each named by users
3. PAVE *processing programs*, PAVE1 to PAVE6
4. PAVE *data transfer files* among processing programs, PAVEFT1 to PAVEFT5
5. PAVE *file service programs*: PAVEC, PAVER, and PAVES

Items 1 and 4 are *data files*; the remainder are *program files*. Item 2 is a set of programs used to store input data. Items 1 and 2 use alternative input storage methods (see sections 8.4 and 11.2). Item 3 programs are used for the processing of PAVE inputs to outputs. Processed information is transferred among Item 3 programs by the data file set of Item 4. Item 5 programs are used to service the files in Items 1 and 4.

The management of PAVE system files will vary with system architecture. (Suggestions for adopting PAVE to your hardware are presented in chapter 13.) The file system described here employs two minidiskettes. Each has a separate drive, which will be identified as *left port* and *right port*. This is a typical system for small minicomputers. If storage capacity is sufficient, it is not necessary to employ two separate disk or tape drives to operate the system (see section 13.1).

To work with the specific coding in this book, PAVE processing programs must be stored on a separate minidiskette from input data files and data transfer files. During PAVE runs processing programs are loaded from the right port, and both types of data files from the left port. The remaining two classes of programs may be stored on any minidiskette and loaded from either port. The following is a good arrangement. Store PAVE processing programs PAVE1 to PAVE6 and PAVE file service programs (PAVEC, PAVER, and PAVES) on one minidiskette. Always mount this in the right port. Store PAVE data transfer files PAVEFT1 to PAVEFT5 on another minidiskette, which is always mounted in the left port. If there are a few input data files or input data statement programs, store these on the same minidiskette with PAVEFT1 to PAVEFT5. For additional input data sets, store on separate minidiskettes. For PAVE runs, always mount data file minidiskettes in the left port. If input data files or input data statement programs are stored on different minidiskettes from data transfer files, this will not cause a problem. There is a programmed pause in PAVE1 to change minidiskettes (see section 7.2).

Operating instructions for a PAVE run are given in section 7.2. Information on how to use some auxiliary file service programs will be given here. All service programs are fully interactive with users. Requests for information are displayed on a video screen. The service programs which are available in this book are:

1. PAVEC catalogs disk space for five data transfer files, PAVEFT1 to PAVEFT5

2. PAVER reads and prints the contents of five data transfer files, PAVEFT1 to PAVEFT5.

3. PAVES services input data files. It transfers storage, reads data inputs, renames data files, resets file contents to zero, and prints contents.

PAVEFT series data transfer files are written and read by PAVE1 to PAVE6, but must be cataloged initially by users on a minidiskette. Once a PAVEFT series has been set up it may be used over and over again for successive runs. Data in process, which was stored during previous runs, is simply overwritten with new data during the latest run. Ordinarily, there is no reason for saving partly processed data which appears on these files. Thus only one set of PAVEFT series files is needed to accompany each PAVE1 to PAVE6 processing set. At most, only one PAVEFT series is required for each user.

Auxiliary program PAVEC contains the coding to catalog and reserve disk sectors for data transfer files PAVEFT1 to PAVEFT5. Once PAVEC has been RUN, PAVEFT series files may be accessed by PAVE1 to PAVE6. Upon a RUN command to PAVEC, users are given a choice to enter "0" for cataloging all PAVEFT series files, or "1" for individual file cataloging. The single command "0" runs the whole process of cataloging PAVEFT files. Under individual file choice, on the other hand, users must enter a file name and a *format number*. Format numbers determine the quantity of sectors to be reserved. Choice numbers one to five command sectors required to store the contents of PAVEFT1 to PAVEFT5, respectively. To replace part of a PAVEFT series, use the individual file choice. Alternative file *names* may be entered under individual choice, but they will not work with current PAVE1 to PAVE6 coding.

The only purpose of PAVER is to print the contents of data transfer files PAVEFT1 to PAVEFT5. As mentioned above, users ordinarily have no interest in the contents of these files. If modifications of PAVE1 to PAVE6 are being debugged, however, it may be extremely useful to know what values are being transferred from one processing program to another. Upon a RUN command to PAVER, users must enter a file name and format number. The only file names for current PAVE programs are PAVEFT1 to PAVEFT5. Format numbers 1 to 5 must match those in the file names. Each number dimensions a set of arrays for each record of a corresponding data transfer file.

After user entry of a name and format, the contents of all arrays are printed. Each array is printed separately. Arrays are assembled into records. Each time a different PAVE processing program writes to the same data transfer file, a new record is established. Records are separated by asterisks in PAVER printing. (For a list of records and array names used to transfer values through the PAVEFT series, see Table 13.1.) Values are printed in five columns. Although index numbers of arrays are not printed, it is fairly easy to keep count with ten items every two lines. Users may enter index number benchmarks in the left margin. PAVER prints the contents of only one data transfer file at a time. To print another file, RUN it again.

Users may be interested in printing the contents of PAVEFT1. This file contains nothing but the input data for a run, which must be transferred from PAVE1 to PAVE2 for further processing. The run title is printed first. This is followed by the values in IDs 1 to 99 for system parameters in the first array, values in IDs 100 to 329 for environment, manufacturing, and trading dynamic input sets in the next two arrays, and values in IDs 330 to 579 for R&D, sales, general, administrative, and financial dynamic input sets in the last two arrays. There is only one record in PAVEFT1. Zeros are printed for invalid or unused ID spaces within the above range. IDs themselves are not printed, which makes for a compact presentation. Some users may prefer this layout of inputs to the complete printing under menu choice "10" in PAVE1 (see section 7.2).

PAVES is used for auxiliary servicing of input data files, whereas PAVEC and PAVER operate with data transfer files. PAVE1 contains the ordinary statements for managing input data files. Here files may be established, written with input sets, renamed, maintained, or revised. PAVE1 lacks flexibility, however, for a few special operations. PAVES may be used to transfer input data files from one diskette to another, rename files, revise input data items, reset input contents to zero, and print a set of inputs. PAVE1 will also print complete input sets (menu choice "10"). PAVEC is more compact, however, because it does not print input item descriptions. On the other hand, PAVES does print ID numbers. It also arranges inputs by sections on the same plan as SEQUENTIAL DISPLAYS mode of PAVE1. PAVES printing is thus easier to read than PAVER printing of the contents of PAVEFT1.

Upon command RUN to PAVES, users must identify an input data file. If the file is OLD it must be located in either the left port or right port. After initial file information, a menu of five choices appears. Choice 1 resets all current input values of the chosen file to zero. This of course destroys the current input set. To avoid inadvertent loss of inputs, a warning message appears which requires a second user entry for confirmation. Choice 2 provides for entry of revised values into a file, one ID at a time. This process is interactive with users on the video screen. First, opportunity is given to revise the input set *title*. This is not to be confused with changes in the file *name* in Choice 4 below. The title may be printed, retained, or reentered. Following the title branch, users will enter individual IDs. The current value is displayed for each selected ID. The current value may be revised at the keyboard and is assigned to an input array. Users are recycled through ID value revisions until an input of 0 returns control to the menu. There is an internal check for invalid ID number entries.

Choice 3 prints the whole current set of input values and IDs as described in the preceding paragraph. Choice 4 stores the current inputs on a minidiskette. Users may rename an OLD file and must locate the port where a new file is to stored. Under NEW option PAVES will catalog an additional block of storage. Choices 4 or 5 END a PAVES run. Choice 5 simply ends without storing anything. Except choices 4 or 5, PAVES branches return users to the menu after a previous command has been completed. Choice 5 would be used if operations on a file in PAVES were not to be preserved on a minidiskette.

It is possible to revise some or all input values with menu Choice 1 or Choice 2 in PAVES. PAVES also reads data statements entered at the keyboard or loaded from a data statements program. The preparation of such data statements follows the same rules as described in section 11.2. After an input data file has been loaded by PAVES, data statement values will be read, if any present, in the same manner as in PAVE1. Data statements, if in the work space, will revise the contents of an OLD file, if this be loaded. Reset of inputs to zero (Choice 1) or of individual keyboard input entries (Choice 2) will revise either OLD file contents or data statements. Changing inputs with PAVES is often not wise. PAVES lacks the flexibility and power of PAVE1; for example, the only way to organize the current set of inputs in PAVES is to print the entire set.

There are many places in PAVE1 to PAVE6 where inputs are checked. First, there is rejection of invalid ID numbers under SEQUENTIAL DISPLAYS and INDIVID-UAL INTERACTIVE input modes. Second, ten inputs are overwritten with internal values to prevent aborting a run. Third, contradictory policy inputs are often modified to prevent illogical outputs. Fourth, there are routines to develop internal values which replace nonentries. Despite all this processing there is no complete check for nonoperational input values. Some users may wish to write a program which examines each input in turn for mistakes, prints messages to prompt corrections, and contains interactive statements for revisions.

11.4 | Additional Inputs for Operating Policies

Basic input items were described in section 8.5. Extension of inputs for dynamic sets was examined in section 11.1. There are a number of other inputs, both system parameters and dynamic sets, which optionally may be used to increase precision or represent particular conditions. This section surveys an operating policies group of inputs. Financial and valuation parameters are discussed in Section 11.5. Inputs which control alternative conditions of output runs were examined in sections 8.5 and 9.4; that information is not repeated here. A glossary of all input IDs will be found in the Appendix.

Certain values, not included on the list in section 8.5, may be processed through a simulation. Users may add both initial (ID 13) and continuing (ID 81) PREPAID EXPENSE. If PREPAID EXPENSE is nonzero, accounts subject to payment are adjusted each period for changes in prepaid expense before establishing ACCOUNTS PAYABLE. A continuing level of PREPAID EXPENSE is established as a percentage of annual payments (ID 81). Initial (ID 42) and continuing (ID 82) UNEARNED ADVANCES FROM CUSTOMERS may be processed in a similar manner. SALES are adjusted for changes in CUSTOMER ADVANCES before establishing amounts available for collection. The level of CUSTOMER ADVANCES is maintained with ID 82 as a percentage of SALES.

Two *manufacturing* inventories are available in addition to the three inventories listed in section 8.5. These are GOODS-IN-PROCESS and MANUFACTURING IN-DIRECT SUPPLIES AND EQUIPMENT. Initial condition values are entered into IDs 17 and 19. Continuing levels are established by ID set 162 and ID 220, respectively.

The management of a class of MANUFACTURING FIXED ASSETS and a class of GENERAL FIXED ASSETS, together with DEPRECIATION rates, was examined in section 8.5. In an extended input system five classes of FIXED ASSETS are available in both manufacturing and general input divisions. Thus a total of ten DEPRECIA-TION rates are provided, any of which may be zero. The behavior of all classes is identical to the single classes described in section 8.5. Each class may be treated as a separate group of assets.

Under *initial condition* input division, certain accounts are merged by PAVE before further processing. Extra beginning input values are supplied to accommodate items which may appear in the statements of some firms. ID 11 is a second RECEIV-ABLES account, and is added in PAVE processing to ID 10. IDs 41 and 43 are additional short-term PAYABLES, and are added to ID 40 before further processing. The proceeds from a bond issue are often different from the amount which must be repaid when a debt matures. Such differences are usually entered in a BOND PRE-MIUM (DISCOUNT) account. They may then be amortized over the term of the bonds. In PAVE such a PREMIUM (DISCOUNT) should be entered initially in ID 46. During first-period processing, ID 46 quantity is added algebraically to ID 48. It is not carried by PAVE throughout a simulation, as might occur in an actual accounting procedure.

The amortization of intangibles was discussed in section 8.5. There is provision for entry of additional intangibles, such as ORGANIZATION EXPENSE, in ID 83. An entry in ID 83 is applied to the first period only. It covers initial expenses for a new or reorganized firm. ID 83 amount is amortized along with initial INTANGIBLES (ID 14) by annual amounts per ID 84.

A total set of 24 input IDs is available for SEASONAL-CYCLICAL INDICES (IDs 51 to 74). It is thus possible to assign a different seasonal-cyclical index to every period simulated. The complete index set is normalized and extended to all periods (see section 8.5).

Turning to dynamic input sets for manufacturing, accounts are available for more precision than the basic set of section 8.5. ID set 192, DIRECT SUPERVISION AND SUPPORT PAYROLL, follows the same rules as ID set 182. ID set 202, *% OPERATING EFFICIENCY OF PROCESSING, is assigned an internal value of 100 for nonpositive entries. ID set 202 works in conjunction with ID set 212 to determine $ CAPACITY OF PLANT. ID set 202 is also applied to ID sets 182 and 192 to determine the costs of DIRECT LABOR and DIRECT SUPERVISION. ID 201 is an uncertainty input for ID set 202. ID input set 202 OPERATING EFFICIENCY may range above or below 100%, but nonpositive values are not permissible.

In section 8.5 ID set 252 was used to enter the sum of *manufacturing period expenses*. These expenses may be subdivided. In such cases ID set 252 is assigned to *$ UTILITIES PER PERIOD, and ID sets 242, 262, and 272 to other period expense categories. By adjusting the uncertainty input in ID 251, period expense totals may be varied from run to run. The same extensions of ID set 252 for manufacturing period expenses are available for ID set 452 for general period expenses. There are duplicate categories of period general expenses for manufacturing expenses. These duplicates are in ID sets 442, 464, and 472. ID 451 is an uncertainty input for total general period expense.

Regular manufacturing CAPACITY OF PLANT (ID set 212 as modified by ID set 202), may be extended by OVERTIME LABOR followed by SUBCONTRACTED OPERATIONS. Extensions are activated automatically if CAPACITY is insufficient to meet SALES DEMAND. The amount of extension is controlled by system parameter inputs, and may be zero or positive. ID 75 controls % OVERTIME LIMIT TO DIRECT LABOR and ID 77 controls % INCREMENT OF PLANT CAPACITY FROM SUBCONTRACTED OPERATIONS. There is a hierarchy of extensions. OVERTIME LABOR is applied first, followed by SUBCONTRACT OPERATIONS. If the combination of these is insufficient, ACHIEVED SALES will be reduced from SALES DEMAND. The PREMIUM COST of overtime labor is entered in ID 76. MATERIAL COST PREMIUM, which is applied to all material if any SUBCONTRACT is needed, is entered in ID 78.

RESEARCH AND DEVELOPMENT PAYROLL, in ID set 332 may be separated from other R&D expenses in ID set 342. The control decision of ID 330 (see section 8.5) applies to both of these ID sets.

Inputs are available for both *variable* and *fixed* SALES PAYROLLS (ID sets 352 and 362) and other SALES EXPENSES (ID sets 372 and 382). Inputs are provided as percentages of SALES for general *SERVICE PAYROLL (ID set 422) and *MATERIALS (ID set 402). These allow for treatment of variable expenses in agribusinesses, extractive industries, services, etc. Input uncertainty IDs 421 and 401 are provided for ID sets 422 and 402. Corresponding fixed expenses (period costs) may be entered in ID sets 432 and 412 (see section 8.5).

11.5 | Financial and Valuation System Parameters

System parameter IDs 87 to 98 are used in conjunction with computations of economic values of a firm. PAVE estimates of value are printed in the VALUATION AND SCOPE output division. This division contains both total and per share figures. The number of outstanding shares at the end of each period is printed in RETAINED EARNINGS AND CAPITAL CHANGES statements of FINANCIAL STATEMENTS output division. Users need make no entries in IDs 87 to 98. Internal values of 50, 200, 50, 1, and 50 are inserted for nonentry of IDs 87, 88, 89, 91, and 95, respectively. Nonentry in ID 90 indicates no INITIAL TAX LOSS FOR CARRYFORWARD. Nonentry in the remaining IDs is an indicator for internal computation of the parameter. An exception occurs for IDs 93 and 94 with a deterministic run (ID 3 = 1). In such cases PRICE-EARNINGS MULTIPLES cannot be computed internally and values of 10 are inserted by PAVE.

Computations in PAVE of value and number of shares are quite complex. Since PAVE methods are covered in detail in section 9.2, they will not be repeated here. The purpose of this section is to explore advantages from overwriting internal parameters. Inputs in ID 91 have already been covered in the basic set of section 8.5.

IDs 87, 88, and 95 quantify the need for liquidity and the capacity for short-term borrowing. Refer to ID 530 in Section 9.4 for a description of how cash investment is managed. The criterion of cash sufficiency is ID 87. If % CASH RATIO MINIMUM (see section 4.6) falls below the ID 87 limit, internal routines are activated to obtain more cash. The internal value of ID 87 is 50%. Other positive values may be entered by users. If additional cash is needed to reach the ID 87 limit, efforts are first made by PAVE to borrow short-term funds. If the % CURRENT RATIO MINIMUM in ID 88 is equal or greater than 150 (internal value 200), then this input will be used as a limit to SHORT-TERM BORROWING. Otherwise, SHORT-TERM BORROWING will be computed as an estimated liquidation value of current assets. The liquidation percentage is taken from ID 95 (internal value 50). User choices in IDs 87, 88, and 95 determine cash requirements, the basis for short-term borrowing, and the capacity for short-term borrowing, respectively. If short-term borrowing is insufficient to meet ID 87 liquidity standards, additional capital will be raised by PAVE if ID 530 = 1 (see section 9.4).

ID 89 (internal value 50) is an *effective* income tax rate. A formula for the effective combined rate C of federal (F) and states (S) rates is:

$$C = F + (100 - F) * S/100 \quad \text{where all rates are in percentages}$$

Users may overwrite the internal value of 50 in ID 89 with any positive C less than 100. (The interactions among INCOME, INCOME TAXES, and TAX LOSS CARRYFORWARDS are discussed in section 9.2.)

Parameter IDs 92 to 98 are used for *valuation*. (The process and hierarchy of valuation are explained in section 9.2.) ID 95 (internal value 50) is the percentage of asset liquidation to original cost. It is applied to both SHORT-TERM BORROWING (above) and LIQUIDATION VALUE. For the remaining valuation parameters, non-entry is a signal for *internal computation*. User entry of parameters is a standby power to stabilize valuation. This standby power may be used to test alternatives or to overcome erratic behavior. If a particular simulation covers too short a time span, contains atypical performance, or lacks stability, then it is best to substitute user parameters for internal values. IDs 96, 97, and 98 control GOING-CONCERN VALUATION under risk. These parameters and GOING-CONCERN computations do not apply unless risk is simulated (ID 3 = 1). Users may prefer to enter a REQUIRED RATE OF RETURN in ID 96. This would replace an unsatisfactory internal computation. If there is no internal computation of GOING-CONCERN VALUE (ID 3 = 1), external inputs should be supplied to IDs 93 and 94. Otherwise, MARKET VALUE from PRICE-EARNINGS MULTIPLES will simply receive a default of ten times EARNINGS. To keep the price of new shares a constant over a simulation, make a positive entry in ID 92. Otherwise, the price of incremental shares will vary with the MARKET VALUE from period to period.

12 Comprehensive Cases With Extended Inputs

12.1 | Description of GIFTIQUE
Retailing Case

Two cases are presented in this chapter. GIFTIQUE is a retailing establishment, and HPG PRODUCTS is a manufacturing firm. The principal purpose of these cases is to illustrate an extended system of PAVE inputs. Extended input systems were described in chapter 11, which, in turn, builds on the basic input set described in chapter 8. Chapter 11 should be used as a reference while examining the cases in this chapter. There is a glossary of all PAVE inputs in the Appendix.

Three sections are devoted here to each case. The first section describes the case, the second is a translation to PAVE inputs, and the third is an interpretation of outputs. Thus sections 12.1, 12.2, and 12.3 cover GIFTIQUE, while sections 12.4, 12.5, and 12.6 are concerned with HPG PRODUCTS.

The four cases of chapter 10 contain a great deal of decision making based upon PAVE outputs. Conclusions about cases here build on the information in chapter 10. There is a general description of PAVE outputs in chapter 9.

GIFTIQUE is a retail establishment which sells wedding accessories, gifts, and antiques. It is located on a main street in a midtown shopping area of a major city. Founded 15 years ago as a small, family corporation, the stimulus of the original business was a lack of a central location where wedding gifts and accessories could be purchased. Gradually the business was extended to include gifts for all occasions, and about five years ago the product line was expanded into antiques. The father in the founding family has recently died. Although the mother worked full time over the years in the business, she does not wish to continue in the management, nor to remain affiliated in any capacity. The children do not wish to leave their present occupations to become involved in GIFTIQUE either.

GIFTIQUE has been offered to you for $150,000, which is approximately the current book value of $47,000 paid-in capital and $101,896 retained earnings. For this amount, which must be in cash, you will acquire all the assets and goodwill of the business, including an initial checking account balance of $28,720. You also must assume current trade debt of $30,097, nontrade payables of $3,695, and accrued expense of $36,758. You decide to run a PAVE simulation to help determine the prospects for a profitable investment. You will develop a strategic plan which includes reasonable policies and a conservative assessment of the environment. You are particularly interested in whether further investment is likely to be required in excess of the initial $150,000. This means that you will program for PAVE internal determination of required additional capital. Over the first ten years of its existence, GIFTIQUE earnings increased rapidly. For the past five years, however, the position has been virtually break-even. The present owners blame this situation on the recession of the last few years and failing health of the deceased principal. You decide to project GIFTIQUE's future sales from this year's actual sales of $420,240. This was the last full year of operation under present owners. To the base sales you will apply reasonable expectations for growth and inflation. You decide to study six future years. Since the business has a pronounced seasonal pattern, quarter years will be taken as the period length. The decision is then to simulate 24 future periods, the maximum capacity of PAVE.

A Monte Carlo simulation will be employed to represent uncertainty in the output and to obtain an internal estimate of going-concern value under risk. A full set of outputs is desired, including pro forma financial statements for all periods.

Since the study is an extension of an existing firm, the GIFTIQUE STATEMENT OF CONDITION of December 31, 19___ describes starting conditions for the simulation. The current names of accounts are quite similar to those which appear in PAVE inputs and outputs. Because the firm is to be sold at book value, there is no goodwill to be added during the first period nor an offsetting adjustment to paid-in capital. There are in fact no intangible assets and no amortization expense. The starting condition is reproduced below:

GIFTIQUE
STATEMENT OF CONDITION
December 31, 19___

Current assets:

Cash	$ 28,720
Accounts receivable—trade	29,501
Accounts receivable—other	12,338
Prepaid expense	3,605
Inventory (at cost)	127,310
Total current assets	$201,474

Store equipment and fixtures	$ 43,163	
Less accumulated depreciation	34,997	8,166
Delivery equipment		9,806
Total assets		$219,446
Current liabilities:		
Accounts payable—trade	$ 30,097	
Accounts payable—other	3,695	
Accrued expense	36,758	
Total liabilities		$ 70,550
Stockholders' equity:		
Common stock, no par 3000 shares		
Authorized, 940 issued at		
$50.00 paid-in	$ 47,000	
Retained earnings	101,896	
Total stockholders' equity		$148,896
Total liabilities and stockholders' equity		$219,446

Estimates of the future economic environment are extremely important. No real growth is projected over the next two years. A 1% real growth rate is taken over the third and fourth years, and a 2% rate over the fifth and sixth years. The 1% rate is projected to grow at 5% per year, and the 2% rate at 2% per year. Inflation rates are revised over the same two-year intervals. The starting rate of inflation is 7%, and this rate is projected to decline at a 2% annual rate until the end of the second year. Then a 6% rate of inflation is chosen, which also declines at an annual rate of 2% until the end of the fourth year. An inflation rate of 5.5% is projected over the remainder of the simulation, with no change applied to this last rate. Inflation factors will not be applied to period costs. Instead, growth of cost will be represented by individual inputs.

For GIFTIQUE real economic growth, inflation, and seasonal pattern will not be applied to an industry, but, rather, directly to the sales of the firm. Furthermore, sales of GIFTIQUE are projected to grow at the same rate as the general economy. Uncertainty about sales demand should not exceed 25% of expected sales per period. In respect to seasonal pattern, the fourth quarter, with Christmas holidays, is very strong. Twice as much is sold then as during the next best quarter, which is the second (spring). This is the season of Easter and June brides. Only half as much is sold during the winter and summer quarters as during the spring quarter. Thus, sales vary by four to one from the strongest to the weakest quarters.

The average annual inventory is a little more than half of the cost of sales, or, in other words, the inventory turns a little less than twice per year. The precise historical figure is 57%, and this will be used without change over the simulation. As already indicated, there is a pronounced seasonal pattern of sales. Finished goods purchases are much smoother than sales, but still vary somewhat with the seasonal pattern. Inventory levels move oppositely from sales to provide a smoothing effect on purchases. The deseasonalization of purchases to sales is taken as 25%.

On the average, merchandise costs 50% of sales price with an uncertainty of 12.5% maximum shift. This relation is not expected to change over the study period.

Normally, accounts receivable run 15% of sales, and advertising and promotional activities 11% of sales. These ratios are not expected to change over the span of the simulation. Uncollectible accounts are expected to equal 1% of credit sales. General administrative payroll will begin at $21,250 in the first quarter, and is expected to increase at 6% a year over the six-year study. Indirect supplies and small equipment are estimated at a starting rate of $375 per quarter, utilities $1642.50 per quarter; maintenance $325 per quarter; and taxes, insurance and miscellaneous period expense $4000 per quarter. All of these four period expenses are expected to increase at an annual rate of 1% over the simulation. Rent and associated occupancy costs are currently $5000 per quarter. These are not expected to increase over the next six years because a new lease has just been negotiated. Supplies which vary with sales are expected to remain at 0.1% of sales over the simulation. These supplies are in addition to the indirect supplies estimated above.

The depreciation rate on store equipment and fixtures is 10% double-declining balance, which is taken as appropriate for future planning. GIFTIQUE has just purchased $9806 worth of new delivery equipment, as shown on the preceding statement of condition. The depreciation rate on this equipment is 25% declining balance. New asset purchases are not projected over the six-year simulation.

Certain variabilities are estimated to represent input uncertainty. These are maximum shifts of 25% for accounts receivable, 12.5% for cost of supplies that vary with sales, and 12.5% applied to utilities for that account and other period costs. The inventory of supplies has historically run 20% of the value of supplies used, and this figure is considered suitable for future projection.

Interest rate estimates are 9% short-term and 7% long-term, with no changes over the simulation. Since these rates are uncertain, however, a 25% maximum shift will be applied to the short-term rate and a 12.5% maximum shift to the long-term rate. Initially there is no long-term interest cost, but if additional capital is required, some of this is planned as a fixed obligation (see below).

No dividends are projected over the simulation; the stockholders will all be active participants in the business.

It is estimated that accounts payable balance on the average will equal 8.333% of payments on account over the year.

Currently GIFTIQUE has no long-term debt, but if new capital is required you estimate that it will be possible to raise 25% by sale of preferred stock to the projected investment group. The stated cost of each new share of common stock will be $50, the same as the current stated value for the initial 940 shares. Since the firm is offered to you at book value, goodwill and corresponding capital surplus accounts need not be added. Short-term seasonal loans may be negotiated with a local bank under normal terms.

Some of the most important simulation outputs are estimates of going-concern value. To compute this calls for an investor required rate of return under risk, a long-term growth rate, and a rate of return on incremental assets. All of these parameters may be calculated internally by the program from other data, but you decide to input an investor required rate of return as 15%. This meets your personal objectives. The remaining two parameters are to be computed internally. Since GIFTIQUE's assets consist mostly of merchandise, which is readily salable at a discount, the value of assets in liquidation is estimated at 70%.

12.2 | Input Set for
GIFTIQUE Case

The assembly of inputs for GIFTIQUE is organized in Table 12.1. Six input divisions are required, but only the first two ID sets in Division 4, MANUFACTURING OR TRADE ITEMS, are used. Each division is discussed in turn.

Among INPUT/OUTPUT system choices, there are 24 periods under ID 1 and 4 periods per year (quarters) under ID 2. A statistical simulation was specified and a sample size of 12 was entered under ID 3. From Table 8.2 the Student's t-value is then 3.1 for output confidence intervals of 99% with 11 degrees of freedom (one less than sample size of 12). The internal default random generator seed number argument of 0 is adequate, so no entry is made in ID 4. Under ID 5 class of firm, trading type 1 is selected for a retail establishment. This means that PAVE will include logic for finished goods inventories, here purchased merchandise. Partly finished goods-in-process will not be included; this inventory appears only for manufacturing (ID 5 equals 2). The full extent of output printing will be elected. By specifying ID 6 with value 0, VALUATION AND SCOPE output division will be printed first. After each print a menu appears to select another output division number. Successive entry of output numbers 1, 2, and 3 will print the remaining three output divisions.

Note that zero entry and nonentry are completely equivalent for PAVE inputs in all sections of Table 12.1. Nonentries appear as zeros in the table, which is a reproduction of a PAVE print.

In the INITIAL CONDITION input division, entries simply replicate the initial balance sheet of GIFTIQUE (see section 12.1). It is sometimes necessary to consolidate values or adjust account names from a particular firm to the PAVE input system, but such transformations are minimal here. Note that cents are omitted from account values for both inputs and outputs of PAVE.

Table 12.1.
INPUT SET FOR GIFTIQUE

GIFTIQUE

INPUT/OUTPUT SYSTEM CHOICES
!! THESE INPUTS CONTROL OTHER DISPLAYS!!

```
 1 TOTAL NUMBER OF PERIODS (MAX 24) . . .      24
 2 NO. OF PERIODS PER YEAR . . . .             4
 3 SAMPLE SIZE--DETERMINISTIC=1/STAT.=2 TO 12. 12
 4 SEED NO.--STANDARD RANDOM SERIES=0 . . .    0
 5 FRAME: SERVICE=0/TRADE=1/MFG=2/ENVRT ONLY=3 1
 6 OUTPUT DIVISION PRINT 1ST FROM LIST BELOW:  0
   VALUATION 1ST AND FINAL YEARS, SCOPE    =0
   STATISTICAL SUMMARY FROM FINAL PERIOD   =1
   FINANCIAL STATEMENTS FOR ALL PERIODS    =2
   SELECTED ACCOUNTS FOR ALL PERIODS       =3
```

INITIAL CONDITION--CURRENT AND INTANGIBLE ASSETS
(START BAL SHEET; NEW FIRM--OMIT/SKELETON)

```
 9 $ CASH AND MARKETABLE SECURITIES . . .          28720
10 $ TRADE ACCOUNTS AND NOTES RECEIVABLE . .       29501
11 $ NONTRADE ADVANCES AND ACCRUED RECEIVABLES     12338
12 $ RESERVE FOR UNCOLLECTIBLE ACCOUNTS . .        3605
13 $ PREPAID EXPENSE AND DEFERRED CHARGES .        0
14 $ INTANGIBLES: ORGAN EXP., PATENT, GOODWILL     0
15 $ INVENTORY OF GENERAL SUPPLIES/SMALL EQPT.     0
16 $ INVENTORY OF MFG OR TRADE FINISHED GOODS.     127310
```

INITIAL CONDITION--GENERAL FIXED ASSETS

```
30 $ CLASS 1 AT COST BASIS. . . . .          43163
31 $ CLASS 2 AT COST BASIS . . . .           9806
32 $ CLASS 3 AT COST BASIS . . . .           0
33 $ CLASS 4 AT COST BASIS . . . .           0
34 $ CLASS 5 AT COST BASIS . . . .           34997
35 $ CLASS 1 RESERVE FOR DEPRECIATION .      0
36 $ CLASS 2 RESERVE FOR DEPRECIATION .      0
37 $ CLASS 3 RESERVE FOR DEPRECIATION .      0
38 $ CLASS 4 RESERVE FOR DEPRECIATION .      0
39 $ CLASS 5 RESERVE FOR DEPRECIATION .      0
```

INITIAL CONDITION--LIABILITIES AND OWNERS' EQUITY
(TOTAL ASSETS, EQUITIES, AND BALANCE
CHECK IN NEXT DISPLAY)

```
40 $ TRADE ACCOUNTS AND NOTES PAYABLE . .         30097
41 $ NONTRADE ACCTS, DIVIDENDS, TAXES PAYABLE.    3695
42 $ UNEARNED ADVANCES FROM CUSTOMERS . .         0
43 $ ACCRUED EXPENSE AND LIABILITIES. . .         36758
44 $ SHORT-TERM DEBT AND LOANS PAYABLE . .        0
45 $ LONG-TERM OBLIGATIONS AT FACE OR STATED .    0
46 $ BOND (PREFERRED STOCK) PREMIUM (DISCOUNT)    0
47 $ PAID-IN OWNER EQUITY CAPITAL. . . .          47000
48 $ RETAINED EARNINGS . . . . .                  101896
```

INITIAL CONDITION (STARTING BALANCE SHEET) TOTALS

```
   TOTAL ASSETS. . . . .       $ 219446
   TOTAL LIABILITIES . . .     $ 70550
   TOTAL OWNERS' EQUITY . .    $ 148896
```

% ANNUAL REAL GROWTH RATE OF ECONOMY

```
102 % BASE VALUE APPLIED IN PERIOD 1 . . .         0
103 % ANNUAL CHANGE TO PERIODS FROM 1ST BASE       0
104 % LAST PERIOD NO., 1ST SCHEDULE (ALL=0).       8
105 % 2ND BASE VALUE NEXT PERIOD (CONTINUE=-1).    1
106 % ANNUAL CHANGE TO PERIODS FROM 2ND BASE       5
107 % LAST PERIOD NO., 2ND SCHEDULE (ALL=0).       16
108 % 3RD BASE VALUE NEXT PERIOD (CONTINUE=-1).    2
109 % ANNUAL CHANGE TO PERIODS FROM 3RD BASE       2

110    INFLATE PERIOD COSTS--NO=0/YES=1            0
```

% ANNUAL AVERAGE INFLATION RATE

```
112 % BASE VALUE APPLIED IN PERIOD 1 . . .         7
113 % ANNUAL CHANGE TO PERIODS FROM 1ST BASE       -2
114 % LAST PERIOD NO., 1ST SCHEDULE (ALL=0).       8
115 % 2ND BASE VALUE NEXT PERIOD (CONTINUE=-1).    6
116 % ANNUAL CHANGE TO PERIODS FROM 2ND BASE       -2
117 % LAST PERIOD NO., 2ND SCHEDULE (ALL=0).       16
118 % 3RD BASE VALUE NEXT PERIOD (CONTINUE=-1).    5.5
119 % ANNUAL CHANGE TO PERIODS FROM 3RD BASE       0
```

Table 12.1 (continued)

```
120 SALES--% INDUSTRY SHARE=0/$ PER PERIOD=1.              0
* NET SALES DEMAND AVAILABLE TO FIRM
  121  *% MAX CHANGE FROM MEAN VALUE . . . .               0
  122  % BASE VALUE APPLIED IN PERIOD 1 . . .             100
  123  % ANNUAL CHANGE TO PERIODS FROM 1ST BASE .           0

130 $ INDUSTRY SALES FOR BASE (PRIOR) YEAR  .          420240
*% ANNUAL INDUSTRY GROWTH COMPARED TO ECONOMY
  131  *% MAX CHANGE FROM MEAN VALUE . . . .              25
  132  % BASE VALUE APPLIED IN PERIOD 1 . . .              0
  133  % ANNUAL CHANGE TO PERIODS FROM 1ST BASE .           0

SEASONAL/CYCLICAL INDICES--1ST SET STOPS AT 1ST ZERO
  51 INDEX 1  . . . . . . . . . .                        .5
  52 INDEX 2  . . . . . . . . . .                        .1
  53 INDEX 3  . . . . . . . . . .                        .5
  54 INDEX 4  . . . . . . . . . .                        .2
  55 INDEX 5  . . . . . . . . . .                         0
  56 INDEX 6  . . . . . . . . . .                         0
  57 INDEX 7  . . . . . . . . . .                         0
  58 INDEX 8  . . . . . . . . . .                         0
  59 INDEX 9  . . . . . . . . . .                         0
  60 INDEX 10 . . . . . . . . . .                         0
  61 INDEX 11 . . . . . . . . . .                         0
  62 INDEX 12 . . . . . . . . . .                         0

140 INITIAL GOODS INVY'S--COST % OF SELL PRICE            50
*DIRECT PURCHASED MATERIAL OR GOODS AS % OF SALES
  141  *% MAX CHANGE FROM MEAN VALUE . . . .             12.5
  142  % BASE VALUE APPLIED IN PERIOD 1 . . .             50
  143  % ANNUAL CHANGE TO PERIODS FROM 1ST BASE .           0

150 % DESEASONALIZE GOODS PRODUCTION/PURCHASE             25
FINISHED GOODS INVENTORY LEVEL AS % ANNUAL COST GOODS
  152  % BASE VALUE APPLIED IN PERIOD 1 . . .             57
  153  % ANNUAL CHANGE TO PERIODS FROM 1ST BASE .           0


ADVERTISE/PROMOTE/MISC SALES EXPENSE AS % OF SALES
  372  % BASE VALUE APPLIED IN PERIOD 1 . . .             11
  373  % ANNUAL CHANGE TO PERIODS FROM 1ST BASE .           0

390 UNCOLLECTIBLE ACCOUNTS . . . . . . . .                 1

*ACCOUNTS RECEIVABLE LEVEL AS % OF ANNUAL SALES
  391  *% MAX CHANGE FROM MEAN VALUE . . . .              25
  392  % BASE VALUE APPLIED IN PERIOD 1 . . .             15
  393  % ANNUAL CHANGE TO PERIODS FROM 1ST BASE .           0

*DIRECT SERVICE/OFFICE MATERIALS AS % OF SALES
  401  *% MAX CHANGE FROM MEAN VALUE . . . .             12.5
  402  % BASE VALUE APPLIED IN PERIOD 1 . . .             .1
  403  % ANNUAL CHANGE TO PERIODS FROM 1ST BASE .           0

$ INDIRECT SERVICE/OFFICE SUPPLIES/SMALL EQPT PERIOD
  412  $ BASE VALUE APPLIED IN PERIOD 1 . . .            375
  413  % ANNUAL CHANGE TO PERIODS FROM 1ST BASE .           1

$ GENERAL ADMINISTRATIVE/INDIRECT SERV. PAYROLL PERIOD
  432  $ BASE VALUE APPLIED IN PERIOD 1 . . .          21250
  433  % ANNUAL CHANGE TO PERIODS FROM 1ST BASE .           6

$ SPACE, RENT, OR OCCUPANCY PER PERIOD--GENERAL
  442  $ BASE VALUE APPLIED IN PERIOD 1 . . .           5000
  443  % ANNUAL CHANGE TO PERIODS FROM 1ST BASE .           0

**$ UTILITIES OR ALL INDIRECT COSTS PER PERIOD--GENERAL
  451  *% MAX CHANGE FROM MEAN VALUE . . . .             12.5
  452  $ BASE VALUE APPLIED IN PERIOD 1 . . .          1642.5
  453  % ANNUAL CHANGE TO PERIODS FROM 1ST BASE .           1

$ MAINTENANCE PER PERIOD--GENERAL
  462  $ BASE VALUE APPLIED IN PERIOD 1 . . .            325
  463  % ANNUAL CHANGE TO PERIODS FROM 1ST BASE .           1
```

Table 12.1 (continued)

```
$ TAXES, INSURANCE, LABOR RELA'N, MISC PERIOD--GENERAL
  472  $ BASE VALUE APPLIED IN PERIOD 1 . . .         4000
  473  % ANNUAL CHANGE TO PERIODS FROM 1ST BASE          1

  480  % DEPREC'N YRLY DECLINE BAL GENERAL CLASS 1      20

$ GENERAL FIXED ASSETS CLASS 1 NET CHANGES PER PERIOD
  482  $ BASE VALUE APPLIED IN PERIOD 1 . . .            0
  483  % ANNUAL CHANGE TO PERIODS FROM 1ST BASE          0

  490  % DEPREC'N YRLY DECLINE BAL GENERAL CLASS 2      25

$ GENERAL FIXED ASSETS CLASS 2 NET CHANGES PER PERIOD
  492  $ BASE VALUE APPLIED IN PERIOD 1 . . .            0
  493  % ANNUAL CHANGE TO PERIODS FROM 1ST BASE          0

GENERAL ADMINISTRATIVE SYSTEM PARAMETERS
  79  GENL SUPPLIES INV'Y LEVEL AS % ANNUAL USAGE       20
  80  ACCTS PAYABLE LEVEL AS % OF ANNUAL ACCT PAY'   8.333
  81  PREPAID EXPENSE LEVEL AS % OF ANNUAL PAY'TS        0
  82  ADVANCES BY CUSTOMERS AS % OF ANNUAL SALES         0
  83  $ ORGAN EXP./GOODWILL INCURRED IN PERIOD 1.        0
  84  % AMORTIZ'N OF INTANGIBLES YRLY, NOT PERIOD        0

  530  INTERNAL COMPUTE REQD INVEST--NO=0/YES=1.         1

$ OWNER NET CASH INVESTMENT PLANNED CHANGE PER PERIOD
  531   EARN ON NEAR CASH AS % SHORT-TERM INT RATE       0

  532  $ BASE VALUE APPLIED IN PERIOD 1 . . .            0
  533  % ANNUAL CHANGE TO PERIODS FROM 1ST BASE          0

  540  % LONG-TERM OBLIGA'S IN REQD ADDED INVEST        25

$ LONG-TERM OBLIGATIONS PLANNED NET CHANGE PER PERIOD
  542  $ BASE VALUE APPLIED IN PERIOD 1 . . .            0
  543  % ANNUAL CHANGE TO PERIODS FROM 1ST BASE          0


*% SHORT-TERM INTEREST RATE ANNUAL
  561    *% MAX CHANGE FROM MEAN VALUE . . .            25
  562  % BASE VALUE APPLIED IN PERIOD 1 . . .            9
  563  % ANNUAL CHANGE TO PERIODS FROM 1ST BASE          0

*% LONG-TERM INTEREST RATE ANNUAL
  571    *% MAX CHANGE FROM MEAN VALUE . .            12.5
  572  % BASE VALUE APPLIED IN PERIOD 1 . . .            7
  573  % ANNUAL CHANGE TO PERIODS FROM 1ST BASE          0

FINANCIAL AND VALUATION SYSTEM PARAMETERS
  87  % CASH RATIO MIN, BELOW WHICH CASH DEMANDED       50
  88  % CURRENT RATIO MIN FROM SHORT-TERM LOANS:       200
  89  % COMBINED EFFECTIVE INCOME TAX RATE (<100)       50
  90  $ INITIAL TAX LOSS CREDIT FOR CARRY FORWARD        0
  91  NO. 1ST PERIOD OWNER EQUITY UNITS (1/SHARE)      940
  92  $ ADDED SHARE COST--INTERNAL COMPUTATION=0.       50
  93  PRICE-EARNINGS MULTIPLE YR 1--INTER'L. COMP=0      0
  94  PRICE-EARN MULTIPLE FINAL YR--INTER'L COMP=0       0
  95  % ASSETS AVERAGE REALIZED IN LIQUIDATION .        70
  96  % INVESTOR REQD RATE RETURN YR--INTL. COMP=0      15
  97  % LONG-TERM AVG GROWTH RATE YR--INTL COMP=0        0
  98  % RETURN ON INCREM'L ASSETS YR--INTL. COMP=0       0
```

In the ENVIRONMENT input division, dynamic input sets follow the specific information given in the case. The 0, 0, 8 entries in IDs 102, 103, 104, for example, supply information on no real growth through the second year or eighth period. Real growth starts at 1% in quarter 9 (ID 105 = 1), and increases at a rate of 5% per year (about 1.25% per quarter) per ID 106 until quarter 16 (end of fourth year) per ID 107. The 2% rate (ID 108) starts at quarter 17 and increases at a 2% rate per ID 109 to the end of the simulation. The dynamic input ID set 112 for annual inflation follows the same rules as real growth above in ID set 102. Inputs follow case information directly. Since inflation adjustments will not be applied to period costs, ID 110 = 0.

Since GIFTIQUE sales are expected to grow at the same rate as the economy, the appropriate entry in ID 132 is 0. This rate could have been adjusted up or down for greater or smaller comparative growth of GIFTIQUE with the economy. ID 120 = 0 because a share of industry, in this case 100% in ID 122, will be used to project GIFTIQUE sales. ID 122 must be entered as 100 because the base sales of 420240 in ID 130 are prior year sales of the firm, not of an industry. Obviously GIFTIQUE is going to obtain a 100% share of its own sales. Although both ID sets 122 and 132 are dynamic inputs, each has only one value throughout the simulation. Thus single entries are sufficient. A 25% maximum shift is entered in ID 131 to model uncertainty about GIFTIQUE's sales; remember that industry sales are taken as GIFTIQUE sales for this case. By the same token there is no variability associated with the 100% in ID 122; ID 121 is zero or nonentry.

Four seasonal indexes are required for the four quarters. Entries reflect case information. Thus the value of ID 54 is twice that in ID 52, and the latter in turn is twice those in IDs 51 and 53. Any set of positive numbers which maintain these proportions would be acceptable; here the inputs average to one and will not require internal normalization. Nonentry in ID 55 signals the end of the index series.

In MANUFACTURING OR TRADE ITEMS division, an average of 57% of annual sales will be required in merchandise inventory. This entry in ID 152 follows directly from case information. The ratio holds constant over the simulation so the value of ID 153 is 0. The entry of 50 in ID 142 establishes cost of goods at 50% of selling price, again unchanged over the simulation. Thus goods are purchased at a discount of 50% off average sales price, or the mean markup is 100%. Initial finished goods inventories are also priced at 50% of sales value (ID 140). The 12.5% maximum shift entered in ID 141 models uncertainty about the relation between cost and selling price of merchandise. The 25% entry in ID 150 indicates that seasonal adjustment of finished goods inventory will move oppositely from sales to partially remove seasonal peaks from purchases of goods.

In the R&D, SALES, GENERAL AND ADMINISTRATIVE ITEMS input division, less than half of the available categories are required for GIFTIQUE. Unneeded expenses are simply left blank. Entries in ID set 372 and 392 reproduce case estimates precisely. Although both are dynamic input sets, the unchanging percentages over the simulation make one entry sufficient in each. General administrative payroll begins at $21,250 in the first quarter per ID 432. The rate of increase is 6% per year (about 1½ per quarter) in ID 433. Entries in IDs 412, 452, 462, and 472 behave in a similar manner except that the corresponding annual rates of growth are 1% per year in IDs 413, 453, 463, and 473. In all five of the above dynamic input sets, the initial schedule continues unchanged to the end of the simulation. The numbers used are transferred directly from the case. The values 0.1 for ID 402 and 5000 for ID 442 come directly from the case and are unchanged over the simulation. Total supplies are the sum of direct in ID set 402 and indirect in ID set 412.

Depreciation rates are 20% in ID 480 for equipment in *Class 1 fixed assets* (10% double-declining balance in the case), and 25% for delivery equipment in ID 490 for *Class 2 fixed assets*. Percentage maximum shifts for input uncertainty are also specified in the case. They appear in IDs 391, 401, and 451. The 12.5% in ID 451 is applied directly to utilities in ID set 452, but has been adjusted to reflect uncertainty about the group of period expenses. A value of 1 was entered in the percentage of uncollectible accounts for ID 390 because this was GIFTIQUE's estimate. Supplies in inventory average 20% of annual usage, which is the figure entered in ID 79. Accounts payable average 8.333% of annual credit payments (ID 80). Average vendor terms are then 30 days. Although there was prepaid expense in INITIAL CONDITION, no level has been specified for future planning (ID 81 = 0). There are also no intangibles (IDs 83 and 84 are 0).

In FINANCIAL AND VALUATION CONTROL ITEMS division, 9% and 7% specified short-term and long-term interest rates are entered in IDs 562 and 572. Here the rates do not change over the simulation, hence single entries suffice. These rates are uncertain, however; thus maximum shifts of 25% are entered in ID 561 and 12.5% in ID 571. GIFTIQUE plans only a checking account so the ID 531 entry is zero. There are no preplanned additional owner nor debt long-term capital additions, hence IDs 532 and 542 are zero. To put it another way, all required capital additions are to be determined internally by the program. An entry of 1 in ID 530 establishes this decision. The policy of no dividends or withdrawals per period is emphasized by an entry of zero in ID 552. If new capital is raised internally, 25% will be in fixed obligations (ID 540).

The case states that GIFTIQUE will seek short-term bank credit under normal conditions for seasonal financing. Parameters of credit policy are IDs 87, 88, and 95. Nonentry in IDs 87 and 88 activates default values of 50% and 2 to 1 for cash and current ratios. Borrowing on liquidation value of current assets is set at a limit of 70% per input in ID 95. The three ratios provide short-term borrowing limits. There is no initial tax loss carryforward, so ID 90 is zero.

Financial parameter IDs 91 and 92 are concerned with share pricing on new capital additions. These parameters are used to determine the number of new shares required, and to compute certain valuation information on a per share basis. The starting number of shares is 940 in ID 91 per case information. If additional shares are added, the paid-in figure per share, again from the case, is $50 in ID 92. For GIFTIQUE any new shares are priced the same as the initial 940 shares, but in general this need not be the case. The initial and terminal price-earnings multiple parameters in IDs 93 and

94 allow a user to estimate market values in the output. This simple valuation procedure may be compared with results from internal valuation routines. Since there is no specific information in the case about price-earnings multiples, internal computations will apply to GIFTIQUE. Thus entries are not required in IDs 93 and 94.

Parameter IDs 95 to 98 are used for internal valuation. The ID 95 input figure of 70% for liquidation of assets comes directly from the case. The values in IDs 96 to 98 will be computed internally unless they are overwritten (with nonzero entries) by a user. It was stated in the case that internal calculations would be used except for investors' rate of return under risk in ID 96. This internal value is overwritten with a user input of 15% per case specification.

12.3 | Output Interpretations of GIFTIQUE Case

For a simulation of GIFTIQUE, in accordance with the input set previously developed, all four output divisions are reproduced in Table 12.2. Referring first to VALUATION AND SCOPE output division, mean rates of return on owners' equity are close to a break-even level the first year, but improve to a modest figure by the final year (Year 6). Confidence limits of this mean suggest that sufficient precision has been obtained to draw some useful inferences. Mean sales, earnings, and owners' equity increase slowly but steadily over the six-year duration. Risk appears modest.

Insolvencies do not occur, but this is scarcely surprising, since required additional capital, if any, is determined internally. On the average, in fact, $40,898 additional owner paid-in capital will be required and $13,633 in long-term obligations. Most of this will be added in the first year, with a smaller amount the second year. *Earnings* and *cash flow* improve over the six-year duration. To analyze capital additions, see CASH FORECASTS, RETAINED EARNINGS AND CAPITAL CHANGES, and CONDITION statements in FINANCIAL STATEMENTS output division. The matter of required additional capital is one of the major questions on which you are seeking more information.

Returning to method of valuation in VALUATION AND SCOPE division, going-concern economic value is negative at present, and may reach a small positive figure ($41,908) after six years. How can this value be negative when earnings are positive? The answer is simple. Substantial capital additions in early years do not earn enough to repay their cost. Thus mean return on incremental assets is only 8.44% against a cost of 15%. This means that a negative return to current owners of new capital is more than enough to offset a capitalization of the current level of earnings at 15%. At the end of the simulation, on the other hand, rates of return improve and new capital needs are reduced to a long-term growth rate of 7.63%. This permits a small positive going-concern value. Note that the 15% cost of capital was a user requirement. It was an input from ID 96, and was not figured internally.

— Table 12.2. —
OUTPUT FOR GIFTIQUE

```
************************
  VALUATION AND SCOPE
************************
GIFTIGUE
  24 PERIODS OVER  6.00 YEARS;  4.00 PERIODS PER YEAR, EACH  0.25 YEARS
******  SCOPE OF FIRM -- INITIAL SHARES 940 -- FINAL SHARES 1667 -- EOP = END OF PERIOD ******
     99 % CONFIDENCE LIMITS FOR MEANS WITH SAMPLE SIZE 12
```

		MEAN	STANDARD DEVIATION	99 % LOWER CONFIDENCE	99 % UPPER CONFIDENCE
SALES	TOTAL	FIRST YEAR	454,051	7,008	432,327	475,776
		FINAL YEAR	640,216	10,421	607,912	672,520
	PER SHARE	FIRST YEAR	483.03	7.46	459.92	506.14
		FINAL YEAR	384.05	6.25	364.67	403.43
EARNINGS	TOTAL	FIRST YEAR	15,719	1,145	12,171	19,267
		FINAL YEAR	38,863	2,025	32,586	45,140
	PER SHARE	FIRST YEAR	16.72	1.22	12.95	20.50
		FINAL YEAR	23.31	1.21	19.55	27.08
RETURN ON OWNERS' EQUITY %	TOTAL	FIRST YEAR	1.59	1.28	-2.38	5.56
		FINAL YEAR	11.00	0.69	8.86	13.15
OWNERS' EQUITY	TOTAL	AT EOP 1	138,676	2,060	132,291	145,060
		END OF RUN	334,031	6,738	313,145	354,918
	PER SHARE	AT EOP 1	147.53	2.19	140.73	154.32
		END OF RUN	200.38	4.04	187.85	212.91
TOTAL ASSETS	TOTAL	AT EOP 1	206,171	6,705	185,384	226,957
		END OF RUN	480,270	16,822	428,123	532,417
	PER SHARE	AT EOP 1	219.33	7.13	197.22	241.44
		END OF RUN	288.10	10.09	256.82	319.39
CASH AND MARKETABLE SECURITIES	TOTAL	AT EOP 1	32,406	2,235	25,476	39,335
		END OF RUN	80,650	9,580	50,953	110,347
	PER SHARE	AT EOP 1	34.47	2.38	27.10	41.85
		END OF RUN	48.38	5.75	30.57	66.19

```
TECHNICAL INSOLVENCY DID NOT OCCUR
LEGAL INSOLVENCY DID NOT OCCUR
```

Table 12.2 (continued)

****** METHODS OF VALUATION ******

	FIRST YEAR OR EOP 1	FINAL YEAR OR END	FIRST YEAR PER SHARE	FINAL YEAR PER SHARE
MARKET VALUE WITH PRICE-EARNINGS MULTIPLES	76,824	189,950	81.72	113.95
PRICE-EARNINGS MULTIPLES	5	5		
GOING CONCERN ECONOMIC VALUE UNDER RISK	-87,658	41,908	-93.26	25.14
LIQUIDATION VALUE TO OWNERS	76,824	189,950	81.72	113.95
LIQUIDATION VALUE OF TANGIBLE ASSETS	144,319	336,189	153.53	201.67
FIXED ASSETS AT BOOK VALUE WITH INTANGIBLES	16,951	4,468	18.03	2.68
TAX LOSS CARRYFORWARD--INITIAL & END OF RUN	0	0		

****** PARAMETERS OF GOING-CONCERN VALUATION ******

	APPLIED EOP 1	APPLIED END OF RUN
INVESTORS' REQUIRED RATE OF RETURN %	15.00	15.00
INFLATION RATE %	7.00	5.50
LONG-TERM FIRM GROWTH RATE WITH INFLATION %	7.63	7.63
LONG-TERM REAL GROWTH RATE OF THE ECONOMY %	2.07	2.07
MEAN RATE OF RETURN ON INCREMENTAL ASSETS %	8.44	8.44

Table 12.2 (continued)

```
**********************************
FINANCIAL SUMMARY FROM FINAL PERIOD
**********************************
```

GIFTIGUE

24 PERIODS OVER 6.00 YEARS; 4.00 PERIODS PER YEAR, EACH 0.25 YEARS
UNDEFINED RATIOS APPEAR '####+--'; YEARLY VALUES ARE EXTRAPOLATED FROM THE FINAL PERIOD; 0 VALUES OMITTED

99 % CONFIDENCE LIMITS FOR MEANS WITH SAMPLE SIZE 12

	MEAN	STANDARD DEVIATION	99 % LOWER CONFIDENCE	99 % UPPER CONFIDENCE	MINIMUM	MAXIMUM
****** SCOPE OF FIRM ******						
FIRM'S SHARE OF INDUSTRY %	100.00	0.00	100.00	100.00	100.00	100.00
NET SALES OR REVENUE PER YEAR	1,332,009	32,505	1,231,243	1,432,774	1,146,824	1,506,120
CASH AND MARKETABLE SECURITIES	80,650	9,580	50,952	110,348	29,285	137,963
TOTAL ASSETS	480,270	16,822	428,121	532,418	377,469	581,603
TOTAL OWNERS EQUITY	334,031	6,738	313,143	354,918	287,380	368,281
****** RATIO ANALYSIS OF PROFITABILITY ******						
GROSS MARGIN ON SALES %	49.49	0.80	47.01	51.97	45.33	54.76
NET OPERATING MARGIN ON SALES %	25.26	0.90	22.47	28.05	20.95	29.05
OPERATING EARNING POWER %	70.69	3.48	59.90	81.47	57.27	92.22
OPERAT'G EFFIC'Y OR CAP'L TURNS	2.79	0.07	2.57	3.00	2.44	3.20
RETURN ON OWNERS' EQUITY %	57.42	3.34	47.06	67.77	38.79	73.17
****** RATIO ANALYSIS OF FINANCIAL CONDITION ******						
CASH RATIO %	72.41	12.39	34.00	110.81	49.60	191.46
ACID TEST OR QUICK RATIO %	273.24	36.46	160.21	386.26	137.97	509.33
CURRENT RATIO %	463.98	62.33	270.75	657.20	207.47	862.83
DEBT TO TANGIBLE ASSETS %	29.25	3.29	19.05	39.44	13.91	48.57
DEBT TO TANGIBLE OWNER EQUITY %	45.05	7.30	22.42	67.68	16.16	94.45
TIMES INTEREST EARNED RATIO	169.86	48.05	20.90	318.81	22.26	527.05
AVG COLLECTION PERIOD IN DAYS	55.68	1.34	51.52	59.83	47.43	63.34
INVENTORY TURNS PER YEAR	3.51	0.00	3.51	3.51	3.50	3.51

Table 12.2 (continued)

****** SELECTED FINANCIAL SUMMARY VALUES ******

	1,332	33	1,229	1,434	1,147	1,506
INDUSTRY SALES PER YR--000 OMIT						
COST OF SALES PER YEAR	672,313	17,547	617,917	726,708	535,491	738,427
GROSS PROFIT PER YEAR	659,696	20,793	595,237	724,154	557,832	775,327
OPERATING INCOME PER YEAR	338,080	17,610	283,489	392,671	256,785	433,716
NET INCOME BEFORE TAX PER YEAR	332,049	16,636	280,477	383,620	255,422	425,479
NET INCOME AFTER TAX PER YEAR	189,899	8,855	162,448	217,349	142,860	243,399
CASH+MKT SECURITIES+ACCTS RECV	284,034	13,764	241,365	326,702	220,183	383,795
TOTAL INVENTORIES	191,768	4,995	176,283	207,252	152,818	210,569
TOTAL CURRENT ASSETS	475,802	16,822	423,653	527,950	373,001	577,135
NET TANGIBLE FIXED ASSETS	4,468	0	4,468	4,468	4,468	4,468
ACCOUNTS PAYABLE	76,427	3,938	64,219	88,634	43,230	91,130
SHORT-TERM LOANS AND NOTES	56,180	20,799	-8,296	120,656	0	205,612
LONG-TERM FIXED OBLIGATIONS	13,633	1,649	8,521	18,744	4,320	23,053
TOTAL LIABILITIES	146,239	21,046	80,996	211,481	52,504	282,500
TOTAL PAID-IN OWNERS' EQUITY	87,898	4,947	72,562	103,233	59,960	116,158

Table 12.2 (continued)

```
*********************************************
   FINANCIAL STATEMENTS PROJECTED FOR ALL PERIODS
*********************************************

ADMIN   ADMINISTRATIVE        DEPRC   DEPRECIATION        GEN    GENERAL
AMORT   AMORTIZATION          EOP     END OF PERIOD       INVY   INVENTORY
BOP     BEGINNING OF PERIOD   GEN     GENERAL             MFG    MANUFACTURING
MISC    MISCELLANEOUS         PURCH   PURCHASES OF        R&D    RESEARCH AND DEVELOPMENT

24 PERIODS OVER  6.00 YEARS;  4.00 PERIODS PER YEAR, EACH  0.25 YEARS

VALUES ARE ACCOUNT MEANS; ACCOUNT OMITTED WHEN ALL VALUES 0
HEADINGS ARE: PERIOD NO. AND YEAR/MONTH; OR CUMULATIVE *FOR YEAR NO.*

GIFTIGUE
```

```
*********************************************
ENVIRONMENTAL ANALYSES OF FIRM
*********************************************
```

INDUSTRY BASE SALES--000S OMITTED; YEAR= 420 -- PERIOD= 105

	1 0/ 3	2 0/ 6	3 0/ 9	4 1/ 0	*FOR YEAR 1*	5 1/ 3
INFLATION RATE ANNUAL %	7.00	6.96	6.93	6.89	6.95*	6.86
REAL ECONOMY GROWTH ANNUAL %	0.00	0.00	0.00	0.00	0.00*	0.00
INDUSTRY TOTAL GROWTH %	7.00	6.96	6.93	6.89	6.95*	6.86
SEASONAL/CYCLICAL INDICES	0.50	1.00	0.50	2.00	1.00*	0.50
INDUSTRY SALES--000S OMITTED	54	109	54	237	454*	59
FIRM'S INDUSTRY SHARE %	100.00	100.00	100.00	100.00	100.00*	100.00
FIRM SALES DEMAND AVAILABLE	53,688	109,210	54,460	236,694	454,052*	58,733

```
*********************************************
ENVIRONMENTAL ANALYSES OF FIRM   (CONTINUED)
*********************************************
```

	6 1/ 6	7 1/ 9	8 2/ 0	*FOR YEAR 2*	9 2/ 3	10 2/ 6
INFLATION RATE ANNUAL %	6.83	6.79	6.76	6.81*	6.00	5.97
REAL ECONOMY GROWTH ANNUAL %	0.00	0.00	0.00	0.00*	1.00	1.01
INDUSTRY TOTAL GROWTH %	6.83	6.79	6.76	6.81*	7.06	7.04
SEASONAL/CYCLICAL INDICES	1.00	0.50	2.00	1.00*	0.50	1.00
INDUSTRY SALES--000S OMITTED	113	60	241	473*	60	122
FIRM'S INDUSTRY SHARE %	100.00	100.00	100.00	100.00*	100.00	100.00
FIRM SALES DEMAND AVAILABLE	112,667	60,343	240,930	472,673*	60,170	122,485

Table 12.2 (continued)

ENVIRONMENTAL ANALYSES OF FIRM (CONTINUED)
****

	11 2/9	12 3/0	3/0 *FOR YEAR 3*	13 3/3	14 3/6	15 3/9
INFLATION RATE ANNUAL %	5.94	5.91	5.96*	5.88	5.85	5.82
REAL ECONOMY GROWTH ANNUAL %	1.02	1.04	1.02*	1.05	1.06	1.08
INDUSTRY TOTAL GROWTH %	7.03	7.01	7.04*	6.99	6.98	6.96
SEASONAL/CYCLICAL INDICES	0.50	2.00	1.00*	0.50	1.00	0.50
INDUSTRY SALES--000S OMITTED	66	255	503*	65	131	68
FIRM'S INDUSTRY SHARE %	100.00	100.00	100.00*	100.00	100.00	100.00
FIRM SALES DEMAND AVAILABLE	65,604	255,224	503,483*	64,897	130,772	67,831

ENVIRONMENTAL ANALYSES OF FIRM (CONTINUED)
****

	16 4/0 *FOR YEAR 4*	4*	17 4/3	18 4/6	19 4/9	20 5/0
INFLATION RATE ANNUAL %	5.79	5.84*	5.50	5.50	5.50	5.50
REAL ECONOMY GROWTH ANNUAL %	1.09	1.07*	2.00	2.01	2.02	2.03
INDUSTRY TOTAL GROWTH %	6.94	6.97*	7.61	7.62	7.63	7.64
SEASONAL/CYCLICAL INDICES	2.00	1.00*	0.50	1.00	0.50	2.00
INDUSTRY SALES--000S OMITTED	278	542*	68	137	75	279
FIRM'S INDUSTRY SHARE %	100.00	100.00*	100.00	100.00	100.00	100.00
FIRM SALES DEMAND AVAILABLE	278,280	541,780*	68,119	136,627	74,542	279,318

ENVIRONMENTAL ANALYSES OF FIRM (CONTINUED)
****

	FOR YEAR 5	21 5/3	22 5/6	23 5/9	24 6/0 *FOR YEAR 6*	6*
INFLATION RATE ANNUAL %	5.50*	5.50	5.50	5.50	5.50	5.50*
REAL ECONOMY GROWTH ANNUAL %	2.02*	2.04	2.05	2.06	2.07	2.06*
INDUSTRY TOTAL GROWTH %	7.63*	7.65	7.66	7.67	7.68	7.67*
SEASONAL/CYCLICAL INDICES	1.00*	0.50	1.00	0.50	2.00	1.00*
INDUSTRY SALES--000S OMITTED	559*	80	148	79	333	640*
FIRM'S INDUSTRY SHARE %	100.00*	100.00	100.00	100.00	100.00	100.00*
FIRM SALES DEMAND AVAILABLE	558,606*	79,679	148,340	79,195	333,002	640,216*

Table 12.2 (continued)

GIFTIQUE

****
INCOME STATEMENTS
****

	1 O/3	2 O/6	3 O/9	4 1/0	*FOR YEAR 1*	5 1/3
FIRM NET SALES ACHIEVED	53,688	109,210	54,460	236,694	454,052*	58,733
-COST OF SALES	26,974	53,312	28,077	117,327	225,690*	29,417
GROSS PROFIT ON SALES	26,714	55,898	26,383	119,367	228,362*	29,317
DIRECT ADVERTISE, MISC SALES	5,906	12,013	5,991	26,036	49,946*	6,461
TOTAL SALES EXPENSE	5,906	12,013	5,991	26,036	49,946*	6,461
PERIOD GEN ADMIN PAYROLL	21,250	21,562	21,878	22,199	86,889*	22,525
PURCH GEN SUPPLIES	770	532	385	772	2,459*	291
+BOP GEN SUPPLIES INVY	0	342	389	344	0*	496
-EOP GEN SUPPLIES INVY	342	389	344	496	496*	350
DIRECT GEN SUPPLIES USED	53	110	53	242	458*	59
PERIOD GEN SUPPLIES USED	375	376	377	378	1,506*	379
SPACE AND RENT--GEN	5,000	5,000	5,000	5,000	20,000*	5,000
UTILITIES--GEN	1,671	1,663	1,629	1,646	6,609*	1,660
MAINTAIN EQUIPMENT--GEN	325	326	327	327	1,305*	328
MISC PERIOD ADMIN EXP--GEN	4,000	4,010	4,020	4,030	16,060*	4,040
DEPRC ON FIXED ASSETS--GEN	1,021	962	907	855	3,745*	806
UNCOLLECTIBLE ACCOUNTS	622	786	859	1,313	3,580*	1,628
TOTAL GEN AND ADMIN EXP	34,317	34,795	35,049	35,991	140,152*	36,425
TOTAL OPERATING EXPENSE	40,223	46,808	41,040	62,027	190,098*	42,885
SALES MARGIN OVER DIRECT EXP	19,734	42,812	19,432	92,233	174,211*	21,991
NET OPERATING INCOME	-13,509	9,090	-14,657	57,339	38,263*	-13,569
-INTEREST, SHORT-TERM	1,207	1,729	1,487	2,200	6,623*	120
-INTEREST, LONG-TERM FIXED	13	32	38	118	201*	197
NET INCOME BEFORE INCOME TAX	-14,730	7,329	-16,182	55,021	31,438*	-13,886
-INCOME TAXES	0	0	0	15,719	15,719*	0
NET INCOME AFTER INCOME TAX	-14,730	7,329	-16,182	39,302	15,719*	-13,886

Table 12.2 (continued)

INCOME STATEMENTS (CONTINUED)
****

	6 1/ 6	7	8 2/ 0	*FOR YEAR 2*	9 2/ 3	10 2/ 6
FIRM NET SALES ACHIEVED	112,667	60,343	240,930	472,073*	60,170	122,485
-COST OF SALES	55,689	30,693	120,511	236,310*	30,463	60,050
GROSS PROFIT ON SALES	56,978	29,650	120,419	236,364*	29,708	62,435
DIRECT ADVERTISE, MISC SALES	12,393	6,638	26,502	51,994*	6,619	13,473
TOTAL SALES EXPENSE	12,393	6,638	26,502	51,994*	6,619	13,473
PERIOD GEN ADMIN PAYROLL	22,856	23,191	23,531	92,103*	23,877	24,227
PURCH GEN SUPPLIES	537	403	765	1,996*	299	557
+BOP GEN SUPPLIES INVY	350	394	354	496*	497	354
-EOP GEN SUPPLIES INVY	394	354	497	497*	354	405
DIRECT GEN SUPPLIES USED	113	62	240	474*	60	122
PERIOD GEN SUPPLIES USED	380	381	382	1,522*	383	383
SPACE AND RENT--GEN	5,000	5,000	5,000	20,000*	5,000	5,000
UTILITIES--GEN	1,681	1,634	1,662	6,637*	1,686	1,719
MAINTAIN EQUIPMENT--GEN	329	330	331	1,318*	332	332
MISC PERIOD ADMIN EXP--GEN	4,050	4,060	4,070	16,220*	4,080	4,091
DEPRC ON FIXED ASSETS--GEN	760	716	675	2,957*	637	600
UNCOLLECTIBLE ACCOUNTS	786	918	1,331	4,663*	1,690	857
TOTAL GEN AND ADMIN EXP	35,954	36,292	37,222	145,893*	37,743	37,332
TOTAL OPERATING EXPENSE	48,347	42,930	63,724	197,886*	44,362	50,805
SALES MARGIN OVER DIRECT EXP	43,712	22,234	93,002	180,939*	22,393	48,239
NET OPERATING INCOME	8,631	-13,280	56,695	38,477*	-14,654	11,630
-INTEREST COST, SHORT-TERM	550	425	1,471	2,566*	5	235
-INTEREST, LONG-TERM FIXED	199	198	218	812*	236	238
NET INCOME BEFORE INCOME TAX	7,882	-13,903	55,007	35,100*	-14,896	11,157
-INCOME TAXES	127	0	17,423	17,550*	0	867
NET INCOME AFTER INCOME TAX	7,755	-13,903	37,584	17,550*	-14,896	10,290

Table 12.2 (continued)

INCOME STATEMENTS (CONTINUED)
****

	11 2/9	12 3/0	*FOR YEAR 3*	13 3/3	14 3/6	15 3/9
FIRM NET SALES ACHIEVED	65,604	255,224	503,483*	64,897	130,772	67,831
-COST OF SALES	32,025	128,565	251,103*	32,082	65,627	33,831
GROSS PROFIT ON SALES	33,580	126,659	252,382*	32,815	65,145	34,000
DIRECT ADVERTISE, MISC SALES	7,216	28,075	55,383*	7,139	14,385	7,461
TOTAL SALES EXPENSE	7,216	28,075	55,383*	7,139	14,385	7,461
PERIOD GEN ADMIN PAYROLL	24,582	24,943	97,629*	25,309	25,680	26,057
PURCH GEN SUPPLIES	407	794	2,057*	300	568	409
+BOP GEN SUPPLIES INVY	405	361	497*	513	362	413
-EOP GEN SUPPLIES INVY	361	513	513*	362	413	366
DIRECT GEN SUPPLIES USED	67	256	505*	66	129	69
PERIOD GEN SUPPLIES USED	384	385	1,535*	386	387	388
SPACE AND RENT--GEN	5,000	5,000	20,000*	5,000	5,000	5,000
UTILITIES--GEN	1,650	1,719	6,774*	1,686	1,663	1,694
MAINTAIN EQUIPMENT--GEN	333	334	1,331*	335	336	337
MISC PERIOD ADMIN EXP--GEN	4,101	4,111	16,383*	4,121	4,131	4,142
DEPRC ON FIXED ASSETS--GEN	566	534	2,337*	503	474	447
UNCOLLECTIBLE ACCOUNTS	976	1,365	4,888*	1,853	918	1,074
TOTAL GEN AND ADMIN EXP	37,659	38,647	151,381*	39,260	38,720	39,208
TOTAL OPERATING EXPENSE	44,876	66,721	206,764*	46,398	53,104	46,669
SALES MARGIN OVER DIRECT EXP	25,731	97,795	194,158*	25,108	50,157	26,022
NET OPERATING INCOME	-11,296	59,938	45,618*	-13,583	12,041	-12,670
-INTEREST COST, SHORT-TERM	24	1,446	1,710*	0	30	51
-INTEREST, LONG-TERM FIXED	237	238	949*	238	238	240
NET INCOME BEFORE INCOME TAX	-11,558	58,254	42,957*	-13,822	11,773	-12,961
-INCOME TAXES	0	20,612	21,479*	0	1,289	0
NET INCOME AFTER INCOME TAX	-11,558	37,642	21,478*	-13,822	10,484	-12,961

Table 12.2 (continued)

INCOME STATEMENTS   (CONTINUED)
****

	16 4/ 0 *FOR YEAR	4*	17 4/ 3	18 4/ 6	19 4/ 9	20 5/ 0
FIRM NET SALES ACHIEVED	278,280	541,780*	68,119	136,627	74,542	279,318
-COST OF SALES	139,589	271,129*	34,551	68,856	36,975	141,357
GROSS PROFIT ON SALES	138,691	270,651*	33,568	67,771	37,568	137,960
DIRECT ADVERTISE, MISC SALES	30,611	59,596*	7,493	15,029	8,200	30,725
TOTAL SALES EXPENSE	30,611	59,596*	7,493	15,029	8,200	30,725
PERIOD GEN ADMIN PAYROLL	26,440	103,486*	26,828	27,221	27,621	28,026
PURCH GEN SUPPLIES	845	2,122*	286	584	414	830
+BOP GEN SUPPLIES INVY	366	513*	538	366	422	372
-EOP GEN SUPPLIES INVY	538	538*	366	422	372	534
DIRECT GEN SUPPLIES USED	283	547*	68	137	72	274
PERIOD GEN SUPPLIES USED	389	1,550*	390	391	392	393
SPACE AND RENT--GEN	5,000	20,000*	5,000	5,000	5,000	5,000
UTILITIES--GEN	1,714	6,757*	1,715	1,726	1,763	1,734
MAINTAIN EQUIPMENT--GEN	337	1,345*	338	339	340	341
MISC PERIOD ADMIN EXP--GEN	4,152	16,546*	4,162	4,173	4,183	4,194
DEPRC ON FIXED ASSETS--GEN	422	1,846*	398	375	354	334
UNCOLLECTIBLE ACCOUNTS	1,560	5,405*	1,888	955	1,125	1,492
TOTAL GEN AND ADMIN EXP	40,298	157,486*	40,786	40,318	40,851	41,788
TOTAL OPERATING EXPENSE	70,908	217,079*	48,279	55,347	49,051	72,513
SALES MARGIN OVER DIRECT EXP	107,375	208,662*	25,609	52,230	28,942	106,627
NET OPERATING INCOME	67,783	53,571*	-14,712	12,424	-11,483	65,447
-INTEREST COST, SHORT-TERM	1,069	1,150*	0	33	52	851
-INTEREST, LONG-TERM FIXED	240	956*	239	238	238	237
NET INCOME BEFORE INCOME TAX	66,474	51,464*	-14,951	12,153	-11,773	64,359
-INCOME TAXES	24,443	25,732*	0	1,115	0	23,779
NET INCOME AFTER INCOME TAX	42,031	25,732*	-14,951	11,039	-11,773	40,579

Table 12.2 (continued)

INCOME STATEMENTS (CONTINUED)
****

	FOR YEAR 5	21 5/3	22 5/6	23 5/9	24 6/0	*FOR YEAR 6*
FIRM NET SALES ACHIEVED	558,606*	79,679	148,340	79,195	333,002	640,216*
-COST OF SALES	281,739*	39,827	71,782	39,177	168,078	318,864*
GROSS PROFIT ON SALES	276,867*	39,852	76,558	40,017	164,924	321,351*
DIRECT ADVERTISE, MISC SALES	61,447*	8,765	16,317	8,711	36,630	70,423*
TOTAL SALES EXPENSE	61,447*	8,765	16,317	8,711	36,630	70,423*
PERIOD GEN ADMIN PAYROLL	109,696*	28,437	28,855	29,278	29,708	116,278*
PURCH GEN SUPPLIES	2,114*	320	597	420	923	2,260*
+BOP GEN SUPPLIES INVY	538*	534	379	434	379	534*
-EOP GEN SUPPLIES INVY	534*	379	434	379	579	579*
DIRECT GEN SUPPLIES USED	551*	80	147	78	327	632*
PERIOD GEN SUPPLIES USED	1,566*	394	395	396	397	1,582*
SPACE AND RENT--GEN	20,000*	5,000	5,000	5,000	5,000	20,000*
UTILITIES--GEN	6,938*	1,756	1,730	1,758	1,734	6,978*
MAINTAIN EQUIPMENT--GEN	1,358*	342	342	343	344	1,371*
MISC PERIOD ADMIN EXP--GEN	16,712*	4,204	4,215	4,225	4,236	16,880*
DEPRC ON FIXED ASSETS--GEN	1,461*	315	297	280	264	1,156*
UNCOLLECTIBLE ACCOUNTS	5,460*	2,037	1,087	1,209	1,764	6,097*
TOTAL GEN AND ADMIN EXP	163,743*	42,566	42,069	42,567	43,774	170,976*
TOTAL OPERATING EXPENSE	225,190*	51,330	58,386	51,279	80,404	241,399*
SALES MARGIN OVER DIRECT EXP	213,408*	30,692	59,796	30,948	127,703	249,139*
NET OPERATING INCOME	51,676*	-11,479	18,172	-11,261	84,520	79,952*
-INTEREST COST, SHORT-TERM	936*	0	0	0	1,270	1,270*
-INTEREST, LONG-TERM FIXED	952*	239	239	239	238	955*
NET INCOME BEFORE INCOME TAX	49,788*	-11,718	17,933	-11,501	83,012	77,726*
-INCOME TAXES	24,894*	0	3,326	0	35,537	38,863*
NET INCOME AFTER INCOME TAX	24,894*	-11,718	14,607	-11,501	47,475	38,863*

Table 12.2 (continued)

```
GIFTIQUE
*****************************************
COST OF GOODS SOLD SCHEDULES
*****************************************
```

	1 0/ 3	2 0/ 6	3 0/ 9	4 1/ 0	*FOR YEAR 1*	5 1/ 3
COST OF FINISHED GOODS	22,801	51,727	34,698	122,615	231,841*	31,468
+BOP FINISHED GOODS INVY	127,310	123,137	121,551	128,172	127,310*	133,460
-EOP FINISHED GOODS INVY	123,137	121,551	128,172	133,460	133,460*	135,511
COST OF GOODS SOLD	26,974	53,312	28,077	117,327	225,690*	29,417

```
COST OF GOODS SOLD SCHEDULES (CONTINUED)
*****************************************
```

	6 1/ 6	7 1/ 9	8 2/ 0	*FOR YEAR 2*	9 2/ 3	10 2/ 6
COST OF FINISHED GOODS	47,149	43,833	117,480	239,930*	34,522	55,824
+BOP FINISHED GOODS INVY	135,511	126,971	140,112	133,460*	137,081	141,140
-EOP FINISHED GOODS INVY	136,914	140,112	137,081	137,081*	141,140	136,914
COST OF GOODS SOLD	55,689	30,693	120,511	236,310*	30,463	60,050

```
COST OF GOODS SOLD SCHEDULES (CONTINUED)
*****************************************
```

	11 2/ 9	12 3/ 0	*FOR YEAR 3*	13 3/ 3	14 3/ 6	15 3/ 9
COST OF FINISHED GOODS	41,303	128,615	260,264*	32,292	68,802	40,301
+BOP FINISHED GOODS INVY	136,914	146,193	137,081*	146,243	146,453	149,629
-EOP FINISHED GOODS INVY	146,193	146,243	146,243*	146,453	149,629	156,098
COST OF GOODS SOLD	32,025	128,565	251,103*	32,082	65,627	33,831

```
COST OF GOODS SOLD SCHEDULES (CONTINUED)
*****************************************
```

	16 4/ 0	*FOR YEAR 4*	17 4/ 3	18 4/ 6	19 4/ 9	20 5/ 0
COST OF FINISHED GOODS	142,272	283,667*	36,138	65,479	48,772	133,362
+BOP FINISHED GOODS INVY	156,098	146,243*	158,782	160,369	156,992	168,789
-EOP FINISHED GOODS INVY	158,782	158,782*	160,369	156,992	168,789	160,794
COST OF GOODS SOLD	139,589	271,129*	34,551	68,856	36,975	141,357

```
COST OF GOODS SOLD SCHEDULES (CONTINUED)
*****************************************
```

	FOR YEAR 5	21 5/ 3	22 5/ 6	23 5/ 9	24 6/ 0	*FOR YEAR 6*
COST OF FINISHED GOODS	283,751*	62,437	52,042	54,359	180,422	349,260*
+BOP FINISHED GOODS INVY	158,782*	160,794	183,404	163,664	178,845	160,794*
-EOP FINISHED GOODS INVY	160,794*	183,404	163,664	178,845	191,189	191,189*
COST OF GOODS SOLD	281,739*	39,827	71,782	39,177	168,078	318,864*

Table 12.2 (continued)

GIFTIQUE

```
****************************************
CASH FORECASTS AND FLOW ANALYSES
****************************************
```

	1 0/3	2 0/6	3 0/9	4 1/0	*FOR YEAR 1*	5 1/3
CASH RECEIPTS FROM SALES	61,570	77,785	84,993	129,999	354,347*	161,194
PAYMENTS ON ACCOUNT	95,129	62,470	59,789	124,303	341,691*	86,306
PAYMENTS ON PAYROLLS	21,250	21,562	21,878	22,199	86,889*	22,525
TOTAL OPERATING PAYMENTS	116,379	84,032	81,667	146,502	428,580*	108,831
NET CASH FLOW ON OPERATIONS	-54,809	-6,247	3,326	-16,502	-74,232*	52,362
NET CHANGE SHORT-TERM CREDIT	53,703	22,929	-11,186	32,757	98,203*	-92,899
+ REQUIRED LONG OBLIGATIONS	1,503	658	21	9,114	11,296*	0
-INTEREST, INCOME TAX COST	1,220	1,761	1,525	18,038	22,544*	317
TOTAL NET CASH FLOW	-824	15,578	-9,364	7,332	12,722*	-40,853
+ REQUIRED OWNERS' EQUITY	4,509	1,973	62	27,343	33,887*	0
+BOP CASH AND SECURITIES	28,720	32,406	49,956	40,654	28,720*	75,328
CASH AND SECURITIES EOP	32,406	49,956	40,654	75,328	75,328*	34,475

Table 12.2 (continued)

CASH FORECASTS AND FLOW ANALYSES (CONTINUED)
****

	6 1/6	7 1/9	8 2/0	*FOR YEAR 2*	9 2/3	10 2/6
CASH RECEIPTS FROM SALES	77,796	90,917	131,785	461,692*	167,266	84,879
PAYMENTS ON ACCOUNT	63,842	64,978	124,507	339,633*	86,960	71,510
PAYMENTS ON PAYROLLS	22,856	23,191	23,531	92,103*	23,877	24,227
TOTAL OPERATING PAYMENTS	86,698	88,169	148,038	431,736*	110,837	95,737
NET CASH FLOW ON OPERATIONS	-8,902	2,748	-16,253	29,955*	56,429	-10,858
NET CHANGE SHORT-TERM CREDIT	18,798	-5,243	46,737	-32,607*	-65,357	10,327
+ REQUIRED LONG OBLIGATIONS	0	0	2,253	2,253*	0	0
-INTEREST, INCOME TAX COST	875	623	19,111	20,926*	242	1,340
TOTAL NET CASH FLOW	9,021	-3,119	13,625	-21,325*	-9,170	-1,871
+ REQUIRED OWNERS' EQUITY	0	0	6,758	6,758*	0	0
+BOP CASH AND SECURITIES	34,475	43,496	40,377	75,328*	60,760	51,590
CASH AND SECURITIES EOP	43,496	40,377	60,760	60,760*	51,590	49,719

CASH FORECASTS AND FLOW ANALYSES (CONTINUED)
****

	11 2/9	12 3/0	*FOR YEAR 3*	13 3/3	14 3/6	15 3/9
CASH RECEIPTS FROM SALES	96,606	135,089	483,840*	183,495	90,850	106,337
PAYMENTS ON ACCOUNT	67,006	132,437	357,913*	90,130	80,216	71,190
PAYMENTS ON PAYROLLS	24,582	24,943	97,629*	25,309	25,680	26,057
TOTAL OPERATING PAYMENTS	91,588	157,380	455,542*	115,439	105,896	97,248
NET CASH FLOW ON OPERATIONS	5,018	-22,291	28,298*	68,056	-15,046	9,089
NET CHANGE SHORT-TERM CREDIT	-9,520	62,720	-1,830*	-63,766	1,356	992
+ REQUIRED LONG OBLIGATIONS	0	84	84*	0	0	0
-INTEREST, INCOME TAX COST	262	22,295	24,139*	238	1,557	291
TOTAL NET CASH FLOW	-4,764	18,218	2,413*	4,052	-15,248	9,790
+ REQUIRED OWNERS' EQUITY	0	253	253*	0	0	0
+BOP CASH AND SECURITIES	49,719	44,955	60,760*	63,426	67,477	52,230
CASH AND SECURITIES EOP	44,955	63,426	63,426*	67,477	52,230	62,019

Table 12.2 (continued)

CASH FORECASTS AND FLOW ANALYSES (CONTINUED)
****

	16 4/.0	*FOR YEAR 4*	17 4/3	18 4/6	19 4/9	20 5/0
CASH RECEIPTS FROM SALES	154,426	535,108*	186,873	94,554	111,420	147,700
PAYMENTS ON ACCOUNT	143,070	384,606*	98,397	79,931	76,558	140,349
PAYMENTS ON PAYROLLS	26,440	103,486*	26,828	27,221	27,621	28,026
TOTAL OPERATING PAYMENTS	169,510	488,093*	125,225	107,153	104,178	168,375
NET CASH FLOW ON OPERATIONS	-15,084	47,015*	61,649	-12,598	7,241	-20,675
NET CHANGE SHORT-TERM CREDIT	45,198	-16,220*	-47,545	1,487	823	36,028
+ REQUIRED LONG OBLIGATIONS	0	0*	0	0	0	0
-INTEREST, INCOME TAX COST	25,752	27,838*	239	1,386	290	24,868
TOTAL NET CASH FLOW	4,362	2,956*	13,865	-12,497	7,774	-9,515
+ REQUIRED OWNERS' EQUITY	0	0*	0	0	0	0
+BOP CASH AND SECURITIES	62,019	63,426*	66,381	80,246	67,749	75,523
CASH AND SECURITIES EOP	66,381	66,381*	80,246	67,749	75,523	66,009

CASH FORECASTS AND FLOW ANALYSES (CONTINUED)
****

	FOR YEAR 5	21 5/3	22 5/6	23 5/9	24 6/0	*FOR YEAR 6*
CASH RECEIPTS FROM SALES	540,547*	201,681	107,636	119,687	174,633	603,637*
PAYMENTS ON ACCOUNT	395,235*	113,943	81,104	76,625	177,800	449,472*
PAYMENTS ON PAYROLLS	109,696*	28,437	28,855	29,278	29,708	116,278*
TOTAL OPERATING PAYMENTS	504,931*	142,380	109,958	105,903	207,508	565,749*
NET CASH FLOW ON OPERATIONS	35,617*	59,301	-2,322	13,784	-32,875	37,888*
NET CHANGE SHORT-TERM CREDIT	-9,207*	-38,338	0	0	56,180	17,842*
+ REQUIRED LONG OBLIGATIONS	0*	0	0	0	0	0*
-INTEREST, INCOME TAX COST	26,783*	239	3,565	240	37,045	41,089*
TOTAL NET CASH FLOW	-373*	20,724	-5,886	13,545	-13,741	14,642*
+ REQUIRED OWNERS' EQUITY	0*	0	0	0	0	0*
+BOP CASH AND SECURITIES	66,381*	66,009	86,733	80,846	94,391	66,009*
CASH AND SECURITIES EOP	66,009*	86,733	80,846	94,391	80,650	80,650*

Table 12.2 (continued)

GIFTIQUE

****
RETAINED EARNINGS AND CAPITAL CHANGES
****

	1 0/ 3	2 0/ 6	3 0/ 9	4 1/ 0	*FOR YEAR 1*	5 1/ 3
BOP OWNER PAID-IN CAPITAL	47,000	51,509	53,482	53,544	47,000*	80,887
+OWNER NET INVESTMENT	4,509	1,973	62	27,343	33,887*	0
EOP OWNER PAID-IN CAPITAL	51,509	53,482	53,544	80,887	80,887*	80,887
BOP RETAINED EARNINGS	101,896	87,166	94,496	78,314	101,896*	117,615
+NET INCOME	-14,730	7,329	-16,182	39,302	15,719*	-13,886
EOP RETAINED EARNINGS	87,166	94,496	78,314	117,615	117,615*	103,729
EOP TOTAL OWNERS' EQUITY	138,676	147,978	131,858	198,502	198,502*	184,616
EOP NO. SHARES OUTSTANDING	940	979	980	1,527	1,107*	1,527
NET INCOME PER SHARE	-15.67	7.49	-16.51	25.74	1.05*	-9.09
EOP OWNERS' EQUITY PER SHARE	147.53	151.15	134.55	129.99	129.99*	120.90

RETAINED EARNINGS AND CAPITAL CHANGES (CONTINUED)
****

	6 1/ 6	7 1/ 9	8 2/ 0	*FOR YEAR 2*	9 2/ 3	10 2/ 6
BOP OWNER PAID-IN CAPITAL	80,887	80,887	80,887	80,887*	87,645	87,645
+OWNER NET INVESTMENT	0	0	6,758	6,758*	0	0
EOP OWNER PAID-IN CAPITAL	80,887	80,887	87,645	87,645*	87,645	87,645
BOP RETAINED EARNINGS	103,729	111,485	97,582	117,615*	135,165	120,269
+NET INCOME	7,755	-13,903	37,584	17,550*	-14,896	10,290
EOP RETAINED EARNINGS	111,485	97,582	135,165	135,165*	120,269	130,559
EOP TOTAL OWNERS' EQUITY	192,371	178,468	222,810	222,810*	207,914	218,204
EOP NO. SHARES OUTSTANDING	1,527	1,527	1,662	1,561*	1,662	1,662
NET INCOME PER SHARE	5.08	-9.10	22.61	9.50*	-8.96	6.19
EOP OWNERS' EQUITY PER SHARE	125.98	116.88	134.06	134.06*	125.10	131.29

Table 12.2 (continued)

RETAINED EARNINGS AND CAPITAL CHANGES (CONTINUED)
****

	11 2/9	12 3/0	*FOR YEAR 3*	13 3/3	14 3/6	15 3/9
BOP OWNER PAID-IN CAPITAL	87,645	87,645	87,645*	87,898	87,898	87,898
+OWNER NET INVESTMENT	0	253	253*	0	0	0
EOP OWNER PAID-IN CAPITAL	87,645	87,898	87,898*	87,898	87,898	87,898
BOP RETAINED EARNINGS	130,559	119,002	135,165*	156,644	142,823	153,307
+NET INCOME	-11,558	37,642	21,478*	-13,822	10,484	-12,961
EOP RETAINED EARNINGS	119,002	156,644	156,644*	142,823	153,307	140,346
EOP TOTAL OWNERS' EQUITY	206,646	244,542	244,542*	230,720	241,204	228,243
EOP NO. SHARES OUTSTANDING	1,662	1,667	1,663*	1,667	1,667	1,667
NET INCOME PER SHARE	-6.95	22.58	12.86*	-8.29	6.29	-7.78
EOP OWNERS' EQUITY PER SHARE	124.34	146.70	146.70*	138.40	144.69	136.92

RETAINED EARNINGS AND CAPITAL CHANGES (CONTINUED)
****

	16 4/0	*FOR YEAR 4*	17 4/3	18 4/6	19 4/9	20 5/0
BOP OWNER PAID-IN CAPITAL	87,898	87,898*	87,898	87,898	87,898	87,898
+OWNER NET INVESTMENT	0	0*	0	0	0	0
EOP OWNER PAID-IN CAPITAL	87,898	87,898*	87,898	87,898	87,898	87,898
BOP RETAINED EARNINGS	140,346	156,644*	182,376	167,425	178,464	166,691
+NET INCOME	42,031	25,732*	-14,951	11,039	-11,773	40,579
EOP RETAINED EARNINGS	182,376	182,376*	167,425	178,464	166,691	207,270
EOP TOTAL OWNERS' EQUITY	270,274	270,274*	255,323	266,362	254,588	295,168
EOP NO. SHARES OUTSTANDING	1,667	1,667*	1,667	1,667	1,667	1,667
NET INCOME PER SHARE	25.21	15.43*	-8.97	6.62	-7.06	24.34
EOP OWNERS' EQUITY PER SHARE	162.13	162.13*	153.16	159.79	152.72	177.07

Table 12.2 (continued)

RETAINED EARNINGS AND CAPITAL CHANGES (CONTINUED)
****

	FOR YEAR 5	21 5/ 3	22 5/ 6	23 5/ 9	24 6/ 0	*FOR YEAR 6*
BOP OWNER PAID-IN CAPITAL	87,898*	87,898	87,898	87,898	87,898	87,898*
+OWNER NET INVESTMENT	0*	0	0	0	0	0*
EOP OWNER PAID-IN CAPITAL	87,898*	87,898	87,898	87,898	87,898	87,898*
BOP RETAINED EARNINGS	182,376*	207,270	195,552	210,160	198,659	207,270*
+NET INCOME	24,894*	-11,718	14,607	-11,501	47,475	38,863*
EOP RETAINED EARNINGS	207,270*	195,552	210,160	198,659	246,133	246,133*
EOP TOTAL OWNERS' EQUITY	295,168*	283,450	298,057	286,556	334,031	334,031*
EOP NO. SHARES OUTSTANDING	1,667*	1,667	1,667	1,667	1,667	1,667*
NET INCOME PER SHARE	14.93*	-7.03	8.76	-6.90	28.48	23.31*
EOP OWNERS' EQUITY PER SHARE	177.07*	170.04	178.80	171.90	200.38	200.38*

Table 12.2 (continued)

```
GIFTIQUE
**************************************
CONDITION STATEMENTS (BALANCE SHEETS)          EOP ALL COLUMNS EXCEPT FIRST
**************************************
```

	START BOP 1	1 0/3	2 0/6	3 0/9	4 1/0*	5 1/3
****** ASSETS ******						
CASH AND MARKET SECURITIES	28,720*	32,406	49,956	40,654	75,328*	34,475
+ACCOUNTS RECEIVABLE GROSS	41,839*	33,957	65,382	34,849	141,543*	39,083
-UNCOLLECTIBLES RESERVE	0*	622	1,408	2,266	3,579*	5,207
CASH+SECURITIES+ACCT RECV	70,559*	65,741	113,931	73,237	213,293*	68,351
PREPAID EXPENSE	3,605*	0	0	0	0*	0
FINISHED GOODS INVENTORY	127,310*	123,137	121,551	128,172	133,460*	135,511
SUPPLIES INVENTORY--GEN	0*	342	389	344	496*	350
TOTAL INVENTORIES	127,310*	123,479	121,940	128,516	133,956*	135,861
TOTAL CURRENT ASSETS	201,474*	189,220	235,871	201,752	347,248*	204,212
GEN FIXED ASSETS AT COST:						
CLASS 1	43,163*	43,163	43,163	43,163	43,163*	43,163
CLASS 2	9,806*	9,806	9,806	9,806	9,806*	9,806
GEN FIXED ASSETS DEPRC RESERVES:						
CLASS 1	34,997*	35,405	35,793	36,162	36,512*	36,844
CLASS 2	0*	613	1,187	1,726	2,231*	2,705
GEN FIXED ASSETS AT BOOK	17,972*	16,951	15,988	15,081	14,226*	13,420
TOTAL ASSETS	219,445*	206,171	251,859	216,834	361,475*	217,632

Table 12.2 (continued)

CONDITION STATEMENTS (BALANCE SHEETS) (CONTINUED)

	START BOP 1	1 0/ 3	2 0/ 6	3 0/ 9	4 1/ 0*	5 1/ 3
****** LIABILITIES AND OWNERS' EQUITY ******						
ACCOUNTS PAYABLE	70,550*	12,289	25,089	17,349	53,474*	16,415
SHORT-TERM LOANS AND NOTES	0*	53,703	76,632	65,446	98,203*	5,305
TOTAL CURRENT LIABILITIES	70,550*	65,992	101,721	82,795	151,677*	21,720
LONG-TERM OBLIGATIONS	0*	1,503	2,161	2,181	11,296*	11,296
TOTAL LIABILITIES	70,550*	67,495	103,882	84,976	162,973*	33,016
TOTAL OWNERS' EQUITY	148,896*	138,676	147,978	131,858	198,502*	184,616
LIABILITIES & OWNER EQUITY	219,446*	205,171	251,859	216,834	361,475*	217,632

Table 12.2 (continued)

CONDITION STATEMENTS (BALANCE SHEETS) (CONTINUED)
****

****** ASSETS ******

	6 1/6	7 1/9	8 2/0*	9 2/3	10 2/6	11 2/9
CASH AND MARKET SECURITIES	43,496	40,377	60,760*	51,590	49,719	44,955
+ACCOUNTS RECEIVABLE GROSS	73,954	43,380	152,525*	45,430	83,036	52,035
-UNCOLLECTIBLES RESERVE	5,993	6,912	8,243*	9,932	10,790	11,766
CASH+SECURITIES+ACCT RECV	111,456	76,845	205,042*	87,087	121,965	85,224
PREPAID EXPENSE	0	0	0*	0	0	0
FINISHED GOODS INVENTORY	126,971	140,112	137,081*	141,140	136,914	146,193
SUPPLIES INVENTORY--GEN	394	354	497*	354	405	361
TOTAL INVENTORIES	127,365	140,466	137,578*	141,494	137,319	146,554
TOTAL CURRENT ASSETS	238,821	217,311	342,620*	228,581	259,284	231,777
GEN FIXED ASSETS AT COST:						
CLASS 1	43,163	43,163	43,163*	43,163	43,163	43,163
CLASS 2	9,806	9,806	9,806*	9,806	9,806	9,806
GEN FIXED ASSETS DEPRC RESERVES:						
CLASS 1	37,160	37,460	37,746*	38,016	38,274	38,518
CLASS 2	3,148	3,564	3,955*	4,320	4,663	4,985
GEN FIXED ASSETS AT BOOK	12,660	11,944	11,269*	10,632	10,032	9,466
TOTAL ASSETS	251,482	229,255	353,889*	239,214	269,316	241,244

Table 12.2 (continued)

CONDITION STATEMENTS (BALANCE SHEETS) (CONTINUED)

****** LIABILITIES AND OWNERS' EQUITY ******

	6 1/ 6	7 1/ 9	8 2/ 0*	9 2/ 3	10 2/ 6	11 2/ 9
ACCOUNTS PAYABLE	23,712	20,632	51,935*	17,512	26,998	20,003
SHORT-TERM LOANS AND NOTES	24,103	18,860	65,597*	240	10,567	1,046
TOTAL CURRENT LIABILITIES	47,815	39,491	117,531*	17,751	37,564	21,049
LONG-TERM OBLIGATIONS	11,296	11,296	13,548*	13,548	13,548	13,548
TOTAL LIABILITIES	59,110	50,787	131,079*	31,300	51,112	34,597
TOTAL OWNERS' EQUITY	192,371	178,468	222,810*	207,914	218,204	206,646
LIABILITIES & OWNER EQUITY	251,482	229,255	353,889*	239,214	269,316	241,244

Table 12.2 (continued)

CONDITION STATEMENTS (BALANCE SHEETS) (CONTINUED)
****

****** ASSETS ******	12 3/0*	13 3/3	14 3/6	15 3/9	16 4/0*	17 4/3
CASH AND MARKET SECURITIES	63,426*	67,477	52,230	62,019	66,381*	80,246
+ACCOUNTS RECEIVABLE GROSS	172,170*	53,572	93,494	54,988	178,841*	60,086
-UNCOLLECTIBLES RESERVE	13,130*	14,984	15,901	16,975	18,535*	20,423
CASH+SECURITIES+ACCT RECV	222,465*	106,066	129,823	100,032	226,687*	119,909
PREPAID EXPENSE	0*	0	0	0	0*	0
FINISHED GOODS INVENTORY	146,243*	146,453	149,629	156,098	158,782*	160,369
SUPPLIES INVENTORY--GEN	513*	362	413	366	538*	366
TOTAL INVENTORIES	146,756*	146,815	150,042	156,464	159,320*	160,735
TOTAL CURRENT ASSETS	369,221*	252,880	279,865	256,496	386,007*	280,645
GEN FIXED ASSETS AT COST:						
CLASS 1	43,163*	43,163	43,163	43,163	43,163*	43,163
CLASS 2	9,806*	9,806	9,806	9,806	9,806*	9,806
GEN FIXED ASSETS DEPRC RESERVES:						
CLASS 1	38,750*	38,971	39,181	39,380	39,569*	39,749
CLASS 2	5,286*	5,568	5,833	6,082	6,314*	6,533
GEN FIXED ASSETS AT BOOK	8,933*	8,430	7,955	7,508	7,086*	6,688
TOTAL ASSETS	378,154*	261,310	287,820	264,003	393,093*	287,332

Table 12.2 (continued)

CONDITION STATEMENTS (BALANCE SHEETS) (CONTINUED)

	12 3/ 0*	13 3/ 3	14 3/ 6	15 3/ 9	16 4/ 0*	17 4/ 3
****** LIABILITIES AND OWNERS' EQUITY ******						
ACCOUNTS PAYABLE	56,213*	16,957	31,627	19,780	61,641*	18,377
SHORT-TERM LOANS AND NOTES	63,766*	0	1,356	2,347	47,545*	0
TOTAL CURRENT LIABILITIES	119,980*	16,957	32,983	22,128	109,186*	18,377
LONG-TERM OBLIGATIONS	13,633*	13,633	13,633	13,633	13,633*	13,633
TOTAL LIABILITIES	133,612*	30,590	46,616	35,760	122,819*	32,009
TOTAL OWNERS' EQUITY	244,542*	230,720	241,204	228,243	270,274*	255,323
LIABILITIES & OWNER EQUITY	378,154*	261,310	287,820	264,003	393,093*	287,332

Table 12.2 (continued)

CONDITION STATEMENTS (BALANCE SHEETS) (CONTINUED)
****

	18 4/6	19 4/9	20 5/0*	21 5/3	22 5/6	23 5/9
****** ASSETS ******						
CASH AND MARKET SECURITIES	67,749	75,523	66,009*	86,733	80,846	94,391
+ACCOUNTS RECEIVABLE GROSS	102,159	65,281	196,899*	74,896	115,600	75,108
-UNCOLLECTIBLES RESERVE	21,378	22,503	23,995*	26,032	27,120	28,329
CASH+SECURITIES+ACCT RECV	148,530	118,301	238,912*	135,596	169,326	141,170
PREPAID EXPENSE	0	0	0*	0	0	0
FINISHED GOODS INVENTORY	156,992	168,789	160,794*	183,404	163,664	178,845
SUPPLIES INVENTORY--GEN	422	372	534*	379	434	379
TOTAL INVENTORIES	157,414	169,161	161,328*	183,783	164,098	179,224
TOTAL CURRENT ASSETS	305,944	287,462	400,240*	319,379	333,424	320,394
GEN FIXED ASSETS AT COST:						
CLASS 1	43,163	43,163	43,163*	43,163	43,163	43,163
CLASS 2	9,806	9,806	9,806*	9,806	9,806	9,806
GEN FIXED ASSETS DEPRC RESERVES:						
CLASS 1	39,919	40,082	40,236*	40,382	40,521	40,653
CLASS 2	6,737	6,929	7,109*	7,277	7,435	7,584
GEN FIXED ASSETS AT BOOK	6,312	5,959	5,625*	5,310	5,013	4,732
TOTAL ASSETS	312,256	293,420	405,865*	324,689	338,437	325,126

Table 12.2 (continued)

CONDITION STATEMENTS (BALANCE SHEETS) (CONTINUED)

****** LIABILITIES AND OWNERS' EQUITY ******

	18 4/ 6	19 4/ 9	20 5/ 0*	21 5/ 3	22 5/ 6	23 5/ 9
ACCOUNTS PAYABLE	30,775	22,890	58,726*	27,607	26,747	24,938
SHORT-TERM LOANS AND NOTES	1,487	2,310	38,338*	0	0	0
TOTAL CURRENT LIABILITIES	32,262	25,199	97,064*	27,607	26,747	24,938
LONG-TERM OBLIGATIONS	13,633	13,633	13,633*	13,633	13,633	13,633
TOTAL LIABILITIES	45,895	38,832	110,697*	41,239	40,379	38,570
TOTAL OWNERS' EQUITY	266,362	254,588	295,168*	283,450	298,057	286,556
LIABILITIES & OWNER EQUITY	312,256	293,420	405,865*	324,689	338,437	325,126

Table 12.2 (continued)

```
CONDITION STATEMENTS (BALANCE SHEETS) (CONTINUED)
******************************************

                                       24   6/ 0*

******  ASSETS  ******

CASH AND MARKET SECURITIES             80,650*
+ACCOUNTS RECEIVABLE GROSS            233,477*
  -UNCOLLECTIBLES RESERVE              30,093*

CASH+SECURITIES+ACCT RECV             284,034*

PREPAID EXPENSE                             0*

FINISHED GOODS INVENTORY              191,189*
SUPPLIES INVENTORY--GEN                   579*

TOTAL INVENTORIES                     191,768*

TOTAL CURRENT ASSETS                  475,802*


GEN FIXED ASSETS AT COST:
        CLASS 1                        43,163*
        CLASS 2                         9,806*

GEN FIXED ASSETS DEPRC RESERVES:
        CLASS 1                        40,779*
        CLASS 2                         7,722*

GEN FIXED ASSETS AT BOOK                4,468*


TOTAL ASSETS                          480,270*

CONDITION STATEMENTS (BALANCE SHEETS) (CONTINUED)


                                       24   6/ 0*

******  LIABILITIES AND OWNERS' EQUITY  ******

ACCOUNTS PAYABLE                       76,427*
SHORT-TERM LOANS AND NOTES             56,180*

TOTAL CURRENT LIABILITIES             132,606*

LONG-TERM OBLIGATIONS                  13,633*

TOTAL LIABILITIES                     146,239*


TOTAL OWNERS' EQUITY                  334,031*

LIABILITIES & OWNER EQUITY            480,270*
```

Table 12.2 (continued)

GIFTIQUE

```
******************************
    SELECTED ACCOUNTS FOR ALL PERIODS
******************************
```

CONDITION ITEMS ARE END-OF-PERIOD; 99 % CONFIDENCE LIMITS FOR MEANS WITH SAMPLE SIZE 12

	1 0/3	2 0/6	3 0/9	4 1/0*	5 1/3	6 1/6
INDUSTRY SALES--000 OMIT						
MEANS	54	109	54	237*	59	113
STANDARD DEVIATIONS	1	3	2	6*	2	3
LOWER CONFIDENCE LIMITS	49	99	49	217*	53	102
UPPER CONFIDENCE LIMITS	58	120	60	257*	64	123
FIRM'S INDUSTRY SHARE %						
MEANS	100.00	100.00	100.00	100.00*	100.00	100.00
STANDARD DEVIATIONS	0.00	0.00	0.00	0.00*	0.00	0.00
LOWER CONFIDENCE LIMITS	100.00	100.00	100.00	100.00*	100.00	100.00
UPPER CONFIDENCE LIMITS	100.00	100.00	100.00	100.00*	100.00	100.00
FIRM NET SALES ACHIEVED						
MEANS	53,688	109,210	54,460	236,694*	58,733	112,667
STANDARD DEVIATIONS	1,474	3,336	1,912	6,409*	1,728	3,338
LOWER CONFIDENCE LIMITS	49,117	98,868	48,533	216,825*	53,376	102,319
UPPER CONFIDENCE LIMITS	58,258	119,551	60,387	256,563*	64,091	123,015
COST OF SALES						
MEANS	26,974	53,312	28,077	117,327*	29,417	55,689
STANDARD DEVIATIONS	839	1,923	906	4,213*	961	1,831
LOWER CONFIDENCE LIMITS	24,374	47,352	25,267	104,267*	26,439	50,011
UPPER CONFIDENCE LIMITS	29,574	59,272	30,887	130,387*	32,395	61,367
GROSS PROFIT ON SALES						
MEANS	26,714	55,898	26,383	119,367*	29,317	56,978
STANDARD DEVIATIONS	812	1,727	1,100	2,799*	896	1,846
LOWER CONFIDENCE LIMITS	24,195	50,543	22,972	110,690*	26,540	51,255
UPPER CONFIDENCE LIMITS	29,232	61,252	29,794	128,044*	32,094	62,701
TOTAL OPERATING EXPENSE						
MEANS	40,223	46,808	41,040	62,027*	42,885	48,347
STANDARD DEVIATIONS	170	393	227	720*	228	388
LOWER CONFIDENCE LIMITS	39,695	45,588	40,335	59,794*	42,177	47,144
UPPER CONFIDENCE LIMITS	40,751	48,027	41,744	64,261*	43,594	49,550
NET OPERATING INCOME						
MEANS	-13,509	9,090	-14,657	57,339*	-13,569	8,631
STANDARD DEVIATIONS	671	1,398	891	2,207*	694	1,504
LOWER CONFIDENCE LIMITS	-15,590	4,756	-17,418	50,498*	-15,720	3,969
UPPER CONFIDENCE LIMITS	-11,428	13,424	-11,896	64,181*	-11,417	13,292
NET INCOME AFTER TAX						
MEANS	-14,730	7,329	-16,182	39,302*	-13,886	7,755
STANDARD DEVIATIONS	650	1,282	801	1,498*	688	1,455
LOWER CONFIDENCE LIMITS	-16,743	3,356	-18,666	34,657*	-16,018	3,246
UPPER CONFIDENCE LIMITS	-12,716	11,302	-13,698	43,946*	-11,755	12,265

Table 12.2 (continued)

CASH AND MARKET SECURITIES						
MEANS	32,406	49,956	40,654	75,328*	34,475	43,496
STANDARD DEVIATIONS	2,235	5,429	4,263	3,294*	6,327	4,299
LOWER CONFIDENCE LIMITS	25,476	33,126	27,439	65,118*	14,861	30,170
UPPER CONFIDENCE LIMITS	39,335	66,787	53,869	85,539*	54,089	56,822
CASH+SECURITIES+ACCT RECV						
MEANS	65,741	113,931	73,237	213,293*	68,351	111,456
STANDARD DEVIATIONS	3,145	8,365	5,590	8,712*	5,762	5,127
LOWER CONFIDENCE LIMITS	55,992	88,000	55,907	186,284*	50,489	95,562
UPPER CONFIDENCE LIMITS	75,489	139,862	90,566	240,301*	86,212	127,351
TOTAL INVENTORIES						
MEANS	123,479	121,940	128,516	133,956*	135,861	127,365
STANDARD DEVIATIONS	3,829	4,386	4,139	4,797*	4,003	4,178
LOWER CONFIDENCE LIMITS	111,608	108,342	115,684	119,084*	123,452	114,412
UPPER CONFIDENCE LIMITS	135,350	135,538	141,348	148,828*	148,270	140,318
TOTAL CURRENT ASSETS						
MEANS	189,220	235,871	201,752	347,248*	204,212	238,821
STANDARD DEVIATIONS	6,705	12,025	9,383	12,812*	6,344	7,585
LOWER CONFIDENCE LIMITS	168,433	198,594	172,665	307,531*	184,545	215,307
UPPER CONFIDENCE LIMITS	210,007	273,148	230,840	386,966*	223,879	262,335
TOTAL ASSETS						
MEANS	206,171	251,859	216,834	361,475*	217,632	251,482
STANDARD DEVIATIONS	6,705	12,025	9,383	12,812*	6,344	7,585
LOWER CONFIDENCE LIMITS	185,384	214,583	187,746	321,757*	197,965	227,967
UPPER CONFIDENCE LIMITS	226,957	289,136	245,921	401,192*	237,299	274,996
TOTAL CURRENT LIABILITIES						
MEANS	65,992	101,721	82,795	151,677*	21,720	47,815
STANDARD DEVIATIONS	4,534	11,076	8,703	6,629*	5,313	9,923
LOWER CONFIDENCE LIMITS	51,935	67,386	55,817	131,126*	5,250	17,053
UPPER CONFIDENCE LIMITS	80,049	136,056	109,773	172,228*	38,190	78,576
TOTAL LIABILITIES						
MEANS	67,495	103,882	84,976	162,973*	33,016	59,110
STANDARD DEVIATIONS	4,980	11,098	8,779	7,623*	4,168	8,463
LOWER CONFIDENCE LIMITS	52,057	69,479	57,760	139,341*	20,094	32,874
UPPER CONFIDENCE LIMITS	82,933	138,285	112,192	186,604*	45,937	85,347
TOTAL OWNERS' EQUITY						
MEANS	138,676	147,978	131,858	198,502*	184,616	192,371
STANDARD DEVIATIONS	2,060	2,711	3,081	6,371*	6,342	7,003
LOWER CONFIDENCE LIMITS	132,229	139,572	122,306	178,751*	164,957	170,663
UPPER CONFIDENCE LIMITS	145,060	156,383	141,409	218,253*	204,275	214,080
ALL FIXED ASSETS AT BOOK	16,951	15,988	15,081	14,226*	13,420	12,660

Table 12.2 (continued)

	7 1/9	8 2/0*	9 2/3	10 2/6	11 2/9	12 3/0*
INDUSTRY SALES--000 OMIT						
MEANS	60	241*	60	122	66	255*
STANDARD DEVIATIONS	1	6*	2	4	2	8*
LOWER CONFIDENCE LIMITS	56	222*	54	110	61	232*
UPPER CONFIDENCE LIMITS	64	260*	66	134	71	279*
FIRM'S INDUSTRY SHARE %						
MEANS	100.00	100.00*	100.00	100.00	100.00	100.00*
STANDARD DEVIATIONS	0.00	0.00*	0.00	0.00	0.00	0.00*
LOWER CONFIDENCE LIMITS	100.00	100.00*	100.00	100.00	100.00	100.00*
UPPER CONFIDENCE LIMITS	100.00	100.00*	100.00	100.00	100.00	100.00*
FIRM NET SALES ACHIEVED						
MEANS	60,343	240,930*	60,170	122,485	65,604	255,224*
STANDARD DEVIATIONS	1,340	6,055*	1,914	3,870	1,585	7,559*
LOWER CONFIDENCE LIMITS	56,190	222,159*	54,238	110,490	60,690	231,792*
UPPER CONFIDENCE LIMITS	64,496	259,701*	66,103	134,481	70,519	278,656*
COST OF SALES						
MEANS	30,693	120,511*	30,463	60,050	32,025	128,565*
STANDARD DEVIATIONS	1,036	4,057*	1,102	1,830	865	4,006*
LOWER CONFIDENCE LIMITS	27,482	107,933*	27,047	54,376	29,342	116,147*
UPPER CONFIDENCE LIMITS	33,903	133,089*	33,878	65,724	34,707	140,983*
GROSS PROFIT ON SALES						
MEANS	29,650	120,419*	29,708	62,435	33,580	126,659*
STANDARD DEVIATIONS	677	3,132*	978	2,671	983	4,351*
LOWER CONFIDENCE LIMITS	27,553	110,710*	26,677	54,155	30,531	113,172*
UPPER CONFIDENCE LIMITS	31,748	130,128*	32,738	70,716	36,628	140,146*
TOTAL OPERATING EXPENSE						
MEANS	42,930	63,724*	44,362	50,805	44,876	66,721*
STANDARD DEVIATIONS	153	705*	234	449	181	870*
LOWER CONFIDENCE LIMITS	42,455	61,537*	43,635	49,415	44,315	64,023*
UPPER CONFIDENCE LIMITS	43,405	65,911*	45,089	52,196	45,436	69,419*
NET OPERATING INCOME						
MEANS	-13,280	56,695*	-14,654	11,630	-11,296	59,938*
STANDARD DEVIATIONS	590	2,608*	773	2,267	840	3,575*
LOWER CONFIDENCE LIMITS	-15,109	48,609*	-17,049	4,604	-13,901	48,855*
UPPER CONFIDENCE LIMITS	-11,450	64,781*	-12,259	18,656	-8,691	71,021*
NET INCOME AFTER TAX						
MEANS	-13,903	37,584*	-14,896	10,290	-11,558	37,642*
STANDARD DEVIATIONS	593	1,493*	768	1,821	832	2,080*
LOWER CONFIDENCE LIMITS	-15,740	32,954*	-17,276	4,645	-14,136	31,193*
UPPER CONFIDENCE LIMITS	-12,066	42,213*	-12,515	15,935	-8,979	44,032*

Table 12.2 (continued)

CASH AND MARKET SECURITIES						
MEANS	40,377	60,760*	51,590	49,719	44,955	63,426*
STANDARD DEVIATIONS	5,344	7,832*	7,678	5,850	7,558	8,270*
LOWER CONFIDENCE LIMITS	23,811	36,481*	27,789	31,583	21,525	37,789*
UPPER CONFIDENCE LIMITS	56,943	85,039*	75,390	67,854	68,384	89,062*
CASH+SECURITIES+ACCT RECV						
MEANS	76,845	205,042*	87,087	121,965	85,224	222,465*
STANDARD DEVIATIONS	5,049	12,674*	7,254	5,296	7,679	12,396*
LOWER CONFIDENCE LIMITS	61,193	165,753*	64,601	105,547	61,420	184,036*
UPPER CONFIDENCE LIMITS	92,498	244,331*	109,574	138,383	109,028	260,895*
TOTAL INVENTORIES						
MEANS	140,466	137,578*	141,494	137,319	146,554	146,756*
STANDARD DEVIATIONS	4,729	4,619*	4,447	4,176	3,952	4,562*
LOWER CONFIDENCE LIMITS	125,805	123,259*	127,710	124,373	134,303	132,613*
UPPER CONFIDENCE LIMITS	155,126	151,898*	155,278	150,265	158,804	160,898*
TOTAL CURRENT ASSETS						
MEANS	217,311	342,620*	228,581	259,284	231,777	369,221*
STANDARD DEVIATIONS	7,359	15,835*	7,421	6,660	8,061	16,261*
LOWER CONFIDENCE LIMITS	194,499	293,532*	205,575	238,639	206,788	318,812*
UPPER CONFIDENCE LIMITS	240,124	391,709*	251,587	279,930	256,767	419,630*
TOTAL ASSETS						
MEANS	229,255	353,889*	239,214	269,316	241,244	378,154*
STANDARD DEVIATIONS	7,359	15,835*	7,421	6,660	8,061	16,261*
LOWER CONFIDENCE LIMITS	206,443	304,801*	216,208	248,671	216,255	327,745*
UPPER CONFIDENCE LIMITS	252,068	402,978*	262,220	289,962	266,233	428,563*
TOTAL CURRENT LIABILITIES						
MEANS	39,491	117,531*	17,751	37,564	21,049	119,980*
STANDARD DEVIATIONS	6,971	17,348*	2,572	6,858	2,970	18,905*
LOWER CONFIDENCE LIMITS	17,881	63,753*	9,779	16,304	11,841	61,375*
UPPER CONFIDENCE LIMITS	61,101	171,309*	25,724	58,824	30,257	178,584*
TOTAL LIABILITIES						
MEANS	50,787	131,079*	31,300	51,112	34,597	133,612*
STANDARD DEVIATIONS	5,970	16,895*	2,412	6,159	3,518	18,229*
LOWER CONFIDENCE LIMITS	32,281	78,706*	23,824	32,019	23,693	77,102*
UPPER CONFIDENCE LIMITS	69,293	183,453*	38,775	70,206	45,502	190,122*
TOTAL OWNERS' EQUITY						
MEANS	178,468	222,810*	207,914	218,204	206,646	244,542*
STANDARD DEVIATIONS	7,004	6,171*	6,187	5,356	5,510	6,512*
LOWER CONFIDENCE LIMITS	156,756	203,679*	188,735	201,599	189,565	224,353*
UPPER CONFIDENCE LIMITS	200,180	241,941*	227,093	234,809	223,728	264,730*
ALL FIXED ASSETS AT BOOK	11,944	11,269*	10,632	10,032	9,466	8,933*

Table 12.2 (continued)

	13 3/ 3	14 3/ 6	15 3/ 9	16 4/ 0*	17 4/ 3	18 4/ 6
INDUSTRY SALES--000 OMIT						
MEANS	65	131	68	278*	68	137
STANDARD DEVIATIONS	2	4	3	8*	2	5
LOWER CONFIDENCE LIMITS	60	118	60	253*	60	121
UPPER CONFIDENCE LIMITS	70	144	76	304*	76	152
FIRM'S INDUSTRY SHARE %						
MEANS	100.00	100.00	100.00	100.00*	100.00	100.00
STANDARD DEVIATIONS	0.00	0.00	0.00	0.00*	0.00	0.00
LOWER CONFIDENCE LIMITS	100.00	100.00	100.00	100.00*	100.00	100.00
UPPER CONFIDENCE LIMITS	100.00	100.00	100.00	100.00*	100.00	100.00
FIRM NET SALES ACHIEVED						
MEANS	64,897	130,772	67,831	278,280*	68,119	136,627
STANDARD DEVIATIONS	1,634	4,227	2,680	8,161*	2,486	4,952
LOWER CONFIDENCE LIMITS	59,831	117,668	59,522	252,982*	60,412	121,275
UPPER CONFIDENCE LIMITS	69,963	143,876	76,139	303,578*	75,826	151,979
COST OF SALES						
MEANS	32,082	65,627	33,831	139,589*	34,551	68,856
STANDARD DEVIATIONS	752	1,988	1,578	4,514*	1,135	2,496
LOWER CONFIDENCE LIMITS	29,751	59,465	28,939	125,594*	31,032	61,119
UPPER CONFIDENCE LIMITS	34,413	71,788	38,723	153,583*	38,070	76,593
GROSS PROFIT ON SALES						
MEANS	32,815	65,145	34,000	138,691*	33,568	67,771
STANDARD DEVIATIONS	1,205	2,536	1,211	4,738*	1,488	2,776
LOWER CONFIDENCE LIMITS	29,080	57,283	30,245	124,002*	28,953	59,165
UPPER CONFIDENCE LIMITS	36,550	73,008	37,754	153,380*	38,182	76,377
TOTAL OPERATING EXPENSE						
MEANS	46,398	53,104	46,669	70,908*	48,279	55,347
STANDARD DEVIATIONS	202	477	334	954*	273	552
LOWER CONFIDENCE LIMITS	45,774	51,625	45,633	67,951*	47,433	53,636
UPPER CONFIDENCE LIMITS	47,023	54,584	47,706	73,866*	49,126	57,057
NET OPERATING INCOME						
MEANS	-13,583	12,041	-12,670	67,783*	-14,712	12,424
STANDARD DEVIATIONS	1,034	2,089	896	3,910*	1,243	2,256
LOWER CONFIDENCE LIMITS	-16,788	5,564	-15,446	55,661*	-18,565	5,430
UPPER CONFIDENCE LIMITS	-10,378	18,518	-9,894	79,904*	-10,859	19,419
NET INCOME AFTER TAX						
MEANS	-13,822	10,484	-12,961	42,031*	-14,951	11,039
STANDARD DEVIATIONS	1,016	1,769	887	1,901*	1,234	1,898
LOWER CONFIDENCE LIMITS	-16,972	5,002	-15,711	36,137*	-18,776	5,154
UPPER CONFIDENCE LIMITS	-10,671	15,966	-10,211	47,925*	-11,126	16,923

Table 12.2 (continued)

CASH AND MARKET SECURITIES					
MEANS	67,477	62,019	66,381*	80,246	67,749
STANDARD DEVIATIONS	7,871	7,592	6,414*	9,185	11,285
LOWER CONFIDENCE LIMITS	43,076	38,483	46,497*	51,772	32,766
UPPER CONFIDENCE LIMITS	91,879	85,555	86,266*	108,720	102,732
CASH+SECURITIES+ACCT RECV					
MEANS	106,066	100,032	226,687*	119,909	148,530
STANDARD DEVIATIONS	8,609	7,499	9,280*	9,016	8,837
LOWER CONFIDENCE LIMITS	79,379	76,784	197,919*	91,959	121,136
UPPER CONFIDENCE LIMITS	132,753	123,279	255,455*	147,860	175,924
TOTAL INVENTORIES					
MEANS	146,815	156,464	159,320*	160,735	157,414
STANDARD DEVIATIONS	3,434	6,843	5,140*	4,505	5,695
LOWER CONFIDENCE LIMITS	136,171	135,252	143,386*	146,768	139,761
UPPER CONFIDENCE LIMITS	157,459	177,676	175,254*	174,702	175,068
TOTAL CURRENT ASSETS					
MEANS	252,880	256,496	386,007*	280,645	305,944
STANDARD DEVIATIONS	9,073	10,673	13,153*	10,291	8,804
LOWER CONFIDENCE LIMITS	224,753	223,409	345,234*	248,742	278,650
UPPER CONFIDENCE LIMITS	281,008	289,582	426,780*	312,548	333,238
TOTAL ASSETS					
MEANS	261,310	264,003	393,093*	287,332	312,256
STANDARD DEVIATIONS	9,073	10,673	13,153*	10,291	8,804
LOWER CONFIDENCE LIMITS	233,183	230,917	352,320*	255,429	284,963
UPPER CONFIDENCE LIMITS	289,437	297,090	433,866*	319,235	339,550
TOTAL CURRENT LIABILITIES					
MEANS	16,957	22,128	109,186*	18,377	32,262
STANDARD DEVIATIONS	1,505	4,825	16,694*	2,653	4,174
LOWER CONFIDENCE LIMITS	12,292	7,169	57,435*	10,152	19,324
UPPER CONFIDENCE LIMITS	21,623	37,087	160,938*	26,602	45,200
TOTAL LIABILITIES					
MEANS	30,590	35,760	122,819*	32,009	45,895
STANDARD DEVIATIONS	2,320	5,211	15,691*	3,533	3,880
LOWER CONFIDENCE LIMITS	23,399	19,605	74,178*	21,058	33,868
UPPER CONFIDENCE LIMITS	37,780	51,915	171,460*	42,960	57,922
TOTAL OWNERS' EQUITY					
MEANS	230,720	228,243	270,274*	255,323	266,362
STANDARD DEVIATIONS	7,145	7,763	7,511*	7,820	7,284
LOWER CONFIDENCE LIMITS	208,572	204,178	246,991*	231,082	243,782
UPPER CONFIDENCE LIMITS	252,869	252,308	293,557*	279,564	288,941
ALL FIXED ASSETS AT BOOK	8,430	7,508	7,086*	6,688	6,312

Table 12.2 (continued)

	19 4/9	20 5/0*	21 5/3	22 5/6	23 5/9	24 6/0*
INDUSTRY SALES--000 OMIT						
MEANS	75	279*	80	148	79	333*
STANDARD DEVIATIONS	2	8*	3	4	3	8*
LOWER CONFIDENCE LIMITS	68	254*	72	136	71	308*
UPPER CONFIDENCE LIMITS	81	304*	88	161	87	358*
FIRM'S INDUSTRY SHARE %						
MEANS	100.00	100.00*	100.00	100.00	100.00	100.00*
STANDARD DEVIATIONS	0.00	0.00*	0.00	0.00	0.00	0.00*
LOWER CONFIDENCE LIMITS	100.00	100.00*	100.00	100.00	100.00	100.00*
UPPER CONFIDENCE LIMITS	100.00	100.00*	100.00	100.00	100.00	100.00*
FIRM NET SALES ACHIEVED						
MEANS	74,542	279,318*	79,679	148,340	79,195	333,002*
STANDARD DEVIATIONS	2,104	8,010*	2,619	3,937	2,518	8,126*
LOWER CONFIDENCE LIMITS	68,021	254,485*	71,560	136,137	71,388	307,811*
UPPER CONFIDENCE LIMITS	81,064	304,150*	87,798	160,544	87,001	358,193*
COST OF SALES						
MEANS	36,975	141,357*	39,827	71,782	39,177	168,078*
STANDARD DEVIATIONS	1,394	4,428*	1,657	2,080	1,329	4,387*
LOWER CONFIDENCE LIMITS	32,652	127,630*	34,690	65,334	35,057	154,479*
UPPER CONFIDENCE LIMITS	41,297	155,085*	44,964	78,231	43,297	181,677*
GROSS PROFIT ON SALES						
MEANS	37,568	137,960*	39,852	76,558	40,017	164,924*
STANDARD DEVIATIONS	1,052	3,886*	1,268	2,474	1,338	5,198*
LOWER CONFIDENCE LIMITS	34,308	125,914*	35,922	68,890	35,869	148,809*
UPPER CONFIDENCE LIMITS	40,827	150,006*	43,781	84,226	44,165	181,039*
TOTAL OPERATING EXPENSE						
MEANS	49,051	72,513*	51,330	58,386	51,279	80,404*
STANDARD DEVIATIONS	267	958*	289	467	299	936*
LOWER CONFIDENCE LIMITS	48,224	69,542*	50,434	56,939	50,351	77,502*
UPPER CONFIDENCE LIMITS	49,878	75,484*	52,227	59,833	52,206	83,306*
NET OPERATING INCOME						
MEANS	-11,483	65,447*	-11,479	18,172	-11,261	84,520*
STANDARD DEVIATIONS	849	2,968*	1,023	2,077	1,067	4,403*
LOWER CONFIDENCE LIMITS	-14,114	56,248*	-14,650	11,735	-14,568	70,872*
UPPER CONFIDENCE LIMITS	-8,853	74,647*	-8,308	24,609	-7,954	98,168*
NET INCOME AFTER TAX						
MEANS	-11,773	40,579*	-11,718	14,607	-11,501	47,475*
STANDARD DEVIATIONS	845	2,174*	1,018	1,115	1,064	2,214*
LOWER CONFIDENCE LIMITS	-14,392	33,841*	-14,874	11,151	-14,800	40,612*
UPPER CONFIDENCE LIMITS	-9,155	47,318*	-8,562	18,064	-8,201	54,337*

Table 12.2 (continued)

CASH AND MARKET SECURITIES						
MEANS	75,523	66,009*	86,733	80,846	94,391	80,650*
STANDARD DEVIATIONS	8,181	6,980*	10,432	8,235	11,359	9,580*
LOWER CONFIDENCE LIMITS	50,164	44,369*	54,393	55,318	59,179	50,953*
UPPER CONFIDENCE LIMITS	100,883	87,648*	119,072	106,375	129,602	110,347*
CASH+SECURITIES+ACCT RECV						
MEANS	118,301	238,912*	135,596	169,326	141,170	284,034*
STANDARD DEVIATIONS	8,345	8,418*	9,491	8,957	9,794	13,764*
LOWER CONFIDENCE LIMITS	92,432	212,816*	106,174	141,558	110,808	241,366*
UPPER CONFIDENCE LIMITS	144,171	265,008*	165,018	197,094	171,532	326,702*
TOTAL INVENTORIES						
MEANS	169,161	161,328*	183,783	164,098	179,224	191,768*
STANDARD DEVIATIONS	6,366	5,044*	6,809	4,745	6,069	4,995*
LOWER CONFIDENCE LIMITS	149,425	145,693*	162,675	149,386	160,412	176,283*
UPPER CONFIDENCE LIMITS	188,897	176,963*	204,892	178,809	198,037	207,252*
TOTAL CURRENT ASSETS						
MEANS	287,462	400,240*	319,379	333,424	320,394	475,802*
STANDARD DEVIATIONS	9,087	11,427*	10,179	10,774	9,310	16,822*
LOWER CONFIDENCE LIMITS	259,293	364,817*	287,825	300,025	291,533	423,655*
UPPER CONFIDENCE LIMITS	315,631	435,663*	350,934	366,823	349,255	527,949*
TOTAL ASSETS						
MEANS	293,420	405,865*	324,689	338,437	325,126	480,270*
STANDARD DEVIATIONS	9,087	11,427*	10,179	10,774	9,310	16,822*
LOWER CONFIDENCE LIMITS	265,252	370,441*	293,134	305,038	296,265	428,123*
UPPER CONFIDENCE LIMITS	321,589	441,288*	356,244	371,836	353,988	532,417*
TOTAL CURRENT LIABILITIES						
MEANS	25,199	97,064*	27,607	26,747	24,938	132,606*
STANDARD DEVIATIONS	4,830	16,007*	3,867	3,087	2,626	22,183*
LOWER CONFIDENCE LIMITS	10,227	47,444*	15,617	17,178	16,798	63,840*
UPPER CONFIDENCE LIMITS	40,172	146,684*	39,596	36,316	33,077	201,373*
TOTAL LIABILITIES						
MEANS	38,832	110,697*	41,239	40,379	38,570	146,239*
STANDARD DEVIATIONS	4,962	14,797*	4,141	3,963	2,591	21,046*
LOWER CONFIDENCE LIMITS	23,449	64,825*	28,403	28,093	30,537	80,995*
UPPER CONFIDENCE LIMITS	54,216	156,568*	54,075	52,666	46,603	211,482*
TOTAL OWNERS' EQUITY						
MEANS	254,588	295,168*	283,450	298,057	286,556	334,031*
STANDARD DEVIATIONS	7,085	7,698*	8,069	7,943	8,125	6,738*
LOWER CONFIDENCE LIMITS	232,626	271,303*	258,435	273,432	261,370	313,145*
UPPER CONFIDENCE LIMITS	276,551	319,033*	308,465	322,682	311,743	354,918*
ALL FIXED ASSETS AT BOOK	5,959	5,625*	5,310	5,013	4,732	4,468*

Since the assets of GIFTIQUE are mostly monetary or in salable merchandise, liquidation values are high. In fact, liquidation value consistently exceeds going-concern value, or GIFTIQUE is worth more dead than alive! In this case, price earnings multiples of 5 are internally derived from liquidation values. As the higher of two internally computed values, liquidation values replace going-concern values as sources of market values.

Needless to say, this simulation was a factor in convincing you not to accept the family's current offer to sell. It should be mentioned that one set of decisions from a PAVE run does not stand alone. Some of the policies could be altered and the sensitivity of earnings projections tested. For GIFTIQUE, however, the first output does not encourage extensive analysis of alternatives, at least not to meet your requirements.

Although the general investment picture emerges rather sharply from VALUATION AND SCOPE, some analysis will be undertaken on the remaining output divisions. Recall that the FINANCIAL SUMMARY is an annualized extrapolation of the final 24th quarter. For GIFTIQUE the fourth quarter is the high sales quarter; four times as much is sold as in the lowest quarters. This peak seasonal pattern will exaggerate annualized figures, a fact to keep in mind during analysis. In FINANCIAL SUMMARY and FINANCIAL STATEMENTS, accounts with all zero values are simply omitted.

The FINANCIAL SUMMARY provides a statistical output of important values and ratios. There is no variability on items where randomization was not applied during input, such as firm's share of industry or net tangible fixed assets. Appropriate levels of cash, total assets, and owners' equity are maintained at all times. This occurs because internal routines insure that enough new capital will be raised despite lack of profitability.

In the ratio analysis of profitability section, ratios suggest results superior to the average indicated in VALUATION AND SCOPE. The reason for this again is the sales surge in the fourth quarter; ratio analysis is confined to the fourth quarter. The same may be said of liquidity ratios of financial condition. For each run these must at least approach the minimum level. For cash ratio, compare minimum output of 49.6% with default input 50%, and for current ratio, minimum output of 207.47% with default input 200% (2 to 1). Again, average figures are much higher because variability (standard deviation) is quite high.

Continuing with the FINANCIAL SUMMARY, extrapolated annual mean net income after tax is a respectable $189,899, whereas the actual mean income from VALUATION AND SCOPE was only $38,863. Again, the former is exaggerated from the seasonal peak. Notice the substantial variability of net income in the FINANCIAL SUMMARY output.

In FINANCIAL STATEMENTS output division, all statements are concerned with flows except the last set, CONDITION STATEMENTS. Flow statements for GIFTIQUE add columns for annual figures in addition to columns for each quarter. There are six annual columns which occur after each set of four quarters.

In the ENVIRONMENTAL ANALYSES, the seasonal pattern is repeated over all 24 periods. Like VALVO (see Table 10.2), the seasonal inputs were normalized at input, hence do not require further adjustment. Here industry sales are identical to sales of the firm because the firm's share of industry was entered at 100%. The annual figures for all ratios (two decimal places in ENVIRONMENTAL ANALYSES) are means of the preceding four quarterly figures.

Firm net sales demand at the end of ENVIRONMENTAL ANALYSES and firm net sales achieved at the beginning of INCOME STATEMENTS are identical. This will hold unless certain conditions occur under manufacturing option when ID 5 equals 2. A trade option was elected here (ID 5 = 1 from section 12.2). (See also the ECOFURN case in section 10.4.)

The arrangement of statements is conventional and there is no need to discuss all the accounts in detail. Referring to INCOME STATEMENTS, note that mean net operating income, net income before taxes, and net income after taxes fluctuate substantially in response to the seasonal pattern. Sales contribution margin is the difference between net sales achieved and the sum of expense accounts which vary with sales. Interest on short-term loans varies directly with short-term credit from quarter to quarter. The latter in turn responds to seasonal needs for cash. Interest on long-term debt increases steadily over the quarters because new capital is required during early quarters, and 25% of this new capital is in fixed obligations.

COST OF GOODS SOLD SCHEDULES reconcile purchases of merchandise (cost of finished goods) with finished goods inventories and the cost of goods sold. As mentioned in the discussion of inputs (section 12.2), inventory levels here would move oppositely from sales to partially stabilize the level of purchases (cost of finished goods) over the quarters. The only PAVE schedules which are not used in GIFTIQUE are COST OF GOODS MANUFACTURED.

The CASH FORECASTS statements present computations which are used internally to compute required additional investment. Planned change in long-term obligations and planned change in owner paid-in capital are zero and not printed because the input decision was to determine any additional capital needs internally. Internal computations are shown under additions to required long-term obligations and additions to required owners' equity. Notice that total net cash flow gives the change in cash position during a period after changes in *debt* capital, but before *owner* capital changes, either planned or internal (required). The final net cash flow after all capital changes, not shown as a separate account, is used to compute the ending cash condition, cash and securities EOP. Acronyms BOP and EOP stand for "beginning of period" and "end of period."

In PAVE, capital changes are incorporated in separate statements, RETAINED EARNINGS AND CAPITAL CHANGES. Both planned and additional required changes are printed for owner paid-in capital. Net income is added, and dividends or withdrawals deducted, from retained earnings. Owner equity number of shares outstanding EOP are printed for each period. For GIFTIQUE this is 940 EOP 1 (ID 91). Additions to required owners' equity are divided by $50 from ID 92 to obtain additional shares each period. Per share values are printed under net income per share and owners' equity per share. For the former, annual figures are the means of quarterly means; for the latter, annual figures EOP simply repeat fourth quarter period EOPs.

CONDITION STATEMENTS (or BALANCE SHEETS) account values are EOP except for the first column. This column gives the beginning condition of the firm or, in other words, balance sheet values at the start of the first period. This column is a copy of INITIAL CONDITION input division after some account adjustments and consolidations. For GIFTIQUE, periods at the end of each year are marked with asterisks.

Mean figures for each period in SELECTED ACCOUNTS output division are identical with the corresponding figures for the same periods in FINANCIAL STATEMENTS. In this last output division, however, users may also examine the standard deviation and confidence interval limits of the mean. Annual figures are not available for this output division.

12.4 | Description of HPG PRODUCTS Manufacturing Case

HPG PRODUCTS manufactures and sells specialized relays for electric power generating equipment. HPG has about a 10% market share in a small industry whose annual sales are currently running around $13 million. HPG sales are made directly to large industrial customers who manufacture and service electric generating systems. Currently, HPG is not earning satisfactory profits, but rapid growth is expected over the next few years. HPG believes that it can maintain or slightly increase its market share, which means that HPG sales could increase substantially.

HPG management has developed a strategic plan which will be translated into next year's budgeting process. The key question is whether these plans are likely to turn the company around into a profitable, viable concern. In order to study this question, management has decided to project HPG's intermediate-term future. You are employed to run a PAVE simulation. You consult with HPG executives to determine policies, details of the strategic plan, and projected information. The agreed conditions and decision variables of the simulation are organized below into PAVE input sections.

Input/output system choices

Twelve quarters will be simulated. A moderate seasonal pattern will be included over a three-year projected performance.

A statistical (Monte Carlo) simulation will be obtained from a small sample of size 10. The selected sample size will produce 95% confidence limits for output means.

Executives desire full analyses, both the environment and internal performance of the firm. Complete FINANCIAL SUMMARY and FINANCIAL STATEMENTS for all periods are desired.

Apart from small periodic additions to long-term debt, HPG has no plans to raise new external capital. Executives would like the simulation to determine if additional funds are likely to be required, and if so at what times and in what amounts.

Inflation adjustments will be applied to all costs.

Initial conditions

The initial condition of the firm is to be entered from the following current statement:

HPG Products
INITIAL CONDITIONS
December 31, 19____

Current assets:		
Cash and marketable securities		$ 250,000
Accounts receivable—trade	$1,000,000	
Accounts receivable—other	100,000	
Accounts receivable for uncollectibles	10,000	1,090,000
Inventories:		
Direct materials	$ 200,000	
Goods-in-process	375,000	
Finished goods	50,000	
Manufacturing supplies	1,000	
General supplies	1,000	627,000
Total current assets		$1,967,000
Fixed Assets:		
Plant machinery and equipment		
at cost	$ 85,000	
Less accumulated depreciation	6,500	$ 78,500
Plant office and test equipment		
at cost	92,000	
Less accumulated depreciation	7,250	84,750
General office equipment at cost	30,000	
Less accumulated depreciation	2,600	27,400
Delivery equipment at cost	16,000	
Less accumulated depreciation	3,000	13,000
Unamortized intangible expense		$ 10,000
Total fixed assets		$ 213,650
Total assets		$2,180,650

Current liabilities:

Accounts payable—trade	$ 10,000	
Accounts payable—other	5,000	
Short-term loans and notes	4,000	
Total current liabilities		$ 19,000
Bonds payable		940,000
Total liabilities		$ 959,000

Stockholders' equity:

Common Stock, 50,000		
Shares authorized and outstanding,		
no par paid in	677,950	
Retained earnings	543,700	
Total stockholders' equity		$1,221,650
Total liabilities and stockholders' equity		2,180,650

Environment of economy and industry to sales demand available to firm

HPG top management has agreed on the following economic forecasting values and parameters.

The economic real growth rate is projected to start at 1% annually and grow at 0.7% annually (about 0.0175% quarterly) for three quarters. Starting with the fourth quarter, no real growth is expected for the remainder of the simulation.

The expected real inflation rate starts at 6% annually. During the remainder of the simulation it is expected to grow 1% per year (about 0.25% per quarter).

The industry should experience much more rapid growth than the economy, in fact about 20% more.

HPG's market share of industry is expected to remain at or slightly less than 20%. Temporary reductions in the projected 20% level are anticipated as about 0.25% during the second quarter, and again from the original 20% level, about 0.25% during the fourth quarter. All other quarters are taken at 20%.

Industry base sales in 1977, prior to the start of the simulation, are $13,000,000 annually.

Maximum shifts of 20% for industry sales and 17.5% for HPG's market share were agreed upon to represent uncertainty.

The moderate seasonal pattern is represented by decimal fractions 0.1, 0.11, 0.09, and 0.1 for the four quarters. This schedule starts with the first quarter of the calendar year. Since the seasonal pattern is moderate, inventory policy is not used to smooth production as compared to sales.

Manufacturing items

An analysis of historical manufacturing expense items, and projection into the future, leads to the following table of inputs. Expenses shown are unchanged over the simulation, except for inflation adjustment, unless otherwise indicated. Percentage figures (if any), printed to the right of the base figures, indicate annual growth above inflation over the simulation for periods beyond the first quarter. A few items have more complex schedules, which are detailed following the table.

Capacity of plant in sales dollars at 100% efficiency	$1,000,000
Finished goods inventory level as % of annual cost of goods (see below)	40%
Goods-in-process inventory level as % of annual cost of goods	50%
Direct materials and supplies inventory level as % of usage	40%
Direct labor payroll as % of sales	10%
Supervision and inspection payroll as % of sales	1.4%, 0.1%
Direct material and supplies as % of sales (see below)	12%
Percent operating efficiency	100%
Indirect manufacturing payroll per period	$10,000, 2%
Indirect manufacturing supplies and small tools used per period	$ 2,000, 0.5%
Rent per period for the plant	$ 8,000, 1%
Utilities per period for the plant	$20,000, 20%
Maintenance per period for the plant	$10,000, 5%
Taxes, insurance, labor relations, and miscellaneous expense per period for the plant	$ 1,000, 6%
Plant machinery and equipment additions per period	$ 1,000, 1%
Plant office and test equipment additions per period	$ 1,000, 1%

After the first period, finished goods inventory is cut from 40% to 30% of cost of goods, and then grows at 3% per year through the sixth period (quarter). Starting with the seventh period, inventory is projected at 40% of sales, but from that point on declines at a rate of 3% per year (about 0.75% per quarter). The rate of 12% shown for direct purchased material applies only to the first period. Starting with period 2 there is a substantial rise to 15%, which continues to grow at 5% annually (about 1.25% quarterly) to the end of the simulation.

It should be noted that manufacturing is in a separate location from the sales and general office. For this reason the simulation will use separate period expense schedules for these facilities.

Some additional parameters for manufacturing expense inputs are given in this paragraph. Depreciation rates are 10% per year double-declining balance on both classes of manufacturing fixed assets. To represent uncertainty of manufacturing expense, it has been agreed with management to apply maximum shifts of 5.5%, 6.25%, 5%, and 2% to operating efficiency, direct labor, direct material, and plant utilities, respectively. Indirect manufacturing supplies in inventory are expected to average 5% of annual usage. The overtime limit which may be applied while maintaining good labor relations is 6%. Overtime premium cost is 50%. Currently, the capacity of the plant is so high that the possibility of needing to extend production in any way is extremely remote.

Research and development, sales, general and administrative items

The analysis of expense below uses the same tabular form as described for MANU-FACTURING items above:

R&D payroll per period	$20,000, 6%
R&D period expense other than payrolls (see below)	$25,000, 20%
Accounts receivable as % of annual sales (see below)	2.5%
Sales salaries and commissions payroll as % of sales	1.0%
Indirect sales payroll per period	$20,000, 6%
Advertising, promotion, and miscellaneous sales expense as % of sales	3.0%
Advertising, promotion, and miscellaneous sales period expense	$20,000, 6%
Service and office payroll as % of sales	8.0%
Administrative payroll per period	$15,000, 4%
Office supplies as % of sales	1.25%
Indirect office supplies and small equipment per period	$10,000, 8%
Rent per period for the office	$30,000
Utilities per period for the office	$10,000, 16%
Maintenance per period for the office	$10,000, 7%
Taxes, insurance, labor relations, and miscellaneous expense per period for the office	$12,000, 8%
General office equipment additions per period (see below)	$10,000
Delivery equipment additions per period	$ 2,000

Initial $25,000 R&D period expense grows at 20% per year (about 5% per quarter) through the fourth quarter. After this it remains at $30,000 per period.

A new credit policy is expected to reduce accounts receivable. Except for accumulation of uncollectible accounts, the projected receivable will virtually be zero at the end of each quarter following the first.

The general office equipment class of assets is increased by $10,000 in the first period, $12,000 in the second period, and none thereafter.

Some additional parameters for general expenses are required. Office equipment uses 7%, and delivery equipment uses 20% double-declining balance annual depreciation rates. To represent uncertainties of general expenses, you have agreed with management to apply maximum shifts of 25%, 3.75%, 2.5%, and 12.5% to accounts receivable, office payroll, office supplies, and office utilities, respectively. Office supplies in inventory are expected to average 10% of annual usage. Uncollectible accounts are expected to average 1.2% of collections. Accounts payable are expected to remain about 10% of generated annual credit from HPG vendors.

At the beginning of the simulation HPG had $10,000 of unamortized intangibles which had been capitalized. Top management expects to add $100,000 more to this category during the first simulation quarter for licenses and patents. The amortization rate over the simulation will be $40,000 per year, or $10,000 per quarter, until intangibles are written off.

Financial and valuation parameters

HPG does expect to earn a 4% average return on its cash and marketable securities. Short-term interest cost rate is estimated at 20% per year, and long-term interest cost at 8% per year. The above three rates are not to be changed over the simulation.

Under current contract with investment bankers, HPG will add $10,000 to its long-term debt each quarter for the next 24 quarters (12 quarters during the current simulation).

Dividends are projected at $10,000 per quarter for the next year and a half (6 quarters), and $15,000 per quarter thereafter.

To simulate uncertainty of interest costs, 12.5% and 8.75% maximum shifts are agreed upon for short- and long-term rates, respectively.

HPG uses short-term credit regularly. Borrowing takes place when the cash ratio is expected to fall below 50%. On the other hand, banks will not advance funds unless a 2 to 1 current ratio is maintained.

The combined federal, state, and local effective income tax rate is estimated at 50%.

HPG does not plan to float new common stock issues over the simulation period. As previously noted, the simulation is to determine if additional long-term capital is needed. If any such capital is required, 20% is to be assigned to debt.

Fifty thousand shares of common stock are outstanding at the beginning of the simulation. Additional shares, if required, are to be given a paid-in value of $25 each.

Price-earnings multiple inputs, to be used for valuation, are 10 at the beginning of the simulation and 15 for the last year. The latter figure has been increased because an improving profit figure is anticipated toward the end of the simulation time span.

Overall, the estimated value of assets upon liquidation is estimated at 40% of book value.

Parameters for internal going-concern value computations are to be determined by the program; they will not be overwritten with user inputs.

12.5 | Input Set for HPG PRODUCTS Case

The information on the HPG PRODUCTS case of the preceding section was organized according to PAVE input divisions. There is almost a direct transfer to a PAVE input set as reproduced in Table 12.3. A few points of interpretation will be noted.

Table 12.3.

INPUT SET FOR HPG PRODUCTS

HPG PRODUCTS

INPUT/OUTPUT SYSTEM CHOICES
!! THESE INPUTS CONTROL OTHER DISPLAYS!!

```
 1 TOTAL NUMBER OF PERIODS (MAX 24) . . .          12
 2 NO. OF PERIODS PER YEAR . . . . .                4
 3 SAMPLE SIZE--DETERMINISTIC=1/STAT.=2 TO 12.     10
 4 SEED NO.--STANDARD RANDOM SERIES=0               0
 5 FRAME: SERVICE=0/TRADE=1/MFG=2/ENVRT ONLY=3      2
 6 OUTPUT DIVISION PRINT 1ST FROM LIST BELOW:       0
   VALUATION 1ST AND FINAL YEARS, SCOPE    =0
   STATISTICAL SUMMARY FROM FINAL PERIOD   =1
   FINANCIAL STATEMENTS FOR ALL PERIODS    =2
   SELECTED ACCOUNTS FOR ALL PERIODS       =3
```

INITIAL CONDITION--CURRENT AND INTANGIBLE ASSETS
(START BAL SHEET; NEW FIRM--OMIT/SKELETON)

```
 9 $ CASH AND MARKETABLE SECURITIES . . .        250000
10 $ TRADE ACCOUNTS AND NOTES RECEIVABLE .       100000
11 $ NONTRADE ADVANCES AND ACCRUED RECEIVABLES   100000
12 $ RESERVE FOR UNCOLLECTIBLE ACCOUNTS . . .     10000
13 $ PREPAID EXPENSE AND DEFERRED CHARGES . .         0
14 $ INTANGIBLES; ORGAN EXP., PATENT, GOODWILL    10000
15 $ INVENTORY OF GENERAL SUPPLIES/SMALL EQPT      1000
16 $ INVENTORY OF MFG OR TRADE FINISHED GOODS.    50000
17 $ INVENTORY OF MFG GOODS-IN-PROCESS .         375000
18 $ INVENTORY OF MFG DIRECT MAT'L & SUPPLIES.   200000
19 $ INVENTORY OF MFG PERIOD SUPPLIES & EQPT.      1000
```

INITIAL CONDITION--MANUFACTURING FIXED ASSETS

```
20 $ CLASS 1 AT COST BASIS . . . . .             85000
21 $ CLASS 2 AT COST BASIS . . . . .             92000
22 $ CLASS 3 AT COST BASIS . . . . .                 0
23 $ CLASS 4 AT COST BASIS . . . . .                 0
24 $ CLASS 5 AT COST BASIS . . . . .              6500
25 $ CLASS 1 RESERVE FOR DEPRECIATION .           7250
26 $ CLASS 2 RESERVE FOR DEPRECIATION .              0
27 $ CLASS 3 RESERVE FOR DEPRECIATION .              0
28 $ CLASS 4 RESERVE FOR DEPRECIATION .              0
29 $ CLASS 5 RESERVE FOR DEPRECIATION .              0
```

INITIAL CONDITION--GENERAL FIXED ASSETS

```
30 $ CLASS 1 AT COST BASIS . . . . .             30000
31 $ CLASS 2 AT COST BASIS . . . . .             16000
32 $ CLASS 3 AT COST BASIS . . . . .                 0
33 $ CLASS 4 AT COST BASIS . . . . .                 0
34 $ CLASS 5 AT COST BASIS . . . . .              2600
35 $ CLASS 1 RESERVE FOR DEPRECIATION             3000
36 $ CLASS 2 RESERVE FOR DEPRECIATION                0
37 $ CLASS 3 RESERVE FOR DEPRECIATION                0
38 $ CLASS 4 RESERVE FOR DEPRECIATION                0
39 $ CLASS 5 RESERVE FOR DEPRECIATION                0
```

INITIAL CONDITION--LIABILITIES AND OWNERS' EQUITY
(TOTAL ASSETS, EQUITIES, AND BALANCE
CHECK IN NEXT DISPLAY)

```
40 $ TRADE ACCOUNTS AND NOTES PAYABLE           10000
41 $ NONTRADE ACCTS, DIVIDENDS, TAXES PAYABLE.   5000
42 $ UNEARNED ADVANCES FROM CUSTOMERS
43 $ ACCRUED EXPENSE AND LIABILITIES.            4000
44 $ SHORT-TERM DEBT AND LOANS PAYABLE.        940000
45 $ LONG-TERM OBLIGATIONS AT FACE OR STATED
46 $ BOND (PREFERRED STOCK) PREMIUM (DISCOUNT) 677950
47 $ PAID-IN OWNER EQUITY CAPITAL.             543700
48 $ RETAINED EARNINGS
```

```
INITIAL CONDITION (STARTING BALANCE SHEET) TOTALS

           TOTAL ASSETS.  .  .  .  .    $ 2180650

           TOTAL LIABILITIES .  .  .    $  959000

           TOTAL OWNERS' EQUITY  .  .   $ 1221650
```

% ANNUAL REAL GROWTH RATE OF ECONOMY

```
102 % BASE VALUE APPLIED IN PERIOD 1 .                 1
103 % ANNUAL CHANGE TO PERIODS FROM 1ST BASE .        .7
104 % LAST PERIOD NO., 1ST SCHEDULE (ALL=0).           3
105 % 2ND BASE VALUE NEXT PERIOD (CONTINUE=-1)         0
106 % ANNUAL CHANGE TO PERIODS FROM 2ND BASE           0
107 % LAST PERIOD NO., 2ND SCHEDULE (ALL=0).           0
108 % 3RD BASE VALUE NEXT PERIOD (CONTINUE=-1)         0
109 % ANNUAL CHANGE TO PERIODS FROM 3RD BASE           0
```

Table 12.3 (continued)

110   INFLATE PERIOD COSTS--NO=0/YES=1 . . .   1

% ANNUAL AVERAGE INFLATION RATE

112 % BASE VALUE APPLIED IN PERIOD 1   6
113 % ANNUAL CHANGE TO PERIODS FROM 1ST BASE .   1

120 SALES--% INDUSTRY SHARE=0/$ PER PERIOD=1.   0

* NET SALES DEMAND AVAILABLE TO FIRM
121   *% MAX CHANGE FROM MEAN VALUE . .   17.5

122 % BASE VALUE APPLIED IN PERIOD 1 . . .   20
123 % ANNUAL CHANGE TO PERIODS FROM 1ST BASE   -1
124   LAST PERIOD NO., 1ST SCHEDULE (CONTINUE=-1).   2
125   2ND BASE VALUE NEXT PERIOD (ALL=0). .   20
126 % ANNUAL CHANGE TO PERIODS FROM 2ND BASE   -1
127   LAST PERIOD NO., 2ND SCHEDULE (ALL=0). .   4
128   3RD BASE VALUE NEXT PERIOD (CONTINUE=-1).   20
129 % ANNUAL CHANGE TO PERIODS FROM 3RD BASE   0

130 $ INDUSTRY SALES FOR BASE (PRIOR) YEAR   13000000

*% ANNUAL INDUSTRY GROWTH COMPARED TO ECONOMY
131   *% MAX CHANGE FROM MEAN VALUE . .   20

132 % BASE VALUE APPLIED IN PERIOD 1 . . .   20
133 % ANNUAL CHANGE TO PERIODS FROM 1ST BASE .   0

SEASONAL/CYCLICAL INDICES--1ST SET STOPS AT 1ST ZERO
51 INDEX 1 1
52 INDEX 2 11
53 INDEX 3 09
54 INDEX 4 1
55 INDEX 5   0
56 INDEX 6   0
57 INDEX 7   0
58 INDEX 8   0
59 INDEX 9   0
60 INDEX 10   0
61 INDEX 11   0
62 INDEX 12   0

140 INITIAL GOODS INVY'S--COST % OF SELL PRICE   60

*DIRECT PURCHASED MATERIAL OR GOODS AS % OF SALES
141   *% MAX CHANGE FROM MEAN VALUE . .   5

142 % BASE VALUE APPLIED IN PERIOD 1 . . .   12
143 % ANNUAL CHANGE TO PERIODS FROM 1ST BASE   0
144   LAST PERIOD NO., 1ST SCHEDULE (ALL=0). .   1
145   2ND BASE VALUE NEXT PERIOD (CONTINUE=-1).   15
146 % ANNUAL CHANGE TO PERIODS FROM 2ND BASE   5
147   LAST PERIOD NO., 2ND SCHEDULE (ALL=0). .   0
148   3RD BASE VALUE NEXT PERIOD (CONTINUE=-1).   0
149 % ANNUAL CHANGE TO PERIODS FROM 3RD BASE   0

150 % DESEASONALIZE GOODS PRODUCTION/PURCHASE   0

FINISHED GOODS INVENTORY LEVEL AS % ANNUAL COST GOODS
152 % BASE VALUE APPLIED IN PERIOD 1 . . .   40
153 % ANNUAL CHANGE TO PERIODS FROM 1ST BASE   0
154   LAST PERIOD NO., 1ST SCHEDULE (ALL=0). .   1
155   2ND BASE VALUE NEXT PERIOD (CONTINUE=-1).   30
156 % ANNUAL CHANGE TO PERIODS FROM 2ND BASE   3
157   LAST PERIOD NO., 2ND SCHEDULE (ALL=0). .   6
158   3RD BASE VALUE NEXT PERIOD (CONTINUE=-1).   40
159 % ANNUAL CHANGE TO PERIODS FROM 3RD BASE   -3

GOODS-IN-PROCESS INVENT'Y LEVEL AS % ANNUAL COST GOODS
162 % BASE VALUE APPLIED IN PERIOD 1 . . .   50
163 % ANNUAL CHANGE TO PERIODS FROM 1ST BASE   0

DIRECT MATERIAL INVENTORY LEVEL AS % ANNUAL USAGE
172 % BASE VALUE APPLIED IN PERIOD 1 . . .   40
173 % ANNUAL CHANGE TO PERIODS FROM 1ST BASE   0

*DIRECT LABOR PAYROLL AS % OF SALES
181   *% MAX CHANGE FROM MEAN VALUE . .   6.25

182 % BASE VALUE APPLIED IN PERIOD 1 . . .   10
183 % ANNUAL CHANGE TO PERIODS FROM 1ST BASE   0

DIRECT SUPERVISION AND SUPPORT PAYROLL AS % OF SALES
192 % BASE VALUE APPLIED IN PERIOD 1 . . .   1.4
193 % ANNUAL CHANGE TO PERIODS FROM 1ST BASE   .1

Table 12.3 (continued)

```
*% OPERATING EFFICIENCY OF PROCESSING  .  .  .  .
   201 %  *% MAX CHANGE FROM MEAN VALUE  .  .  .        5.5
   202 $  BASE VALUE APPLIED IN PERIOD 1  .  .  .        100
   203 %  ANNUAL CHANGE TO PERIODS FROM 1ST BASE  .        0

$ CAPACITY OF PLANT PER PERIOD, 100% EFFIC'Y, SALES $
   212 $  BASE VALUE APPLIED IN PERIOD 1  .  .  .   10000000
   213 %  ANNUAL CHANGE TO PERIODS FROM 1ST BASE  .        0

220 MFG SUPPLIES INV'Y LEVEL AS % ANNUAL USAGE           5

$ INDIRECT SUPPLIES/SMALL EQPT USED PER PERIOD
   222 $  BASE VALUE APPLIED IN PERIOD 1  .  .  .       2000
   223 %  ANNUAL CHANGE TO PERIODS FROM 1ST BASE  .      .05

$ INDIRECT MFG PAYROLL PER PERIOD
   232 $  BASE VALUE APPLIED IN PERIOD 1  .  .  .      10000
   233 %  ANNUAL CHANGE TO PERIODS FROM 1ST BASE  .        2

$ SPACE, RENT OR OCCUPANCY PER PERIOD--MFG
   242 $  BASE VALUE APPLIED IN PERIOD 1  .  .  .      -8000
   243 %  ANNUAL CHANGE TO PERIODS FROM 1ST BASE  .        1

**$ UTILITIES OR ALL INDIRECT COSTS PER PERIOD--MFG
   251 %  *% MAX CHANGE FROM MEAN VALUE  .  .  .          2
   252 $  BASE VALUE APPLIED IN PERIOD 1  .  .  .      20000
   253 %  ANNUAL CHANGE TO PERIODS FROM 1ST BASE  .       20

$ MAINTENANCE PER PERIOD--MFG
   262 $  BASE VALUE APPLIED IN PERIOD 1  .  .  .      10000
   263 %  ANNUAL CHANGE TO PERIODS FROM 1ST BASE  .        5

$ TAXES, INSURANCE, LABOR RELA'N, MISC PER PERIOD--MFG
   272 $  BASE VALUE APPLIED IN PERIOD 1  .  .  .       1000
   273 %  ANNUAL CHANGE TO PERIODS FROM 1ST BASE  .        6


280 % DEPREC'N PER YR DECLINING BAL MFG CLASS 1         20
$ MFG FIXED ASSETS CLASS 1 NET CHANGES PER PERIOD
   282 $  BASE VALUE APPLIED IN PERIOD 1  .  .  .       1000
   283 %  ANNUAL CHANGE TO PERIODS FROM 1ST BASE  .        1

290 % DEPREC'N PER YR DECLINING BAL MFG CLASS 2         20
$ MFG FIXED ASSETS CLASS 2 NET CHANGES PER PERIOD
   292 $  BASE VALUE APPLIED IN PERIOD 1  .  .  .       1000
   293 %  ANNUAL CHANGE TO PERIODS FROM 1ST BASE  .        1

MANUFACTURING EXPENSE SYSTEM PARAMETERS
   75 %  OVERTIME LIMIT TO REGULAR DIRECT LABOR  .        6
   76 %  OVERTIME PREMIUM COST  .  .  .                  50
   77 %  INCR PLANT CAPAC'Y FROM SUBCONTRACT OPERN        0
   78 %  MAT'L COST PREMIUM IF SUBCONTRACT OPERA'N        0

330 R&D EXPENSES--% SALES=0/$ PER PERIOD=1  .            1
RESEARCH AND DEVELOPMENT PAYROLL
   332 $  BASE VALUE APPLIED IN PERIOD 1  .  .  .      20000
   333 %  ANNUAL CHANGE TO PERIODS FROM 1ST BASE  .        6

RES & DVLPT MATERIAL/CONTRACTS/MISC EXPENSE PER PERIOD
   342 $  BASE VALUE APPLIED IN PERIOD 1  .  .  .      25000
   343 %  ANNUAL CHANGE TO PERIODS FROM 1ST BASE  .       20
   344 %  LAST PERIOD NO., 1ST SCHEDULE (ALL=0).          4
   345 $  2ND BASE VALUE NEXT PERIOD (CONTINUE=-1).   30000
   346 %  ANNUAL CHANGE TO PERIODS FROM 2ND BASE  .        0
   347 %  LAST PERIOD NO., 2ND SCHEDULE (ALL=0).          0
   348 $  3RD BASE VALUE NEXT PERIOD (CONTINUE=-1).       0
   349 %  ANNUAL CHANGE TO PERIODS FROM 3RD BASE  .        0
```

Table 12.3 (continued)

```
SALES SALARIES/COMMISSIONS PAYROLL AS % OF SALES
     *% MAX CHANGE FROM MEAN VALUE  .  .  .        1
352 % BASE VALUE APPLIED IN PERIOD 1  .  .  .
353 % ANNUAL CHANGE TO PERIODS FROM 1ST BASE  .    0

$ INDIRECT SALES PAYROLL PER PERIOD               20000
362 $ BASE VALUE APPLIED IN PERIOD 1  .  .  .
36.3 % ANNUAL CHANGE TO PERIODS FROM 1ST BASE  .    6

ADVERTISE/PROMOTE/MISC SALES EXPENSE AS % OF SALES
372 % BASE VALUE APPLIED IN PERIOD 1  .  .  .       3
373 % ANNUAL CHANGE TO PERIODS FROM 1ST BASE  .     0

$ ADVERTISE/PROMOTE/MISC SALES EXPENSE PER PERIOD
382 $ BASE VALUE APPLIED IN PERIOD 1  .  .  .     20000
383 % ANNUAL CHANGE TO PERIODS FROM 1ST BASE  .     6

390 % UNCOLLECTIBLE ACCOUNTS  .  .  .  .           1.2

*ACCOUNTS RECEIVABLE LEVEL AS % OF ANNUAL SALES
391   *% MAX CHANGE FROM MEAN VALUE  .  .           25
392 % BASE VALUE APPLIED IN PERIOD 1  .  .  .       2.5
393 % ANNUAL CHANGE TO PERIODS FROM 1ST BASE  .     0
394 LAST PERIOD NO., 1ST SCHEDULE (ALL=0).          1
395 2ND BASE VALUE NEXT PERIOD (CONTINUE=-1).       0
396 % ANNUAL CHANGE TO PERIODS FROM 2ND BASE        0
397 LAST PERIOD NO., 2ND SCHEDULE (ALL=0).          0
398 3RD BASE VALUE NEXT PERIOD (CONTINUE=-1).       0
399 % ANNUAL CHANGE TO PERIODS FROM 3RD BASE        0

*DIRECT SERVICE/OFFICE MATERIALS AS % OF SALES
401   *% MAX CHANGE FROM MEAN VALUE  .  .           2.5
402 % BASE VALUE APPLIED IN PERIOD 1  .  .  .       1.25
403 % ANNUAL CHANGE TO PERIODS FROM 1ST BASE  .     0

$ INDIRECT SERVICE/OFFICE SUPPLIES/SMALL EQP'T PERIOD
412 $ BASE VALUE APPLIED IN PERIOD 1  .  .  .     10000
413 % ANNUAL CHANGE TO PERIODS FROM 1ST BASE  .     8


*DIRECT SERVICE/OFFICE PAYROLL AS % OF SALES
421   *% MAX CHANGE FROM MEAN VALUE  .  .  .        3.75
422 % BASE VALUE APPLIED IN PERIOD 1  .  .  .       8
423 % ANNUAL CHANGE TO PERIODS FROM 1ST BASE  .     0

$ GENERAL ADMINISTRATIVE/INDIRECT SERV. PAYROLL PERIOD
432 $ BASE VALUE APPLIED IN PERIOD 1  .  .  .     15000
433 % ANNUAL CHANGE TO PERIODS FROM 1ST BASE  .     4

$ SPACE, RENT, OR OCCUPANCY PER PERIOD--GENERAL
442 % BASE VALUE APPLIED IN PERIOD 1  .  .  .     30000
443 % ANNUAL CHANGE TO PERIODS FROM 1ST BASE  .     0

*$ UTILITIES OR ALL INDIRECT COSTS PER PERIOD--GENERAL
451   *% MAX CHANGE FROM MEAN VALUE  .  .  .        12.5
452 % BASE VALUE APPLIED IN PERIOD 1  .  .  .     10000
453 % ANNUAL CHANGE TO PERIODS FROM 1ST BASE  .     16

$ MAINTENANCE PER PERIOD--GENERAL
462 % BASE VALUE APPLIED IN PERIOD 1  .  .  .     10000
463 % ANNUAL CHANGE TO PERIODS FROM 1ST BASE  .     7

$ TAXES, INSURANCE, LABOR RELA'N, MISC PERIOD--GENERAL
472 % BASE VALUE APPLIED IN PERIOD 1  .  .  .     12000
473 % ANNUAL CHANGE TO PERIODS FROM 1ST BASE  .     8

480 % DEPREC'N YRLY DECLINE BAL GENERAL CLASS 1     14

$ GENERAL FIXED ASSETS CLASS 1 NET CHANGES PER PERIOD
482 $ BASE VALUE APPLIED IN PERIOD 1  .  .  .     10000
483 % ANNUAL CHANGE TO PERIODS FROM 1ST BASE  .     1
484 LAST PERIOD NO., 1ST SCHEDULE (ALL=0).        12000
485 2ND BASE VALUE NEXT PERIOD (CONTINUE=-1).       0
486 % ANNUAL CHANGE TO PERIODS FROM 2ND BASE        2
487 LAST PERIOD NO., 2ND SCHEDULE (ALL=0).          0
488 3RD BASE VALUE NEXT PERIOD (CONTINUE=-1).       0
489 % ANNUAL CHANGE TO PERIODS FROM 3RD BASE        0
```

Table 12.3 (continued)

```
*%  SHORT-TERM INTEREST RATE ANNUAL
561     *% MAX CHANGE FROM MEAN VALUE . . .          12.5
562  %  BASE VALUE APPLIED IN PERIOD 1 . . .           20
563  %  ANNUAL CHANGE TO PERIODS FROM 1ST BASE .        0

*%  LONG-TERM INTEREST RATE ANNUAL
571     *% MAX CHANGE FROM MEAN VALUE . . .          8.75
572  %  BASE VALUE APPLIED IN PERIOD 1 . . .            8
573  %  ANNUAL CHANGE TO PERIODS FROM 1ST BASE .        0

FINANCIAL AND VALUATION SYSTEM PARAMETERS
87  %  CASH RATIO MIN, BELOW WHICH CASH DEMANDED       50
88  %  CURRENT RATIO MIN FROM SHORT-TERM LOANS .      200
89  %  COMBINED EFFECTIVE INCOME TAX RATE (<100)       50
90  $  INITIAL TAX LOSS CREDIT FOR CARRY FORWARD    50000
91     NO. 1ST PERIOD OWNER EQUITY UNITS (1/SHARE)     25
92  $  ADDED SHARE COST--INTERNAL COMPUTATION=0.       10
93     PRICE-EARNINGS MULTIPLE YR j--INTER'L COMP=0     15
94     PRICE-EARN MULTIPLE FINAL YR--INTER'L COMP=0     40
95  %  ASSETS AVERAGE REALIZED IN LIQUIDATION           0
96  %  INVESTOR REQD RATE RETURN YR--INTL COMP=0         0
97  %  LONG-TERM AVG GROWTH RATE YR--INTL COMP=0         0
98  %  RETURN ON INCREM'L ASSETS YR--INTL COMP=0         0
```

```
490  %  DEPREC'N YRLY DECLINE BAL GENERAL CLASS 2      40

$ GENERAL FIXED ASSETS CLASS 2 NET CHANGES PER PERIOD
492  $  BASE VALUE APPLIED IN PERIOD 1 . .           2000
493  %  ANNUAL CHANGE TO PERIODS FROM 1ST BASE .        0

GENERAL ADMINISTRATIVE SYSTEM PARAMETERS

79     GENL SUPPLIES INV'Y LEVEL AS % ANNUAL USAGE      10
80     ACCTS PAYABLE LEVEL AS % OF ANNUAL ACCT PAY'     10
81     PREPAID EXPENSE LEVEL AS % OF ANNUAL SALES        0
82     ADVANCES BY CUSTOMERS AS % OF ANNUAL SALES   100000
83  $  ORGAN EXP./GOODWILL INCURRED IN PERIOD 1.     40000
84  $  AMORTIZ/N OF INTANGIBLES YRLY, NOT PERIOD

530    INTERNAL COMPUTE REQD INVEST--NO=0/YES=1.         1

$ OWNER NET CASH INVESTMENT PLANNED CHANGE PER PERIOD
531    EARN ON NEAR CASH AS % SHORT-TERM INT RATE       20
532  $  BASE VALUE APPLIED IN PERIOD 1 . .               0
533  %  ANNUAL CHANGE TO PERIODS FROM 1ST BASE .         0

540    LONG-TERM OBLIGA'S IN REQD ADDED INVEST          20

$ LONG-TERM OBLIGATIONS PLANNED NET CHANGE PER PERIOD
542  $  BASE VALUE APPLIED IN PERIOD 1 . .           10000
543  %  ANNUAL CHANGE TO PERIODS FROM 1ST BASE .         0

550    DIVIDENDS--% EARNINGS=0/$ PER PERIOD=1 . .        1

DIVIDENDS OR WITHDRAWLS PER PERIOD

552  $  BASE VALUE APPLIED IN PERIOD 1 . .           10000
553  %  ANNUAL CHANGE TO PERIODS FROM 1ST BASE           0
554    LAST PERIOD NO., 1ST SCHEDULE (ALL=0).            6
555  $  2ND BASE VALUE NEXT PERIOD (CONTINUE=-1).    15000
556  %  ANNUAL CHANGE TO PERIODS FROM 2ND BASE           0
557    LAST PERIOD NO., 2ND SCHEDULE (ALL=0).            0
558  $  3RD BASE VALUE NEXT PERIOD (CONTINUE=-1).        0
559  %  ANNUAL CHANGE TO PERIODS FROM 3RD BASE           0
```

For the INPUT/OUTPUT SYSTEM CHOICES division, a small sample specification was entered as ID 3 = 10. Then a Student's t-statistic of about 2.3 accompanies a 95% confidence interval column and nine degrees of freedom (see Table 8.2).

Since HPG is a manufacturing firm, an entry of 2 is required in ID 5.

A full output set will be obtained for HPG PRODUCTS. An entry of 0 in ID 6 will print VALUATION AND SCOPE, the first output division. Subsequent commands of 1, 2, and 3 will print the remaining three output divisions.

For INITIAL CONDITIONS input division, entries correspond to the December 31 statement of INITIAL CONDITION given in the case. Two classes for both manufacturing (plant) and general fixed assets are listed on this statement. These fixed asset classes are used throughout the simulation.

In ENVIRONMENT OF ECONOMY AND INDUSTRY OF SALES AVAILABLE TO FIRM input division, information from the case may be transferred directly to dynamic input ID sets 102, 112, 121, and 131. The operation of these sets was described in detail in section 12.2 for the GIFTIQUE case. Here there will be an inflation adjustment to period costs (ID 110 = 1). An industry analysis will be used (ID 120 = 0). Industry sales are subject to three growth rates in ID sets 102, 112, and 132; and to a seasonal adjustment per IDs 51 to 54. Industry sales grow from a base of $13,000,000 per ID 130. HPG PRODUCTS sales are computed as a market share of industry per ID set 122. Uncertainty about industry sales is entered in ID 131; uncertainty about HPG market share in ID 121.

Seasonal indexes may be transferred directly from the case to IDs 51 to 54. These will be internally normalized by PAVE to a mean of one.

Dynamic input set entries in the MANUFACTURING ITEM section follow the tabulated information in the case. Nonentry in ID 150 means that inventories will not be adjusted oppositely from the seasonal pattern of sales in order to stabilize production.

The depreciation rates in IDs 280 and 290 are entered as 20 because of the double-declining balance specification.

Notice that expense entries in both MANUFACTURING and GENERAL sections are divided into categories "variable with sales" and "fixed per period." This distinction should be followed when organizing expenses for any PAVE simulation.

For R&D, SALES, GENERAL, AND ADMINISTRATIVE EXPENSE, inputs again follow the tabulated information from the case. An entry of 1 in ID 330 indicates dollar period inputs for R&D. The depreciation rates in IDs 480 and 490 are entered at 14 and 40 from the double-declining balance specification. The two categories each for MANUFACTURING and GENERAL fixed assets are implemented with "net addition" inputs for ID sets 282, 292, 482, and 492. Corresponding depreciation rate inputs appear under IDs 280, 290, 480, and 490.

Inputs for office supplies inventory (10 in ID 79) and intangible assets follow directly from case information. Additional organization expense of $100,000 the first year is entered in ID 83, and $40,000 per year amortization in ID 84.

Accounts payable are maintained at 10% of annual vendor credit to HPG (ID 80). Input uncertainties for elements of general expense are maximum shifts of 25% for accounts receivable (ID 391), 2.5% for variable office supplies (ID 401), and 12.5% for utilities and other period expenses in ID 451. Uncollectible accounts are estimated at 1.2% of credit sales in ID 390.

In FINANCIAL AND VALUATION PARAMETERS division there are no *planned* sales of new common stock, hence nonentry is correct for ID 532.

Interest rates in IDs 562 for short term and 572 for long term are entered directly from case data. Uncertainty inputs for interest rates appear in IDs 561 and 571. The mean rate of return on cash and marketable securities balances of HPG was given in the case as 4%. This is 20% of the short-term rate of 20% in ID 562. Thus 20 is the correct entry in ID 531.

There is a planned long-term debt addition in ID 542 of $10,000 per period. This amount will be added every period. The above item is the only planned long-term capital addition.

Dividend inputs correspond to case data. An entry of 1 in ID 550 indicates that dividend inputs will be in dollar amounts instead of percentages of earnings. The dollar entries appear in ID set 552.

If additional capital is required from internal computation, 20% of this capital is to be raised with long-term debt. The relevant entry is in ID 540.

Short-term borrowing limit parameters IDs 87, 88, and 95 follow case specifications. Note that IDs 87, 88, and 89 have values in the case which are identical with PAVE internal default values. ID 95, however, is assigned a new value of 40.

The 50,000 starting common shares entered in ID 91 appear both in the statement of INITIAL CONDITION (section 12.4) and in the financial parameters description of the case. The $25 cost of additional shares and price-earnings multiples of 10 and 15 must be entered in IDs 92, 93, and 94, respectively. These are different from internal default parameters.

There are no entries in IDs 96, 97, and 98 because internal computation of these parameters is specified in the case.

12.6 | Output Interpretations of HPG PRODUCTS Case

Outputs are printed in Table 12.4 and will be discussed by division. The VALUATION AND SCOPE division provides overall information on the HPG management's key question: "Is the firm likely to become a profitable operation in the intermediate term?" Note that no insolvencies occurred during the simulation.

Outputs confirm that growth expectations are sufficient to improve the current earnings position. Solid values and profitability are projected. Risks are quite low under the input assumptions of the case.

Table 12.4.
OUTPUT FOR HPG PRODUCTS

```
*********************
  VALUATION AND SCOPE
*********************
HPG PRODUCTS

12 PERIODS OVER  3.00 YEARS;  4.00 PERIODS PER YEAR, EACH  0.25 YEARS

******  SCOPE OF FIRM -- INITIAL SHARES 50000 --- FINAL SHARES 50000 -- EOP = END OF PERIOD ******

      95 % CONFIDENCE LIMITS FOR MEANS WITH SAMPLE SIZE 10
```

			MEAN	STANDARD DEVIATION	95 % LOWER CONFIDENCE	95 % UPPER CONFIDENCE
SALES	TOTAL	FIRST YEAR	3,081,829	62,732	2,937,545	3,226,113
		FINAL YEAR	4,945,534	53,365	4,822,795	5,068,273
	PER SHARE	FIRST YEAR	61.64	1.25	58.75	64.52
		FINAL YEAR	98.91	1.07	96.46	101.37
EARNINGS	TOTAL	FIRST YEAR	382,551	29,894	313,794	451,307
		FINAL YEAR	851,810	45,495	747,171	956,450
	PER SHARE	FIRST YEAR	7.65	0.60	6.28	9.03
		FINAL YEAR	17.04	0.91	14.94	19.13
RETURN ON OWNERS' EQUITY %	TOTAL	FIRST YEAR	25.10	1.87	20.80	29.39
		FINAL YEAR	32.87	1.46	29.51	36.23
OWNERS' EQUITY	TOTAL	AT EOP 1	1,143,034	16,672	1,104,689	1,181,379
		END OF RUN	2,881,654	60,780	2,741,861	3,021,447
	PER SHARE	AT EOP 1	22.86	0.33	22.09	23.63
		END OF RUN	57.63	1.22	54.84	60.43
TOTAL ASSETS	TOTAL	AT EOP 1	2,422,053	34,093	2,343,639	2,500,467
		END OF RUN	4,148,191	32,779	4,072,798	4,223,583
	PER SHARE	AT EOP 1	48.44	0.68	46.87	50.01
		END OF RUN	82.96	0.66	81.46	84.47
CASH AND MARKETABLE SECURITIES	TOTAL	AT EOP 1	988,775	20,101	942,543	1,035,006
		END OF RUN	1,805,133	59,155	1,669,077	1,941,189
	PER SHARE	AT EOP 1	19.78	0.40	18.85	20.70
		END OF RUN	36.10	1.18	33.38	38.82

```
TECHNICAL INSOLVENCY DID NOT OCCUR
LEGAL INSOLVENCY DID NOT OCCUR
```

Table 12.4 (continued)

****** METHODS OF VALUATION ******

	FIRST YEAR OR EOP 1	FINAL YEAR OR END	FIRST YEAR PER SHARE	FINAL YEAR PER SHARE
MARKET VALUE WITH PRICE-EARNINGS MULTIPLES	3,825,506	12,777,157	76.51	255.54
PRICE-EARNINGS MULTIPLES	10	15		
GOING CONCERN ECONOMIC VALUE UNDER RISK	25,063,091	33,894,275	501.26	677.89
LIQUIDATION VALUE TO OWNERS	-350,198	392,739	-7.01	7.85
LIQUIDATION VALUE OF TANGIBLE ASSETS	928,821	1,659,276	18.57	33.19
FIXED ASSETS AT BOOK VALUE WITH INTANGIBLES	307,104	160,524	6.14	3.21
TAX LOSS CARRYFORWARD--INITIAL & END OF RUN	0	0		

****** PARAMETERS OF GOING-CONCERN VALUATION ******

	APPLIED EOP 1	APPLIED END OF RUN
INVESTORS' REQUIRED RATE OF RETURN %	11.23	8.67
INFLATION RATE %	6.00	6.17
LONG-TERM FIRM GROWTH RATE WITH INFLATION %	6.33	6.33
LONG-TERM REAL GROWTH RATE OF THE ECONOMY %	0.00	0.00
MEAN RATE OF RETURN ON INCREMENTAL ASSETS %	27.19	27.19

Table 12.4 (continued)

```
***********************************
  FINANCIAL SUMMARY FROM FINAL PERIOD
***********************************
```

HPG PRODUCTS

12 PERIODS OVER 3.00 YEARS; 4.00 PERIODS PER YEAR, EACH 0.25 YEARS
UNDEFINED RATIOS APPEAR '###--'; YEARLY VALUES ARE EXTRAPOLATED FROM THE FINAL PERIOD; O VALUES OMITTED

95 % CONFIDENCE LIMITS FOR MEANS WITH SAMPLE SIZE 10

	MEAN	STANDARD DEVIATION	95 % LOWER CONFIDENCE	95 % UPPER CONFIDENCE	MINIMUM	MAXIMUM
****** SCOPE OF FIRM ******						
FIRM'S SHARE OF INDUSTRY %	19.41	0.37	18.55	20.26	17.90	21.35
NET SALES OR REVENUE PER YEAR	5,080,054	152,680	4,728,890	5,431,218	4,419,888	5,873,684
CASH AND MARKETABLE SECURITIES	1,805,133	59,155	1,669,076	1,941,189	1,524,270	2,053,015
TOTAL ASSETS	4,148,191	32,779	4,072,799	4,223,582	4,006,784	4,289,497
TOTAL OWNERS' EQUITY	2,881,654	60,780	2,741,860	3,021,448	2,553,111	3,113,803
****** RATIO ANALYSIS OF PROFITABILITY ******						
GROSS MARGIN ON SALES %	76.41	7.01	60.28	92.53	43.12	100.00
NET OPERATING MARGIN ON SALES %	42.61	6.65	27.31	57.90	10.28	65.87
OPERATING EARNING POWER %	50.58	7.10	34.25	66.91	13.39	80.01
OPERAT'G EFFIC'Y OR CAP'L TURNS	1.23	0.04	1.13	1.32	1.04	1.41
RETURN ON OWNERS' EQUITY %	35.67	4.76	24.72	46.61	9.46	55.70
****** RATIO ANALYSIS OF FINANCIAL CONDITION ******						
CASH RATIO %	1,106.23	168.51	718.65	1,493.80	409.61	1,814.32
ACID TEST OR QUICK RATIO %	1,106.23	168.51	718.65	1,493.80	409.61	1,814.32
CURRENT RATIO %	2,453.90	367.47	1,608.71	3,299.08	973.45	3,631.89
DEBT TO TANGIBLE ASSETS %	30.59	1.00	28.29	32.89	27.41	36.31
DEBT TO TANGIBLE OWNER EQUITY %	44.34	2.13	39.44	49.23	37.76	57.00
TIMES INTEREST EARNED RATIO	25.63	3.53	17.51	33.74	7.14	39.41
INVENTORY TURNS PER YEAR	0.60	0.18	0.18	1.01	0.00	1.44

Table 12.4 (continued)

****** SELECTED FINANCIAL SUMMARY VALUES ******

INDUSTRY SALES PER YR--000 OMIT	26,196	707	24,569	27,822	23,409	31,105
COST OF SALES PER YEAR	1,260,976	378,591	390,216	2,131,735	0	3,027,353
GROSS PROFIT PER YEAR	3,819,077	290,930	3,149,938	4,488,216	2,295,326	4,979,753
OPERATING INCOME PER YEAR	2,109,354	300,554	1,418,079	2,800,628	547,365	3,280,270
NET INCOME BEFORE TAX PER YEAR	2,091,207	300,426	1,400,227	2,782,186	523,566	3,257,953
NET INCOME AFTER TAX PER YEAR	1,045,604	150,213	700,114	1,391,093	261,783	1,628,976
CASH+MKT SECURITIES+ACCTS.RECV	1,805,133	59,155	1,669,076	1,941,189	1,524,270	2,053,015
TOTAL INVENTORIES	2,182,533	51,056	2,065,104	2,299,961	1,887,063	2,415,006
TOTAL CURRENT ASSETS	3,987,666	32,779	3,912,274	4,063,057	3,846,260	4,128,973
NET TANGIBLE FIXED ASSETS	160,524	0	160,524	160,524	160,524	160,524
ACCOUNTS PAYABLE	206,537	33,822	128,746	284,327	112,988	395,282
LONG-TERM FIXED OBLIGATIONS	1,060,000	0	1,060,000	1,060,000	1,060,000	1,060,000
TOTAL LIABILITIES	1,266,537	33,822	1,188,746	1,344,327	1,172,988	1,455,282
TOTAL PAID-IN OWNERS' EQUITY	677,950	0	677,950	677,950	677,950	677,950

Table 12.4 (continued)

```
**************************************
  FINANCIAL STATEMENTS PROJECTED FOR ALL PERIODS
**************************************
```

ADMIN	ADMINISTRATIVE	DEPRC	DEPRECIATION	GEN	GENERAL
AMORT	AMORTIZATION	EOP	END OF PERIOD	INVY	INVENTORY
BOP	BEGINNING OF PERIOD	GEN	GENERAL	MFG	MANUFACTURING
MISC	MISCELLANEOUS	PURCH	PURCHASES OF	R&D	RESEARCH AND DEVELOPMENT

12 PERIODS OVER 3.00 YEARS; 4.00 PERIODS PER YEAR, EACH 0.25 YEARS

VALUES ARE ACCOUNT MEANS; ACCOUNT OMITTED WHEN ALL VALUES 0
HEADINGS ARE: PERIOD NO. AND YEAR/MONTH; OR CUMULATIVE *FOR YEAR NO.*

HPG PRODUCTS

```
**************************************
  ENVIRONMENTAL ANALYSES OF FIRM
**************************************
```

INDUSTRY BASE SALES--000S OMITTED; YEAR= 13000 -- PERIOD= 3250

	1 0/ 3	2 0/ 6	3 0/ 9	4 1/ 0	*FOR YEAR 1*	5 1/ 3
INFLATION RATE ANNUAL %	6.00	6.01	6.03	6.04	6.02*	6.06
REAL ECONOMY GROWTH ANNUAL %	1.00	1.00	1.00	0.00	0.75*	0.00
INDUSTRY TOTAL GROWTH %	28.47	28.49	28.51	27.25	28.18*	27.27
SEASONAL/CYCLICAL INDICES	1.00	1.10	0.90	1.00	1.00*	1.00
INDUSTRY SALES--000S OMITTED	3,338	4,196	3,579	4,422	15,535*	4,399
FIRM'S INDUSTRY SHARE %	19.47	19.62	20.28	19.90	19.82*	20.34
FIRM SALES DEMAND AVAILABLE	651,992	823,877	727,282	878,677	3,081,828*	895,948

```
**************************************
  ENVIRONMENTAL ANALYSES OF FIRM  (CONTINUED)
**************************************
```

	6 1/ 6	7 1/ 9	8 2/ 0	*FOR YEAR 2*	9 2/ 3	10 2/ 6
INFLATION RATE ANNUAL %	6.08	6.09	6.11	6.09*	6.12	6.14
REAL ECONOMY GROWTH ANNUAL %	0.00	0.00	0.00	0.00*	0.00	0.00
INDUSTRY TOTAL GROWTH %	27.29	27.31	27.33	27.30*	27.34	27.36
SEASONAL/CYCLICAL INDICES	1.10	0.90	1.00	1.00*	1.00	1.10
INDUSTRY SALES--000S OMITTED	5,226	4,510	5,407	19,542*	5,682	6,787
FIRM'S INDUSTRY SHARE %	19.37	20.91	19.59	20.05*	20.28	20.13
FIRM SALES DEMAND AVAILABLE	1,011,608	942,255	1,059,344	3,909,155*	1,149,768	1,361,196

Table 12.4 (continued)

```
ENVIRONMENTAL ANALYSES OF FIRM   (CONTINUED)
*********************************
```

	11	2/ 9	12	3/ 0	*FOR YEAR 3*
INFLATION RATE ANNUAL %		6.15		6.17	6.15*
REAL ECONOMY GROWTH ANNUAL %		0.00		0.00	0.00*
INDUSTRY TOTAL GROWTH %		27.38		27.40	27.37*
SEASONAL/CYCLICAL INDICES		0.90		1.00	1.00*
INDUSTRY SALES--000S OMITTED		5,748		6,549	24,766*
FIRM'S INDUSTRY SHARE %		20.24		19.41	20.02*
FIRM SALES DEMAND AVAILABLE		1,164,557		1,270,013	4,945,534*

Table 12.4 (continued)

HPG PRODUCTS
****
INCOME STATEMENTS
****

	1 0/3	2 0/6	3 0/9	4 1/0	*FOR YEAR 1*	5 1/3
FIRM NET SALES ACHIEVED	651,992	823,877	727,282	878,677	3,081,828*	895,948
-COST OF SALES	409,872	104,993	226,243	287,501	1,028,609*	284,279
GROSS PROFIT ON SALES	242,120	718,884	501,040	591,177	2,053,221*	611,668
R&D PAYROLL	20,293	20,894	21,513	22,152	84,852*	22,810
R&D MATERIAL AND MISC EXP	25,367	25,940	28,613	30,390	111,310*	32,278
TOTAL R&D EXPENSE	45,660	47,835	50,126	52,541	196,162*	55,088
DIRECT SALES PAYROLL	6,520	8,239	7,273	8,787	30,819*	8,959
PERIOD SALES PAYROLL	20,293	20,894	21,513	22,152	84,852*	22,810
DIRECT ADVERTISE, MISC SALES	19,560	24,716	21,818	26,360	92,454*	26,878
PERIOD ADVERTISE, MISC SALES	20,293	20,894	21,513	22,152	84,852*	22,810
TOTAL SALES EXPENSE	66,667	74,743	72,118	79,451	292,979*	81,458
DIRECT SERVICE PAYROLL	52,387	65,159	58,393	70,344	246,283*	71,603
PERIOD GEN ADMIN PAYROLL	15,220	15,596	15,982	16,378	63,176*	16,785
PURCH GEN SUPPLIES	24,616	21,821	19,541	23,095	89,073*	23,032
+BOP GEN SUPPLIES INVY	1,000	7,319	8,326	7,962	1,000*	8,873
-EOP GEN SUPPLIES INVY	7,319	8,326	7,962	8,873	8,873*	9,116
DIRECT GEN SUPPLIES USED	8,150	10,318	9,047	10,951	38,466*	11,170
PERIOD GEN SUPPLIES USED	10,147	10,496	10,858	11,232	42,733*	11,620
SPACE AND RENT--GEN	30,440	30,888	31,343	31,807	124,478*	32,278
UTILITIES--GEN	9,985	10,712	11,376	12,042	44,115*	12,475
MAINTAIN EQUIPMENT--GEN	10,147	10,472	10,807	11,154	42,580*	11,512
MISC PERIOD ADMIN EXP--GEN	12,176	12,595	13,029	13,479	51,279*	13,944
DEPRC ON FIXED ASSETS--GEN	2,538	2,956	3,181	3,181	11,856*	3,180
AMORT OF INTANGIBLES	10,000	10,000	10,000	10,000	40,000*	10,000
UNCOLLECTIBLE ACCOUNTS	20,138	10,652	8,727	10,544	50,061*	10,751
TOTAL GEN AND ADMIN EXP	181,329	189,844	182,744	201,112	755,029*	205,319
TOTAL OPERATING EXPENSE	293,656	312,422	304,987	333,104	1,244,169*	341,864
SALES MARGIN OVER DIRECT EXP	155,502	610,453	404,509	474,735	1,645,199*	493,057
NET OPERATING INCOME	-51,536	406,462	196,052	258,073	809,051*	269,804
+INTEREST & FINANCE INCOME	2,539	9,958	9,643	10,767	32,907*	11,792
-INTEREST COST, SHORT-TERM	0	0	0	0	0*	0
-INTEREST, LONG-TERM FIXED	18,874	13,151	19,383	19,451	76,859*	19,747
NET INCOME BEFORE INCOME TAX	-67,871	397,270	186,312	249,390	765,101*	261,849
-INCOME TAXES	599	164,101	93,156	124,695	382,551*	132,395
NET INCOME AFTER INCOME TAX	-68,469	233,169	93,156	124,695	382,551*	129,453

Table 12.4 (continued)

INCOME STATEMENTS (CONTINUED)
****

	6 1/6	7 1/9	8 2/0	*FOR YEAR 2*	9 2/3	10 2/6
FIRM NET SALES ACHIEVED	1,011,608	942,255	1,059,344	3,909,155*	1,149,768	1,361,196
-COST OF SALES	346,119	363,747	254,094	1,248,239*	426,553	458,449
GROSS PROFIT ON SALES	665,490	578,508	805,250	2,660,916*	723,215	902,747
R&D PAYROLL	23,488	24,188	24,909	95,395*	25,653	26,420
R&D MATERIAL AND MISC EXP	32,757	33,245	33,741	132,021*	34,246	34,760
TOTAL R&D EXPENSE	56,246	57,433	58,651	227,418*	59,899	61,180
DIRECT SALES PAYROLL	10,116	9,423	10,593	39,091*	11,498	13,612
PERIOD SALES PAYROLL	23,488	24,188	24,909	95,395*	25,653	26,420
DIRECT ADVERTISE, MISC SALES	30,348	28,268	31,780	117,274*	34,493	40,836
PERIOD ADVERTISE, MISC SALES	23,488	24,188	24,909	95,395*	25,653	26,420
TOTAL SALES EXPENSE	87,441	86,066	92,192	347,157*	97,296	107,287
DIRECT SERVICE PAYROLL	80,633	76,037	85,153	313,426*	92,519	108,147
PERIOD GEN ADMIN PAYROLL	17,202	17,630	18,069	69,686*	18,520	18,983
PURCH GEN SUPPLIES	25,383	24,026	26,813	99,254*	28,450	32,011
+BOP GEN SUPPLIES INVY	9,116	9,857	9,681	8,873*	10,427	11,108
-EOP GEN SUPPLIES INVY	9,857	9,681	10,427	10,427*	11,108	12,320
DIRECT GEN SUPPLIES USED	12,621	11,765	13,198	48,754*	14,454	17,022
PERIOD GEN SUPPLIES USED	12,022	12,438	12,869	48,949*	13,315	13,777
SPACE AND RENT--GEN	32,757	33,245	33,741	132,021*	34,246	34,760
UTILITIES--GEN	13,214	13,815	14,835	54,339*	15,550	16,085
MAINTAIN EQUIPMENT--GEN	11,883	12,265	12,661	48,321*	13,070	13,492
MISC PERIOD ADMIN EXP--GEN	14,426	14,925	15,442	58,737*	15,978	16,533
DEPRC ON FIXED ASSETS--GEN	3,179	3,178	3,177	12,714*	3,176	3,175
AMORT OF INTANGIBLES	10,000	10,000	10,000	40,000*	10,000	10,000
UNCOLLECTIBLE ACCOUNTS	12,139	11,307	12,712	46,909*	13,797	16,334
TOTAL GEN AND ADMIN EXP	220,075	216,606	231,858	873,858*	244,625	268,308
TOTAL OPERATING EXPENSE	363,762	360,105	382,700	1,448,431*	401,820	436,775
SALES MARGIN OVER DIRECT EXP	531,772	453,016	664,525	2,142,370*	570,251	723,130
NET OPERATING INCOME	301,728	218,403	422,550	1,212,485*	321,395	465,972
+INTEREST & FINANCE INCOME	12,873	14,450	13,034	52,149*	13,339	14,876
-INTEREST COST, SHORT-TERM	0	0	0	0*	0	0
-INTEREST, LONG-TERM FIXED	19,909	20,066	20,193	79,915*	20,441	20,701
NET INCOME BEFORE INCOME TAX	294,692	212,787	415,390	1,184,718*	314,292	460,147
-INCOME TAXES	145,875	106,393	207,695	592,358*	157,146	230,074
NET INCOME AFTER INCOME TAX	148,817	106,393	207,695	592,358*	157,146	230,074

Table 12.4 (continued)

```
INCOME STATEMENTS   (CONTINUED)
********************
```

	11 2/ 9	12 3/ 0	*FOR YEAR 3*
FIRM NET SALES ACHIEVED	1,164,557	1,270,013	4,945,534*
-COST OF SALES	337,699	315,244	1,537,945*
GROSS PROFIT ON SALES	826,858	954,769	3,407,589*
R&D PAYROLL	27,210	28,026	107,309*
R&D MATERIAL AND MISC EXP	35,283	35,814	140,103*
TOTAL R&D EXPENSE	62,493	63,840	247,412*
DIRECT SALES PAYROLL	11,646	12,700	49,456*
PERIOD SALES PAYROLL	27,210	28,026	107,309*
DIRECT ADVERTISE, MISC SALES	34,937	38,100	148,366*
PERIOD ADVERTISE, MISC SALES	27,210	28,026	107,309*
TOTAL SALES EXPENSE	101,003	106,852	412,438*
DIRECT SERVICE PAYROLL	93,006	102,202	395,874*
PERIOD GEN ADMIN PAYROLL	19,459	19,947	76,909*
PURCH GEN SUPPLIES	28,051	31,322	119,834*
+BOP GEN SUPPLIES INVY	12,320	11,535	10,427*
-EOP GEN SUPPLIES INVY	11,535	12,245	12,245*
DIRECT GEN SUPPLIES USED	14,580	15,860	61,916*
PERIOD GEN SUPPLIES USED	14,256	14,752	56,100*
SPACE AND RENT--GEN	35,283	35,814	140,103*
UTILITIES--GEN	17,623	17,667	66,925*
MAINTAIN EQUIPMENT--GEN	13,928	14,379	54,869*
MISC PERIOD ADMIN EXP--GEN	17,107	17,702	67,320*
DEPRC ON FIXED ASSETS--GEN	3,175	3,175	12,701*
AMORT OF INTANGIBLES	10,000	0	30,000*
UNCOLLECTIBLE ACCOUNTS	13,975	15,240	59,346*
TOTAL GEN AND ADMIN EXP	252,392	256,739	1,022,064*
TOTAL OPERATING EXPENSE	415,888	427,431	1,681,914*
SALES MARGIN OVER DIRECT EXP	672,689	785,907	2,751,977*
NET OPERATING INCOME	410,970	527,338	1,725,675*
+INTEREST & FINANCE INCOME	16,322	16,686	61,223*
-INTEREST COST, SHORT-TERM	0	0	0*
-INTEREST, LONG-TERM FIXED	20,913	21,223	83,278*
NET INCOME BEFORE INCOME TAX	406,380	522,802	1,703,621*
-INCOME TAXES	203,190	261,401	851,811*
NET INCOME AFTER INCOME TAX	203,190	261,401	851,811*

Table 12.4 (continued)

MFG PRODUCTS

```
*******************************************
COST OF GOODS MANUFACTURED SCHEDULES
*******************************************
```

	1 O/ 3	2 O/ 6	3 O/ 9	4 1/ 0	*FOR YEAR 1*	5 1/ 3
PURCH DIRECT MFG MATERIAL	514,713	57,058	40,575	199,289	811,635*	120,675
+BOP DIRECT MATERIAL INVY	200,000	439,823	366,580	267,160	200,000*	295,284
-EOP DIRECT MATERIAL INVY	439,823	366,580	267,160	295,284	295,284*	266,639
DIRECT REGULAR MATERIAL USED	274,890	130,302	139,994	171,166	716,352*	149,319
PURCH PERIOD SUPPLIES	1,435	2,065	2,096	2,127	7,723*	2,159
+BOP PERIOD SUPPLIES INVY	1,000	406	412	418	1,000*	424
-EOP PERIOD SUPPLIES INVY	406	412	418	424	424*	431
PERIOD SUPPLIES USED	2,029	2,059	2,090	2,121	8,299*	2,153
DIRECT LABOR PAYROLL	232,406	85,357	91,134	110,159	519,056*	96,414
DIRECT SUPERVISION PAYROLL	32,395	12,165	12,951	15,484	72,995*	13,392
PERIOD MFG ADMIN PAYROLL	10,147	10,347	10,552	10,761	41,807*	10,975
SPACE AND RENT--MFG	8,117	8,257	8,400	8,545	33,319*	8,694
UTILITIES--MFG	20,332	21,523	22,957	24,367	89,179*	25,796
MAINTAIN EQUIPMENT--MFG	10,147	10,422	10,706	10,997	42,272*	11,297
MISC PERIOD ADMIN EXP--MFG	1,015	1,045	1,076	1,108	4,244*	1,140
DEPRC ON FIXED ASSETS--MFG	8,213	7,905	7,614	7,339	31,071*	7,080
COST OF GOODS INTO PROCESS	599,691	289,384	307,473	362,048	1,558,596*	326,260
+BOP GOODS-IN-PROCESS INVY	375,000	341,566	499,144	549,600	375,000*	593,553
-EOP GOODS-IN-PROCESS INVY	341,566	499,144	549,600	593,553	593,553*	617,911
COST OF FINISHED GOODS	633,125	131,806	257,016	318,095	1,340,042*	301,902

Table 12.4 (continued)

COST OF GOODS MANUFACTURED SCHEDULES (CONTINUED)
****

	6 1/6	7 1/9	8 2/0	*FOR YEAR 2*	9 2/3	10 2/6
PURCH DIRECT MFG MATERIAL	197,086	435,418	121,812	874,991*	252,538	323,611
+BOP DIRECT MATERIAL INVY	266,639	289,190	445,913	295,284*	389,478	407,308
-EOP DIRECT MATERIAL INVY	289,190	445,913	389,478	389,478*	407,308	458,971
DIRECT REGULAR MATERIAL USED	174,535	278,695	178,247	780,796*	234,709	271,947
PURCH PERIOD SUPPLIES	2,192	2,225	2,258	8,834*	2,292	2,327
+BOP PERIOD SUPPLIES INVY	431	437	444	424*	450	457
-EOP PERIOD SUPPLIES INVY	437	444	450	450*	457	464
PERIOD SUPPLIES USED	2,185	2,218	2,251	8,807*	2,285	2,320
DIRECT LABOR PAYROLL	110,862	179,049	110,271	496,596*	147,085	164,273
DIRECT SUPERVISION PAYROLL	15,212	24,593	15,488	68,685*	20,550	23,274
PERIOD MFG ADMIN PAYROLL	11,193	11,416	11,644	45,228*	11,877	12,115
SPACE AND RENT--MFG	8,845	8,999	9,156	35,694*	9,316	9,479
UTILITIES--MFG	27,354	29,051	31,037	113,238*	32,866	34,866
MAINTAIN EQUIPMENT--MFG	11,606	11,923	12,250	47,076*	12,586	12,931
MISC PERIOD ADMIN EXP--MFG	1,174	1,209	1,245	4,768*	1,283	1,321
DEPRC ON FIXED ASSETS--MFG	6,835	6,605	6,388	26,908*	6,184	5,993
COST OF GOODS INTO PROCESS	369,801	553,759	377,977	1,627,797*	478,741	538,518
+BOP GOODS-IN-PROCESS INVY	617,911	630,829	672,571	593,553*	754,630	775,617
-EOP GOODS-IN-PROCESS INVY	630,829	672,571	754,630	754,630*	775,617	823,176
COST OF FINISHED GOODS	356,882	512,017	295,918	1,466,719*	457,754	490,960

Table 12.4 (continued)

```
COST OF GOODS MANUFACTURED SCHEDULES   (CONTINUED)
*******************************************
```

	11 2/ 9	12 3/ 0	*FOR YEAR 3*
PURCH DIRECT MFG MATERIAL	215,489	225,721	1,017,359*
+BOP DIRECT MATERIAL INVY	458,971	443,710	389,478*
-EOP DIRECT MATERIAL INVY	443,710	474,674	474,674*
DIRECT REGULAR MATERIAL USED	230,750	194,758	932,164*
PURCH PERIOD SUPPLIES	2,362	2,398	9,379*
+BOP PERIOD SUPPLIES INVY	464	471	450*
-EOP PERIOD SUPPLIES INVY	471	478	478*
PERIOD SUPPLIES USED	2,355	2,391	9,351*
DIRECT LABOR PAYROLL	137,011	116,142	564,511*
DIRECT SUPERVISION PAYROLL	19,351	16,153	79,328*
PERIOD MFG ADMIN PAYROLL	12,358	12,606	48,956*
SPACE AND RENT--MFG	9,646	9,815	38,256*
UTILITIES--MFG	37,099	39,687	144,518*
MAINTAIN EQUIPMENT--MFC	13,287	13,652	52,456*
MISC PERIOD ADMIN EXP--MFG	1,361	1,401	5,366*
DEPRC ON FIXED ASSETS--MFG	5,813	5,644	23,634*
COST OF GOODS INTO PROCESS	469,029	412,249	1,898,537*
+BOP GOODS-IN-PROCESS INVY	823,176	903,126	754,630*
-EOP GOODS-IN-PROCESS INVY	903,126	977,811	977,811*
COST OF FINISHED GOODS	389,079	337,564	1,675,357*

Table 12.4 (continued)

HPG PRODUCTS

```
****************************
COST OF GOODS SOLD SCHEDULES
****************************
```

	1 0/3	2 0/6	3 0/9	4 1/0	*FOR YEAR 1*	5 1/3
COST OF FINISHED GOODS	633,125	131,806	257,016	318,095	1,340,042*	301,902
+BOP FINISHED GOODS INVY	50,000	273,253	300,066	330,840	50,000*	361,434
-EOP FINISHED GOODS INVY	273,253	300,066	330,840	361,434	361,434*	379,057
COST OF GOODS SOLD	409,872	104,993	226,243	287,501	1,028,609*	284,279

```
COST OF GOODS SOLD SCHEDULES  (CONTINUED)
****************************
```

	6 1/6	7 1/9	8 2/0	*FOR YEAR 2*	9 2/3	10 2/6
COST OF FINISHED GOODS	356,882	512,017	295,918	1,466,719*	457,754	490,960
+BOP FINISHED GOODS INVY	379,057	389,821	538,091	361,434*	579,914	611,116
-EOP FINISHED GOODS INVY	389,821	538,091	579,914	579,914*	611,116	643,626
COST OF GOODS SOLD	346,119	363,747	254,094	1,248,239*	426,553	458,449

```
COST OF GOODS SOLD SCHEDULES  (CONTINUED)
****************************
```

	11 2/9	12 3/0	*FOR YEAR 3*
COST OF FINISHED GOODS	389,079	337,564	1,675,357*
+BOP FINISHED GOODS INVY	643,626	695,006	579,914*
-EOP FINISHED GOODS INVY	695,006	717,325	717,325*
COST OF GOODS SOLD	337,699	315,244	1,537,945*

Table 12.4 (continued)

HPG PRODUCTS

****
CASH FORECASTS AND FLOW ANALYSES
****

	1 O/3	2 O/6	3 O/9	4 1/0	*FOR YEAR 1*	5 1/3
CASH RECEIPTS FROM SALES	1,658,046	877,032	718,555	868,133	4,121,766*	885,196
PAYMENTS ON ACCOUNT	508,529	494,553	259,179	351,917	1,614,178*	378,044
PAYMENTS ON PAYROLLS	389,662	238,652	239,311	276,217	1,143,842*	263,747
TOTAL OPERATING PAYMENTS	898,191	733,204	498,490	628,134	2,758,019*	641,792
NET CASH FLOW ON OPERATIONS	759,855	143,828	220,065	240,000	1,363,748*	243,405
NET CHANGE SHORT-TERM CREDIT	-4,000	0	0	0	-4,000*	0
PLAN CHANGE LONG OBLIGATIONS	10,000	10,000	10,000	10,000	40,000*	10,000
+INTEREST & FINANCE INCOME	2,539	9,958	9,643	10,767	32,907*	11,792
-INTEREST, INCOME TAX COST	19,473	183,252	112,540	144,146	459,411*	152,142
-DIVIDENDS, OWNER DRAWINGS	10,147	10,296	10,448	10,602	41,493*	10,759
TOTAL NET CASH FLOW	738,775	-29,761	116,721	106,019	931,754*	102,295
+BOP CASH AND SECURITIES	250,000	988,775	959,013	1,075,735	250,000*	1,181,754
CASH AND SECURITIES EOP	988,775	959,013	1,075,735	1,181,754	1,181,754*	1,284,048

Table 12.4 (continued)

CASH FORECASTS AND FLOW ANALYSES (CONTINUED)
****

	6 1/ 6	7 1/ 9	8 2/ 0 *FOR YEAR 2*	9 2/ 3	10 2/ 6
CASH RECEIPTS FROM SALES	999,469	930,948	1,046,632	3,862,245*	1,135,971	1,344,862
PAYMENTS ON ACCOUNT	401,863	581,125	496,639	1,857,671*	460,795	569,342
PAYMENTS ON PAYROLLS	292,194	366,523	301,037	1,223,501*	353,355	393,243
TOTAL OPERATING PAYMENTS	694,057	947,648	797,676	3,081,173*	814,149	962,585
NET CASH FLOW ON OPERATIONS	305,412	-16,700	248,956	781,073*	321,821	382,277
NET CHANGE SHORT-TERM CREDIT	0	0	0	0*	0	0
PLAN CHANGE LONG OBLIGATIONS	10,000	10,000	10,000	40,000*	10,000	10,000
+INTEREST & FINANCE INCOME	12,873	14,450	13,034	52,149*	13,339	14,876
-INTEREST, INCOME TAX COST	165,784	126,460	227,889	672,275*	177,587	250,774
-DIVIDENDS, OWNER DRAWINGS	10,919	16,623	16,871	55,172*	17,123	17,380
TOTAL NET CASH FLOW	151,582	-135,332	27,231	145,776*	150,449	138,998
+BOP CASH AND SECURITIES	1,284,048	1,435,630	1,300,298	1,181,754*	1,327,529	1,477,978
CASH AND SECURITIES EOP	1,435,630	1,300,298	1,327,529	1,327,529*	1,477,978	1,616,977

CASH FORECASTS AND FLOW ANALYSES (CONTINUED)
****

	11 2/ 9	12 3/ 0 *FOR YEAR 3*
CASH RECEIPTS FROM SALES	1,150,582	1,254,773	4,886,188*
PAYMENTS ON ACCOUNT	537,704	507,177	2,075,018*
PAYMENTS ON PAYROLLS	347,251	335,801	1,429,650*
TOTAL OPERATING PAYMENTS	884,955	842,978	3,504,667*
NET CASH FLOW ON OPERATIONS	265,627	411,796	1,381,521*
NET CHANGE SHORT-TERM CREDIT	0	0	0*
PLAN CHANGE LONG OBLIGATIONS	10,000	10,000	40,000*
+INTEREST & FINANCE INCOME	16,322	16,686	61,223*
-INTEREST, INCOME TAX COST	224,102	282,624	935,087*
-DIVIDENDS, OWNER DRAWINGS	17,641	17,907	70,051*
TOTAL NET CASH FLOW	50,206	137,951	477,604*
+BOP CASH AND SECURITIES	1,616,977	1,667,182	1,327,529*
CASH AND SECURITIES EOP	1,667,182	1,805,133	1,805,133*

Table 12.4 (continued)

HPG PRODUCTS

****
RETAINED EARNINGS AND CAPITAL CHANGES
****

	1 0/3	2 0/6	3 0/9	4 1/0	*FOR YEAR 1* 1*	5 1/3
BOP OWNER PAID-IN CAPITAL	677,950	677,950	677,950	677,950	677,950*	677,950
EOP OWNER PAID-IN CAPITAL	677,950	677,950	677,950	677,950	677,950*	677,950
BOP RETAINED EARNINGS	543,700	465,084	687,957	770,665	543,700*	884,758
+NET INCOME	-68,469	233,169	93,156	124,695	382,551*	129,453
-DIVIDENDS PAID	10,147	10,296	10,448	10,602	41,493*	10,759
EOP RETAINED EARNINGS	465,084	687,957	770,665	884,758	884,758*	1,003,452
EOP TOTAL OWNERS' EQUITY	1,143,034	1,365,907	1,448,615	1,562,708	1,562,708*	1,681,402
EOP NO. SHARES OUTSTANDING	50,000	50,000	50,000	50,000	50,000*	50,000
NET INCOME PER SHARE	-1.37	4.66	1.86	2.49	7.64*	2.59
DIVIDENDS PER SHARE	0.20	0.21	0.21	0.21	0.83*	0.22
EOP OWNERS' EQUITY PER SHARE	22.86	27.32	28.97	31.25	31.25*	33.63

RETAINED EARNINGS AND CAPITAL CHANGES (CONTINUED)
****

	6 1/6	7 1/9	8 2/0	*FOR YEAR 2* 2*	9 2/3	10 2/6
BOP OWNER PAID-IN CAPITAL	677,950	677,950	677,950	677,950*	677,950	677,950
EOP OWNER PAID-IN CAPITAL	677,950	677,950	677,950	677,950*	677,950	677,950
BOP RETAINED EARNINGS	1,003,452	1,141,349	1,231,120	884,758*	1,421,945	1,561,968
+NET INCOME	148,817	106,393	207,695	592,358*	157,146	230,074
-DIVIDENDS PAID	10,919	16,623	16,871	55,172*	17,123	17,380
EOP RETAINED EARNINGS	1,141,349	1,231,120	1,421,945	1,421,945*	1,561,968	1,774,662
EOP TOTAL OWNERS' EQUITY	1,819,299	1,909,070	2,099,895	2,099,895*	2,239,918	2,452,612
EOP NO. SHARES OUTSTANDING	50,000	50,000	50,000	50,000*	50,000	50,000
NET INCOME PER SHARE	2.98	2.13	4.15	11.85*	3.14	4.60
DIVIDENDS PER SHARE	0.22	0.33	0.34	1.11*	0.34	0.35
EOP OWNERS' EQUITY PER SHARE	36.39	38.18	42.00	42.00*	44.80	49.05

Table 12.4 (continued)

```
RETAINED EARNINGS AND CAPITAL CHANGES (CONTINUED)
**************************************

                                 11    2/ 9    12    3/ 0  *FOR YEAR  3*

BOP OWNER PAID-IN CAPITAL            677,950          677,950          677,950*
EOP OWNER PAID-IN CAPITAL            677,950          677,950          677,950*

BOP RETAINED EARNINGS             1,774,662        1,960,210        1,421,945*
   +NET INCOME                      203,190          261,401          851,811*
   -DIVIDENDS PAID                   17,641           17,907           70,051*
EOP RETAINED EARNINGS             1,960,210        2,203,704        2,203,704*

EOP TOTAL OWNERS' EQUITY          2,638,160        2,881,654        2,881,654*

EOP NO. SHARES OUTSTANDING           50,000           50,000           50,000*

NET INCOME PER SHARE                   4.06             5.23            17.03*
DIVIDENDS PER SHARE                    0.35             0.36             1.40*
EOP OWNERS' EQUITY PER SHARE          52.76            57.63            57.63*
```

Table 12.4 (continued)

HFG PRODUCTS
****
CONDITION STATEMENTS (BALANCE SHEETS)
****

****** ASSETS ******	*START BOP 1*	1 0/3	2 0/6	3 0/9	4 1/0*	5 1/3
CASH AND MARKET SECURITIES	250,000*	988,775	959,013	1,075,735	1,181,754*	1,284,048
+ACCOUNTS RECEIVABLE GROSS	1,100,000*	93,946	40,790	49,518	60,062*	70,813
-UNCOLLECTIBLES RESERVE	10,000*	30,138	40,790	49,518	60,062*	70,813
CASH+SECURITIES+ACCT RECV	1,340,000*	1,052,582	959,013	1,075,735	1,181,754*	1,284,048
DIRECT MATERIAL INVY--MFG	200,000*	439,823	366,580	267,160	295,284*	266,639
PERIOD SUPPLIES INVY--MFG	1,000*	406	412	418	424*	431
GOODS-IN-PROCESS INVY--MFG	375,000*	341,566	499,144	549,600	593,553*	617,911
FINISHED GOODS INVENTORY	50,000*	273,253	300,066	330,840	361,434*	379,057
SUPPLIES INVENTORY--GEN	1,000*	7,319	8,326	7,962	8,873*	9,116
TOTAL INVENTORIES	627,000*	1,062,367	1,174,527	1,155,980	1,259,569*	1,273,154
TOTAL CURRENT ASSETS	1,967,000*	2,114,949	2,133,541	2,231,715	2,441,322*	2,557,202
MFG FIXED ASSETS AT COST:						
CLASS 1	85,000*	86,015	87,047	88,097	89,165*	90,252
CLASS 2	92,000*	93,015	94,047	95,097	96,165*	97,252
MFG FIXED ASSETS DEPRC RESERVES:						
CLASS 1	6,500*	10,450	14,254	17,920	21,456*	24,868
CLASS 2	7,250*	11,513	15,614	19,562	23,365*	27,032
MFG FIXED ASSETS AT BOOK	163,250*	157,066	151,226	145,712	140,509*	135,603
GEN FIXED ASSETS AT COST:						
CLASS 1	30,000*	40,147	52,502	52,502	52,502*	52,502
CLASS 2	16,000*	18,029	20,089	22,178	24,299*	26,450
GEN FIXED ASSETS DEPRC RESERVES:						
CLASS 1	2,600*	3,737	5,227	6,882	8,478*	10,019
CLASS 2	3,000*	4,401	5,867	7,394	8,978*	10,618
GEN FIXED ASSETS AT BOOK	40,400*	50,038	61,496	60,404	59,344*	58,315
UNAMORTIZED INTANGIBLES	10,000*	100,000	90,000	80,000	70,000*	60,000
TOTAL ASSETS	2,180,650*	2,422,053	2,436,262	2,517,831	2,711,175*	2,811,120

Table 12.4 (continued)

CONDITION STATEMENTS (BALANCE SHEETS) (CONTINUED)

	START BOP 1	1 0/3	2 0/6	3 0/9	4 1/0*	5 1/3
****** LIABILITIES AND OWNERS' EQUITY ******						
ACCOUNTS PAYABLE	15,000*	329,019	110,355	99,216	168,467*	139,718
SHORT-TERM LOANS AND NOTES	4,000*	0	0	0	0*	0
TOTAL CURRENT LIABILITIES	19,000*	329,019	110,355	99,216	168,467*	139,718
LONG-TERM OBLIGATIONS	940,000*	950,000	960,000	970,000	980,000*	990,000
TOTAL LIABILITIES	959,000*	1,279,019	1,070,355	1,069,216	1,148,467*	1,129,718
TOTAL OWNERS' EQUITY	1,221,650*	1,143,034	1,365,907	1,448,615	1,562,708*	1,681,402
LIABILITIES & OWNER EQUITY	2,180,650*	2,422,053	2,436,262	2,517,831	2,711,175*	2,811,120

Table 12.4 (continued)

CONDITION STATEMENTS (BALANCE SHEETS) (CONTINUED)
****

****** ASSETS ******

	6 1/6	7 1/9	8 2/0*	9 2/3	10 2/6	11 2/9
CASH AND MARKET SECURITIES	1,435,630	1,300,298	1,327,529*	1,477,978	1,616,977	1,667,182
+ACCOUNTS RECEIVABLE GROSS	82,953	94,260	106,972*	120,769	137,103	151,078
-UNCOLLECTIBLES RESERVE	82,953	94,260	106,972*	120,769	137,103	151,078
CASH+SECURITIES+ACCT RECV	1,435,630	1,300,298	1,327,529*	1,477,978	1,616,977	1,667,182
DIRECT MATERIAL INVY--MFG	289,190	445,913	389,478*	407,308	458,971	443,710
PERIOD SUPPLIES INVY--MFG	437	444	450*	457	464	471
GOODS-IN-PROCESS INVY--MFG	630,829	672,571	754,630*	775,617	823,176	903,126
FINISHED GOODS INVENTORY--MFG	389,821	538,091	579,914*	611,116	643,626	695,006
SUPPLIES INVENTORY--GEN	9,857	9,681	10,427*	11,108	12,320	11,535
TOTAL INVENTORIES	1,320,134	1,666,699	1,734,900*	1,805,605	1,938,557	2,053,848
TOTAL CURRENT ASSETS	2,755,765	2,966,997	3,062,428*	3,283,583	3,555,533	3,721,030
MFG FIXED ASSETS AT COST:						
CLASS 1	91,357	92,482	93,627*	94,791	95,976	97,182
CLASS 2	98,357	99,482	100,627*	101,791	102,976	104,182
MFG FIXED ASSETS DEPRC RESERVES:						
CLASS 1	28,165	31,353	34,438*	37,427	40,324	43,137
CLASS 2	30,571	33,988	37,292*	40,487	43,582	46,582
MFG FIXED ASSETS AT BOOK	130,978	126,623	122,524*	118,668	115,045	111,644
GEN FIXED ASSETS AT COST:						
CLASS 1	52,502	52,502	52,502*	52,502	52,502	52,502
CLASS 2	28,634	30,851	33,100*	35,383	37,700	40,053
GEN FIXED ASSETS DEPRC RESERVES:						
CLASS 1	11,506	12,941	14,326*	15,662	16,951	18,196
CLASS 2	12,310	14,054	15,846*	17,685	19,571	21,502
GEN FIXED ASSETS AT BOOK	57,320	56,358	55,431*	54,538	53,680	52,858
UNAMORTIZED INTANGIBLES	50,000	40,000	30,000*	20,000	10,000	0
TOTAL ASSETS	2,994,063	3,189,978	3,270,383*	3,476,789	3,734,259	3,885,531

Table 12.4 (continued)

CONDITION STATEMENTS (BALANCE SHEETS) (CONTINUED)

****** LIABILITIES AND OWNERS' EQUITY ******

	6 1/ 6	7 1/ 9	8 2/ 0*	9 2/ 3	10 2/ 6	11 2/ 9
ACCOUNTS PAYABLE	174,763	270,908	150,488*	206,871	241,647	197,371
SHORT-TERM LOANS AND NOTES	0	0	0*	0	0	0
TOTAL CURRENT LIABILITIES	174,763	270,908	150,488*	206,871	241,647	197,371
LONG-TERM OBLIGATIONS	1,000,000	1,010,000	1,020,000*	1,030,000	1,040,000	1,050,000
TOTAL LIABILITIES	1,174,763	1,280,908	1,170,488*	1,236,871	1,281,647	1,247,371
TOTAL OWNERS' EQUITY	1,819,299	1,909,070	2,099,895*	2,239,918	2,452,612	2,638,160
LIABILITIES & OWNER EQUITY	2,994,063	3,189,978	3,270,383*	3,476,789	3,734,259	3,885,531

Table 12.4 (continued)

```
CONDITION STATEMENTS (BALANCE SHEETS) (CONTINUED)
*******************************************

                                 12    3/ 0*

******  ASSETS  ******

CASH AND MARKET SECURITIES       1,805,133*
+ACCOUNTS RECEIVABLE GROSS         166,318*
  -UNCOLLECTIBLES RESERVE          166,318*

CASH+SECURITIES+ACCT RECV        1,805,133*


DIRECT MATERIAL INVY--MFG          474,674*
PERIOD SUPPLIES INVY--MFG              478*
GOODS-IN-PROCESS INVY--MFG         977,811*
FINISHED GOODS INVENTORY           717,325*
SUPPLIES INVENTORY--GEN             12,245*

TOTAL INVENTORIES                2,182,533*

TOTAL CURRENT ASSETS             3,987,666*


MFG FIXED ASSETS AT COST:
        CLASS 1                     98,409*
        CLASS 2                    105,409*

MFG FIXED ASSETS DEPRC RESERVES:
        CLASS 1                     45,870*
        CLASS 2                     49,493*

MFG FIXED ASSETS AT BOOK           108,454*


GEN FIXED ASSETS AT COST:
        CLASS 1                     52,502*
        CLASS 2                     42,440*

GEN FIXED ASSETS DEPRC RESERVES:
        CLASS 1                     19,396*
        CLASS 2                     23,476*

GEN FIXED ASSETS AT BOOK            52,070*


UNAMORTIZED INTANGIBLES                  0*

TOTAL ASSETS                     4,148,191*


******  LIABILITIES AND OWNERS' EQUITY  ******

ACCOUNTS PAYABLE                   206,537*
SHORT-TERM LOANS AND NOTES               0*

TOTAL CURRENT LIABILITIES          206,537*

LONG-TERM OBLIGATIONS            1,060,000*

TOTAL LIABILITIES                1,266,537*


TOTAL OWNERS' EQUITY             2,881,654*

LIABILITIES & OWNER EQUITY       4,148,191*
```

Table 12.4 (continued)

HPG PRODUCTS

```
*********************************
  SELECTED ACCOUNTS FOR ALL PERIODS
*********************************
```

CONDITION ITEMS ARE END-OF-PERIOD; 95 % CONFIDENCE LIMITS FOR MEANS WITH SAMPLE SIZE 10

	1 0/ 3	2 0/ 6	3 0/ 9	4 1/ 0*	5 1/ 3	6 1/ 6
INDUSTRY SALES--000 OMIT						
MEANS	3,338	4,196	3,579	4,422*	4,399	5,226
STANDARD DEVIATIONS	89	109	90	104*	87	142
LOWER CONFIDENCE LIMITS	3,132	3,945	3,371	4,183*	4,200	4,899
UPPER CONFIDENCE LIMITS	3,544	4,447	3,787	4,660*	4,599	5,553
FIRM'S INDUSTRY SHARE %						
MEANS	19.47	19.62	20.28	19.90*	20.34	19.37
STANDARD DEVIATIONS	0.44	0.42	0.40	0.44*	0.39	0.40
LOWER CONFIDENCE LIMITS	18.44	18.66	19.35	18.89*	19.43	18.45
UPPER CONFIDENCE LIMITS	20.49	20.58	21.20	20.92*	21.24	20.30
FIRM NET SALES ACHIEVED						
MEANS	651,992	823,877	727,282	878,677*	895,948	1,011,608
STANDARD DEVIATIONS	28,824	29,391	28,528	23,759*	29,596	31,176
LOWER CONFIDENCE LIMITS	585,696	756,279	661,667	824,032*	827,877	939,904
UPPER CONFIDENCE LIMITS	718,288	891,475	792,898	933,323*	964,018	1,083,313

Table 12.4 (continued)

COST OF SALES						
MEANS	409,872	104,993	226,243	287,501*	284,279	346,119
STANDARD DEVIATIONS	7,717	27,572	39,321	42,869*	41,868	34,769
LOWER CONFIDENCE LIMITS	392,123	41,577	135,803	188,902*	187,982	266,151
UPPER CONFIDENCE LIMITS	427,621	168,408	316,682	386,099*	380,577	426,087
GROSS PROFIT ON SALES						
MEANS	242,120	718,884	501,040	591,177*	611,668	665,490
STANDARD DEVIATIONS	21,112	19,351	37,662	35,329*	44,934	35,257
LOWER CONFIDENCE LIMITS	193,562	674,378	414,417	509,919*	508,321	584,399
UPPER CONFIDENCE LIMITS	290,677	763,391	587,663	672,434*	715,015	746,580
TOTAL OPERATING EXPENSE						
MEANS	293,656	312,422	304,987	333,104*	341,864	363,762
STANDARD DEVIATIONS	4,166	4,156	4,198	3,246*	4,514	4,529
LOWER CONFIDENCE LIMITS	284,074	302,863	295,332	325,639*	331,483	353,344
UPPER CONFIDENCE LIMITS	303,237	321,981	314,643	340,568*	352,246	374,180
NET OPERATING INCOME						
MEANS	-51,536	406,462	196,052	258,073*	269,804	301,728
STANDARD DEVIATIONS	16,955	17,955	36,770	35,534*	43,335	33,474
LOWER CONFIDENCE LIMITS	-90,532	365,166	111,480	176,345*	170,134	224,738
UPPER CONFIDENCE LIMITS	-12,540	447,759	280,624	339,801*	369,474	378,717
NET INCOME AFTER TAX						
MEANS	-68,469	233,169	93,156	124,695*	129,453	148,817
STANDARD DEVIATIONS	16,672	4,377	18,468	17,713*	22,707	16,263
LOWER CONFIDENCE LIMITS	-106,815	223,102	50,680	83,956*	77,228	111,412
UPPER CONFIDENCE LIMITS	-30,124	243,236	135,633	165,434*	181,679	186,221

Table 12.4 (continued)

CASH AND MARKET SECURITIES						
MEANS	988,775	959,013	1,075,735	1,181,754*	1,284,048	1,435,630
STANDARD DEVIATIONS	20,101	29,661	15,094	17,460*	30,721	28,079
LOWER CONFIDENCE LIMITS	942,543	890,794	1,041,017	1,141,597*	1,213,391	1,371,050
UPPER CONFIDENCE LIMITS	1,035,006	1,027,233	1,110,452	1,221,911*	1,354,706	1,500,211
CASH+SECURITIES+ACCT RECV						
MEANS	1,052,582	959,013	1,075,735	1,181,754*	1,284,048	1,435,630
STANDARD DEVIATIONS	16,997	29,661	15,094	17,460*	30,721	28,079
LOWER CONFIDENCE LIMITS	1,013,490	890,794	1,041,017	1,141,597*	1,213,391	1,371,050
UPPER CONFIDENCE LIMITS	1,091,674	1,027,233	1,110,452	1,221,911*	1,354,706	1,500,211
TOTAL INVENTORIES						
MEANS	1,062,367	1,174,527	1,155,980	1,259,569*	1,273,154	1,320,134
STANDARD DEVIATIONS	50,778	39,176	32,859	32,400*	35,747	38,236
LOWER CONFIDENCE LIMITS	945,578	1,084,422	1,080,405	1,185,049*	1,190,935	1,232,191
UPPER CONFIDENCE LIMITS	1,179,156	1,264,632	1,231,556	1,334,088*	1,355,373	1,408,077
TOTAL CURRENT ASSETS						
MEANS	2,114,949	2,133,541	2,231,715	2,441,322*	2,557,202	2,755,765
STANDARD DEVIATIONS	34,093	11,884	23,934	23,990*	30,747	24,690
LOWER CONFIDENCE LIMITS	2,036,535	2,106,207	2,176,666	2,386,145*	2,486,484	2,698,978
UPPER CONFIDENCE LIMITS	2,193,363	2,160,874	2,286,764	2,496,500*	2,627,920	2,812,551
TOTAL ASSETS						
MEANS	2,422,053	2,436,262	2,517,831	2,711,175*	2,811,120	2,994,063
STANDARD DEVIATIONS	34,093	11,884	23,934	23,990*	30,747	24,690
LOWER CONFIDENCE LIMITS	2,343,639	2,408,929	2,462,782	2,655,998*	2,740,402	2,937,276
UPPER CONFIDENCE LIMITS	2,500,457	2,463,595	2,572,880	2,766,352*	2,881,838	3,050,850
TOTAL CURRENT LIABILITIES						
MEANS	329,019	110,355	99,216	168,467*	139,718	174,763
STANDARD DEVIATIONS	17,453	10,682	10,538	25,216*	17,955	20,222
LOWER CONFIDENCE LIMITS	288,877	85,787	74,979	110,470*	98,422	128,253
UPPER CONFIDENCE LIMITS	369,162	134,924	123,452	226,465*	181,014	221,274
TOTAL LIABILITIES						
MEANS	1,279,019	1,070,355	1,069,216	1,148,467*	1,129,718	1,174,763
STANDARD DEVIATIONS	17,453	10,682	10,538	25,216*	17,955	20,222
LOWER CONFIDENCE LIMITS	1,238,877	1,045,787	1,044,979	1,090,470*	1,088,422	1,128,253
UPPER CONFIDENCE LIMITS	1,319,162	1,094,924	1,093,452	1,206,465*	1,171,014	1,221,274
TOTAL OWNERS' EQUITY						
MEANS	1,143,034	1,365,907	1,448,615	1,562,708*	1,681,402	1,819,299
STANDARD DEVIATIONS	16,672	16,809	19,371	29,894*	22,075	31,269
LOWER CONFIDENCE LIMITS	1,104,689	1,327,247	1,404,062	1,493,951*	1,630,629	1,747,380
UPPER CONFIDENCE LIMITS	1,181,379	1,404,567	1,493,169	1,631,465*	1,732,175	1,891,219
ALL FIXED ASSETS AT BOOK	150,038	151,496	140,404	129,344*	118,315	107,320

Table 12.4 (continued)

	7 1/9	8 2/0*	9 2/3	10 2/6	11 2/9	12 3/0*
INDUSTRY SALES--000 OMIT						
MEANS	4,510	5,407*	5,682	6,787	5,748	6,549*
STANDARD DEVIATIONS	110	85*	140	200	144	177*
LOWER CONFIDENCE LIMITS	4,258	5,212*	5,360	6,327	5,416	6,142*
UPPER CONFIDENCE LIMITS	4,762	5,603*	6,003	7,246	6,080	6,955*
FIRM'S INDUSTRY SHARE %						
MEANS	20.91	19.59*	20.28	20.13	20.24	19.41*
STANDARD DEVIATIONS	0.37	0.41*	0.43	0.50	0.44	0.37*
LOWER CONFIDENCE LIMITS	20.06	18.64*	19.29	18.99	19.22	18.56*
UPPER CONFIDENCE LIMITS	21.76	20.54*	21.26	21.28	21.25	20.26*
FIRM NET SALES ACHIEVED						
MEANS	942,255	1,059,344*	1,149,768	1,361,196	1,164,557	1,270,013*
STANDARD DEVIATIONS	25,670	28,859*	28,973	35,837	42,847	38,170*
LOWER CONFIDENCE LIMITS	883,215	992,968*	1,083,130	1,278,771	1,066,008	1,182,222*
UPPER CONFIDENCE LIMITS	1,001,296	1,125,720*	1,216,405	1,443,621	1,263,106	1,357,804*
COST OF SALES						
MEANS	363,747	254,094*	426,553	458,449	337,699	315,244*
STANDARD DEVIATIONS	31,953	48,074*	68,667	65,745	61,050	94,648*
LOWER CONFIDENCE LIMITS	290,255	143,524*	268,620	307,236	197,285	97,554*
UPPER CONFIDENCE LIMITS	437,240	364,663*	584,486	609,663	478,113	532,934*
GROSS PROFIT ON SALES						
MEANS	578,508	805,250*	723,215	902,747	826,858	954,769*
STANDARD DEVIATIONS	28,429	31,421*	59,046	52,719	49,697	72,733*
LOWER CONFIDENCE LIMITS	513,122	732,981*	587,409	781,493	712,555	787,484*
UPPER CONFIDENCE LIMITS	643,894	877,519*	859,021	1,024,000	941,161	1,122,054*
TOTAL OPERATING EXPENSE						
MEANS	360,105	382,700*	401,820	436,775	415,888	427,431*
STANDARD DEVIATIONS	3,697	3,985*	4,302	4,780	6,072	5,705*
LOWER CONFIDENCE LIMITS	351,602	373,534*	391,926	425,780	401,922	414,310*
UPPER CONFIDENCE LIMITS	368,607	391,867*	411,714	447,769	429,854	440,552*
NET OPERATING INCOME						
MEANS	218,403	422,550*	321,395	465,972	410,970	527,338*
STANDARD DEVIATIONS	27,444	32,775*	59,613	53,418	49,071	75,138*
LOWER CONFIDENCE LIMITS	155,283	347,167*	184,286	343,110	298,107	354,520*
UPPER CONFIDENCE LIMITS	281,524	497,933*	458,504	588,834	523,833	700,157*
NET INCOME AFTER TAX						
MEANS	106,393	207,695*	157,146	230,074	203,190	261,401*
STANDARD DEVIATIONS	13,610	16,294*	29,871	26,734	24,449	37,553*
LOWER CONFIDENCE LIMITS	75,090	170,220*	88,443	168,585	146,958	175,028*
UPPER CONFIDENCE LIMITS	137,697	245,171*	225,850	291,562	259,421	347,773*

Table 12.4 (continued)

CASH AND MARKET SECURITIES						
MEANS	1,300,298	1,327,529*	1,477,978	1,616,977	1,667,182	1,805,133*
STANDARD DEVIATIONS	43,350	51,105*	36,077	25,772	46,239	59,155*
LOWER CONFIDENCE LIMITS	1,200,593	1,209,986*	1,395,000	1,557,701	1,560,832	1,669,077*
UPPER CONFIDENCE LIMITS	1,400,003	1,445,071*	1,560,956	1,676,252	1,773,533	1,941,189*
CASH+SECURITIES+ACCT RECV						
MEANS	1,300,298	1,327,529*	1,477,978	1,616,977	1,667,182	1,805,133*
STANDARD DEVIATIONS	43,350	51,105*	36,077	25,772	46,239	59,155*
LOWER CONFIDENCE LIMITS	1,200,593	1,209,986*	1,395,000	1,557,701	1,560,832	1,669,077*
UPPER CONFIDENCE LIMITS	1,400,003	1,445,071*	1,560,956	1,676,252	1,773,533	1,941,189*
TOTAL INVENTORIES						
MEANS	1,666,699	1,734,900*	1,805,605	1,938,557	2,053,848	2,182,533*
STANDARD DEVIATIONS	52,086	48,039*	30,284	55,076	59,247	51,056*
LOWER CONFIDENCE LIMITS	1,546,901	1,624,403*	1,735,951	1,811,882	1,917,580	2,065,105*
UPPER CONFIDENCE LIMITS	1,786,498	1,845,390*	1,875,259	2,065,232	2,190,115	2,299,961*
TOTAL CURRENT ASSETS						
MEANS	2,966,997	3,062,428*	3,283,583	3,555,533	3,721,030	3,987,666*
STANDARD DEVIATIONS	36,056	31,094*	37,836	50,242	48,040	32,779*
LOWER CONFIDENCE LIMITS	2,884,069	2,990,912*	3,196,561	3,439,977	3,610,537	3,912,274*
UPPER CONFIDENCE LIMITS	3,049,926	3,133,945*	3,370,606	3,671,090	3,831,523	4,063,058*
TOTAL ASSETS						
MEANS	3,189,978	3,270,383*	3,476,789	3,734,259	3,885,531	4,148,191*
STANDARD DEVIATIONS	36,056	31,094*	37,836	50,242	48,040	32,779*
LOWER CONFIDENCE LIMITS	3,107,050	3,198,866*	3,389,767	3,618,702	3,775,038	4,072,798*
UPPER CONFIDENCE LIMITS	3,272,907	3,341,899*	3,563,812	3,849,815	3,996,024	4,223,583*
TOTAL CURRENT LIABILITIES						
MEANS	270,908	150,488*	206,871	241,647	197,371	206,537*
STANDARD DEVIATIONS	27,593	19,740*	20,177	34,689	34,610	33,822*
LOWER CONFIDENCE LIMITS	207,444	105,085*	160,463	161,862	117,769	128,747*
UPPER CONFIDENCE LIMITS	334,372	195,890*	253,279	321,432	276,974	284,326*
TOTAL LIABILITIES						
MEANS	1,280,908	1,170,488*	1,236,871	1,281,647	1,247,371	1,266,537*
STANDARD DEVIATIONS	27,593	19,740*	20,177	34,689	34,610	33,822*
LOWER CONFIDENCE LIMITS	1,217,444	1,125,085*	1,190,463	1,201,862	1,167,769	1,183,747*
UPPER CONFIDENCE LIMITS	1,344,372	1,215,890*	1,283,279	1,361,432	1,326,974	1,344,326*
TOTAL OWNERS' EQUITY						
MEANS	1,909,070	2,099,895*	2,239,918	2,452,612	2,638,160	2,881,654*
STANDARD DEVIATIONS	28,625	34,891*	31,493	46,950	41,094	60,780*
LOWER CONFIDENCE LIMITS	1,843,234	2,019,646*	2,167,484	2,344,626	2,543,644	2,741,861*
UPPER CONFIDENCE LIMITS	1,974,907	2,180,144*	2,312,352	2,560,597	2,732,676	3,021,447*
ALL FIXED ASSETS AT BOOK	96,358	85,431*	74,538	63,680	52,858	52,070*

Market values from price-earnings multiples merely reflect initial and terminal annual earnings. Note that the multiples themselves (user inputs) were raised from 10 to 15 between the first and final years. The simulation confirms that this was reasonable because performance improves over the simulated time span.

Compare printed going-concern value with market value. The former are much higher because they are the result of relatively low investor required rates of return (11.23% and 8.67%), reasonable long-term growth rate at 6.33%, and a rate of return on incremental assets at a high 27.19% as compared to investor required rates. Market values in this case simply follow from user inputs of multiples. Outputs suggest that risk may have been understated. Run the case again with more risk and check decrease of going-concern values.

The 50,000 initial shares (data input) are not increased during the simulation because no additional amount of equity is required (see below).

The principal thing to notice in FINANCIAL SUMMARY FROM FINAL PERIOD is the *variability* of important financial output amounts and ratios. With the uncertainty parameters which have been chosen for inputs, and the small sample size of 10, the range of values for some items is considerable.

The cash ratio is maintained at a minimum of 409.61% (minimum input parameter of 50% is never reached), hence short-term borrowing is not required. The original $4000 is never renewed. One thing HPG PRODUCTS turns up with from this simulation is plenty of cash!

Since the last quarter of the simulation is neutral to seasonal-cyclical indexes (has normalized index of one), the annualized figures for the FINANCIAL SUMMARY are not biased here as they were in the GIFTIQUE case. Sales figures for the final year still do not correspond exactly between VALUATION AND SCOPE and FINANCIAL SUMMARY. This occurs because the former still combines the last four quarters, whereas the latter is an extrapolation of the last quarter only.

Referring to FINANCIAL STATEMENTS output division, note that seasonal-cyclical indexes in ENVIRONMENTAL ANALYSES have been internally normalized from the original inputs. Mean industry sales dollars increased by more than 50% over the simulation period, whereas the mean firm's industry share remained in the 19% to 21% range.

In the INCOME STATEMENTS, gross profit increases rapidly over time. Gross profit is the difference between net sales achieved in the INCOME STATEMENT and *total cost of goods sold* from COST OF GOODS SCHEDULES. Net sales achieved (from INCOME STATEMENTS) is precisely equal to net sales demand (from ENVIRONMENTAL ANALYSES). This means that plant capacity is always sufficient to meet production needs. The capacity input parameter ID 212 value of $10,000,000 is almost double the final mean going annual rate of sales demand at $5,080,054 (see FINANCIAL SUMMARY).

Excess plant capacity is further demonstrated by expense accounts in COST OF GOODS MANUFACTURED SCHEDULES. Overtime premium payroll is always zero, although 6% was permitted from input policy ID 330.

COST OF GOODS MANUFACTURED SCHEDULES are included only for manufacturing firms such as HPG. Total cost of goods into process is the account which brings together the direct and period expenses for each period. Note that direct regular material used and period supplies used are reconciled with inventories and purchases in the first few accounts of COST OF GOODS MANUFACTURED SCHEDULES.

The input specification for inventory levels in PAVE is a percentage of usage. The central question is: What value of stock is required to support a required annual flow? The reciprocal of this input stock to flow ratio (after converting percentage inputs to decimals) is inventory turnover. Thus an inventory stock level input of 25% in PAVE is identical with 4 turns per year.

There are five inventory classes in PAVE. All appear in both flow statements and statements of condition. In all cases the derivation of usage is shown in flow statements. This derivation is the sum of replenishment (purchases or cost) plus a change in inventory levels. All five inventory classes are active in HPG PRODUCTS. Three are derived in COSTS OF GOODS MANUFACTURED SCHEDULES, one is derived for finished goods in COST OF GOODS SOLD SCHEDULES, and one is derived for non-manufacturing materials and supplies in INCOME STATEMENTS.

A user may verify his input inventory policies by computing EOP inventory levels each period. There are two reasons why inventory levels in FINANCIAL STATE-MENTS might not conform precisely to user inputs. If a replenishment (purchase or cost) would be driven negative to satisfy an input specification of EOP level, then the EOP level will be reset enough lower to increase replenishment to 0. This does not occur on the average for HPG PRODUCTS.

Inventories of goods-in-process and *finished goods* will not correspond to input percentages of cost of goods sold. The reason is that these inventory levels are established on the basis of current period costs, whereas cost of goods sold also reflects the valuation of inventories from costs of prior periods. To put it another way, costing routines in PAVE are essentially FIFO. Inventories EOP are always valued at current costs, whereas cost of goods sold absorbs historical cost. These facts about inventory pricing in PAVE will help with the analysis of particular output situations.

Cost of finished goods is transferred from COST OF GOODS MANUFACTURED SCHEDULES to COST OF GOODS SOLD SCHEDULES. The latter schedules, which reconcile cost with finished goods inventories, are used under both manufacturing and trading options. As previously noted, cost of goods sold account is transferred to INCOME STATEMENTS to compute gross profit. The logic of purchases, usage, and inventories for direct materials and goods-in-process is presented in COST OF GOODS MANUFACTURED SCHEDULES. The logic of finished goods or merchandise always appears in COST OF GOODS SOLD SCHEDULES.

In CASH FORECASTS note that growth and seasonal pattern sometimes combine to produce a negative mean cash flow. This is not serious; there is sufficient cash balance to maintain more than adequate liquidity. Income does grow fast enough to supply cash needs internally. Except for a $10,000 quarterly addition to long-term debt, there are no long-term or short-term external additions to capital.

A further examination of expected risk, on a period-by-period basis, may be performed from outputs in SELECTED ACCOUNTS division.

After a thorough analysis of the simulation, HPG PRODUCTS management was encouraged by their strategic plan and took steps to implement first year policies. The HPG PRODUCTS simulation paints a portrait of a successful growth company. As mentioned earlier, risk may be somewhat understated. Moderate increases in risk, however, would not be likely to alter significantly HPG PRODUCT's strategic plan.

PART III

PAVE Model Documentation

Part III is for persons who must adapt PAVE programs to some particular hardware, or become otherwise involved with the structure of PAVE software. If PAVE has been set up on a particular computer system, users need not be concerned with the information given in this part.

Chapter 13 contains a general description of PAVE software design. There is information about the file arrangements, input/output devices, capacity requirements, and speed of processing. There are notes on the BASIC language of PAVE and how to modify PAVE BASIC for various dialects. Alternative display systems are provided.

Chapter 14 presents a detailed documentation of the current set of PAVE programs. A section is devoted to a line-by-line explanation of each processing program. A final section documents three PAVE service programs. The coding of PAVE programs is given in figures 14.1 to 14.9 at the end of the chapter. Also at the end of chapter 14, a set of 18 tables organizes and describes the scalars and arrays of the PAVE system.

13 The Structure of PAVE Programs

13.1 | Specification of the PAVE Programs and Data Files

Chapter 13 contains information to help users adapt the PAVE system to their own equipment. This section summarizes the arrangement and size of PAVE programs and data files. Among different hardware configurations, communication with storage media is likely to be a most important source of variation. For this reason section 13.2 is devoted to an explanation of the file management as coded in this book. Suggestions are made for adaptation to other storage modes. Control of outputs, both video displays and printing, is another area of difference among BASIC interpreters. The statements used here, and adjustments for other BASICs, are summarized in section 13.3. There are thousands of minor variations among BASIC language interpreters. Wang BASIC, a language of considerable power, is used in this book. Nevertheless, an effort has been made to minimize departures from a fundamental Dartmouth BASIC. For economy of coding and speed of processing, some advanced BASIC statements appear in PAVE coding. These statements are explained in section 13.4. Simple BASIC language alternatives are presented for adaptations to less sophisticated interpreters. PAVE interacts with video displays. Among equipments there are differences in control over positioning display lines and the cursor (location indicator for next entry). The control of video displays is discussed in section 13.5. Instructions are given for more sophistication than the coding in this book. PAVE may be adapted to time-sharing systems whose terminals do not have video displays. Suggestions for such adaptations are included in section 13.6. By using the notes in this chapter users may be able to reuse PAVE coding for different equipment without rewriting the logic of the entire system.

For a PAVE run with all outputs printed, six programs, PAVE1 to PAVE6, are chained in turn. Five data transfer files, PAVEFT1 to PAVEFT5, are used to transfer data bases in process among PAVE1 to PAVE6. Figure 13.1 presents a flow chart of the system. Each of the PAVEFT files provides all the data required by a following PAVE program. Each PAVEFT data file receives information from one or more PAVE

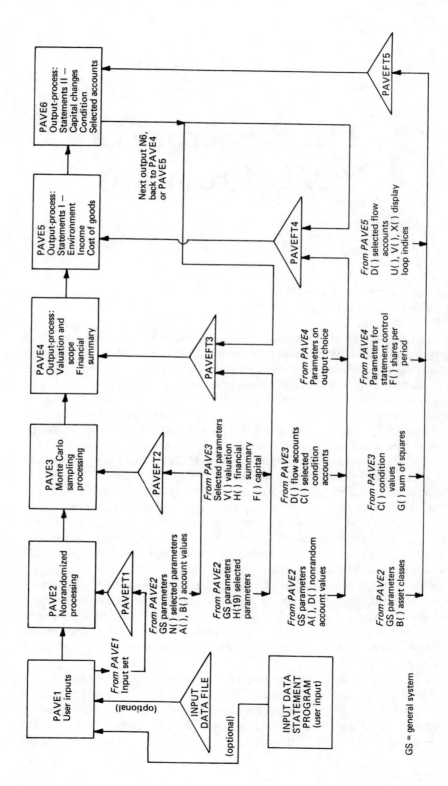

Figure 13.1 Flow chart of PAVE programs and data files

PAVE1
User inputs

PAVE2
Nonrandomized processing

PAVE3
Monte Carlo sampling processing

PAVE4
Output-process:
Valuation and scope
Financial summary

PAVE5
Output-process:
Statements I –
Environment
Income
Cost of goods

PAVE6
Output-process:
Statements II –
Capital changes
Condition
Selected accounts

PAVEFT1

PAVEFT2

PAVEFT3

PAVEFT4

PAVEFT5

From PAVE1
Input set

INPUT DATA FILE
(optional)

(optional)

INPUT DATA STATEMENT PROGRAM
(user input)

From PAVE2
GS parameters
N( ) selected parameters
A( ), B( ) account values

From PAVE2
GS parameters
H(19) selected parameters

From PAVE2
GS parameters
A( ), D( ) nonrandom
account values

From PAVE2
GS parameters
B( ) asset classes

From PAVE3
Selected parameters
V( ) valuation
H( ) financial summary
F( ) capital

From PAVE3
D( ) flow accounts
C( ) selected
condition accounts

From PAVE3
C( ) condition values
G( ) sum of squares

From PAVE4
Parameters on
output choice

From PAVE4
Parameters for
statement control
F( ) shares per period

From PAVE5
D( ) selected flow accounts
U( ), V( ), X( ) display
loop indices

Next output N6,
back to PAVE4
or PAVE5

GS = general system

programs. A *record* is set up each time a PAVE program *writes* information to a PAVEFT data file. A total of 12 records are written during a complete PAVE run. In addition, 6 program files and 5 data transfer files must be read into the work space. This means that files are accessed a total of 23 times during one complete PAVE run. Random access to storage is useful but not essential under these conditions. The layout of records and variables used to transfer information among PAVE programs is given in Table 13.1.

Table 13.1

RECORDS, ARRAYS, AND FIELDS USED TO TRANSFER INFORMATION AMONG PAVE PROGRAMS WITH PAVEFT FILES

Records are numbered in order for each transfer file.

The number of numeric fields for each record and transfer file is given on the right side of each transfer file title line.

Dimensions are shown with arrays. The suffix @ indicates that the number of a *single* array element is being listed, and not a whole dimensioned array.

For description of arrays, which often change several times between PAVE1 and PAVE6, see tables 14.10 to 14.18.

Transfers to PAVE2 from PAVEFT1 (579)

#1	WRITE	PAVE1	N$64,N(99), P(230),Q(250)
	READ	PAVE2	Same as above
		PAVER	N$64,I(1,99),J(1,200),0(1,30),R(1,200),Y(1,50)

Transfers to PAVE3 from PAVEFT2 (947)

#1	WRITE	PAVE2	M,N,N5,N(53),B(3,25),A(34,24)
	READ	PAVE3	Same as above
		PAVER	I(1,131),J(1,240),0(1,240),R(1,240),Y(1,96)

Transfers to PAVE4 from PAVEFT3 (1(#1) + 23(#2) + 181(#3) = 205)

#1	WRITE	PAVE2	N(6)@
	or WRITE	PAVE6	N6
	READ	PAVE4	N6
		PAVER	I(1,1)
#2	WRITE	PAVE2	N$64,M,N,N3,N5,H(19)
	READ	PAVE4	N$64,M,N,N3,N5,N(19)
		PAVER	N$64,I(1,4),J(1,5),O(1,5),R(1,5),Y(1,4)
#3	WRITE	PAVE3	M(12),V(6,2),H(33,4),F(25)
	READ	PAVE4	G(12),V(6,2),H(33,4),F(25)
		PAVER	I(1,12),J(1,6),O(1,6),R(1,132),Y(1,25)

Table 13.1. (continued)

Transfers to PAVE5 from PAVEFT4 (558(#1) + 1038(#2) + 3(#3) = 1599)

#1	WRITE	PAVE2	N$64,M,N,N3,N5,P(31)@,A(7,24),D(15,24),B(1,25)
	READ	PAVE5	N$64,M,N,N3,N5,I1,A(22,24),B(1,25)
		PAVER	N$64,I(1,5),J(1,240),O(1,240),R(1,48),Y(1,25)
#2	WRITE	PAVE3	C(6,25),D(37,24)
	READ	PAVE5	Same as above
		PAVER	I(1,150),J(1,240),O(1,240),R(1,240),Y(1,168)
#3	WRITE	PAVE4	N6,N(2)@,N(3)@
or	WRITE	PAVE6	N6,S1,R1
	READ	PAVE5	N6,S1,R
		PAVER	I(1,3)

Transfer to PAVE6 from PAVEFT5 (606(#1) + 734(#2) + 29(#3) + 290(#4) = 1659)

#1	WRITE	PAVE2	N$64,M,N,N3,N5,N(49)@,N(50)@,B(24,25)
	READ	PAVE6	N$64,M,N,N3,N5,I1,I2,B(24,25)
		PAVER	N$64,I(1,6),J(1,250),O(1,250),R(1,50),Y(1,50)
#2	WRITE	PAVE3	C(14,25),G(16,24)
	READ	PAVE6	Same as above
		PAVER	I(1,100),J(1,250),O(1,240),R(1,120),Y(1,24)
#3	WRITE	PAVE4	T,P,N(2)@,N(3)@,F(25)
	READ	PAVE6	R,P,S1,R1,F(25)
		PAVER	I(1,29)
#4	WRITE	PAVE5	N6,Z,D(10,24),V(6),V(6),X(36)
	READ	PAVE6	Same as above
		PAVER	I(1,2),J(1,240),O(1,6),R(1,6),Y(1,36)

Since PAVE is a complex model, care has been taken in the matching of program design to minicomputer capacity. The coding in this book will operate immediately on a Wang PCS-II with a user memory of 32K (32,768) bytes. On minidiskettes of 5¼ inch diameter and 89,600 bytes (87.5K), the set of PAVE programs require 69K bytes of storage, and the set of PAVEFT data files 51.5K bytes. This means that two mini-diskettes are required to operate the system, which is the basis of programming here. Allow at least 1.5K on each minidiskette for cataloging of files and internal control. Many of the latest minicomputers, such as a Wang PCS-II, are equipped with twin disk drives. If one moves to standard floppy disks, then only one drive is necessary to operate the whole PAVE system.

The following statistical information will help to relate PAVE requirements to the capacities of various equipment configurations:

Byte size is 8 bits.

Each numeric variable requires a base of 8 bytes (64 bits).

Each alphnumeric variable requires a base of 1 byte per character.

Printed outputs from cases in this book are rounded from a *precision* of 13 significant digits. The system will function down to 6-digit precision (see input warning in section 9.5 for low precision).

The number range required for PAVE is 10^{-26} to 10^{26}.

Maximum numeric single array dimension is (250).

Maximum numeric double array dimension is (39,24).

Maximum size of alphanumeric variable is 64 characters.

Maximum alphanumeric array dimension is 17.

Range of statement line numbers is 10 to 9920.

Maximum statement line length is 64 characters and spaces.

Video displays require 15 lines of 64 characters.

Printer minimum is 110 characters per line.

Maximum print lines per sheet is 59.

Characters are limited to numbers, capital letters, and standard symbols.

For each PAVE program, the list below shows RAM (random access memory) capacity required to run the program. This figure is followed by the space required to store the program on a minidiskette. The figures exclude *remarks* (REM) statements space. For a RUN, core space must be assigned for scalar and array variables, in addition to the space taken up by the program itself.

PAVE1, to run 28K, to store 22.75K

PAVE2, to run 25.5K, to store 6.5K

PAVE3, to run 29.5K, to store 7.75K

PAVE4, to run 13.25K, to store 11.75K

PAVE5, to run 24.25K, to store 10.25K

PAVE6, to run 25.25K, to store 10K

For each PAVEFT data transfer file, the following space is required for storage on a minidiskette:

PAVEFT1, to store 6K

PAVEFT2, to store 9.5K

PAVEFT3, to store 3.5K

PAVEFT4, to store 16K

PAVEFT5, to store 16.5K

In the RAM requirements for PAVE programs listed above, five types of space economies, which may be unavailable on some systems, were included:

1. The BASIC interpreter was hard-wired; it did not occupy RAM. Allow 4K to 5K extra if the interpreter is software in RAM.

2. Several statements are often compressed onto one line number. Some BASIC interpreters will accept only one statement per line (see section 13.3). Full decomposition should require 1K to 2K additional RAM.

3. Most BASIC language *words* which are used in statements and commands are compressed into one byte (8 bits) in Wang internal character code. This feature saves a substantial amount of RAM. It is difficult to estimate how much more space would be needed for particular equipment without this feature, but it would be at least 1K to 2K.

4. On Wang BASIC one may specify the maximum number of characters for each alphanumeric scalar or array variable. Other BASIC interpreters often use block lengths, such as multiples of 16 characters. Here available lengths do not exceed actual requirements, an economy which often is not available on other equipment.

5. Program codings in chapter 14 includes remarks (REM) statements. These are not required on any BASIC to run programs, and are excluded from RAM requirements above. Add 1K to 2K if REM statements are present in operating programs.

On many systems 40K or 48K of RAM will be required to run PAVE rather than the 32K for Wang computers. If *input data statement programs* are used, there must be enough RAM to LOAD these along with PAVE1 (see section 11.2 and Figure 11.1). Such a program may occupy 5K to 7K of RAM.

The time required for a PAVE run depends upon a number of variables:

1. Processing speed (this can vary by a factor of 20 or more)

2. Access speed to storage—random or sequential access, average access time, and transfer rate

3. Input display speed on video screen

4. Sophistication of cursor control on video screen

5. Speed of line printer

6. Conditions of PAVE run
    (a) Sample size (ID 3)—avoid large samples
    (b) Number of periods simulated (ID 1)
    (c) Extent of OUTPUT (ID 6)—FINANCIAL STATEMENTS output division takes the longest to print

Given all the sources of variation, it is difficult to make any general statement about run time. The range in minicomputers may go from a couple of minutes to an hour. Slow equipment need not pose a major problem. Once inputs are complete, a run does not require further attention until an output printing has been reached.

The following run times have been observed while simulating a manufacturing firm on various Wang units:

WANG PCS-II, 20 to 40 minutes

WANG 2200 VP with mounted twin minidiskette drives, 5 to 15 minutes

WANG MVP system, 2 to 5 minutes

13.2 | PAVE System of Communication with Files

There are numerous references in the remainder of this chapter to the syntax of statements in PAVE programs. Complete coding of programs PAVE1 to PAVE6 and three auxiliary programs will be found in figures 14.1 to 14.9.

The following is the syntax of statements for file management within PAVE programs.

1. To access an existing *data* file for either READ or WRITE:
   2480 DATA LOAD DC OPEN F Y$ or
   590 DATA LOAD DC OPEN F "PAVEFT5"

2. To open or access a *new data* file for WRITE:
   5870 DATA SAVE DC OPEN F 23, Z$

3. To access a *data* file space under a *new* name:
   5860 SCRATCH F Y$
   5862 DATA SAVE DC OPEN F Y$, Z$

4. To READ *records* from an accessed *data* file:
   202 DATA LOAD DC C( ), D( )
   210 DATA LOAD DC N6, S1, R

5. To WRITE *records* to an accessed *data* file:
   685 DBACKSPACE BEG   or
   688 DSKIP 3
   690 DATA SAVE DC N(6)
   692 DATA SAVE DC N$, M, N, N3, N5, H( )
   695 DATA SAVE DC END

6. To *close* a *data* file which has been accessed for READ or WRITE:
   170 DATA SAVE DC CLOSE

7. To LOAD or CHAIN another PAVE *program*:
   1630 LOAD DC R "PAVE6"   or
   4300 LOAD DC R "PAVE1" 2450

Data files in PAVE are accessed by either *alpha variable* or *name*, as illustrated by Y$ in 2480 or "PAVEFT5" in 590. Only one data file is accessed at a time in PAVE, an important simplification. For this reason file identification is not required for READ, WRITE, or CLOSE statements. The symbol F relates to the left port, and the symbol R to the right port. The letters DC refer to "disk." For one file at a time under Wang syntax, *accessing* a new file automatically closes a previous open file. For this reason DATA SAVE DC CLOSE is not required between all file changes. It is used here at the end of each program and to signal the end of a block of file reading or writing.

In statement 5870, 23 sectors of space must be reserved for a new input data file, with a name stored in Z$. Each input data file requires 23 sections, or 5.75K bytes, on a minidiskette. Statement 5860 renders an old file, named Y$, unaccessible to be accessed by program statements. Statement 5860 is necessary before the space of Y$ may be accessed under a file name Z$. Z$ will have the same storage capacity as Y$; both are used for input data. Statements are not available in Wang BASIC to UNSAVE (eliminate) data files from minidiskettes. This would be a useful interactive option in the input data file management of PAVE1.

The content of a data file is divided into records. Each separate DATA SAVE DC statement writes a new record, and each separate DATA LOAD DC statement reads from a different record. Statements 202 and 210 READ two records; statements 690 and 692 WRITE two records. Each record contains a string of fields. Fields may be scalar numerics or alphas, or members of arrays, as illustrated in the above statements. Symbols such as C( ), D( ), or H( ) are macroinstructions to READ or WRITE all the fields of an array into a record. Field N(6) in a list, on the other hand, is a single N( ) array element. On most BASICs, single or double FOR . . . NEXT loops would be used to READ or WRITE arrays. This ordinary system is not feasible in PAVE Wang BASIC because each DATA LOAD or DATA SAVE in a loop would create a separate record. Since every record occupies at least 0.25K or one sector, on a minidiskette, it is not economical in PAVE to establish multiple records to store arrays. In PAVE each input data file has only one record. The maximum number of records in a PAVEFT series data transfer file is four. The layout of records, variable names, and fields in PAVEFT series files is shown in Table 13.1.

To save space, the same array is often used consecutively for different sets of data. Statements like MAT REDIM C(6,25) appear frequently to resize arrays, particularly before or after DATA LOAD or DATA SAVE statements. An original *dimension* (DIM) statement must establish a maximum size for each array. If REDIM is not available on your BASIC, simply leave each array at its maximum size. Under some syntaxes this might result in transferring unused elements (fields) between files, but in PAVE this is not a serious degradation of efficiency. In all BASICs data may be read out of a file under different variable names than it was read in. As shown in Table 13.1, this occurs occasionally in PAVE.

Whenever a data file is accessed, the pointer resets to the first field. Since all PAVE data files are READ (DATA LOAD) from the beginning, no complexities arise. With DATA SAVE (WRITE) statements, however, one needs to move either to the beginning or the end of a file. It is not necessary in PAVE to count records or to locate a particular record in a file. Note that if a DATA SAVE is executed at a particular record, it will simply write over and destroy any previous contents of that record. In Statement 685 an input data file had previously been read into RAM. The pointer is now at the end of the file. DBACKSPACE BEG resets the pointer to the beginning. This is necessary because revised inputs are to be stored in this file; the previous data are to be destroyed. In Statement 688 a new record is to be written to a data transfer file which has just been accessed. Three previously written records on this file must not be destroyed. DSKIP 3 is an instruction to move the pointer to the end of the previous data by skipping over 3 records which were previously written.

After a set of DATA SAVE statements is completed, Statement 695 instruction DATA SAVE DC END is always inserted. This sets an end-of-file marker in the record space past the last currently written records. Such a marker is not actually needed to process PAVE because there are a fixed number of records in each data file; END OF FILE conditional branches are not required. Such branches do appear, however, in the file service program PAVER (see sections 11.3 and 14.7).

Statement 1630 simply replaces the current program in RAM with another chained program, in this case PAVE6. All variable values are wiped out. Although a COMMON variable space is available in Wang BASIC to hold values between programs, PAVE depends entirely on data files to transfer processed variables from one program to another. A COMMON variable space was avoided because it is unavailable to most BASIC interpreters. Statement 4300 loads PAVE1 for a rerun, but only statement lines 2470 and higher will be replaced on the previous program. Also, program execution will start at line 2470 of PAVE1 instead of at the lowest line number. This is a convenient feature for PAVE reruns because some initial questions are bypassed. If such a feature is unavailable on your BASIC, simply chain in all of PAVE1. Very little time will be lost if initial questions are repeated.

13.3 | Control of Displays and Printing

There are probably more differences among BASIC syntaxes on PRINT instructions than in any other area. Also, computers differ in the power to control video displays. The PRINT choices in PAVE are described in this section for both video displays and line printers. Means of adjustment to other systems are suggested.

A position for editing of inputs on a video display is usually indicated by a flashing character or a flashing horizontal line. The term cursor may be applied to a flashing line. Three levels of control over video displays, in ascending order of power, are the following:

1. Information is first printed on the bottom line. As additional lines are printed at the bottom, earlier lines "roll up" to the top. After the display is full, lines disappear through the top as new lines are added at the bottom.

2. There is a BASIC statement available to CLEAR SCREEN and HOME CURSOR. Upon this instruction the PRINT position is shifted to the upper left-hand corner of the display. Print lines then start at the top and work down through the display. When a screen is full further printing will lead to "roll up" as described above.

3. In addition to CLEAR SCREEN and HOME CURSOR, statements may be available to position the cursor at any location on the video screen. Then INPUTS and PRINT changes may be shifted around the screen without reprinting the entire display.

PAVE programs (chapter 14) are written at the second level, even though third level control is available on Wang BASIC. The CLEAR SCREEN and HOME CURSOR instruction is print HEX (03). If this instruction is not available, add PRINT statements to line space between displays so that each display is positioned appropriately on the video screen. The majority of displays in PAVE are exactly fifteen lines each. If your video screen has 15 print lines, no instructions will be required between displays. With 16 print lines, one PRINT statement will be required between displays, etc. Some PAVE displays, such as individual inputs or warning statements, have less than 15 lines. Add PRINT statements to line space with the following small subroutine:

```
6000 REM 10** SUB—LINE SPACE TO POSITION DISPLAYS
6010 FOR I = 1 TO K
6020 PRINT
6030 NEXT I
6040 RETURN
```

Between displays the number of line spaces is assigned to K. Control is passed to the subroutine with GOSUB 6010.

The speed and quality of video displays may be improved if program statements are used to control cursor position. Instructions for doing this with Wang BASIC syntax are given in section 13.5. These instructions are presented as changes and additions to the standard PAVE1 program in section 14.1.

BASIC input and output statements are the same in PAVE for either video screens or line printers. SELECT statements are used for each shift between the two devices:

```
300 SELECT PRINT 005(64)    for video display screen
440 SELECT PRINT 215(110)   for line printer
```

The figures in parentheses are the number of positions per line specified for each device.

Numeric variable displays in PAVE use either *packed print zones* or formatting with image statements. The former is employed when numeric variables appear within printed sentences. The latter is applied to columns of figures in tables and statements. Packed zones in PAVE BASIC provide one space on either side of unsigned numbers. The spacing may require adjustment for other BASIC syntaxes. On most BASICs the PRINT instructions of PAVE will not output floating-point numbers with exponents. Numeric outputs are usually rounded to integers of two decimal places. To save space, prefix "$" is omitted from statement fields.

IMAGE statements differ among BASICS. In PAVE the following symbols occur.

1. The beginning of a set of IMAGE STATEMENT fields is signaled by "%" instead of ":" symbol. A colon is used in PAVE to separate multiple statements on the same line (see section 13.4).

2. The prefix "-" to a numeric field is a signal to omit a sign from positive number outputs, and to prefix a minus sign to negative outputs.

3. Commas have been supplied within image formats of numeric fields. These improve readability of outputs. For other BASICs this feature may not be available. If not, then remove commas from IMAGE STATEMENTS.

4. To avoid problems in some BASICs, reliance has not been placed upon PRINT-USING statements to round numbers before printing. Separate INT function expressions have been coded for this purpose.

5. To print columns of titles and statement values, several IMAGE STATEMENTS have often been combined on the same line with close-packed zoning. The syntax for this is a semicolon at the end of each PRINTUSING statement. A line is terminated with

```
1000 PRINTUSING [Image statement no.] ," "
```

The accompanying image statement has one position

```
1200 %#
```

If this syntax is not available, a separate IMAGE STATEMENT must be coded for every required line layout.

6. PRINT or TAB statements are never combined with PRINTUSING statements on the same output line in PAVE. Such a combination is not allowed on some BASICs.

To save space, a statement which combines PRINT with INPUT is sometimes used:

```
2500 INPUT "ENTER 'NEW' FILE NAME",Z$
```

For BASICs without this combined statement, substitute:

```
2500 PRINT "ENTER 'NEW' FILE NAME';
2505 INPUT Z$
```

The instruction PRINT HEX (OC) line spaces print paper to the top of the next sheet. This instruction appears whenever a new statement is started, or when printing of one statement might overflow 59 lines per sheet of paper. Since outputs are of variable lengths, PRINT HEX (OC) is controlled by maximum printing per statement. Considerable blank paper may be generated with short statements. PRINT HEX (OC), and the branches from it, may be optionally eliminated.

After a user input, keying of EXECUTE, X/C, or CONTROL/C returns control to the computer. In PAVE user inputs are sometimes present to " " (blanks) or "0" prior to entry. Then keying EXECUTE without a user entry will pass through the INPUT statement while retaining the original input value. This may save response time in working through an interactive sequence (series of questions). In order to proceed, some syntaxes of other BASICs require a user input prior to EXECUTE. If this is the case, substitute a prescribed user input symbol for each PAVE direct EXECUTE choice.

On PAVE1 displays, users may sometimes enter either numbers for values or characters for display control. Such inputs are first treated as a set of characters in V\$. If a numeric branch is reached, however, an instruction CONVERT V\$ TO V transforms contents to numeric. If this instruction is not available, use numeric symbols to replace P, *, /, //, or " " (blank) characters.

If a nonnumeric character were entered by mistake in a V\$ numeric value input branch, the program would abort when CONVERT V\$ TO V statement is reached. To prevent this a function test, IF NUM (V\$)>=9 THEN 6270, has been inserted. Function NUM counts the number of characters in V\$ which comprise a legal BASIC number, including trailing spaces. There are nine positions to input characters, thus all of them must be numeric to pass the test and to continue to line 6270. Otherwise, control is recycled for a new input. If NUM function is not available substitute an ON ERROR or WHEN ERROR branch.

The instruction PRINT HEX(07) sounds a buzzer along with a warning or error message display. PRINT HEX(07) may be omitted.

13.4 | Notes on BASIC Statements used in PAVE

To save space and speed processing, some statements are used in PAVE that are not available on all BASICs. File management and printing statements were presented in sections 13.2 and 13.3. Other special statement features are discussed in this section. Methods of removing special features are given. The list of features is

Line compression

Dimensioning of character variables

Marked subroutines

Branching out of subroutines

Branching out of loops

Multiple assignment statements

Library functions

To save space, several statements in PAVE are often compressed onto one line. Compressed statements are always separated by a colon and one trailing space. Line length in PAVE is 64 characters or less. This includes line number and one trailing space. Decompression is simple because there is no branching to compressed statements. Intermediate line numbers may be easily assigned to such statements, since PAVE line numbers are incremented by 10.

Two compressed statements, followed by one uncompressed statement are:

```
2820 M9=V(5,1)*N(11): IF N(11)<>0 THEN 2850: GOSUB 4630: M9=P9
2830 IF L9<P9 THEN 2840: M9=L9
2840 N(11)=M9/V(5,1)
```

Decompress by writing each statement on a separate line:

```
2820 M9=V(5,1)*N(11)
     IF N(11)<>0 THEN 2850
     GOSUB 4630
     M9=P9
2830 IF L9<P9 THEN 2840
     M9=L9
2840 N(11)=M9/V(5,1)
```

Assign intermediate line numbers to compressed statements:

```
2820 M9=V(5,1)*N(11)
2822 IF N(11)<>0 THEN 2850
2825 GOSUB 4630
2827 M9=P9
2830 IF L9<P9 THEN 2840
2835 M9=L9
2840 N(11)=M9/V(5,1)
```

Alphanumeric (character) scalar and array variables are each dimensioned in PAVE to precise maximum length. This saves core space and is accomplished with a trailing number in dimension (DIM) statements. Thus H$(4)31 is a 4-element array with maximum length of 31 characters per element, and C$1 is a scalar with only one character. Many BASICs use standard lengths, or blocks of standard lengths, such as 16 or 18 characters per block. In such cases review the contents of each character variable to improve the efficiency of fit to standard lengths.

Unmarked subroutine calls in PAVE, such as GOSUB 4630, branch to a line number per standard BASIC syntax. A second class of "marked" subroutines, such as GOSUB '2(X,Y,Z), is used in PAVE to pass values from a main program to a subroutine. This syntax does not require a subroutine line number. Use of marked subroutine reduces coding. The syntax is shown on the following page.

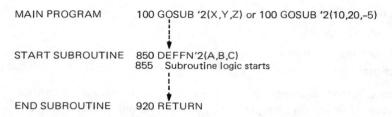

MAIN PROGRAM   100 GOSUB '2(X,Y,Z) or 100 GOSUB '2(10,20,-5)

START SUBROUTINE   850 DEFFN'2(A,B,C)
                    855   Subroutine logic starts

END SUBROUTINE   920 RETURN

In this case the values in X, Y, and Z, or constants (10, 20, and -5), are assigned to variables A, B, and C in the subroutine. Control branches to line 850. The special syntax is easily replaced by assignment statements and an unmarked subroutine call:

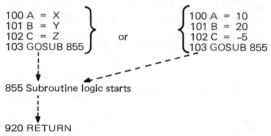

```
100 A = X  ⎫              ⎧ 100 A = 10
101 B = Y  ⎬    or        ⎨ 101 B = 20
102 C = Z  ⎭              ⎩ 102 C = -5
103 GOSUB 855            103 GOSUB 855
```

855 Subroutine logic starts

920 RETURN

If control branches out of a subroutine without reaching a RETURN statement, the stored line numbers of return to the main program may not be cleared out of memory. In some, but not all BASICs, repeated branching out will pile up these stored line numbers, and eventually cause an overflow. To avoid this in PAVE, the statement RETURN CLEAR has been inserted in each branch out of a subroutine before reaching the RETURN statement at the end:

```
6080 IF C>=A THEN 6090
6083 RETURN CLEAR
6086 GO TO 5660
6090 RETURN
```

If C<A, then control branches out of the subroutine to line 5660. Statement RETURN CLEAR has been inserted in the branch path. Check the syntax of your BASIC.

The same accumulation problem of stored line numbers may occur with repeated branching out before the end (NEXT statement) of FOR . . . NEXT loops. In PAVE the stored line numbers (of FOR statements) are cleared by inserting extra NEXT statements in branch-out paths.

```
380 FOR I = 1 TO 24
385 IF N(50 + I)>0 THEN 400
390 Z = I - 1
392 I = 24
395 NEXT I
397 GOTO 410
400 Z1 = Z1 + N(50 + I)
405 NEXT I
```

If N(50 + I)>0 then control branches to line 400 and the main loop is completed on line 405. Otherwise, there is a branch out of the loop on lines 392 to 397. On line 392 the I index is reset to its terminal value of 24. Then the branch statement NEXT I on line 395 will complete the loop and clear line number 380 stored in memory. Per statement 397, control then bypasses the rest of the loop to line 410. Caution: Multiple NEXT statements are not allowed in some BASICs. Check your own syntax.

Multiple assignments are separated by commas in PAVE. Thus

220 F(1), S, F(39) = F(32)

would appear as

220 F(1) = S = F(39) = F(32)

in some BASIC syntaxes.

The system-defined functions used in PAVE are ABS, INT, LOG, NUM, SGN, and SQR. Subject to the notes below, these functions are standard. Function INT is always used for rounding, if required, before printing. Function LOG is a *natural* logarithm. If the argument X in RND(X) is zero, the *first* number of the random list is always produced. If X is nonzero, the next number of the list is produced. Nonentry in ID 4, SEED NUMBER, retains the internal default of zero, which initializes random numbers with RND(0). This means that successive runs of PAVE will use the same series of random numbers. In comparisons among runs there will be an increase in efficiency with reduction of between-treatment variance. To develop a new stream of random numbers between runs, users should enter any nonzero value in ID 4. The use of NUM function for testing inputs was explained in section 13.3.

13.5 | Alternative Methods of Display

If instructions are available to locate the cursor anywhere on the screen, updating and inputting of video displays will become faster and more flexible. Two methods of improvement are given in this section. Video displays are not available on some systems. Suggestions for modifying PAVE to meet this limitation are given at the close of the section.

Returning to improved video control, all modifications in this section are related to PAVE1B, the basic PAVE1 program, which is documented in section 14.2. Only changes are given here. PAVE1X modification has the same display and input system as PAVE1B. Moving "X" marker columns on each side of displays identify IDs in turn for inputs. New ID values are entered at the bottom. This display method is shown in Figure 13.2. In contrast to PAVE1B, PAVE1X does not reprint the entire display for each input shift. Instead, only the Xs and input values are reprinted in new positions. This speeds up inputs and reduces eye strain. Modification PAVE1C follows the same changes as PAVE1X, but a flashing cursor is substituted for "X" markers at the current ID for input. Inputs are made at the right of the line which describes an ID. Current values of IDs for input are printed at the bottom of the display. The PAVE1C method is shown in Figure 13.3.

Cursor positions are 0 to 15 vertically (16 lines) and 0 to 63 horizontally (64 characters and spaces). Special bytes are used for cursor control. Each byte is identified by a hexdigit pair:

01 home cursor

03 clear screen and home cursor

08 backspace, or move cursor left one space

09 nondestructive space, or move cursor right one space

0A move cursor down one line

0C move cursor up one line

0D carriage return to leftmost position

A string of cursor control instructions may be assembled into a HEX statement. Thus HEX(010A0A0A) would move the cursor to the fourth line down from the top. In

Figure 13.2 Input display with X markers identification

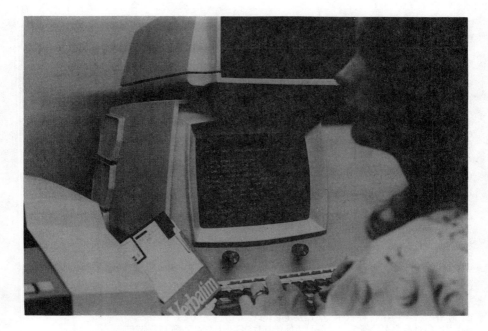

Figure 13.3 Input display with flashing cursor identification

PAVE1X and PAVE1C, vertical cursor position instructions are assembled into U$, horizontal forward position with W$, and horizontal backspace into B$. Function SRT is used to obtain subsets of character variables. Thus STR (U$, 1, 14) applies to the characters in U$ starting in position one and moving to the right for a total of 14 characters. Statement INIT places the character in its argument in *every* position of an alpha variable or a STR subset of it. The cursor may be moved to a specific location by application of subsets (STR functions) of U$, W$, an B$.

Cursor control variables U$, W$, and B$ may be initialized with hexidigits for PAVE1X and PAVE1C modifications. Add dimensions X(12), B$12, U$17, and W$62 to DIM statements. Array X$(12)1 may be eliminated. Add the following statement:

```
2725 U$=HEX(010D): INIT(OA) STR(U$,3): INIT(09)W$: INIT(08)B$
```

Each display of PAVE1X is printed only once during inputs to it. This means that X$( ) markers will not be printed by display subroutines. Instead, markers will be printed in the display control subroutine SUB'1. Display printing subroutines will determine the line number (0 to 14) for each ID number of a display to be printed in SUB'1. This number is stored in X( ).

For PAVE1X and PAVE1C, insert the following line changes in the three PRINT INPUT DISPLAY subroutines:

```
6320 PRINT " ";J+K;B$(J);TAB(52);N(J+K): X(J)=J: NEXT J
6390 PRINT" ";J+K;C$;C(J);B$(J);TAB(52);N(J+K): X(J)=J
6430 PRINT HEX(03): H=0: X=P+2: IF P>3 THEN 6440:X=L (1)+6
6440 D$(1),D$(4),D$(7)=G$(X): IF C$(1)<>" " THEN 6450: H=2
6445 GOTO 6460
6450 PRINT " ";K+1;C$(1);" ";F$;TAB(52);L(1): X(1)=0: PRINT
6460 PRINT A$;" ";F$;H$: IF C$(2) <>" " THEN 6470: H=H+1
6465 GOTO 6480
6470 PRINT " ";K+2;" ";C$(2);TAB(52);L(2): X(2)=3-H
6510 PRINT " ";K+J;D$(J-2);" ";C$(J);TAB(52);L(J): X(J)=J+2-H
```

Control of cursor position and printing of "X" markers must be moved to SUB'1 of PAVE1X. Make the following changes:

```
6060 IF Z4 <10 THEN 6100: PRINT : PRINT
6070 to 6090 delete
6105 IF V$ <>"P" THEN 6115: SELECT PRINT 005(64): V$=" "
6110 GOTO 6100
6115 GOSUB 6870
6120 I=C
6130 I1=I: IF I <>2 THEN 6135: I1=I-Y
6135 A1=I1+K: V=L(I1): IF P >2 THEN 6140: V=N(A1)
6140 PRINT STR (U$,1,X(I1)+1); "X";W$;"X"
6145 PRINT STR (U$,1,15); TAB(63); HEX(0D); TAB(14): "EXIT=//,";
6150 PRINT " PRINT=P; OR VALUE OF ID "; A1;" ";: V$=" "
6155 INPUT V$: IF V$ <>" " THEN 6160: GOSUB 6890: GOTO 6260
6200 IF V$ <>"*" THEN 6220: GOSUB 6890
6205 IF I >A THEN 6210: I=B: GOTO 6130
6210 I=I-1: GOTO 6130
6220 IF NUM(V$) >=9 THEN 6230: PRINT HEX(07): GOTO 6135
6252 IF P <> 3 THEN 6256: IF I1 <>1 THEN 6256: GOSUB 6430
6254 GOSUB 6870
6256 GOSUB 6890
```

For PAVE1X, add the following cursor control subroutine at the end of PAVE1B:

```
6860 REM 23**SUBS—PRINT INPUT INFO; CURSOR RESTORES INPUT VALUE
6870 PRINT STR (U$,1,14); "FWD='EXC', BACK=*, NEXT DISPLAY OR";
6880 PRINT " ID=/,": RETURN
6890 PRINT STR (U$,1,X(I1)+1); " "; STR(W$,1,50);TAB(14);B$;V
6900 RETURN : END
```

PAVE1C differs from PAVE1X only in a few cursor control lines of SUB'1 and SUB'23 for INPUT DISPLAY CONTROL. Make these changes to lines previously listed for PAVE1X changes:

```
6140 PRINT STR(U$,1,15); TAB(63); HEX(0D); TAB(14); "EXIT=//,";
6145 PRINT " PRINT=P.   ID "; A1; " = ";V
6150 PRINT STR(U$,1,X(I1)+1);W$; TAB(12); B$;: V$=" "
```

For PAVE1C, replace the *last two* lines of SUB'23 in PAVE1X above with the following single line:

```
6890 PRINT STR(U$,1,X(I1)+1);W$;TAB(12);B$;V: RETURN : END
```

An interesting modification, PAVE1U, *underlines* the variable description for input instead of printing markers. This type of display is shown in Figure 13.4. The instructions for underlining are so specialized that they are not given here.

Video screens may not be available, particularly when computing with portable terminals. All PAVE display instructions will work on line printers, but unless modified, input processing would become very slow. Under such conditions it is suggested that printing of menus, starting on line 2880 of PAVE1 and on line 3570 of PAVE6, become subject to user choice.

A more serious problem arises with SEQUENTIAL DISPLAYS input mode of PAVE1. If no video screen is available, displays should not be reprinted in full for each input. Instead, print each line in order for ID description and current value, one line at a time. Return control to a user for INPUT at the end of each line. Key 'EXECUTE' to print the next line. User input "P" may be used to recycle printing of displays for further revision, as in video inputs of PAVE1. On displays for dynamic input sets, branch away from printing remaining IDs if zero or nonentry occurs in ID –4 or ID –7 positions. Under such input conditions entries in following digit positions will be disregarded. A branch like this is already in place for ID –4 (5th

Figure 13.4 Input display with underlining identification

ID description) with PAVE1 menu item Z4 = 10, PRINT ALL INPUTS. See lines 6490 and 6500 of PAVE1. The SELECTIVE INTERACTIVE input requires only a little printing, and should not require modification if there is no video screen.

13.6 | Adaptations to Time-Sharing

If PAVE is time-shared, more than one set of data transfer files must be accessible among programs. There is no provision for multiple transfer file sets in the PAVE coding of chapter 14. Several methods are available to add this feature. For a small number of terminals, duplicate sets of PAVE program files and PAVEFT data files, all with different file names, may be supplied for each terminal. This consumes a lot of storage space.

For large systems, it is best if users assign an individual name to a set of transfer files for each run. Only one name need be entered because the PAVE programs may add serial numbers to identify individual files. Coding should be added to UNSAVE each file as soon as read. A WHEN ERROR or ON ERROR branch should also be supplied to UNSAVE files when a RUN is aborted. If these precautions are not followed, obsolete files are likely to pile up in storage. A difficulty with the above method is that users must input the data transfer file name six times during each PAVE RUN. In addition to an original input, five chained programs must receive information about which transfer file to access.

If COMMON storage is available, multiple file name entry may be eliminated. The statements for such a time-sharing system are given below. Set up COMMON storage for five data transfer files under array J$( ):

```
2065 COM J$(5)8
```

In place of *disk change* statements in PAVE1, substitute the following instructions to enter a data transfer file set name:

```
5910 INPUT "ENTER DATA TRANSFER FILE SET NAME, 2-7 STRING",J$(1)
```

The user-supplied name must contain between 2 and 7 characters. A loop is next added to PAVE1. This loop assigns digits 1 to 5 in the first trailing position beyond the input file name. The five revised file names are stored in J$( ). The STR function to do this was described in section 13.5. The LEN function determines the number of characters in the input name, here 2 to 7, exclusive of trailing blanks. In the coding below, LEN is used to determine the position of digits 1 to 5. These digits are added to the file name by the STR function. COMMON storage and character variable functions are often available in minicomputer BASICs.

```
5913 FOR I=1 TO 5
5916 J$(I)=J$(1)
5920 CONVERT I TO STR(J$(I),LEN(J$(I))+1,1),(#)
5925 NEXT I
```

Five user file names are now stored in J$(1) to J$(5). All that remains is to change in PAVE1 to PAVE6 the DATA LOAD statements for transfer files. In each of these "PAVEFT1" must be changed to J$(1), "PAVEFT2" to J$(2), etc. In PAVE1, for example, substitute

5940 DATA LOAD DC OPEN F J$(1)

14 Documentation of PAVE Programs

14.1 | Arrangement of Documentation

Detailed explanations of BASIC coding of the standard set of PAVE programs are given in this chapter. A section is devoted to each of the six chained PAVE programs. A final section is concerned with PAVE service programs. These are PAVEC to establish data transfer files, PAVER to print the contents of data transfer files, and PAVES to service input data files. The coding itself is presented in figures 14.1 to 14.9. A complete variable list has been compiled for each program. These are presented in tables 14.1 to 14.9. Additional tabulations of arrays are referenced in the text. Users who wish to become involved with detailed coding will probably refer back and forth among the coding sheets, variable lists, and explanations. For this purpose it is suggested that figures and tables be copied from the book. In this chapter all figures and tables have been assembled together at the end.

An overview of PAVE logic is not presented in this chapter. Section 13.1 explains the PAVE system of programs and files. Figure 13.1 displays a flow chart of the whole PAVE set. Notes on BASIC syntax used in this book will be found in sections 13.2 to 13.4. Alternative displays and adaptations are discussed in sections 13.5 and 13.6.

The explanation of coding here follows a uniform pattern in all sections. Statement line numbers are given in the left margin. General headings identify major divisions of logic. Remarks (REM) statements in PAVE programs also indicate the organization of processing.

14.2 | PAVE1 Documentation

INITIALIZE SYSTEM AND PRINT INSTRUCTIONS

2010– SELECT video screen with 64 character line; home *cursor*; PRINT program
2050 title on video screen.

2060–	DATA statement flag pair signals end of DATA statement READ loop (see
2090	2550). DIMENSION arrays and alpha variables.

The relation between input IDs and array addresses is as follows:

IDs 1 to 99 in N(1) to N(99) for *system parameters*.

IDs 100 to 329 in P(1) to P(230) for *environment*, *trade*, and *manufacturing dynamic* input sets.

IDs 330 to 579 in Q(1) to Q(250) for *research and development*, *sales*, *general administration*, and *financial dynamic* input sets.

See Table 14.10 for a list of input titles, IDs, and corresponding array addresses.

2100	Enter option T to PRINT condensed instructions at the terminal.
2110	If T=0, bypass PRINT of instructions. Otherwise branch to SUB 6830 for *line printer* ON warning and SELECT *line printer*.
2120– 2430	PRINT condensed PAVE input-output instructions on *line printer*.
2440	Line space and SELECT video screen.
2450– 2460	Enter Option T to PRINT *policy reminder statements* (POLREMS) along with SEQUENTIAL DISPLAYS inputs.

CHOOSE, NAME, AND READ INPUT DATA FILES

2470	On RERUN option in PAVE4 or PAVE6, PAVE1 processing starts here. Line space and SELECT video screen.
2490	INPUT Z1 from 4 *input data file* choices.
2500– 2530	ON input file choice Z1:

Z1=0 bypass file open to DATA statements READ at (2550)

Z1=1 or 2, enter name and OPEN old file Y$. READ inputs from it (2510 and 2520). N$ is title, N( ) is array of *system parameters*, P( ) and Q( ) are arrays of *dynamic input sets*. Branch to DATA statement READ at 2550 for *old* file only (Z1=1).

Z1=2 or 3, enter new file name Z$ in 2530

2550– 2560	READ data statements. A1 is an input ID number, and A2 is the corresponding input value. Flag to discontinue is ID number value. Flag to discontinue if ID number A1=0. If there is a DATA statement or DATA statement program present with nonzero IDs in A1 address, it will automatically be read. If there are no nonzero DATA statements then the first DATA statement encountered is line 2060. The flag A1=0 on this line will cause DATA statement READ to be bypassed.

Indicator W is set to 4 if nonzero A1 is read, otherwise W=0. If A1 is less than 100 for *system parameter*, then A2 is assigned to N(A1).

2570– Otherwise, if A1 is less than 330, then A2 is assigned to A(A1–99); other-
2580 wise A2 is assigned to Q(A1–329). The READ and assignment of (A1, A2)
pairs continues in a loop (2550 to 2580) until the first A1=0 flag READ is
encountered. A1=0 leads to branch out from READ and assign. Arrays P( )
and Q( ) are used for inputs of *dynamic sets*.

The correspondence between individual input IDs in A1 and elements of input arrays N( ), P( ) and Q( )is given in columns of Table 14.10 (see also
2060 above and general explanation in section 11.1). Note relations between
ID groups and P( ) and Q( ) units digit positions for *dynamic sets*. For these
arrays the "1" position is for associated parameters, the "2" position usually
for uncertainty input components, and the "3" to "0" or "ten" positions
for dynamic input values proper.

Note that DATA statements follow the READ of *"old" input data file*, if
any. Thus DATA statements will overwrite an *input file*.

2590 Z1, the file choice index, remains equal to 4 *if and only if* there is *no input
file* (Z1 input=0), and nonzero A1 DATA statements have been READ. Revised values of Z1 now are:

Z1=0, *no input file* nor nonzero *DATA statements*
Z1=1, *old* input file only, with or without DATA statements
Z1=2, both *old* and *new* input files, with or without DATA statements
Z1=3, *new* input file only, with or without DATA statements
Z1=4, *no input file* but DATA statements have been read

Each *input data file* (but not input DATA statement programs) includes a
title under N$64. If there is no title, N$ is preset to a blank.

2600– INPUT V$ title option. For V$="D" option to display title on video screen,
2630 recycle to option after display. For V$="I" option, INPUT new or revised
title.

2650– Default input values are supplied to 10 IDs after *old* input file, optionally
2720 overwritten by *DATA statements*, but before new user entries at keyboard.

2730– Assign character strings in *displays* which do not change: prefixes in D$( )
2830 and last two elements G$( ), class numbers under first five elements of G$( ),
titles under C$( ), and uncertainty input title S$.

MENU FOR CONTROL OF INPUTS

2850 Reset to blanks the titles C$(1), C$(2), F$, and H$, which are unused on
some input displays. This is prior to new *menu* choice. Bypass to *menu* display except Z4=10 for PRINT all inputs.

2860 For Z4=10, add one to display section counter Z2, line space, and bypass
menu display routine unless Z2 counter reaches 7. In such case all input
displays have been presented, and return to *menu*.

2870   SELECT video screen, and home *cursor*. Scalar Z controls POLREM display. If T=1 then POLREMS will be displayed unless Z4=10 for input PRINT. In the latter case Z remains at 0 (see 3020).

2880–   Display menu; user selects INPUT menu choice under Z4.
3010

INITIALIZATION AND CONTROL FOR PRINT ALL INPUTS

3020   The input displays section is located with variable Z2. Initially set Z2=Z4. Except for Z4=10 with PRINT all inputs, Z2 equals Z4. Then branch to type of firm (frame) check at 3040. Otherwise Z2 starts at first output division (Z2=1) and omit POLREMS (Z=0).

        Branch to SUB 6830 for line printer ON warning and SELECT line printer.

3030   This statements continues to initiate Z=10 for PRINT all inputs. PRINT title N$ and line space.

CHECK AND MESSAGES FOR INAPPLICABLE INPUT DIVISIONS

3040   In this section inapplicable input divisions are rejected for SEQUENTIAL DISPLAYS or PRINT all inputs. Home *cursor*. Reset input variable V$ to a blank.

        Branch according to type of firm (frame) in N(5). If frame is *manufacturing* or *trade*, all input sections apply; bypass directly to menu multiple branch at 3140.

3050   This is an input check for service frame N(5)=0. Except for *manufacturing* and *trade* input division Z2=4, which does not apply to N(5)=0, transfer to multiple branch at 3140. Otherwise, if Z4=10 for PRINT all inputs, return to pick up next input division at 2860.

3060   Otherwise, continue error routine for Input Division 4 with service frame. PRINT error message for this incorrectly chosen input division.

3070–   Continue input section error routine. Line space and sound error bell
3090   HEX(07). Upon INPUT of blank in V$ (EXECUTE to operate V$ preset value on 3040), return control to *menu* at 2850. This permits user to select another input division.

3100–   Check of *environment frame* (N(5)=3) for inapplicable input divisions starts
3110   here. The only relevant input divisions for N(5)=3 are Z2=1 or 3; in such case transfer control to multiple branch 3140. Otherwise, if Z4=10 for PRINT all inputs, return to pick up next input division at 2850. If Z2>6, a choice other than input division or PRINT all inputs, transfer control to multiple branch 3140.

3120–   Otherwise N(5)=3 is inapplicable to chosen input division (2, 4, 5, or 6).
3130   PRINT error message for this incorrect input division and branch to further error routine on 3070 to 3090.

SEQUENTIAL INPUT DISPLAYS VALUE ASSIGNMENTS

Each of 6 input divisions has a set of displays (see section 8.3 for list). The SEQUENTIAL DISPLAY input divisions are reached from the first 6 branches per Z2 on 3140. Inapplicable divisions have already been eliminated (3040 to 3130). Displays appear in order within each input division.

A$ is the main title of each display.

Displays are divided into two types, *system parameters* and *dynamic input sets*. Each display loops through a set of input IDs.

B$( ) is assigned to subtitles for *system parameters*. Blanks may be assigned to B$( ) for line spacing.

C$(1) and C$(2) are titles of related IDs assigned to *dynamic sets* (if used). Otherwise, they remain as present blanks. Parameters C$(3) to C$(10) are preassigned for subtitles of dynamic sets (2750 to 2820). These titles are always used for dynamic sets.

All display composition and input routines are controlled by SUB '1(K,P) at 5970. Display PRINTS are processed by SUBs controlled from SUB '1.

K is a counter which links each ID to its display line within display loops. See Table 14.10 for a complete list.

P is display PRINT control parameter:

P=1 for *system parameters* except those with numbered classes (PRINT SUB 6290).

P=2 for *system parameter* with numbered (indexed) classes (PRINT SUB 6370).

P=3 to 5 for *dynamic sets* (PRINT SUB 6430):

P=3 for variable prefix in D$(1), D$(4), and D$(7). The prefix, either "%" or "$", depends upon other input choices.

P=4 for "%" input prefix in above D$( ) elements.

P=5 for "$" input prefix in above D$( ) elements.

A is starting loop index for PRINT input IDs in a display.

B is ending loop index for PRINT input IDs in a display. A and B are preset for each call of SUB '1 with *system parameters*, but are determined within SUB '1 for *dynamic sets*.

At the end of each input division in SEQUENTIAL DISPLAYS, control is returned to the *menu* at 2850. This return appears on lines 3290, 3930, 4240, 4690, 5240, and 5580.

Lines 3160 to 5580 provide information for SEQUENTIAL DISPLAYS. This information furnishes titles of inputs, parameters for SUB '1 control and PRINT display SUBs, and branching both within and among displays. This branching particularly depends upon the frame input N(5). *Initial conditions balance* and text for option to PRINT POLREMS are also contained within these line numbers. The latter are discussed as separate divisions below. Further notes on particular displays are given below. The display information is used also with INDIVIDUAL INTERACTIVE input mode (Z4=7), and for PRINT all inputs (Z4=10).

3140   The first six branch menu choices go to the start of SEQUENTIAL DISPLAY input divisions. Branch 7 goes to INDIVIDUAL INTERACTIVE ID routine, Branch 8 to continue the RUN, and Branch 9 to END with PAVE1. This END occurs after writing input sets to data files (if elected). Menu choice 10 to PRINT all inputs branched off at 3110.

3430–   This display of *initial condition* is shortened from 11 items if the frame is
3450   not *manufacturing* (N(5) less than 2), except for INDIV. INTERACT. Z2=7. For trade N(5)=1, 3 inventories are removed; and for service N(5)=0, a fourth inventory is removed.

3460   Initial *manufacturing assets* display is bypassed for N(5) less than 2.

3490–   *System parameter* displays with *numbered classes* use PRINT SUB 6370
3520   (P=2), and require additional display variables. Array C( ) is the class number. Exactly 5 classes, both for "cost basis" and "reserve for depreciation," are printed here. C\$ is assigned to a word in the display, here "CLASS".

3530–   Except for *manufacturing* bypass from 3460, *manufacturing initial fixed*
3550   *assets* are displayed first with K=18 from 3480. The same assignments (3490 to 3530) are used again for *general initial fixed assets* with a new title and K=28 (3550). Branch away from initial fixed assets displays after *general fixed assets* check of K=28 on line 3530.

INITIAL CONDITIONS CHECK

3700   This routine is reached twice. First, it appears at the end of SEQUENTIAL DISPLAYS inputs of *initial condition* (from 3680). Second, it is the first stop after a RUN decision for further processing (3140). Sums of initial *assets* and *liabilities*, S1 and S2, are preset to 0. The number of initial assets added together depends upon the frame N(5) branching. For environment only (N(5)=3), bypass to end of inputs.

3710   For *manufacturing* frame (N(5)=2), 5 classes of initial fixed assets at cost less reserves are aggregated (inputs from 3480).

3720   For *manufacturing*, 3 initial inventories are aggregated (input from 3400).

3730   For *trade* and *manufacturing* (N(5)=1 or 2), one additional initial inventory N(16) is added in (input at 3390).

3740–   Add all remaining initial assets. This includes 5 classes of *general* initial fixed
3750   assets at cost less reserves (N(5)=0 to 2).

3760–   Add all initial liabilities into S2 and initial owners' equity items into S3.
3770   Round S1, S2, and S3 to the nearest integer.

3780   Two line spaces are added for PRINT all inputs Z4=10. The *initial condition summary* (3800 to 3840) is included for Z4=10.

3790   For other menu items (Z4<10) home *cursor* and preset input V$ to a blank. Except for SEQUENTIAL DISPLAYS (Z2=2), or Z4=10 from 3780, *initial condition summary* will not be printed.

3800–   Display *initial condition summary* on video screen. Initial assets must balance initial equities within $1 to proceed with processing. If this condition is not met, branch to *unbalance* routine starting at 3880.

3870   Otherwise, branch starts for initial balance satisfied. If Z2 is RUN from menu, branch to 5800 for continued processing. For Z4=10, PRINT all inputs, return to pick up next input division at 2850. For Z2=2 (initial conditions input division), branch to 3910 for further processing of displays.

3880–   Start *initial conditions unbalance* branch. PRINT amount of unbalance
3900   S1-S2-S3. For Z4=10 pick up next input division at 2850. Otherwise sound *error bell* HEX(07) and proceed to further processing.

3910–   Processing of *initial conditions display* starts here. The display may start with *initial conditions summary* if routed from Z2=2 at 3870. *Unbalance* will be displayed, if it was encountered (3880), except Z4=10 (see 3890).

        If V$ not "P," branch to display choice at 3920. If V$ were "P" for line printer, SELECT video screen, redisplay initial conditions on video screen by return to 3790.

3920–   Otherwise display input choice V$. If V$ remains a blank (command EXE-
3930   CUTE), return to menu at 2850. Otherwise, V$ = "P" to record *initial conditions* on line printer. Branch to SUB 6830 printer ON warning and SELECT line printer. Return to 3800 for PRINT *initial conditions* on *line printer*.

POLREM PRINT OPTION

POLREMS will be presented as separate displays if Z=1; otherwise POLREM routines are bypassed. POLREMS are never printed with complete input sets under Z4=10 menu item (Z=0 at 3020). POLREM displays are located at the beginning of Input Divisions 3 (line 3950), 5 (line 4700), and 6 (line 5250). POLREMS are located after the first two dynamic sets, for N(5)=2 *manufacturing*, in Input Division 4 (line 4330). The above line numbers branch past POLREMS if Z=0.

After POLREMS have been displayed, there are *line printer* and *continue* input displays options in SUB 6750.

SEQUENTIAL INPUT DISPLAYS VALUE ASSIGNMENT (CONTINUED)

4150   Title S$ is assigned to C$(2) whenever an uncertainty component is available to a *dynamic input set* (prefix * in title).

If *dollars per period* option is chosen for *sales demand* with P(21)=1 input, then remaining sets of Input Division 3 are inapplicable; return to *menu* for next input choice.

4190–
4230   There are two displays of *seasonal/cyclical indexes*, with 12 inputs in each. The first (K=50) is always displayed unless P(21)=0 (4150). Q is a parameter of index number change between the two displays. The numbers in (C) are *indexes* 1 to 12 for the *first* display, and 13 to 24 for the *second* display.

4240   If the previous display (4210 to 4230) were the *second* with K=62, then Input Division 3 ends; return to *menu*. Otherwise, if last index N(62) of *first* display were 0, *second* display is inapplicable, and also return to *menu*.

4250–
4260   Otherwise, set K and Q parameters for *second* set of *seasonal/cyclical indexes*. Return to 4210 for remaining value assignments for *second* display.

4320   *Dynamic input sets* of Division 4 end here for *trade* frame N(5)=1. Under such condition return to menu at 2850. Otherwise, continue with *manufacturing* inputs.

4620   SUB '2 counts *manufacturing fixed asset classes* and controls SUB 6670. SUB '2 assigns display parameters for asset net changes *dynamic input sets*. The same SUB '2 is used for *general fixed asset classes* (5150). SUB '2 again controls SUB 6670.

4890   Inputs to the *second* (K=339) R & D *dynamic input set* (% of sales or $ per period) depend upon the choice in Q(1) or C$(1) made for the first R & D dynamic set at 4860 (K=329). P is preset at 4 for *% of sales*. If Q(1)=0 this stands; otherwise reset P to 5 for *$ per period*.

5150   See SUB '2 note at 4620.

INDIVIDUAL INTERACTIVE INPUT ID SELECTION

5600–
5620   Reset display titles to blanks, since they are often omitted. Preset ID number A1 to 0. Home *cursor*. INPUT ID under A1. Entry of A1=0, or EXECUTE to retain A1=0, is flag to terminate INDIVIDUAL IDs. In such cash branch back to *menu* to 2850.

5630–
5660   The remainder of INDIVIDUAL ID logic is concerned with location of display parameter set for INPUT ID, and branch to error message routine (5680 and 5690) for invalid ID entries.

On 5630 to 5660 the branches of displays for *system parameter* inputs are located. Lines for *dynamic input* displays are 5700 to 5780.

IDs above 579 (5630) are *invalid*; branch to *error message*. IDs above 99 are *dynamic input sets*; branch to locate these displays at 5700 to 5780.

Remaining statements move progressively through IDs 1 to 98, and branch to line with display parameters for A1 ID INPUT. If a display is not found the ID INPUT is invalid; proceed to *error message*.

5680–
5690

This is invalid ID *error routine*. Sound error bell HEX(07). Reset ID number A1 to 0. PRINT *error message*. INPUT new ID number under A1. Return to locate display for ID (5620).

5700–
5780

Locate display for *dynamic input sets*. An integer index U (range 1 to 48) is assigned to each *dynamic set* of 10 IDs which contains the INPUT ID A1. Single and multiple branch statements are used to locate the display parameter line number for each value of U.

Fixed asset net changes are processed for *manufacturing* (U=19 to 23 on line 5730), and for *general* (U=39 to 43 or line 5770). Parameter S+1=1 to 5 is the *fixed asset class number*. Parameter Q is 0 for *manufacturing* and 10 for *general*. Fixed asset display parameters are processed in SUB 6670.

Invalid ID numbers within *dynamic input sets* are not identified here. Instead they are detected in SUB '1, which in such case will return control to 5680.

WRITE FINAL SET OF INPUTS TO INPUT DATA FILES

5800

Count fixed asset classes in SUB '2(Q): first for *manufacturing* with Q=0, and then for *general* with Q=10. This is a final count of fixed asset classes after all inputs have been completed.

5810

At this point all keyboard inputs and input changes have been completed. Branch for Z1 set of 5 values, 0 to 4 (see 2590). If Z1=0 or 4 for no *input data file*, branch to further processing at 5890.

5820–
5830

Start branch for *old* input file, Z1=1 or 2. PRINT *old* file name. If not *old and new* for Z1=2, INPUT *old* file choice in Z3. For Z3=0, *old* file remains the SAME, branch to further processing at 5890.

5840

Otherwise reset pointer to beginning of *old* file and branch to WRITE inputs to file at 5880.

5850

Start *old and new* file branch from 5820 with INPUT *old* file choice Z3. For Z3=1 to RETAIN *old* file, there is no more processing of *old* file; branch to opening *new* file at 5870.

5860

Otherwise SCRATCH *old* file and *recatalog* it under *new* file name Z$. Branch to WRITE inputs to *new* file at 5880.

5870

Branch to catalog *new* file starts here. Catalog *new* file under name Z$. This branch is reached from Z1=3 at 5810 or Z1=2 and Z3=1 at 5850.

5880

SAVE complete input set in *input data file* (*old* from 5840, *new* name for *old* file from 5860, or new file from 5870). Set end-of-file marker.

5890   Continue RUN unless Z2 *menu* choice is 9. In the latter case END. Note that *input data files* have been serviced prior to an END processing with PAVE1 inputs (Z2=9).

WRITE TO TRANSFER FILE FOR NEXT CHAINED PROGRAM PAVE2

5900–
5920   If *input data files* or *input data programs* are on a separate minidiskette from *data transfer files* among programs, disks must be changed in *left port* at this point. A message is displayed and a user INPUT required. The sequence is bypassed for no *input data file* nor *program* (Z1=0). Otherwise, INPUT V\$ is preset to a blank, and command EXECUTE will resume processing. This provides a user-controlled pause to change minidiskettes. If no *mini-diskette* change is required, supply EXECUTE to resume processing.

5940–
5950   OPEN "PAVEFT1" *data transfer file* for inputs to PAVE2 (this file must have been previously cataloged). WRITE complete input set to file. Set end-of-file marker. CLOSE file. CHAIN next program PAVE2. All statements and variable addresses of PAVE1 have now been deleted from the work space. PAVE2 statements are in the work space. PAVE2 will start to run and READ input data from PAVEFT1.

SUB '1–INPUT DISPLAY AND USER ENTRY CONTROL

This SUB is used to process displays for both SEQUENTIAL DISPLAYS and INDIVIDUAL INTERACTIVE input modes.

5970   The following parameters are transferred:

    K links IDs to display lines (see preamble to 3140 and Table 14.10).
    P controls display SUB and prefix of printing (see preamble to 3140).

Parameters A and B, beginning and ending line numbers of IDs in displays, are transferred in for *system parameter displays*; they are determined internally for *dynamic input sets*.

Preset Y to 0; Y determines whether ID in C\$(2) position will be skipped during indexing as a blank. For *system parameter* displays (P less than 3), branch to 6030.

Dynamic set display control starts here and ends at 6060. Preset A to 1, and B will always be 10.

5980   If C\$(2) is blank, A must be increased one line and Y is set to 1.

5990   If C\$(1) is blank, A must be increased one line and Y is reset to 0.

    The following values now hold:
    C\$(1) and C\$(2) neither used (both blank):
      A=3, Y=0
    C\$(1) used, C\$(2) blank: A=2, Y=1. This is the only case where a line
      must be skiped *between* adjacent IDs.
    C\$(1) blank, C\$(2) used: A=2, Y=0
    C\$(1) and C\$(2) both used: A=1, Y=0

6000–   Branch to 6020 for transfer Q( ) inputs into L( ) if K is 329 or greater. Other-
6020   wise P( ) inputs are transferred into L( ). Note P( ) and Q( ) are the input
        arrays for *dynamic input sets*. The local array L( ) is for printing and trans-
        ferring dynamic set values within displays.

6030   The initial display line number location for input is given by C. Parameter
        C is preset to A for *menu* items 1 to 6 (SEQUENTIAL DISPLAYS). In such
        case branch to next routine at 6060. Otherwise C must be reset and checked
        for INDIVIDUAL INTERACTIVE ID input mode. First set C line number
        in display to line position for A1 input ID. If C is three or more, all ID
        numbers are valid, branch to final check at 6050. Otherwise add Y to C. Y
        is 1 only if C$(2) is blank, or C=2 is invalid ID. Now C will be 3 only if
        C$(2) were blank and C$(1) valid.

6040   If C is less than 3 proceed to final check. Otherwise the C$(2) invalid condi-
        tion from 6030 above holds. Reduce C to 1.

6050   If C is not less than A the input A1 ID is valid. Otherwise, branch to *error
        routine* for invalid IDs at 5680 under INDIV. INTERACT. mode.

        Note detection procedure for invalid IDs from 6030 to 6050:

           C$(1), C$(2) blank; A=3, Y=0; input C=1 or 2 fails test at 6050
           C$(1) blank; A=2; Y=0; input C=1 fails test on 6050; C=2 passes test
           C$(2) blank; A=2; Y=1; input C to C+1 on 6030.
             If input C=1, then passes test in 6050. If input C=2 so C+1=3 on 6030,
             then recompute C−2=1 on line 6040, and fails test on 6050.
             Neither C$(1) nor C$(2) blank; A=1; Y=0; input C=1 or 2 passes test
             on 6050.

6060   If PRINT all inputs Z4=10, line space and bypass assignment of markers to
        input ID.

        Lines 6070 to 6090 are concerned with location and marking on ID line in
        a display. Prior to printing display, assign "X" to input ID line marker array
        X$( ). For all other lines except active ID, X$( ) is a blank. The line for the
        marker is given by index I1, whereas I is the sequential index of input IDs
        from initial value C. Values of I, along with K, are given for all IDs in Table
        14.10. When a given display is first printed the marker is set at C from 6030.

6070–   Preset index I to C for first input ID of display (top item for I1 is set equal
6080   to I). This equality stands unless, for second line (I=2), C$(2) were blank
        and C$(1) were a valid ID. In such case Y=1 and I1 is reduced to 1. This
        means that the first ID will appear on the top subtitle C$(1) position, and
        the second (blank) C$(2) position will be skipped, while cycling ID inputs
        through displays. Line 6070 is the return point for an ID on the first line
        of a display; line 6080 is the return point for redisplay with next I index.

6090   Assign to A1 the input ID from position I1 and parameter K. Replace blank
        by "X" in X$( ) at I1 line position. Preset input variable V$ to a blank. This

is the return point for repeating a display input for an input error or *line printer* option.

6100   For dynamic input sets, P=3, 4, 5, see preamble of 3140. Branch to one of three SUBs to PRINT display. Upon RETURN skip additional printing and cycling for inputs if Z4=10 for PRINT all inputs.

6110–   Reset X$(I1) to blank for next display. If V$ INPUT were "P" for *line*
6120   *printer*, then SELECT video screen and return to beginning of *display control*.

6130–   Display information at bottom of video screen for user input to V$, either
6150   *value* of ID in A1 (6090), or *symbol*. V$ remains blank for user EXECUTE without an input. In such case branch to cycle next ID at 6260.

6160   If V$="P" branch to SUB 6830 for line printer ON warning and SELECT *line printer*. Branch to 6100 to print display on *line printer*. Note close of line printer routine under 6110 to 6120 above.

6170–   If V$="/" and Z2=SEQUENTIAL input divisions 1 to 6, RETURN for next
6180   display. If Z2=7 for INDIV. INTERACT., RETURN for next ID.

6190   If V$="//" return to *menu* at 2850 for new input division choice.

6200–   If V$="*" for back up ID one line, and line index I is not on top line (I
6210   exceeds A), reduce I line index by one, or back up a line. Return to video display control at 6080. Otherwise (I=A on top line), reset I=B to bottom line and return to 6080.

6220   At this point processing is complete for all valid nonnumerical symbols in V$. These are EXECUTE with V$ blank, P, /, //, and *. The only other valid V$ entry is a *numerical value* for the ID in A1. NUM function checks for at least 9 numerical symbols, including trailing blanks. Otherwise there is an input error. Sound *error bell* HEX(07) and return to *repeat* input display at 6090.

6230–   If V$ consists of valid numerical characters, CONVERT to numerical vari-
6250   able V. Assign V to value of ID in N(A1) for *system parameters* (P=1 or 2) or L(I1) for *dynamic sets* (P exceeds 2). *Dynamic set* inputs are also assigned to appropriate P( ) or Q( ) input array elements with K value as switch between.

6260   Line of display update for input ID starts here. Reset C to A, the starting line number position for ID inputs. This is necessary if original C were set to some ID from INDIV. INTERACT. input mode. Add one to I for new ID line position. If I exceeds the bottom ID line number in B, branch to reset top ID line at 6070 before repeating display. Otherwise, return to beginning of loop to process next I at 6080.

6270   Reset parameters unused on some displays to blanks. SUB '1 ends.

SUBS TO PRINT DISPLAYS

There are three: *System parameters nonindexed* at 6290, *system parameters indexed* (*initial fixed assets* and *seasonal/cyclical indexes*) at 6370, and *dynamic input sets* at 6430.

6290–
6300

Start *system parameter* nonindexed display PRINT. Home *cursor*. PRINT title A$. If first ID is on top subtitle line (A=1), bypass extended title. Otherwise, loop through subtitle lines in B$( ) not associated with input IDs.

6310–
6320

Start ID PRINT and INPUT lines (from A to B). PRINT left-hand X$( ) marker, ID number J+K, subtitle of input in B$( ), value of ID in N(J+K), and right-hand X$( ) marker. Markers X$( )will be blank except on line for input, where Xs will be printed.

6330–
6350

SUB ends if B=12, which is the bottom line. Otherwise, loop through subtitle lines in B$( ) not associated with input IDs. SUB 6290 ends.

6370

Start *system parameter* indexed display PRINT. Home cursor. PRINT title A$. If first ID is on top subtitle line (A=1), bypass a line space.

6380–
6410

PRINT lines for IDs from A to B. Print left X$( ) marker, ID number J+K, C$ subtitle, index number C( ), remainder of subtitle in B$( ), value of ID in N(J+K), and right X$( ) marker. Line space if B is not bottom subtitle line 12. Note either 10 or 12 ID lines are used on this SUB. Thus there are either 2 line spaces or none. SUB 6370 ends.

6430

Start *dynamic input sets* display PRINT. Home *cursor*. X is index of prefix G$(6)="%" and G$(7)="$". Preset X to 6 for P=4, or 7 for P=5. This stands unless P=3. If P=3 then prefix depends on inputs 0 or 1 in position L(1).

6440

Set input amount prefixes in D$( ) to G$(X). Bypass top ID line if C$(1) is blank.

6450

Otherwise print top ID line; left X$( ) marker, ID number K+J, ID subtitle in C$( ), class number (often blank) in F$ (see 6720), value of ID in L( ), and right X$( ) marker. There is always one line space after nonempty top ID line.

6460

Print title A$ of dynamic input set. Sometimes F$ is not blank for a class number. The title sometimes has a nonblank trailing phrase in H$ (see 6720). If C$(2) is blank, branch to main ID loop.

6470

Otherwise print second ID line (same item plan as 6450 except that F$ is never used).

6480–
6530

PRINT ID lines from 3 to 10 (always used). These have the same item plan as 6470. SUB 6430 ends after this loop. On 6490, for Z=10 for PRINT all inputs only, and for the fifth line only, if L(5) is less than one, or greater that or equal to the number of periods simulated, the remainder of the IDs are bypassed and *not* printed. If L(5) meets above conditions, further inputs to the *dynamic set* are inoperative (see section 11.1). This bypass usually reduces the length of all inputs PRINT by a substantial amount.

SUB '2–COUNT FIXED ASSET CLASSES AND DISPLAY CONTROL

SUB '2 is used to count *fixed asset* classes twice. The first count occurs when *fixed asset net changes* displays are called, in which case SUB '2 (6560) transfers control to SUB 6670 for display titles and parameters. The second count occurs at the end of inputs. *Manufacturing* and *general* fixed asset classes are processed in the same SUBs, but with different IDs.

The following is a summary of count conditions for *fixed asset* classes:

1. The counter S is the sum of fixed asset classes which are nonzero in *initial condition* plus additional classes (if any) which have nonzero inputs for *fixed asset net changes dynamic sets*.
2. Under SEQUENTIAL DISPLAYS input mode, one more *net changes* display under S+1 will be presented than the current count from above. The first nonentry in a *net changes* display will end the input sets and the class count.
3. Under INDIV. INTERACT. input mode, users may call up any valid ID in any fixed asset class. Parameter S is initialized at 0 and displays are presented under S+1 class input count.

6550   Start SUB '2(Q) where Q=0 for *manufacturing* and Q=10 for *general* fixed asset classes. Number of fixed asset classes equals S+1 for calling up *displays*, but S for final count. Preset S=0 for first class display. Maximum classes are 5 with S=4 on display input and S=5 for final count of classes. Then S=5 is a signal to branch away from count.

6560   Lines 6560 to 6580 count fixed asset classes with *initial condition* nonzero. If S=5, branch to final count in N(49) for *manufacturing* or N(50) for *general* at 6650. Parameter Q determines which N( ) element is updated. If Z4 exceeds 7, inputs are complete, hence bypass display control to next line 6570. Otherwise, branch to SUB 6670 for *fixed asset net changes* display control in class S+1.

6570   If initial condition of fixed assets were 0 in class of N( ), branch to next check on current inputs to this class starting at 6590. Otherwise, for Z4 menu choice *less* than 10 to PRINT all inputs, branch to counter and recycle loop for next class. If Z4=10, PRINT the display for fixed asset class by branching to parameter control in SUB 6670.

6580   Add one to counter S. Recycle for next class. Note cycle of counts and display calls in 6560 to 6580 continues until an *initial condition* of an asset class is zero. The count of fixed assets with nonzero initial condition is now in S. For SEQUENTIAL inputs there is a display call even if initial condition is zero. For Z4=10 PRINT all inputs, there is a display only for nonzero initial condition in this section (see also 6620).

6590   Lines 6590 to 6640 determine number of fixed asset classes, in addition to those in 6560 to 6580 for nonzero *initial condition*, which contains nonzero entries in *fixed asset net changes*. Check ID line positions 3 to 5 for nonzero inputs. If all these positions have 0 inputs, nonzero inputs in further IDs will be inapplicable. Complete loop and branch to 6650 for final count.

6600   If any of above positions are nonzero in P( ) or Q( ), with array separation determined by passed parameter Q, then branch out of ID loop to cycle through next class (6620).

6610   Otherwise complete loop. If no nonzero inputs, branch to 6650 for final asset count.

6620   Given nonzero inputs in 6600 complete loop (I=5). Except with Z4=10 for PRINT all inputs, go to 6630 to continue fixed asset class cycle. Otherwise, PRINT display in SUB 6670 for Z4=10.

6630   Add one to fixed asset classes. If S has reached 5, branch to final count at 6650. If Z4 exceeds 7 do not PRINT display, hence bypass to next line 6640. Otherwise branch to SUB 6670 for *fixed asset net changes* display for class S+1. Unless S+1 reaches 5, one more display is printed for SEQUEN-TIAL input than for Z=10 PRINT all inputs (compare 6580).

6640   Return to 6590 to check *fixed asset net changes* in next class.

6650   Record final fixed asset classes count in N(49) for *manufacturing* or N(50) for *general*.

SUB–FIXED ASSET ADDITIONS INPUT DISPLAY

6670   SUB for display titles and parameters of *fixed asset net changes* starts. If Q=10 branch to second title in A$; otherwise, assign *manufacturing* title to A$.

6680–
6690   Assign *manufacturing* depreciation subtitle to C$(1). Branch to display processing at 6720.

6700–
6710   Repeat title A$ and subtitle C$(1) assignments as in 6670 to 6680. Here subtitles apply to *general* classes of fixed asset.

6720   Assign class number S+1 to F$ and title trailing phrase to H$.

6730   Assign parameters K and P to SUB '1 (Q and S determine the value of K). SUB 6670 ends.

SUBS–POLREM PRINT: LINE PRINTER CONTROL AND 'ON' WARNING

6750–
6760   SUB for *policy reminder statement* (POLREM) PRINT control starts. If V$ input control were "P" for *line printer*, then reselect video screen, reset V$ to a blank, and branch to restore video screen display at 6810.

6770–
6780   Otherwise reset V$ to a blank and PRINT options for INPUT in V$. These options follow video display of POLREMS, which appear in order among SEQUENTIAL DISPLAY parameter assignments (ranging from 3960 to 5290).

6790 If V$="//" return to next *menu* choice at 2850.

6800 If V$="P" branch to SUB 6830 line printer ON warning and SELECT *line printer*.

6810 To restore video display after *line printer* from 6760, or after SELECT *line printer* from 6800, return to multiple branching statement of Z2 at 3140. This will PRINT POLREMS again (either on *line printer* or restored to video screen per previous statements). This occurs because POLREMS appear at the beginning of input divisions. The exception is Z2=4 input division, where POLREMS start at 4330.

6820 EXECUTE command, without an input from 6780 in V$, branches control to 6820. Then SUB 6750 for POLREM print control ends and the next input display set will be printed. POLREMS will not be displayed under *menu* Z2=7 INDIV. INTERACT. because POLREM line numbers will never be selected. POLREMS will not be displayed under Z4=10 for PRINT all inputs because here Z=0 (3020). SUB 6750 ends.

6830– SUB for *line printer* ON warning on video screen, and SELECT *line printer*,
6850 starts. PRINT warning on video display. SELECT *line printer*. Line space twice. SUB 6830 ends. PAVE1 ends.

14.3 | PAVE2 Documentation

INITIALIZE SYSTEM AND DETERMINE INFLATION FACTORS

PAVE2 is used to process values over periods without uncertainty inputs, and to preprocess values with uncertainty.

30– SELECT video screen; home *cursor*. PRINT program title. DIMENSION
90 arrays and alpha variables. OPEN PAVEFT1 *data transfer file* from PAVE1, and READ input set into N( ) for *system parameters*, and into P( ) and Q( ) for *dynamic sets*. Transfer much used system control N( ) parameters to scalar variables. N2 is a period growth compounding factor, the reciprocal of number of periods N. Initialize H(1) and H(10) to 0 (see 1160).

100 SUB '1 *converts* input system for *dynamic sets* to values for each period at 1160. Parameter Z is 1 for *manufacturing* or *environment* sets from P( ), or Z is 0 for *general* or *financial* sets from Q( ). Parameter X is 0 for *percentage of sales* inputs, or X is 1 for *period inputs* subject to inflation adjustment.

The passed parameters into SUB '1 are:

F = Index of first element of P( ) or Q( ) for *dynamic sets*.

E = Index of output arrays: 1 for A( ) and 2 for D( )

A(K,I) is for flow accounts to be processed in PAVE3—these have uncertainty-adjusted, nonconstant values or are totals. Account number is K, and period number is I=1 to M.

D(K,I) is for nonrandom flow accounts. In contrast to A( ), these are transferred directly to PAVE5 for FINANCIAL STATEMENT outputs, or are not processed in PAVE3. D(3,I) is first used as an *inflation adjustment* factor for period amount items in PAVE2 (120). When this adjustment process is complete, D(3,I) receives *industry growth compared to economy* at 360, and finally *industry total growth* at 460.

D(4,I) is first used in *every* call of SUB '1 to collect values for each period. When the SUB '1 processing is complete, D(4,I) is reassigned to *seasonal/cyclical indexes* at 430.

D(6,I) to D(10,I) are *general fixed asset net changes* (5 classes). Results are first transferred into B( ) (see 1400). *Net changes* are summed into A(14,I); then the above D( ) elements are reused for *expense accounts*.

D(11,I) to D(15,I) follow the same pattern as D(6,I) to D(10,I), but for *manufacturing fixed asset net additions*. The sum is applied to A(28,I), and D( ) elements are reused.

L = index of A( ) or D( ) *output* arrays.

R = index of final adjustment of period values (see 1280).

Table 14.11 organizes the indices of all arrays processed in PAVE2. Dynamic input set IDs and descriptions are related to A( ), B( ) and D( ) in PAVE2. Transfers of these arrays to other PAVE processing programs are shown in Table 14.11.

At 100 determine *real growth* D(1,I) and *inflation* D(2,I) percentages for each period in SUB '1. These inputs may be used with all frames (N5). In this section auxiliary parameters Z=1 and X=0.

120	Preset *inflation adjustment factors* (IAFs) in D(3,I) for all periods to one. If P(11) input is 0 for no adjustment; above values stand.
130–140	Otherwise compute factor in W for period, using input inflation percentage D(2,I). The IAFs are *cumulative* over periods on an annually compounded basis. The exponent N2 adjusts for compounding over periods not one year in length. Accumulation takes place from successive products Z*W. Parameter Z is used here to store prior period factor; D(3,I) is the final IAF for Period I.

CONVERT DYNAMIC INPUT SETS TO VALUES FOR ALL PERIODS

160	For N5 is 3 for *environment only*, bypass *manufacturing* and *general* input sets. Note *real growth* and *inflation* has already been *determined* (see 100).

Reset Z to 0 for *general* and *financial* inputs.

Fixed asset net changes are processed in SUB '2 at 1370, which SUB in turn calls SUB '1. Parameter Z separates P( ) and Q( ) inputs (see 100). The parameters passed to SUB '2 are:

A = Index of Class 1 first element of P( ) or Q( ) input set, *less ten* (compare F in SUB '1 at 100).

B = Index of Class 1 output array D( ) *less one* for net changes each period.

C = Index of Class 1 output array B( ) *less one* for fixed assets at cost.

D = Index of A( ) for *total* net fixed asset changes

Y = Index of B( ) for *total* net fixed assets at *book* value.

B(K, I+1) is array for *condition* accounts. Account number is K. Beginning-of-period (BOP) number is I=1 to M, whereas end-of-period (EOP) number is I+1=2 to M+1. Maximum second dimension is 25.

For a description of arrays B( ), A( ) and D( ), see Table 14.11. When X is determined by input choices, its value is injected ahead of the *dynamic set* to which it applies (see 100). This call of SUB '2 is for *general* fixed assets.

170–   Process all *dynamic input sets* for *general* (nonmanufacturing) values each
250   period in SUB '1. Nonentered sets will yield zero outputs for all periods.

270   Reset Z to 1 for *manufacturing* and *trade* accounts. Bypass manufacturing accounts to *sales demand* (350) under *service* frame N5=0.

        Process *manufacturing* fixed assets in SUB '2

280–   Process all *dynamic input sets* for *manufacturing* and *trade* in SUB '1. Six
330   of these are processed in a K loop. There are no *trade* accounts beyond the K loop hence bypass SUB '1 *manufacturing* input processing if N5 is 1 (300) for *trade*.

350   Start processing *net sales demand available* in SUB '1 for all frames (values of N5). Here X is determined by input choice P(21). If X=1 for *direct sales $ per period*, the remaining *environmental* accounts are inapplicable, hence bypass to 510.

360   Otherwise process *industry growth compared to economy* in SUB '1. This is the second use of output array D(3,I) (cf. 120).

SEASONAL/CYCLICAL INDEX SET

370   Continue *environmental* analysis with *seasonal/cyclical* index set processing in 370 to 430. If N(51) is 0 there is no seasonal adjustment; reset parameters to 1 and bypass to 410 the processing of 380 to 400.

380–   *Sum* of indices and *count* of nonzero indices is at lines 380 to 400. The
390   index *counter* Z is preset to 24 maximum and the *sum* Z1 to 0 minimum. Loop through 24 indices. Branch to cumulation sum at 400 as long as input N( ) exceeds 0.

        Otherwise the processing stops at 390. Reset final count in Z to number of nonzero N( ) values and branch to further index processing.

400   Accumulate sum of indexes in Z1. Index summation and counting loop ends.

410   *Mean* of index set is A1/Z. The nonzero *normalized* (mean of 1) index set is repeated over all periods, hence the STEP Z loop.

420   For each STEP in loop, check each index for exceeding the total number of periods M, or I+J greater than M+2. If this occurs, terminate loops and index processing.

430   Otherwise, store *normalized* index in D(4,I). Prior use of D(4,I) in SUB '1 has been previously completed. Normalization (mean of indexes is 1) is computed from division of each positive input index from N( ) by the mean Z1.

INDUSTRY GROWTH, SALES DEMAND, AND DESEASONALIZATION

450   Store *industry base sales*, factored to one period duration, in Z.

       Store input *deasonalization* percentage N(51), as a decimal, in P.

       Initialize Q, now an *inventory class discriminator*, to 0.

       Loop through all periods.

460   Compute *industry total growth rate* in D(3,I). Prior uses of D(3,I) as IAFs from 120 and *industry growth compared to economy* from 360, have at this point been completed.

       Total industry growth (annual) is the compound of three annual component growths:

> Total growth D(3,I) = (1 + Real economic growth D(1,I))
>   x (1 + Inflation growth D(2,I))
>   x (1 + Industry to economy comparison growth D(3,I)) – 1

470   Industry sales before seasonal adjustment *each period* in Z are compounded from prior period sales Z and *annual* sales growth in D(3,I). Exponent N2 is a compounding factor for period durations not one year.

       Seasonal/cyclical index D(4,I) is assigned to W.

       Industry sales—before randomization in PAVE3—are assigned to A(2,I). This value is the product of Z and seasonal factor W.

       A *deseasonalization* factor Z1 is preset as a negative compliment to W.

480–
490   *Deseasonalization* input P operates on *two* inventory input factors:

> A(21,I) Finished goods
> A(23,I) Goods-in-process

These inventory factors will be applied to extrapolated annual sales per policy inputs. Without further adjustment, therefore, inventory levels will shift with both industry growth in D(3,I) and seasonal/cyclical indexes in D(4,I).

Three types of *deseasonalization* effects are available from P:

If P>0, both inventories are simply deseasonalized from division by W at 490.

If P=0, *finished goods* inventory will swing oppositely from sales by some amount to deseasonalize *cost of finished goods*, thus acting to stabilize goods production or purchases (490). For P=1 or N(51)=100

$$A(21,I) = \frac{A(21,I)}{W} - 1 + \frac{1}{W}$$

The full seasonalization factor of sales is now applied to move inventory oppositely from sales. This input of P=1 (N(15)=100) will probably over-compensate, since two inventories (BOP and EOP) determine the demand for goods. Complete compensation will require some trials. Input N(51) around 50 as a most likely starting point.

Since Q=0, goods-in-process factor A(23,I) is simply deseasonalized with P>0, the same as for P=0.

If P<0, inventory exhibits a seasonal pattern in phase with sales. For P=-1 or N(51)=-100, and with reset of P at 480,

$$A(21,I) = \frac{A(21,I)}{W} + A(21,I) - \frac{A(21,I)}{W}$$

and all deseasonalization of inventory has been removed.

The same adjustment applies to A(32,I) from reset of Q at 480.

PREPROCESSING OF ACCOUNT VALUES

A( ) and B( ) accounts for all periods are processed as far as possible in PAVE2 before transfer to PAVE3 or PAVE5. There are two reasons for this: the latter two programs use more work space than PAVE2, and PAVE3 processing must be repeated over a Monte-Carlo sample (except for N3=1).

510   For N5=3 for *environment* only, further processing is not required, branch to WRITE outputs. *Initial intangibles* are transferred to B(4,1) and are also added to *total general fixed assets* in B(3,1). Tangible fixed assets have been summed into B(3,1) in SUB '2 (1380).

520   Intangibles amortization N(84) is factored to a *period* basis with N2. *Long-term obligations* and *paid-in owner equity* are preset to initial condition values in Z1 and Z. Initial *manufacturing supplies* are stored in B(1,1).

530   An I loop is used to compute or check for all periods several values which are not subject to uncertain inputs. Such values may be processed in PAVE2 instead of PAVE3.

Period amortization D(11,I) is preset to input N(84). Then
> Intangibles EOP B(4,I+1) = Intangibles BOP B(4,I)
> - Amortization N(84)

Additional *organization expense for the first period only* N(83) is also added in. This is reset to 0 before the end of Period 1 loop (560).

540   If *intangibles* EOP exceeds 0, above computation stands. Otherwise reset EOP to 0 and recompute D(11,I) to amortize all remaining *intangibles* for that period (including N(83) if nonzero).

550   *Amortization* D(11,I) is added to *total depreciation and amortization* in A(16,I). *First period organization expense* N(83) is added to *total net asset changes* in A(14,I).

560   For each period *intangibles EOP* B(4,I+1) are added to *total fixed assets at book EOP* B(3,I+1). Compare this total to initial conditions (510). Reset N(83) to 0 since its use in first-period loop is complete (see 530).

570   Adjust two interest rates to a period basis.

590   Certain summations, which do not have uncertainty components, if performed here, reduce array and computation requirements in PAVE3. Array A(8,I) is the sum of indirect sales and general administrative payrolls. Array A(12,I) is the sum of nonrandom period general expense, including indirect advertising.

600–   The cummulative amounts over periods of *long-term obligations* in Z1 and
610   *paid-in owner capital* in Z cannot be permitted to go negative. These amounts were initialized in 520.

If *planned changes* in A(18,I) maintain Z1 in excess of 0, continue. Otherwise recompute A(18,I) for 0 value of Z1. Reset Z1 to 0. The same procedure is used for Z. If planned changes in A(33,I) maintain Z positive, continue processing. Otherwise, recompute A(33,I) for 0 value of Z, and reset Z to 0.

630   A triple branch separates routines for *service* at 690, *service and trade* at 700, and three frames (including *manufacturing* but not *environment* only) at 640.

640–   EOP inventory level of *indirect manufacturing supplies* B(1,I+1) equals in-
660   put factor P(121) times supplies usage in A(22,I). Factor N supplies annual basis. Initial inventory value was established at 520.

Supplies purchases D(12,I) = EOP inventory level
> + usage A(22,I) - BOP inventory level

If purchases exceed 0, the formula stands, otherwise reset purchases D(12,I) to 0 and recompute EOP inventory level B( ) at 660. This is a default for the B( ) computation on 640.

670   Add *indirect supplies* purchases D( ) to total *manufacturing net asset changes* in A(28,I). Sum nonrandom *period manufacturing expense* into A(26,I).

680   All accounts are used for *manufacturing* frame, bypass reset to 0 at 690 and 700.

690   *Finished goods* or *material purchases*, and *finished goods inventories*, are reset to 0 for *service* (N5=1 at 630); they are used only for *manufacturing* or *trade*.

700–   Reset *manufacturing* accounts to 0 for *service* or *trade* firms (branch from
710   630). End preprocessing loop over periods.

ADJUST AND WRITE OUTPUTS TO TRANSFER FILES

730–   Open PAVEFT5 for transfer of parameters and STATEMENTS OF CONDI-
740   TION values B( ) to PAVE6. All transfer PAVEFT series files must have been previously cataloged. WRITE values to PAVEFT5. Set end-of-file marker.

750   In the VALUATION output division of PAVE4, quantities are aggregated over the *first* and *final* years of simulation. Three parameters to control this process are developed here:

H(1) is an interpolation factor in the event number of periods per year N is not an integer. It is used for valuation adjustment in PAVE4. If N is an integer, H(1) will be 1.

N(52) is the *ending* period number of the *first* year. It is used in PAVE3 for aggregation.

N(53) is the *beginning* period number of the *final* year. It is also used in PAVE3 for aggregation.

Preset H(1) to N; N(52) to *first* period, and N(53) to *final* period. These values stand if one-period duration exceeds a year. Then H(1) will reduce one-period values to one-year equivalency. In the above event branch past further changes.

760   Otherwise reset H(1) to duration of run, N(52) to *last* period, and N(53) to *first* period. These values stand if *run* duration does not *exceed* one year; branch past further changes.

770   Otherwise reset H(1) to adjustment factor by which N exceeds its integer value. Then N(52) and N(53) are set to the period numbers, giving the largest integral number of periods not exceeding one-year duration, from the beginning and the end of the simulation. If N were input as an integer, which is the common case, then H(1) is 1, and N(52) and N(53) are merely the numbers of periods which occur at one year, counting *forward* from the *first*, and *backward* from the *final*.

790–   Assign parameters into H( ) for use in PAVE4; OPEN PAVEFT3 for transfer
850   of parameters into PAVE4. Opening of a new file *closes* the previous open file (PAVEFT5 at 730). WRITE *two* records to PAVEFT4, N(6) and the set

of remaining parameters. *Output division* choice N(6) is written separately because it may be subject to new user inputs in PAVE4 or PAVE6. Set end-of-file marker.

870–
1010

New values are transferred into N(K) array, K=1 to S1, from previous N( ), P( ), and Q( ) inputs. Parameters N(52) and N(53) were developed at 750 to 770. Parameters N( ) revised are used for Monte Carlo sample processing in PAVE3.

Consolidate input *initial condition* values into N(1) to N(14) to conform to PAVE *output* CONDITION STATEMENTS accounts.

Reset initial goods inventories in N(15) and N(16) from *cost* to *sales* value levels. This is needed for processing demand for production or purchases in PAVE3.

Reassign remaining parameters to N( ) revised. Factor 0.01 converts percentage inputs to decimals for processing. Factor N2 reduces annual inputs to amounts per period.

1020

REDIMENSION revised N( ) for transfer of values to PAVE3. Only the first three asset accounts of B( ) are required in PAVE3, hence REDIMENSION.

1040–
1050

For sample size N3 of 1, a *deterministic* simulation option without uncertainty inputs, reset 12 *uncertainty* input components to N( ) to 0.

1060–
1070

Open PAVEFT2 for transfer of parameters into PAVE3. WRITE most used control parameters, parameter array N( ), reduced asset accounts in B( ), and flow values of A( ) (see 100 and Table 14.11) into PAVEFT2. Set end-of-file marker.

1090–
1140

Seven flow account inputs developed for all periods in A( ) are not randomized in PAVE3, and thus may be transferred directly to PAVE5. B( ) is redimensioned a second time (see 1020).

Open PAVEFT4 for transfer of parameters and arrays into PAVE5. Write values to PAVEFT4. Set end-of-file marker. CLOSE file. CHAIN next program PAVE3.

SUB '1–DETERMINE VALUES FOR ALL PERIODS FROM DYNAMIC INPUT SETS

1160

Start SUB '1 with the following passed variables:

F = index number of first element of input P( ) or Q( ) dynamic sets. This element is two less than the first dynamic input in the units position −3. (see explanation of *dynamic input sets* in sections 8.2 and 11.1).

E = indicator of *output* array: 1=A( ) array, 2=D( ) array (see also 100).

L = index number of A( ) or D( ) *output* array.

R = indicator of decimal, annual, and inflation adjustments (see also 1280). D(4,I), I=1 to M, is the array used to collect generated values over all periods (see also 100). This is the first use of D(4,I).

Current values of X and Z are also relevant to processing in SUB '1. If X=0, an input is *percent of sales*; otherwise X=1 and the input is *dollars per period*. Z=0 for Q( ) input set and Z=1 for P( ) input set. Start J loop to transfer P( ) and Q( ) inputs to H( ) processing array. H(1) to H(10) set is reused in this SUB '1 to collect *dynamic set inputs*. Elements H(1) and H(10) always remain as 0 benchmark values. The first base value H(2) is transferred from Q(−3), etc.

1170   If Z=0 then Q( ) to H( ) transfer stands. Otherwise, for Z=1, overwrite H( ) with corresponding P( ) values.

1180   End transfer J loop H( ) from Q( ) or P( ). Start main processing loop for inputs. This is a 3-STEP loop for J=1, J=4, and J=7:

   J=1   Always 0, used for initiation of growth values and periods.
   J=2   1st base value.
   J=3   Growth rate of 1st base value.
   J=4   Last period number of 1st base schedule.
   J=5   2nd base value at period H(4)+1; input (−1) is a signal to obtain the new base value from the amount in the period number of H(4), but use a new J=6 growth rate.
   J=6   Growth rate of 2nd base value.
   J=7   Last period number of 2nd base schedule.
   J=8   3rd base value at period H(7)+1; (−1) signal as above applies to amount in period number of H(7).
   J=9   Growth rate of 3rd base value.
   J=10   Always 0, signals last growth schedule to continue to end of simulation (see 1210).

   For STEP 1, J=1 loop, the (−1) signal does not apply; an input (−1) to J=2 will be interpreted as a base value; bypass (−1) processing at 1190.

1190   If 2nd or 3rd bases not equal to (−1) bypass special processing. Otherwise, the 2nd or 3rd base is computed on the preceding value D(4,H(J)), where H(J) is the last period number of preceeding base. Base D( ) is multiplied by the new growth factor compounded amount. The exponent N2 adjusts for compounding over periods not a year in length.

1200–   Start check for *last period number* (J+3) position for end of growth in this
1210   STEP. If H(J+3)>M reset period number to M at 1210. The period number which ends any STEP must be at least one more than the period number which ended the preceding STEP. Otherwise, the new period number is reset to M at 1210. Thus negative or 0 period number inputs will always be reset to M because they can never exceed the preceding period number stored. Note that the initial reference period number is 0, and was stored in H(1) at 90.

1220   Start processing period values within a STEP. If base value in (J+1)=0, branch to no-growth loop at 1260. If growth value in (J+2)=0, also branch to no-growth loop at 1260.

1230   Growth loop processing starts. Assign base value to correct period number of D(4,I) array. If H(J+3) is not at least two periods more than H(J), bypass growth calculations to STEP summary at 1270.

1240   Start loop for growth over periods in current STEP. Loop goes from 2 periods beyond last period of preceding STEP to period at end of this STEP. Assign growing values to D(4,I). Compute compounded annual growth rate using N2 as exponent for period duration. Multiply growth rate by preceding D( ) period value.

1250   End growth loop over periods for STEP; bypass to summary of STEPS at 1270.

1260   Process loop for repeated value assignments to D(4,I) without growth.

1270   STEP summary starts. If last period number is less than M, recycle to next STEP at 1280. Otherwise, reset J index to maximum value, which will end loop at this STEP at 1280.

1280   End loop of up to 3 STEPS. Start loop to process adjustments of period values in D(4,I) array. Branch on value of processing indicator R. Choices of indicator R:

R=1 No adjustments.

R=2 Convert percent to decimal only.

R=3 Convert percent to decimal and annualize rate.

R=4 Provide inflation adjustment factor.

R=5 Either *percent to decimal conversion* or *inflation* adjustment, depending on value of X. This feature is used for *net sales demand*, *R&D expense* and *dividends*.

1290   Start branch for adjustment based on indicator X for R=5. (X=0 for % of *sales or earnings*, and X=1 for *$ per period*). If X=0 branch to *% sales adjustment*; otherwise, continue processing to inflation adjustment.

1300   Start branch R=4 for inflation adjustment to *$ per period*. The input D(4,I) is adjusted with *inflation factor* D(3,I). Branch to end of adjustments at 1330.

1310   Start branch R=3 for combined *annualizing* factor and *decimal conversion*. Value on this line receives annual adjustment.

1320   Start branch R=2 for *decimal conversion*. This receives some values directly (R=2), some from 1310 (R=3), and some from line 1290 (R=5).

1330   Start final processing after adjustments. This line receives values from preceding line (R=2, 3 and 5 (for X=0)), values from 1300 for R=4, and R=5 (for X=1). Control passes directly to this line for R=1. If indicator E=1 for A( ) then branch to 1340; otherwise, D(4,I) is assigned to D(L,I). Go to end of I loop over periods at 1350.

1340   Assign D(4,I) to A(L,I).

1350   Loop I for adjustments over periods ends. SUB '1 ends.

SUB '2—DETERMINE FIXED ASSET BALANCES AND DEPRECIATION

This SUB is used to process 0 to 5 classes of both *manufacturing* and *general* fixed assets and depreciation rates. It is called once during the processing of each of these input divisions.

Initial conditions are transferred from N( ) to B( ) arrays at 1380 and 1390 as follows:

> Classes 1 to 5 *manufacturing* fixed assets at cost from N(20) to N(24), to B(15,1) to B(19,1).
> Classes 1 to 5 *manufacturing* fixed assets reserve for depreciation from N(25) to N(29), to B(20,1) to B(24,1).
> Classes 1 to 5 *general* fixed assets at cost, from N(30) to N(34), to B(5,1) to B(9,1).
> Classes 1 to 5 *general* fixed assets reserve for depreciation, from N(35) to N(39), to B(10,1) to B(14,1).

1370   Passed parameters into SUB '2 are:

> A = Index of *first* class from P( ) *manufacturing* or Q( ) *general* inputs, *less* 10.
> B = Index of *first* class, *less* one, for D( ) *fixed asset net changes* input.
> C = Index of *first* class, *less* one, for B( ) *fixed asset at cost* accounts.
> D = Index of A( ) for *total* net fixed asset changes.
> Y = Index of B( ) for *total* net fixed assets at *book* value.

Parameter Z=0 for *general* classes and Z=1 for *manufacturing* classes applies to SUB '2. Parameter N(49) is the *number* or *manufacturing*, and N(50) the *number* of *general*, fixed asset classes.

Bypass SUB '2 if 0 classes of assets.

1380   Start K loop for number of fixed asset classes. *Initial* fixed assets at cost are transferred into B( ) from *initial* input in N( ) (see preamble). The basic K loop is over classes. After initialization, there is a nested loop over period.

1390   Initial *depreciation reserve* for class in B( ) is transferred from initial input in N( ).

Total initial *net assets* (book value) BOP 1 are accumulated over classes in B(Y,1) as sum of previous classes *plus* initial *cost* of current class less initial *reserve* in that class.

This ends initialization by individual classes and for total initial *book* value.

1400 Obtain *net asset changes* for *each* period with SUB '1 into D( ). Parameter H, from A and class K, establishes index of class from P( ) or Q( ).

Reestablish H as the array elements in P( ) or Q( ) which are depreciation *rates per period*, converted from percents to decimals. Parameter Z is used to switch between P( ) and Q( ).

1410 If H>1 then the routine will cycle endlessly. The default of 1 prevents this for inputs in excess of 100. Such inputs would always be invalid, but might be entered in error.

1420 Start loop over periods (for each class of depreciation and fixed asset changes).

1430 Depreciation Z1 = Depreciation rate transformed to decimals at 1400 x (BOP cost – BOP reserve + ½ of Net asset changes)

1440 Fixed assets at cost EOP = Fixed asset at cost BOP
+ Net fixed asset changes

Fixed assets reserve EOP = Fixed assets reserve BOP
+ Depreciation this period Z1

1450 If *fixed assets at cost EOP* exceeds *reserve EOP* then update of fixed assets is consistent and complete per formulas at 1430 and 1440. Branch to summary total at 1470.

1460 Otherwise user net *fixed asset changes* D( ) is recomputed so that *reserve* does not exceed *cost* of fixed assets. The formulas are as follows:

Asset cost EOP = Reserve EOP = Reserve BOP
+ Depreciation for period

Allowable net change for period = Reserve BOP
– Asset cost BOP + Depreciation

Again:

Depreciation = Depreciation rate
x (Asset cost BOP – Reserve BOP + ½ of Net changes)

Combining the above two formulas:

$$\text{Allowable net change} = \frac{(\text{Depreciation rate} - 1)(\text{Asset cost BOP} - \text{Reserve BOP}}{(1 - .5\ (\text{Depreciation rate}))}$$

With revised *net change* in D( ) return to 1430.

Recompute *depreciation* in Z1, and *fixed assets at cost* and *fixed asset reserves* in B( ).

1470– Compute *total net changes* in A(D,I), *total depreciation* in A(D+2,I), and
1480 *total book value of fixed assets* in B(Y,I+1). These are summed over all classes K for each period. Periods I loop ends, and classes K loop ends.

1490 SUB '2 ends. PAVE2 ends.

14.4 | PAVE3 Documentation

INITIALIZE SYSTEM; START SAMPLE AND PERIOD LOOPS

PAVE3 is used to process Monte Carlo samples over periods where uncertainty inputs will vary the period outputs and totals. Outputs not subject to uncertainty, and preprocessing prior to uncertainty, were developed in PAVE2.

The following are major arrays used for processing in PAVE3:

N( ) for system parameters in PAVE2 (see Table 14.12)
L(K,1) for BOP, and L(K,2) for EOP, processing of *condition* accounts in PAVE2 (see Table 14.13)
F( ) for flow values and accounts during periods (see Table 14.14)
C( ) for cumulative sums of condition values from L( ) (see Table 14.13)
D( ) for cumulative sums of flow values from F( ) (see Table 14.14)
T( ), E( ), and G( ) for totals and sums of squares from L( ) or F( ) (see Table 14.15)
U( ) and H( ) for financial summary accounts (see Table 14.16)

30–90	SELECT video screen; home *cursor*. PRINT program title. A *runs complete count* will be displayed at the end of each sample loop below the title (see 1550). DIMENSION arrays.

OPEN PAVEFT2 *data transfer file* from PAVE2 and READ inputs. System parameters and uncertainty inputs are stored in N( ). The following are arrays of inputs for all periods, which are used for further processing:

A( ) are flow accounts
B( ) are summation condition accounts

See Table 14.11 for a description of the elements of these arrays.

100	Initial conditions, N(1) to N(14) from PAVE2 are transferred as sums over sample size N(19) into C(K,1) (see Table 14.12).

A starting *random number* is generated in X from *seed* N(20). If N(20) argument is 0, a repeat series of numbers is produced. If N(20) is positive, the next random number of a series is produced.

120	Start sample J loop. Period I loop (starts at 150) is nested into sample replication J loop. Reset insolvency I1, I2 indicators. Reset summation array W( ) for *first* and *final* year values.
130	Assign initial condition values to L(K,2) array. Such EOP values are reassigned to L(K,1), at the beginning of each period loop, for BOP values of current period (see Table 14.13).

Branch to SUB 1690 for totals in T( ) of quick assets, current assets, inventories, and current liabilities (see Table 14.15). These are BOP totals of assets, which are needed for Period 1 processing. Period index I is set to 0 in order to pick up BOP value of B( ) at 1700. Reset first period summation factor H to 1.

150–
160

Start I loop over periods 1 to M. This loop is nested within sample J loop (see 120). Reset L1, M1 overtime and material extension factors to 1.

Transfer EOP condition set in L( ) from prior period to BOP in L( ) this period. Note initial conditions of Period 1 from 130. Reset EOP conditions in L( ) and flow values in F( ) to 0.

170

Assign some input flow accounts from A( ) to F( ); the latter for processing during period (see tables 14.11 and 14.14).

Randomize purchased *direct material* or *goods for sale* in SUB '1 at 1730. Parameters are passed to Y for the mean value element of F( ), and to Z for the maximum shift input element of N( ). The output of SUB '1 is stored in the same F( ) element as the mean value input.

SALES ANALYSIS

Sales *achieved* output F(1) is equal to sales *demand* output F(32) [D(23,I)] unless all three of the following pertain:

a. Frame is *manufacturing* (N5=2).
b. Sales demand exceeds *manufacturing* capacity.
c. Sales demand exceeds manufacturing capacity after full extension with both *overtime labor* and *subcontracted* operations.

If condition c. applies then F(32) remains as *sales demand*, but F(1) and S are recomputed as *sales achieved* from final plant capacity.

190

Sales *achieved* F(32) is set initially to nonrandom sales *demand*. A(1,I) is either *% of market* or *$ sales per period*. Randomize *sales demand* (% market or $ sales) in SUB '1. If A(1,I) is *$ sales per period*, or N(33)=1, then bypass further processing; F(32) is now final sales *demand*.

200

Sales *demand* based on *market penetration of industry* starts here. Randomize *industry sales*; F(3) is now industry sales output. Set F(2), E(2) for *% market output* equal to F(32), and adjust to percentages for output printing. E( ) is a transfer array for sums of squares to be accumulated in G( ) (see Table 14.15).

210

Reassign F(32) to *sales* demand as product of *industry sales* F(3) and F(32) *market penetration*. Note that *market penetration* percent for printing was previously assigned to F(2). Now F(3) and E(1) are divided by 1000 for printing.

220

Sales achieved F(1) and S, and *gross profit* F(39), are initially set equal to *sales demand* F(32). F(39) will be changed later if N5=1 or 2 (trade or manufacturing on line 470). F(1) and S may be changed per conditions noted above. Further processing depends on frame. Manufacturing (N5=0) follows immediately, trade (N5=1) bypasses to finished goods, service (N5=2) skips over all goods cost and inventories, and environment only (N5=3) is now complete for account processing and goes to period summary.

DEMAND FOR MANUFACTURING GOODS INTO PROCESS AT SALES PRICING

Manufacturing goods inventories and goods flows are first computed at sales pricing. This is done to translate sales demand into a demand for goods to be put into process.

Goods into process are used to develop direct manufacturing costs. When period manufacturing costs are added to above, total manufacturing cost per period is obtained. A comparison between total manufacturing cost and sales values of goods into process provides a basis for revaluing manufacturing goods inventories at cost, a first-in-first-out (FIFO) cost method. All output inventory values are at cost.

Inventories are processed through SUB '2. The EOP inventory level is established as a percent of annual usage. Amount to replenish is the difference between EOP and BOP levels, plus outflow demand.

Manufacturing goods inventories are first valued at sales level to establish demand for goods, and later repriced at cost. Manufacturing materials inventories are computed from usage of materials.

Trade or merchandising goods inventories are valued directly at cost from demand for goods at cost. Supplies inventories are valued from usage.

240 Establish *finished goods* EOP inventory level L(15,2) and finished goods to be transferred into inventory F(33), both at sales pricing levels. Both L(15,2) level and F(33) finished goods are based upon sales demand F(1). Processing is in SUB '2 (see 1790). SUB '2 establishes EOP level and flow into inventory. Its inputs are listed at 1790. Establish *goods-in-process* EOP inventory level L(16,2) and *goods to be put into process* F(34) with SUB '2.

EOP finished goods L(15,2) = Sales F(1)
  x Inventory level factor F(21)

Demand for finished goods F(33)
  = EOP fin. goods inventory L(15,2)
  – BOP fin. goods inventory L(15,1) + Sales F(1)

EOP goods-in-process L(16,2) = Sales F(1)
  x Inventory level factor F(23)

Goods into process F(34)
  = EOP goods-in-process inventory L(16,2)
  – BOP goods-in-process inventory L(16,1)
  + Demand for finished goods F(33)

OVERTIME LABOR, SUBCONTRACTING, AND SALES ACHIEVED ADJUSTMENTS, IF REQUIRED FOR MANUFACTURING

In this routine C1 starts as *sales capacity* of plant; then is reset to *sales achieved* for further processing of manufacturing costs.

250   Randomize plant operating efficiency in SUB '1 from input parameter F(31). *Plant capacity* C1 is the product of capacity input A(32,I) and *operating efficiency* F(31).

If *goods into process at sales price level* F(34), or in other words goods which must be put into process to meet sales demand, exceed capacity, then branch to extended capacity routines starting on line 280.

270   Otherwise capacity is sufficient. Then reset C1 to demand for goods into process. Branch to manufacturing cost section start at line 350.

280   This section starts routines when extended capacity is needed. Inputs L1 and M1 are used to extend labor and subcontract capacity, respectively. Each was initialized at 1 for general processing (line 150), but is reset to inputs N(21) and N(23) if extensions are required in this section. Original percentage inputs N(75) and N(77) were converted in PAVE2 to factors greater than or equal to 1. No extensions will occur if N(21) and N(23) equal minimum values of one, or in other words inputs N(75) and N(77) were zero.

Set L1 initially to maximum value given by input. If extended capacity C1*L1 is less than sales demand F(34), branch to further extension on line 290. In such case L1 remains at its maximum value. Otherwise, reset L1 to actual labor extension (overtime needed) factor, and branch to manufacturing cost section (line 350). In this path demand for extra capacity has been met.

290   In this branch, after maximum overtime from line 280, capacity is still insufficient to meet demand.

Maximum subcontract extension factor M1 is first applied. If capacity is still insufficient to meet demand F(34), M1 remains at maximum, and branch to line 310 for further processing. Otherwise, reset M1 to actual required subcontract extension. Revised M1 factor is the quotient of demand F(34) by extended capacity C1*L1.

300   From above, with capacity now sufficient, branch to line 350 for further manufacturing costs.

310   This branch from 310 to 330 is reached only if extended capacity is insufficient to meet sales demand. The total hierarchy of events is:
1. If capacity is sufficient to meet sales demand set capacity equal to demand and proceed to manufacturing cost (line 270 to line 350).
2. Add overtime labor (line 280 to line 350).

3. Add subcontract materials on top of maximum overtime labor (line 280 to line 350).
4. Reduce *achieved sales* from *sales demand* after maximum overtime labor and subcontract extensions have been applied (lines 310 to 330).

Now goods put into process F(34) is reset to the lower *sales achievable* level from extended capacity C1*L1*M1.

The order must be from overtime through subcontract to reduced sales achievement. By varying input parameters N(75) and N(77) users may select or reject particular capacity extensions.

320   Sales achieved outputs F(1) and S are recomputed from revised F(34). The purpose of the formula is to convert from revised F(34) of *goods into process* to a *revised sales* from goods inventories under assumption that previously established closing goods inventories are adjusted at input specified levels with the scaled down levels of revised sales. All inventory and production pricing here remains at sales levels.

Sales = BOP inventory finished goods
   + BOP inventory goods-in-process
   + Goods into process – EOP inventory finished goods
   – EOP inventory goods into process

Now EOP inventory levels *revised* (rev.) must be scaled down from *original* levels (orig.) by proportionate sales reduction:

EOP inventory fin. goods rev.
   = EOP inventory fin. goods orig.
   x Sales achieved/Sales demand orig.

Substitution of the last two formulas in the first gives the formula on line 320. Revised sales achieved F(1) and S are expressed in terms of revised F(34) goods into process and the revised EOP inventory levels.

330   EOP inventories L(15,2) and L(16,2) for finished goods and goods-in-process are revised for lower sales achieved, as described above. This ends the adjustments of capacity and achieved sales.

COMPUTATION OF MANUFACTURING COST

350   F(19) is the *percent of sales in direct material* or *purchased goods*. The former specification is for *manufacturing* (on this line), and the latter for *trade* (line 460). F(19) was randomized on line 170. *Direct material used* (cost for period) F(35) equals the product of *goods into process* C1, factor F(19), and *capacity extension* factors L1 and M1. There is no extension if the last two factors equal one (inputs N(75) and N(77) were 0). F(33), which was previously *demand for finished goods* at sales pricing, is reset to zero. At this point F(33) will denote *direct material premium* (if any) from

subcontract operations. If M1 does not exceed one, or no subcontract extension is signaled, F(33) remains at zero.

360   Otherwise subcontract operations cost premium F(33) equals total *direct material cost* F(35) times the input subcontract premium factor N(24). Note that subcontract premium is applied to *all* material, not just a portion used to extend capacity.

370   Total *direct material* cost is transferred to F(19) as the sum of *regular cost* F(35) plus *subcontract premium* F(33). Direct manufacturing material *inventories* and *purchases* are computed at cost from SUB '2. The closing *materials inventory* L(8,2) level is established from usage F(19) (which includes a subcontract premium, if any), and input parameter F(25). In the same subroutine F(25) becomes *purchases of direct material* output from *inventories* and *usage* F(19).

EOP direct material inventory L(8,2)
=   Direct material used F(19)
x   Inventory level factor F(25)

Purchases of direct material F(25)
=   EOP material inventory L(8,2)
–   BOP material inventory L(8,1)
+   Direct material used F(19)

380   *Direct labor* as a percent of sales F(27) input is randomized in SUB '1. Then F(27) becomes total *direct labor* for the period. It is the product of *goods into process demand* C1, *overtime labor extension* factor L1, and *labor factor of sales* F(27). Division by F(31) adjusts F(27) for plant efficiency. A default value of 100 has been applied to F(31). This prevents division by 0 from nonentry.

Utilities F(24) are randomized.

390   *Direct supervisory labor* F(29) is the product of *goods into process demand* C1, overtime extension factor L1, and input supervisory factor of sales F(29). Again there is division by F(31) for plant efficiency adjustment.

Overtime labor cost output F(31) (this address was formerly used for plant efficiency factor input) is equal to the sum of direct labor F(27) and supervision F(29) times overtime premium input N(22), and times the increment of overtime hours was previously included in both F(27) and F(29) (380 and 390). Only the *premium cost* is computed here in F(31). Premium cost (L1–1) is a proportion of the total labor in factor L1.

410   All manufacturing direct and period costs are summed into F(36) as the actual total cost of *goods into process* for the period.

420   F(38), the *ratio* of goods into process at *cost* to goods into process at *sales* value level, is preset to 1, its maximum value. This factor is used to reprice manufacturing goods inventories.

      If sales value of goods into process F(34) exceeds the cost value F(36), then goods inventories remain priced at sales level. In other words goods are never priced above the sales level.

      If cost is below sales value, then this ratio is stored in F(38).

440   Goods-in-process inventories and transfers to finished goods are repriced at cost levels in SUB '2. L(7,2) is *EOP goods-in-process inventory at cost* as a fraction of the same inventory L(16,2) at sales pricing per factor F(38). *Cost of finished goods* F(34) is the difference between BOP and EOP inventories plus the cost of goods into process F(36). F(34) was used previously for *goods into process* at sales value level.

      EOP goods-in-process inventory at cost L(7,2)
      = EOP goods-in-process inventory at sales price L(16,2)
      x Factor F(34)

      Cost of finished goods F(34) = EOP goods-in-process inventory L(7,2)
      – BOP goods-in-process inventory L(7,1) + Goods into process F(36)

450   Manufacturing finished goods inventory level at cost L(6,2), and final cost of goods sold F(37), are computed in SUB '2. Inputs for L(6,2) *EOP finished goods manufacturing inventory* are that inventory at sales value L(15,2) and the cost proportioning factor F(38). *Cost of goods sold* is the difference between BOP and EOP *finished goods inventories* and the *cost of finished goods*. The latter input is F(34) from the preceding formula.

      EOP fin. goods inventory at cost L(6,2)
      = EOP fin. goods inventory at sales price L(15,2)
      x Factor F(38)

      Cost of goods sold F(37) = EOP fin. goods inventory L(6,2)
      – BOP fin. goods inventory L(6,1) + Cost of fin. goods F(34)

      For manufacturing frame (N5=2), branch around the computation of *trade inventories* on line 460 to the computation of *gross profit* on line 470.

TRADE INVENTORIES, COST, AND GROSS PROFIT

460   This line is reached from branch on line 220 for *trading* or merchandising option (N5=1). The *cost of goods sold* F(37) equals sales achieved S times cost of a fraction of sales. The latter factor is input parameter F(19). F(37) is also used for *cost of goods sold* in manufacturing (line 450), and F(19) as *cost of purchased direct material* (350 and 370). The different specifications for F(34), F(37) and F(19) do not occur simultaneously. F(19) input was previously randomized in SUB '1 on line 170.

      Trading *finished goods inventories* and *cost of goods purchased* are computed at cost with SUB '2. Closing levels of finished goods inventory F(6,2)

—the same address is used in manufacturing—are computed as the product of *cost of goods sold* F(37) and an input factor F(21). *Cost of goods purchased* F(34)—again the same address as manufacturing—is computed as the difference between EOP and BOP (F(6,2) and F(6,1)) *finished goods inventories* plus the value of *cost of goods sold* F(37).

EOP fin. goods inventory at cost L(6,2)
   = Cost of goods sold F(37) x Inventory level factor F(21)

Cost of goods purchased F(34) = EOP fin. goods inventory L(6,2) - BOP fin. goods inventory L(6,1) + Cost of goods sold F(37)

F(34) is transferred to F(25) to facilitate closing loop transfers.

470   The E( ) array stores significant values for summing into statistics for *selected accounts* output division and G( ) sums of squares. In this case E(4) is properly indexed from F(37) *cost of goods sold*.

F(39), E(5) are assigned to *gross profit* as the difference between *achieved sales* S and *cost of goods sold* F(37). This line and gross profit are reached for either *manufacturing* or *trading* firms. The line is bypassed for *service* frame (branch to 490 on line 220), which does not compute a cost of goods for sale nor employ finished goods inventories. The *gross profit default* value in F(39) at 220, which applies unchanged to *service* frame, was initially set equal to sales in F(32). Thus for all frames F(39) is the *revenue* from which further expenses and financial adjustments will lead to *net income*.

GENERAL EXPENSE PROCESSING

490   *Randomize* direct service material, direct service labor, and general utilities or period expense in SUB '1.

500   Transfer R&D expenses to F( ) from input A( ). If these inputs were *$ per period* from input N(40) equal to 1, branch past further processing.

510   Otherwise, recompute R&D expenses with F(40) and F(41) as factors of sales.

520   Compute other direct, general expenses as multiples of sales S.

540   Total service material and supplies used in F(38) is the sum of *direct* F(11) and *indirect* F(6) usage. Service *supplies inventory EOP* in L(5,2) and *purchases* F(42) are computed in SUB '2 from input usage F(38) and input inventory level factor N(25).

EOP service supplies inventory L(5,2) = Supplies used F(38) x inventory level factor N(25)

Purchases of service material and supplies F(42)
   = EOP supplies inventory L(5,2) - BOP supplies inventory L(5,1)
   + Supplies used F(38)

550   *Randomize* long-term interest *rate* F(17) in SUB '1. Interest cost on long-term obligations at this point is equal to the BOP obligations in L(12,1)

plus one-half the *planned* net changes in $A(33,I)$, all multiplied by the interest rate in $F(17)$.

PREPAID EXPENSE AND ACCOUNTS PAYABLE

Expenses are divided into two groups, *cash* and *account*. *Payrolls*, *income taxes*, *interest* payments, and *dividends* are assigned to *cash*, or are paid in full by the end of the current period. All other expenses, *fixed asset net changes*, and *intangible additions* during the first period, are assigned to open vendor *account*.

Processing of *account expenses* to *payments on account* proceeds through two adjustments. The first is changes in *prepaid expense* balance, and the second is *accounts payable balance*. Thus there are two steps between expense generation and cash disbursement.

570   Total *account expenses* are summed under T. The figure includes fixed asset additions, intangible additions (Period 1), and purchases of materials and supplies ($F(14)$, $F(28)$, and $F(42)$).

580   Payrolls are summed under $F(44)$.

590   Expenses, and payments subject to prepayment $F(45)$, are taken as the sum of account items T and payrolls $F(44)$.

$F(46)$ is set equal to account items T for entry into SUB '2. SUB '2 computes EOP *prepaid expense* and adjusted accounts subject to payment:

EOP prepaid expense $L(4,2)$
= Expense subject to prepayment $F(45)$
x Prepaid level factor input $N(27)$

Available for payment of payables $F(47)$ = Prepaid EOP $L(4,2)$ – Prepaid BOP $L(4,1)$ + Account items $F(46)$

600   SUB '2 computes accounts payable and payments on account.

EOP payables $L(9,2)$ = Available for account payments $F(47)$ x Vendor account credit factor $N(26)$

Payments on payables $F(45)$ = BOP payables $L(9,1)$ – EOP payables $L(9,2)$ + Available for payment of payables $F(47)$

ADVANCES FROM CUSTOMERS AND ACCOUNTS RECEIVABLE

Sales are adjusted by changes in unearned customer advances to obtain accounts available for collection. Collections are adjusted from above by changes in accounts receivable balances. The processing from sales to collections thus adjusts first for changes in unearned customer advances (liabilities of the firm to customers), and then for changes in accounts receivable.

Uncollectible account expense is computed as a percentage of accounts available for collection (unadjusted collections). Final collections are adjusted net of this expense. Each period's uncollectibles are added to both accounts receivable gross and to a reserve for uncollectibles. The latter is not closed to the former over the simulation. Thus net receivables subject to collection are always equal to the gross less the reserve.

620   SUB '2 computes EOP unearned advances and revenue available for collection:

EOP unearned advances $L(10,2)$ = Sales x Advances input factor $N(28)$

Available for collection $F(46)$ = Advances EOP – Advances BOP + Sales $F(1)$

Input parameter $F(9)$, for accounts receivable as a fraction of sales, is randomized in SUB '1.

630   Accounts receivable BOP $L(2,1)$ is reduced to net value. In other words uncollectible reserve BOP $L(3,1)$ is subtracted before using $L(2,1)$ as an input to collections. The $L(3,1)$ component is not collectible. SUB '2 computes for each period EOP accounts receivable and collections before adjustment for uncollectible accounts expense:

EOP accounts receivable $L(2,2)$ = Available for collection $F(46)$ x Input factor $F(9)$

Unadjusted collections $F(9)$ = BOP receivables $L(2,2)$ – EOP receivables $L(2,1)$ + Available for collection $F(46)$

Note that $F(9)$ goes into SUB '2 as a receivables input factor, and comes out as unadjusted collections. This does not interfere because the output use is not developed until the input use has been completed.

640   Uncollectible account expense $F(4)$ equals unadjusted collections $F(9)$ times uncollectible input factor $N(41)$.

Final collections $F(9)$ equals *unadjusted* $F(9)$ less *uncollectibles expense* $F(4)$. Increase uncollectibles reserve EOP $L(3,2)$ from BOP reserve $L(3,1)$ by new uncollectible expense this period $F(4)$.

650   EOP accounts receivable $L(2,2)$ from line 630 was computed net of reserve $L(3,2)$. The reserve is added back in for final $L(2,2)$.

TOTAL EXPENSE, INVESTMENT INCOME, AND INCOME BEFORE INCOME TAXES

670–   The sum of total *operating expense* is developed on two lines in $F(46)$.
680

Net income on operations $F(47)$, $E(7)$ is *gross profit* $F(39)$, or *sales* in *service* frame (see 220), less operating expense $F(46)$.

690   *Randomize* short-term interest rate $F(15)$ in SUB '1. The final short-term rate is set equal to R1. The *rate of return* on monetary assets R4 is taken as a fraction of R1 per input factor $N(47)$. Variables $F(15)$ and $F(16)$ are now reset to 0, prior to other assignments.

700   *Interest income* is taken at rate R4 of BOP cash assets L(1,1) plus one-half of net changes in owner equity capital F(18) and long-term obligations in A(33,I). This income will require adjustment if there are further cash changes (990). Net changes to capital are assigned on average to be effective over one half a period.

710   *Total income before income taxes* F(48) equals operating income F(47), plus interest income F(38), less interest cost on long-term debt F(43). Again, cash changes will require further adjustments (1030). The purpose of computing F(48) here is to derive a tentative income tax rate (730).

INCOME TAXES AND DIVIDENDS TENTATIVE COMPUTATION

Income taxes are computed twice: first, tentatively in order to obtain a *marginal tax rate*, and, second, for the final *output cost*. The *marginal tax rate*, which is either the input parameter or zero, is used to adjust to an after-tax effect basis for required *capital additions*, *short-term borrowing* and *permanent capital*.

Dividends are computed as a cash outflow component of *net cash flow* and tentative *EOP cash* balance. Per user input choice, *dividends* will be computed from either a dollar input schedule or from a percentage of earnings schedule (net income after income taxes). For the latter option dividends must be computed twice: first, as a component of tentative *net cash flow* and *EOP cash balance*, and, second, after a final determination of *net income after taxes*.

730   Input combined effective *income tax rate* N(31) is assigned to R. Tentative *income taxes* F(6) are the product of the difference between *net income before income taxes* this run F(48) and *tax loss carryforward* L(17,1), and rate R. Last period's closing *tax loss carryforward* L(17,2) was assigned to L(17,1) this period on line 160.

740   If F(6) is greater than 0 the above computation stands. Otherwise *income taxes* F(6) and rate R, which is now the *marginal tax rate*, are reset to 0. In other words, taxes and the rate cannot be negative.

750   Tentative *net income after income taxes* F(8) is *income before taxes* F(48) less *income taxes* F(6).

Dividends F(12) are initially set equal to the input schedule for the period A(34,I).

If the dividend computation parameter N(49) equals 1, above becomes the value applied to output summation routines; bypass recomputation of dividends as a percent of earnings.

760–   Otherwise A(34,I) and F(12) will be *dividend* input factors, and must be
800   multiplied by tentative *net income after income taxes* F(8). If the product F(12) above is positive its value stands. Otherwise F(12) is reset to zero. In other words *dividends* F(12) must be nonnegative.

The tentative computation of *marginal tax rate* R, *income taxes* F(6), *net income after income taxes* F(8), and *dividends* F(12) ends at this point. Tentative *net cash flow* after income taxes and dividends F(14) is computed on lines 780 and 790. This figure includes net changes in debt A(33,I), but not in owner investment F(18). Tentative *EOP cash balance* L(1,2) is computed on line 800. This equals *BOP cash balance* L(1,1) plus net cash flow F(14) and owner planned net investment F(18).

SHORT-TERM BORROWING

The general order of events is:

1. If projected *EOP cash* is negative branch to capital-raising routines.
2. If projected cash is positive check adequacy from input minimum cash ratio unless accounts payable EOP are zero. In the latter case *cash ratio* may be undefined, and any cash balance is considered adequate.
3. The input minimum *cash ratio* is the basis of *short-term borrowing* unless it exceeds 0.9. In the latter case *short-term borrowing* is not an efficient means to improve *cash ratio*; bypass *short-term borrowing* to permanent capital additions.
4. Check projected against minimum input *cash ratios*. If projected exceeds minimum, no added capital is required. This check is bypassed if *EOP cash* is negative or *EOP payables* are zero.
5. Compute borrowing capacity, first from *liquidation of current assets*. Then, if input *current ratio* limit not less than 1.5, check *cash ratio* to limit of specified *current ratio*. User controls priority of these borrowing options by the input current ratio parameter N(30).
6. Compute *short-term borrowing* required to meet specified minimum *cash ratio*. If required borrowing exceeds limit from 5., *short-term borrowing* is set equal to this limit. Then branch to permanent capital additions; otherwise, required borrowing stands and cash balance is now adequate.

Some general conditions of *short-term borrowing*:

1. Amounts are borrowed for only one period, and are assumed borrowed BOP. Previous borrowings appear EOP in preceding period *statements of condition*. They are repaid BOP in the next period.
2. Full interest on short-term borrowings is charged over one period for borrowing during that period.
3. BOP conditions are used to determine borrowing capacity for any period.

820　　If *EOP cash* L(1,2) is currently negative, branch to next borrowing step at 830. Otherwise check *EOP payables* L(9,2). If nonpositive, cash position is taken as adequate because *cash ratio* would be undefined with no other current liabilities. Branch to line 1010, which bypasses further capital raising. With positive payables proceed to next borrowing step.

830   If input required *cash ratio* N(29) exceeds 0.9, *short-term borrowing* is not
       a feasible means to improve the *cash ratio*. Branch to permanent capital
       additions, which starts at line 910. If cash is negative bypass line 850 ad-
       equacy test—additional capital is automatically required.

840   If projected EOP *cash ratio* exceeds input minimum parameter N(29), cash
       will be adequate. Bypass capital raising to line 1010.

850   *Short-term borrowing* capacity Q calculation starts here. Compute first as
       liquidation percentage N(32) of net current assets. If the input current ratio
       N(30), as a borrowing limit, is less than 1.5, then above *short-term borrow-
       ing* capacity stands, and branch to 870.

860   Otherwise, compute borrowing capacity, still as Q, from minimum current
       ratio limit N(30). The formula for deriving Q comes from:

$$N(30) = \frac{\text{Total current assets } T(3) - \text{Short-term borrowing } L(11,1)}{Q + \text{Total current liabilities } T(5) - \text{Short-term borrowing } L(11,1)}$$

       Solve above for Q.

       This Q is based on BOP current ratio after previous period's *short-term
       borrowing* has been repaid.

870   If capacity Q is negative, branch to permanent capital additions at 910.

880   Compute L(11,2) tentative *short-term borrowings required* to meet input
       cash ratio parameter N(29). Note here that *required* computation projects
       to the end of the period whereas *capacity* was based upon BOP. The formula
       for L(11,2) comes from:

$$N(29) = \frac{L(1,2) + L(11,2)}{L(9,2) + L(10,2) + L(11,2)}$$

       Solve for L(11,2).

890   If *required short-term borrowing* L(11,2) is less than *capacity* Q, capital is
       sufficient; progress to final period computations on line 980. Otherwise, set
       L(11,2) equal to capacity Q. As much as possible has now been borrowed.

REQUIRED PERMANENT CAPITAL ADDITIONS

These are divided into two classes, *owner equity* and *long-term obligations*
(long-term debt and preferred stock). Each class is subdivided into *planned*
(user input) under F(18) equity and A(33,I) debt, and *required*. The
latter are derived internally under F(15) equity and F(16) debt if input
parameter N(46) is one. If N(46) input is 0, then no additional capital is
raised internally.

The *planned* amounts may be any sign, but are not permitted to drive EOP
accounts below zero *before* required additions (if any) are included (PAVE2,
lines 600 to 610). The *required* additions are always nonnegative.

Interest income F(38) is computed on the *BOP cash balance* L(1,1) plus
one half the sum of four capital addition accounts (F(18), A(33,I), F(15)

and F(16)), and short-term borrowings L(11,2). In effect interest income is computed on the average cash balance based on BOP values (lines 700 and 990). Interest income is not permitted to go negative (line 1010).

Interest on long-term obligations F(43) is computed on BOP balance plus one-half the *planned* additions (line 550) and one-half the *required* additions (line 960).

The permanent capital additions routine may be reached only through *short-term borrowing* routines. Branches occur to permanent capital if either *short-term borrowing* will not reach the required input *cash ratio* N(29) or if available borrowing capacity has not been specified.

910   If input decision parameter N(46) equals 0, then internal routines for raising required additional capital will be bypassed to final computations at 980. In such cases negative cash and net worth may appear in the outputs.

920   Otherwise there is a computation of required additional capital Q to reach specified input minimum cash ratio N(29) from formula:

$$N(29) = \frac{L(1,2) + L(11,2) + Q}{L(9,2) + L(10,2) + L(11,2)}$$

Solve for Q.

Note that *short-term borrowing EOP* may be either positive or zero, depending on branch taken from *short-term borrowing* routine. Note also that prior period L(K,2) series were reset to zero at beginning of this period (160).

L is the adjustment factor from actual added capital to required cash effect Q. Permanent capital, unlike short-term borrowing, is assumed available at the middle of the period when raised. Q will then earn R4 times 0.5 as an additional cash input, but this is reduced by the tax rate factor (1-R) after income taxes. Division of Q by factor L gives the *actual* added equity capital to be raised F(15) in order to obtain the *cash effect* Q.

940   The above amount stands as long as N(48), the proportion of added required capital to be raised in fixed obligations, does not exceed zero. Otherwise, separate components of debt and equity must be computed because cash effects of income taxes are different, and fixed obligations require interest payments.

950   The fixed obligations component F(16) is derived from the following:

F(16) debt *required cash effect* = F(16) *actual* x (Long-term interest rate F(17) x (1 - R))

$$\frac{F(16) \text{ debt actual}}{F(15) \text{ owner equity actual}} = \frac{N(48)}{1-N(48)} \quad \text{to preserve input proportions}$$

Total cash effect required Q = F(16) debt *effect* + F(15) owner equity
= F(16) debt effect + F(15) *actual* x L

But F(15) *actual* = F(16) *actual* x $\dfrac{1-N(48)}{N(48)}$ from proportioning

Then Q = F(16) *actual* x (1–F(17)) x (1–R)) + F(16) *actual* x $\dfrac{1-N(48)}{N(48)}$ x L

Solution of above for F(16) gives the required fixed obligations *actual* component.

960   The owner equity component, *actual* addition F(15), must fulfill the appropriate proportion with *actual* debt above, per the proportioning formula previously given.

Interest on *long-term obligations* F(43) is increased by one-half the required debt addition F(16).

FINAL ADJUSTMENTS OF BORROWING, INTEREST INCOME, INCOME TAXES, AND DIVIDENDS

980   The final *unadjusted short-term borrowing* L(1,2) was determined from line 890. The actual amount to be borrowed is increased by interest cost and decreased by income tax savings. Both of above affect cash flow. The final value of L(11,2) is net of these effects as given in the formulas below:

Cash effect L(11,2) = Actual L(11,2)
- Interest cost on actual L(11,2) = L(11,2)
- L(11,2) x R1

The cash effect of interest rate R1 after income taxes = Actual R1 x (1 – tax rate R)

Actual L(11,2) is determined from above formulas.

F(17) is the interest expense computed on actual L(11,2) *short-term borrowings* with interest rate R1.

990   Interest income F(38) is increased by the rate of return R4 times one-half of the capital additions to cash balances. The capital additions are required owner equity F(15), added required long-term obligations F(16), and L(11,2) short-term borrowings.

1010   Interest income F(38) cannot be negative. If not greater than 0, reset to 0.

1020   EOP long-term obligations L(12,2) is taken as BOP in L(12,1) plus planned changed A(33,I) and required additions F(16).

EOP paid-in owner equity L(13,2) is taken as BOP in L(13,1) plus planned changes F(18) and required additions F(15).

If N(46) were 0 to bypass required capital routines on 910 to 960, then both F(15) and F(16) will be 0.

1030   The final computation of *net income before income taxes* F(48) starts with *net income from operations* F(47). F(47) was first used for this quantity on line 680; previously it applied to a different use, amounts available for processing through accounts payable (lines 590 and 600). To obtain the final value of F(48), adjust F(47) for final values of *interest income* F(38), *interest cost on long-term obligations* F(43), and *interest expense on short-term borrowing* F(17). Initialize *tax loss carryforward* L(17,2) to zero. This address still holds the loss from the preceding run, which was previously transferred to L(17,1) on line 160.

Income subject to income taxes T is the difference between *income this period* F(48) and the *BOP tax loss carryforward* L(17,1).

1040 *Income taxes* F(6) are T times the input tax rate N(31). If T is nonnegative the above value stands. Under these conditions the *loss carryforward* will be less than F(48), and will be completely absorbed this period; thus the preset of L(17,2) to zero also stands. Otherwise (T nonpositive), *income taxes* F(6) must be reset to 0. Also *tax loss carryforward* L(17,2) is credited with the negative residual net income.

1050 Final *net income after income taxes*, F(8) and E(8), is *income before taxes* F(48) less *income taxes* F(6).

If the input *dividend* choice parameter N(49) equals 1, then the original computation of dividends F(12) per input dollar schedule A(34,1), as developed on line 750, stands.

1060 Otherwise, *dividends* are computed a second time (the first calculation was on line 760), as the product of *net income after taxes* F(8) and the input schedule factor A(34,I).

If above F(12) is positive, it stands.

Otherwise *dividends* F(12) are reset to 0; negative *dividends* are not permitted.

FINAL CASH FLOW, CASH BALANCE, AND TECHNICAL INSOLVENCY

1080– Total *net cash flow* N(14) is recomputed a second time on two lines (com-
1090 pare 780, 790). There are possible changes in income taxes, dividends, interest income, interest expense, and capital additions.

1100 PAVE computes probabilities of both *technical* and *legal* insolvency, and the *mean* number of the period (if any) when either of these events *first* occurs.

Here *Technical insolvency* is defined as a negative *EOP cash* balance, or L(1,2) less than 0. *Legal insolvency* is defined as a negative *EOP owner's equity*, T(7)=L(13,2)+L(14,2), the sum of *paid-in capital* and *retained earnings*.

For a sample size N(19) equal to one (*deterministic* run), *probability of an insolvency*, if it occurs, will always be *one*.

For internal computation of *required additional investment* choice (input N(46)=1), PAVE will specify permanent capital sources of cash, in addition to *short-term borrowing*. Short-term borrowing is always attempted if cash is inadequate. *Technical insolvency* is not possible if PAVE is commanded to raise sufficient capital. *Legal insolvency* under such choice is possible but unlikely. To study questions of insolvency, input ID 530 (N(46) in PAVE3) equal to zero.

Final computation of EOP *cash* balance L(1,2) is BOP *cash* balance L(1,1) plus *total net cash flow* F(14), plus *planned owner equity net investments* F(18) from input schedule A(18,I), plus *required additional owner permanent capital* F(15). Changes in short-term borrowing and long-term fixed obligations were included in the F(14) net cash flow.

If EOP *cash* L(1,2) is nonnegative, *technical insolvency* does not occur, and parameter changes are bypassed.

1110   Otherwise, *technical insolvency* parameters are adjusted *if* the *initial* period of technical insolvency is being simulated. Indicator I1 was set to 0 before the first period of each sample run (120). It is reset to one after an initial *technical insolvency* has been encountered (1110).

Thus if I1 equals one, a *technical insolvency* has already taken place during some prior period, and insolvency logic is bypassed to 1130. For the first insolvency during this sample run, the period number I is added to accumulator M(1).

Counter M(2) is increased by one.

I1 is reset to one, which will bypass further changes in M(1) and M(2), whether or not there are additional insolvencies, for any subsequent periods.

Accumulators M(1) and M(2) are transferred to PAVE4, where final computation and printing occurs. If final M(1) and M(2) values are zero, a message is printed that *technical insolvency* did not occur. Otherwise, division by *sample size* converts M(1) to *mean* period number of first occurrence, and M(2) to *proportion (probability)* of occurrences out of the sample size.

TOTAL EOP CONDITION ACCOUNTS AND LEGAL INSOLVENCY

1130–   EOP retained earnings L(14,2) equals BOP amount L(14,1) plus net income
1140   after tax F(8) less dividends paid F(12).

Branch to SUB 1690 for totals in T( ) of quick assets, current assets, inventories and current liabilities. These are BOP totals for the period.

Account totals for a period are stored in T( ) (see Table 14.15).

T(6) is total liabilities, T(4) is total assets, and T(7) is total owners' equity.

1150   Sum of *first* period *total liabilities* in M(8) and sum of *first* period *total assets* in M(6) are needed for printing in PAVE4. Reset of H to 0 prevents

T(6) and T(4) from accumulating values in periods other than the first. H is reset to 1 prior to the next sample replication (130).

1170   If EOP *owners' equity* T(7) is nonpositive, go to legal insolvency processing on line 1180.

Otherwise *rate of return on owners' equity* Q for the period I is computed as the quotient of *net income after income taxes* F(8) and EOP *owners' equity* T(7).

Branch past *legal insolvency* processing to line 1190.

1180   If *owners' equity* T(7) from line 1120 were *nonpositive*, then *rate of return on owners' equity* Q is reset to 0; or rate of return is not computed on *nonpositive equity*.

The logic of *legal insolvency* is identical with that described for *technical insolvency* under line 1110 above. I2 has been set to 0 before the first period of each sample run. It is reset to one after the first *legal insolvency*, if it occurs. Subsequent *legal insolvencies*, if they occur, will bypass remaining statements on this line.

M(3) is the period accumulator which corresponds to M(1) on line 1110.

Counter M(4) corresponds to M(2) on line 1110.

I2 is reset to one after the first occurrence of *legal insolvency*, if any, during each sample run.

Processing and printing of *legal insolvency* is completed in PAVE4. The process is similar to that described above under 1100 and 1110 for *technical insolvency*.

FIRST AND FINAL YEAR SALES, INCOME, AND RATE OF RETURN

The values are as follows (the second index of V is 1 for *sum* and 2 for *sum of squares*):

	FIRST YEAR	FINAL YEAR
Sales	W(1),V(1,1),V(1,2)	W(4),V(4,1),V(4,2)
Earnings	W(2),V(2,1),V(2,2)	W(5),V(5,1),V(5,2)
Rate return on owners' equity	W(3),V(3,1),V(3,2)	W(6),V(6,1),V(6,2)

The simple and squared sums are computed in PAVE3. They are processed into *means* and *standard deviations* under V( ) array in PAVE4 with an interpolation factor N(1). This factor was computed in PAVE2. It is different from unity when year ends do not correspond to period ends within the simulation. The *last* period number of the *first* year N(52) and the *first* period number of the final year N(53) are also computed in PAVE2. The *means* and *standard deviations* are printed in PAVE4. These amounts are used for further computations in PAVE4, particularly for *going-concern* value.

First and *final* year figures differ from other *annual* figures in PAVE in the following ways:

For each sample run, V( ) is summed over the specific periods which make up the *first year*, counting forward from the first period, and the *final* year, counting backward from the final period. This routine is the only source of standard deviations over time spans different from one period.

The annualized statistics in FINANCIAL SUMMARY FROM FINAL PERIOD in H( ) array are extrapolations from the *final* period; no other period values are added in.

The annual columns in FINANCIAL STATEMENTS are sums of the means for periods that constitute each simulated year, starting from the beginning. Thus *first year mean* sales and earnings will agree between VALUATION output and STATEMENTS output. The *final year* figures will agree only if the last period coincides with an end-of-year point, counting from the beginning. For example, assume 12 periods are simulated, and each period is a quarter year long. Then the simulation ends after 3 years have elapsed from the beginning. In this case *final year* sales in VALUATION will correspond to sales "for year 3" in STATEMENTS. If 13 periods of a quarter length were simulated, however, the *final year* under VALUATION will sum periods 10-13, but the last annual totals under STATEMENTS will still sum periods 9-12.

1190–
1200   If the current simulated period number I exceeds the *last* period number of the *first* year N(52), bypass additions to *first* year totals and proceed to *final* year computations on line 1210.

Otherwise, add sales S, earnings F(8), and rate of return on owners' equity Q to *first* year totals W(1), W(2), and W(3).

Note if *owners' equity* T(7) at 1170 were nonpositive, then *rate of return on owners' equity* Q was set to 0 at 1180. Thus periods with negative owners' equity can make no contribution to positive rate of return.

1210–
1220   If period number I is less than the *first* period number of the *final* year N(53), bypass additions to *final* year totals. Control then passes to next section at 1240.

Otherwise, add sales S, earnings F(8), and rate of return on owners' equity Q to *final* year totals W(4), W(5) and W(6). See note on Q equal to 0 at 1190.

SUMS AND SUMS OF SQUARES OVER SAMPLE FOR EACH PERIOD

1240–
1290   Sums over sample J loop are accumulated for each period I for flow values in D( ) from F( ) (see Table 14.14), and for EOP condition values in C( ) from L(K,2) (see Table 14.13).

Two F( ) array transfers are required to accommodate assignment loops.

Array E( ) is used to accumulate *selected accounts* from both F( ) and L(K,2) (see also 200). The squares of E( ) over *sample* J loop are accumulated for each period I in G( ) (see Table 14.15).

Arrays D( ) and C( ) are used in PAVE5 and PAVE6 to compute *mean* values for statements. Array G( ) is used in PAVE6 to derive selected *standard deviations* and *confidence interval limits*.

Period loop I ends.

1310–
1360

Array V( ) stores 33 financial summary values for printing in PAVE4 (see Table 14.16). Since the period loop ended at 1290, only the final period values will be present in S, F( ), T( ), and L(K,2). Thus final values will be stored in U( ). The N factor is used to obtain *annual* extrapolations, where so defined.

Key accounts are stored in U(1) to U(5), and U(19) to U(33).

Some new final period values are assigned to T(1), T(3), T(4), and T(6). This reassignment facilitates a check loop for negative denominators at 1380.

1380–
1460

Elements U(6) to U(18) are *financial ratios* during the final period. A loop K checks for 7 denominators in T( ) equal to 0 before ratios are computed. If a 0 denominator is formed, it is reset to a small positive number 10^{-25}. This will cause the final ratio in U( ) to become very large and overflow the print field in PAVE4. Overflow symbols are used to indicate undefined ratios in PAVE4.

After the denominator check, appropriate financial ratios are computed in U(6) to U(18) (see section 4.6).

At 1460, except for a service firm with N5=0, S is reset to *cost of goods sold* F(37) in order to compute inventory turns in U(18).

M(9) is used to accumulate the sum of final *tax loss carryforwards* L(17,2) for printing of the *mean* in PAVE4.

SUMMATION OF ANNUAL SUMMARY VALUES

1480

At the close of each sample run in J loop, W(1) to W(3) contain totals for the *first* year, and W(4) to W(6) for the *final* year. For each year there are 3 values for this sample run. Add the W(K) for cumulative sums in V( ) over the simulation. V(K,1) is used for simple sums and V(K,2) for sums of squares. For descriptions of W( ) and V( ), see preamble to 1190.

1490–
1510

Over the J loop, sum U(1) into H(K,1) and U(K) squared into H(K,2) (see Table 14.16). For the first replication, J equals 1, *min* value of U(K) in H(K,3) and *max* value of U(K) in H(K,4) are set equal to initial U(K). This initializes the *sort* routine at 1520 to 1550, and bypasses the sort for a sample size of 1 (deterministic). For J equals 1 for first replication, bypass sort to 1550.

1520– Sort routine starts at 1520 for *min* and *max* values of U( ) over sample
1540   J replications.

If U(K) in this replication exceeds the current *max* in H(K,4) branch to 1540. Otherwise, check if U(K) equals or exceeds the current *min* in H(K,3). If U(K) exceeds H(K,3), branch to end of routine at 1550. In such cases there is neither a new *max* nor a new *min*.

Otherwise, at 1530 U(K) is a new *min*; reset H(K,3) to new min. Branch to end of routine at 1550.

If U(K) exceeded the current *max* H(K,4) in 1520, control branched to 1540, where H(K,4) is reset to the new *max*.

1550   Determination of statistices in H( ) for PAVE4 from U( ) ends. Print the sample number J, of replication just ended, on video screen. Sample J loop ends.

ASSIGN AND WRITE OUTPUTS TO TRANSFER FILES

1570   REDIMENSION and reassign F( ) for transfer of *owner paid-in equity* C(13,I+1) to PAVE4 for number of share computations.

1580– Assign EOP 1 selected accounts to M( ) for transfer to PAVE4 for VALUA-
1620   TION AND SCOPE outputs (see Table 14.12).

OPEN and WRITE to PAVEFT3 for transfer of values to PAVE4. Skip *two* records written to PAVEFT3 by PAVE2. Set end-of-file marker for PAVEFT3.

OPEN and WRITE to PAVEFT5 for transfer of values to PAVE6. Condition account C( ) and sum-of-squares G( ) arrays are required. Skip *one* record written to PAVEFT5 by PAVE2. Set end-of-file marker for PAVEFT5.

1630– Reassign for all periods 5 values in C( ) which are needed by PAVE5. C(1,I)
1660   already has the correct value. REDIMENSION C( ) to exclude all but the first 6 values for each period.

OPEN and WRITE to PAVEFT4 for transfer of values to PAVE5. Revised C( ) and all D( ) array values are required. Skip *one* record written to PAVEFT4 by PAVE2. Set end-of-file marker for PAVEFT4. CLOSE file.

1670   CHAIN next program PAVE4.

SUB–TOTALS FOR CONDITION ACCOUNTS

1690– These totals in T( ) were placed in a SUB because preceding period totals
1710   are used in processing before new totals are generated. Initial totals are called at 130. Final totals are called at 1130. These are used as preceding totals for the next period I loop.

SUB '1–TRIANGULAR RANDOM GENERATOR

1730   The passed variables are:

   Y = central value input element of F in F(Y)

   Z = maximum percent shift from central value element per input in N(Z)

Variable X is a generated random number. In the BASIC used here a nonzero argument of RND function generates the next random number of a series. The *seed*, or initial *argument* N(20), was used in RND function at 100. If N(20) were 0, its default value, a duplicate series of random numbers would be generated for each run of PAVE3. If N(20) were nonzero, each series of random numbers X will be different.

The *random process generator* here uses an *inverse transformation method* explained in section 3.4. Random numbers X are used as cumulative probabilities of a *triangular distribution* to inversely generate the corresponding random variables in F(Y).

Random numbers X less than 0.5 generate values in F(Y) *output* at 1750 which are in the range

$$F(Y)' - f(N(Z)) < = F(Y) < F(Y)'$$

where F(Y)' symbolizes the *input* central value in F(Y), and $f(N(Z))$ the maximum shift in F(Y)' per uncertainty input N(Z).

Random numbers X greater than or equal to 0.5 generate *output* values in F(Y) at 1740 in the range

$$F(Y)' < = F(Y) < = F(Y)' + f(N(Z))$$

1760–   Negative generated values in F(Y) are reset to 0. SUB ends.
1770

SUM '2–FLOW AND CONDITION ACCOUNTING LOGIC

1790   The passed variables are:

   A = Index of L(A,2) and L(A,1) for EOP and BOP condition accounts.
   B = Index of flow account F(B) from which L(A,1) level is determined.
   C = Input factor of L(A,2) level from F(B) flow value.
   D = Index of F(D) solution *output* flow from *input* flow F(E) and change in condition of L( ) from A.
   E = Index of F(E) *input* flow used to determine *output* flow F(D).
   F = Computation factor (+1) or (–1) determines direction of change to compute F(D).

Note that the individual formulas for each call of SUB '2 are given on the lines of branching.

EOP condition L(A,2) equals flow account F(B) times input factor C.

1800   *Output* flow F(D) equals an input flow F(E) times the difference in EOP
        and BOP condition accounts L( ). The sign of change in condition is deter-
        mined by factor F.

        Negative *outputs* in F(D) are invalid. If positive branch to end of SUB '2
        at 1820.

1810   Otherwise the *output* F(D) is reset to 0. The closing condition L(A,2) is
        then reset to maintain the logic of L( ) and F( ). If F(D) is 0, then EOP
        L(A,2) must equal the algebraic sum of BOP L(A,1) and *input* flow F(E).
        The revised L(A,2) is a default for an input C incompatible with account
        conditions in L( ).

1820   SUB '2 ends. PAVE3 ends.

14.5 | PAVE4 Documentation

INITIALIZE SYSTEM AND READ INPUTS

2470–   PAVE4 is used to compute t-statistics, number of shares outstanding, and
2520   economic valuation of the firm. PAVE4 also controls PRINT for output
        divisions FINANCIAL SUMMARY FROM FINAL PERIOD (N6=1) and
        VALUATION AND SCOPE (N6=0).

        SELECT video screen; home *cursor*; PRINT PAVE4 title; dimension arrays
        and alpha scalar variables.

2540–   OPEN PAVEFT3 and read inputs from PAVE2 and PAVE3. If other than
2560   an initial output division has been called, there will be a revised input in N6,
        which may have been called from PAVE6. The principal input arrays to
        PAVE4 are:

        N( ) for system parameters and selected first or final year values from
            PAVE2 (see Table 14.17).
        G( ) for sums and sums of squares of first and final year values from
            PAVE3 (see Table 14.12).
        V( ) for first and final year *earnings, owners' equity*, and *rates of return
            on owners equity*; statistics from PAVE3 (see preamble to line 1190
            in section 14.4).
        H( ) for summary value statistics from final period. These are generated
            in PAVE3 (see Table 14.16).

        The most important parameters of PAVE4 are:
        M = number of periods
        N = number of periods per year
        N3 = sample size (N3=1 for nonstatistical outputs)
        N5 = frame (service = 0, trade = 1, manufacturing = 2, and environ-
              ment only = 3)
        N6 = output division (VALUATION = 0, FINANCIAL SUMMARY
              = 1, STATEMENTS = 2, SELECTED ACCOUNTS = 3)

2570 Redimension H( ) to allow for 3 additional summary values, needed for processing in PAVE4, which were not READ from PAVE3.

COMPUTE MEANS AND STANDARD DEVIATIONS OF SUMMARY ITEMS

2590 Compute means of 6 values returned to V(K,1) for *first* and *final* year of VALUATION AND SCOPE output division. Factor N(1) is an interpolator from periods to years (see PAVE2, 750 to 770). If N3=1, bypass *standard deviation* computations, which are inapplicable.

2600 Compute *standard deviations* of 6 values for *first* and *final* years for VALUATION AND SCOPE output division. The variance numerator is assigned to V; N(1) is an interpolation factor.

2610 For V positive, continue. Otherwise, reset V to 0. This step prevents aborting from square root of negative V at 2620.

2620 Compute *standard deviations*.

2630 VALUATION AND SCOPE loop for V(K,1) and V(K,2) ends. Compute means from sums for *total liabilities EOP 1* in G(8) and *final tax loss carryforward* in G(9).

2640 Assign 3 inputs from G( ) to extended H( ) for sums and sums of squares. Then the G( ) items will be included in *mean* and *standard deviation computations* in 2660 to 2680.

2650 Bypass *standard deviation* and *t-statistic* computations for *sample size* N3=1. For N3=1, *mean* equals *sum* for H( ); there is no interpolation factor.

2660 For 36 items in H( ), compute *means*, which are returned to H(K,1), and compute numerators for *variance* formula, which are first stored in V.

2670 If V is less than 0 it is reset to 0. This protects against aborting the program with square root of a negative number at 2680.

2680 Complete computation of 36 *standard deviations*, which are returned to H(K,2). Output of 2660 to 2680 is used principally in FINANCIAL SUMMARY output division.

DETERMINATION OF CONFIDENCE LEVEL AND STUDENT'S t-STATISTIC

Values are supplied internally from user selection of sample size N3. The coding is a combination of table look up for small N3 and interpolated formulas. Except for very small or large N3, output rotates through 90%, 95%, 98%, and 99% confidence (risk) levels as sample size is increased. Thus any reasonable combination of risk level and precision (t-statistic) may be selected by appropriate choice of N3.

P output confidence level, or 100 minus risk percentage.

T output t-statistic, used in PAVE4 and PAVE6 to compute confidence interval limits.

P( )   array stores table values of percentage confidence levels. Percentages in PAVE are 80, 90, 95, 98, and 99.

T( )   array stores table values of t-statistics or parameters to develop t-statistics. The same array T( ) is used later in PAVE4 to hold FINAN-CIAL SUMMARY values.

2700   Set array T( ) equal to 4 initial table values for sample size N3 of 2 to 5.

2710   Set array P( ) equal to 4 initial table values for sample size N3 of 2 to 5.

Adjustment term K is set to 1.

If sample size N3 is less than 6, i.e., from 2 to 5, then branch to final computation of T and P on line 2770. In this case sample size will be reduced by one (K=1) to relate the table values of lines 2700 and 2710 to output values of T and P.

2720   A formula for T is presented as a decreasing numerical approximation function of sample size N3. This approximation is used for N3   23.

The above approximation is coupled with confidence level P( ) of 99%. In other words, all sample sizes of 24 or greater are associated with 99% confidence level.

If sample size N3 exceeds 23, then the above formula and values of T and P hold as outputs. Branch to next section on line 2810 (lines 2790 and 2800 in following section apply only to N3=1).

2730   Otherwise T(1) to T(3) are reassigned table values for sample sizes 6 through 8.

P(1) to P(4) reassignments of 90, 95, 98, and 99 are used for sample sizes N3 from 6 to 23. P(4) is assigned on line 2740. This assignment has the effect of rotating confidence level choices over increasing sample sizes.

2740   Adjustment term K is set equal to 5 in order to accomodate N3 of 6 to 8. The value assignment to P(4) is a continuation of 2730.

If sample size less than 9, i.e., 6 to 8, then branch to computation of T and P on line 2770.

Otherwise, develop numerical approximation parameters Z and L, which are operational over sample sizes from 9 to 23.

2750   T(1) to T(4) are reassigned parameters which will be used for numerical approximation of t-statistics with degrees of freedom 8 to 22 (sample size N3 to 9 to 23).

2760   T is approximated as a linear combination of L and Z, using also the T( ) reassigned array values from 2750. L takes on rotating integer values from 1 to 4 over N3 range 9 to 23.

P takes on rotating values of 90, 95, 98 and 99, as sample size N3 increases, per the reassignment of P( ) on 2730 and 2740, and the integer values of L.

The numerical approximation of P and T for sample sizes 9 to 23 is now complete; branch to start of statistical processing in next section at 2810.

2770 T and P are assigned table values from T( ) and P( ). The values depend upon sample size N3 and index adjustment factor K. K relates array index to prior tabled values. Branch to statistical valuation processing at 2810.

VALUES TO BE USED FOR ADDITIONAL OWNER SHARES

Economic valuation of a firm is computed for the *first* year and for the *final* year. There are several methods used to compute economic values. If there is only one period simulated, or if total time span simulated does not exceed one year, then first year valuation is identical to final-year valuation. Owner share valuation is based upon computations of *market* value.

There is a hierarchy of *market* valuations. If a *price-earnings multiplier* were a user input, then this factor will be used. If a multiplier is zero or nonentry, then a *market* valuation is attempted using the Modigliani and Miller (MM) theory of earnings capitalization under risk and inflation. In such cases *price-earnings multipliers* are internally computed from the above valuation system. If *liquidation value* exceeds MM value, then *market value* is set equal to *liquidation value*.

The valuation from MM is termed here *going-concern* value. This value is computed and printed in the VALUATION AND SCOPE output division whether or not it is also assigned to *market value* in the hierarchy of the last paragraph. The exception is a sample size (N3) of one. The MM computation in PAVE is based on *investors' required rate of return under risk and inflation*. Risk is computed from variabilities in the output not available from a sample of one, hence for such runs no MM *going-concern value* are computed. If there are no *price-earnings multiplier* inputs with a sample size of one, default values of 10 are supplied internally.

Starting *number of shares* is a user input with internal default of one. These starting shares are assumed to be paid in at some time during the first period. Thus this input is applied to EOP 1 regardless of the amount of either BOP 1 or EOP 1 owners' equity accounts. Permanent capital additions (if any) during the first period do not cause internally generated increases in the number of shares issued.

After the first period, additions of permanent owner equity capital, either input *planned* or internally computed *required* increment, will lead to increases in issued shares. The price of such shares is first computed per positive user input amount per share. If this input is nonpositive, share price is derived from the *market value* at the beginning of each period, as interpolated per the hierarchy above.

The following symbols are used for valuation and share computations with "1" for *first* year and "9" for *final* year:

    N1,N9   numbers of shares issued and outstanding
    L1,L9   liquidation values of assets to owners
    M1,M9   market values, a valuation basis for additional shares
    P1,P9   going-concern or MM values
    R1,R9   investors' required rates of return under risk and inflation

2790   If sample size N3 = 1 then 2790 and 2800 default value check of price-earnings multipliers has been bypassed; the multipliers may be computed internally. A positive input for first year price-earnings multiplier N(10) stands. Otherwise, an internal default of 10 is assigned.

2800   A positive input for final year price-earnings multiplier N(11) stands. Otherwise, an internal default of 10 is assigned. Statements 2790 and 2800 are in a branch for sample size N3 equal to one.

2810   Initialize F(1) as number of shares EOP 1; N1,N9 are also preset to numbers of shares. The EOP 1 number of shares input parameter N(8) has an internal default of one.

For *environment only* N5=3, economic value of the firm and number of shares computations are inapplicable; bypass to PRINT outputs. Then number of shares will be printed as one for output divisions with N5=3.

2820   N2,N8 are value per share factors for EOP 1 and EOP M, used in VALUATION AND SCOPE output printing. Both are first preset for shares EOP 1. L1,L9 are initialized to the computation of final tangible liquidation value to owners. This value is total assets H(4,1) less intangible assets N(6), all multiplied by the factor N(12). The above liquidation *value of tangible assets* less *total liabilities* H(32,1) is tangible liquidation value which would be realized by owners. All the above condition accounts are quantities at the end of the run.

2830   Final *market value* M9 is set equal to final year mean earnings V(5,1) times input multiplier N(11).

If N(11) input were nonzero, then above valuation stands; branch to *first* year computations.

Otherwise control branches to SUB 4670, which computes *going-concern (MM) value* P9 for the final year, and if separable (see 4830 to 4860), a first year going concern value P1.

End of run *market value* M9 is set equal to end of run *going-concern value* P9.

2840   If ending owner *liquidation value* L9 is less than *going-concern value*, M9 remains equal to P9.

Otherwise M9 is reset equal to L9, or *market value* now equals owner *liquidation value*.

2850   Ending price-earnings multiplier N(11) is reset to the final ending market value M9 divided by final year earnings V(5,1). This reset occurs only if N(11) were originally input at zero (note bypass from 2830). This ends the branch for computing end-of-run values M9, L9, and P9. The final value of last year multiplier N(11) has also been determined. L1 and N1 have been initialized as equal to L9 and N9, respectively. Although P1 was initially set equal to P9 in SUB 4670, its final value depends on conditions of run encountered in SUB 4670 (see 4830).

2860   *First* year *market* value M1 is set equal to the product of first year mean earnings V(2,1) and first year input multiplier N(10). If number of periods M exceeds one, processing is transferred to line 2880.

Otherwise the processing for one period depends on whether first year multiplier N(10) is nonzero. If it is nonzero, the initial statement of this line for M1 first year *market value* stands. Control for period one then bypasses the shares per period computation to 2990, since the initial input shares parameter N(8) is the only shares count figure which is relevant.

2870   In this branch number of periods M equals one, and first year multiplier N(10) has an input value of zero. Reset initial market value M1 to equal final value M9.

Reset first year multiplier N(10) equal to final year multiplier N(11).

Branch past shares computations to line 2990 since additional periods are not specified.

2880   Start computation of first-year values for number of periods M greater than one. Compute EOP 1 tangible *liquidation* value to owners L1 from total assets H(35,1), intangibles N(5), liquidation value factor N(12), and total liabilities G(8). The formula corresponds to that for L9 on 2820, but uses EOP 1 values in place of final values. This computation replaces the prior value of L1 equal to L9 (2820).

If N(10) first year multiplier input were nonzero, then the prior computation of initial *market value* M1 on line 2860 stands; *going-concern* revalue is bypassed.

2890   Otherwise lines 2890 and 2920 revalue *market value* to *going-concern value* over the *first* year. This sequence corresponds to lines 2830 to 2850 for the *last* year. GOSUB 4670 computes *going-concern (MM) value* P1 for the first year. Whether P1 is different from P9 depends on whether sufficient periods are separable, as determined in SUB 4670 (line 4830). If SUB 4670 were previously called at 2830, it will be bypassed here from the nonzero value in such case in P9.

2900   First-year *market value* M1 is tentatively set equal to *going-concern MM value* P1.

If EOP 1 *liquidation value* is less then P1, the above value of M1 stands.

Otherwise, first-year *market value* M1 is set equal to EOP 1 *liquidation value of tangible assets to owners* L1.

2910   The first-year price-earnings multiplier N(10) is recomputed as the ratio of *initial market value* P1 to *first-year earnings* V(2,1).

DETERMINE NUMBER OF SHARES OUTSTANDING EOP

2930   Computation of number of shares loop for all periods past the first starts here. First period shares F(1) was set equal to starting shares input N(8) on line 2810. If there were only one period (M=1), this whole routine was by-passed on 2860 or 2870.

The array F( ) input to PAVE4 is cumulative dollar owner equity capital sums for each period from PAVE3 (*paid-in capital* EOP). These sums combine *planned* and internally *required* permanent owner equity capital. The sum array F( ) is used here to output the number of shares for each period. Outputs will be computed for each period past the first.

S is set equal to mean additional dollars for permanent equity capital per period. For example, in the second period (M=2), S equals the difference between paid-in owner capital EOP 2 and EOP 1, or added capital during period 2. Division by N3 sample size determines the mean value; F( ) was input from PAVE3 as sums over the sample size. Inputs F( ) may *decrease* as well as *increase* over periods; but one share is always required (see 2970).

2940   Value factor for a period V is first computed as product of input paid-in cost per share N(9) and number of shares outstanding in the preceding period F(I-1). The reason for this choice of V components is given below (line 2960). Factor V is always the value of existing shares as a basis for valuing capital additions per new share.

If share cost input N(9) is greater than 0, the preceding value factor V stands. Then control transfers to minimum price check on 2960. If N(9) exceeds 0, this means that an *input* price per share will determine the number of additional shares. If N(9)=0, then the number of shares will be computed internally from interpolated changes in market value (M9 and M1) over the preceding period.

2950   For N(9)=0 value factor V is taken as the initial value M1 plus the proportionate increment of value between initial value M1 and final value M9. For period I this is the value V at BOP I, or EOP (I-1). Positive values of V are required for computing the number of additional shares.

2960   If V is greater than the number of shares BOP I, or in other words if existing shares are valued at more than $1 each, then line 2950 computation stands.

Otherwise, the value of existing shares is set to $1 each (equal to share count).

2970   Total shares EOP equals BOP shares plus incremental shares. Incremental number of shares equals additional capital S divided by the going price per share. This going price is V divided by F(I-1). The above arithmetic is combined in factor F(I-1)*S/V. If V was set equal to N(9)*F(I-1) on line 2940, then the computation of incremental shares reduces to S/N(9), or additional owner equity capital divided by price per share.

If the number of shares EOP 1 is greater than one, then the above computation of shares stands.

Otherwise, number of shares is reset to 1. The firm is never permitted less than one share outstanding.

2980   Number of shares is rounded to a whole number.

Number of shares loop ends.

N9 is set equal to final number of shares F(M).

N8 value per share factor EOP M is reset from number of final shares N9 (compare with 2820).

2990   Branch on choice of *output division*. Choices in PAVE4 are N6=0 for VALUATION AND SCOPE to 3570, and N6=1 for FINANCIAL SUMMARY to 3010. Remaining two choices require chaining into PAVE5.

FINANCIAL SUMMARY OUTPUT DIVISION PRINTING

3010–
3030   PRINT *output division* main heading starts. SELECT *line printer* and display printer "ON" warning on video screen with SUB 5170. Sub 4480 prints rows of asterisks above and below division title from passed parameter L for number of asterisks. PRINT firm title input N$.

3040–
3120   PRINT subtitles. For sample size N3=1 at 3070, subtitle information on statistical confidence limits is omitted. Headings for 6 columns of statistical outputs are also omitted. For N3=1 there is one column of up to 33 output items; for N3>1 there are 6 columns of up to 33 output items per column. Titles of columns appear on 3100 to 3120.

3140   PRINT section heading on *Scope of firm*. Three other section headings may be *printed* at 3210, 3280 and 3290, and 3390.

3150–
3540   Up to 33 items (K=1 to 33) may be printed within 4 sections of FINANCIAL SUMMARY. Titles of each are assigned to H$( ). The actual PRINT routine is SUB '1 (line 4510). Information for FINANCIAL SUMMARY is obtained from H( ).

H(K,1) is now the *mean* (2660).

H(K,2) is now the *standard deviation* (2660 to 2680).

H(K,3) and H(K,4) were inputs from PAVE3 as *minimum* and *maximum* values.

SUB '1 loops PRINT 1 to 4 items in each column. Passed parameters to SUB '1 are:

A = starting K index of H( ) for PRINT loop

B = ending K index of H( ) for PRINT loop

Z = indicator of *one* for *dollar* amount with *integer* PRINT, or *two* for two decimal places with *ratios* PRINT

SUB '1 contains a routine (4510 and 4520) which omits items with 0 values.

On 3170 for *environment only* (N5=3), if N(2)=0 for firm sales computed from industry, branch directly to industry sales (3390 to 3410). Beyond this there are no further applicable values at 3410 under N5=3; branch to next output choice at 4270. Returning to 3170, if N(2)=1 there are no further outputs in FINANCIAL SUMMARY; again branch to 4270.

On 3370 start new page (PRINT HEX(OC)) for last section of FINANCIAL SUMMARY except for sample size N3=1. The latter has less headings (3080 to 3120 omitted), and does not require a second page.

On 3410, for *service* frame (N5=0), omit print of *gross profit*, which in such case has the same numerical value as *net sales*. For *service* this account does not provide useful information.

3550   Branch to next output choice.

VALUATION AND SCOPE OUTPUT DIVISION PRINTING—HEADINGS AND SCOPE OF FIRM SECTION

3570–   PRINT main heading using SUB 5170 and SUB 4480 (see 3010 to 3030
3580   explanation).

3590–   PRINT subtitles. Title of firm in N$, period information, title of section
3620   *Scope of firm*, and general information on number of shares (3590 to 3620) are used with all outputs. For sample size N3=1 on 3640, subtitles on statistical information are omitted on 3650 to 3690 (compare 3080 to 3120). Also number of columns reduces from 4 to 1 for nonstatistical output. PRINT phrases are assigned to variables A$, B$, E$, and F$ for all sample sizes.

3710–   The PRINT control routine for *Scope of firm* section is SUB '3 (line 4970).
3810   The *two decimal places* PRINT control routine is SUB '5 (line 5080). SUB '5 is called directly at 3750 for *return on owners' equity*, but indirectly from SUB '3 for the printing of *per share* values. Parameters passed to SUB '3 or SUB '5 are:

A = first year mean

B = first year standard deviation

C = final year mean

D = final year standard deviation

SUB '5 requires additional parameters. Y and Z are per share or rounding factors for *first* and *final* years, and are used in ratio PRINT routine SUB '6. At 3740 Y and Z are rounding factors.

SUB '3 produces one PRINT set of 4 lines of values per call. SUB '3 calls SUB '4 for integer PRINT or SUB '5 for ratio PRINT. Titles of accounts are stored in H$. One column of *means* is printed if N3=1; otherwise 3 additional columns of statistical information are printed. Four items (rows) are printed for each SUB '3 call. These are *total–first year*, *total–final year*, *per share –first year*, and *per share–final year*.

INSOLVENCY INFORMATION PRINTING

3830–
3840

If G(2)=0 there is no *technical insolvency*; PRINT message on 3830 and bypass to legal insolvency output.

3850–
3870

Otherwise, PRINT *technical insolvency* message. The sample proportion of insolvent occurrences is G(2)/N3, and the mean first period of occurrence is G(1)/G(2). Here G(1) is the sum of period numbers of first occurrences.

3880–
3920

Outputs are identical in form to 3830 to 3870, except these outputs apply to *legal insolvency* with input parameters G(3) and G(4) replacing G(1) and G(2).

ECONOMIC VALUATION PRINTING

3940–
3990

PRINT section title *Methods of valuation*, and headings for four columns.

4000–

PRINT routines for *Methods of valuation* are SUB '7 (line 5210) with 4 columns, including *per share* output; or SUB '9 (line 5280) with 2 columns. In each SUB there are pairs of columns for *first year* and *final year*. SUB '7 prints both *total* and *per share* information; SUB '9 *total* information only.

The parameters passed to SUB '7 or SUB '9 are:

A = first year value

C = final year value

Titles of accounts are stored in H$.

For sample size N3=1, bypass *going-concern economic value* on 4030 to 4050. Again for N3=1, the final section PRINT on *parameters of going-concern valuation* is bypassed to 4120 to next output choice.

SUB 4670 for computation of *going-concern values* is included in the flow before PRINT on 4040 and 4050. If values of P1 and P9 were already determined in SUB 4670 from 2830 or 2890, a nonzero *going-concern value* in P9 bypasses another trip through SUB 4670.

4140–
4160

PRINT section title *Parameters of going-concern valuation*, and headings for two columns. This section is bypassed for N3=1 (4120).

4170–   PRINT routines are in SUB '8 (line 5250). Titles are in H$. Parameters
4250   passed to SUB '5 are:

A = EOP 1 parameter value
C = end-of-run parameter value

SELECT NEXT OUTPUT CHOICE AND PROCESS INFORMATION
TRANSFERS

This section is reached after either of two output divisions in PAVE4 have
completed PRINT. The choice variable is N6.

4270–   Select video screen; home *cursor*. Display menu of 6 choices; 4 output divi-
4300   sions, RERUN, or END. INPUT choice in N6.

4320   Upon choice branch to PAVE4 output divisions VALUATION AND SCOPE
        or FINANCIAL SUMMARY with N6=0 or 1, branch to continued processing
        through PAVE5 and PAVE6 for output divisions FINANCIAL STATE-
        MENTS or SELECTED ACCOUNTS with N6=2 or 3, chain back to PAVE1
        for RERUN with N6=4, or branch to END for N6=5.

4330–   Branch for N6=2 or 3 starts here. WRITE 3 parameters needed in PAVE5
4370   to third record of PAVEFT4 data transfer file; set end-of-file marker.

        Write parameters, and F( ) array of number of shares EOP needed in PAVE6,
        to third record of PAVEFT5 data transfer file; set end-of-file marker.

        Close all data transfer files; chain in PAVE5 to continue processing.

4380   RERUN branch for N6=4 is processed here. Chain in PAVE1 for reproces-
        sing. The chained line number of PAVE1 omits for RERUN the preliminary
        user interaction on instructions PRINT and POLREMS.

4390–   All format *image* statements for PAVE4 PRINT sections are grouped to-
4460   gether on these lines.

SUB–PRINT ROW OF ASTERISKS FOR TITLES

4470   A loop is used to print asterisks. Parameter L for number of asterisks is
4490   assigned in main program prior to SUB call. Rows of asterisks are used both
        above and below output division main titles.

SUB '1–COMPUTE AND PRINT FINANCIAL SUMMARY ITEMS

SUB '1 is for PRINT of *one* (N3=1) or *six* (N3>1) columns of information
for each FINANCIAL SUMMARY item in a loop K of 1 to 4 account or
ratio items. For each item the title is stored in H$(K), the input *mean* in
H(K,1), the input *standard deviation* in H(K,2), and input *minimum* and
maximum values in H(K,3) and H(K,4). All these values have been assigned
upon SUB '1 call. For a further explanation see 3150 and Table 14.16. Parameters passed to SUB '1 upon call are:

A = starting K index of H( ) for PRINT loop
B = ending K index of H( ) for PRINT loop
Z = indicator; *one* for *integer* amounts, or *two* for *ratios*

4510– 4520	Pass parameters. Start K loop of items. Start check for 0 values. If mean H(K,1) nonzero, branch to PRINT at 4530. Otherwise, if standard deviation H(K,2) is also 0, branch to end of loop and SUB. If *both* H(K,1) and H(K,2) are 0, item PRINT is omitted; otherwise, branch to PRINT at 4530.
4530	Print title in H$( ). For Z=2 for *ratio*, branch to second routine.
4540	Otherwise, start PRINT for integer (dollar) amounts. Values for PRINT are rounded to nearest integer. Rounded values are stored in T(1), T(2), T(5), and T(6). T( ) was formerly used for Student's t-statistics at 2700 to 2770. Rounded *mean* is stored in T(1). PRINT T(1).
4550	For sample size of 1, or N3=1, PRINT stops after T(1) in first column. Close line with *blank*; branch to end of loop and SUB.
4560– 4580	Otherwise, PRINT five columns from rounded H(K,2) to H(K,4) stored in T( ). *Standard deviation* T(2), and *minimum* and *maximum* values in T(5) and T(6), are PRINT columns as rounded from H( ). *Confidence limits* in T(3) and T(4) are derived from T(1) and T(2) with Student's t-statistics T (from 2700 to 2770). Branch to end of loop and SUB.
4590– 4640	Processing is identical to 4540 to 4580, except this is PRINT branch for *ratios*. Values in T( ) are rounded to two decimal places (hundredths), instead of to integers. This branch is reached from indicator Z equals 2 at 4530.
4650	End of K loop; end of SUB '1.

SUB–GOING-CONCERN VALUE FROM INVESTOR REQUIRED RATES OF RETURN UNDER RISK AND INFLATION

4670	This computation is performed only once for each processing of PAVE4. If a test for nonzero P9 is passed, repeat calls of SUB 4670 will be bypassed at 2890 and 4030.
	Control branches to SUB '2, which computes an *investors' required rate of return* under risk and inflation. Inputs at 4670 to SUB '2 are *standard deviation* (V(6,2) at 2600 to 2620) and *mean* (V(6,1) at 2590) of *last* year *rate of return on owners' equity*, and final *inflation* rate N(18).
	Initially both *first* year R1, and *final* year R9, *investor required rates of return* under risk and inflation, are set equal to R, the output required rate of return from SUB '2.
4680	The long-term growth rate of the industry G is first set equal to user input N(14). Several checks and transformations of G are intended to prevent excessive value since G is applied over an indefinitely long future.

If long-term growth rate input N(14) were nonzero, the above value of G is retained for further processing.

Otherwise, G is set equal to N(19). The latter is the last period total industry growth rate, as computed internally in PAVE2. Input N(14) at zero is the indicator for such internal computation.

4690   If industry inputs were not entered (ID 120=1, or industry growth is otherwise 0), then G is again 0, and a second default value is applied. This default is the sum of final economic *real* growth rate in N(16) and *inflation* rate in N(18). Regardless of choice, a component from inflation will always be applied to G (except nonzero user input in N(14)).

4700   Prior value assigned to G must be less than 75% of the value of *investors' required rate of return* R9 for its value to stand. Otherwise, G is reset to 75% of R9. Values of G which exceed 75% of *investors' required rate of return* behave unstably in growth capitalizations. As growth becomes excessive, or G approaches R, valuation approaches infinity.

4710   In another check G should not in the long run assume a level which is excessive to the general growth of the economy. If G does not exceed the sum of final real *economic* growth N(16) and final *inflation* rate N(18), there is no further downward adjustment.

If G does exceed the *economy growth* rate N(16) plus N(18), then it is replaced by its simple *mean* with the economy rate. The mean is an approximation for an asymptotic decline of G toward the long-term inflated growth rate of the economy.

4720   Negative growth rates do not work in the formulas under some conditions.

If negative, G is reset to 0. At this point the development of long-term industry growth rate G is complete.

4730   Routines for computing useable *rate of return on incremental assets* R5 start here. R5 is first set equal to user input parameter N(15).

If this input N(15) is nonzero the initial value of R5 stands; and control branches to line 4790, which bypasses internal recomputation of R5. Input N(15) at zero is the indicator for such internal computation.

Internal computation of R5 starts with the next statement. If total final assets H(4,1) are negative, there is no current return on incremental assets. Then control branches to line 4780 where R5 is reset to 0.

4740   R5 rate of return on incremental assets is set equal to final year *mean* earnings V(5,1) divided by final value of assets H(4,1). This is a return on total, not incremental, assets, but is initialized as a default if incremental assets are not suitable.

If the above value of R5 is negative, or in other words earnings V(5,1) are negative, a return on assets is not realized and control transfers to line 4780 where R5 is reset to 0.

If there is only one period (M=1), the default F5 *return on total assets* must be used from the first statement on this line; branch to next parameter processing.

4750 If not more than one year is simulated (M $\leq$ N), then again there is insufficient time base for incremental assets. Again, the default R5 *return on total assets* from line 4740 is used; branch to next parameter processing.

4760 If incremental assets during the simulation, computed as H(4,1) final assets less H(35,1) assets EOP 1, are less than 5% of the absolute value of final assets, again incremental assets cannot be used as a base for rate of return. Less than 5% growth of assets is so small that rate of return calculations are likely to be unstable or excessive. Again, *return on total assets* default R5 from line 4740 stands; branch to next parameter processing.

4770 Assuming none of the above default conditions, with R5 equal to *zero* or *rate of return on total assets*, R5 *rate on return on incremental assets* becomes:

$$R5 = \frac{\text{Final year earnings V(5,1) - First year earnings V(2,1)}}{\text{Final EOP assets H(4,1) - Assets EOP 1 H(35,1)}}$$

If R5   0, from above, then this value stands; branch to next parameter processing.

4780 Otherwise, R5=0; R5 is not permitted to go negative, which would produce unrealistic combinations in MM formulas. This zero default for R5 is also reached if final assets H(4,1) are negative (4730), or if *rate of return on total assets* is negative (4740).

4790 For the MM formulas it is necessary to input the incremental assets themselves as well as the rate of return on them. EOP 1 and end-of-run (EOP M) values for total assets are assigned to Q2 and Q5 respectively. First Q2 and Q5 are preset to 0. In general (Q5-Q2) is the amount of incremental assets acquired during the simulation.

The zero values for both Q2 and Q5 are unchanged if final assets H(4,1) are less than initial assets H(35,1). In such case branch to valuation formula on 4820.

4800 If EOP 1 assets H(35,1) are negative, then Q2 remains at zero; branch to compute Q5. Otherwise, Q2 is reset to equal EOP 1 assets.

4810 If final EOP assets H(4,1) are negative, then Q5 remains at 0; branch to valuation.

Otherwise, Q5 is reset to equal final EOP M assets. Negative assets, Q2 or Q5, are not permitted in formula calculation at 4820.

4820   The formula for *going-concern value* from capitalized earnings and earnings growth (MM), at the end of the simulation, is given below. Initially this value is set equal to both first year P1 and final year P9. The growth horizon in the formula is the long-term future past the end of the simulation. In other words, this is a final valuation from the simulation.

$$P9, P1 = \frac{V(5,1)}{R9} + \frac{(Q5)(G)(R5-R9)}{R9(R9-G)}$$

The first term is the long-term capitalization at rate R9 on the *final* year earnings $V(5,1)$. The second term is the benefit to current owners of *incremental earnings* on *incremental assets*. Incremental assets are the product of final asset level Q5 times the growth rate G. Current owners receive an incremental rate (which may be positive, negative, or zero) of the excess of R5, which Q5 times G assets can earn, over R9, which is the assets' market cost of capital. The long-term capitalization of the numerator is accomplished by R9 factor in the denominator. The (R9–G) factor in the denominator expresses long-run valuation under growth.

4830   If only one period were simulated, the computation above is the only source of going-concern value; branch to end of SUB 4670. If the total number of periods of simulation M does not exceed the number of periods per year N, then the span of the simulation does not exceed a year. Again, a second estimate of *going-concern value* is not available; branch to end of SUB 4670.

4840   Otherwise a second estimate of value, for the first year simulated, is computed. Return to SUB '2 for an estimate of R1, the investors' *required rate of return* under risk and inflation during the first year of the simulation. Inputs to SUB '2 are *standard deviation* ($V(3,2)$ at 2600 to 2620) and *mean* ($V(3,1)$ at 2590) of *first* year *rate of return on owners' equity*, and EOP 1 *inflation* rate N(17).

R1 is reset equal to the new R generated by the second call of SUB '2.

4850–   The formula for *going-concern value* during the first year of the simulation
4860   P1 is given on these two lines. This formula is more complex than the one for P9 at 4820 because two growths are encountered. The first is growth during the simulation; the second is projected growth into the indefinite future from the end of the simulation.

$$P1\ Value = \frac{V(2,1)}{R1} + \frac{(Q5-Q2)(R5-R1)}{R1(1+R1)^{0.5(M/N-1)}} + \frac{G*Q5(R5-R9)}{R9(R9-G)(1+R1)^{M/N-1}}$$

The first and third terms are value components similar to those described for the formula on line 4820. The left term is the long-term capitalization of the *first* year (current) earnings. The general capitalization rate is now R1 instead of R9. The third term is identical to that of line 4820 except that here generated future value must be adjusted back to the *present*. On line 4820 a *future* value was generated at the time of the *end* of the simulation. Here, however, the long-run value from growth in the third term must be given a present value. The expression (1+R1), in the denominator, is the present value factor at rate R1. The exponent M/N–1 is the span of the simulation minus one year. The middle term expresses value to beginning owners of incremental assets (Q5–Q2) acquired during the simulation. They receive return R5 on assets at a cost of capital R1. The incremental benefits from (Q5–Q2) are capitalized indefinitely at rate R1 (in the denominator). This capitalization has a present value given by (1+R1) factor with the exponent 0.5(M/N–1). Half the span of the simulation reduced by one year is taken as the mean time at which payoffs from (Q5–Q2) occur.

P1 is assigned a *going-concern value* for the first year simulated, replacing its earlier equality to P9 (line 4820). The formula for P1 is developed on two lines because of its length.

4870   The estimates of *going-concern value* in P9 and P1 end; SUB 4670 ends.

SUB '2– INVESTORS' REQUIRED RATE OF RETURN UNDER RISK AND INFLATION

4890   Values transferred in (for either *final* or *first* year) are:

S = *Standard deviation* of *mean* rate of *return on owners' equity*

A = *Mean* rate of *return on owners' equity*

I0 = *Inflation* rate

Reset S to *variance* of *return on owners' equity*, not variance of its mean.

Preset V to minimum variance operational in LOG formula of 4910.

If actual variance S exceeds minimum V, continue processing. Otherwise, reset S to V, and continue processing.

4900   The output investors' *required rate of return* R is preset to input parameter N(13).

If input parameter N(13) is significantly above zero (above 0.001), its value stands, and control transfers to the end of SUB '2. Otherwise, N(13) at 0 is an indicator to proceed with *internal* computation. If the *mean* rate of return on owners' equity A is nonpositive, branch to maximum default value at 4930.

4910   Otherwise a LOG formula is used to compute R:

$$R = \frac{0.43429 \ (\text{LOG S}) + 2.7249}{17.74} + I0 + 0.018$$

The *natural* LOG is taken of the *variance* of the rate of return on owners' equity. The variance (originally a standard deviation) of the *rate of return on owners' equity* is used here as an estimate of *risk*. *Inflation* rate I0 is added directly to the *required rate of return*. The addition of rate 0.018 is an empirical adjustment for a fundamental, real interest rate.

4920   The maximum *required rate of return* R on risky input A (with high S) is asymptotic to the formula for R on line 4910. If computed R is less than this maximum, 0.268 + I0, then computed R stands.

4930   Otherwise R is set equal to maximum rate of return above. This rate is also a default for nonpositive mean rate of return from 4900.

4940   Rate of return R must also not be zero, as it is used for division in P9 and P1 formulas (4820, 4850, and 4860). To prevent an undefined or unstable operation, R must exceed .001. If it does the value of R stands, and control passes to the end of SUB '2 at 4950.

Otherwise, R is reset to a minimum default *required rate of return* of 0.001.

4950   SUB '2 ends; return to computation of *going-concern values* P9 or P1 in SUB 4670.

SUB '3–PRINT CONTROL OF SCOPE SECTION IN VALUATION OUT-PUT DIVISION

4970   SUB '3 controls PRINT of 4 lines of values (see 3710). It controls SUB '4 for PRINT 2 lines of integer (*total*) values, and controls SUB '5 for PRINT 2 more lines of *per share* values with two decimal places.

Parameters passed to SUB '3 or SUB '5 are:

   A = *first* year *mean*
   B = *first* year *standard deviation*
   C = *final* year *mean*
   D = *final* year *standard deviation*

PRINT titles in H$, E$, and A$ for first line.

4980   Call SUB '4 for first line *total* value PRINT.

Parameters passed SUB '4 are:

   A or C for *mean*
   B or D for *standard deviation*

These are transferred to W and X in SUB '4.

PRINT titles or blanks for second line.

Call SUB '4 for second line *total* value PRINT.

4990   For *environment only* N5=3, only the first account, *sales*, is available to print in VALUATION AND SCOPE division. For N5=3 branch back to *next output choice* at 4270. This will occur after *sales* from the first call of SUB '3.

5000   PRINT titles for third line. Assign *first* and *final* year *per share* factors to Y and Z as auxiliary parameters for SUB '5.

5010 Call SUB '5 to PRINT two lines of *per share* values. SUB '5 has the same variables for passed parameters as SUB '3.

SUB '3 ends.

SUB '4—PRINT INTEGER VALUE LINE FOR SCOPE SECTION OF VALUATION OUTPUTS

5030 Two passed parameters for SUB '4 were listed under 4980.

Titles PRINT was completed in SUB '3. PRINT rounded *mean* value.

5040 For N3=1, branch to RETURN after PRINT of blank to terminate line. In this case only one column is printed.

5050 Otherwise PRINT *standard deviation* and *confidence limits* of *mean*. These values are computed and rounded.

5060 SUB '4 ends.

SUB '5—PRINT CONTROL OF RATIOS FOR SCOPE SECTION OF VALUATION OUTPUTS

5080 SUB '5 is called directly in SCOPE output PRINT for 2 lines of ratios for *rate of return on owners equity* (3750), and also from SUB '3 (4970).

Four passed parameters to SUB '5 are listed at 4970.

Titles PRINT, for *first* line of ratios PRINT in SUB '5, is supplied either in SUB '3 or on line 3740.

Auxiliary parameters required by SUB '5 are:

Y = factor for per share value *first* year
Z = factor for per share value *final* year

Division by *number of shares* is not required for the SUB '5 call at 3750. Values of 100 are supplied there to convert Y and Z to one.

Call SUB '6 for first line of *ratio* print.
Parameters passed to SUB '6 are:

W = *mean* value (before factoring by Y)
X = *standard deviation* value (before factoring by Y)
Y = Factor for per share computation (input Y or Z)

5090 PRINT titles for second line. Call SUB '6 for second line of ratios PRINT.
SUB '5 ends.

SUB '6—PRINT RATIO VALUES FOR SCOPE SECTION OF VALUATION OUTPUTS

5110 Passed parameters to SUB '6 are listed at 5080. SUB '6 processing is similar to SUB '4 except that *per share* division may take place with factor Y, and PRINT values are rounded to two decimal places.

PRINT rounded mean value.

5120 Branch for N3=1; explanation is identical to 5040.

5130–   Otherwise PRINT *standard deviation* and *confidence limits* of *mean*. SUB
5150   '6 ends.

SUB–PRINTER 'ON' WARNING AND SELECTION

5170–   SELECT *video* screen; home *cursor*; *display* instruction and warning message
5180   for *line* printer.

5190   SELECT *line* printer; scroll to top of sheet; SUB 5170 ends.

SUB '7–PRINT 4 COLUMNS FOR METHODS OF VALUATION

5210   SUB '7 PRINT gives 4 columns of figures; SUBs '8 and '9 give 2 columns.

The parameters passed to SUBs '7, '8, and '9 are:

A = *first* year or EOP 1 value
C = *final* year or end-of-run (EOP M) value

PRINT title.

5220   PRINT *first* and *final total* values after rounding.

5230   PRINT *per share first* and *final* year values, using factors N2 and N8 (see
2820 and 2980), and rounding to two decimal places. SUB '7 ends.

SUB '8–PRINT 2 COLUMNS OF RATIO FIGURES FOR PARAMETERS
OF GOING-CONCERN VALUE

5250   All values in *parameters* section of VALUATION AND SCOPE division are
printed with SUB '8.

See passed parameters under 5210. PRINT title.

5260–   PRINT *first* and *final* ratios. Multiplication by 1E4 (or 10,000) converts
5270   output to *percentages* as well as rounding to two decimal places. A blank
field is used between columns here. SUB '8 ends.

SUB '9–PRINT 2 COLUMNS OF INTEGERS FOR METHODS OF
VALUATION

5280   As compared to SUB '7, SUB '9 PRINT gives only the first 2 columns.

See passed parameters under 5210. PRINT title.

5290   PRINT *first* and *final* rounded integer values. SUB '9 ends.

5300   PAVE4 ends.

14.6 | PAVE5 Documentation

PAVE5 is used to PRINT 3 to 5 statements out of the set in FINANCIAL
STATEMENTS output division. Two final statements of this division require chaining into PAVE6.

The principal account arrays in PAVE5 are:

A( )   for *flow* values which are transferred from PAVE2 under reduced A( ), or D( ). These values are *not* sums over sample replications.

C( )   for *condition* accounts needed in PAVE5; transferred as replication *sums* from PAVE3.

D( )   for *flow* accounts transferred as replication *sums* from PAVE3.

Table 14.18 lists the elements of account arrays for PAVE5 statements PRINT.

30–
60   SELECT video screen; home *cursor*; PRINT program title; DIMENSION arrays and alpha scalar variables.

80–
110   READ 3 records from PAVEFT4 data transfer file into scalar control parameters and arrays. The records are transferred variables from PAVE2, PAVE3, and PAVE4 or PAVE6. The last record comes from PAVE4 for *initially* specified outputs, but from either PAVE4 or PAVE6 for subsequent output choices. PAVE5 call depends upon prior output division: from PAVE4 for N6 division choice 0 or 1; PAVE6 for choice 2 or 3 (see description of N6 below).

Arrays C( ) and D( ) are redimensioned to reduced size (line 80) in order to receive a correct number of input items from PAVE2. They are redimensioned again back to full size at 110.

System parameters transferred from PAVE2 are:

N\$ =   title of run for PRINT at top of statements
M   =   number of periods
N   =   number of periods per year
N3 =   sample size (nonstatistical = 1)
N5 =   frame (service = 0, trade = 1, manufacturing = 2, environment only = 3)
I1   =   industry sales for base year (input P(31) from ID 130)

System parameters transferred from PAVE4 or PAVE6 are:

N6 =   output division choice (VALUATION AND SCOPE = 0, FINANCIAL SUMMARY = 1, FINANCIAL STATEMENTS = 2, SELECTED ACCOUNTS = 3)
S1 =   net sales demand indicator (% sales = 0/\$ per period = 1) (input P(21) from ID 120)
R   =   R&D expense indicator (% sales = 0/\$ per period = 1) (input Q(1) from ID 330)

Computation factors from N3, R, and I1 are developed at 110: N9 is reciprocal of N3, R inputs 0 or 1 are interchanged, and I1 is converted to "000s omitted."

120   B$ is given a "continuation" subtitle for statement displays beyond the initial display.

Final period single B( ) account from PAVE2 is transferred to a C array for SUB '3 (2380) PRINT. The other periods of B( ) are assigned in a loop (600). B( ) is also converted to an equivalent sum over sample replications.

INDEXING PARAMETERS FOR PRINT COLUMNS

Parameters must be developed to index displays of PRINT columns for each statement. ALL PAVE5 statements are *flow* statements and use the same column arrangements, headings, and display system.

Statements form must meet the following conditions:

1. *Annual summary* columns are added at the end of each year if both
   a. Period duration is one-half year or less, $N>=2$.
   b. Total length of simulation is not less than a year, $M/N>=1$.

2. *Total* required account value print columns are 1 to 36 from sum of *period* columns (M=1 to 24) and separate *annual* columns (C=0 to 12 with at least 2 periods per year for separate PRINT of annual columns).

3. Each *statement* is organized as follows:
   a. Divided into *tableaus* or *displays*.
   b. Each *display* repeats account titles in left column and prints from 1 to 6 account value columns.
   c. Only the last display has less than 6 value columns.
   d. Total displays range from 1 to 6.

4. The following are important display parameters:
   M = Number of period columns (1 to 24 range)
   C = Number of annual columns (0 to 12 range)
   I = Index of total PRINT columns over all displays (1 to M+C range).
   $X(I)$ = Control integer for column time intervals:
             $X(I) = 1$ to M+1 for *period* columns; $X(I) = 26$ to 25+C for *annual* columns, where $X(I) = 26$ for *Year 1* column, 27 for *Year 2* column, etc.
   Z = Number of displays (1 to 6 range)
   J = Index of displays (1 to Z range)
   $U(J)$ = Total columns index I for *first* column of display J
   $V(J)$ = Total column index I for *last* column of display J

The values developed in 140 to 210 for column control arrays X( ), U( ), and V( ) are used not only for all statements in PAVE5, but also are transferred at 1820 to PAVEFT5 for use in CAPITAL CHANGES statements of PAVE6

140   Assign INTEGER value to N1 for number of periods per year.

Then N1 is the number of *period* PRINT columns between each *annual* column.

Preset annual columns C to 0.

If less than 2 periods per year (period duration exceeds ½ year) above C=0 stands and there are no annual columns.

Otherwise, annual columns is INTEGER of M/N. Note that simulation duration less than a year retains C=0.

150   Compute total number of displays Z from sum of M and C.

Preset accumulators W, V1, U1, and Y; start J loop through displays.

170   First column number display, U(J) and U1, is incremented by 6 for each display. Then initial –5 in U1 leads to a U(J) series of values, 1, 7, 13, etc.

Last column number of display V(J) and V1 is *tentatively* incremented by 6 for each display. This series runs 6, 12, 18, etc.

If tentative V(J) is less than highest column number M+C, value stands.

Otherwise, V(J) is reset to highest column number.

180   Start nested I loop of columns within a display.

Y is a counter of period columns past the last *annual* column.

Y is set to 0 to indicate an annual column.

The first column is *always* Period 1; hence preset of Y to 1 at 150. Branch to 200 if *annual* column from Y equal to 0.

Otherwise, set X(I) equal to *period* number. W is counter of annual columns; initially there are no annual columns, hence preset W=0 at 150. The period number in X(I) is total column count I less number of annual columns W up to current I.

Increment Y count for *period* column just processed. The count of Y determines when next annual column is required.

190   If no *annual* columns, or count of Y is not up to total *period* columns between *annual* columns per N1, branch past annual column routines at 200 to next I index.

Otherwise, if Y is not less than N1, last *period* column before *annual* column has just been processed on 170 and 180. Reset Y to 0 so next column will be processed as *annual* at Y text on 180.

200   This is *annual* column branch. Update W to number of annual columns. Apply year number plus 25 in X(I).

Reset Y to 1 for first *period* column past annual.

210   End I loop for columns in displays; end J loop for displays.

For SELECTED ACCOUNTS output division (N6=3), all statements PRINT in PAVE5 is bypassed. Branch to transfer of information to PAVE6.

PRINT FROM 3 TO 5 FINANCIAL STATEMENTS

230–   Home *cursor*; display instruction and warning message for *line* printer.
240
SELECT line printer.

250–   PRINT main title FINANCIAL STATEMENTS output division and general
380   explanatory information headings.

SUB '0 at 1970 prints a row of asterisks. The passed parameters are:

T1 = Spaces in margin to left of title. The FINANCIAL STATEMENTS division heading is indented more than individual statement headings.

L   = Number of asterisks or length of row.

Rows of asterisks are printed above and below division title (250 and 270), and above and below *each* statement title. On repeat displays of statements the top row of asterisks is omitted. *Scroll to top of page* (HEX(OC) at 250) for this heading and each new set of financial statements.

400–   PRINT ENVIRONMENT ANALYSES statements. All statements follow
580   the same plan. The N$ title is printed followed by the statements title, under-lined and overlined with asterisk rows (SUB '0). The statements title is stored in A$.

At 430, *base industry sales* PRINT is bypassed for no industry analysis with S1=1. Otherwise, *base industry sales* for *year* (I1) and *period* are computed, rounded, and printed.

There is a J loop of displays for each statement (450 here). SUB 2010 is used to print *period* and *year* headings for each display.

Account titles are stored in H$. The following SUBs are called to PRINT a line of 1 to 6 columns of values:

SUB '1 for A( ) with *flow* values *not* sums over sample replications.
SUB '2 for D( ) with *flow* values as replication *sums*.
SUB '3 for C( ) *condition* accounts as *sums*. Two lines, BOP and EOP conditions, are printed by this SUB.

The parameters passed to these SUBs are:

T = Indicator for print loops
        T = 1 for *percentage* or ratio with 2 decimal places printed (different use in SUB '3; see 2380)
        T = 2 for *dollar* integers (different use in SUB '3; see 2380)
Q = account index of A( ), D( ), or C( )

On 480, for *no* industry analysis, accounts between PRINT of *real growth rate* and *PRINT firm sales demand* are inapplicable, and are bypassed.

Scroll to top of page (HEX(OC)) checks occur frequently. These checks differ because statements are often of different length from variations in type of run. On 540, if on last display, bypass *scroll*. For displays J=2 or 5, *scroll*. But if either is last display, there is no scroll. Note that each *new* statement begins with a *scroll*.

At the end of each display (here 570), but bypassed for the last display (J=Z at 540); statement title A$, continue message in B$, and *one* row of asterisks (SUB '0) are printed. This sequence is used as a continuation title for all displays except the first.

600– 650	Certain summation accounts for totals of INCOME STATEMENTS, not precomputed and transferred from PAVE2 or PAVE3, are developed here in a loop over all periods.

The single B( ) account from PAVE2 is transferred to C( ). It is converted to a sum with N3, so it may be processed in SUB '3. The conversion is completed with B(1,M+1) at 120.

Account indexes already printed on ENVIRONMENTAL ANALYSES are used here again as totals for INCOME STATEMENTS. Examples are indexes 8 to 11 for A( ); and 23 for D( ). The A( ) conversions are transformed into *means* through factor N9, the D( ) into sums through factor N3.

The factor R in 640 will include total *R&D expense*, now in A(9,I), in *sales margin over direct expense* D(39,I), only if A(9,I) were taken as variable with sales.

670– 1060	INCOME STATEMENTS are printed in 670 to 1060. A HEX(OC) scrolls paper to the top for each set of displays at the start of a new group of statements.

A J loop controls displays following the N$ titles PRINT. SUB 2010 gives PRINT of *period* and year headings, which provides similar information for all displays.

For *service frame* N5=0, *cost of sales* and *gross profit* accounts are inapplicable, and are *bypassed* (710).

Except for last display J=Z, each display scrolls a new page (1040) and PRINTs a *continuation title* (1050). See additional PRINT explanations under 400 to 580.

A triple branch relates statements PRINT to frame choice N5. For *service* N5=0, the next two statements are bypassed; for *trade* N5=1, only the next is bypassed; and for *manufacturing* N5=3, none are bypassed.

1080–   The sequence of printing of COST OF GOODS MANUFACTURED SCHE-
1440   DULES on 1080 to 1320 is identical to summary description of INCOME
        STATEMENTS at 670 to 1060, and additional explanations at 400 to 580.

        PRINT of COST OF GOODS SOLD is identical to above except that for
        these short statements *scroll* to top of page is activated only after nonfinal
        fifth display (the sixth display, if used, is printed on a new sheet).

1460–   An I loop over periods totals accounts for CASH FORECASTS, which were
1480   not transferred as totals from PAVE3 (compare 600 to 650). Account ele-
        ments of D( ) are revised from previous statements. All values are SUMS
        over sample replications.

1500–   PRINT of CASH FORECASTS uses the same system as previous statements
1720   (see 670 to 1060, and 400 to 580). At 1680 there is a scroll at the end of
        each *odd-numbered* display (2 displays per sheet except for first).

        PROCESS INFORMATION TRANSFERS

        From end of PAVE5 information is always transferred to PAVE6 to com-
        plete the PRINT of FINANCIAL STATEMENTS.

1740–   Certain *flow* value *sums* are required for SELECTED ACCOUNTS in PAVE6.
1790   These are transferred for all periods in an I loop to low order indices of D( )
        (see Table 14.18). *Gross profit* $D(5,I)$ is set to 0 for service N5=0 (1770).
        Gross profit and *operating income* $D(7,I)$ are also reset to 0 for environment
        only N5=3 (1780).

1810–   Reduce D( ) DIMENSION for transfer of SELECTED ACCOUNT values
1830   to PAVE6.

        WRITE to PAVEFT5 for transfer to PAVE6: output choice parameter N6;
        reduced array D( ) values; and display control arrays U( ), V( ), and X( )
        (see preamble to 140).

        Set end-of-file marker, CLOSE files; chain next program PAVE6.

1840–   All *format* image statements for PAVE5 PRINT are grouped together in
1950   these lines.

        SUB '(0)—PRINT ROW OF ASTERISKS FOR TITLES

1970–   SUB '0 uses a K loop for one row of asterisks with the following passed
1980   parameters:

        T1 = indented left margin to *title* and asterisk rows
        L   = number of asterisks PRINT (length of row)

        SUB—PRINT PERIOD AND YEAR HEADINGS FOR DISPLAYS

        These headings appear at the top of each display in FINANCIAL STATE-
        MENTS. They are the same set for all statements, but different for each
        display within statements. For explanation of U(J), V(J) and X(J), see pre-
        amble to 140.

2000   Skip account title area with PRINT blank in field.

Start loop of 1 to 6 columns of values with index I.

2010   Value X=X(I)/N is elapsed years at the end of each *period* when X(I) is a period number. INT(X) is the counter of preceding years.

If X(I) exceeds 25, the *column* is a *year* instead of a *period*, branch to alternate heading for years.

2020–   Otherwise, print *period number*, *preceding year number* and *month number*.
2030

Branch to next columns heading.

2040   PRINT heading for *years* column. Number of year equals X(I)–25.

2050   Loop I for columns ends. PRINT trailing blank to complete PRINT line. This is always done at the end of a set of column printing to shift from a loop through sequential fields on a line to a line space at end.

SUB 2000 ends.

SUB '1—PRINT FLOW VALUE FROM A( ) NOT SAMPLE REPLICATION SUMS

2070   Passed parameters to SUB '1 are:

        T = indicator 1 for ratios PRINT with two decimal places, or 2 for PRINT integers

        Q = account index of A( )

Loop over periods I bypasses PRINT for all 0 values. If value in A(I,Q) is 0, continue check loop.

2080   Otherwise, terminate loop and branch to print because nonzero value has been found.

2090   At end of loop all values were zeros; do not PRINT; branch to RETURN.

2100   Start PRINT with account title in H$. Move to account values loop with I from U(J) to V(J) (see preamble to 140). Note range of I index has shifted from use in 2070 to 2090. Now I indexes PRINT columns over set of statement displays instead of periods.

2110   If *annual* column is reached (signaled by X(I)>25), branch to this routine at 2150. Otherwise, PRINT values are for a *period*.

If *integer* value PRINT, branch to that routine at 2130.

2120   Otherwise, compute rounded ratio in P and PRINT P. Note that the correct period number has been stored in X(I). Branch to accumulation of values over periods in P(Q) at 2140. P(Q) is saved to PRINT *annual* aggregates when the next *annual* column is reached. It is necessary to store each *account line* of a given statement separately, since the last column of a display often does not coincide with the end of a year. Then P(Q) values must be carried over to the next display.

2130   Integer values are rounded and PRINT with P in this branch. Progress to accumulation the same as 2120.

2140   Accumulate A(Q,I) values in P(Q) and branch to next column.

2150   *Annual* columns valuation and PRINT starts. For integer values, branch to 2170.

         Otherwise round and PRINT *mean* annual ratio.

2160   After *annual* PRINT column branch to *reset* P(Q) to 0 at 2180.

2170   PRINT annual *total* from P(Q) and progress to *reset* at 2180.

2180–   Reset *annual* value in P(Q); display column I loop ends. PRINT trailing blank
2200   to line space (see 2050).

         If not *final* display, branch from 2190 to RETURN. This switches control back to main program and initiates the next display.

         Otherwise, reset P(Q) to 0. If this is not done, and the final statement column is *period* rather than *annual*, then residual values in P(Q) would in some cases be transferred to another statement.

SUB '2—PRINT FLOW VALUES FROM D( ) SUMS OF SAMPLE REPLICATIONS

2220–   Processing and passing of parameters is similar to SUB '1 (2070 to 2200
2360   above) except for the following adjustments:

         Q is the index of D( ) in place of A( ). Then D( ) is tested for all 0 values bypass (2220 to 2240).

         The factor N9 is included in the computation of P at 2270 and 2290. This factor obtains *means* in P from *sums* in D( ).

         Accumulations over periods for annual columns are stored in Z( ) and D( ). It is necessary to keep Z( ) separate from P( ) with A( ), since both A( ) and D( ) indices often appear in the same statements and displays.

SUB '3—PRINT CONDITION VALUES FROM C( ) SUMS OF SAMPLE REPLICATIONS

2380–   The passed parameters to SUB '3 are:
2400

         T = Indicator of prefix printing: Standard EOP second-line title 1/
               Special title used only with EOP cash = 2
         Q = Account index of C( )

         SUB '3 prints *two* lines of *condition* values per call, BOP and EOP; SUB '1 and SUB '2 each print *one* line of *flow* values. All values printed by SUB '3 are rounded integers.

         Annual columns in SUB '3 PRINT *annual* BOP and EOP values. The *annual* BOP value is stored in K(Q,1) from N–1 periods behind the period just before the annual column. The *annual* EOP value is the same as the preceding period value, and is stored in K(Q,2).

For all periods, M+1 *condition* values are required: BOP values are stored for X(I) period number values 1 to M, and EOP values for X(I) period number values 2 to M+1. The range of X(I) values for periods is now 1 to 25, but as before, 26 to 37 is the counter range for *annual* values.

The check and bypass PRINT for 0 values of C(Q,I) over all periods is the same as 2070 to 2090, but now M+1 period values are checked. Again the I index here is different from the I index of columns used in the remainder of SUB '3.

2410   Start *first* line BOP condition values PRINT (2410 to 2460); PRINT account title. Start PRINT loop for account values in columns of display.

2420   If X(I) exceeds 25, branch to *annual* column routine.

2430   Otherwise PRINT *mean* (factor N9) BOP value in C( ) with X(I) BOP index.

2440   If I index, and also *period* number, is less than the *last* period number of the *first* year, then a BOP value is not stored for *annual* column; branch to next column of *first* line PRINT.

Otherwise store BOP value for *annual* column in K(Q,1). The value stored is one year ago, which is the value of C( ) for N-1 periods back. Branch to next column.

2450   PRINT *annual* stored BOP value as *mean* of K(Q,1).

2460–   *First* line BOP condition values loop ends. PRINT trailing blank to line space.
2480

Start *second* line EOP values PRINT (2460 to 2530).

For T=1, account title print repeats routine of 2410, but with EOP values. Progress to value column loop at 2490.

Otherwise for T=2, used only for EOP *cash*, line space and PRINT title on 2470. Branch to value column loop at 2490.

2490   Start PRINT loop for *second* line EOP account values; branch for *annual* columns to 2520.

2500   Set P to *mean* EOP value in C( ) with (X(I)+1) EOP index; PRINT P.

2510   Set *annual* EOP stored value K(Q,2) equal to most recent *period* EOP value in P.

Branch to I loop index for next value column.

2520   In *annual* column branch PRINT value EOP in K(Q,2). Progress to 2530 for next EOP value column.

2530   *Second* PRINT line loop I for EOP columns ends. PRINT trailing blank to line space.

Note that K(Q,1) and K(Q,2) need not be reset to 0. They are not accumulators and receive correct values during period just prior to *annual* columns.

2540   SUB '3 ends; PAVE5 ends.

14.7 | PAVE6 Documentation

INITIALIZE SYSTEM AND READ INPUTS

PAVE6 provides PRINT of two remaining STATEMENTS (CAPITAL CHANGES and CONDITION at 2770 to 3390 in FINANCIAL STATEMENTS output division N6=2), and entire PRINT of SELECTED ACCOUNTS output division (N6=3) (3410 to 4110). PRINT of 3 to 5 other FINANCIAL STATEMENTS is in PAVE5, but PAVE6 is always chained in from PAVE5 because accounts are processed there for PAVE6.

The principal account arrays of PAVE6 are:

From PAVE2:

B( )   for *condition* accounts, values without uncertainty (see also Table 14.11). B( ) account indexes are:

1, indirect *manufacturing* supplies inventory

2, total *manufacturing* fixed assets at *book* value

3, total *general* fixed assets at *book* value plus intangibles *unamortized*

4, intangible *unamortized* balance

5 to 9,   classes of *general* fixed assets (5) at cost

10 to 14,   classes of *reserves* (5) for *general* fixed assets

15 to 19,   classes of *manufacturing* fixed assets (5) at cost

20 to 24,   classes of reserves (5) for *manufacturing* fixed assets

From PAVE3:

C( ) for *condition* accounts statistical sums (see Table 14.13)

Further values in C( ) are developed internally. The indexes of these are:

15, total monetary assets

16, total inventories

17, total current assets

18, total assets

19, total current liabilities

20, total liabilities

21, total owners' equity

22, total liabilities and owners' equity

From 3480 C( ) is used for *sums* and *means* (3510) of 17 SELECTED ACCOUNTS. From this point C( ) applies to both *flow* and *condition* accounts (see Table 14.15).

G( ) for *sums of squares* for SELECTED ACCOUNTS (see Table 14.15).

From PAVE4:

F( ) for number of shares outstanding at the end of each period.

Following PRINT of CAPITAL CHANGES statements, F( ) is assigned to *months* in period headings for CONDITION STATEMENTS.

D( ) for *flow* values statistical sums needed for CAPITAL CHANGES statements and SELECTED ACCOUNTS (see Table 14.18).

U( ), V( ), and X( ) control PRINT value columns of displays (see preamble to 140 in section 14.6).

System parameters transferred from PAVE2 are:

N$, *title of run* for PRINT at top of statements
M, number of periods per year
N3, sample size (nonstatistical = 1)
N5, frame (service = 0, trade = 1, manufacturing = 2, environment only = 3)
I1, number of *manufacturing* fixed asset classes (originally N(49))
I2, number of *general* fixed asset classes (originally N(50))

System parameters transferred from PAVE4 are:

T, Student's t-statistic for computation of confidence limits
P, confidence probability
S1, industry sales indicator: % share of industry = 0/$ direct firm sales per period = 1; P(21) or ID 120 originally, N(2) in PAVE4
R1, R&D expense indicator: % sales = 0/$ per period = 1; Q(1) or ID 330 originally, N(3) in PAVE4

System parameters transferred from PAVE5 are:

N6, Output division choice (VALUATION AND SCOPE = 0, FINANCIAL SUMMARY = 1, FINANCIAL STATEMENTS = 2, SELECTED ACCOUNTS = 3)
Z, Number of displays per statement in FINANCIAL STATEMENTS output PRINT

2490– SELECT video screen; home *cursor*; PRINT PAVE6 program title; DIMEN-
2580 SION arrays and alpha scalar variables. OPEN and READ 4 records of PAVEFT5 data transfer file. These records come from PAVE2, PAVE3, PAVE4, and PAVE5 (see preceding descriptions of arrays and system parameters). C( ) and D( ) must be REDIMENSIONED (2540) for READ correct fields from PAVE3. They are REDIMENSIONED back to original size at 2580.

CLOSE input data transfer file PAVEFT5.

Factor N9 for *mean* values is the reciprocal of sample size N3.

ASSIGN TITLES AND VALUES TO CONDITION ACCOUNTS

2600–2640	Titles are assigned to *accounts* in C$( ), which are used for *both* CONDITION STATEMENTS and SELECTED ACCOUNTS.

2660–
2730 Account totals sums are required for both CONDITION STATEMENTS and SELECTED ACCOUNTS. These were not available from C( ) transfers from PAVE3. The I loop to M+1 is for *condition* values from BOP 1 to EOP M (index M+1).

C(15,I) is used to develop *total monetary assets* internally.

C(16,I) sums total inventories. The classes of applicable inventories depends on the frame; hence N5+1 branch at 2670.

B( ) terms are multiplied by N3 to convert to sums for adding to other sum totals.

2740–
2750 B(3,I) is restated at *total general fixed assets at book value*. The *unamortized intangibles* component is removed.

Except for BOP 1 bypass, *owners' equity* values are transferred to D( ). This facilitates SUB '2 call for *owners' equity per share* at 2900.

Totals loop over periods ends.

For SELECTED ACCOUNTS (N6=3), branch to 3410.

Display line printer information and warning on video screen; SELECT line printer from SUB 5080.

For *environment only* frame N5=3, bypass PAVE6 FINANCIAL STATEMENTS to *next output choice* routine.

PRINT CAPITAL CHANGES STATEMENTS

2770–
2950 PRINT displays of CAPITAL CHANGES statements. The processing system is identical to statements in PAVE5 (see 400 to 580, and 670 to 1060, in section 14.6) except for different variable assignments in A$, B$, and H$. J and Z are the same as in PAVE5.

SUB '0 is used to print a row of asterisks above and below the main title on first display (2770 and 2790), and as an underline for subsequent displays (2940).

SUB 4390 prints calendar headings for each display in an identical fashion to SUB 2000 in PAVE5 (section 14.6).

For CAPITAL CHANGES statements there is a *scroll to top of next sheet* after each even-numbered display (2910) (2 displays per sheet).

The SUBs used to print lines of values are as follows:

SUB '1 for *period* and *annual* integer *condition* values for C( ) BOP. The only passed parameter is Q, account index of C( ).

SUB '2 for *period* and *annual* values for D( ) *flows* array and F( ) number of EOP shares array.

The passed parameters from SUB '2 are E and Q:

E is index of computation and printing:
  1 = means of integer flows
  2 = EOP values of outstanding shares with F( )
  3 = per share PRINT with two decimal places
  Q is account index of D( )

SUB '3 for *period* and *annual* integer *condition* values for C( ) EOP. The only passed parameter is Q, account index of C( ).

In PAVE5 SUB '1 and SUB '3 above were combined in SUB '3 (2380 to 2540 in PAVE5). This is not feasible in PAVE6 because BOP and EOP pair of PRINT lines are not always together as in PAVE5.

PRINT CONDITION STATEMENTS

2970–
3010
The main title, with 2 rows of asterisks from SUB '0, is similar to CAPITAL CHANGES above. There is an explanatory remark to the right of the main title (2990) and an "assets" subtitle (3010).

The column arrangement differs from all previous statements because *separate* annual columns are not printed. The first value PRINT column, however, is BOP 1; all other columns are EOP indexed. Number of displays Z, and column number indices I for the last display U(Z) and V(Z), are recomputed in SUB 4910.

Revised calendar headings for CONDITION printing are developed in SUB 4460.

3020–
3380
H$ receives account titles, some of which were previously assigned to C$ (2600 to 2640).

Each line of integer value columns uses SUB '4 at 4940 for PRINT. The following variables are passed:

E is indicator of printing, computation, and array name:
  1 = C( ) for source with H$ title
  2 = B( ) for source with H$ title
  3 = B( ) for source with *class number* of fixed assets subtitle
  Q = Account number index of B( ) or C( ) array

On 3060 inapplicable inventories under frame N5 are bypassed from triple branch N5+1.

The same bypass occurs at 3190 for I2=0 with *general* fixed asset classes. The K loops (3150, 3160 to 3170 3210, and 3220 to 3230) print subtitles accessed from within SUB '4.

Each CONDITION display occupies exactly two pages. Note the *scroll to next page* HEX(OC) at 3270. This occurs just prior to repeating the main CONDITION STATEMENTS title in A$ (this time not underlined by an asterisks row), continuation phrase in B$, and subtitle of 3280.

3390   End J display loop for end of CONDITION STATEMENTS. Branch to *next output choice* routine.

ASSIGN TITLES AND VALUES FOR SELECTED ACCOUNTS

3410–   SELECTED ACCOUNTS output division process and PRINT starts. The
3470   following control parameters are developed for SELECTED ACCOUNTS:

    C   first statistic display line for each account
    D   last statistic display line for each account
    G   first account block to be printed
    H   last account block to be printed
    I   index of periods or columns for each display line
    I0   indicator to process (I0=0) or bypass (I0=1) initial set of values (values are assigned on 3410 to 3550).
    I3   scroll to top of page for display of 17 accounts indicated by I3=1
    J   index of displays from 1 to Z
    K   index of accounts to be printed in vertical blocks
    L   index of display lines for each account
    Q   1. Numerator of standard deviations (3520 to 3540)
           2. Value to be rounded and printed (3990 to 4040)
    R   bypass indicator (R=1) for main title on repeat account runs while within SELECTED ACCOUNTS output division
    S   INPUT statistical display by number, and heading PRINT choice by sign (minus sign omits headings)
    U   statistical display choice, absolute value of S, used to set C and D for statistical outputs
    W   INPUT account number choice

Reset R to 0 to PRINT title on first division call. Within PAVE6, lines 3410 to 3550 are only executed *once*. Bypass indicator I0 is reset to 1 at 3550.

Assign remaining titles of SELECTED ACCOUNTS to C$( ). This extends assignments at 2600 to 2640.

3480–   Compute amount *sums* needed for SELECTED ACCOUNTS in C( ) by I
3500   loop over all periods. This includes change of account indexes to conform to numbers 1 to 17 used for menu, C$( ) titles, and G( ) sums of squares (see Table 14.15).

Here C( ) is no longer just a *condition* array; it is used for all SELECTED ACCOUNTS, both *flow* and *condition*. The index of condition accounts is reduced by *one* because now the I period index conforms to EOP condition values, not BOP values as formerly.

3510   Sixteen indexed C( ) accounts are factored by N9 from *sums* to *means*. The 17th account, *all fixed assets at book*, has no uncertainty. It was derived from B( ) which is not a sample sum array. There is no *standard deviation* computation in 3520 to 3540 for this account.

3520–   For sample size N3=1, computation of *standard deviations* of SELECTED
3540   ACCOUNTS is bypassed.

        Otherwise a *variance* numerator is computed in Q from C( ) and G( ).

        Q is reset to 0, if negative, to avoid aborting the program at 3540.

        Convert G( ) to *standard deviations* of SELECTED ACCOUNTS.

3550   Loop K to 16 account *means* and *standard deviations* over all accounts ends.
        Loop I over periods ends. Reset I0 to 1 to bypass 3410 to 3550 on future
        runs in PAVE6.

        USER COMMAND PARAMETERS FOR SELECTED ACCOUNTS

3570   SELECT video screen; home *cursor*; preset user INPUT variables W and S
        to 0.

3580–   Display *menu* and *instructions*. Account titles are printed from C$(K). User
3660   provides INPUT of W and S.

        SET SELECTED ACCOUNTS RANGE PARAMETERS

3680   If W exceeds 17 (INPUT instruction gives entry of 99), branch to *next out-
        put choice* routine. The same occurs for INPUT of S=0.

3690   Preset account limits G and H to account W. This stands for PRINT one
        account.

        Otherwise, if W=0 for PRINT 17 accounts, reset G and H. Set page control
        I3 to 1 for *scroll* with extensive printing.

3700   Preset statistical display line limits for each account to one line. For no un-
        certainty (N3=1) this preset stands and subtitles in S$( ), lines 3720 to 3740,
        are also bypassed.

3710   Otherwise, set U to the input choice from S (U disregards sign of S).

        If U is three or more, first display line of account will be the *first* statistic
        (C=1 for *mean*). Then D is *second* or *fourth* statistic, which is transformed
        from U=3 or 4.

3720–   Assign display of account subtitles in S$( ). Subtitle S$(1) is set at 3830
3740   because it must be reset for each display (see 3960).

        PRINTED SELECTED ACCOUNTS OUTPUT DIVISION TITLE

3750   Start PRINT of titles for SELECTED ACCOUNTS output division.

3760   If R=1 the title is skipped. The title is printed only once on first call in
        PAVE6 of SELECTED ACCOUNTS output division. Upon first call (3410)
        R has been reset to 0. At the end of first statement R is reset to 1 (4110).

        Similarly to SELECTED ACCOUNTS main title; column and display
        controls Z, U(Z), and V(Z) need only be processed once. This is done in
        SUB 4910.

        Scroll to sheet top (HEX(OC)) for start of SELECTED ACCOUNTS.

3770–   A *negative* INPUT to S omits all titles.
3820
         Otherwise, PRINT run title N$, overline of asterisks in SUB '0, output
         division title, an underline of asterisks in SUB '0, and a subtitle.

         Bypass statistical information subtitle at 3800 if N3=1.

         CONTROL OF SCROLL UP AND HEADINGS FOR DISPLAYS

3830–   Start display loop J. Assign subtitle to S$(1).
3840
         The purpose of the next routine to 3870 is to *scroll* up (3860) if a PRINT
         set for *one* account has just followed a PRINT set of 17 accounts.

         The scroll up is not required if a first statement with main title were just
         printed (R=0).

         Branch to *scroll* up for 17 accounts PRINT with G not equal to H.

         Otherwise, again bypass *scroll* up except on first display J=1.

         Otherwise, again bypass *scroll* up unless 17 accounts immediately preceded
         the current single account PRINT, in which case I3=1.

3850   Reset I3 to 0. This means *scroll* up will be bypassed for all future *single*
         account PRINT. I3 cannot be reset to 1 unless 17 account PRINT is again
         called (3690).

3860   Line with branch for *scroll* up instruction.

3870   Bypass *calendar* column headings for negative S input. Otherwise, PRINT
         column headings with SUB 4460.

         SELECTED ACCOUNTS PRINT LOOP

3880–   Start K loop of *accounts*. The *account title* C$(K) is printed unless the dis-
3890   play is not the first (J=1) *and* there is only *one* account. Account titles are
         always printed for 17 account displays, but only for the first display of
         periods with single account displays.

3900–   Check loop I for 0 values all periods. If all are 0 and loop is completed at
3940   3910, progress to message at 3920, and branch to end of account loop
         at 4110.

         Otherwise, if nonzero value found at 3900, branch to further PRINT at
         3940. This ends I loop. Start L loop of lines of statistics for each account.

3950–   Branch to reset of S$(1) to blank for nonstatistical output (N3=1). Also
3960   branch to 3960 for K=17 for *all fixed assets* account. Account K=17 has
         no uncertainty and no statistical subtitles. Thus S$(1) subtitle is converted
         to a blank for N3=1 or account K=17.

         If K=17 only one line of values is printed. After the first line (L not equal
         to 1) branch to end of L loop.

| 3970– | PRINT subtitle for line of statistics. Start I loop for columns of values over |
| 3980 | periods from U(J) to V(J) in display J. |

Branch to required information per L number of statistical PRINT line.

| 3990– | Compute statistic in Q from C( ) or G( ) per L index. The statistics in 4010 |
| 4020 | and 4020 are *confidence limits* from the mean in C( ), the standard deviation in G( ), and t-statistic in T. |

| 4030– | PRINT rounded integers in 4030 except for *account* K=2 for *firm's industry* |
| 4040 | *share*. This account is a percentage to be printed with two decimal places at 4040. |

| 4050– | Asterisk suffix control *end-of-year* columns starts here. With less than 2 |
| 4060 | periods per year there are no asterisks printed, so bypass. |

Otherwise, an asterisk indicator is developed in F, which is usually 0 for only the last period of a year. One cannot rely on the similar F( ) indicators available from heading PRINT in SUB 4390 because this routine may be bypassed (S 0).

If F greater than 0, branch to 4070. Otherwise, PRINT asterisk suffix to account value in column.

| 4070 | Value columns loop I ends. PRINT trailing blank for line space. |

| 4080 | Loop L for statistical item PRINT lines per account ends. |

| 4090– | This routine *scrolls* up a page, PRINT HEX(OC), in the middle of a 17 |
| 4100 | account PRINT routine. Bypass for *one* account (G=H). Bypass also if only one or two statistical item lines are printed (U=1 or 2). In the latter cases all 17 items will fit on one page. |

Otherwise, *scroll* up only for *account* K=8. There will be a new page after 8 accounts out of 17 have been printed.

| 4110 | Loop K of accounts ends. Set R to 1, which will bypass repeat PRINT of main title while within SELECTED ACCOUNTS division (3680). |

Display loop J ends. Branch back to SELECTED ACCOUNTS menu. Exit from SELECTED ACCOUNTS is accomplished with menu INPUTS of W 17 or S=0.

NEXT OUTPUT CHOICE

| 4130– | SELECT video screen; home *cursor*; display next output choices. User IN- |
| 4160 | PUT is to N6, whose values 0 to 3 correspond to call numbers of 4 output PRINT divisions. |

| 4170 | Per value of N6 branch back to PAVE4 for output divisions 0 and 1, to PAVE5 for start of FINANCIAL STATEMENTS division 2, and to start of division in PAVE6 for SELECTED ACCOUNTS (N6=3). The latter is the only output division which starts in PAVE6. |

4190– For N6=0 or 1, WRITE new value of N6 in first record of PAVEFT3 for
4200   input to PAVE4; CLOSE files and chain in PAVE4.

4210– For N6=2, WRITE new values of 3 parameters needed at the start of FINAN-
4230   CIAL STATEMENTS. These parameters are written to PAVEFT4 for input
       to PAVE5; CLOSE files and chain in PAVE5.

4240   This is the *rerun* branch. Chain in PAVE1 at its line 2470, which bypasses
       initial user instructions and POLREM choice.

4250– All *format* image statements for PAVE6 PRINT are grouped together on
4340   these lines.

       SUB '0–ASTERISK ROW PRINT

4360– The passed variables are T1 for left indent and L for number of asterisks
4370   (length of row).

       Loop K prints L asterisks. SUB ends. This SUB is identical to SUB 1970 in
       PAVE5 (see Section 14.6).

       SUB–FLOW HEADINGS, PERIOD AND CUMULATIVE

4390– This SUB is identical to SUB 2000 in PAVE5. The required arrays are U(J),
4440   V(J), and X(J), which were transferred to PAVE6 (2570) from computa-
       tions in PAVE5 (see 140 to 210 in section 14.6 for PAVE5).

       For an explanation of this SUB, see section 14.6, lines 2000 to 2050.

       SUB–CONDITION AND SELECTED ACCOUNT HEADINGS

4460   This SUB prints headings for either CONDITION STATEMENTS or
       SELECTED ACCOUNTS. The SUB also stores *number of months* in F( )
       for all periods. F(I) will be 0 for year-end periods, which is used as an in-
       dicator to PRINT an asterisk suffix on end-of-year value columns of CONDI-
       TION STATEMENTS (5040). The same feature is not operational for
       SELECTED ACCOUNTS because here the PRINT of headings may be by-
       passed (3870 and 4050).

       Calendar column headings developed in SUB 4460 differ from *flow* state-
       ment headings at 4390 because the latter may add separate *annual* columns.
       The CONDITION STATEMENTS headings differ from SELECTED AC-
       COUNTS by one extra column which is added in the first position of the
       STATEMENTS. This is "START BOP 1" heading, and in effect moves all
       the columns, including year-end period columns with asterisks, one position
       to the right for CONDITION STATEMENTS (N6=2) as compared to
       SELECTED ACCOUNTS (N6=3). The adjustment is computed internally
       in SUB 4460 from the value of N6.

       The following parameters are used in SUB 4460:
       A   U(J) value for of first display
       B   Column shift control for calendar adjustments between CONDI-
             TION STATEMENTS and SELECTED ACCOUNTS.
       F(I) Number of month for each column or period index I

For calendar headings, skip over *account* title PRINT; preset A to first column index and B to 0.

4470–
4480
Above values of A and B stand for SELECTED ACCOUNTS.

Otherwise, for CONDITION STATEMENTS, B is reset to 1, and for *first display only*, PRINT BOP 1 heading; reset A to 2, and F(1) to 0.

Reset of B to 1 has the effect of moving all columns over one position for CONDITION STATEMENTS. For first display of CONDITION STATE-MENTS, calendar heading PRINT starts with second column (A=2). Reset F(1)=0 is used to supply asterisk suffixes for *first* column BOP 1 account values.

4490–
4500
Start display loop I from A to V(J). Compute *year number* in A1, and *month number* in A2. A2 is rounded in F(I). The period number is I–B, where each period number is moved one column to the right for B=1 with CONDITION STATEMENTS. The column number remains in I. For SELECTED ACCOUNTS, *period* and *column* numbers are identical.

PRINT *period number*, *year number*, and *month number*.

4510
For less than 2 periods per year (6-month maximum duration), or N less than 2, bypass asterisk suffix PRINT for headings or column values.

Otherwise, PRINT asterisk suffix if F(I)=0, which indicates that the period is year-end.

4520
Loop I for display headings end. PRINT trailing blank to line space. SUB 4460 ends.

SUB '1–PRINT PERIOD AND ANNUAL BOP CONDITION INTEGER VALUES IN FLOW STATEMENTS

4540–
4560
The passed parameter is Q, which is account index of C( ). Start I loop for nonzero value check of M+1 periods (including BOP 1).

K(Q–12,1) is used to store *annual* column BOP values. Subtraction of 12 reduces the K( ) account index.

For 0 value in C( ), continue loop at 4560.

Otherwise, complete loop at 4550, and branch to account PRINT line at 4570.

If I loop ends with all 0 values, branch to end of SUB at 4630. In such case no values will be printed.

4570
PRINT account title in H$. Start loop I through account value columns in display J. Note new use of I.

4580
For *annual* column value in X(I), branch to annual PRINT at 4610.

4590
Otherwise, store rounded integer *mean* (with factor F9) of *condition* value in F and PRINT.

4600   Start update of stored *beginning of year* value. Bypass computations for period before *last* period of *Year 1* (I less than N). In this case there will be no *annual* column, and no beginning of year value is stored.

Otherwise, store value N-1 periods back in a low index account value of K( ) for *beginning of year* value.

Branch to next column at 4630.

4610   PRINT beginning of year value stored from previous column at 4600. Factor N9 converts this rounded integer to a *mean* value.

4620   Loop I of PRINT BOP value columns ends; PRINT trailing blank for line space.

4630   SUB '1 ends.

SUB '2–PRINT PERIOD AND ANNUAL FLOW VALUES FROM ACCOUNT ARRAY D( ) OF NUMBER OF SHARES F( )

4650   Passed parameters to SUB '2 are:

      E index of computation and printing:
        1 = means of integer flows from D( )
        2 = EOP values of outstanding shares from F( )
        3 = per share PRINT with 2 decimal places
      Q is account index of D( )
      R is a term used to reduce account storage index in Z( )

Bypass nonzero value check in I loop for Q index of 1. This index is assigned to F( ) number of shares PRINT, which is never 0.

Start nonzero value check over all periods for D(Q,I).

4660   If D(Q,I) is 0, branch to 4670 to continue I loop.

Otherwise, complete I loop and branch to PRINT at 4680.

4670   Complete I loop. Branch to end of SUB '2 for all 0 values; in such case account is not printed.

4680   PRINT account title in H$. Start loop I through account value columns for display J. Note new use of I.

4690   For *annual* period per X(I), branch to 4750. Otherwise, branch on E indicator.

4700   Start branch for *means* of *integer* flows. Store rounded mean (factor F9) in F. PRINT F.

Set Z( ) storage index adjustment R to 7. Bypass to 4740 for accumulation of values for *sum* of periods in *annual* column.

4710   Start *branch* for number of shares. PRINT number of shares from F( ). Accumulate number of shares for *mean* of *annual* column in Z(5).

Branch to next column.

4720   Start *branch* for *mean* of *per share* value with *two* decimal places. Store rounded *mean* (factor F9) in F. PRINT F.

4730   Reset R to 4 for storing *per share* accounts in Z( ).

If Q account index is not 11, branch to 4740 for accumulation of period values for *sum* over periods in *annual* column.

If Q is 11 *EOP per share* value is to be printed, not a *sum* over periods. Then the Z(7) accumulation of previous periods is reset to 0. This means that only the immediately prior period value will be stored in Z( ) for this account.

4740   Accumulate *values* in Z( ) for PRINT of annual columns.

Branch to next column.

4750   *Annual* column PRINT starts. Branch on E indicator.

4760   Start branch for period *sums* of *integer annual* values. PRINT *sum* of period values in *annual* column from Z( ).

Branch to reset accumulator Z( ) to 0 at 4790.

4770   Start branch for *mean* number of shares in *annual* column. PRINT rounded *mean* of shares in Z(5).

Reset accumulator Z(5) to 0.

Branch to next column.

4780   Start branch for period *sums* of *per share* annual values. PRINT *sum* in *annual* column from Z( ).

4790   Reset Z( ) to 0 from 4760 to 4780. This is done after PRINT of *annual* column, but before the start of period accumulations for the next annual column.

4800   Column PRINT loop ends; PRINT trailing blank for line space.

4810   SUB '2 ends.

SUB '3 PRINT PERIOD AND ANNUAL EOP INTEGER CONDITION VALUES IN FLOW STATEMENT

4830   The passed parameter is Q, account index of C( ).

Array K(R,2), with R=3 or Q-12, is used to store *annual* column EOP values (compare with 4600 for BOP values).

PRINT account title H$. There is no loop for nonzero value check because EOP owners' equity accounts should always be printed.

4840   Preset R account index to 3. This stands if Q=21. Otherwise, R is reset to (Q-12).

4850   Start I loop through account value columns in display J.

Branch to *annual* column PRINT for annual value in X(I).

4860   Assign rounded *mean* (factor N9) integer value to F from C( ). PRINT F.

4870   Assign latest period *mean* value to K(R,2) as current *annual* EOP value. Branch to next column.

4880   *Annual* EOP value PRINT column starts. PRINT value previously stored in K(R,2).

4890   Loop I over PRINT EOP value columns ends. PRINT trailing blank for line space.

SUB '3 ends.

SUB–COLUMN INDEXES FOR FINAL DISPLAY

4910   This SUB is used to index the final display of CONDITION STATEMENTS or SELECTED ACCOUNTS. Each such display will use the U(J) and V(J) column indexes transferred from PAVE5 (2570) except the *final* display. This final display will usually have less columns, and under one situation, one more column, than CAPITAL CHANGES STATEMENTS. The latter statements have possible extra columns for annual flows. The PAVE5 input U(J) and V(J) are used without change for CAPITAL CHANGES STATEMENTS.

The value in N6 (2 or 3 here) is used to adjust for differences in the number of displays and columns between CONDITION STATEMENTS and SELECTED ACCOUNTS. The latter has one less column (see 4460).

Recompute number of displays Z (six columns per display, except in some cases the final display).

Compute U(Z) and V(Z) *final* display column indexes with M and N6 as arguments. SUB 4910 ends.

SUB '4 PRINT CONDITION INTEGER VALUES IN CONDITION STATEMENTS

4930   The passed parameters are:

E is indicator of printing, computation, and array:
    1 = C( ) for source with sum of sample runs
    2 = B( ) for source with item value and H$ account title
    3 = B( ) for source with item value and *class* number of *fixed assets* subtitle.
Q = account number index of B( ) or C( ) array

Start J loop for nonzero value check of M+1 periods (including BOP 1).

If E exceeds 1 to indicate B( ) accounts, branch to B( ) check.

4940   Otherwise, check C( ). If 0 value, branch to 4970 to continue check loop.

Otherwise, for nonzero value found, branch to 4960 to terminate I loop and branch again to PRINT values.

4950 This is nonzero check for *fixed asset* branch with B( ). If 0 value, branch to 4970 to continue check loop.

Otherwise, progress to 4960 for loop termination of PRINT.

4960 Terminate I loop with nonzero value. If E=3 branch to PRINT at 4980.

Otherwise, branch to PRINT at 4990.

4970 Terminate nonzero value check I loop. If all zero values, branch to SUB end at 5060. In this case the account will not be printed.

4980 Start PRINT for E=3 branch. PRINT *fixed asset* class number K (see 3150 to 3170, and 3210 to 3230) in subtitle image statement (4300) with final blank to space the field.

Branch past account title PRINT to value column print.

4990 For E=1 or 2, PRINT account title H$.

5000 Start loop I through account value columns of display J. Note new use of index I.

Branch to 5020 if E=1 for C( ) array sums.

Otherwise, round B( ) integer value in F for E=2 or 3.

5010 Bypass *mean* value computation in 5020.

5020 Branch for E=1 starts. F is rounded integer *mean* value (factor N9) from C( ).

5030 PRINT F from any of the E branches.

Asterisk suffix for periods at *end-of-year* begins. For period duration more than six months (less than two periods per year in N) bypass asterisk suffix. In such case year-end periods will not be identified.

5040 If the month stored in F( ) (see 4500) is nonzero, bypass asterisk. Periods at end-of-year carry zero-numbered months in headings (see 4460).

Apply asterisk suffix to all values in end-of-year columns with F(I)=0.

5050 Columns loop I ends; PRINT trailing blank to line space.

5060 SUB '4 ends.

SUB—LINE PRINTER 'ON' INFORMATION AND SELECT LINE PRINTER

5070– This SUB is called once either at the PAVE6 continuation of FINANCIAL
5090 STATEMENTS or at beginning of SELECTED ACCOUNTS output divisions.

Home *cursor*; PRINT on video screen information and warning on *line* printer.

5100 SUB 5080 ends.

5110 PAVE6 and processing through PAVE programs ends.

14.8 | PAVE Service Programs
| Documentation

PAVEC–CATALOG PAVEFT TYPE DATA TRANSFER FILES

PAVEC program catalogs PAVEFT series *data transfer files* for PAVE processing programs. The diskette for PAVEFT files must be in the LEFT port; PAVEC may be loaded from either port. PAVE programs LOAD, READ, and WRITE to PAVEFT files; but PAVEFT files must be cataloged separately before a first PAVE run. Once a set of 5 PAVEFT type files has been cataloged, they may be overwritten indefinitely with new runs of PAVE.

PAVEC will catalog all transfer files under PAVEFT1 to PAVEFT5 names with one instruction. Alternatively, transfer files, with the same record structures, may be cataloged one at a time under user selected names. User selected *data transfer* file names are not operational in the current PAVE programs.

9820   Dimension for 5 PAVEFT series file names Q$( ), 5 sector reservations J( ), and file name Q$.

9830–   Preset 5 file names and assign 5 sector reservations for each of the 5 data
9850   transfer files.

9860   SELECT video screen; home *cursor*.

9870   Enter choice for catalog all PAVEFT files, or one file at a time, under user selected name; INPUT variable is N7.

9880   Preset file number index N8 to one.

    If choice N7 is for "all files," N8=1 stands; branch to cataloging at 9910.

9890   Otherwise, user enters his own file name Q$ and structure number N8. Structure N8 selects required number of sector records, as previously stored in J( ).

9900   User's file name is transferred to Q$(N8) for cataloging statement in 9910.

9910   Catalog file on LEFT diskette under name Q$(N8) with J(N8) sectors. For N7=0, N8=1 initially and PAVEFT1 will be cataloged from preset Q$(1). If N7=1, then 9910 is reached in direct sequence. Index N8 is a user input and Q$(N8) has been overwritten with user name Q$. If N7=1, branch to 9930 END of PAVEC. This completes user individual file catalog.

9920   Otherwise, increase N8 index by 1.

    When N8 reaches 6, branch to END.

    Otherwise return to catalog next PAVEFT series file under N7=0 option.

9930   END of PAVEC.

PAVER–PRINT CONTENTS OF PAVEFT TYPE DATA TRANSFER FILES

The purpose of PAVER is to PRINT the contents of a PAVEFT series file. These files, PAVEFT1 to PAVEFT5, transfer data from one PAVE program to another during processing.

Ordinarily a user is not concerned with the contents of these files. There are two occasions, however, when such contents may need to be exhibited:

1. PAVEFT1 contains in order the complete set of user inputs at the completion of PAVE1, which is the user interactive input program. PAVER will PRINT these inputs in compact form, without ID numbers or descriptions. The menu item in PAVE1 to PRINT all inputs, on the other hand, does include ID numbers and descriptions. As an intermediate exhibit, PAVES will PRINT all inputs with ID numbers, but without descriptions.

2. One may need to examine the contents of PAVEFT files if programming is interrupted during processing, if a defective sector or diskette develops, or if debugging of the PAVE programs becomes necessary.

PAVER must be RUN separately for each *data transfer* file whose contents are to be printed. Structure number inputs 1 to 5 correspond to digits in the name of PAVEFT series programs. Ordinarily the *name* input will be PAVEFT1 to PAVEFT5. There is provision for alternate names of transfer files, but they will not work with the current set of PAVE programs.

The diskette with *data transfer* (PAVEFT series) files must be mounted in the LEFT port.

In a PAVER PRINT of file contents, a title identifies each printed file by name. Every record is printed in a separate block. Three asterisks mark the beginning of a new record.

Numerical values in a record are printed 5 elements per line. This facilitates user identification and marking of array elements, which are not printed by PAVER. The layout of arrays is for PAVER printing, and printed blocks follow the original PAVEFT arrays only roughly. See Table 13.1 for a comparison between arrays used in PAVE programs and those in PAVER.

9620   Dimension 5 arrays to LOAD and PRINT records from PAVEFT data transfer files. Dimension one alpha variable for title of run, which is transferred in some PAVEFT files.

9630   SELECT video screen; home *cursor*.

9640   INPUT *file name* and *structure number*. The file name Q$ is printed by PAVER and used to LOAD and READ a file from LEFT port. Structure number N8, with inputs 1 through 5, selects fields and *records* in PAVER which correspond to the structures of PAVEFT1 to PAVEFT5 with the same suffix numbers.

9650   Select *line* printer with width for 5 columns of numerics (see below). PRINT file name heading.

9660   LOAD selected PAVEFT data transfer file. Branch to one of five *record* and
        field configurations. Each record is controlled by a marked SUB. Three
        such SUBs handle all type field configurations in PAVEFT records. For the
        original array and scalar layout of each record, see Figure 13.1. Here 5
        arrays (9620) are used to store and PRINT all numeric fields. Usually, except
        for total number of numeric fields, PAVER array dimensions do not cor-
        respond to the original transferred PAVE arrays.

9680   Call control SUBs in order for each *record*. The passed variables are *redimen-
        sions* for LOAD and PRINT numeric elements of *record*:

        SUB '1 has an alpha field for title of firm, and is followed by 5 matrix
        fields for numerics.

        SUB '2 has 5 matrix fields for numerics, but omits the initial alpha field
        of SUB '1.

        SUB '3 has one matrix field for numerics; it is used for short numeric
        records of 1 to 29 values.

        One I( ) array is used for SUB '3, and 5 arrays (9620) for SUB '1 and SUB '2.
        The matrices are dimensioned as row vectors; each with "one" as the first
        index and the required number of values in the second index. Since the
        printer has been dimensioned for 80 characters, or 5 numeric fields of 16
        positions each, precisely 5 values will be printed per line until the contents
        of each matrix has been displayed.

        The matrices for each *record* of each PAVEFT file are presented in order.
        SUBs control an IF END of file check. All the PAVEFT files have end-of-file
        trailer records. When this record is reached, control branches to the end of
        the program (line 9930).

9760   Start SUB '1. Transfer in REDIMENSIONS of 5 arrays. Transfer control to
        PRINT heading and REDIMENSION array SUB 9870.

9770   LOAD title N$, and numerics into 5 arrays, from PAVEFT file.

        Check if end-of-file record has been READ. If it has, branch to END
        as all records on PAVEFT file have now been read and printed. Otherwise,
        CONTINUE.

9780   PRINT firm title.

        Transfer to PRINT array SUB 9910.

        RETURN to process another *record*. End of SUB '1.

9800–   Start SUB '2. The operation of SUB '2 is identical to SUB '1 on lines 9670
9820   to 9780 except that a title is neither LOADED nor PRINTED. It uses the
        same nested SUBs.

9840   Start SUB '3. The operation of SUB '3 is similar to SUB '1 and SUB '2 but
        there is only one array, and all REDIMENSION and PRINT operations are
        contained in SUB '3 rather than by transfer to nested SUBs.

PRINT asterisks as *record* heading.

REDIMENSION array I( ) for PAVEFT record.

9850   LOAD record from PAVEFT file.

BRANCH to END if this *record* is end-of-file.

PRINT array I( ).

RETURN to process another *record*. End of SUB '3.

9870   Start PRINT heading and REDIMENSION SUB.

PRINT asterisks as *record* heading.

9880   REDIMENSION 5 arrays I( ), J( ), O( ), R( ), Y( ) to hold PAVEFT *records*.

9890   RETURN to marked SUB to LOAD and PRINT *record* into REDIMEN-SIONED arrays.

9910   Start PRINT array SUB.

PRINT 5 matrix arrays I( ), J( ), O( ), R( ), Y( ) on this line and line 9920.

9920   RETURN to process the next *record*.

9930   CLOSE all files; END.

PAVES—SERVICE INPUT DATA FILES FOR PAVE SYSTEM

PAVES services only *input data files* for PAVE programs, whereas auxiliary programs PAVEC and PAVER service only *data transfer files* among PAVE programs.

Most servicing of *input data files* may be managed directly in the first PAVE input program PAVE1. Users may set up, revise, rename, display, or PRINT inputs of *input data files* with PAVE1. There are some operations, however, which are not available in PAVE1. These include transferring *input data files* from one port or input device to another, reinitializing all input values to 0, and PRINT of contents in compact form (see PAVES menu at 8120 to 8160).

8020   DIMENSION input arrays, array for printing V$, run title N$, and file names Y$ and Z$.

8030   SELECT two input device addresses, which are assigned to #1 and #2 of variable A.

SELECT video display; home *cursor*.

8040   INPUT file management choices to Z:

    Z=0   *old* file only to be READ and processed.

    Z=1   *old* file to be READ and processed, but *store* after processing under *new* file *name*. Original *old* file name has now been eliminated.

    Z=2   *old* file to be READ, but *store* after processing in *new* file *name*. The original *old* file is not altered.

    Z=3   *new* file to be cataloged, and set of inputs to be stored in it.

8050   Branch if *new* file Z=3; bypass *old* file initial processing to *data statement* routine.

Otherwise user INPUT of *old* file name is stored in Y$.

8060   User enters INPUT number A of device address for *old* file.

8070   LOAD *old* file; READ run title in N$, and numeric inputs in N( ), P( ) and Q( ).

8090–   Read *data statements* (either entered at keyboard or from loaded *data state-*
8100   *ment program*). Each data pair (C,D,) is for one ID number and its corresponding value (see section 11.2). C=0, or C<1 (8100), is a flag to *end* READ
of data pairs and branch out of loop. C=0 is not a valid ID for inputs.

SUB 8780 assigns data values in D to input arrays. Note that *data statements*
are READ after *old input data files*. Thus values of individual IDs of *input
data files* may be overwritten at the keyboard. There is also an *individual
interactive* mode for inputs in PAVES (menu choice 3 at 8140). This input
mode will overwrite both *data statement* and *data file* inputs.

The *data statement* operation of PAVES is identical to PAVE1 (see sections
11.2 and 14.2).

8120–   Enter *menu* processing choice number in Q, and branch on Q (8170):
8170

Q=1   Reset all inputs to 0; destroys current contents of *old* file or other
inputs currently in the workspace.

Q=2   Revise individual inputs; this is an interactive mode for processing
input IDs one at a time.

Q=3   PRINT current input set. This prints IDs and values in rows of 5.
ID descriptions are not printed. The extent of printing is between
full information in PAVE1 (menu choice 10), and a skeleton
PRINT of PAVEFT1 in PAVER. For a compact exhibit, the
PRINT here is preferable to PAVER.

Q=4   Store current input set (now in work space) in a file as specified
by choice Z (8040). Then the PAVES run ends.

Q=5   END. This writes to no files, and any input changes made during
PAVES processing will be lost. END here is different from 9=END
in PAVE1; the latter *does* WRITE current inputs to files.

8190   Start branch Q=1 to *reset inputs to 0*; home *cursor*; reset Q to 0.

8200   PRINT confirming message in Q to erase current inputs. This is a precaution
against accidental destruction of input set.

8210–   Unless Q=1, return to menu.
8230

Otherwise, reset title N4 to blank. In I loops the contents of N( ), P( ), and
Q( ) input arrays are reset to 0. Return to menu.

8250   Start branch Q=2 for *individual interactive* inputs; home *cursor*.

After a *title of run* processing, this branch allows entry of input IDs one at a time. Entry of 0 for an ID is the signal to terminate entries and return to the menu. The current value in each ID is printed and users must enter a revised value. This input system is inferior to the INDIVIDUAL INTER-ACTIVE input mode (menu choice 7) in PAVE1. The latter locates a display which shows ID descriptions and surrounding values. Note also that PAVE1 may be used for input changes in files either during or apart from simulation runs.

8260–8270	Reset T to 0. Branch on choice of run title processing in T. 'EXECUTE' to *pass* will simply bypass the title to first ID entry.
8280	PRINT title in N$ branch for T=1. After PRINT, return to *title of run* choices.
8290–8300	INPUT *new* title in N$ branch T=2. N$ here is preset to a blank. 'EXECUTE' to *pass* will retain the blank and destroy any previous title. After title entry progress to individual ID entry.
8310	Home *cursor*; INPUT individual ID number in C.
8320	If C=0 return to menu. Otherwise, transfer C to appropriate N( ), P( ), or Q( ) input array index in SUB 8780. The current value of input array element is stored there in E.
8330	Current value for ID of C is displayed as E.
8340	INPUT revised value in D for ID of C. Return to SUB 8780, which assigns current value to input array.

Following INPUT, return to 8310 for next ID in C. Individual IDs will recycle until INPUT C=0 returns control to the menu at 8120. Note that only one input value is processed per cycle.

8360–8370	Start branch Q=3 for *PRINT all inputs*. Display *line* printer ON information and warning. SELECT 98 columns of *line* printer. There are six print fields of 16 characters each, and a seventh field of 2 positions to terminate PRINT loops with a line space.
8380	*Scroll* to top of page; PRINT run title in N$.
8390–8420	Divisions to PRINT IDs and values are controlled by SUBs '1 and '2. Separate PRINT blocks are assigned to each of 6 input divisions. In each input division there are one or two blocks. The first block is for *dynamic input set* IDs (SUB '2, not applicable to the first two input divisions), and the second is for *system parameters* (SUB '1 applicable to all 6 input divisions). *System parameters* of the second input division, INITIAL CONDITION, are sub-divided into two blocks, both SUB '1. The two blocks are ASSETS, and LIABILITIES AND OWNERS' EQUITY. For a discussion of input divisions and ID types, see sections 8.2 and 8.3.

The variables passed to both SUB '1 and SUB '2 are:

M = First ID number of PRINT block
N = Final ID number of PRINT block

SUB '1 and SUB '2 calls are arranged in correct order for an entire input set, the same order as input displays of menu choice 10 in PAVE1. ID numbers and values are printed on lines in order of their units digits, −1 to −5, or −6 to −0 ("tens" position). Thus there is a maximum of 5 IDs per PRINT line. PRINT lines with *all* 0 values are completely omitted.

8430   At the end of INPUT PRINT, SELECT again the video screen. Return to menu.

8450   Start branch Q=4 of closing routine for processing *input data files*.

Also If not just an *old* file Z=0, branch to OPEN new file or rename.

Otherwise reset pointer of old file to beginning of file; branch to WRITE file routine. Revised inputs will now overwrite original inputs.

8460   INPUT *new* (or revised) file name in Z$. If not a *rename* (Z=1), branch to OPEN new file at 8480.

8470   Otherwise SCRATCH old file and OPEN again under *new* name; branch to WRITE file routine.

8480   This routine is reached only if a *new* file is to be cataloged (Z=2 or 3).

INPUT device address for new file in A. This was preassigned to #1 or #2 at 8030.

8490   OPEN new file at address A. The new file is assigned 23 sectors, which is correct for one complete set of input data. The new file name is Z$ (8460).

8500   WRITE complete set of inputs in N$, N( ), P( ), and Q( ) to *old* file (Z=0), *old* file renamed (Z=1), or *new* file (Z=2 or 3).

Set end-of-file marker on file just written.

8510   CLOSE *all* input data files; END PAVES processing.

This branch is reached either from Q=5 at 8160 of menu, or at the close of branch Q=4 above from 8500. Thus for menu choices 4 or 5 PAVES will terminate; for all other choices there is a return to menu after previous Q choice has been completed. A choice 5=END in PAVES will *not* write to files before termination. In PAVE1, on the other hand, choice 9=END *will* write inputs to files (if previously chosen).

8530   SUB '1 starts for control of PRINT of *system parameters* (see 8390). Passed variables M and N are *first* and *final* IDs of a SUB '1 call for a block of inputs.

K is set to the ID number position at the *first value column* of the *first* PRINT line. The "units" digit of an ID position number K for the first column must be −1 for a *first* ID number M of −1 to −5, or −6 for a first

ID number of −6 to −0 ("tens" position). For example, the following (M,K) pairs are established by the function of M: (1,1), (3,1), (5,1), (6,6), (9,6), (10,6), (11,11), (330,326), (331,331), (333,331), (335,331), (336,336), (340,336), etc.

8540 Loop I processes a set of IDs from K to N. The STEP 5 assigns 5 value column positions per PRINT line. R is the number of *leading blanks* before the *first* ID column value PRINT. R produces blanks only on the *first* PRINT line because negative R, as I increases beyond the first line, is reset to 0. Note that K is an ID number position, and need not itself be a valid ID number. In the latter case, per values in M and R, a blank will be assigned to the field position of K.

8550 T is the number of *trailing blanks* after the *last* ID value column PRINT. T produces blanks only on the *last* PRINT line because negative T, as I decreases above the *final* line, is reset to 0.

8560 Compute the number of ID value PRINT columns S on each PRINT line. This is 5 less the sum of numbers of *leading* and *trailing* blanks.

Transfer control and line PRINT parameters to SUB '3. This SUB '3 performs the input printing. The I index, always the first column ID position, is also used by SUB '3.

Loop I through IDs ends. SUB '1 ends.

8580– SUB '2 starts for control of PRINT of *dynamic input sets* (see 8390). Passed
8600 variables M and N are *first* and *final* IDs of a SUB '2 call for a block of inputs.

Dynamic input sets could be processed by SUB '1, but SUB '2 provides an additional feature. The first ID of a *dynamic input set* in −0 digit position (if nonzero in SUB '3) is printed on a *separate line* from the last four IDs −6 to −9 digit positions of the *preceding* dynamic input set.

Loop L processes one *dynamic input set* (10 IDs) through 3 PRINT lines in SUB '3. In other words, SUB '3 is called 3 times for each *dynamic input set* (L loop). From the uniform digit pattern of dynamic input ID assignments, blank and printed column are fixed for each PRINT line (SUB '3 call). Thus the first call requires 4 *leading* blanks (R=4, S=1, T=0), the second call has no blanks, and the third call has one *trailing* blank (T=1). Prior to each SUB '3 call, index I is adjusted from the L loop index, which rises by 10 each loop, to the correct ID numbers for the *first* column positions.

Loop L for dynamic input set IDs for PRINT block ends. SUB '2 ends.

8620 SUB '3 starts for PRINT one input line. Each input line PRINT is controlled by SUB '1 for *system parameters* or by SUB '2 for *dynamic input sets*.

SUB '3 ends.

8740– SUB '4 PRINTS columns of *leading* or *trailing* blanks upon call at both the
8760 beginning and end of a PRINT line from SUB '3.

The parameter X for number of blank columns is passed from SUB '3 as R for *leading*, or T for *trailing*.

If X=0, there are no blanks upon a call of SUB '4; branch to RETURN at end of SUB '4.

Otherwise, PRINT X blank fields in J loop.

SUB '4 ends at end of J loop.

8780–   SUB starts which assigns input values in N( ), P( ), or Q( ) arrays. The input
8800   parameters are ID number in C, and corresponding assigned value in D. SUB 8780 is called for both the reading of *data statement* pairs (8100), and for *individual interactive input*. It is called twice by the latter, first at 8320 to obtain the current value in E, and secondly at 8340 to assign a revised value to D.

Branch to correct input array per ID number input in C. When the array line is located (8780 to 8800), first assign the current value to E; then reassign D to the array. This is the sequence required for *individual interactive processing* menu branch Q=2 (8310 to 8340).

Only one ID number and value pair may be processed at a time in SUB 8780.

8810   After a value assignment branch to 8810 where SUB 8780 ends.

END of PAVES.

Figure 14.1 PAVE1 coding

```
2010 REM **C.L.HUBBARD, R.A.PETERSON JR, F.J.GANOE
2020 REM **PAVE1 WANG--SYSTEM INPUTS; MOVING "X" BASIC
2030 REM 1**DIMENSIONS, INSTRUCTIONS OPTION, POLREM OPTION
2040 SELECT PRINT 005(64): PRINT HEX(03)
2050 PRINT "PAVE1 INPUTS; PLANNING AND VALUATION OF ENTERPRISES"
2060 PRINT : DATA 0,0
2070 DIM N(99),P(230),Q(250),C(12),L(12)
2080 DIM B$(12)44,C$(10)42,D$(8)1,G$(7)1,X$(12)1
2090 DIM A$54,C$7,F$1,H$23,N$64,S$42,V$9,Y$8,Z$8
2100 INPUT "PRINT INPUT/OUTPUT INSTRUCTIONS--NO=0/YES=1",T
2110 PRINT : IF T=0 THEN 2450: GOSUB 6830
2120 PRINT "    MOUNT YOUR INPUT FILES/PAVE TRANSFER FILES IN";
2130 PRINT " LEFT PORT; PAVE PROGRAM DISK IN RIGHT PORT."
2140 PRINT "   TO START; LOAD DCR (PAVE1 IN QUOTES) & LOAD DCF";
2150 PRINT " (YOUR DATA STATE'T FILE NAME IN QUOTES), IF ANY."
2160 PRINT "   YOUR OPTIONAL RECORD FILES MANAGED INTERACTIVE."
2170 PRINT "   INPUT ID NOS.--SYST PARAMS 1 TO 98; INPUTS OVER";
2180 PRINT " PERIODS IN SETS OF 10; 100 TO 109,...,570 TO 579."
2190 PRINT "   $ PREFIX FOR PERIOD AMTS EXCEPT IDS 84,130 YRLY."
2200 PRINT "   % PREFIX FOR RATES, TIME RATES ALWAYS YEARLY."
2210 PRINT "   * PREFIX UP TO 12 RANDOM DISTRIBUTED OVER PERDS."
2220 PRINT "   ID NO. DIGITS FOR INPUTS OVER PERIODS ALL ON";
2230 PRINT " SAME PLAN--DESCRIPTION PRINTED ON DISPLAYS."
2240 PRINT "   ORDER OF INPUT PROCESS--READ 'OLD' USER FILE";
2250 PRINT " (IF ANY), READ DATA STATE'T FILE (IF ANY MERGED),"
2260 PRINT "ASSIGN DEFAULT SET FOR 0/NONENTRY, DISPLAY INPUTS,";
2270 PRINT " OVERWRITE REVISED INPUTS, REDISPLAY/REENTER, RUN."
2280 PRINT "   'OLD' USER FILE OPTIONS--SAME/REVISE/RENAME AND";
2290 PRINT " REVISE; 'NEW' USER FILE GETS FINAL INPUT SET."
2300 PRINT "   INPUT DISPLAYS SEQUENTIAL IN SECTION CHOICE, OR";
2310 PRINT " BY INDIVIDUAL ID NO. SELECTION."
2320 PRINT "   DISPLAY CONTROL SIGNALS--'EXECUTE' FOR NEXT ID,";
2330 PRINT " '*' FOR PRIOR ID, '/' FOR NEXT DISPLAY OR ID NO.,"
2340 PRINT " '///' FOR EXIT TO CONTROL, 'P' FOR PRINT DISPLAY."
2350 PRINT "   PRINCIPAL PROCESSING OPTIONS ARE:"
2360 PRINT "DETERMINISTIC OR MONTE CARLO RANDOM SAMPLE SIMUL'N."
2370 PRINT "ADJUSTS ACCTS & INVENTORIES FOR MFG/TRADE/SERVICE";
2380 PRINT " FRAMES; OR ECON/INDUSTRY ENVRT TO FIRM SALES ONLY."
2390 PRINT "INTERNAL BACKUP DETERMINE REQD CASH & INVESTMENT."
2400 PRINT "USER SELECTS SEQUENCE OF OUTPUTS FROM 1ST & FINAL";
2410 PRINT " YRS VALUATION & SCOPE, FINAN'L STAT SUMMARY OF"
2420 PRINT "FINAL PERIOD, FIN STATE'S ALL PERIODS, SELECTED";
2430 PRINT " ACCTS ALL PERIODS, REVISE INPUTS/RERUN OUTPUTS."
2440 PRINT : PRINT : SELECT PRINT 005(64): PRINT HEX(03)
2450 PRINT "DISPLAY POLICY REMINDERS (POLREMS) WITH INPUT"
2460 INPUT "   SECTIONS--NO=0/YES=1",T
2470 PRINT : PRINT : SELECT PRINT 005(64): PRINT HEX(03)
2480 REM 2**INPUT FILE OPTIONS
2490 PRINT "INPUT FILES CHOICE--NONE=0/OLD=1/OLD & NEW=2/NEW=3";
```

Figure 14.1 (continued)

```
2500 INPUT Z1: ON Z1+1 GOTO 2550,2510,2510,2530
2510 INPUT "ENTER 'OLD' FILE NAME",Y$: DATA LOAD DC OPEN F Y$
2520 DATA LOAD DC N$,N(),P(),Q(): IF Z1<2 THEN 2550
2530 INPUT "ENTER 'NEW' FILE NAME",Z$
2540 REM 3**READ DATA STATEMENTS (IF ANY)
2550 READ A1,A2: IF A1=0 THEN 2590: W=4: IF A1>99 THEN 2570
2560 N(A1)=A2: GOTO 2550
2570 IF A1>329 THEN 2580: P(A1-99)=A2: GOTO 2550
2580 Q(A1-329)=A2: GOTO 2550
2590 Z1=Z1+(1-SGN(Z1))*W: PRINT : IF N$<>" " THEN 2600: N$=" "
2600 V$=" ": PRINT "RUN TITLE; FIRM NAME/INFO--DISPLAY=D,";
2610 INPUT " INPUT=I, PASS='EXEC'",V$: PRINT
2620 IF V$<>"D" THEN 2630: PRINT N$: PRINT : GOTO 2600
2630 IF V$<>"I" THEN 2650: INPUT N$: PRINT
2640 REM 4**ASSIGN DEFAULT VALUES TO SELECTED 0/NONENTRY INPUTS
2650 FOR I=1 TO 3: IF N(I)>0 THEN 2660: N(I)=1
2660 NEXT I: IF N(87)>0 THEN 2670: N(87)=50
2670 IF N(88)>0 THEN 2680: N(88)=200
2680 IF N(89)>0 THEN 2690: N(89)=50
2690 IF N(91)>0 THEN 2700: N(91)=1
2700 IF N(95)>0 THEN 2710: N(95)=50
2710 IF P(41)>0 THEN 2720: P(41)=60
2720 IF P(103)>0 THEN 2730: P(103)=100
2730 D$(2),D$(5),D$(8),G$(6)="%": G$(7)="$"
2740 G$(1)="1": G$(2)="2": G$(3)="3": G$(4)="4": G$(5)="5"
2750 C$(3)="BASE VALUE APPLIED IN PERIOD 1 . . . ."
2760 C$(4)="ANNUAL CHANGE TO PERIODS FROM 1ST BASE ."
2770 C$(5)="LAST PERIOD NO., 1ST SCHEDULE (ALL=0). ."
2780 C$(6)="2ND BASE VALUE NEXT PERIOD (CONTINUE=-1)."
2790 C$(7)="ANNUAL CHANGE TO PERIODS FROM 2ND BASE ."
2800 C$(8)="LAST PERIOD NO., 2ND SCHEDULE (ALL=0). ."
2810 C$(9)="3RD BASE VALUE NEXT PERIOD (CONTINUE=-1)."
2820 C$(10)="ANNUAL CHANGE TO PERIODS FROM 3RD BASE ."
2830 S$=" *% MAX CHANGE FROM MEAN VALUE . . . ."
2840 REM 5**CENTRAL CONTROL OF INPUT DISPLAYS AND PROCESS
2850 C$(1),C$(2),F$,H$=" ": IF Z4<10 THEN 2870
2860 Z2=Z2+1: PRINT : PRINT : IF Z2<7 THEN 3040
2870 SELECT PRINT 005(64): PRINT HEX(03): Z=T
2880 PRINT "    LIST OF CONTROL OPTIONS FOR INPUTS AND PROCESS:"
2890 PRINT : PRINT "1=INPUT/OUTPUT SYSTEM CHOICES SEQUENCE"
2900 PRINT "    !!-THESE INPUTS CONTROL OTHER DISPLAYS-!!"
2910 PRINT "2=INITIAL CONDITIONS (BALANCE SHEET) SEQUENCE"
2920 PRINT "3=ENVRT OF ECONOMY/INDUSTRY TO FIRM SALES SEQUENCE"
2930 PRINT "4=MANUFACTURING OR TRADE ITEMS SEQUENCE"
2940 PRINT "5=R&D, SALES, GENERAL ADMINISTRATION ITEMS SEQUENCE"
2950 PRINT "6=FINANCIAL AND VALUATION CONTROL ITEMS SEQUENCE"
2960 PRINT "7=SELECT INDIVIDUAL ID NO. FOR ENTRY OR REENTRY"
2970 PRINT "8=RUN PROGRAMS AND PRINT OUTPUTS; INPUTS COMPLETE"
2980 PRINT "9=END ALL INPUTS AND PROCESSING AT THIS POINT"
2990 PRINT "10=PRINT ALL CURRENT INPUTS (SOME 0 VALUES OMITTED)"
```

Figure 14.1 (continued)

```
3000 REM 6**SELECT DISPLAY/PROCESS OPTION; INAPPLICABLE MESSAGE
3010 PRINT : INPUT "ENTER NO. ABOVE FOR CONTROL OPTION",Z4
3020 Z2=Z4: IF Z4<10 THEN 3040: Z2=1: Z=0: GOSUB 6830
3030 PRINT N$: PRINT : PRINT
3040 PRINT HEX(03): V$=" ": ON N(5)+1 GOTO 3050,3140,3140,3100
3050 IF Z2<>4 THEN 3140: IF Z4>9 THEN 2860
3060 PRINT "MFG OR TRADE ITEMS DO NOT APPLY TO SERVICE FRAME"
3070 PRINT : PRINT : PRINT HEX(07)
3080 INPUT "SELECT ANOTHER INPUT CHOICE: PRESS 'EXECUTE'",V$
3090 GOTO 2850
3100 IF Z2=1 THEN 3140
3110 IF Z2=3 THEN 3140: IF Z4>9 THEN 2860: IF Z2>6 THEN 3140
3120 PRINT "THIS SECTION DOES NOT APPLY TO ENVIRONMENT ONLY RUN"
3130 GOTO 3070
3140 ON Z2 GOTO 3160,3300,3950,4270,4700,5250,5600,3700,5800
3150 REM 7**DISPLAYS; INPUT/OUTPUT SYSTEM AND INITIAL ASSETS
3160 A$="INPUT/OUTPUT SYSTEM CHOICES"
3170 B$(1)="   !! THESE INPUTS CONTROL OTHER DISPLAYS!!"
3180 B$(2)=" "
3190 B$(3)="TOTAL NUMBER OF PERIODS (MAX 24) . . . ."
3200 B$(4)="NO. OF PERIODS PER YEAR . . . . . . ."
3210 B$(5)="SAMPLE SIZE--DETERMINISTIC=1, STAT.<=20. ."
3220 B$(6)="SEED NO.--STANDARD RANDOM SERIES=0 . . ."
3230 B$(7)="FRAME: SERVICE=0/TRADE=1/MFG=2/ENVRT ONLY=3"
3240 B$(8)="OUTPUT SECTION PRINT 1ST (FROM LIST BELOW):"
3250 B$(9)="   VALUATION 1ST AND FINAL YEARS, SCOPE  =0"
3260 B$(10)="   STATISTICAL SUMMARY FROM FINAL PERIOD =1"
3270 B$(11)="   FINANCIAL STATEMENTS FOR ALL PERIODS  =2"
3280 B$(12)="   SELECTED ACCOUNTS FOR ALL PERIODS     =3"
3290 A=3: B=8: GOSUB '1(-2,1): GOTO 2850
3300 A$="INITIAL CONDITION--CURRENT AND INTANGIBLE ASSETS"
3310 B$(1)=" (START BAL SHEET: NEW FIRM--OMIT/SKELETON)"
3320 B$(2)=" $ CASH AND MARKETABLE SECURITIES . . . ."
3330 B$(3)="$ TRADE ACCOUNTS AND NOTES RECEIVABLE . ."
3340 B$(4)="$ NONTRADE ADVANCES AND ACCRUED RECEIVABLES"
3350 B$(5)="$ RESERVE FOR UNCOLLECTIBLE ACCOUNTS  . ."
3360 B$(6)="$ PREPAID EXPENSE AND DEFERRED CHARGES . ."
3370 B$(7)="$ INTANGIBLES: ORGAN EXP., PATENT, GOODWILL"
3380 B$(8)="$ INVENTORY OF GENERAL SUPPLIES/SMALL EQPT."
3390 B$(9)="$ INVENTORY OF MFG OR TRADE FINISHED GOODS."
3400 B$(10)="$ INVENTORY OF MFG GOODS-IN-PROCESS . . ."
3410 B$(11)="$ INVENTORY OF MFG DIRECT MAT'L & SUPPLIES."
3420 B$(12)="$ INVENTORY OF MFG PERIOD SUPPLIES & EQPT"
3430 A=2: B=12: IF Z2=7 THEN 3460: IF N(5)>1 THEN 3460
3440 B=9: B$(10),B$(11),B$(12)=" ": IF N(5)>0 THEN 3460
3450 B=8: B$(9)=" "
3460 GOSUB '1(7,1): IF N(5)<2 THEN 3540
3470 REM 8**DISPLAYS; LOOPS FOR INITIAL ASSETS, INITIAL EQUITIES
3480 A$="INITIAL CONDITION--MANUFACTURING FIXED ASSETS": K=18
3490 B$(1),B$(12)=" ": C$="$ CLASS": FOR I=2 TO 6: C(I)=I-1
```

Figure 14.1 (continued)

```
3500 B$(I)="AT COST BASIS . . . . . . .": NEXT I
3510 FOR I=7 TO 11: C(I)=I-6
3520 B$(I)="RESERVE FOR DEPRECIATION . . .": NEXT I
3530 A=2: B=11: GOSUB '1(K,2): IF K=28 THEN 3560
3540 A$="INITIAL CONDITION--GENERAL FIXED ASSETS"
3550 K=28: GOTO 3490
3560 A$="INITIAL CONDITION--LIABILITIES AND OWNERS' EQUITY"
3570 B$(1)="   (TOTAL ASSETS, EQUITIES, AND BALANCE"
3580 B$(2)="    CHECK IN NEXT DISPLAY)": B$(3)=" "
3590 B$(4)="$ TRADE ACCOUNTS AND NOTES PAYABLE . . ."
3600 B$(5)="$ NONTRADE ACCTS, DIVIDENDS, TAXES PAYABLE."
3610 B$(6)="$ UNEARNED ADVANCES FROM CUSTOMERS . . ."
3620 B$(7)="$ ACCRUED EXPENSE AND LIABILITIES. . . ."
3630 B$(8)="$ SHORT-TERM DEBT AND LOANS PAYABLE . . ."
3640 B$(9)="$ LONG-TERM OBLIGATIONS AT FACE OR STATED ."
3650 B$(10)="$ BOND (PREFERRED STOCK) PREMIUM (DISCOUNT)"
3660 B$(11)="$ PAID-IN OWNER EQUITY CAPITAL. . . . ."
3670 B$(12)="$ RETAINED EARNINGS . . . . . . . ."
3680 A=4: B=12: GOSUB '1(36,1)
3690 REM 9**ADD INITIAL ASSETS AND EQUITIES; PRINT TOTALS
3700 S1,S2=0: ON N(5)+1 GOTO 3740,3730,3710,5800
3710 FOR I=1 TO 5: S1=S1+N(I+19)-N(I+24): NEXT I
3720 S1=S1+N(17)+N(18)+N(19)
3730 S1=S1+N(16)
3740 S1=S1+N(9)+N(10)+N(11)-N(12)+N(13)+N(14)+N(15)
3750 FOR I=1 TO 5: S1=S1+N(I+29)-N(I+34): NEXT I
3760 FOR I=40 TO 46: S2=S2+N(I): NEXT I: S3=INT(N(47)+N(48)+.5)
3770 S1=INT(S1+.5): S2=INT(S2+.5)
3780 IF Z4<10 THEN 3790: PRINT : PRINT : GOTO 3800
3790 PRINT HEX(03): V$=" ": IF Z2>6 THEN 3860
3800 PRINT "INITIAL CONDITION (STARTING BALANCE ";
3810 PRINT "SHEET) TOTALS": PRINT : PRINT
3820 PRINT TAB(17);"TOTAL ASSETS. . . . . . $";S1: PRINT
3830 PRINT TAB(17);"TOTAL LIABILITIES . . . $";S2: PRINT
3840 PRINT TAB(17);"TOTAL OWNERS' EQUITY . . $";S3: PRINT
3850 REM 10**INITIAL CONDITIONS BALANCE WITH ERROR MESSAGE
3860 PRINT : IF ABS(S1-S2-S3)>1 THEN 3880
3870 IF Z2<>2 THEN 5800: IF Z4>9 THEN 2850: GOTO 3910
3880 PRINT "UNBALANCE: ASSETS $";S1;"EXCEED EQUITIES $";S2+S3;
3890 PRINT "BY $";S1-S2-S3: IF Z4>9 THEN 2850: PRINT : PRINT
3900 PRINT HEX(07)
3910 IF V$<>"P" THEN 3920: SELECT PRINT 005(64): GOTO 3790
3920 INPUT "'EXECUTE' FOR EXIT TO CONTROL OR 'P' FOR PRINT",V$
3930 IF V$<>"P" THEN 2850: GOSUB 6830: GOTO 3800
3940 REM 11**DISPLAYS; DYNAMIC INPUTS, AND OPTIONAL POLREMS
3950 IF Z=0 THEN 4090
3960 PRINT "POLREM: WHAT OVERALL SOCIAL GROWTH? SEGMENT GROWTH?"
3970 PRINT "  HOW MUCH INFLUENCE FROM STATE OF BUSINESS CYCLE?"
3980 PRINT "POLREM: LINK INDUSTRY TO SOCIETY ON TECHNICAL,"
3990 PRINT "  ECONOMIC, SOCIAL-CULTURAL, POLITICAL ENVIRONMENTS"
```

Figure 14.1 (continued)

```
4000 PRINT "POLREM: WHAT GROWTH OF ECONOMY, REAL AND INFLATION?"
4010 PRINT "  COMPARE INDUSTRY TO ECONOMY--GROWTH AND CYCLICAL,"
4020 PRINT "  INFLATION SENSITIVITY, INTERNATIONAL OPPORTUNITY"
4030 PRINT "POLREM: FIRM'S ACTUAL/LATENT COMPARATIVE ADVANTAGE?"
4040 PRINT "  LOCATE COMPETITIVE NICHE; DEFINE MISSION/SCOPE;"
4050 PRINT "  RELATE TO R&D, PRODUCT MIX, PRICING POLICY"
4060 PRINT "POLREM: FORECAST INDUSTRY SALES, TREND & SEASONAL-"
4070 PRINT "  CYCLICAL; DOES FIRM PROJECTED PRICING AND SHARE"
4080 PRINT "  OF MARKET JUSTIFY INVESTMENT?": GOSUB 6750
4090 A$="% ANNUAL REAL GROWTH RATE OF ECONOMY": GOSUB '1(99,4)
4100 A$="% ANNUAL AVERAGE INFLATION RATE"
4110 C$(1)="   INFLATE PERIOD COSTS--NO=0/YES=1  . ."
4120 GOSUB '1(109,4)
4130 A$="* NET SALES DEMAND AVAILABLE TO FIRM"
4140 C$(1)="SALES--% INDUSTRY SHARE=0/$ PER PERIOD=1."
4150 C$(2)=S$: GOSUB '1(119,3): IF P(21)>0 THEN 2850
4160 A$="*% ANNUAL INDUSTRY GROWTH COMPARED TO ECONOMY"
4170 C$(1)="$ INDUSTRY SALES FOR BASE (PRIOR) YEAR  ."
4180 C$(2)=S$: GOSUB '1(129,4)
4190 A$="SEASONAL/CYCLICAL INDICES--1ST SET STOPS AT 1ST ZERO"
4200 K=50: Q=0
4210 C$="INDEX": FOR I=1 TO 12: C(I)=I+Q
4220 B$(I)=". . . . . . . . . . . .": NEXT I
4230 A=1: B=12: GOSUB '1(K,2)
4240 IF K=62 THEN 2850: IF N(62)=0 THEN 2850
4250 A$="SEASONAL/CYCLICAL INDICES--2ND SET STOPS AT 1ST ZERO"
4260 K=62: Q=12: GOTO 4210
4270 A$="*DIRECT PURCHASED MATERIAL OR GOODS AS % OF SALES"
4280 C$(1)="INIT'L GOODS INVY'S--COST % OF SELL PRICE"
4290 C$(2)=S$: GOSUB '1(139,4)
4300 A$="FINISHED GOODS INVENTORY LEVEL AS % ANNUAL COST GOODS"
4310 C$(1)="% DESEASONALIZE GOODS PRODUCTION/PURCHASE"
4320 GOSUB '1(149,4): IF N(5)=1 THEN 2850
4330 IF Z=0 THEN 4400: PRINT HEX(03)
4340 PRINT "POLREM: WHAT TRANSFORMS OF RESOURCES IN OPERATIONS?"
4350 PRINT "  WHAT MIX MAKE OR BUY? FABRICATE OR ASSEMBLE?"
4360 PRINT "  HOW DEPLOY CAPITAL FOR SPACE, EQPT., INVENTORIES?"
4370 PRINT "POLREM: WHAT LABOR & SUPERV.? WHAT SYSTEM OF MAT'L,"
4380 PRINT "  PRODUCTION, INVENTORY, PURCHASE, QUALITY CONTROL?"
4390 GOSUB 6750
4400 A$="GOODS-IN-PROCESS INVENT'Y LEVEL AS % ANNUAL COST GOODS"
4410 GOSUB '1(159,4)
4420 A$="DIRECT MATERIAL INVENTORY LEVEL AS % ANNUAL USAGE"
4430 GOSUB '1(169,4)
4440 A$="*DIRECT LABOR PAYROLL AS % OF SALES"
4450 C$(2)=S$: GOSUB '1(179,4)
4460 A$="DIRECT SUPERVISION AND SUPPORT PAYROLL AS % OF SALES"
4470 GOSUB '1(189,4)
4480 A$="*% OPERATING EFFICIENCY OF PROCESSING"
4490 C$(2)=S$: GOSUB '1(199,4)
```

Figure 14.1 (continued)

```
4500 A$="$ CAPACITY OF PLANT PER PERIOD, 100% EFFIC'Y, SALES $"
4510 GOSUB '1(209,5)
4520 A$="$ INDIRECT SUPPLIES/SMALL EQPT USED PER PERIOD"
4530 C$(1)="MFG SUPPLIES INV'Y LEVEL AS % ANNUAL USE."
4540 GOSUB '1(219,5)
4550 A$="$ INDIRECT MFG PAYROLL PER PERIOD": GOSUB '1(229,5)
4560 A$="$ SPACE, RENT OR OCCUPANCY PER PERIOD--MFG"
4570 GOSUB '1(239,5)
4580 A$="*$ UTILITIES OR ALL INDIRECT COSTS PER PERIOD--MFG"
4590 C$(2)=S$: GOSUB '1(249,5)
4600 A$="$ MAINTENANCE PER PERIOD--MFG": GOSUB '1(259,5)
4610 A$="$ TAXES, INSURANCE, LABOR RELA'N, MISC PER PERIOD--MFG"
4620 GOSUB '1(269,5): GOSUB '2(0)
4630 A$="MANUFACTURING EXPENSE SYSTEM PARAMETERS"
4640 B$(1),B$(2),B$(3)=" ": FOR I=8 TO 12: B$(I)=" ": NEXT I
4650 B$(4)="% OVERTIME LIMIT TO REGULAR DIRECT LABOR  ."
4660 B$(5)="% OVERTIME PREMIUM COST . . . . . . . . ."
4670 B$(6)="% INCR PLANT CAPAC'Y FROM SUBCONTRACT OPERN"
4680 B$(7)="% MAT'L COST PREMIUM IF SUBCONTRACT OPERA'N"
4690 A=4: B=7: GOSUB '1(71,1): GOTO 2850
4700 IF Z=0 THEN 4850
4710 PRINT "POLREM: R&D ON UNIQUE TIME, PLACE, FEATURE, COST"
4720 PRINT "  ADVANTAGE. WHAT STAGES OF RESEARCH? DEVLPT? WHAT"
4730 PRINT "  MKT RESEARCH OR TESTING ON OLD OR NEW PRODUCTS?"
4740 PRINT "POLREM: WHAT EXCLUSIVE FEATURES? DIFFERENTIATE"
4750 PRINT "  PRODUCTS/MKTS. TECHNICAL/ETHICAL/STYLE IMPLICA-"
4760 PRINT "  TIONS; TYPE AND STAGE OF PRODUCT LIFE CYCLE"
4770 PRINT "POLREM: COMPARE MERCHANDISE/PROMOTE/ADVERTISE"
4780 PRINT "  POLICIES WITH PRICING/INDUSTRY STATE/SHARE OF MKT"
4790 PRINT "POLREM: DISTRIB'N & SALES COMPENS'N IN RESPECT TO"
4800 PRINT "  PROFIT, CREDIT, INVESTMENT, LEAD TIME, CONTROL"
4810 PRINT "POLREM: PLAN ORGAN'N FOR SYSTEMS AND HUMAN CONTROL."
4820 PRINT "  WHAT MGT STYLE? DEGREE CENTRALIZE? PROJECT MGT?"
4830 PRINT "  COST/RESPONSIBILITY CENTERS? EXEC/LABOR DVLP/REL?"
4840 GOSUB 6750
4850 A$="RESEARCH AND DEVELOPMENT PAYROLL"
4860 C$(1)="R&D EXPENSES--% SALES=0/$ PER PERIOD=1  ."
4870 GOSUB '1(329,3)
4880 A$="RES & DVLPT MATERIAL/CONTRACTS/MISC EXPENSE PER PERIOD"
4890 P=4: IF Q(1)=0 THEN 4900: P=5
4900 GOSUB '1(339,P)
4910 A$="SALES SALARIES/COMMISSIONS PAYROLL AS % OF SALES"
4920 GOSUB '1(349,4)
4930 A$="$ INDIRECT SALES PAYROLL PER PERIOD": GOSUB '1(359,5)
4940 A$="ADVERTISE/PROMOTE/MISC SALES EXPENSE AS % OF SALES"
4950 GOSUB '1(369,4)
4960 A$="$ ADVERTISE/PROMOTE/MISC SALES EXPENSE PER PERIOD"
4970 GOSUB '1(379,5)
4980 A$="*ACCOUNTS RECEIVABLE LEVEL AS % OF ANNUAL SALES"
4990 C$(1)="% UNCOLLECTIBLE ACCOUNTS . . . . . . ."
```

Figure 14.1 (continued)

```
5000 C$(2)=S$: GOSUB '1(389,4)
5010 A$="*DIRECT SERVICE/OFFICE MATERIALS AS % OF SALES"
5020 C$(2)=S$: GOSUB '1(399,4)
5030 A$="$ INDIRECT SERVICE/OFFICE SUPPLIES/SMALL EQPT PERIOD"
5040 GOSUB '1(409,5)
5050 A$="*DIRECT SERVICE/OFFICE PAYROLL AS % OF SALES"
5060 C$(2)=S$: GOSUB '1(419,4)
5070 A$="$ GENERAL ADMINISTRATIVE/INDIRECT SERV. PAYROLL PERIOD"
5080 GOSUB '1(429,5)
5090 A$="$ SPACE, RENT, OR OCCUPANCY PER PERIOD--GENERAL"
5100 GOSUB '1(439,5)
5110 A$="*$ UTILITIES OR ALL INDIRECT COSTS PER PERIOD--GENERAL"
5120 C$(2)=S$: GOSUB '1(449,5)
5130 A$="$ MAINTENANCE PER PERIOD--GENERAL": GOSUB '1(459,5)
5140 A$="$ TAXES, INSURANCE, LABOR RELA'N, MISC PERIOD--GENERAL"
5150 GOSUB '1(469,5): GOSUB '2(10)
5160 A$="GENERAL ADMINISTRATIVE SYSTEM PARAMETERS"
5170 B$(1),B$(2),B$(3),B$(10),B$(11),B$(12)=" "
5180 B$(4)="GENL SUPPLIES INV'Y LEVEL AS % ANNUAL USAGE."
5190 B$(5)="ACCTS PAYABLE LEVEL AS % OF ANNUAL ACCT PAY'"
5200 B$(6)="PREPAID EXPENSE LEVEL AS % OF ANNUAL PAY'TS."
5210 B$(7)="ADVANCES BY CUSTOMERS AS % OF ANNUAL SALES ."
5220 B$(8)="$ ORGAN EXP./GOODWILL INCURRED IN PERIOD 1 ."
5230 B$(9)="$ AMORTIZ/N OF INTANGIBLES YRLY, NOT PERIOD."
5240 A=4: B=9: GOSUB '1(75,1): GOTO 2850
5250 IF Z=0 THEN 5310
5260 PRINT "POLREM: OPTIMAL CAPITAL MIX? LIQUIDITY PLAN WITH"
5270 PRINT "  SEASONAL NEEDS? LEASE/SUBCONTRACT REPLACE DEBT?"
5280 PRINT "POLREM: MAX VALUE POLICIES WITH DIVIDENDS, CREDIT,"
5290 PRINT "  CAPITAL DEPLOY, REFINANCE DEBT, INVESTMENT"
5300 GOSUB 6750
5310 A$="$ OWNER NET CASH INVESTMENT PLANNED CHANGE PER PERIOD"
5320 C$(1)="INTERNAL COMPUTE REQD INVEST--NO=0/YES=1."
5330 C$(2)="EARN ON NEAR CASH AS % SHORT-TERM INT RATE"
5340 GOSUB '1(529,5)
5350 A$="$ LONG-TERM OBLIGATIONS PLANNED NET CHANGE PER PERIOD"
5360 C$(1)="% LONG-TERM OBLIGA'S IN REQD ADDED INVEST"
5370 GOSUB '1(539,5)
5380 A$="DIVIDENDS OR WITHDRAWALS PER PERIOD"
5390 C$(1)="DIVIDENDS--% EARNINGS=0/$ PER PERIOD=1  ."
5400 GOSUB '1(549,3)
5410 A$="*% SHORT-TERM INTEREST RATE ANNUAL"
5420 C$(2)=S$: GOSUB '1(559,4)
5430 A$="*% LONG-TERM INTEREST RATE ANNUAL"
5440 C$(2)=S$: GOSUB '1(569,4)
5450 A$="FINANCIAL AND VALUATION SYSTEM PARAMETERS"
5460 B$(1)="% CASH RATIO MIN, BELOW WHICH CASH DEMANDED."
5470 B$(2)="% CURRENT RATIO MIN FROM SHORT-TERM LOANS  ."
5480 B$(3)="% COMBINED EFFECTIVE INCOME TAX RATE (<100)."
5490 B$(4)="$ INITIAL TAX LOSS CREDIT FOR CARRY FORWARD."
```

Figure 14.1 (continued)

```
5500 B$(5)="NO. 1ST PERIOD OWNER EQUITY UNITS (1/SHARE)."
5510 B$(6)="$ ADDED SHARE COST--INTERNAL COMPUTATION=0 ."
5520 B$(7)="PRICE-EARNINGS MULTIPLE YR 1--INTER'L COMP=0"
5530 B$(8)="PRICE-EARN MULTIPLE FINAL YR--INTER'L COMP=0"
5540 B$(9)="% ASSETS AVERAGE REALIZED IN LIQUIDATION.  ."
5550 B$(10)="% INVESTOR REQD RATE RETURN YR--INTL COMP=0"
5560 B$(11)="% LONG-TERM AVG GROWTH RATE YR--INTL COMP=0"
5570 B$(12)="% RETURN ON INCREM'L ASSETS YR--INTL COMP=0"
5580 A=1: B=12: GOSUB '1(86,1): GOTO 2850
5590 REM 12**START INDIVIDUAL ID INPUT SELECTION
5600 C$(1),C$(2),F$,H$=" ": A1=0: PRINT HEX(03)
5610 INPUT "ENTER ID NO. ('EXEC' TO EXIT)",A1
5620 IF A1=0 THEN 2850
5630 IF A1>579 THEN 5680: IF A1>99 THEN 5700: IF A1<7 THEN 3160
5640 IF A1<20 THEN 3300: IF A1<30 THEN 3480: IF A1<40 THEN 3540
5650 IF A1<49 THEN 3560: IF A1<63 THEN 4190: IF A1<75 THEN 4250
5660 IF A1<79 THEN 4630: IF A1<85 THEN 5160: IF A1<99 THEN 5450
5670 REM 13**ID INPUT ERROR; PERIOD INPUT SELECTION
5680 PRINT HEX(07): A1=0: PRINT : PRINT "ID NO. INVALID--";
5690 INPUT "REENTER",A1: GOTO 5620
5700 U=INT(.1*A1-9): IF U>18 THEN 5730: IF U>9 THEN 5720
5710 ON U GOTO 4090,4100,4130,4160,4270,4300,4400,4420,4440
5720 ON U-9 GOTO 4460,4480,4500,4520,4550,4560,4580,4600,4610
5730 IF U>23 THEN 5740: S=U-19: Q=0: GOSUB 6670
5740 IF U>38 THEN 5770: IF U>32 THEN 5760
5750 ON U-23 GOTO 4850,4880,4910,4930,4940,4960,4980,5010,5030
5760 ON U-32 GOTO 5050,5070,5090,5110,5130,5140
5770 IF U>43 THEN 5780: S=U-39: Q=10: GOSUB 6670
5780 ON U-43 GOTO 5310,5350,5380,5410,5430
5790 REM 14**INPUTS COMPLETE; WRITE TO FILES; RUN OPTIONS
5800 GOSUB '2(0): GOSUB '2(10)
5810 ON Z1+1 GOTO 5890,5820,5820,5870,5890
5820 PRINT "'OLD' INPUT FILE ";Y$;: IF Z1>1 THEN 5850
5830 INPUT "--SAME=0/REVISE=1",Z3: IF Z3<1 THEN 5890
5840 DBACKSPACE BEG : GOTO 5880
5850 INPUT   "--UNSAVE=0/RETAIN=1",Z3: IF Z3>0 THEN 5870
5860 SCRATCH F Y$: DATA SAVE DC OPEN F Y$,Z$: GOTO 5880
5870 DATA SAVE DC OPEN F 23,Z$
5880 DATA SAVE DC N$,N(),P(),Q(): DATA SAVE DC END
5890 IF Z2<9 THEN 5900: END
5900 IF Z1=0 THEN 5940: PRINT HEX(03): V$=" "
5910 PRINT "LEFT PORT--REPLACE YOUR INPUT DISK (IF ANY)"
5920 INPUT "   BY PAVE TRANSFER FILE DISK--THEN 'EXECUTE'",V$
5930 REM 15**WRITE INPUTS TO PAVEFT1 FILE, TRANSFER TO PAVE2
5940 DATA LOAD DC OPEN F "PAVEFT1": DATA SAVE DC N$,N(),P(),Q()
5950 DATA SAVE DC END : DATA SAVE DC CLOSE: LOAD DC R "PAVE2"
5960 REM 16**SUB'1--INPUT DISPLAY AND USER ENTRY CONTROL
5970 DEFFN'1(K,P): Y=0: IF P<3 THEN 6030: A=1: B=10
5980 IF C$(2)<>" " THEN 5990: A=A+1: Y=1
5990 IF C$(1)<>" " THEN 6000: A=A+1: Y=0
```

Figure 14.1 (continued)

```
6000 IF K>328 THEN 6020
6010 FOR J=1 TO 10: L(J)=P(J+K-99): NEXT J: GOTO 6030
6020 FOR J=1 TO 10: L(J)=Q(J+K-329): NEXT J
6030 C=A: IF Z2<7 THEN 6060: C=A1-K: IF C>2 THEN 6050: C=C+Y
6040 IF C<=2 THEN 6050: C=C-Y-Y
6050 IF C>=A THEN 6060: RETURN CLEAR : GOTO 5680
6060 IF Z4<10 THEN 6070: PRINT : PRINT : GOTO 6100
6070 I=C
6080 I1=I: IF I<>2 THEN 6090: I1=I-Y
6090 A1=I1+K: X$(I1)="X": V$=" "
6100 ON P GOSUB 6290,6370,6430,6430,6430: IF Z4>9 THEN 6270
6110 X$(I1)=" ": IF V$<>"P" THEN 6130
6120 SELECT PRINT 005(64): GOTO 6090
6130 PRINT "FWD='EXEC', BACK=*, NEXT DISPLAY OR ID=/,"
6140 PRINT TAB(14);"EXIT=//, P=PRINT; OR VALUE OF ID ";A1;" ";
6150 INPUT V$: IF V$=" " THEN 6260
6160 IF V$<>"P" THEN 6170: GOSUB 6830: GOTO 6100
6170 IF V$<>"/" THEN 6190: IF Z2<7 THEN 6270
6180 RETURN  CLEAR : GOTO 5600
6190 IF V$<>"//" THEN 6200: RETURN CLEAR : GOTO 2850
6200 IF V$<>"*" THEN 6220: IF I>A THEN 6210: I=B: GOTO 6080
6210 I=I-1: GOTO 6080
6220 IF NUM(V$)>=9 THEN 6230: PRINT HEX(07): GOTO 6090
6230 CONVERT V$ TO V: IF P>2 THEN 6240: N(A1)=V: GOTO 6260
6240 L(I1)=V: IF K>328 THEN 6250: P(A1-99)=L(I1): GOTO 6260
6250 Q(A1-329)=L(I1)
6260 C=A: I=I+1: IF I>B THEN 6070: GOTO 6080
6270 C$(1),C$(2),F$,H$=" ": RETURN
6280 REM 17**SUB--PRINT INPUT DISPLAY FOR SYSTEM PARAMETERS
6290 PRINT HEX(03): PRINT A$: IF A=1 THEN 6310
6300 FOR J=1 TO A-1: PRINT B$(J): NEXT J
6310 FOR J=A TO B
6320 PRINT X$(J);" ";J+K;B$(J);" ";N(J+K);" ";X$(J): NEXT J
6330 IF B=12 THEN 6350: FOR J=B+1 TO 12: PRINT "      ";B$(J)
6340 NEXT J
6350 RETURN
6360 REM 18**SUB--PRINT INPUT DISPLAY FOR INDEXED PARAMETERS
6370 PRINT HEX(03): PRINT A$: IF A=1 THEN 6380: PRINT
6380 FOR J=A TO B
6390 PRINT X$(J);" ";J+K;C$;C(J);B$(J);TAB(50);N(J+K);" ";X$(J)
6400 NEXT J: IF B=12 THEN 6410: PRINT
6410 RETURN
6420 REM 19**SUB--PRINT INPUT DISPLAY OVER DYNAMIC INPUTS
6430 PRINT HEX(03): X=P+2: IF P>3 THEN 6440: X=L(1)+6
6440 D$(1),D$(4),D$(7)=G$(X): IF  C$(1)=" " THEN 6460
6450 PRINT X$(1);" ";K+1;C$(1);" ";F$;" ";L(1);" ";X$(1): PRINT
6460 PRINT A$;" ";F$;H$: IF C$(2)=" " THEN 6480
6470 PRINT X$(2);" ";K+2;" ";C$(2);" ";L(2);" ";X$(2)
6480 PRINT : FOR J=3 TO 10
6490 IF Z4<10 THEN 6510: IF J<>5 THEN 6510
```

Figure 14.1 (continued)

```
6500 IF L(J)<1 THEN 6530: IF L(J)>=N(1) THEN 6530
6510 PRINT X$(J);" ";K+J;D$(J-2);" ";C$(J);" ";L(J);" ";X$(J)
6520 NEXT J
6530 RETURN
6540 REM 20**SUB'2--COUNT FIXED ASSET CLASSES; CYCLE DISPLAYS
6550 DEFFN'2(Q): S=0
6560 IF S=5 THEN 6650: IF Z4>7 THEN 6570: GOSUB 6670
6570 IF N(20+Q+S)=0 THEN 6590: IF Z4<10 THEN 6580: GOSUB 6670
6580 S=S+1: GOTO 6560
6590 FOR I=3 TO 5
6600 IF P(180+10*S+I)*(10-Q)+Q(150+10*S+I)*Q<>0 THEN 6620
6610 NEXT I: GOTO 6650
6620 I=5: NEXT I: IF Z4<10 THEN 6630: GOSUB 6670
6630 S=S+1: IF S=5 THEN 6650: IF Z4>7 THEN 6640: GOSUB 6670
6640 GOTO 6590
6650 N(49+.1*Q)=S: RETURN
6660 REM 21**SUB--FIXED ASSET ADDITIONS INPUT DISPLAYS
6670 IF Q=10 THEN 6700: A$="$ MFG FIXED ASSETS CLASS"
6680 C$(1)="% DEPREC'N PER YR DECLINING BAL MFG CLASS"
6690 GOTO 6720
6700 A$="$ GENERAL FIXED ASSETS CLASS"
6710 C$(1)="% DEPREC'N YRLY DECLINE BAL GENERAL CLASS"
6720 F$=G$(S+1): H$=" NET CHANGES PER PERIOD"
6730 GOSUB '1(Q*20+279+10*S,5): RETURN
6740 REM 22**SUBS--POLREM PRINT; PRINTER 'ON' WARNING
6750 IF V$<>"P" THEN 6770: SELECT PRINT 005(64): V$=" "
6760 GOTO 6810
6770 V$=" ": PRINT : PRINT "'EXECUTE' FOR INPUTS, '///' FOR";
6780 INPUT " EXIT, 'P' FOR PRINT",V$
6790 IF V$<>"//" THEN 6800: RETURN CLEAR : GOTO 2850
6800 IF V$<>"P" THEN 6820: GOSUB 6830
6810 RETURN CLEAR : IF Z2=4 THEN 4330: PRINT HEX(03): GOTO 3140
6820 RETURN
6830 PRINT HEX(03): PRINT " !!--PRINTER 'ON'?  'SELECT' LITED?";
6840 PRINT "  PLUGGED INTO COMPUTER?--!!"
6850 SELECT PRINT 215(110): PRINT : PRINT : RETURN : END
```

Figure 14.2 PAVE2 coding

```
10 REM **C.L.HUBBARD, R.A.PETERSON JR, F.J.GANOE
20 REM **PAVE2 WANG--SYSTEM NONRANDOMIZED PROCESSING PHASE
30 SELECT PRINT 005(64): PRINT HEX(03)
40 PRINT "PAVE2 NONRANDOMIZED PROCESSING IN PROGRESS"
50 DIM N(99),P(230),Q(250),A(34,24),D(15,24),B(24,25),H(19),N$64
60 REM 1**READ INPUT FILE PAVEFT1; CONVERT ENVT INPUTS TO PER'DS
70 DATA LOAD DC OPEN F "PAVEFT1": DATA LOAD DC N$,N(),P(),Q()
80 DATA SAVE DC CLOSE: M=N(1): N=N(2): N2=1/N: N3=N(3)
90 N5=N(5): H(1),H(10)=0
100 Z=1: GOSUB '1(1,2,1,1): GOSUB '1(11,2,2,1)
```

Figure 14.2 (continued)

```
110 REM 2**INFLATION FACTORS OVER PERIODS
120 FOR I=1 TO M: D(3,I)=1: IF P(11)=0 THEN 140
130 W=(1+.01*D(2,I))↑N2: Z,D(3,I)=Z*W
140 NEXT I
150 REM 3**GENERAL ASSETS AND INPUTS PROCESSING FOR ALL PERIODS
160 IF N5>2 THEN 350: Z=0: GOSUB '2(141,5,4,14,3): X=Q(1)
170 GOSUB '1(1,1,3,5): GOSUB '1(11,1,4,5): GOSUB '1(21,1,5,2)
180 GOSUB '1(31,2,5,4): GOSUB '1(41,1,7,2): GOSUB '1(51,2,6,4)
190 GOSUB '1(61,1,9,3): GOSUB '1(71,1,11,2): GOSUB '1(81,1,6,4)
200 GOSUB '1(91,1,13,2): GOSUB '1(101,2,7,4)
210 GOSUB '1(111,2,8,4): GOSUB '1(121,1,10,4)
220 GOSUB '1(131,2,9,4): GOSUB '1(141,2,10,4)
230 GOSUB '1(201,1,18,1): GOSUB '1(211,1,33,1): X=Q(221)
240 GOSUB '1(221,1,34,5): GOSUB '1(231,1,15,2)
250 GOSUB '1(241,1,17,2)
260 REM 4**MFG ASSETS AND INPUTS PROCESSING FOR ALL PERIODS
270 Z=1: IF N5<1 THEN 350: GOSUB '2(171,10,14,28,2)
280 GOSUB '1(41,1,19,2): FOR K=1 TO 3
290 GOSUB '1(10*K+41,1,2*K+19,3): GOSUB '1(10*K+71,1,2*K+25,2)
300 NEXT K: IF N5<2 THEN 350: GOSUB '1(111,1,32,4)
310 GOSUB '1(121,1,22,4): GOSUB '1(131,1,20,4)
320 GOSUB '1(141,2,13,4): GOSUB '1(151,1,24,4)
330 GOSUB '1(161,2,14,4): GOSUB '1(171,2,15,4)
340 REM 5**SALES & INDUSTRY INPUTS; SEASON-CYCLICAL INDEX SET
350 X=P(21): GOSUB '1(21,1,1,5): IF X>0 THEN 510
360 GOSUB '1(31,2,3,1)
370 IF N(51)>0 THEN 380: N(51),Z,Z1=1: GOTO 410
380 Z1=0: Z=24: FOR I=1 TO 24: IF N(50+I)>0 THEN 400
390 Z=I-1: I=24: NEXT I: GOTO 410
400 Z1=Z1+N(50+I): NEXT I
410 Z1=Z1/Z: FOR I=1 TO M STEP Z: FOR J=1 TO Z
420 IF I+J<M+2 THEN 430: J=Z: NEXT J: I=M: NEXT I: GOTO 450
430 D(4,I+J-1)=N(50+J)/Z1: NEXT J: NEXT I
440 REM 6**INDUSTRY GROWTH & SALES, DESEASONALIZATION FACTORS
450 Z=P(31)*N2: P=.01*N(51): Q=0: FOR I=1 TO M
460 D(3,I)=(100+D(1,I))*(100+D(2,I))*(100+D(3,I))*1E-4-100
470 Z=Z*(1+.01*D(3,I))↑N2: W=D(4,I): A(2,I)=W*Z: Z1=1-1/W
480 IF P>=0 THEN 490: Q=A(23,I)*P: P=A(21,I)*P
490 A(21,I)=A(21,I)/W-Z1*P: A(23,I)=A(23,I)/W-Z1*Q: NEXT I
500 REM 7**INTANGIBLE ACCOUNTS; ADD TO ASSET ACCOUNTS
510 IF N5>2 THEN 730: B(4,1)=N(14): B(3,1)=B(3,1)+N(14)
520 N(84)=N(84)*N2: Z1=N(47): Z=N(45): B(1,1)=N(19)
530 FOR I=1 TO M: D(11,I)=N(84): B(4,I+1)=B(4,I)+N(83)-N(84)
540 IF B(4,I+1)>0 THEN 550: B(4,I+1)=0: D(11,I)=B(4,I)+N(83)
550 A(16,I)=A(16,I)+D(11,I): A(14,I)=A(14,I)+N(83)
560 B(3,I+1)=B(3,I+1)+B(4,I+1): N(83)=0
570 A(15,I)=N2*A(15,I): A(17,I)=N2*A(17,I)
580 REM 8**SUM INDIRECT PAYROLLS, NONRANDOM EXP; DEBT ADDITIONS
590 A(8,I)=D(5,I)+D(7,I): A(12,I)=D(6,I)+D(8,I)+D(9,I)+D(10,I)
600 Z1=Z1+A(18,I): IF Z1>0 THEN 610: A(18,I)=A(18,I)-Z1: Z1=0
```

Figure 14.2 (continued)

```
610 Z=Z+A(33,I): IF Z>0 THEN 630: A(33,I)=A(33,I)-Z: Z=0
620 REM 9**MFG SUPPLIES & ADD TO ASSET ADDITIONS; NONRANDOM EXP
630 ON N5+1 GOTO 690,700,640
640 B(1,I+1)=P(121)*.01*N*A(22,I)
650 D(12,I)=B(1,I+1)+A(22,I)-B(1,I): IF D(12,I)>0 THEN 670
660 D(12,I)=0: B(1,I+1)=B(1,I)-A(22,I)
670 A(28,I)=A(28,I)+D(12,I): A(26,I)=D(13,I)+D(14,I)+D(15,I)
680 GOTO 710
690 A(19,I),A(21,I)=0
700 FOR K=22 TO 31: A(K,I)=0: NEXT K: A(20,I)=0
710 NEXT I
720 REM 10**WRITE PAVEFT5 FOR PAVE6; 1ST & FINAL YR INTERPOLATE
730 DATA LOAD DC OPEN F "PAVEFT5"
740 DATA SAVE DC N$,M,N,N3,N5,N(49),N(50),B(): DATA SAVE DC END
750 H(1)=N: N(52)=1: N(53)=M: IF N<=1 THEN 790
760 H(1)=N/M: N(52)=M: N(53)=1: IF N>=M THEN 790
770 H(1)=N/INT(N): N(52)=INT(N): N(53)=M+1-N(52)
780 REM 11**ADJUST OUTPUTS IN H() FOR PAVEFT3 FOR PAVE4
790 H(2)=P(21): H(3)=Q(1)
800 H(4)=B(2,2)+B(3,2): H(5)=B(4,2): H(6)=B(4,M+1)
810 FOR K=7 TO 15: H(K)=N(K+83): NEXT K: H(16)=D(1,M)
820 H(17)=D(2,1): H(18)=D(2,M): IF X>0 THEN 830: H(19)=D(3,M)
830 FOR K=12 TO 19: H(K)=H(K)*.01: NEXT K
840 DATA LOAD DC OPEN F "PAVEFT3": DATA SAVE DC N(6)
850 DATA SAVE DC N$,M,N,N3,N5,H(): DATA SAVE DC END
860 REM 12**REASSIGN N() TO INPUT PARAMETERS PAVEFT2 FOR PAVE3
870 N(1)=N(9): N(2)=N(10)+N(11): N(3)=N(12): N(20)=N(4)
880 N(4)=N(13): FOR K=5 TO 8: N(K)=N(K+10): NEXT K
890 N(9)=N(40)+N(41)+N(43): N(10)=N(42): N(11)=N(44)
900 N(12)=N(45): N(13)=N(47): N(14)=N(48)-N(46)
910 N(15)=N(16)*100/P(41): N(16)=N(17)*100/P(41): N(17)=N(90)
920 N(18)=B(4,M+1): N(19)=N3: N(21)=N(75)*.01+1: N(22)=N(76)*.01
930 N(23)=N(77)*.01+1: N(24)=N(78)*.01: FOR K=25 TO 28
940 N(K)=N(K+54)*N*.01: NEXT K: N(29)=N(87)*.01: N(30)=N(88)*.01
950 N(31)=N(89)*.01: N(32)=N(95)*.01: N(33)=P(21)
960 N(34)=P(22)*.01: N(35)=P(32)*.01: N(36)=P(42)*.01
970 N(37)=P(82)*.01: N(38)=P(102)*.01: N(39)=P(152)*.01
980 N(40)=Q(1): N(41)=Q(61)*.01: N(42)=Q(62)*.01
990 N(43)=Q(72)*.01: N(44)=Q(92)*.01: N(45)=Q(122)*.01
1000 N(46)=Q(201): N(47)=Q(202)*.01: N(48)=Q(211)*.01
1010 N(49)=Q(221): N(50)=Q(232)*.01*N2: N(51)=Q(242)*.01*N2
1020 MAT REDIM N(53): MAT REDIM B(3,25)
1030 REM 13**RESET SHIFTS TO 0 IF 1 RUN; WRITE PAVEFT2 FOR PAVE3
1040 IF N3>1 THEN 1060: FOR K=34 TO 39: N(K)=0: NEXT K
1050 N(42),N(43),N(44),N(45),N(50),N(51)=0
1060 DATA LOAD DC OPEN F "PAVEFT2"
1070 DATA SAVE DC M,N,N5,N(),B(),A(): DATA SAVE DC END
1080 REM 14**TRANSFERS FOR REDUCED A(); WRITE PAVEFT4 FOR PAVE5
1090 FOR I=1 TO M: A(1,I)=A(6,I): A(2,I)=A(16,I): A(3,I)=A(18,I)
1100 A(4,I)=A(33,I): A(5,I)=A(22,I): A(6,I)=A(20,I)
```

Figure 14.2 (continued)

```
1110 A(7,I)=A(30,I): NEXT I: DATA LOAD DC OPEN F "PAVEFT4"
1120 MAT REDIM A(7,24),B(1,25)
1130 DATA SAVE DC N$,M,N,N3,N5,P(31),A(),D(),B()
1140 DATA SAVE DC END : DATA SAVE DC CLOSE: LOAD DC R "PAVE3"
1150 REM 15**SUB'1--ADJUSTED VALUES ALL PERIODS, DYNAMIC INPUTS
1160 DEFFN'1(F,E,L,R): FOR J=2 TO 9: H(J)=Q(J+F)
1170 IF Z=0 THEN 1180: H(J)=P(J+F)
1180 NEXT J: FOR J=1 TO 7 STEP 3: IF J<4 THEN 1200
1190 IF H(J+1)<>-1 THEN 1200: H(J+1)=D(4,H(J))*(1+.01*H(J+2))^N2
1200 IF H(J+3)>M THEN 1210: IF H(J+3)>=H(J)+1 THEN 1220
1210 H(J+3)=M
1220 IF H(J+1)=0 THEN 1260: IF H(J+2)=0 THEN 1260
1230 D(4,H(J)+1)=H(J+1): IF H(J)+2>H(J+3) THEN 1270
1240 FOR I=H(J)+2 TO H(J+3): D(4,I)=D(4,I-1)*(1+.01*H(J+2))^N2
1250 NEXT I: GOTO 1270
1260 FOR I=H(J)+1 TO H(J+3): D(4,I)=H(J+1): NEXT I
1270 IF H(J+3)<M THEN 1280: J=7
1280 NEXT J: FOR I=1 TO M: ON R GOTO 1330,1320,1310,1300,1290
1290 IF X=0 THEN 1320
1300 D(4,I)=D(4,I)*D(3,I): GOTO 1330
1310 D(4,I)=D(4,I)*N
1320 D(4,I)=D(4,I)*.01
1330 IF E=1 THEN 1340: D(L,I)=D(4,I): GOTO 1350
1340 A(L,I)=D(4,I)
1350 NEXT I: RETURN
1360 REM 16**SUB'2--FIXED ASSET AND DEPRECIATION CLASSES
1370 DEFFN'2(A,B,C,D,Y): IF N(50-Z)<1 THEN 1490
1380 FOR K=1 TO N(50-Z): B(C+K,1)=N(10*Y-1+K)
1390 B(C+5+K,1)=N(10*Y+4+K): B(Y,1)=B(Y,1)+B(C+K,1)-B(C+5+K,1)
1400 H=10*K+A: GOSUB '1(H,2,B+K,4): H=.01*N2*(Z*P(H)+(1-Z)*Q(H))
1410 IF H<1 THEN 1420: H=1
1420 FOR I=1 TO M
1430 Z1=H*(B(C+K,I)-B(C+5+K,I)+.5*D(B+K,I))
1440 B(C+K,I+1)=B(C+K,I)+D(B+K,I): B(C+5+K,I+1)=B(C+5+K,I)+Z1
1450 IF B(C+K,I+1)>=B(C+5+K,I+1) THEN 1470
1460 D(B+K,I)=(H-1)*(B(C+K,I)-B(C+5+K,I))/(1-.5*H): GOTO 1430
1470 A(D,I)=A(D,I)+D(B+K,I): A(D+2,I)=A(D+2,I)+Z1
1480 B(Y,I+1)=B(Y,I+1)+B(C+K,I+1)-B(C+K+5,I+1): NEXT I: NEXT K
1490 RETURN : END
```

Figure 14.3 PAVE3 coding

```
10 REM **C.L.HUBBARD, R.A.PETERSON JR, F.J.GANOE
20 REM **PAVE3 WANG--SYSTEM STATISTICAL PROCESSING PHASE
30 SELECT PRINT 005(64): PRINT HEX(03)
40 PRINT "PAVE3 STATISTICAL PROCESSING: RUNS COMPLETED COUNT---"
50 DIM A(34,24),B(3,25),C(14,25),D(37,24),E(16),F(48),G(16,24)
60 DIM H(33,4),L(17,2),M(12),N(53),T(7),U(33),V(6,2),W(6)
70 REM 1**READ PAVEFT2 INPUTS FROM PAVE2; START CONDITION TO C()
```

Figure 14.3 (continued)

```
80 DATA LOAD DC OPEN F "PAVEFT2"
90 DATA LOAD DC M,N,N5,N(),B(),A(): DATA SAVE DC CLOSE
100 FOR K=1 TO 14: C(K,1)=N(K)*N(19): NEXT K: X=RND(N(20))
110 REM 2**START SAMPLE RUN LOOP; INITIALIZE AT TIME ZERO
120 FOR J=1 TO N(19): I1,I2=0: FOR K=1 TO 6: W(K)=0: NEXT K
130 FOR K=1 TO 17: L(K,2)=N(K): NEXT K: I=0: GOSUB 1690: H=1
140 REM 3**START LOOP THRU PERIODS; PROCESS INPUTS INTO F()
150 FOR I=1 TO M: L1,M1=1: FOR K=1 TO 16: L(K,1)=L(K,2)
160 L(K,2),F(K),F(K*2),F(K*3)=0: NEXT K : L(17,1)=L(17,2)
170 FOR K=5 TO 31: F(K)=A(K,I): NEXT K: GOSUB '1(19,36)
180 REM 4**INDUSTRY AND FIRM SALES, % MARKET SHARE
190 F(32)=A(1,I): GOSUB '1(32,34): IF N(33)>0 THEN 220
200 F(3)=A(2,I): GOSUB '1(3,35): F(2),E(2)=F(32)*100
210 F(32)=F(32)*F(3): F(3),E(1)=F(3)*1E-3
220 F(1),S,F(39)=F(32): ON N5+1 GOTO 490,460,240,1190
230 REM 5**MFG INVENTORIES AT SALES LEVELS; CHECK CAPACITY
240 GOSUB '2(15,1,F(21),33,1,1): GOSUB '2(16,1,F(23),34,33,1)
250 GOSUB '1(31,38): C1=A(32,I)*F(31): IF F(34)>C1 THEN 280
260 REM 6**OVERTIME, MATERIAL PREMIUM & REVISE CAPACITY BRANCHES
270 C1=F(34): GOTO 350
280 L1=N(21): IF F(34)>C1*L1 THEN 290: L1=F(34)/C1: GOTO 350
290 M1=N(23): IF F(34)>C1*L1*M1 THEN 310: M1=F(34)/(C1*L1)
300 GOTO 350
310 F(34)=C1*L1*M1
320 F(1),S=(F(34)+L(15,1)+L(16,1))*S/(S+L(15,2)+L(16,2))
330 L(15,2)=L(15,2)*S/F(32): L(16,2)=L(16,2)*S/F(32)
340 REM 7**DIRECT MATERIAL INVENTORY & PURCHASE; MFG EXPENSE
350 F(35)=C1*L1*M1*F(19): F(33)=0: IF M1<=1 THEN 370
360 F(33)=F(35)*N(24)
370 F(19)=F(35)+F(33): GOSUB '2(8,19,F(25),25,19,1)
380 GOSUB '1(27,37): F(27)=C1*L1*F(27)/F(31): GOSUB '1(24,39)
390 F(29)=C1*L1*F(29)/F(31): F(31)=(F(27)+F(29))*N(22)*(L1-1)/L1
400 REM 8**COST OF GOODS INTO PROCESS; RATIO OF COST TO SALES
410 F(36)=F(27)+F(29)+F(31)+F(19)+F(24)+F(30)+F(20)+F(26)+F(22)
420 F(38)=1: IF F(34)<F(36) THEN 440: F(38)=F(36)/F(34)
430 REM 9**MFG & TRADE GOODS--COST, INVENTORIES, GROSS PROFIT
440 GOSUB '2(7,38,L(16,2),34,36,-1)
450 GOSUB '2(6,38,L(15,2),37,34,-1): GOTO 470
460 F(37)=S*F(19): GOSUB '2(6,37,F(21),34,37,1): F(25)=F(34)
470 E(4)=F(37): F(39),E(5)=S-F(37)
480 REM 10**GENERAL EXPENSE PROCESSING
490 GOSUB '1(11,43): GOSUB '1(13,44): GOSUB '1(10,45)
500 F(40)=A(3,I): F(41)=A(4,I): IF N(40)>0 THEN 520
510 F(40)=F(40)*S: F(41)=F(41)*S
520 F(5)=F(5)*S: F(7)=F(7)*S: F(11)=F(11)*S: F(13)=F(13)*S
530 REM 11**SUPPLIES INVENTORY, TENTATIVE L-T DEBT & INTEREST
540 F(38)=F(11)+F(6): GOSUB '2(5,38,N(25),42,38,1)
550 GOSUB '1(17,51): F(43)=(L(12,1)+.5*A(33,I))*F(17)
560 REM 12**PAYABLES, CASH EXPENSE, AND PREPAID EXPENSE
570 T=F(26)+F(28)+F(24)+F(25)+F(41)+F(7)+F(42)+F(10)+F(14)+F(12)
```

Figure 14.3 (continued)

```
580 F(44)=F(27)+F(29)+F(31)+F(20)+F(40)+F(5)+F(8)+F(13)
590 F(45)=T+F(44): F(46)=T: GOSUB '2(4,45,N(27),47,46,1)
600 GOSUB '2(9,47,N(26),45,47,-1)
610 REM 13**ADVANCES, RECEIVABLES, UNCOLLECTIBLES
620 GOSUB '2(10,1,N(28),46,1,1): GOSUB '1(9,42)
630 L(2,1)=L(2,1)-L(3,1): GOSUB '2(2,46,F(9),9,46,-1)
640 F(4)=F(9)*N(41): F(9)=F(9)-F(4): L(3,2)=L(3,1)+F(4)
650 L(2,2)=L(2,2)+L(3,2)
660 REM 14**INVEST INCOME, TOTAL EXPENSE, INCOME BEFORE TAX
670 F(46)=F(40)+F(41)+F(5)+F(7)+F(13)+F(8)+F(10)+F(38)
680 F(46),E(6)=F(46)+F(12)+F(16)+F(4): F(47),E(7)=F(39)-F(46)
690 GOSUB '1(15,50): R1=F(15): R4=R1*N(47): F(15),F(16)=0
700 F(38)=R4*(L(1,1)+.5*(F(18)+A(33,I)))
710 F(48)=F(47)+F(38)-F(43)
720 REM 15**TENTATIVE TAXES, INCOME AFTER TAX, DIVIDENDS
730 R=N(31): F(6)=(F(48)-L(17,1))*R
740 IF F(6)>0 THEN 750: R,F(6)=0
750 F(8)=F(48)-F(6): F(12)=A(34,I): IF N(49)>0 THEN 780
760 F(12)=F(12)*F(8): IF F(12)>0 THEN 780: F(12)=0
770 REM 16**TENTATIVE NET CASH FLOW AND EOP BALANCE
780 F(14)=F(9)+F(38)+A(33,I)-L(11,1)-F(44)-F(45)-F(43)-F(6)
790 F(14)=F(14)-F(12)
800 L(1,2)=L(1,1)+F(14)+F(18)
810 REM 17**SHORT-TERM BORROWING
820 IF L(1,2)<0 THEN 830: IF L(9,2)<=0 THEN 1010
830 IF N(29)>.9 THEN 910: IF L(1,2)<0 THEN 850
840 IF L(1,2)/(L(9,2)+L(10,2))>=N(29) THEN 1010
850 Q=N(32)*(L(2,1)-L(3,1)+T(2)): IF N(30)<1.5 THEN 870
860 Q=(T(3)-L(11,1)-(T(5)-L(11,1))*N(30))/(N(30)-1)
870 IF Q<=0 THEN 910
880 L(11,2)=(N(29)*(L(9,2)+L(10,2))-L(1,2))/(1-N(29))
890 IF L(11,2)< Q THEN 980: L(11,2)= Q
900 REM 18**ADDITIONAL REQUIRED CAPITAL, OWNER AND DEBT
910 IF N(46)<1 THEN 980
920 Q=N(29)*(L(9,2)+L(10,2)+L(11,2))-L(1,2)-L(11,2)
930 IF Q<0 THEN 980: L=1+.5*R4*(1-R): F(15)=Q/L
940 IF N(48)<=0 THEN 980
950 F(16)=Q*N(48)/((1-N(48))*L+N(48)*(1-F(17)*(1-R)))
960 F(15)=(1-N(48))*F(16)/N(48): F(43)=F(43)+.5*F(16)*F(17)
970 REM 19**ADJUST SHORT-TERM BORROWING AND INTEREST
980 L(11,2)=L(11,2)/(1-R1*(1-R)): F(17)=L(11,2)*R1
990 F(38)=F(38)+R4*.5*(F(15)+F(16)+L(11,2))
1000 REM 20**CAPITAL BALANCES; RECOMPUTE INCOME TAX, DIVIDENDS
1010 IF F(38)>0 THEN 1020: F(38)=0
1020 L(12,2)=L(12,1)+A(33,I)+F(16): L(13,2)=L(13,1)+F(18)+F(15)
1030 F(48)=F(47)+F(38)-F(43)-F(17): L(17,2)=0: T=F(48)-L(17,1)
1040 F(6)=T*N(31): IF T>=0 THEN 1050: F(6)=0: L(17,2)=-T
1050 F(8),E(8)=F(48)-F(6): IF N(49)>0 THEN 1080
1060 F(12)=F(8)*A(34,I): IF F(12)>0 THEN 1080: F(12)=0
1070 REM 21**FINAL CASH FLOW & EOP BALANCE, TECHNICAL INSOLVENCY
```

Figure 14.3 (continued)

```
1080 F(14)=F(9)+F(38)+A(33,I)+F(16)-L(11,1)+L(11,2)-F(44)-F(45)
1090 F(14)=F(14)-F(17)-F(43)-F(6)-F(12)
1100 L(1,2)=L(1,1)+F(14)+F(18)+F(15): IF L(1,2)>=0 THEN 1130
1110 IF I1>0 THEN 1130: M(1)=M(1)+I: M(2)=M(2)+1: I1=1
1120 REM 22**TOTAL RETAINED EARNINGS, ASSETS, LIABILITIES
1130 L(14,2)=L(14,1)+F(8)-F(12): GOSUB 1690: T(6)=T(5)+L(12,2)
1140 T(4)=T(3)+B(2,I+1)+B(3,I+1): T(7)=L(13,2)+L(14,2)
1150 M(8)=M(8)+T(6)*H: M(6)=M(6)+T(4)*H: H=0
1160 REM 23**LEGAL INSOLVENCY, 1ST/FINAL YR SALES/INCOME/RETURN
1170 IF T(7)<=0 THEN 1180: Q=F(8)/T(7): GOTO 1190
1180 Q=0: IF I2>0 THEN 1190: M(3)=M(3)+I: M(4)=M(4)+1: I2=1
1190 IF I>N(52) THEN 1210: W(1)=W(1)+S: W(2)=W(2)+F(8)
1200 W(3)=W(3)+Q
1210 IF I<N(53) THEN 1240: W(4)=W(4)+S: W(5)=W(5)+F(8)
1220 W(6)=W(6)+Q
1230 REM 24**SUMS & SUMS SQUARES OVER PERIOD, END PERIOD LOOP
1240 FOR K=1 TO 17: D(K,I)=D(K,I)+F(K): NEXT K: F(28)=F(24)
1250 F(30)=F(25): FOR K=18 TO 37
1260 D(K,I)=D(K,I)+F(K+9): NEXT K: FOR K=1 TO 14
1270 C(K,I+1)=C(K,I+1)+L(K,2): NEXT K: E(3)=S: E(9)=L(1,2)
1280 FOR K=1 TO 7: E(K+9)=T(K): NEXT K: FOR K=1 TO 16
1290 G(K,I)=G(K,I)+E(K)*E(K): NEXT K: NEXT I
1300 REM 25**ESTABLISH FINAL PERIOD SUMMARY NONRATIO VALUES
1310 U(1)=F(2): U(2)=S*N: U(3)=L(1,2): U(4)=T(4): U(5)=T(7)
1320 U(19)=F(3)*N: U(20)=F(37)*N: U(21)=F(39)*N: U(22)=F(47)*N
1330 U(23)=F(48)*N: U(24)=F(8)*N: U(25)=T(1)
1340 U(26)=T(2): U(27)=T(3): T(4)=T(4)-N(18): U(28)=T(4)-T(3)
1350 U(29)=L(9,2): U(30)=L(11,2): U(31)=L(12,2): U(32)=T(6)
1360 U(33)=L(13,2): T(1)=S: T(3)=F(17)+F(43): T(6)=T(7)-N(18)
1370 REM 26**RESET 0 DENOMINATORS FOR OVERLOW, COMPUTE RATIOS
1380 FOR K=1 TO 7: IF T(K)<>0 THEN 1390: T(K)=1E-25
1390 NEXT K: U(6)=F(39)*100/T(1): U(7)=F(47)*100/T(1)
1400 U(8)=F(47)*100*N/T(4): U(9)=S*N/T(4): U(10)=F(8)*100*N/T(7)
1410 U(11)=L(1,2)*100/T(5): U(12)=U(25)*100/T(5)
1420 U(13)=U(27)*100/T(5): U(14)=U(32)*100/T(4)
1430 U(15)=U(32)*100/T(6): U(16)=(F(47)+F(38))/T(3)
1440 U(17)=(L(2,2)-L(3,2))*365/(T(1)*N)
1450 IF N5<1 THEN 1460: S=F(37)
1460 U(18)=S*N/T(2): M(9)=M(9)+L(17,2)
1470 REM 27**STATISTICS--1ST & FINAL YR, FINAL PERIOD SUMMARY
1480 FOR K=1 TO 6: V(K,1)=V(K,1)+W(K): V(K,2)=V(K,2)+W(K)*W(K)
1490 NEXT K: FOR K=1 TO 33: H(K,1)=H(K,1)+U(K)
1500 H(K,2)=H(K,2)+U(K)*U(K): IF J>1 THEN 1520
1510 H(K,3),H(K,4)=U(K): GOTO 1550
1520 IF U(K)>H(K,4) THEN 1540: IF U(K)>=H(K,3) THEN 1550
1530 H(K,3)=U(K): GOTO 1550
1540 H(K,4)=U(K)
1550 NEXT K: PRINT TAB(J+5);J: NEXT J
1560 REM 28**WRITE PAVEFT3,PAVEFT4,PAVEFT5 FOR PAVE4,PAVE5,PAVE6
1570 MAT REDIM F(25): FOR I=1 TO M+1: F(I)=C(13,I): NEXT I
```

Figure 14.3 (continued)

```
1580 M(5)=C(13,2)+C(14,2): M(7)=C(1,2): M(10)=G(16,1)
1590 M(11)=G(13,1): M(12)=G(9,1): DATA LOAD DC OPEN F "PAVEFT3"
1600 DSKIP 2: DATA SAVE DC M(),V(),H(),F()
1610 DATA SAVE DC END : DATA LOAD DC OPEN F "PAVEFT5": DSKIP 1
1620 DATA SAVE DC C(),G(): DATA SAVE DC END
1630 FOR I=1 TO M+1: FOR K=2 TO 5: C(K,I)=C(K+3,I): NEXT K
1640 C(6,I)=C(11,I): NEXT I: MAT REDIM C(6,25)
1650 DATA LOAD DC OPEN F "PAVEFT4": DSKIP 1
1660 DATA SAVE DC C(),D(): DATA SAVE DC END : DATA SAVE DC CLOSE
1670 LOAD DC R "PAVE4"
1680 REM 29**SUB--TOTAL INVENTORIES, CUR ASSETS, CUR LIAB'S
1690 T(1)=L(1,2)+L(2,2)-L(3,2)
1700 T(2)=L(5,2)+L(6,2)+L(7,2)+L(8,2)+B(1,I+1)
1710 T(3)=T(1)+L(4,2)+T(2): T(5)=L(9,2)+L(10,2)+L(11,2): RETURN
1720 REM 30**SUB'1--TRIANGULAR RANDOM GENERATOR
1730 DEFFN'1(Y,Z): X=RND(1): IF X<.5 THEN 1750
1740 F(Y)=F(Y)*(1+N(Z)-N(Z)*SQR(2-2*X)): GOTO 1760
1750 F(Y)=F(Y)*(1+N(Z)*SQR(2*X)-N(Z))
1760 IF F(Y)>0 THEN 1770: F(Y)=0
1770 RETURN
1780 REM 31**SUB'2--FLOW AND POSITION LOGIC AND DEFAULTS
1790 DEFFN'2(A,B,C,D,E,F): L(A,2)=F(B)*C
1800 F(D)=F*L(A,2)-F*L(A,1)+F(E): IF F(D)>0 THEN 1820
1810 F(D)=0: L(A,2)=L(A,1)-F*F(E)
1820 RETURN : END
```

Figure 14.4 PAVE4 coding

```
2470 REM **C.L.HUBBARD, R.A.PETERSON JR, F.J.GANOE
2480 REM **PAVE4 WANG--VALUATION, AND FINANCIAL SUMMARY OUTPUTS
2490 SELECT PRINT 005(64): PRINT HEX(03)
2500 PRINT "PAVE4 VALUATION, FINANCIAL SUMMARY--PROCESS, OUTPUT"
2510 DIM F(25),G(12),H(36,4),N(19),P(4),T(6),V(6,2),H$(4)31
2520 DIM A$10,B$10,E$5,F$9,H$44,N$64
2530 REM 1**READ PAVEFT3 INPUTS FROM PAVE2, PAVE3
2540 DATA LOAD DC OPEN F "PAVEFT3": MAT REDIM H(33,4)
2550 DATA LOAD DC N6: DATA LOAD DC N$,M,N,N3,N5,N()
2560 DATA LOAD DC G(),V(),H(),F(): DATA SAVE DC CLOSE
2570 MAT REDIM H(36,4)
2580 REM 2**SUMMARY ITEM MEANS AND STANDARD DEVIATIONS
2590 FOR K=1 TO 6: V(K,1)=V(K,1)*N(1)/N3: IF N3<2 THEN 2630
2600 V=N(1)*N(1)*V(K,2)-N3*V(K,1)*V(K,1)
2610 IF V>0 THEN 2620: V=0
2620 V(K,2)=SQR(V/(N3*(N3-1)))
2630 NEXT K: G(8)=G(8)/N3: G(9)=G(9)/N3
2640 FOR K=1 TO 3: H(K+33,1)=G(K+4): H(K+33,2)=G(K+9): NEXT K
2650 IF N3<2 THEN 2790
2660 FOR K=1 TO 36: H(K,1)=H(K,1)/N3: V=H(K,2)-N3*H(K,1)*H(K,1)
2670 IF V>0 THEN 2680: V=0
```

Figure 14.4 (continued)

```
2680 H(K,2)=SQR(V/(N3*(N3-1))): NEXT K
2690 REM 3**T-STATISTIC & CONFIDENCE PROBABILITY PER SAMPLE SIZE
2700 T(1)=3.1: T(2)=2.9: T(3)=2.4: T(4)=2.8
2710 P(1)=80: P(2),P(3)=90: P(4)=95: K=1: IF N3<6 THEN 2770
2720 T=2.6+.1*INT(60/N3): P=99: IF N3>23 THEN 2810
2730 T(1)=2: T(2)=2.4: T(3)=2.9: P(1)=90: P(2)=95: P(3)=98
2740 P(4)=99: K=5: IF N3<9 THEN 2770: Z=INT((N3-1)/4): L=N3-4*Z
2750 T(1)=1.9: T(2)=2.3: T(3)=2.8: T(4)=3.1
2760 T=T(L)-Z*.1+.2: P=P(L): GOTO 2810
2770 T=T(N3-K): P=P(N3-K): GOTO 2810
2780 REM 4**COMPUTE VALUE TO BE USED WITH NUMBER OF SHARES
2790 IF N(10)>0 THEN 2800: N(10)=10
2800 IF N(11)>0 THEN 2810: N(11)=10
2810 F(1),N1,N9=N(8): IF N5>2 THEN 2990
2820 N2,N8=100/N1: L9,L1=(H(4,1)-N(6))*N(12)-H(32,1)
2830 M9=V(5,1)*N(11): IF N(11)<>0 THEN 2860: GOSUB 4670: M9=P9
2840 IF L9<P9 THEN 2850: M9=L9
2850 N(11)=M9/V(5,1)
2860 M1=V(2,1)*N(10): IF M>1 THEN 2880: IF N(10)<>0 THEN 2990
2870 M1=M9: N(10)=N(11): GOTO 2990
2880 L1=(H(35,1)-N(5))*N(12)-G(8): IF N(10)<>0 THEN 2930
2890 IF P9<>0 THEN 2900: GOSUB 4670
2900 M1=P1: IF L1<P1 THEN 2910: M1=L1
2910 N(10)=M1/V(2,1)
2920 REM 5**DETERMINE NUMBER OF SHARES EACH PERIOD FROM VALUE
2930 FOR I=2 TO M: S=(F(I+1)-F(I))/N3
2940 V=N(9)*F(I-1): IF N(9)>0 THEN 2960
2950 V=M1+(M9-M1)*(I-2)/(M-1)
2960 IF V>F(I-1) THEN 2970: V=F(I-1)
2970 F(I)=F(I-1)*(1+S/V): IF F(I)>=1 THEN 2980: F(I)=1
2980 F(I)=INT(F(I)+.5): NEXT I: N9=F(M): N8=100/N9
2990 ON N6+1 GOTO 3570,3010,4330,4330
3000 REM 6**START FINANCIAL SUMMARY--PRINT HEADINGS
3010 GOSUB 5170: L=35: GOSUB 4480
3020 PRINT TAB(10);"FINANCIAL SUMMARY FROM FINAL PERIOD"
3030 GOSUB 4480: PRINT : PRINT N$: PRINT
3040 PRINTUSING 4390,M,M/N,N;: PRINTUSING 4400,1/N
3050 PRINT "    UNDEFINED RATIOS APPEAR '####-- '; YEARLY";
3060 PRINT " VALUES ARE EXTRAPOLATED FROM THE FINAL PERIOD;";
3070 PRINT " 0 VALUES OMITTED": IF N3<2 THEN 3140
3080 PRINT : PRINT TAB(12);P;"% CONFIDENCE LIMITS FOR MEANS";
3090 PRINT " WITH SAMPLE SIZE";N3: PRINT
3100 PRINT TAB(38);"MEAN       STANDARD  ";P;"% LOWER  ";
3110 PRINT P;"% UPPER    MINIMUM     MAXIMUM"
3120 PRINT TAB(48);"DEVIATION  CONFIDENCE   CONFIDENCE"
3130 REM 7**FINALIZE AND PRINT FINANCIAL SUMMARY WITH GOSUB'1
3140 PRINT : PRINT : PRINT "******  SCOPE OF FIRM  ******"
3150 PRINT : H$(1)="FIRM'S SHARE OF INDUSTRY %": GOSUB '1(1,1,2)
3160 H$(1)="NET SALES OR REVENUE PER YEAR": GOSUB '1(2,2,1)
```

Figure 14.4 (continued)

```
3170 PRINT : IF N5<3 THEN 3180: IF N(2)<1 THEN 3390: GOTO 4270
3180 H$(1)="CASH AND MARKETABLE SECURITIES"
3190 H$(2)="TOTAL ASSETS": H$(3)="TOTAL OWNERS' EQUITY"
3200 GOSUB '1(3,5,1): PRINT
3210 PRINT "****** RATIO ANALYSIS OF PROFITABILITY  ******"
3220 PRINT : IF N5<1 THEN 3240: H$(1)="GROSS MARGIN ON SALES %"
3230 GOSUB '1(6,6,2)
3240 H$(1)="NET OPERATING MARGIN ON SALES %"
3250 H$(2)="OPERATING EARNING POWER %"
3260 H$(3)="OPERAT'G EFFIC'Y OR CAP'L TURNS"
3270 H$(4)="RETURN ON OWNERS' EQUITY %": GOSUB '1(7,10,2): PRINT
3280 PRINT "****** RATIO ANALYSIS OF FINANCIAL CONDITION";
3290 PRINT "  ******": PRINT : H$(1)="CASH RATIO %"
3300 H$(2)="ACID TEST OR QUICK RATIO %": H$(3)="CURRENT RATIO %"
3310 GOSUB '1(11,13,2): PRINT
3320 H$ (1)="DEBT TO TANGIBLE ASSETS %"
3330 H$(2)="DEBT TO TANGIBLE OWNER EQUITY %"
3340 H$(3)="TIMES INTEREST EARNED RATIO": GOSUB '1(14,16,2)
3350 PRINT : H$(1)="AVG COLLECTION PERIOD IN DAYS"
3360 H$(2)="INVENTORY TURNS PER YEAR": GOSUB '1(17,18,2)
3370 IF N3<2 THEN 3380: PRINT HEX(0C)
3380 PRINT
3390 PRINT "******  SELECTED FINANCIAL SUMMARY VALUES  ******"
3400 PRINT : H$(1)="INDUSTRY SALES PER YR--000 OMIT"
3410 GOSUB '1(19,19,1): IF N5>2 THEN 4270: IF N5<1 THEN 3440
3420 PRINT : H$(1)="COST OF SALES PER YEAR"
3430 H$(2)="GROSS PROFIT PER YEAR": GOSUB '1(20,21,1)
3440 PRINT : H$(1)="OPERATING INCOME PER YEAR"
3450 H$(2)="NET INCOME BEFORE TAX PER YEAR"
3460 H$(3)="NET INCOME AFTER TAX PER YEAR": GOSUB '1(22,24,1)
3470 PRINT : H$(1)="CASH+MKT SECURITIES+ACCTS RECV"
3480 H$(2)="TOTAL INVENTORIES": H$(3)="TOTAL CURRENT ASSETS"
3490 H$(4)="NET TANGIBLE FIXED ASSETS": GOSUB '1(25,28,1)
3500 PRINT : H$(1)="ACCOUNTS PAYABLE"
3510 H$(2)="SHORT-TERM LOANS AND NOTES"
3520 H$(3)="LONG-TERM FIXED OBLIGATIONS": GOSUB '1(29,31,1)
3530 PRINT : H$(1)="TOTAL LIABILITIES"
3540 H$(2)="TOTAL PAID-IN OWNERS' EQUITY": GOSUB '1(32,33,1)
3550 GOTO 4270
3560 REM 8**PRINT VALUATION AND SCOPE HEADINGS
3570 GOSUB 5170: L=19: GOSUB 4480
3580 PRINT TAB(10);"VALUATION AND SCOPE": GOSUB 4480: PRINT
3590 PRINT N$: PRINT : PRINTUSING 4390,M,M/N,N;
3600 PRINTUSING 4400,1/N: PRINT : PRINT
3610 PRINT "******  SCOPE OF FIRM -- INITIAL SHARES";N1;
3620 PRINT "-- FINAL SHARES";N9;"-- EOP = END OF PERIOD  ******"
3630 A$="FIRST YEAR": B$="FINAL YEAR": E$="TOTAL"
3640 F$="PER SHARE": PRINT : IF N3<2 THEN 3710
3650 PRINT TAB(12);P;"% CONFIDENCE LIMITS FOR MEANS";
```

Figure 14.4 (continued)

```
3660 PRINT " WITH SAMPLE SIZE";N3: PRINT
3670 PRINT TAB(65);"MEAN        STANDARD  ";P;"% LOWER  ";P;
3680 PRINT "% UPPER"
3690 PRINT TAB(74);"DEVIATION  CONFIDENCE  CONFIDENCE": PRINT
3700 REM 9**PRINT SCOPE OUTPUTS FOR VALUATION SECTION
3710 H$="SALES": GOSUB '3(V(1,1),V(1,2),V(4,1),V(4,2))
3720 H$="EARNINGS": GOSUB '3(V(2,1),V(2,2),V(5,1),V(5,2))
3730 H$="RETURN ON OWNERS' EQUITY %": PRINT
3740 PRINTUSING 4440,H$,E$,A$;: Y,Z=100
3750 GOSUB '5(100*V(3,1),100*V(3,2),100*V(6,1),100*V(6,2))
3760 A$="AT EOP 1": B$="END OF RUN": H$="OWNERS' EQUITY"
3770 GOSUB '3(H(34,1),H(34,2),H(5,1),H(5,2))
3780 H$="TOTAL ASSETS"
3790 GOSUB '3(H(35,1),H(35,2),H(4,1),H(4,2))
3800 H$="CASH AND MARKETABLE SECURITIES"
3810 GOSUB '3(H(36,1),H(36,2),H(3,1),H(3,2))
3820 REM 10**PROCESS AND PRINT INSOLVENCY INFORMATION
3830 PRINT : PRINT : IF G(2)>0 THEN 3850
3840 PRINT "TECHNICAL INSOLVENCY DID NOT OCCUR": GOTO 3880
3850 PRINT "TECHNICAL INSOLVENCY OCCURRED WITH PROBABILITY";
3860 PRINT INT(100*G(2)/N3+.5)*.01;"-- ON AVERAGE BEGAN DURING";
3870 PRINT " PERIOD";INT(10*G(1)/G(2)+.5)*.1
3880 IF G(4)>0 THEN 3900
3890 PRINT "LEGAL INSOLVENCY DID NOT OCCUR": GOTO 3940
3900 PRINT "LEGAL INSOLVENCY OCCURRED WITH PROBABILITY";
3910 PRINT INT(100*G(4)/N3+.5)*.01;"-- ON AVERAGE BEGAN DURING";
3920 PRINT " PERIOD";INT(10*G(3)/G(4)+.5)*.1
3930 REM 11**OUTPUT ON METHODS OF VALUATION
3940 PRINT HEX(0C): PRINT
3950 PRINT "******  METHODS OF VALUATION  ******": PRINT
3960 PRINT TAB(52);"FIRST YEAR   FINAL YEAR   FIRST YEAR";
3970 PRINT "   FINAL YEAR"
3980 PRINT TAB(53);"OR EOP 1      OR END      PER SHARE";
3990 PRINT "     PER SHARE": PRINT
4000 H$="MARKET VALUE WITH PRICE-EARNINGS MULTIPLES"
4010 GOSUB '7(M1,M9): H$="PRICE-EARNINGS MULTIPLES"
4020 GOSUB '9(N(10),N(11)): IF N3<2 THEN 4060
4030 IF P9<>0 THEN 4040: GOSUB 4670
4040 H$="GOING CONCERN ECONOMIC VALUE UNDER RISK"
4050 GOSUB '7(P1,P9)
4060 PRINT : H$="LIQUIDATION VALUE TO OWNERS": GOSUB '7(L1,L9)
4070 H$="LIQUIDATION VALUE OF TANGIBLE ASSETS"
4080 GOSUB '7(L1+G(8),L9+H(32,1))
4090 PRINT : H$="FIXED ASSETS AT BOOK VALUE WITH INTANGIBLES"
4100 GOSUB '7(N(4),H(28,1)+N(6))
4110 H$="TAX LOSS CARRYFORWARD--INITIAL & END OF RUN"
4120 GOSUB '9(N(7),G(9)): PRINT : PRINT : IF N3<2 THEN 4270
4130 REM 12**OUTPUT FOR PARAMETERS OF GOING-CONCERN VALUE
4140 PRINT "******  PARAMETERS OF GOING-CONCERN VALUATION";
4150 PRINT "  ******": PRINT
```

Figure 14.4 (continued)

```
4160 PRINT TAB(53);"APPLIED EOP 1";TAB(76);"APPLIED END OF RUN"
4170 PRINT : H$="INVESTORS' REQUIRED RATE OF RETURN %"
4180 GOSUB '8(R1,R9): H$="INFLATION RATE %"
4190 GOSUB '8(N(17),N(18))
4200 H$="LONG-TERM FIRM GROWTH RATE WITH INFLATION %"
4210 GOSUB '8(G,G)
4220 H$="LONG-TERM REAL GROWTH RATE OF THE ECONOMY %"
4230 GOSUB '8(N(16),N(16))
4240 H$="MEAN RATE OF RETURN ON INCREMENTAL ASSETS %"
4250 GOSUB '8(R5,R5)
4260 REM 13**SELECT NEXT OUTPUT OPTION
4270 SELECT PRINT 005(64): PRINT HEX(03)
4280 PRINT "NEXT OUTPUT: VALUATION=0, FINANCIAL SUMMARY=1,";
4290 PRINT " STATEMENTS=2"
4300 INPUT "     SELECTED ACCOUNTS=3, RERUN=4, END=5",N6
4310 REM 14**PAVE4 OUTPUTS TO PAVEFT4, PAVEFT5 FOR PAVE5, PAVE6
4320 ON N6+1 GOTO 3570,3010,4330,4330,4380,5300
4330 DATA LOAD DC OPEN F "PAVEFT4": DSKIP 2
4340 DATA SAVE DC N6,N(2),N(3): DATA SAVE DC END
4350 DATA LOAD DC OPEN F "PAVEFT5": DSKIP 2
4360 DATA SAVE DC T,P,N(2),N(3),F()
4370 DATA SAVE DC END : DATA SAVE DC CLOSE: LOAD DC R "PAVE5"
4380 LOAD DC R "PAVE1" 2470
4390 %      ## PERIODS OVER###.## YEARS; ##.## PERIODS PER YEAR
4400 %, EACH###.## YEARS
4410 %###############################
4420 %-####,###,###
4430 %-#####,###.##
4440 %############################### #########  ############
4450 %####################################################
4460 %##############
4470 REM 15**SUB--PRINT ROW OF ASTERISKS FOR MAJOR TITLES
4480 PRINT TAB(10);: FOR K=1 TO L: PRINT "*";: NEXT K
4490 PRINT : RETURN
4500 REM 16**SUB'1--FINAL COMPUTE AND PRINT FINANCIAL SUMMARY
4510 DEFFN'1(A,B,Z): FOR K=A TO B: IF H(K,1)<>0 THEN 4530
4520 IF H(K,2)=0 THEN 4650
4530 PRINTUSING 4410,H$(K-A+1);: IF Z>1 THEN 4590
4540 T(1)=INT(H(K,1)+.5): PRINTUSING 4420,T(1);
4550 IF N3>1 THEN 4560: PRINTUSING 4460," ": GOTO 4650
4560 T(2)=INT(H(K,2)+.5): T(5)=INT(H(K,3)+.5)
4570 T(6)=INT(H(K,4)+.5): T(3)=T(1)-T(2)*T: T(4)=T(1)+T(2)*T
4580 PRINTUSING 4420,T(2);T(3);T(4);T(5);T(6): GOTO 4650
4590 T(1)=.01*INT(100*H(K,1)+.5): PRINTUSING 4430,T(1);
4600 IF N3>1 THEN 4610: PRINTUSING 4460," ": GOTO 4650
4610 T(2)=.01*INT(100*H(K,2)+.5)
4620 T(5)=.01*INT(100*H(K,3)+.5): T(6)=.01*INT(100*H(K,4)+.5)
4630 T(3)=T(1)-T(2)*T: T(4)=T(1)+T(2)*T
4640 PRINTUSING 4430,T(2);T(3);T(4);T(5);T(6)
4650 NEXT K: RETURN
```

Figure 14.4 (continued)

```
4660 REM 17**SUB--GOING CONCERN VALUE FROM REQD RATES OF RETURN
4670 GOSUB '2(V(6,2),V(6,1),N(18)): R1,R9=R
4680 G=N(14): IF G<>0 THEN 4700: G=N(19)
4690 IF G<>0 THEN 4700: G=N(18)+N(16)
4700 IF G<.75*R9 THEN 4710: G=.75*R9
4710 IF G<N(16)+N(18) THEN 4720: G=.5*(G+N(16)+N(18))
4720 IF G>0 THEN 4730: G=0
4730 R5=N(15): IF R5<>0 THEN 4790: IF H(4,1)<=0 THEN 4780
4740 R5=V(5,1)/H(4,1): IF R5<=0 THEN 4780: IF M=1 THEN 4790
4750 IF M<=N THEN 4790
4760 IF H(4,1)-H(35,1)<.05*ABS(H(4,1)) THEN 4790
4770 R5=(V(5,1)-V(2,1))/(H(4,1)-H(35,1)): IF R5>0 THEN 4790
4780 R5=0
4790 Q2,Q5=0: IF H(4,1)<H(35,1) THEN 4820
4800 IF H(35,1)<0 THEN 4810: Q2=H(35,1)
4810 IF H(4,1)<0 THEN 4820: Q5=H(4,1)
4820 P9,P1=V(5,1)/R9+Q5*G*(R5-R9)/(R9*(R9-G))
4830 IF M=1 THEN 4870: IF M<=N THEN 4870
4840 GOSUB '2(V(3,2),V(3,1),N(17)): R1=R
4850 P1=V(2,1)/R1+(Q5-Q2)*(R5-R1)/(R1*(1+R1)^((M/N-1)*.5))
4860 P1=P1+G*Q5*(R5-R9)/(R9*(R9-G)*(1+R1)^(M/N-1))
4870 RETURN
4880 REM 18**SUB'2--REQUIRED RATE OF RETURN, FIRST OR FINAL YEAR
4890 DEFFN'2(S,A,I0): S=S*S*N3: V=.001885: IF S>V THEN 4900: S=V
4900 R=N(13): IF N(13)>.001 THEN 4950: IF A<=0 THEN 4930
4910 R=(.43429*LOG(S)+2.7249)/7.784+I0+.018
4920 IF R<.268+I0 THEN 4940
4930 R=.268+I0
4940 IF R>.001 THEN 4950: R=.001
4950 RETURN
4960 REM 19**SUB'3--PRINT CONTROL OF SCOPE IN VALUATION DIVIS'N
4970 DEFFN'3(A,B,C,D): PRINT : PRINTUSING 4440,H$,E$,A$;
4980 GOSUB '4(A,B): PRINTUSING 4440," "," ",B$;: GOSUB '4(C,D)
4990 PRINT : IF N5<3 THEN 5000: RETURN CLEAR : GOTO 4270
5000 PRINTUSING 4440," ",F$,A$;: Y=N2: Z=N8
5010 GOSUB '5(A,B,C,D): RETURN
5020 REM 20**SUB'4--PRINT INTEGER AMOUNTS, SCOPE IN VALUATION
5030 DEFFN'4(W,X): PRINTUSING 4420,INT(W+.5);
5040 IF N3>1 THEN 5050: PRINTUSING 4460," ": GOTO 5060
5050 PRINTUSING 4420,INT(X+.5);INT(W-X*T+.5);INT(W+X*T+.5)
5060 RETURN
5070 REM 21**SUB'5--PRINT RATIO CONTROL, SCOPE IN VALUA'N DIV'N
5080 DEFFN'5(A,B,C,D): GOSUB '6(A,B,Y)
5090 PRINTUSING 4440," "," ",B$;: GOSUB '6(C,D,Z): RETURN
5100 REM 22**SUB'6--PRINT RATIOS, SCOPE IN VALUATION DIVISION
5110 DEFFN'6(W,X,Y): PRINTUSING 4430,.01*INT(W*Y+.5);
5120 IF N3>1 THEN 5130: PRINTUSING 4460," ": GOTO 5150
5130 PRINTUSING 4430,.01*INT(X*Y+.5);.01*INT((W-X*T)*Y+.5);
5140 PRINTUSING 4430,.01*INT((W+X*T)*Y+.5)
5150 RETURN
```

Figure 14.4 (continued)

```
5160 REM 23**SUB--PRINTER 'ON' WARNING AND SELECTION
5170 SELECT PRINT 005(64): PRINT HEX(03): PRINT " !!--PRINTER";
5180 PRINT " 'ON'?  'SELECT' LITED?  PLUGGED INTO COMPUTER?--!!"
5190 SELECT PRINT 215(110): PRINT HEX(0C): PRINT : RETURN
5200 REM 24**SUB'7--PRINTING SUBROUTINE FOR METHODS OF VALUATION
5210 DEFFN'7(A,C): PRINTUSING 4450,H$;
5220 PRINTUSING 4420,INT(A+.5);INT(C+.5);
5230 PRINTUSING 4430,.01*INT(A*N2+.05);.01*INT(C*N8+.5): RETURN
5240 REM 25**SUBS'8 & 9--PRINT PARAMETERS OF GOING-CONCERN VALUE
5250 DEFFN'8(A,C): PRINTUSING 4450,H$;
5260 PRINTUSING 4430,.01*INT(1E4*A+.5);: PRINTUSING 4460," ";
5270 PRINTUSING 4430,.01*INT(1E4*C+.5): RETURN
5280 DEFFN'9(A,C): PRINTUSING 4450,H$;
5290 PRINTUSING 4420,INT(A+.5);INT(C+.5): RETURN
5300 END
```

Figure 14.5 PAVE5 coding

```
10 REM **C.L.HUBBARD, R.A.PETERSON JR, F.J.GANOE
20 REM **PAVE5 WANG--FINANCIAL STATEMENTS FIRST SECTION OUTPUT
30 SELECT PRINT 005(64): PRINT HEX(03)
40 PRINT "PAVE5 FINANCIAL STATEMENTS FIRST SECTION OUTPUT"
50 DIM A(22,24),B(1,25),C(7,25),D(39,24),U(6),V(6),X(36),P(22)
60 DIM K(7,2),Z(39),A$37,B$13,H$28,N$64
70 REM 1**READ PAVE2, PAVE3, PAVE4 RECORDS FROM PAVEFT4
80 DATA LOAD DC OPEN F "PAVEFT4": MAT REDIM C(6,25),D(37,24)
90 DATA LOAD DC N$,M,N,N3,N5,I1,A(),B(): DATA LOAD DC C(),D()
100 DATA LOAD DC N6,S1,R: DATA SAVE DC CLOSE
110 MAT REDIM C(7,25),D(39,24): N9=1/N3: R=1-R: I1=.001*I1
120 B$="  (CONTINUED)": C(7,M+1)=N3*B(1,M+1)
130 REM 2**PARAMETERS FOR DETERMINING INDICES OF COLUMNS
140 N1=INT(N): C=0: IF N<2 THEN 150: C=INT(M/N)
150 Z=INT((M+C+5)/6): W,V1=0: U1=-5: Y=1: FOR J=1 TO Z
160 REM 3**DETERM PERIOD, CUMUL INDICES X() FOR PRINT COLUMNS
170 U(J),U1=U1+6: V(J),V1=V1+6: IF V1<M+C THEN 180: V(J)=M+C
180 FOR I=U(J) TO V(J): IF Y<1 THEN 200: X(I)=I-W: Y=Y+1
190 IF C=0 THEN 210: IF Y<=N1 THEN 210: Y=0: GOTO 210
200 W=W+1: X(I)=W+25: Y=1
210 NEXT I: NEXT J: IF N6>2 THEN 1740
220 REM 4**PRINTER WARNING ON CRT & STATEMENTS GENERAL HEADING
230 PRINT HEX(03): PRINT " !!--PRINTER 'ON'?  'SELECT' LITED?";
240 PRINT "  PLUGGED INTO COMPUTER?--!!": SELECT PRINT 215(110)
250 PRINT HEX(0C): PRINT : GOSUB '0(10,46): PRINT TAB(10);
260 PRINT "FINANCIAL STATEMENTS PROJECTED FOR ALL PERIODS"
270 GOSUB '0(10,46): PRINT : PRINT "ADMIN  ADMINISTRATIVE";
280 PRINT TAB(38);"DEPRC  DEPRECIATION";TAB(76);"GEN    GENERAL"
290 PRINT "AMORT  AMORTIZATION";TAB(38);"EOP    END OF PERIOD";
300 PRINT TAB(76);"INVY   INVENTORY"
310 PRINT "BOP    BEGINNING OF PERIOD";TAB(38);"GEN    GENERAL";
```

Figure 14.5 (continued)

```
320 PRINT TAB(76);"MFG     MANUFACTURING"
330 PRINT "MISC    MISCELLANEOUS";TAB(38);"PURCH   PURCHASES OF";
340 PRINT TAB(76);"R&D     RESEARCH AND DEVELOPMENT": PRINT
350 PRINTUSING 1840,M,M/N,N;: PRINTUSING 1850,1/N: PRINT
360 PRINT "     VALUES ARE ACCOUNT MEANS; ACCOUNT OMITTED WHEN";
370 PRINT " ALL VALUES 0": PRINT "     HEADINGS ARE: PERIOD NO.";
380 PRINT " AND YEAR/MONTH; OR CUMULATIVE *FOR YEAR NO.*": PRINT
390 REM 5**PRINT ENVIRONMENTAL ANALYSIS
400 PRINT : PRINT N$: PRINT : GOSUB '0(0,30)
410 A$="ENVIRONMENTAL ANALYSES OF FIRM": PRINT A$
420 GOSUB '0(0,30)
430 IF S1>0 THEN 450: PRINT TAB(37);"INDUSTRY BASE SALES--000S";
440 PRINT " OMITTED; YEAR=";INT(I1+.5);"-- PERIOD=";INT(I1/N+.5)
450 FOR J=1 TO Z: GOSUB 2000
460 H$="INFLATION RATE ANNUAL %": GOSUB '1(1,9)
470 H$="REAL ECONOMY GROWTH ANNUAL %": GOSUB '1(1,8)
480 IF S1>0 THEN 530
490 H$="INDUSTRY TOTAL GROWTH %": GOSUB '1(1,10)
500 PRINT : H$="SEASONAL/CYCLICAL INDICES": GOSUB '1(1,11)
510 PRINT : H$="INDUSTRY SALES--000S OMITTED": GOSUB '2(2,3)
520 H$="FIRM'S INDUSTRY SHARE %": GOSUB '2(1,2)
530 PRINT : H$="FIRM SALES DEMAND AVAILABLE": GOSUB '2(2,23)
540 IF J=Z THEN 580: IF ABS(J-3.5)<>1.5 THEN 560
550 PRINT HEX(0C): GOTO 570
560 PRINT
570 PRINT : PRINT A$;B$: GOSUB '0(0,30)
580 NEXT J: IF N5>2 THEN 1740
590 REM 6**SUMMATION OF VALUES FOR INCOME STATEMENTS
600 FOR I=1 TO M: C(7,I)=N3*B(1,I): A(9,I)=N9*(D(31,I)+D(32,I))
610 A(8,I)=N9*(D(5,I)+D(7,I))+A(12,I)+A(13,I)
620 A(10,I)=A(2,I)-A(18,I)
630 D(38,I)=D(37,I)-D(31,I)-D(32,I)-N3*A(8,I)
640 D(39,I)=D(30,I)-R*N3*A(9,I)-D(5,I)-D(7,I)-D(13,I)-D(11,I)
650 D(23,I)=D(30,I)-D(37,I): A(11,I)=N9*(D(8,I)+D(6,I)): NEXT I
660 REM 7**PRINT INCOME STATEMENTS
670 PRINT HEX(0C): PRINT
680 PRINT N$: PRINT : GOSUB '0(0,17): A$="INCOME STATEMENTS"
690 PRINT A$: GOSUB '0(0,17): FOR J=1 TO Z: GOSUB 2000
700 H$="FIRM NET SALES ACHIEVED": GOSUB '2(2,1)
710 IF N5<1 THEN 730: H$="  -COST OF SALES": GOSUB '2(2,28)
720 H$="GROSS PROFIT ON SALES": GOSUB '2(2,30)
730 PRINT : H$="R&D PAYROLL": GOSUB '2(2,31)
740 H$="R&D MATERIAL AND MISC EXP": GOSUB '2(2,32)
750 H$="   TOTAL R&D EXPENSE": GOSUB '1(2,9): PRINT
760 H$="DIRECT SALES PAYROLL": GOSUB '2(2,5)
770 H$="PERIOD SALES PAYROLL": GOSUB '1(2,12)
780 H$="DIRECT ADVERTISE, MISC SALES": GOSUB '2(2,7)
790 H$="PERIOD ADVERTISE, MISC SALES": GOSUB '1(2,13)
800 H$="   TOTAL SALES EXPENSE": GOSUB '1(2,8): PRINT
810 H$="DIRECT SERVICE PAYROLL": GOSUB '2(2,13)
```

Figure 14.5 (continued)

```
820 H$="PERIOD GEN ADMIN PAYROLL": GOSUB '1(2,14): PRINT
830 H$="PURCH GEN SUPPLIES": GOSUB '2(2,33)
840 H$="GEN SUPPLIES INVY": GOSUB '3(1,2)
850 H$="DIRECT GEN SUPPLIES USED": GOSUB '2(2,11)
860 H$="PERIOD GEN SUPPLIES USED": GOSUB '1(2,1): PRINT
870 H$="SPACE AND RENT--GEN": GOSUB '1(2,15)
880 H$="UTILITIES--GEN"
890 GOSUB '2(2,10): H$="MAINTAIN EQUIPMENT--GEN": GOSUB '1(2,16)
900 H$="MISC PERIOD ADMIN EXP--GEN": GOSUB '1(2,17): PRINT
910 H$="DEPRC ON FIXED ASSETS--GEN": GOSUB '1(2,10)
920 H$="AMORT OF INTANGIBLES": GOSUB '1(2,18)
930 H$="UNCOLLECTIBLE ACCOUNTS": GOSUB '2(2,4)
940 H$="  TOTAL GEN AND ADMIN EXP": GOSUB '2(2,38): PRINT
950 H$="TOTAL OPERATING EXPENSE": GOSUB '2(2,37)
960 H$="SALES MARGIN OVER DIRECT EXP": GOSUB '2(2,39): PRINT
970 H$="NET OPERATING INCOME": GOSUB '2(2,23)
980 H$="  +INTEREST & FINANCE INCOME": GOSUB '2(2,29)
990 H$="  -INTEREST COST, SHORT-TERM": GOSUB '2(2,17)
1000 H$="  -INTEREST, LONG-TERM FIXED": GOSUB '2(2,34)
1010 H$="NET INCOME BEFORE INCOME TAX": GOSUB '1(2,11): PRINT
1020 H$="  -INCOME TAXES": GOSUB '2(2,6)
1030 H$="NET INCOME AFTER INCOME TAX": GOSUB '2(2,8)
1040 IF J=Z THEN 1060: PRINT HEX(0C): PRINT
1050 PRINT A$;B$: GOSUB '0(0,17)
1060 NEXT J: ON N5+1 GOTO 1460,1340,1080
1070 REM 8**PRINT COST OF GOODS MANUFACTURED SCHEDULES
1080 PRINT HEX(0C): PRINT : PRINT N$: PRINT : GOSUB '0(0,36)
1090 A$="COST OF GOODS MANUFACTURED SCHEDULES": PRINT A$
1100 GOSUB '0(0,36): FOR J=1 TO Z: GOSUB 2000
1110 H$="PURCH DIRECT MFG MATERIAL": GOSUB '2(2,21)
1120 H$="DIRECT MATERIAL INVY": GOSUB '3(1,5)
1130 H$="DIRECT REGULAR MATERIAL USED": GOSUB '2(2,26)
1140 H$="  +CONTRACT ASSEMBLY USED": GOSUB '2(2,24): PRINT
1150 H$="PURCH PERIOD SUPPLIES": GOSUB '1(2,19)
1160 H$="PERIOD SUPPLIES INVY": GOSUB '3(1,7)
1170 H$="PERIOD SUPPLIES USED": GOSUB '1(2,5): PRINT
1180 H$="DIRECT LABOR PAYROLL": GOSUB '2(2,18)
1190 H$="DIRECT SUPERVISION PAYROLL": GOSUB '2(2,20)
1200 H$="OVERTIME PREMIUM PAYROLL": GOSUB '2(2,22)
1210 H$="PERIOD MFG ADMIN PAYROLL": GOSUB '1(2,6): PRINT
1220 H$="SPACE AND RENT--MFG": GOSUB '1(2,20)
1230 H$="UTILITIES--MFG": GOSUB '2(2,19)
1240 H$="MAINTAIN EQUIPMENT--MFG": GOSUB '1(2,21)
1250 H$="MISC PERIOD ADMIN EXP--MFG": GOSUB '1(2,22)
1260 H$="DEPRC ON FIXED ASSETS--MFG": GOSUB '1(2,7): PRINT
1270 H$="COST OF GOODS INTO PROCESS": GOSUB '2(2,27)
1280 H$="GOODS-IN-PROCESS INVY": GOSUB '3(1,4)
1290 H$="COST OF FINISHED GOODS": GOSUB '2(2,25)
1300 IF J=Z THEN 1320: PRINT HEX(0C): PRINT
1310 PRINT A$;B$: GOSUB '0(0,36)
```

Figure 14.5 (continued)

```
1320 NEXT J
1330 REM 9**PRINT COST OF GOODS SOLD SCHEDULES
1340 PRINT HEX(OC): PRINT : PRINT N$: PRINT : GOSUB '0(0,28)
1350 A$="COST OF GOODS SOLD SCHEDULES": PRINT A$: GOSUB '0(0,28)
1360 FOR J=1 TO Z: GOSUB 2000
1370 H$="COST OF FINISHED GOODS": GOSUB '2(2,25)
1380 H$="FINISHED GOODS INVY": GOSUB '3(1,3)
1390 H$="COST OF GOODS SOLD": GOSUB '2(2,28)
1400 IF J=Z THEN 1440: IF J<>5 THEN 1420
1410 PRINT HEX(OC): GOTO 1430
1420 PRINT
1430 PRINT : PRINT A$;B$: GOSUB '0(0,28)
1440 NEXT J
1450 REM 10**SUMMATION OF VALUES FOR CASH FORECAST STATEMENTS
1460 FOR I=1 TO M: D(21,I)=D(36,I)+D(35,I)
1470 D(26,I)=D(9,I)-D(21,I): D(24,I)=C(6,I+1)-C(6,I)
1480 D(18,I)=D(17,I)+D(34,I)+D(6,I): D(20,I)=C(1,I+1)): NEXT I
1490 REM 11**PRINT CASH FLOW STATEMENTS
1500 PRINT HEX(OC): PRINT : PRINT N$: PRINT : GOSUB '0(0,32)
1510 A$="CASH FORECASTS AND FLOW ANALYSES": PRINT A$
1520 GOSUB '0(0,32)
1530 FOR J=1 TO Z: GOSUB 2000: H$="CASH RECEIPTS FROM SALES"
1540 GOSUB '2(2,9): PRINT : H$="PAYMENTS ON ACCOUNT"
1550 GOSUB '2(2,36): H$="PAYMENTS ON PAYROLLS": GOSUB '2(2,35)
1560 H$="   TOTAL OPERATING PAYMENTS": GOSUB '2(2,21): PRINT
1570 H$="NET CASH FLOW ON OPERATIONS": GOSUB '2(2,26): PRINT
1580 H$="NET CHANGE SHORT-TERM CREDIT": GOSUB '2(2,24): PRINT
1590 H$="PLAN CHANGE LONG OBLIGATIONS": GOSUB '1(2,4)
1600 H$="+ REQUIRED LONG OBLIGATIONS": GOSUB '2(2,16)
1610 H$="   +INTEREST & FINANCE INCOME": GOSUB '2(2,29)
1620 H$="   -INTEREST, INCOME TAX COST": GOSUB '2(2,18)
1630 H$="   -DIVIDENDS, OWNER DRAWINGS": GOSUB '2(2,12): PRINT
1640 H$="TOTAL NET CASH FLOW": GOSUB '2(2,14): PRINT
1650 H$="PLAN CHANGE OWNERS' EQUITY": GOSUB '1(2,3)
1660 H$="+ REQUIRED OWNERS' EQUITY": GOSUB '2(2,15): PRINT
1670 H$="CASH AND SECURITIES": GOSUB '3(2,1): PRINT
1680 IF J=Z THEN 1720: IF .5*J=INT(.5*J) THEN 1700
1690 PRINT HEX(OC): GOTO 1710
1700 PRINT
1710 PRINT : PRINT A$;B$: GOSUB '0(0,32)
1720 NEXT J
1730 REM 12**SUMMATION AND D() TRANSFERS FOR PAVE6 STATEMENTS
1740 FOR I=1 TO M: D(4,I)=D(28,I): D(5,I)=D(30,I)
1750 D(6,I)=D(37,I): D(7,I)=D(30,I)-D(37,I)
1760 D(9,I)=N3*A(3,I)+D(15,I): D(10,I)=D(12,I)
1770 IF N5>0 THEN 1780: D(5,I)=0
1780 IF N5<3 THEN 1790: D(5,I),D(7,I)=0
1790 NEXT I
1800 REM 13**PAVE5 OUTPUTS TO PAVEFT5 FOR PAVE6; CHAIN PAVE6
```

Figure 14.5 (continued)

```
1810 MAT REDIM D(10,24): DATA LOAD DC OPEN F "PAVEFT5"
1820 DSKIP 3: DATA SAVE DC N6,Z,D(),U(),V(),X()
1830 DATA SAVE DC END : DATA SAVE DC CLOSE: LOAD DC R "PAVE6"
1840 %    ## PERIODS OVER###.## YEARS; ##.## PERIODS PER YEAR
1850 %, EACH###.## YEARS
1860 %   ## ###/##
1870 %#
1880 % *FOR YEAR###*
1890 %#############################
1900 %-#####,###.##
1910 %-####,###,###
1920 %-#####,###.##*
1930 %-####,###,###*
1940 %  +BOP ####################
1950 %  -EOP ####################
1960 REM 14**SUB'0--PRINT ASTERISK BORDERS FOR MAJOR TITLES
1970 DEFFN'0(T1,L): PRINT TAB(T1);: FOR K=1 TO L: PRINT "*";
1980 NEXT K: PRINT : RETURN
1990 REM 15**SUB--PRINT HEADINGS FOR PERIODS; YR/MO, CUMULATIVE
2000 PRINT : PRINTUSING 1890," ";: FOR I=U(J) TO V(J)
2010 X=X(I)/N: IF X(I)>25 THEN 2040
2020 PRINTUSING 1860,X(I),INT(X+.005),INT(12*(X-INT(X))+.005);
2030 GOTO 2050
2040 PRINTUSING 1880,X(I)-25;
2050 NEXT I: PRINTUSING 1870," ": PRINT : RETURN
2060 REM 16**SUB'1--COMPUTE/PERIOD/CUMULATIVE FOR A()
2070 DEFFN'1(T,Q): FOR I=1 TO M: IF A(Q,I)=0 THEN 2090
2080 I=M: NEXT I: GOTO 2100
2090 NEXT I: GOTO 2200
2100 PRINTUSING 1890,H$;: FOR I=U(J) TO V(J)
2110 IF X(I)>25 THEN 2150: IF T>1 THEN 2130
2120 P=.01*INT(100*A(Q,X(I))+.5): PRINTUSING 1900,P;: GOTO 2140
2130 P=INT(A(Q,X(I))+.5): PRINTUSING 1910,P;
2140 P(Q)=P(Q)+P: GOTO 2190
2150 IF T>1 THEN 2170: PRINTUSING 1920,.01*INT(100*P(Q)/N+.5);
2160 GOTO 2180
2170 PRINTUSING 1930,P(Q);
2180 P(Q)=0
2190 NEXT I: PRINTUSING 1870," ": IF J<Z THEN 2200: P(Q)=0
2200 RETURN
2210 REM 17**SUB'2--COMPUTE/PRINT PERIOD/CUMULATIVE FOR D()
2220 DEFFN'2(T,Q): FOR I=1 TO M: IF D(Q,I)=0 THEN 2240
2230 I=M: NEXT I: GOTO 2250
2240 NEXT I: GOTO 2360
2250 PRINTUSING 1890,H$;: FOR I=U(J) TO V(J)
2260 IF X(I)>25 THEN 2310: IF T>1 THEN 2290
2270 P=.01*INT(100*N9*D(Q,X(I))+.5): PRINTUSING 1900,P;
2280 GOTO 2300
2290 P=INT(N9*D(Q,X(I))+.5): PRINTUSING 1910,P;
```

Figure 14.5 (continued)

```
2300 Z(Q)=Z(Q)+P: GOTO 2350
2310 IF T>1 THEN 2330: PRINTUSING 1920,.01*INT(100*Z(Q)/N+.5);
2320 GOTO 2340
2330 PRINTUSING 1930,Z(Q);
2340 Z(Q)=0
2350 NEXT I: PRINTUSING 1870," ": IF J<Z THEN 2360: Z(Q)=0
2360 RETURN
2370 REM 18**SUB'3--COMPUTE/PRINT PERIOD/CUMULATIVE FOR C()
2380 DEFFN'3(T,Q): FOR I=1 TO M+1: IF C(Q,I)=0 THEN 2400
2390 I=M+1: NEXT I: GOTO 2410
2400 NEXT I: GOTO 2540
2410 PRINTUSING 1940,H$;: FOR I=U(J) TO V(J)
2420 IF X(I)>25 THEN 2450
2430 PRINTUSING 1910,INT(N9*C(Q,X(I))+.5);
2440 IF I<N THEN 2460: K(Q,1)=C(Q,X(I)-N+1): GOTO 2460
2450 PRINTUSING 1930,INT(N9*K(Q,1)+.5);
2460 NEXT I: PRINTUSING 1870," ": IF T<2 THEN 2480: PRINT
2470 PRINTUSING 1890,"CASH AND SECURITIES EOP";: GOTO 2490
2480 PRINTUSING 1950,H$;
2490 FOR I=U(J) TO V(J): IF X(I)>25 THEN 2520
2500 P=INT(N9*C(Q,X(I)+1)+.5): PRINTUSING 1910,P;
2510 K(Q,2)=P: GOTO 2530
2520 PRINTUSING 1930,K(Q,2);
2530 NEXT I: PRINTUSING 1870," "
2540 RETURN : END
```

Figure 14.6 PAVE6 coding

```
2470 REM **C.L.HUBBARD, R.A.PETERSON JR, F.J.GANOE
2480 REM **PAVE6 WANG--FINANCIAL STATEMENTS 2, SELECTED ACCOUNTS
2490 SELECT PRINT 005(64): PRINT HEX(03)
2500 PRINT "PAVE6 FINANCIAL STATEMENTS 2 OR SELECTED ACCOUNTS"
2510 DIM B(24,25),C(22,25),K(3,2),G(16,24),F(25),D(11,24),Z(7)
2520 DIM U(6),V(6),X(36),C$(17)26,S$(4)26,A$37,B$12,H$28,N$64
2530 REM 1**READ PAVE2, PAVE3, PAVE4, PAVE5 RECORDS FROM PAVEFT5
2540 DATA LOAD DC OPEN F "PAVEFT5": MAT REDIM C(14,25),D(10,24)
2550 DATA LOAD DC N$,M,N,N3,N5,I1,I2,B(): DATA LOAD DC C(),G()
2560 DATA LOAD DC T,P,S1,R1,F()
2570 DATA LOAD DC N6,Z,D(),U(),V(),X(): DATA SAVE DC CLOSE
2580 N9=1/N3: MAT REDIM C(22,25),D(11,24): B$=" (CONTINUED)"
2590 REM 2**TITLES FOR STATEMENTS AND SELECTED ACCOUNTS
2600 C$(9)="CASH AND MARKET SECURITIES"
2610 C$(10)="CASH+SECURITIES+ACCT RECV"
2620 C$(11)="TOTAL INVENTORIES": C$(12)="TOTAL CURRENT ASSETS"
2630 C$(13)="TOTAL ASSETS": C$(14)="TOTAL CURRENT LIABILITIES"
2640 C$(15)="TOTAL LIABILITIES": C$(16)="TOTAL OWNERS' EQUITY"
2650 REM 3**SUM C() USED FOR STATEMENTS AND SELECTED ACCOUNTS
2660 FOR I=1 TO M+1: C(15,I)=C(1,I)+C(2,I)-C(3,I)
2670 ON N5+1 GOTO 2700,2690,2680
```

Figure 14.6 (continued)

```
2680 C(16,I)=C(7,I)+C(8,I)+N3*B(1,I)
2690 C(16,I)=C(16,I)+C(6,I)
2700 C(16,I)=C(16,I)+C(5,I): C(17,I)=C(15,I)+C(4,I)+C(16,I)
2710 C(18,I)=C(17,I)+N3*(B(2,I)+B(3,I))
2720 C(19,I)=C(9,I)+C(10,I)+C(11,I): C(20,I)=C(12,I)+C(19,I)
2730 C(21,I)=C(13,I)+C(14,I): C(22,I)=C(20,I)+C(21,I)
2740 B(3,I)=B(3,I)-B(4,I): IF I=1 THEN 2750: D(11,I-1)=C(21,I)
2750 NEXT I: IF N6>2 THEN 3410: GOSUB 5080: IF N5>2 THEN 4130
2760 REM 4**RETAINED EARNINGS AND CAPITAL CHANGES STATEMENTS
2770 PRINT HEX(OC): PRINT : PRINT N$: PRINT : GOSUB '0(0,37)
2780 A$="RETAINED EARNINGS AND CAPITAL CHANGES STATEMENTS"
2790 PRINT A$: GOSUB '0(0,37)
2800 FOR J=1 TO Z: GOSUB 4390: H$="BOP OWNER PAID-IN CAPITAL"
2810 GOSUB '1(13): H$="  +OWNER NET INVESTMENT": GOSUB '2(1,9)
2820 H$="EOP OWNER PAID-IN CAPITAL": GOSUB '3(13): PRINT
2830 H$="BOP RETAINED EARNINGS": GOSUB '1(14)
2840 H$="  +NET INCOME": GOSUB '2(1,8): H$="  -DIVIDENDS PAID"
2850 GOSUB '2(1,10): H$="EOP RETAINED EARNINGS": GOSUB '3(14)
2860 PRINT : H$="EOP TOTAL OWNERS' EQUITY": GOSUB '3(21): PRINT
2870 H$="EOP NO. SHARES OUTSTANDING": GOSUB '2(2,1): PRINT
2880 H$="NET INCOME PER SHARE": GOSUB '2(3,8)
2890 H$="DIVIDENDS PER SHARE": GOSUB '2(3,10)
2900 H$="EOP OWNERS' EQUITY PER SHARE": GOSUB '2(3,11)
2910 IF J=Z THEN 2950: IF .5*J<>INT(.5*J) THEN 2930
2920 PRINT HEX(OC): GOTO 2940
2930 PRINT
2940 PRINT : PRINT A$;B$: GOSUB '0(0,37)
2950 NEXT J
2960 REM 5**CONDITIONS STATEMENTS
2970 PRINT HEX(OC): PRINT : PRINT N$: PRINT : GOSUB '0(0,37)
2980 A$="CONDITION STATEMENTS (BALANCE SHEETS)": PRINT A$;
2990 PRINT TAB(45);"EOP ALL COLUMNS EXCEPT FIRST"
3000 GOSUB '0(0,37): GOSUB 4910: FOR J=1 TO Z: GOSUB 4460
3010 PRINT "****** ASSETS ******": PRINT
3020 H$=C$(9): GOSUB '4(1,1): H$="+ACCOUNTS RECEIVABLE GROSS"
3030 GOSUB '4(1,2): H$="  -UNCOLLECTIBLES RESERVE"
3040 GOSUB '4(1,3): PRINT
3050 H$=C$(10): GOSUB '4(1,15): PRINT : H$="PREPAID EXPENSE"
3060 GOSUB '4(1,4): PRINT : ON N5+1 GOTO 3110,3100,3070
3070 H$="DIRECT MATERIAL INVY--MFG": GOSUB '4(1,8)
3080 H$="PERIOD SUPPLIES INVY--MFG": GOSUB '4(2,1)
3090 H$="GOODS-IN-PROCESS INVY--MFG": GOSUB '4(1,7)
3100 H$="FINISHED GOODS INVENTORY": GOSUB '4(1,6)
3110 H$="SUPPLIES INVENTORY--GEN": GOSUB '4(1,5): PRINT
3120 H$=C$(11): GOSUB '4(1,16): PRINT : H$=C$(12)
3130 GOSUB '4(1,17): IF I1<1 THEN 3190
3140 PRINT : PRINT "MFG FIXED ASSETS AT COST:"
3150 FOR K=1 TO I1: GOSUB '4(3,K+14): NEXT K: PRINT
3160 PRINT "MFG FIXED ASSETS DEPRC RESERVES:": FOR K=1 TO I1
3170 GOSUB '4(3,K+19): NEXT K: PRINT
```

Figure 14.6 (continued)

```
3180 H$="MFG FIXED ASSETS AT BOOK": GOSUB '4(2,2): PRINT
3190 IF I2<1 THEN 3250
3200 PRINT : PRINT : PRINT "GEN FIXED ASSETS AT COST:"
3210 FOR K=1 TO I2: GOSUB '4(3,K+4): NEXT K: PRINT
3220 PRINT "GEN FIXED ASSETS DEPRC RESERVES:": FOR K=1 TO I2
3230 GOSUB '4(3,K+9): NEXT K: PRINT
3240 H$="GEN FIXED ASSETS AT BOOK": GOSUB '4(2,3)
3250 PRINT : PRINT : H$="UNAMORTIZED INTANGIBLES": GOSUB '4(2,4)
3260 PRINT : H$=C$(13): GOSUB '4(1,18)
3270 PRINT HEX(OC): PRINT : PRINT A$;B$: PRINT : GOSUB 4460
3280 PRINT "******  LIABILITIES AND OWNERS' EQUITY  ******"
3290 PRINT : H$="ACCOUNTS PAYABLE": GOSUB '4(1,9)
3300 H$="UNEARNED CUSTOMER ADVANCES": GOSUB '4(1,10)
3310 H$="SHORT-TERM LOANS AND NOTES": GOSUB '4(1,11)
3320 PRINT : H$=C$(14): GOSUB '4(1,19): PRINT
3330 H$="LONG-TERM OBLIGATIONS"
3340 GOSUB '4(1,12): PRINT : H$=C$(15): GOSUB '4(1,20)
3350 PRINT : PRINT : H$=C$(16): GOSUB '4(1,21): PRINT
3360 H$="LIABILITIES & OWNER EQUITY": GOSUB '4(1,22)
3370 IF J=Z THEN 3390: PRINT HEX(OC): PRINT
3380 PRINT A$;B$: GOSUB '0(0,37)
3390 NEXT J: GOTO 4130
3400 REM 6**ARRAY TRANSFERS FOR SELECTED ACCOUNTS PRINTING
3410 R=0: IF I0>0 THEN 3570: C$(1)="INDUSTRY SALES--000 OMIT"
3420 C$(2)="FIRM'S INDUSTRY SHARE %"
3430 C$(3)="FIRM NET SALES ACHIEVED": C$(4)="COST OF SALES"
3440 C$(5)="GROSS PROFIT ON SALES"
3450 C$(6)="TOTAL OPERATING EXPENSE"
3460 C$(7)="NET OPERATING INCOME": C$(8)="NET INCOME AFTER TAX"
3470 C$(17)="ALL FIXED ASSETS AT BOOK"
3480 FOR I=1 TO M: C(9,I)=C(1,I+1): FOR K=10 TO 16
3490 C(K,I)=C(K+5,I+1): NEXT K: C(1,I)=D(3,I): C(2,I)=D(2,I)
3500 C(3,I)=D(1,I): FOR K=4 TO 8: C(K,I)=D(K,I): NEXT K
3510 C(17,I)=B(3,I+1)+B(4,I+1): FOR K=1 TO 16: C(K,I)=C(K,I)*N9
3520 IF N3=1 THEN 3550: Q=G(K,I)-N3*C(K,I)*C(K,I)
3530 IF Q>0 THEN 3540: Q=0
3540 G(K,I)=SQR(Q/(N3*(N3-1)))
3550 NEXT K: NEXT I: I0=1
3560 REM 7**USER COMMANDS FOR SELECTED ACCOUNTS OUTPUT
3570 SELECT PRINT 005(64): PRINT HEX(03): W,S=0
3580 PRINT "    ACCOUNT NOS.--ALL=0, BRANCH TO NEXT OUTPUT=99"
3590 FOR K=1 TO 8: PRINT K;"=";C$(K);TAB(34);K+9;"=";C$(K+9)
3600 NEXT K: PRINT " 9 =";C$(9): PRINT
3610 PRINT "STATISTICS EXTENT NOS.--MINUS SIGN OMITS";
3620 PRINT " YEAR/MONTH HEADINGS": PRINT "    (SD  STANDARD";
3630 PRINT " DEVIATION, CL  CONFIDENCE LIMITS)"
3640 PRINT "MEAN=1,SD=2,MEAN+SD=3,MEAN+SD+CL=4,NONE=0"
3650 PRINT TAB(19);
3660 INPUT "ENTER: ACCOUNT NO., STAT EXTENT NO.",W,S
3670 REM 8**SELECTED ACCOUNTS OUTPUT COMPUTE AND PRINT
```

Figure 14.6 (continued)

```
3680 IF W>17 THEN 4130: IF S=0 THEN 4130
3690 G,H=W: IF W>0 THEN 3700: G=1: H=17: I3=1
3700 C,D=1: IF N3<2 THEN 3750
3710 U=ABS(S): C,D=U: IF U<3 THEN 3720: C=1: D=2*U-4
3720 S$(2)="   STANDARD DEVIATIONS"
3730 S$(3)="   LOWER CONFIDENCE LIMITS"
3740 S$(4)="   UPPER CONFIDENCE LIMITS"
3750 GOSUB 5080
3760 IF R>0 THEN 3830: GOSUB 4910: PRINT HEX(OC): PRINT
3770 IF S<0 THEN 3830: PRINT N$: PRINT : GOSUB '0(10,33)
3780 A$="SELECTED ACCOUNTS FOR ALL PERIODS": PRINT TAB(10);A$
3790 GOSUB '0(10,33): PRINT : PRINT "CONDITION ITEMS ARE END";
3800 PRINT "-OF-PERIOD";: IF N3<2 THEN 3830
3810 PRINT ";";P;"% CONFIDENCE LIMITS FOR MEANS WITH";
3820 PRINT " SAMPLE SIZE";N3: PRINT
3830 FOR J=1 TO Z: S$(1)="   MEANS": IF R=0 THEN 3870
3840 IF G<>H THEN 3860: IF J>1 THEN 3870: IF I3=0 THEN 3870
3850 I3=0
3860 PRINT HEX(OC)
3870 PRINT : IF S<0 THEN 3880: GOSUB 4460
3880 FOR K=G TO H: IF J<2 THEN 3890: IF G=H THEN 3900
3890 PRINT C$(K)
3900 FOR I=1 TO M: IF C(K,I)=0 THEN 3910: GOTO 3940
3910 NEXT I
3920 PRINT "   ALL ACCOUNT VALUES ARE ZERO OR INAPPLICABLE"
3930 GOTO 4110
3940 I=M: NEXT I: FOR L=C TO D
3950 IF N3<2 THEN 3960: IF K<17 THEN 3970: IF L<>1 THEN 4080
3960 S$(1)="  "
3970 PRINTUSING 4290,S$(L);
3980 FOR I=U(J) TO V(J): ON L GOTO 3990,4000,4010,4020
3990 Q=C(K,I): GOTO 4030
4000 Q=G(K,I): GOTO 4030
4010 Q=C(K,I)-T*G(K,I): GOTO 4030
4020 Q=C(K,I)+T*G(K,I)
4030 IF K=2 THEN 4040: PRINTUSING 4310,INT(Q+.5);: GOTO 4050
4040 PRINTUSING 4330,.01*INT(100*Q+.5);
4050 IF N<2 THEN 4070: F=INT(.005+12*(I/N-INT(I/N)))
4060 IF F>0 THEN 4070: PRINTUSING 4270,"*";
4070 NEXT I: PRINTUSING 4270," "
4080 NEXT L
4090 IF G=H THEN 4110: IF U<3 THEN 4110: IF K<>8 THEN 4110
4100 PRINT HEX(OC)
4110 PRINT : NEXT K: R=1: NEXT J: GOTO 3570
4120 REM 9**NEXT OUTPUT OPTION
4130 SELECT PRINT 005(64): PRINT HEX(03): PRINT : PRINT "NEXT";
4140 PRINT " OUTPUT: VALUATION=0, FINANCIAL SUMMARY=1, ";
4150 PRINT "STATEMENTS=2"
4160 INPUT "     SELECTED ACCOUNTS=3, RERUN=4, END=5",N6
4170 ON N6+1 GOTO 4190,4190,4210,3410,4240,5110
```

Figure 14.6 (continued)

```
4180 REM 10**WRITE NEXT OUTPUT DATA TO FILES AND CHAIN PROGRAMS
4190 DATA LOAD DC OPEN F "PAVEFT3": DATA SAVE DC N6
4200 DATA SAVE DC CLOSE: LOAD DC R "PAVE4"
4210 DATA LOAD DC OPEN F "PAVEFT4": DSKIP 2
4220 DATA SAVE DC N6,S1,R1: DATA SAVE DC CLOSE
4230 LOAD DC R "PAVE5"
4240 LOAD DC R "PAVE1" 2470
4250 %###########################
4260 %    ## ###/##
4270 %#
4280 % *FOR YEAR###*
4290 %###########################
4300 %     CLASS #                    #
4310 %-####,###,###
4320 %-####,###,###*
4330 %-#####,###.##
4340 %-#####,###.##*
4350 REM 11**SUB'0--ASTERISK PRINTING FOR TITLES
4360 DEFFN'0(T1,L): PRINT TAB(T1);: FOR K=1 TO L: PRINT "*";
4370 NEXT K: PRINT : RETURN
4380 REM 12**SUB--FLOW HEADINGS, PERIOD AND CUMULATIVE
4390 PRINT : PRINTUSING 4250," ";: FOR I=U(J) TO V(J)
4400 X=X(I)/N: IF X(I)>25 THEN 4430
4410 PRINTUSING 4260,X(I),INT(X+.005),INT(12*(X-INT(X))+.005);
4420 GOTO 4440
4430 PRINTUSING 4280,X(I)-25;
4440 NEXT I: PRINTUSING 4270," ": PRINT : RETURN
4450 REM 13**SUB--CONDITION AND SELECTED ACCOUNTS HEADINGS
4460 PRINT : PRINTUSING 4290," ";: A=U(J): B=0
4470 IF N6>2 THEN 4490: B=1: IF J>1 THEN 4490
4480 PRINT " *START BOP 1*";: A=2: F(1)=0
4490 FOR I=A TO V(J): A1=(I-B)/N: A2=12*((I-B)/N-INT((I-B)/N))
4500 F(I)=INT(A2+.005): PRINTUSING 4260,I-B,INT(A1+.005),F(I);
4510 IF N<2 THEN 4520: IF F(I)>0 THEN 4520: PRINTUSING 4270,"*";
4520 NEXT I: PRINTUSING 4270," ": PRINT : RETURN
4530 REM 14**SUB'1--COMPUTE/PRINT BOP/CUMULATIVE FOR C()
4540 DEFFN'1(Q): FOR I=1 TO M+1: IF C(Q,I)=0 THEN 4560
4550 I=M+1: NEXT I: GOTO 4570
4560 NEXT I: GOTO 4630
4570 PRINTUSING 4250,H$;: FOR I=U(J) TO V(J)
4580 IF X(I)>25 THEN 4610
4590 F=INT(N9*C(Q,X(I))+.5): PRINTUSING 4310,F;
4600 IF I<N THEN 4620: K(Q-12,1)=C(Q,X(I)-N+1): GOTO 4620
4610 PRINTUSING 4320,INT(N9*K(Q-12,1)+.5);
4620 NEXT I: PRINTUSING 4270," "
4630 RETURN
4640 REM 15**SUB'2--COMPUTE/PRINT PERIOD/CUMULATIVE D(), F()
4650 DEFFN'2(E,Q): IF Q=1 THEN 4680: FOR I=1 TO M
4660 IF D(Q,I)=0 THEN 4670: I=M: NEXT I: GOTO 4680
4670 NEXT I: GOTO 4810
```

Figure 14.6 (continued)

```
4680 PRINTUSING 4250,H$;: FOR I=U(J) TO V(J)
4690 IF X(I)>25 THEN 4750: ON E GOTO 4700,4710,4720
4700 F=INT(N9*D(Q,X(I))+.5): PRINTUSING 4310,F;: R=7: GOTO 4740
4710 PRINTUSING 4310,F(X(I));: Z(5)=Z(5)+F(X(I)): GOTO 4800
4720 F=.01*INT(100*N9*D(Q,X(I))/F(X(I))+.5): PRINTUSING 4330,F;
4730 R=4: IF Q<>11 THEN 4740: Z(Q-R)=0
4740 Z(Q-R)=Z(Q-R)+F: GOTO 4800
4750 ON E GOTO 4760,4770,4780
4760 R=7: PRINTUSING 4320,Z(Q-R);: GOTO 4790
4770 PRINTUSING 4320,INT(Z(5)/N+.5);: Z(5)=0: GOTO 4800
4780 R=4: PRINTUSING 4340,Z(Q-R);
4790 Z(Q-R)=0
4800 NEXT I: PRINTUSING 4270," "
4810 RETURN
4820 REM 16**SUB'3--COMPUTE/PRINT EOP/CUMULATIVE FOR C()
4830 DEFFN'3(Q): PRINTUSING 4250,H$;
4840 R=3: IF Q>20 THEN 4850: R=Q-12
4850 FOR I=U(J) TO V(J): IF X(I)>25 THEN 4880
4860 F=INT(N9*C(Q,X(I)+1)+.5): PRINTUSING 4310,F;
4870 K(R,2)=F: GOTO 4890
4880 PRINTUSING 4320,K(R,2);
4890 NEXT I: PRINTUSING 4270," ": RETURN
4900 REM 17**SUB--DISPLAY INDICES FOR CONDITION, SPECIAL ACCTS
4910 Z=INT((M+8-N6)/6): U(Z)=(Z-1)*6+1: V(Z)=M+3-N6: RETURN
4920 REM 18**SUB'4--COMPUTE/PRINT CONDITIONS FOR C(),B()
4930 DEFFN'4(E,Q): FOR I=1 TO M+1: IF E>1 THEN 4950
4940 IF C(Q,I)=0 THEN 4970: GOTO 4960
4950 IF B(Q,I)=0 THEN 4970
4960 I=M+1: NEXT I: IF E>2 THEN 4980: GOTO 4990
4970 NEXT I: GOTO 5060
4980 PRINTUSING 4300,K," ";: GOTO 5000
4990 PRINTUSING 4290,H$;
5000 FOR I=U(J) TO V(J): IF E<2 THEN 5020: F=INT(B(Q,I)+.5)
5010 GOTO 5030
5020 F=INT(N9*C(Q,I)+.5)
5030 PRINTUSING 4310,F;: IF N<2 THEN 5050
5040 IF F(I)<>0 THEN 5050: PRINTUSING 4270,"*";
5050 NEXT I: PRINTUSING 4270," "
5060 RETURN
5070 REM 19**SUB--PRINTER 'ON' WARNING AND SELECT PRINTER
5080 PRINT HEX(03): PRINT " !!--PRINTER'ON'? 'SELECT' LITED?";
5090 PRINT "  PLUGGED INTO COMPUTER?--!!": SELECT PRINT 215(110)
5100 RETURN
5110 END
```

Figure 14.7 PAVEC coding

```
9800 REM **C.L.HUBBARD, R.A.PETERSON JR, F.J.GANOE
9810 REM **PAVEC--CATALOGS PAVEFT TYPE DATA FILES OF PAVE SYSTEM
9820 DIM Q$(5)8,J(5),Q$8
```

Figure 14.7 (continued)

```
9830 Q$(1)="PAVEFT1": Q$(2)="PAVEFT2": Q$(3)="PAVEFT3"
9840 Q$(4)="PAVEFT4": Q$(5)="PAVEFT5"
9850 J(1)=24: J(2)=37: J(3)=13: J(4)=63: J(5)=65
9860 SELECT PRINT 005(64): PRINT HEX(03)
9870 INPUT "CATALOG ALL PAVEFT FILES=0/INDIVIDUAL FILES=1",N7
9880 N8=1: IF N7<1 THEN 9910
9890 INPUT "FILE NAME, FORMAT NO. 1-5 FROM PAVEFTS",Q$,N8
9900 Q$(N8)=Q$
9910 DATA SAVE DC OPEN F J(N8),Q$(N8): IF N7>0 THEN 9930
9920 N8=N8+1: IF N8>5 THEN 9930: GOTO 9910
9930 END
```

Figure 14.8 PAVER coding

```
9600 REM **C.L.HUBBARD, R.A.PETERSON JR, F.J.GANOE
9610 REM **PAVER--PRINT PAVEFT TYPE DATA FILES OF PAVE SYSTEM
9620 DIM I(1,150),J(1,250),O(1,250),R(1,240),Y(1,168),N$64,Q$8
9630 SELECT PRINT 005(64): PRINT HEX(03)
9640 INPUT "FILE NAME, FORMAT NO. 1-5 FROM PAVEFTS",Q$,N8
9650 SELECT PRINT 215(80): PRINT : PRINT : PRINT "***";Q$;"***"
9660 DATA LOAD DC OPEN F Q$: ON N8 GOTO 9680,9690,9700,9710,9730
9670 REM 1**DIMENSIONS OF ARRAYS TO RECEIVE PAVEFT DATA
9680 GOSUB '1(99,200,30,200,50)
9690 GOSUB '2(131,240,240,240,96)
9700 GOSUB '3(1): GOSUB '1(4,5,5,5,4): GOSUB '2(12,6,6,132,25)
9710 GOSUB '1(5,240,240,48,25): GOSUB '2(150,240,240,240,168)
9720 GOSUB '3(3)
9730 GOSUB '1(6,250,250,50,50): GOSUB '2(100,250,240,120,24)
9740 GOSUB '3(29): GOSUB '2(2,240,6,6,36)
9750 REM 2**SUB'1--LOAD AND CONTROL RECORD; TITLE N$ AND 5 ARRAYS
9760 DEFFN'1(A8,B8,C8,D8,E8): GOSUB 9870
9770 DATA LOAD DC N$,I(),J(),O(),R(),Y(): IF END THEN 9930
9780 PRINT N$: PRINT : GOSUB 9910: RETURN
9790 REM 3**SUB'2--LOAD AND CONTROL RECORD; 5 ARRAYS
9800 DEFFN'2(A8,B8,C8,D8,E8): GOSUB 9870
9810 DATA LOAD DC I(),J(),O(),R(),Y(): IF END THEN 9930
9820 GOSUB 9910: RETURN
9830 REM 4**SUB'3--LOAD AND PRINT RECORD; ONE ARRAY
9840 DEFFN'3(A8): PRINT : PRINT "***": MAT REDIM I(1,A8)
9850 DATA LOAD DC I(): IF END THEN 9930: MAT PRINT I: RETURN
9860 REM 5**SUB--PRINT HEADING AND DIMENSION ARRAYS FOR RECORD
9870 PRINT : PRINT "***"
9880 MAT REDIM I(1,A8),J(1,B8),O(1,C8),R(1,D8),Y(1,E8)
9890 RETURN
9900 REM 6**SUB--MATRIX PRINT ARRAY
9910 MAT PRINT I: PRINT : MAT PRINT J: PRINT : MAT PRINT O
9920 MAT PRINT R: PRINT : MAT PRINT Y: RETURN
9930 DATA SAVE DC CLOSE: END
```

Figure 14.9 PAVES coding

```
8000 REM **C.L.HUBBARD. R.A.PETERSON JR, F.J.GANOE
8010 REM **PAVES--SERVICE INPUT DATA FILES FOR PAVE SYSTEM
8020 DIM N(99),P(230),Q(250),V(5),N$64,Y$8,Z$8
8030 SELECT #1 310,#2 810: SELECT PRINT 005(64): PRINT HEX(03)
8040 INPUT "FILE--OLD=0/OLD RENAME=1/OLD TO NEW=2/NEW=3",Z
8050 IF Z>2 THEN 8090: PRINT : INPUT "ENTER OLD FILE NAME",Y$
8060 PRINT : INPUT "LOAD OLD FILE--LEFT PORT=1/RIGHT PORT=2",A
8070 DATA LOAD DC OPEN T #A,Y$: DATA LOAD DC #A,N$,N(),P(),Q()
8080 REM 1**READ DATA STATEMENTS, IF PRESENT
8090 DATA 0,0
8100 READ C,D: IF C<1 THEN 8120: GOSUB 8780: GOTO 8100
8110 REM 2**MENU DISPLAY AND INPUT CHOICE
8120 PRINT HEX(03): PRINT "1=RESET ALL INPUTS TO ZERO"
8130 PRINT : PRINT "2=REVISE INDIVIDUAL INPUTS"
8140 PRINT : PRINT "3=PRINT ALL INPUTS"
8150 PRINT : PRINT "4=STORE INPUTS ON DISK": PRINT
8160 PRINT "5=END": PRINT : PRINT : INPUT "  ENTER MENU NO.",Q
8170 ON Q GOTO 8190,8250,8360,8450,8510
8180 REM 3**RESET INPUTS TO ZERO BRANCH
8190 PRINT HEX(03): Q=0
8200 INPUT "ERASE ALL INPUTS ON FILE--NO=0/YES=1",Q
8210 IF Q<>1 THEN 8120: N$=" ": FOR I=1 TO 99: N(I)=0: NEXT I
8220 FOR I=1 TO 230: P(I)=0: NEXT I: FOR I=1 TO 250: Q(I)=0
8230 NEXT I: GOTO 8120
8240 REM 4**DISPLAY AND REVISE INDIVIDUAL INPUTS
8250 PRINT HEX(03)
8260 T=0: INPUT "INPUT FILE TITLE--'EXEC'=PASS/PRINT=1/ENTER=2",T
8270 ON T+1 GOTO 8310,8280,8290
8280 PRINT HEX(03) : PRINT N$: PRINT : GOTO 8260
8290 PRINT : N$=" ": PRINT "ENTER TITLE ('EXEC' TO PASS)"
8300 PRINT : INPUT N$
8310 PRINT HEX(03): INPUT "ENTER ID NO.--RETURN TO MENU=0",C
8320 IF C<1 THEN 8120: PRINT : GOSUB 8780
8330 PRINT  "CURRENT VALUE OF ID";C;"=";E: PRINT
8340 INPUT "ENTER REVISED VALUE",D: GOSUB 8780: GOTO 8310
8350 REM 5**PRINT ALL INPUTS BRANCH
8360 PRINT HEX(03): PRINT " !!--PRINTER 'ON'?  'SELECT' LITED?";
8370 PRINT "  PLUGGED INTO COMPUTER?--!!": SELECT PRINT 215(98)
8380 PRINT : PRINT N$: PRINT
8390 GOSUB '1(1,6): GOSUB '1(9,39): GOSUB '1(40,48)
8400 GOSUB '2(100,139): GOSUB '1(51,74): GOSUB '2(140,329)
8410 GOSUB '1(75,78): GOSUB '2(330,529): GOSUB '1(79,84)
8420 GOSUB '2(530,579): GOSUB '1(87,98)
8430 SELECT PRINT 005(64): GOTO 8120
8440 REM 6**OPEN NEW FILE AND STORE INPUTS ON DISK BRANCH
8450 PRINT HEX(03): IF Z>0 THEN 8460: DBACKSPACE #A,BEG : GOTO 8500
8460 INPUT "ENTER NEW FILE NAME",Z$: IF Z>1 THEN 8480
8470 SCRATCH T #A,Y$: DATA SAVE DC OPEN T #A,Y$,Z$: GOTO 8500
8480 PRINT : INPUT "LOAD NEW FILE--LEFT PORT=1/RIGHT PORT=2",A
8490 DATA SAVE DC OPEN T #A,23,Z$
```

Figure 14.9 (continued)

```
8500 DATA SAVE DC #A,N$,N(),P(),Q(): DATA SAVE DC #A,END
8510 DATA SAVE DC CLOSE ALL: END
8520 REM 7**SUB'1--DETERMINE PARAMETERS FOR N() INPUTS PRINT
8530 DEFFN'1(M,N): K=5*INT(.005+(M-1)/5)+1: PRINT
8540 FOR I=K TO N STEP 5: R=M-I: IF R>0 THEN 8550: R=0
8550 T=I+4-N: IF T>0 THEN 8560: T=0
8560 S=5-R-T: GOSUB '3(R,S,T): NEXT I: RETURN
8570 REM 8**SUB'2--DETERMINE PARAMETERS FOR P(),Q() INPUTS PRINT
8580 DEFFN'2(M,N): PRINT : FOR L=M TO N STEP 10: I=L-4
8590 GOSUB '3(4,1,0): I=L+1: GOSUB '3(0,5,0): I=L+6
8600 GOSUB '3(0,4,1): NEXT L: RETURN
8610 REM 9**SUB'3--SET VALUES, CHECK ZEROS, PRINT IDS AND FIELDS
8620 DEFFN'3(R,S,T): F=R+1: B=R+S: I1=0: FOR J=F TO B
8630 IF M>99 THEN 8640: V(J)=N(I+J-1): GOTO 8660
8640 IF M>329 THEN 8650: V(J)=P(I+J-100): GOTO 8660
8650 V(J)=Q(I+J-330)
8660 IF V(J)=0 THEN 8670: I1=1
8670 NEXT J: IF I1<1 THEN 8720
8680 IF S>1 THEN 8690: PRINT " ID";I+F-1,: GOTO 8700
8690 PRINT "IDS";I+F-1;"TO";I+B-1,
8700 GOSUB '4(R): FOR J=F TO B
8710 PRINT V(J),: NEXT J: GOSUB '4(T): PRINT " "
8720 RETURN
8730 REM 10**SUB'4--SPACE LEAD AND TRAIL BLANKS IN PRINT COLUMNS
8740 DEFFN'4(X): IF X=0 THEN 8760: FOR J=1 TO X: PRINT " ",
8750 NEXT J
8760 RETURN
8770 REM 12**SUB--READ OR WRITE INDIVIDUAL IDS
8780 IF C>99 THEN 8790: E=N(C): N(C)=D: GOTO 8810
8790 IF C>329 THEN 8800: E=P(C-99): P(C-99)=D: GOTO 8810
8800 E=Q(C-329): Q(C-329)=D
8810 RETURN : END
```

—— Table 14.1 ——
PAVE1 VARIABLE LIST

Initial statement line for each use, except dimensioning, is given at the end of each description.

Dimensions are shown for arrays.

A Line number of first ID in video input display (3290)

A1 ID number from DATA STATEMENTS or INDIVIDUAL INTERACTIVE input modes, and printed in video input displays (2550)

A2 Value in ID of A1, read from DATA STATEMENTS input mode (2550)

B Line number of last ID in video input display (3290)

C Line number of first ID in video display which is marked for input (6030)

I 1. Loop index for nonzero default assignments to input IDs (2650)
   2. Loop index for fixed asset classes initial condition inputs (3490)
   3. Loop index for total initial book value of fixed assets over classes (3710)
   4. Loop index for processing inputs of seasonal/cyclical indexes (4210)
   5. Loop index for trailing blank lines of *manufacturing expense system parameters* displays (4640)
   6. Index for sequence of ID input lines in video input displays (6070)
   7. Loop index for checking first three ID positions for nonzero values in *fixed asset net changes* dynamic input sets (6590)

I1 Index for sequence of ID inputs in video input displays, which has been adjusted from I for skipped ID line which occurs in some dynamic input sets (6080)

J 1. Loop index for transfer of dynamic inputs sets to L( ) from P( ) or Q( ) (6010)
   2. Loop index for printing ID lines of *system parameter* input displays (6300)
   3. Loop index for printing ID lines of *indexed parameter* input displays (6380)
   4. Loop index for printing ID lines of *dynamic sets* input displays (6480)

K Counter links ID number in A1 to line in video display for first input C or print I1; K is passed to SUB '1 (3480)

P Indicator of type of display and print of "%" or "$"; P is passed to SUB '1 (4890)

Q 1. Shift indicator between two displays of *seasonal/cyclical indexes* (4200)

Table 14.1 (continued)

	2. Shift indicator between manufacturing and *general fixed asset net changes* classes, passed to control SUB '2–COUNT FIXED ASSET CLASSES; CYCLE DISPLAYS (5730)
S	Counter of fixed asset classes, either *manufacturing* or *general* (5730)
S1	Total assets for initial condition (3700)
S2	Total liabilities for initial condition (3700)
S3	Total owners' equity for initial condition (3760)
T	1. Choice input to print input/output instructions (2100)
	2. Choice input to print *policy reminder statements* (POLREMS) (2460)
U	Multiple branch integer for video input displays under INDIVIDUAL INTERACTIVE input mode (5700)
V	Value of numerical input from IDs in video input displays, converted from V\$ (6230)
W	Factor for nonzero DATA STATEMENTS input; used in the computation of Z1 (2550)
X	Index of prefix in G\$( ) for dynamic sets in video input displays (6430)
Y	Indicator of skipped ID line for dynamic sets in video input displays (5970)
Z	Indicator of POLREM print from input T or menu choice Z4=10 (2870)
Z1	Input file choice and file management branching indicator (2500)
Z2	Menu number branch control, derived from input menu choice Z4 (2860)
Z3	Input choices and branching for management of *old* files (5830)
Z4	Menu input choice, transferred to Z2 for input divisions and further processing, except with control of Z4=10 for *print all inputs* (2850)
C(12)	Class numbers for *seasonal/cylical* indexes or *fixed assets* (3490)
L(12)	Local array for printing and transferring dynamic input values for video input displays (6010)
N(99)	*System parameter* input values (see Table 14.10); transfer to PAVEFT1 for PAVE2 (2520)
P(230)	*Dynamic set* input values for *environment, trade,* and *manufacturing* (see tables 14.10 and 14.11); transfer to PAVEFT1 for PAVE2 (2500)
Q(250)	*Dynamic set* input values for *research and development, sales, general administration,* and *finance* (see tables 14.10 and 14.11); transfer to PAVEFT1 for PAVE2 (2520)
A\$	Main title of each video input display (3160)

Table 14.1 (continued)

C$	Standard phrase used for ID descriptions of video input displays (3490)
F$	Class number used for ID descriptions of fixed assets in video input displays (2850)
H$	Trailing phrase used for ID descriptions of fixed assets in video input displays (2850)
N$	Title of run input; printed with menu choice Z4=10, and transferred to PAVEFT1 for PAVE2 (2520)
S$	ID description of uncertainty input for dynamic sets; transferred to C$(2) (2830)
V$	User input of nonnumerical, or either numerical or nonnumerical, value (2600)
Y$	*Old* input data file name (2510)
Z$	*New* input data file name (2530)
B$(12)	ID description for *system parameters* in a video input display, including blanks (3170)
C$(10)	ID descriptions for *dynamic sets* in a video display, including blanks (2750)
D$(8)	ID description prefixes for *dynamic sets* in a video display, including blanks (2730)
G$(7)	Number of fixed asset class, transferred to F$, in first five elements; and variable ID description prefix for dynamic sets, transferred to D$( ), in last two elements (2730)
X$(12)	Marker, either "X" or blank, for ID lines in video input displays (6090)

——Table 14.2——
PAVE2 VARIABLE LIST

Initial statement line for each use, except dimensioning, is given at the end of each description.

Dimensions are shown for arrays.

A	Passed to SUB '2 for index *less 10* of Class 1 *fixed asset net changes* from input P( ) or Q( ) (1370)

Table 14.2 (continued)

B	Passed to SUB '2 as index *less one* of output D( ) of Class 1 *fixed asset net changes* each period (1370)
C	Passed to SUB '2 as index *less one* of output B( ) of Class 1 *fixed asset condition* each period (1370)
D	Passed to SUB '2 as index of output A( ) for *total net fixed asset changes* (1370)
E	Passed to SUB '1 as indicator of output array: 1 for A( ) or 2 for D( ) (1160)
F	Passed to SUB '1 as index of first element of *dynamic set* inputs from P( ) and Q( ) (1160)
H	1. Factor of *net asset changes* input from P( ) for *manufacturing* or Q( ) for *general* (1400)
	2. Depreciation rate input from P( ) or Q( ) (1400)
I	1. Loop index over periods for *inflation* adjustment factors (120)
	2. Loop indexes for processing up to 24 *seasonal/cyclical* indexes (380)
	3. Loop index over periods for *industry sales* before randomization (450)
	4. Loop index over periods for processing various expense accounts prior to randomization (530)
	5. Loop index over periods for transfers of A( ) reassignments to PAVEF4 for PAVE5 (1090)
	6. Loop indexes for processing values every period for *dynamic inputs* within a STEP 3 cycle (1240)
	7. Loop index over periods for processing adjustments to *dynamic inputs* (1280)
	8. Loop index over periods for processing *fixed asset net changes, fixed assets condition*, and *depreciation* (1420)
J	1. Nested loop index for assigning set of *seasonal/cyclical indexes* over all periods I (410)
	2. Loop index for assigning items in *dynamic input sets* to H( ) (1160)
	3. Loop index for assigning *dynamic input sets* to values for all periods (1180)
K	1. Loop index for processing six *manufacturing* and *trade* account inputs through SUB '1 for values all periods (280)
	2. Loop index to reset manufacturing accounts to 0 for trade or service frame (N5=0) (700)
	3. Loop indexes to assign N( ) input parameters to H( ) for PAVEFT3 transfer to PAVE4 (810)

Table 14.2 (continued)

	4. Loop indexes to assign N( ) input parameters to new elements of N( ) for PAVEFT2 transfer to PAVE3 (880)
	5. Loop index to reset uncertainty inputs to 0 for N3=1 before transfer to PAVEFT2 for PAVE3 (1040)
	6. Loop index for fixed asset classes in SUB '3 (1380)
L	Passed to SUB '1 as account index for A( ) or D( ) output arrays for *dynamic input sets* processed for all periods (1160)
M	Number of periods from N(1) parameter; transferred to PAVE3, PAVE4, PAVE5, and PAVE6 (80)
N	Number of periods per year from N(2) parameter; transferred to PAVE3, PAVE4, PAVE5, and PAVE6 (80)
N2	Length of a period in years (80)
N3	Sample size from N(3) parameter; transferred to PAVE4, PAVE5, and PAVE6 (80)
N5	Frame from N(5) parameter; transferred to PAVE3, PAVE4, PAVE5, and PAVE6 (90)
P	Deseasonalization factor from N(51) input (450)
Q	Deseasonalization intermediate factor for goods-in-process inventories (450)
R	Passed to SUB '1 as indicator of final adjustment for *dynamic inputs* assigned to all periods (1160)
W	1. *Inflation* factor for processing inflation adjustments over periods (130)
	2. *Seasonal/cyclical index* from D(4,I) for processing total industry growth over periods (470)
X	Indicator for % of base flow value of $ per period, used for final adjustment of input values processed over all periods (160)
Y	Passed to SUB '2 for index of B( ) for *total* net fixed assets at book value (1370)
Z	1. Indicator of transfer for P( ) or Q( ) to H( ) in SUB '1 (100)
	2. Accumulator for inflation factors over periods (130)
	3. Description of use under 1. is restored (160)
	4. Counter for nonzero *seasonal/cyclical indexes* (370)
	5. Industry sales for processing through periods (450)
	6. *Paid-in owner equity* for processing through periods (520)
Z1	1. Sum of *seasonal/cyclical indexes* (370)

Table 14.2 (continued)

	2. Complement of reciprocal of *seasonal/cyclical index*, used for processing *deseasonalization* adjustments (470)
	3. *Long-term obligations* for processing through periods (520)
	4. *Depreciation* for processing in SUB '2 over periods (1430)

A(34,24) 1. Flow and ratio accounts over periods to PAVE3 for processing (see Table 14.11) (470)
2. Reduced set of accounts over periods for direct transfer to statements in PAVE5 (1090)

B(24,25) Condition input accounts for dates 1 to M+1 to PAVE3, or direct transfer for CONDITION STATEMENTS in PAVE5 and PAVE6 (see Table 14.11) (510)

D(15,24) Flow and rate accounts over periods used for intermediate processing in PAVE2 and transferred directly for flow statements in PAVE5 (see Table 14.11) (120)

H(19) 1. *System parameters* for PAVEFT3 transfer to PAVE4 (see Table 14.17) (90)
2. Local array for dynamic set inputs in SUB '1 (1160)

N(99) 1. *System parameter* input values from PAVE1 by PAVEFT1 (see Table 14.10); N(49) and N(50) are transferred to PAVE6 (70)
2. Indexes reassigned to *system parameters* for PAVEFT2 transfer to PAVE3 (see Table 14.12) (750)

P(230) *Dynamic set* input values from PAVE1 by PAVEFT1 for *environment*, *trade*, and *manufacturing* (see tables 14.10 and 14.11); P(31) is transferred to PAVE5 (70)

Q(250) Dynamic set input values from PAVE1 by PAVEFT1 for *research and development, sales, general administration*, and *finance* (see tables 14.10 and 14.11) (70)

N$ Title of run input from PAVE1 by PAVEFT1; transferred to PAVE4, PAVE5, and PAVE6 (70)

—— Table 14.3 ——
PAVE3 VARIABLE LIST

Initial statement line for each use, except dimensioning, is given at the end of each description.

Table 14.3 (continued)

Dimensions are shown for arrays.

A   Passed parameter to SUB '2 for L( ) condition account index (1790)

B   Passed parameter to SUB '2 for input flow F( ) index used to determine EOP condition (1790)

C   Passed parameter to SUB '2 for input factor used with flow F( ) from index B to determine EOP condition (1790)

C1   Demand for goods into process at sales value level (250)

D   Passed parameter to SUB '2 for output or solution flow value in F( ) from input flow F( ) with index E and change in condition from L( ) (1790)

E   Passed parameter to SUB '2 for input flow F( ) index used to determine output flow F( ) with index D (1790)

F   Computation factor of (+1) or (–1) to determine direction of L( ) change in condition for the computation of output flow F( ) with index D (1790)

H   Loop factor over periods limits the storage of total assets in M(6), or total liabilities in M(8), to Period 1 only (130)

I   1. Period index I is set to 0 in order to obtain BOP 1 value of B( ) in 1700 for first call of SUB 1690 (initial condition), which puts totals of condition accounts into L( ) for processing (130)
                 2. Loop index over periods for account processing in PAVE3; nested into J sample replication loop (150)
                 3. Loop index over periods for assigning owner paid-in capital to F( ) (1570)
                 4. Loop index over periods for reassignment of four C( ) account indexes for input to FINANCIAL STATEMENTS in PAVE5 (1630)

I1   Indicator for occurrence of *technical insolvency* (120)

I2   Indicator for occurrence of *legal insolvency* (120)

J   Loop index for Monte Carlo sample replications over all periods with nested I loop (120)

K   1. Loop index for initial conditions transfers from N( ) into C( ) as sums over sample size (100)
                 2. Loop index to reset to 0 six VALUATION AND SCOPE summation accounts over *first* and *final* years in W( ) for next sample replication (120)
                 3. Loop index to assign initial condition accounts in N( ) to L( ) (130)
                 4. Loop index to transfer EOP values in L( ) from last period I to BOP value for this period (150)

Table 14.3 (continued)

5. Loop index to set up 27 flow accounts in F( ) for processing this period I from inputs A( ) (170)
6. Loop indexes at the close of a period to accumulate *flow* sums in D( ), and *condition* sums C( ) or E( ) (1260)
7. Loop index at the close of a period to accumulate sums of squares in G( )
8. Loop index to reset 0 denominator of FINANCIAL SUMMARY account ratios to a small, positive value (1380)
9. Loop index to accumulate sums and sums of squares of *first* and *final* year VALUATION AND SCOPE accounts in V( ) from W( ) (1480)
10. Loop index to accumulate sums and sums of squares, and process minimum and maximum values for FINANCIAL SUMMARY accounts, in H( ) (1490)
11. Loop index for reassignment of four C( ) account indexes for input to FINANCIAL STATEMENTS in PAVE5, and nested into I loop over all periods (1630)

L	Adjustment factor from actual required capital to required cash effect Q (930)
L1	Overtime labor extension factor (150)
M	Number of periods simulated, from PAVE2 (90)
M1	Subcontract assembly extension factor for plant capacity (150)
N	Number of periods per year in simulation, from PAVE2 (90)
N5	Frame of firm, used to control processing, from PAVE2 (90)
Q	1. Computed short-term borrowing capacity (850)
	2. Local variable for required additional cash effect of capital to reach cash ratio or liquidity policy (920)
	3. Local variable for *rate of return on owner's equity* (1170)
R	Combined *effective income tax rate* from N(31), used as marginal tax rate to compute cash effects of capital changes (730)
R1	*Short-term interest rate* randomized (690)
R4	*Rate of return on monetary assets*, taken as a product of R1 and an input factor (690)
S	1. *Net sales demand*, later adjusted in *manufacturing* frame (320) to *net sales achieved* (220)
	2. Reset S equal to *cost of goods sold* F(37) for computation of inventory turns ratio (1450)

Table 14.3 (continued)

T	1. Total purchases processed through vendor open accounts (570) 2. Local variable for income subject to income tax (1030)
X	Generated random number, initial (100) and in SUB '1 (1730) random generator (100)
Y	Mean value to be randomized for input uncertainty, passed to SUB '1 (1730)
Z	Maximum shift uncertainty input, which is applied to randomization of values in SUB '1; passed to SUB '1 (1730)
A(34,24)	*Flow* accounts for all periods from PAVE2; many are applied to local flow array F( ) (see Table 14.11) (90)
B(3,25)	*Condition* accounts for all dates from PAVE2, and needed for processing in PAVE3 (see Table 14.11) (90)
C(14,25)	Cumulative sums of *condition* accounts for all periods, processed in PAVE3 from local array L( ), and transferred to PAVEFT5 for PAVE6 FINANCIAL STATEMENTS; some are also transferred to PAVEFT4 for PAVE5 FINANCIAL STATEMENTS (see Table 14.13) (100)
D(37,24)	Cumulative sums of *flow* values for all periods, processed in PAVE3 from local array F( ), and transferred to PAVEFT4 for PAVE5 FINANCIAL STATEMENTS (see Table 14.14) (1240)
E(16)	Local array which assembles both *flows* and *condition* accounts during processing for 16 SELECTED ACCOUNTS in PAVE6; E( ) is used as a source for G( ) sums of squares (200)
F(48)	1. Flow values and accounts during processing for a period within sample replications, including SUB '1 (see Table 14.14) (160) 2. Total *owner paid-in capital* for all periods, reassigned from C(13,I), and transferred to PAVEFT3 for PAVE4 (1570)
G(16,24)	Sums of squares from E( ) during all periods for 16 accounts in SELECTED ACCOUNTS outputs; transfer to PAVEFT5 for PAVE6 (see Table 14.15) (1290)
H(33,4)	Four statistics for each of 33 accounts in FINANCIAL SUMMARY, accumulated from U( ) after final periods; transfer to PAVEFT3 for PAVE4 (see Table 14.16) (1490)
L(17,2)	*Condition* accounts during processing for a period within sample replications; L(K,1) for BOP, L(K,2) for EOP, K=1 to 17 accounts (see Table 14.13) (130)
M(12)	Array assembles *system parameters* developed in PAVE3 and required for transfer to PAVEFT3 for PAVE4 (1110)

Table 14.3 (continued)

N(53)   *System parameter* inputs from PAVE2 (90)

T(7)   Totals of flows F( ) or condition L( ) accounts during processing for a period within sample replications (see Table 14.15) (850)

U(33)   Accounts and ratios required for FINANCIAL SUMMARY outputs after final periods; statistics are accumulated from U( ) into H( ) (see Table 14.16) (1310)

V(6,2) *First* (K=1,2,3) year and *final* (K=4,5,6) year *sales* (K=1,4), *earnings* (K=2,5), and *rates of return on owners' equity* (K=3,6); *cumulative sums* V(K,1), and *sum of squares* V(K,2); this array is required for VALUATION AND SCOPE outputs in PAVE4; values are accumulated from W( ) during processing; transfer to PAVEFT3 for PAVE4 (1480)

W(6)   First and final year accounts for VALUATION AND SCOPE during processing; statistics are accumulated from W( ) to V( ) after each final period M; accounts for each index are given in V( ) above (120)

——Table 14.4——
PAVE4 VARIABLE LIST

Initial statement line for each use, except dimensioning, is given at the end of each description.

Dimensions are shown for arrays.

A
1. Starting account index of H( ) in K print loop of FINANCIAL SUMMARY, passed to SUB '1 (4510)
2. Passed parameter to SUB '2 for *mean rate of return on owners' equity* (4890)
3. Passed parameter to SUB '3 for *first* year *mean* value printing for control in VALUATION AND SCOPE (4970)
4. Passed parameter to SUB '4 (4980) integer values print from SUB '3, and SUB '6 (5080) ratio values print from SUB '5, for *first* and *mean* values in VALUATION AND SCOPE (4980)
5. First year values passed to SUB '7 for *methods of valuation* section print in VALUATION AND SCOPE (5210)
6. First year values passed to SUB '8 (5250) and SUB '9 (5280) for parameters of going-concern value in section print in VALUATION AND SCOPE (5250)

Table 14.4 (continued)

B
1. Ending account index of H( ) in K print loop of FINANCIAL SUM-MARY, passed to SUB '1 (4510)
2. Passed parameter to SUB '3 (4970) *integer* values and SUB '5 (5080) *ratios* for *first* year *standard deviations* printing control in VALUA-TION AND SCOPE (4970)
3. Passed parameter to SUB '4 (4980) for *integer* values print from SUB '3, and SUB '6 (5080) *ratio* values print from SUB '5 for *first* year standard deviations in VALUATION AND SCOPE (4980)

C
1. *Last* year *mean* values passed to SUB '3 (4970) and SUB '5 (5080) (see A 3.) (4970)
2. *Last* year *mean* values passed to SUB '4 (4980) and SUB '6 (5090) (see A 4.) (4980)
3. *Last* year values passed to SUB '7 (see A 5.) (5210)
4. *Last* year values passed to SUB '8 (5280) and SUB '9 (5280) (see A 5.) (5250)

D
1. Passed parameter to SUB '3 (4970) and SUB '5 (5080) for *last* year standard deviations (see B 2.) (4970)
2. Passed parameter to SUB '4 (4980) and SUB '6 (5090) for *last* year *standard deviations* (see B 3.) (4980)

G
Long-term growth rate (4210)

I
Loop index for number of shares over periods (2930)

I0
Inflation rate passed to SUB '2 for computation of *investors' required rate of return* (4890)

K
1. Loop index for computing *means* and *standard deviations* of *first* and *final* year items V( ) for VALUATION AND SCOPE (2590)
2. Loop index for transfers, and *means* and *standard deviations*, of H( ) accounts in FINANCIAL SUMMARY
3. Adjustment term relates indexes of P( ) for *risk level* and T( ) for Student's t-statistic to prior tabled value in routine for confidence internal parameters (2710)
4. Loop index for asterisk row print SUB 4480, used with titles print (4480)
5. Loop index for print H( ) accounts of FINANCIAL SUMMARY in SUB '1 (4510)

L
1. Computed index of P( ) for *risk level* and T( ) for Student's t-statistic, which arrays are used to develop these parameters for transfer to P and T respectively for printing and computation of confidence limits (2740)

Table 14.4 (continued)

	2. Length of asterisk row print with titles in SUB 4480 (3010)
L1	Liquidation value of assets to owners, EOP 1 (2820)
L9	Liquidation value of assets to owners, EOP M (2820)
M	Number of periods of simulation, from PAVE2 (2550)
M1	Market value of firm, EOP 1 (2860)
M9	Market value of firm, EOP M (2830)
N	Number of periods per year simulated, from PAVE2 (2550)
N1	Number of shares outstanding, EOP 1
N2	Value per share factor for EOP 1 printing of per share figures in VALUATION AND SCOPE (2820)
N3	Sample size, from PAVE2 (2250)
N5	Frame of firm, used to control statement accounts from PAVE2 (2550)
N6	Output division choice from PAVE2 or PAVE6 (from PAVE6 upon user selection of VALUATION AND SCOPE or FINANCIAL SUMMARY after FINANCIAL STATEMENTS or SELECTED ACCOUNTS); transferred to PAVEFT4 for PAVE5 (2550)
N8	Value per share factor for EOP M printing of *per share* figures in VALUATION AND SCOPE (2820)
N9	Number of shares outstanding, EOP M (2810)
P	*Risk level*, computed in confidence level statistics routine, and used for printing; transferred to PAVE6 (2720)
P1	Going-concern value, EOP 1 (2900)
P9	Going-concern value, EOP M (2830)
Q2	Total or incremental assets EOP 1, used in computation of going-concern value (4790)
Q5	Total or incremental assets EOP M, used in computation of going-concern value (4790)
R	Investors' required rate of return, computed in SUB '2 (4670)
R1	Investors' required rate of return, EOP 1 (4180)
R5	Return on assets used in computation of going-concern value (4250)
R9	Investors' required rate of return, EOP M (4180)
S	1. Mean change in equity capital each period (2930)
	2. Passed parameter to SUB '2 for *standard deviation* of *mean rate of return on owners' equity* (4890)

Table 14.4 (continued)

T   Student's t-statistic, computed in confidence level statistics routine, and used to compute confidence limits; transferred to PAVE6 (2720)

V   1. Local variable for variance numerator (2600) of V( ) and variance numerator (2660) of H( ) (2600)
   2. Local variable for value of the firm during share computations (2940)
   3. Minimum value of *investors' required rate of return* in SUB '2 (4890)

W   *Mean* value passed parameter to SUB '4 (5030) for printing *integer* outputs, and to SUB '6 (5110) for printing *ratio* outputs, both in VALUATION AND SCOPE (5030)

X   *Standard deviation* passed parameter to SUB '4 (5030) for printing *integer* outputs, and to SUB '6 (5110) for printing *ratio* outputs, both in VALUATION AND SCOPE (5030)

Y   Rounding and value per share factor for EOP 1 passed to SUB '6 for *ratio* outputs of VALUATION AND SCOPE (3740); Y also received Z for EOP M in SUB '6 (3740)

Z   1. Local variable for computing value of Student's t-statistic used for confidence limits (2740)
   2. Rounding and value per share factor for EOP M passed to SUB '6 for *ratio* outputs of VALUATION AND SCOPE (3740)

F(25)   1. Paid-in owners' equity each date I=1 to M+1 from PAVE3, used to compute number of shares (2560)
   2. Number of shares each period I (F(1) assigned at 2810); transferred to PAVE6 (2940)

G(12)   Sums and sums of squares of *first* year values required in VALUATION AND SCOPE, final tax loss carry forward, and insolvency parameters; from PAVE3 (see Table 14.12) (2560)

H(36,4)   FINANCIAL SUMMARY account statistics. Inputs for 33 accounts from PAVE3 are sums (index 1), sums of squares (index 2), minimum value (index 3), and maximum value (index 4). The first two are converted in PAVE4 to *mean* and *standard deviation* for printing; 3 more H( ) accounts are added in PAVE4. (See Table 14.16) (2540)

N(19)   *System parameters* are selected *first* and *final* year values from PAVE2; N(2) and N(3) are transferred to PAVEFT4 and PAVEFT5 for PAVE5 and PAVE6 (see Table 14.17) (2550)

P(4)   Four *risk levels* used for processing P, which is printed with confidence limits outputs (2710)

Table 14.4 (continued)

T(6)   1. Four *Student's t-statistics* used for processing T, which in turn is a factor for computing confidence limits (2700)
            2. Local arrays for printing 6 output statistics for each H( ) account in SUB '2 for FINANCIAL SUMMARY (4540)

V(6,2)   *First* and *final* year *earnings, owner's equity,* and *rate of return on owner's equity; sum* (index 1) and *sum of squares* (index 2) from PAVE3 are converted to *mean* and *standard deviation.* (2560)

A$ Two successive subtitles for account printing in VALUATION AND SCOPE (3630)

B$ Second two successive subtitles for account printing in VALUATION AND SCOPE (3630)

E$ Subtitle "TOTAL" for account printing in VALUATION AND SCOPE (3630)

F$ Subtitle "PER SHARE" for account printing in VALUATION AND SCOPE (3640)

H$ Account titles for output printing in VALUATION AND SCOPE (3710)

N$ Title of run, used to head output divisions, from PAVE2 (2550)

H$(4)   Titles of accounts in FINANCIAL SUMMARY (3150)

—— Table 14.5 ——
PAVE5 VARIABLE LIST

Initial statement line for each use, except dimensioning, is given at the end of each description.

Dimensions are shown for arrays.

C   Number of annual columns for statement print (140)

I   1. Index for column control loop in print displays (180)
            2. Index for summing account values over periods loop for INCOME STATEMENTS (600)
            3. Index for summing account values over periods loop for CASH FLOW STATEMENTS (1460)
            4. Index over periods for transfer of D( ) account values by PAVEFT5 to PAVE6 (1740)
            5. Index for print headings of columns loop for flow statements (2000)

Table 14.5 (continued)

	6. Loop index for nonzero value check of A( ) in SUB '1 print (2070)

6. Loop index for nonzero value check of A( ) in SUB '1 print (2070)
7. Loop index for print column values of A( ) (2100)
8. Loop index for nonzero value check of D( ) in SUB '2 print (2220)
9. Loop index for print column values of A( ) (2250)
10. Loop index for nonzero value check of C( ) in SUB '2 print (2380)
11. Loop index for print column of BOP values of C( ) (2410)
12. Loop index for print column of EOP values of C( ) (2490)

I1	Industry base sales input and print from PAVE2 (90)
J1	Index of print display loops (150)
K	Index of asterisks print line loop with titles print (1970)
L	Number of asterisks line print parameter, passed to SUB '0 (1970)
M	Number of periods of simulation, from PAVE2 (90)
N	Number of periods per year simulated, from PAVE2 (90)
N1	Integer value of N, used for print column indexing (140)
N3	Sample size, from PAVE2 (90)
N5	Frame of firm used to control statement accounts, from PAVE2 (90)
N6	Output division choice, from PAVE4 or PAVE6; this parameter is transferred to PAVEFT5 for PAVE6 (100)
N9	Reciprocal of N3, used for computing accounts means (110)
P	1. Local value for printing A( ) (2120)
	2. Local value for printing D( ) (2270)
	3. Local value for printing C( ) in EOP loop (2500)
Q	Passed parameter to SUBs '1, '2, and '3 for account index of A( ), D( ), and C( ), respectively.
R	R & D expense choice input from PAVE4 or PAVE6 reset to 1-R (100)
S1	Sales demand choice from PAVE4 or PAVE6 (100)
T	Passed parameter to SUBs '1, '2, and '3 for control of conditions of printing (2070)
T1	Passed parameter to SUB '0 for margin control of asterisk line print (1970)
U1	Processing parameter for left-hand column number of print displays J (150)
V1	Processing parameter for right-hand column number of print displays J (150)
W	Counter for number of annual columns in column control routine (150)

Table 14.5 (continued)

X	Year number in column headings print (2010)
Y	Counter for number of period columns between annual columns in column control routine (150)
Z	Number of account displays for printed statements, transferred to PAVEFT5 for PAVE6 (150)
A(22,24)	Inputs and processing of *flow* accounts for M periods from PAVE2, and without uncertainty (see tables 14.11 and 14.18) (90)
B(1,25)	Input of one *condition* account, *indirect manufacturing materials inventory*, for M+1 dates from PAVE2, and without uncertainty (90)
C(7,25)	Input and processing of *condition* accounts for M+1 dates from PAVE3, and subject to uncertainty. Some accounts are reassigned to PAVE6 (see tables 14.13, 14.15, and 14.18) (80)
D(39,24)	Input and processing of *flow* accounts for M periods from PAVE3, and subject to uncertainty. Some accounts are reassigned to PAVE6 (see tables 14.14 and 14.18) (80)
K(7,2)	Accumulation of BOP and EOP account values Q over periods from C( ) for annual print columns in SUB '3 (2440)
P(22)	Accumulation of *flow* account values Q over periods from A( ) for annual print columns in SUB '1 (2140)
U(6)	Number of first column for print display J, also transferred to PAVEFT5 for PAVE6 (170)
V(6)	Number of last column for print display J, also transferred to PAVEFT5 for PAVE6 (170)
X(36)	Number of period or year for each printed column I of each display J, also transferred to PAVEFT5 for PAVE6 (180)
Z(39)	Accumulate *flow* account values Q over periods from D( ) for annual print columns in SUB '3 (2300)
A$	Main title of each statement in set of FINANCIAL STATEMENTS (410)
B$	Statement continuation display subtitle (120)
H$	Account titles used in FINANCIAL STATEMENTS print (460)
N$	Title of run, used to head statements, and transferred from PAVE2 (90)

——Table 14.6——
PAVE6 VARIABLE LIST

Initial statement line for each use, except dimensioning, is given at the end of each description.

Dimensions are shown for arrays.

A   Index of first column to receive calendar headings in statements print displays (4460)

A1   Year number for column headings in print displays (4490)

A2   Month number for column headings in print displays (4490)

B   Column shift control for calendar headings between CONDITION STATEMENTS and SELECTED ACCOUNTS (4460)

C   First statistic display line number for each SELECTED ACCOUNT (3700)

D   Last statistic display line number for each SELECTED ACCOUNT (3700)

E   1. Print control indicator passed to SUB '2 for D( ) and F( ) flow accounts in CAPITAL CHANGES STATEMENTS (4650)
           2. Print control indicator passed to SUB '4 for C( ) condition accounts in CONDITION STATEMENTS (4930)

F   1. Local variable for control of asterisk indicator for end-of-year columns in SELECTED ACCOUNTS (4050)
           2. Local print variable for BOP *condition* accounts in SUB '1 for CAPITAL CHANGES STATEMENTS (4590)
           3. Local print variable for *flow accounts* in SUB '2 for CAPITAL CHANGES STATEMENTS (4700)
           4. Local print variable for EOP *condition* accounts in SUB '3 for CAPITAL CHANGES STATEMENTS (4860)
           5. Local print variable for *condition* accounts in SUB '4 for CONDITION STATEMENTS (5000)

G   First account number of values in SELECTED ACCOUNTS to print (3690)

H   Last account number of values in SELECTED ACCOUNTS to print (3690)

I   1. Loop index for reassignments of C( ) over periods for STATEMENTS and SELECTED ACCOUNTS (2660)

Table 14.6 (continued)

    2. Loop index for further reassignments of C( ) over periods for SE-LECTED ACCOUNTS (3480)

    3. Loop index for nonzero value check of accounts in SELECTED AC-COUNTS (3900)

    4. Loop index for print columns of values over periods for a display in SELECTED ACCOUNTS (3980)

    5. Loop index for print column headings of CAPITAL CHANGES STATEMENTS in SUB 4390 (4390)

    6. Loop index for compute and print column headings of CONDITION STATEMENTS and SELECTED ACCOUNTS in SUB 4460 (4490)

    7. Loop index for nonzero value check of C( ) for CAPITAL CHANGES print in SUB '1 (4540)

    8. Loop index for print columns of BOP values of C( ) for CAPITAL CHANGES in SUB '1 (4570)

    9. Loop index for nonzero value check of D( ) for CAPITAL CHANGES in SUB '2 print (4650)

   10. Loop index for print columns of flow accounts for CAPITAL CHANGES in SUB '2 (4680)

   11. Loop index for print columns of EOP values of C( ) for CAPITAL CHANGES in SUB '3 (4850)

   12. Loop index for nonzero value check of C( ) for CONDITION STATEMENTS in SUB '4 print (4930)

   13. Loop index for print columns of C( ) in CONDITION STATEMENTS with SUB '4 (5000)

I0   Indicator to process or bypass (on repeat runs in PAVE6) reassignments for SELECTED ACCOUNTS of account titles to C$( ) and account values to C( ) over periods (3410)

I1   Number of *manufacturing* fixed asset classes input from PAVE2 (2550)

I2   Number of *general* fixed asset classes input from PAVE2 (2550)

I3   Indicator to scroll to top of page when printing 17 SELECTED AC-COUNTS (3690)

J   Index of print display loops in both FINANCIAL STATEMENTS and SELECTED ACCOUNTS (2800)

K   1. Loop index of fixed asset class printing in CONDITION STATE-MENTS

         2. Loop index of accounts during reassignment of C( ) values over periods for SELECTED ACCOUNTS (3480)

         3. Video display loop index for user choice of output from SELEC-TED ACCOUNTS (3590)

Table 14.6 (continued)

	4. Loop index of accounts to be printed in SELECTED ACCOUNTS output (3880)
	5. Loop index for print line of asterisks in SUB '0 (4360)
L	1. Loop index of display lines of statistics for each account of SE-LECTED ACCOUNTS print (3940)
	2. Number of asterisks line print parameter, passed to SUB '0 (4360)
M	Number of periods of simulation from PAVE2 (2550)
N	Number of periods per year simulated from PAVE2 (2550)
N3	Sample size from PAVE2 (2550)
N5	Frame of firm used to control statement accounts from PAVE2 (2550)
N6	Output division choice from PAVE5; transferred back to PAVE4 or PAVE5 upon user selection of another output division (2570)
N9	Reciprocal of N3, used for computing account means (2580)
P	Level of confidence from PAVE4, printed with statistical outputs (2560)
Q	1. Numerator of standard deviations for SELECTED ACCOUNTS (3520)
	2. Value to be rounded and printed for SELECTED ACCOUNTS (3990)
	3. Passed parameter to SUBs '1, '2, '3, and '4 for account indexes of C( ) and D( ), used in printing FINANCIAL STATEMENTS (4540)
R	1. Bypass indicator for main title print on repeat runs in SELECTED ACCOUNTS (3410)
	2. Adjustment term between Q index of D( ) *flow* accounts in SUB '2 and index of Z( ) for annual accumulations (4700)
	3. Adjustment term between Q index of C( ) *condition* accounts in SUB '3 and index of K( ) for annual accumulation (4840)
R1	R & D expense indicator from PAVE4, not used in PAVE6, but must be passed back to PAVE5 upon a new user output call in PAVE6 for FINANCIAL STATEMENTS print (2560)
S	User input number for type of statistical display, and heading option, under SELECTED ACCOUNTS (3570)
S1	Sales demand choice from PAVE4, not used in PAVE6, but must be passed back to PAVE5 upon a new user output cell in PAVE6 for FINANCIAL STATEMENTS print (2560)
T	Student's t-statistic for computing confidence intervals in SELECTED ACCOUNTS; transferred from PAVE4 (2560)

Table 14.6 (continued)

T1   Passed parameter to SUB '0 for margin control of asterisks line print (4360)

U   Absolute value of statistical display choice S, used to eliminate sign of S, under user inputs for SELECTED ACCOUNTS (3710)

W   User input of account number choice under SELECTED ACCOUNTS (3570)

X   Year number in column headings print for CAPITAL CHANGES statements (4400)

Z   Number of account displays for printed statements; input from PAVE5 (2570)

B(24,25)   Input and printing of *fixed asset* and *inventory condition* accounts without uncertainty for M+1 dates from PAVE2 (see Table 14.11) (2550)

C(22,25)   Inputs, processing, and printing of *condition* accounts with uncertainty for M+1 dates from PAVE3. Some accounts are reassigned twice in PAVE6, first for FINANCIAL STATEMENTS (2660), and then for SELECTED ACCOUNTS (3480) (see tables 14.13, 14.15, and 14.18) (2540)

D(11,24)   Input and processing of *flow* accounts for M periods from PAVE5, and subject to uncertainty. D(11,I) is assigned on 2740 for printing *EOP owners' equity* in CAPITAL CHANGES statements (see Table 14.18) (2540)

F(25)   Owner shares outstanding each period from PAVE4; I=25 is not used in PAVE6 (2560)

G(16,24)   Sums of squares input from PAVE3 for 16 SELECTED ACCOUNTS (the 17th, FIXED ASSETS AT BOOK, has no uncertainty) (see Table 14.15) (2550)

K(3,2)   Accumulation of C( ) BOP and EOP account values, from index Q, over periods for annual print columns in SUB '1 and SUB '3 (4600)

U(6)   Number of first column for print display J, input from PAVE5 (2570)

V(6)   Number of last column for print display J, input from PAVE5 (2570)

X(36)   Number of period or year for each printed column I of each display J, input from PAVE5 (2570)

Z(7)   Accumulation over periods of D( ) *flow* account values, from index Q, for annual print columns in SUB '2 (4710)

A$ FINANCIAL STATEMENTS and SELECTED ACCOUNTS main title (2780)

Table 14.6 (continued)

B$	Statement continuation display subtitle (2580)
H$	Account titles used in FINANCIAL STATEMENTS print (2800)
N$	Title of run, used to head each statement in FINANCIAL STATE-MENTS, and SELECTED ACCOUNTS output division title; transferred from PAVE2 (2550)
C$(17)	Titles of 17 SELECTED ACCOUNTS (2600)
X$(4)	Titles of 4 statistical display lines in SELECTED ACCOUNTS (3720)

——Table 14.7——
PAVEC VARIABLE LIST

Initial statement line for each use, except dimensioning, is given at the end of each description.

Dimensions are shown for arrays.

N7	Choice: all PAVEFT files=0/individual=1 (9870)
N8	Index number of file to be catalogued (9880)
J(5)	Number of sectors required for each data transfer file (9850)
Q$	Input name of data transfer file (9890)
Q$(5)	Set of PAVEFT data transfer file names (9830)

—— Table 14.8 ——
PAVER VARIABLE LIST

Initial statement line for each use, except dimensioning, is given at the end of each description.

Dimensions are shown for arrays.

A8	REDIM of I( ) to receive record (9760)
B8	REDIM of J( ) to receive record (9760)
C8	REDIM of O( ) to receive record (9760)
D8	REDIM of R( ) to receive record (9760)

Table 14.8 (continued)

E8	REDIM of Y( ) to receive record (9760)
I	for I( ) with MATRIX PRINT statement (9910)
J	for J( ) with MATRIX PRINT statement (9910)
N8	Format number 1 to 5 for records and fields in *data transfer files*, such as PAVEFT1 to PAVEFT5, required for file READ. User inputs N8, which then controls multiple branch to correct set of records. (9640)
O	For O( ) with MATRIX PRINT statement (9910)
R	For R( ) with MATRIX PRINT statement (9920)
Y	For Y( ) with MATRIX PRINT statement (9920)
I(1,150)	Array 1 for record store and print (9770)
J(1,250)	Array 2 for record store and print (9770)
O(1,250)	Array 3 for record store and print (9770)
R(1,240)	Array 4 for record store and print (9770)
Y(1,168)	Array 5 for record store and print (9770)
N$	Title of run to store and print from some records (9770)
Q$	File name for user input and print (9640)

——Table 14.9——
PAVES VARIABLE LIST

Initial statement line for each use, except dimensioning, is given at the end of each description.

Dimensions are shown for arrays.

A	Number of disk port for choosing among input/output devices (8060)
B	Last ID number print column, adjusted from R and S in SUB '3 (8620)
C	1. ID number in data statement READ pair (8100)
	2. ID number for INDIVIDUAL INTERACTIVE input mode (8310)
D	Value of input ID (8100) in *data statement pair*, or *revised* value of ID (8340) for *individual interactive input* (8100)
E	Current value of ID for *individual interactive input* (8330)

Table 14.9 (continued)

F   First ID number print column, adjusted from R in SUB '3 (8620)

I   1. Loop indexes for reset all inputs to 0 of N( ), P( ), and Q( ) (8210)
        2. Loop index in SUB '1 (*system parameters* in N( )) to determine control parameters R, S, and T to print all input IDs in SUB '3. I is the ID number of the first column print position, and is used directly in SUB '3. (8540)
        3. Determine ID number for I in SUB '2 with *dynamic input sets* from P( ) or Q( ). This I controls printing in SUB '3 (8580)

I1   Indicator for nonzero print values; if all values 0 then I1 omits line of 5 values under *print all inputs* (8620)

J   1. Loop index for SUB '3 check of 5 values in print line for all 0 (8620)
        2. Loop index for print line of 5 values in SUB '3 (8700)
        3. Loop index for print leading or trailing blanks in SUB '4 (8740)

K   ID number position at the *first* value line column of the first *print* line in SUB '3 call (8530)

L   Loop index for controlling print line in SUB '3 for *dynamic input sets*. (8580)

M   First ID number passed to SUB '1 or '2 for print control (8530)

N   Last ID number passed to SUB '1 or '2 for print control (8530)

Q   1. User input of menu choice number (8160)
        2. User input number for confirmation to destroy contents of *input data file* (8190)

R   Number of leading blank columns for print line of input values, passed to SUB '3, and through SUB '3 to SUB '4 (8540)

S   Number of print position columns for print line of input values, passed to SUB '3 (8560)

T   1. User choices in processing of *run title* for INDIVIDUAL INTERACTIVE input (8260)
        2. Number of trailing blank columns for print line of input values, passed to SUB '3, and through SUB '3 to SUB '4 (8550)

X   Number of leading or trailing blanks in SUB '4, passed to SUB '4 as R and T from SUB '3 (8740)

Z   User input file choice (8040)

N(99)   *System parameter* input values from *input data file* (see Table 14.10) (8070)

P(230) *Dynamic set* input values for *environment, trade,* and *manufacturing* from *input data file* (see Table 14.10) (8070)

Table 14.9 (continued)

Q(250)	*Dynamic input* set values for *research and development, sales, general administration,* and *finance* from *input data file* (see Table 14.10) (8070)
V(5)	Local array for zero check and print line of up to 5 input values in SUB '3 (8630)
N$	Title of run input from input data file (8070)
Y$	Name of old file (8050)
Z$	Name of new file, or revised name of old file (8460)

───────────────── **Table 14.10** ─────────────────

INPUT IDs, DESCRIPTIONS, ARRAY ELEMENTS, AND LOOP PARAMETERS

NOTE: Internal default values of IDS are zero unless shown in brackets after description.

ID NUMBER	DESCRIPTION	INPUT ARRAY VARIABLE	K INDEX FROM ID NUMBER TO DISPLAY VARIABLE	DISPLAY LOOP INDEX
	SYSTEM PARAMETERS			
	Input/output system choices			
1	Total number of periods (max 24) [1]	N(1)	-2	3
2	Number of periods per year [1]	N(2)	-2	4
3	Sample size—deterministic=1/ statistical=2 to 30 [1]	N(3)	-2	5
4	Seed number—standard random series=0	N(4)	-2	6
5	Frame: service=0/trade=1/ manufacturing=2/environment only=3	N(5)	-2	7
6	Output section and print first: Valuation and scope first and final years=0 Statistical summary from final period=1			

Table 14.10 (continued)

ID NUMBER	DESCRIPTION	INPUT ARRAY VARIABLE	K INDEX FROM ID NUMBER TO DISPLAY VARIABLE	DISPLAY LOOP INDEX
	SYSTEM PARAMETERS (continued)			
	Financial statements for all periods=2			
	Selected accounts for all periods=3	N(6)	-2	8
Initial condition—current and intangible assets				
9	$ Cash and marketable securities	N(9)	7	2
10	$ Trade accounts and notes receivable	N(10)	7	3
11	$ Nontrade credit, advances, and accrued receivables	N(11)	7	4
12	$ Reserve for uncollectible accounts	N(12)	7	5
13	$ Prepaid expense and deferred charges	N(13)	7	6
14	$ Intangibles: organization expense, patents, goodwill, leasehold improvements	N(14)	7	7
15	$ Inventory of general supplies, small tools, and small equipment	N(15)	7	8
16	$ Inventory of manufacturing or trade finished goods	N(16)	7	9
17	$ Inventory of manufacturing goods-in-process	N(17)	7	10
18	$ Inventory of manufacturing direct material and supplies	N(18)	7	11
19	$ Inventory of manufacturing indirect material and supplies	N(19)	7	12
Initial condition—manufacturing fixed assets				
20-14	$ Class 1 to 5 manufacturing fixed assets at cost basis	N(20)-N(24)	18	2-6
25-29	$ Class 1 to 5 manufacturing fixed assets reserve for depreciation	N(25)-N(29)	18	7-11

Table 14.10 (continued)

ID NUMBER	DESCRIPTION	INPUT ARRAY VARIABLE	K INDEX FROM ID NUMBER TO DISPLAY VARIABLE	DISPLAY LOOP INDEX
SYSTEM PARAMETERS (continued)				
Initial condition—general fixed assets				
30-34	$ Class 1 to 5 general fixed assets at cost basis	N(30)-N(34)	28	2-6
35-39	$ Class 1 to 5 general fixed assets reserve for depreciation	N(35)-N(39)	28	7-11
Initial condition—liabilities and owner's equity				
40	$ Trade accounts and notes payable	N(40)	36	4
41	$ Nontrade accounts, dividends, and taxes payable	N(41)	36	5
42	$ Unearned advances from customers	N(42)	36	6
43	$ Accrued expense and liabilities	N(43)	36	7
44	$ Short-term debt and loans payable	N(44)	36	8
45	$ Long-term obligations at face or stated value	N(45)	36	9
46	$ Bond (and preferred stock) premium (discount)	N(46)	36	10
47	$ Paid-in owner equity capital	N(47)	36	11
48	$ Retained earnings	N(48)	36	12
Seasonal/cyclical indexes, first set				
51-62	Seasonal/cyclical indexes, first set	N(51)-N(62)	50	1-12
Seasonal/cyclical indexes, second set				
63-74	Seasonal/cyclical indexes, second set	N(63)-N(74)	62	1-12
Manufacturing expense system parameters				
75	% Overtime limit to regular direct labor payroll	N(75)	71	4
76	% Overtime premium cost	N(76)	71	5
77	% Increase in plant capacity limit from subcontract operations	N(77)	71	6
78	% Material cost premium to be applied to subcontract operations	N(78)	71	7

Table 14.10 (continued)

ID NUMBER	DESCRIPTION	INPUT ARRAY VARIABLE	K INDEX FROM ID NUMBER TO DISPLAY VARIABLE	DISPLAY LOOP INDEX
	SYSTEM PARAMETERS (continued)			
General administration system parameters				
79	General supplies inventory level as % of annual sales	N(79)	75	4
80	Accounts payable level as % of annual account payments	N(80)	75	5
81	Prepaid expense level as % of annual payments	N(81)	75	6
82	Advances by customers as % of annual sales	N(82)	75	7
83	$ Organization expense, goodwill, and intangibles added in Period 1	N(83)	75	8
84	$ Amortization of intangibles yearly, not per period	N(84)	75	9
Financial and valuation system parameters				
87	% Cash ratio minimum, below which cash demanded [50]	N(87)	86	1
88	% Current ratio minimum from short-term loans [200]	N(88)	86	2
89	% Combined effective income tax rate (less than 100) [50]	N(89)	86	3
90	$ Initial tax loss credit for carry forward	N(90)	86	4
91	Number of first period owner equity units (1/share of firm) [1]	N(91)	86	5
92	$ Added share cost—internal computation=0	N(92)	86	6
93	Price-earnings multiple final year—internal computation=0	N(93)	86	7
94	Price—earnings multiple year 1—internal computation=0	N(94)	86	8
95	% Assets values on average realized in liquidation [50]	N(95)	86	9

Table 14.10 (continued)

ID NUMBER	DESCRIPTION	INPUT ARRAY VARIABLE	K INDEX FROM ID NUMBER TO DISPLAY VARIABLE	DISPLAY LOOP INDEX
SYSTEM PARAMETERS (continued)				
96	% Investor required rate of return per year—internal computation=0	N(96)	86	10
97	% Long-term average growth rate per year—internal computation=0	N(97)	86	11
98	% Return per year on incremental assets—internal computation=0	N(98)	86	12
DYNAMIC INPUT SETS OVER PERIODS				
Environment of economy and industry to sales of firm inputs over periods				
102-109	% Annual real growth rate of economy Parameter set over periods	P(3)-P(10)	99	3-10
110	Inflate period costs—NO=0/YES=1	P(11)	109	1
112-119	% Annual average inflation rate Parameter set over periods	P(13)-P(20)	109	3-10
120	Sales demand—% industry share=0/ $ per period=1	P(21)	119	1
121	* Net sales demand available to firm *% Maximum change from mean value	P(22)	119	1
122-129	Parameter set over periods	P(23)-P(30)	119	3-10
130	$ Industry sales for base (prior) year, not period	P(31)	129	1
131	*% Annual industry growth compared to economy *% Maximum change from mean value	P(32)	129	1
132-139	Parameter set over periods	P(33)-P(40)	129	3-10
Manufacturing or trade inputs over periods				
140	Initial goods inventories—cost % of selling price [60]	P(41)	139	1

Table 14.10 (continued)

ID NUMBER	DESCRIPTION	INPUT ARRAY VARIABLE	K INDEX FROM ID NUMBER TO DISPLAY VARIABLE	DISPLAY LOOP INDEX
	DYNAMIC INPUT SETS OVER PERIODS (continued)			
	*Direct purchased material or goods as % of sales			
141	*% Max change from mean value	P(42)	139	2
142-149	Parameter set over periods	P(43)-P(50)	139	3-10
150	% Deseasonalize goods production or purchase	P(51)	149	1
	Finished goods inventory level as % of annual cost of goods sold			
152-159	Parameter set over periods	P(53)-P(60)	149	3-10
Manufacturing inputs over periods				
	Goods-in-process inventory level as % of annual cost of goods sold			
162-169	Parameter set over periods	P(63)-P(70)	159	3-10
	Direct material inventory level as % of annual usage			
172-179	Parameter set over periods	P(73)-P(80)	169	3-10
	*Direct labor payroll as % of sales			
181	*% Max change from mean value	P(82)	179	2
182-189	Parameter set over periods	P(83)-P(90)	179	3-10
	Direct supervision and support payroll as % of sales			
192-199	Parameter set over periods	P(93)-P(100)	189	3-10
	*% Operating efficiency of processing 100 in ID 202			
201	*% Max change from mean value	P(102)	199	2
202-209	Parameter set over periods	P(103)-P(110)	199	3-10
	$ Capacity of plant per period in sales $ at 100% efficiency			

Table 14.10 (continued)

ID NUMBER	DESCRIPTION	INPUT ARRAY VARIABLE	K INDEX FROM ID NUMBER TO DISPLAY VARIABLE	DISPLAY LOOP INDEX
	DYNAMIC INPUT SETS OVER PERIODS (continued)			
212-219	Parameter set over periods	P(113)-P(120)	209	3-10
220	Manufacturing supplies inventory level as % of annual usage	P(121)	219	1
	$ Indirect supplies and small equipment used per period—manufacturing			
222-229	Parameter set over periods	P(123)-P(130)	219	3-10
	$ Indirect manufacturing payroll per period			
232-239	Parameter set over periods	P(133)-P(140)	229	3-10
	$ Space, rent or occupancy per period—manufacturing			
242-249	Parameter set over periods	P(143)-P(150)	239	3-10
	*$ Utilities or all indirect cost per period—manufacturing			
251	*% Max change from mean value	P(152)	249	2
252-259	Parameter set over periods	P(153)-P(160)	249	3-10
	$ Maintenance per period—manufacturing			
262-269	Parameter set over periods	P(163)-P(170)	259	3-10
	$ Taxes, insurance, labor relations, and miscellaneous expense per period—manufacturing			
272-279	Parameter set over periods	P(173)-P(180)	269	3-10
{ 280 to 320	% Depreciation per year on declining balance for manufacturing fixed assets class 1 to 5	{ P(181) to P(221)	{ 279 to 319	1
	$ Manufacturing fixed assets Class 1 to 5 net changes per period			
{ 282-289 to 322-329	Parameter set over periods	{ P(183)-P(190) to P(223)-P(230)	{ 279 to 319	3-10

Table 14.10 (continued)

ID NUMBER	DESCRIPTION	INPUT ARRAY VARIABLE	K INDEX FROM ID NUMBER TO DISPLAY VARIABLE	DISPLAY LOOP INDEX
	DYNAMIC INPUT SETS OVER PERIODS (continued)			
	Research and development, sales, and general administrative inputs over periods			
330	Research and development expenses— % sales=0/$ per period=1	Q(1)	329	1
332-339	Research and development payroll Parameter set over periods	Q(3)-Q(10)	329	3-10
342-349	Research and development material, contracts, and miscellaneous expense per period Parameter set over periods	Q(13)-Q(20)	339	3-10
352-359	Sales salaries and commissions payroll as % of sales Parameter set over periods	Q(23)-Q(30)	349	3-10
362-369	$ Indirect sales payroll per period Parameter set over periods	Q(33)-Q(40)	359	3-10
372-379	Advertising, promotion, and miscellaneous sales expense as % of sales Parameter set over periods	Q(43)-Q(50)	369	3-10
382-389	$ Advertising, promotion, and miscellaneous sales expense per period Parameter set over periods	Q(53)-Q(60)	379	3-10
390	% Uncollectible accounts	Q(61)	389	1
391	*Accounts receivable level as % of annual sales *% Max change from mean value	Q(62)	389	2
392-399	Parameter set over periods *Direct service and office materials as % of sales	Q(63)-Q(70)	389	3-10

Table 14.10 (continued)

ID NUMBER	DESCRIPTION	INPUT ARRAY VARIABLE	K INDEX FROM ID NUMBER TO DISPLAY VARIABLE	DISPLAY LOOP INDEX
DYNAMIC INPUT SETS OVER PERIODS (continued)				
401	*% Max change from mean value	Q(72)	399	2
402-409	Parameter set over periods	Q(73)-Q(80)	399	3-10
	$ Indirect service, office supplies, and small equipment per period			
412-419	Parameter set over periods	Q(83)-Q(90)	409	3-10
	* Direct service and office payroll as % of sales			
421	*% Max change from mean value	Q(92)		
422-429	Parameter set over periods	Q(93)-Q(100)	419	2
	$ General administrative and indirect service payroll per period			
432-439	Parameter set over periods	Q(103)-Q(110)	429	3-10
	$ Space, rent, or occupancy per period—general			
442-449	Parameter set over periods	Q(113)-Q(120)	439	3-10
	*$ Utilities or all indirect costs per period—general			
451	*% Max change from mean value	Q(122)	449	2
452-459	Parameter set over periods	Q(123)-Q(130)	449	3-10
	$ Maintenance per period—general			
462-469	Parameter set over periods	Q(133)-Q(140)	459	3-10
	$ Taxes, insurance, travel, labor relations, legal, and miscellaneous expense per period—general			
472-479	Parameter set over periods	Q(143)-Q(150)	469	3-10
480 to 520	% Depreciation per year on declining balance for general fixed assets Class 1 to 5	Q(151) to Q(191)	479 to 519	1

Table 14.10 (continued)

ID NUMBER	DESCRIPTION	INPUT ARRAY VARIABLE	K INDEX FROM ID NUMBER TO DISPLAY VARIABLE	DISPLAY LOOP INDEX
	$ General fixed assets Class 1 to 5 net changes per period			
482-489 to 522-529	Parameter set over periods	Q(153)-Q(160) to Q(193)-Q(200)	479 to 519	3-10
Financial and valuation control inputs over periods				
530	Internal computation of required investment—NO=0/YES=1	Q(201)	529	1
	$ Owner net cash investment planned change per period			
531	Earn on near-cash as % of short-term interest rate	Q(202)	529	2
532-539	Parameter set over periods	Q(203)-Q(210)	529	3-10
540	% Long-term obligations in required added investment	Q(211)	539	1
	$ Long-term obligations planned net change per period			
542-549	Parameter set over periods	Q(213)-Q(220)	539	3-10
550	Dividends—% Earnings=0/$ per period=1	Q(221)	549	1
	Dividends or withdrawals per period			
552-559	Parameter set over periods	Q(223)-Q(230)	549	3-10
	*% Short-term interest rate annual			
561	*% Max change from mean value	Q(232)	559	2
562-569	Parameter set over periods	Q(233)-Q(240)	559	3-10
	*% Long-term interest rate annual			
571	*% Max change from mean value	Q(242)	569	2
572-579	Parameter set over periods	Q(243)-Q(250)	569	3-10

Table 14.11

DESCRIPTION OF ACCOUNT ARRAYS IN PAVE2 AND TRANSFERS TO FOLLOWING PAVE PROGRAMS

Array Plan:

A( )   for flows and ratio inputs to PAVE3 for processing
D( )   for flows and rates inputs direct to PAVE5
B( )   for condition inputs to PAVE3 or direct to PAVE6
   * indicates uncertainty
   # indicates account index was previously assigned to another use in PAVE2

INPUT ID SET NUMBER	INPUT ARRAY SET IN PAVE1, WRITE PAVEFT1 FOR PAVE2	DESCRIPTION	PAVE2 ARRAYS	PROCESS IN PAVE3, WRITE PAVEFT3	PRINT IN PAVE5, WRITE PAVEFT5	PRINT IN PAVE6
		Environment				
102	P(3)	% Annual real growth rate of economy	D(1,I)		A(8,I)	
112	P(13)	% Annual average inflation rate	D(2,I)		A(9,I)	
121	P(22)	* Net sales demand available to firm	A(1,I)	A(1,I)		
131	P(32)	*% Annual industry growth compared to economy	D(3,I)#			
		Industry combined annual growth rate	D(3,I)#	A(2,I)	A(10,I)	
		Industry sales before randomization	A(2,I)			
		Seasonal/cyclical index set	D(4,I)#		A(11,I)	
		Set of inflation adjustment factors from D(2,I)	D(3,I)			

Manufacturing and Trade

Line	Prompt	Item				
141	P(42)	*Direct purchased material or goods as % of sales	A(19,I)	A(19,I)		
152	P(53)	Finished goods inventory level as % of annual cost of goods sold	A(21,I)	A(21,I)		

Manufacturing Only

Line	Prompt	Item				
162	P(63)	Goods-in-process inventory level as % of annual cost of goods sold	A(23,I)	A(23,I)		
172	P(73)	Direct material inventory level as % of annual usage	A(25,I)	A(25,I)		
181	P(82)	*Direct labor payroll as % of sales	A(27,I)	A(27,I)		
192	P(93)	Direct supervision and support payroll as % of sales	A(29,I)	A(29,I)		
201	P(102)	*% Operating efficiency of processing	A(31,I)	A(31,I)		
212	P(113)	$ Capacity of plant per period in sales $ at 100% efficiency	A(32,I)	A(32,I)		
222	P(123)	$ Indirect supplies and small equipment used per period—manufacturing	A(22,I)	A(22,I)	A(5,I)	
232	P(133)	$ Indirect manufacturing payroll per period	A(20,I)	A(20,I)	A(6,I)	
242	P(143)	$ Indirect manufacturing supplies purchases	D(12,I)		A(19,I)	
251	P(152)	$ Indirect manufacturing supplies inventory	B(1,I+1)	B(1,I+1)	B(1,I+1)	B(1,I+1)
262	P(163)	$ Space, rent or occupancy per period—manufacturing	D(13,I)		A(20,I)	
272	P(173)	*$ Utilities or all indirect costs per period—manufacturing	A(24,I)	A(24,I)	A(21,I)	
		$ Maintenance per period—manufacturing	D(14,I)		A(22,I)	
		$ Taxes, insurance, labor relations, and miscellaneous expense per period—manufacturing	D(15,I)			
		$ Total nonrandom period expense, manufacturing	A(26,I)	A(26,I)		
282 to 322	P(183) to P(223)	$ Manufacturing fixed assets Class 1 to 5 net changes per period	D(11,I)# to D(15,I)#			

Table 14.11 (continued)

INPUT ID	SET NUMBER	INPUT ARRAY SET IN PAVE1, WRITE PAVEFT1 FOR PAVE2	DESCRIPTION	PAVE2 ARRAYS	PROCESS IN PAVE3, WRITE PAVEFT3	PRINT IN PAVE5, WRITE PAVEFT5	PRINT IN PAVE6
			$ Total net manufacturing fixed asset additions plus indirect supplies purchases	A(28,I)	A(28,I)		
			$ Total depreciation on manufacturing fixed assets	A(30,I)	A(30,I)	A(7,I)	
			$ Manufacturing fixed assets at cost (0 to 5 classes)	B(15,I+1) to B(19,I+1)			B(15,I+1) to B(19,I+1)
			$ Manufacturing fixed asset reserves (0 to 5 classes)	B(20,I+1) to B(24,I+1)			B(20,I+1) to B(24,I+1)
			$ Total manufacturing fixed assets at book value	B(2,I+1)	B(2,I+1)		
			Research and Development				
332	Q(3)		Research and development payroll	A(3,I)	A(3,I)		
342	Q(13)		Research and development materials, contracts, and miscellaneous expense per period	A(4,I)	A(4,I)		
			Sales				
352	Q(23)		Sales salaries and commissions payroll as % of sales	A(5,I) D(5,I)	A(5,I)		
262	Q(33)		$ Indirect sales payroll per period			A(12,I)	

No.	Q	Description			
372	Q(43)	Advertising, promotion, and miscellaneous sales expense as % of sales		A(7,I)	A(7,I)
382	Q(53)	$ Advertising, promotion, and miscellaneous sales expense per period	D(6,I)		A(13,I)
391	Q(62)	* Accounts receivable level as % of annual sales	A(9,I)	A(9,I)	
		General Administration			
401	Q(72)	* Direct service and office materials as % of sales	A(11,I)	A(11,I)	
412	Q(83)	$ Indirect service, office supplies, and small equipment per period	A(6,I)	A(6,I)	A(1,I)
421	Q(92)	* Direct service and office payroll as % of sales	A(13,I) D(7,I)	A(13,I)	A(14,I)
432	Q(103)	$ Sum of indirect sales and administrative payrolls	A(8,I)		A(15,I)
442	Q(113)	$ Space, rent, or occupancy per period–general			
451	Q(122)	* $ Utilities or all indirect costs per period–general	A(10,I) D(9,I)	A(10,I)	
462	Q(133)	$ Maintenance per period–general			A(16,I)
472	Q(143)	$ Taxes, insurance, travel, labor relations, legal, and miscellaneous expenses per period–general	D(10,I)		A(17,I)
		$ Total nonrandom period expense including advertising	A(12,I) D(11,I)	A(12,I)	
		$ Amortization of intangibles			A(18,I)
482 to 522	Q(153) to Q(193)	$ General fixed assets Class 1 to 5 net changes per period	D(6,I)# to D(10,I)#		
		$ Total net general fixed asset additions including intangibles	A(14,I)	A(14,I)	
		$ Total depreciation on general fixed assets including amortization of intangibles	A(16,I)	A(16,I)	A(2,I)

Table 14.11 (continued)

INPUT ID SET NUMBER	INPUT ARRAY SET IN PAVE1, WRITE PAVEFT1 FOR PAVE2	DESCRIPTION	PAVE2 ARRAYS	PROCESS IN PAVE3, WRITE PAVEFT3	PRINT IN PAVE5, WRITE PAVEFT5	PRINT IN PAVE6
		Financial				
532	Q(203)	$ Owner net cash investment planned change per period	A(18,I)	A(18,I)	A(3,I)	
542	Q(213)	$ Long term obligations planned net changes per period	A(33,I)	A(33,I)	A(4,I)	
552	Q(223)	Dividends or withdrawals per period	A(34,I)	A(34,I)		
561	Q(232)	*% Short-term interest rate annual	A(15,I)	A(15,I)		
571	Q(242)	*% Long-term interest rate annual	A(17,I)	A(17,I)		
		$ General fixed assets at cost (0 to 5 classes)	B(5,I+1) to B(9,I+1)			B(5,I+1) to B(9,I+1)
		$ General fixed asset reserves (0 to 5 classes)	B(10,I+1) to B(14,I+1)			B(10,I+1) to B(14,I+1)
		$ Total general fixed assets at book value including intangibles	B(3,I+1)	B(3,I+1)		
		$ Unamortized intangible balance	B(4,I+1)			

————————Table 14.12————————
SYSTEM PARAMETER ASSIGNMENTS IN PAVE3

Input parameters to PAVE3 from PAVE2 are assigned to 3 scalars and N( ) array.
  * indicates uncertainty input

PAVE3 scalar or array element	Description	PAVE1 and PAVE2 array elements, and input IDs
M	Total number of periods	N(1) = ID 1
N	Number of periods per year	N(2) = ID 2
N5	Frame (service=0, trade=1, manufacturing=2, environment only=3)	N(5) = ID 5
N(1)	Cash and marketable securities BOP 1	N(9) = ID 9
N(2)	Accounts receivable BOP 1	N(10)+N(11)
N(3)	Reserve for uncollectible accounts BOP 1	N(12) = ID 12
N(4)	Prepaid expense BOP 1	N(13) = ID 13
N(5)	Inventory of general supplies BOP 1	N(15) = ID 15
N(6)	Inventory of finished goods (manufacturing or trade) BOP 1	N(16) = ID 16
N(7)	Inventory of manufacturing goods-in-process BOP 1	N(17) = ID 17
N(8)	Inventory of manufacturing direct materials BOP 1	N(18) = ID 18
N(9)	Accounts payable BOP 1	N(40)+N(41)+N(43)
N(10)	Unearned advances from customers BOP 1	N(42) = ID 42
N(11)	Short-term debt BOP 1	N(44) = ID 44
N(12)	Long-term obligations BOP 1	N(45) = ID 45
N(13)	Paid-in owner equity capital BOP 1	N(47) = ID 47
N(14)	Retained earnings BOP 1	N(48)–N(46)
N(15)	Manufacturing finished goods inventory at sales value BOP 1	N(16)*100/P(41)
N(16)	Manufacturing goods-in-process inventory at sales value BOP 1	BOP 1 N(17)*100/P(41)
N(17)	Initial tax loss carry forward BOP 1	N(90) = ID 90
N(18)	Final balance of intangibles EOP M	B(4, M+1)

Table 14.12 (continued)

PAVE3 scalar or array element	Description	PAVE1 and PAVE2 array elements, and input IDs
N(19)	Sample size	N(3) = N3 = ID 3
N(20)	Random generator seed number	N(4) = N4 = ID 4
N(21)	% overtime limit to regular direct labor	N(75) = ID 75
N(22)	% overtime limit labor premium cost	N(76) = ID 76
N(23)	% increment to plant capacity from subcontracting	N(77) = ID 77
N(24)	% material cost premium with subcontracting	N(78) = ID 78
N(25)	General supplies inventory level as % of annual usage	N(79) = ID 79
N(26)	Accounts payable level as % of annual payments	N(80) = ID 80
N(27)	Prepaid expense level as % of annual payments	N(81) = ID 81
N(28)	Advances by customers as % of annual sales	N(82) = ID 82
N(29)	% cash ratio minimum	N(87) = ID 83
N(30)	% current ratio minimum	N(88) = ID 84
N(31)	% combined effective income tax rate	N(89) = ID 89
N(32)	% assets average realized in liquidation	N(95) = ID 95
N(33)	Sales demand—% of industry=0/$ per period=1	P(21) = ID 120
N(34)	*% max shift—net sales demand	P(22) = ID 121
N(35)	*% max shift—annual industry sales	P(32) = ID 131
N(36)	*% max shift—purchased direct manufacturing material or trade goods	P(42) = ID 141
N(37)	*% max shift—direct manufacturing labor	P(82) = ID 181
N(38)	*% max shift—operating efficiency	P(102) = ID 201
N(39)	*% max shift—utilities and period expense, manufacturing	P(152) = ID 251
N(40)	R&D expense—% of sales=0/ $ per period=1	Q(4) = ID 330
N(41)	% uncollectible accounts	Q(61) = ID 390

Table 14.12 (continued)

PAVE3 scalar or array element	Description	PAVE1 and PAVE2 array elements, and input IDs
N(42)	*% max shift—accounts receivable balance	Q(62) = ID 391
N(43)	*% max shift—direct purchased general material	Q(72) = ID 401
N(44)	*% max shift—direct general labor	Q(92) = ID 421
N(45)	*% max shift—utilities and period expense, general	Q(122) - ID 451
N(46)	Internal computation of required additional investment—NO=0/YES=1	Q(201) = ID 530
N(47)	Earn on near cash as % of short-term interest rate	Q(202) = ID 531
N(48)	% long-term obligations in required additional investment	Q(211) = ID 540
N(49)	Dividends—% of earnings=0/$ per period=1	Q(221) = ID 550
N(50)	*% max shift—short-term interest rate	Q(232) = ID 561
N(51)	*% max shift—long-term interest rate	Q(242) = ID 571
N(52)	Period number at end of *first* year	Process in PAVE2
N(53)	Period number at beginning of *final* year	Process in PAVE2
B(1,I)	Inventory of manufacturing indirect supplies	B(1,1) from N(19) = ID 19
B(2,I)	Total net fixed assets, manufacturing	Process in PAVE2
B(3,I)	Total net fixed assets, general	Process in PAVE2

Parameter arrays to PAVE4 from PAVE3

These same elements appear in G( ) of PAVE4, which are transferred from M( ) in PAVE3

M(1)	Sum of first periods for technical insolvency
M(2)	Count of runs with technical insolvency
M(3)	Sum of first periods for legal insolvency
M(4)	Count of runs with legal insolvency
M(5)	Sum of owners' equity EOP 1
M(6)	Sum of total assets EOP 1

Table 14.12 (continued)

PAVE3 scalar or array element	Description	PAVE1 and PAVE2 array elements, and input IDs
M(7)	Sum of cash EOP 1 from C(1,2)	
M(8)	Sum of total liabilities EOP 1	
M(9)	Sum of final tax loss carry forwards from L(17,2)	
M(10)	Sum of squares of owners' equity EOP 1 from G(16,1)	
M(11)	Sum of squares of total assets EOP 1 from G(13,1)	
M(12)	Sum of squares of cash EOP 1 from G(9,1)	

———————— Table 14.13 ————————
ARRAYS FOR PROCESSING CONDITION ACCOUNTS IN PAVE3

L( ) is used to process condition accounts for each period in Monte Carlo sample replications of PAVE3.

L(K,1) is condition BOP.

L(K,2) is condition EOP.

C(K,I+1) is used to accumulate sums for each period I (BOP=I, EOP=I+1), for transfer to PAVE6.

The following are descriptions of K indexes (first 14 for C( ) and all 17 for L( )):

1   Cash and marketable securities
2   Accounts receivable
3   Reserve for uncollectible accounts
4   Prepaid expense
5   General supplies inventory

6   *Manufacturing* or *trade* finished goods inventory at cost
7   *Manufacturing* goods-in-process inventory at cost
8   *Manufacturing* direct material inventory
9   Accounts payable
10   Unearned advances from customers

11   Short-term debt
12   Long-term obligations
13   Total paid-in owner capital
14   Retained earnings

Table 14.13 (continued)

15   *Manufacturing* finished goods inventory at sales value

16   *Manufacturing* goods-in-process inventory at sales value

17   Tax loss carry forward

C( )   index is changed to 6 from 11 for WRITE to PAVE5 from PAVE3

———————— Table 14.14 ————————

ARRAYS FOR PROCESSING FLOW ACCOUNTS IN PAVE3

F(K) is used to process flow accounts for each period in Monte Carlo sample replications, where K is the account index.

The same index number is assigned among 1 to 3 different accounts in succession. Multiple uses are shown on separate lines in the same order as assignments in PAVE3.

The first use is always an *input,* and the last an *output.*

The following are descriptions of K indexes:

1   Sales demand available to firm preset $(F(1)=S=F(32))$
     Sales achieved by firm

2   Firm's market share of industry for output printing from F(32)

3   Industry sales before randomization from A(2,1)
     Industry sales after randomization

4   Uncollectible accounts expense

5   Sales and commission payroll as % of sales from A(5,I)
     Sales and commission payroll expense

6   Indirect service material used from A(6,I)
     Income taxes

7   Advertising and promotion expense as % of sales from A(7,I)
     Direct advertising and promotion expense

8   Sales indirect and general administrative payroll per period from A(8,I)
     Net income after income taxes (earnings)

9   Accounts receivable as % of sales before randomization from A(9,I)
     Accounts receivable randomized before deduction of collectible accounts
     Collections on accounts receivables

10   Utilities or all indirect expense, general, before randomization, from A(10,I)
      Utilities or all indirect expense, general, after randomization

Table 14.14 (continued)

11   Direct service material as % of sales before randomization from A(11,I)
      Direct service material as % of sales after randomization
      Direct service material expense

12   Total nonrandomized sales period expense from A(12,I)
      Dividends paid

13   Direct service labor payroll as % of sales before randomization from A(13,I)
      Direct service labor payroll as % of sales after randomization
      Direct service labor payroll expense

14   Total general fixed assets at book value and intangible assets from A(14,I)
      Total net cash flow

15   Short-term % interest rate before randomization from A(15,I)
      Short-term % interest rate after randomization
      Required additional owner equity capital

16   Total depreciation on general fixed assets, plus amortization of intangibles,
         from A(16,I)
      Required additional long-term obligations

17   Long-term % interest rate before randomization from A(17,I)
      Long-term % interest rate after randomization
      Interest expense on short-term debt

18   Planned owner equity capital changes from A(18,I)

19   Purchased direct material or goods as % of sales before randomization from
         A(19,I)
      Purchased direct material or goods as % of sales after randomization
      Total manufacturing material used, direct plus premium for subcontract
         operations

20   Indirect manufacturing payroll from A(20,I)

21   Finished goods inventory as % of sales from A(21,I)

22   Indirect manufacturing supplies usage from A(22,I)

23   Goods-in-process inventory as % of sales from A(23,I)

24   Utilities or all indirect expense, manufacturing, before randomization from
         A(24,I)
      Utilities or all indirect expense, manufacturing, after randomization

25   Direct material inventory of % of usage from A(25,I)
      Purchases of direct material

Table 14.14 (continued)

26   Total nonrandomized general period expense from A(26,I)

27   Direct labor payroll as % of sales before randomization from A(27,I)
Direct labor payroll as % of sales after randomization
Direct labor payroll expense

28   Total manufacturing fixed assets at book value plus indirect supplies purchases from A(28,I)
Utilities or all indirect expense, manufacturing (transferred from F(24) at summation)

29   Factory supervision and support payroll as % of sales from A(29,I)
Factory supervision and support payroll expense

30   Total depreciation on manufacturing fixed assets from A(30,I)
Purchases of direct material (transferred from F(25) at summation)

31   Operating efficiency % before randomization from A(31,I)
Operating efficiency % after randomization
Overtime premium cost of direct manufacturing payrolls

32   Sales demand input, as firm's market share of industry or direct firm sales, before randomization, from A(1,I)
Sales demand input, firm's market share of industry or direct firm sales, after randomization
Sales demand available to firm

33   Cost of finished goods, manufacturing, at sales value level
Premium cost of subcontract operations in manufacturing

34   Cost of goods into process at sales value level
Cost of finished goods for manufacturing or trade

35   Direct manufacturing material used

36   Cost of goods into process, manufacturing

37   Cost of goods sold, manufacturing or trade

38   Ratio of cost value level to sales value level, manufacturing
Service material used, direct F(11) plus indirect F(6)
Interest income

39   Sales demand available to firm preset $(F(39) = F(1) = S = F(32))$
Gross profit on sales, manufacturing or trade

40   Research and development payroll as % of sales or period expense from A(3,I)
Research and development payroll expense

Table 14.14 (continued)

41   Research and development, except payroll, as % of sales or period expense
        from A(4,I)
        Research and development, except payroll, expense

42   Purchases of service material

43   Indirect cost on long-term obligations

44   Total payments on payrolls

45   Total expense available for prepaid expense
        Payments on accounts payable

46   Total generated accounts payables before adjustment for prepaid expense
        Total sales available for accounts receivable after adjustment for unearned
           advances from customers
        Total operating expense

47   Total generated accounts payable after adjustment for prepaid expense
        Net income on oeprations

48   Total income before income taxes

In the output summations:

F(1) to F(17) are summed in D(1,I) to D(17,I)
F(27) to F(46) are summed in D(18,I) to D(37,I)

——————————— Table 14.15 ———————————

ARRAYS FOR TOTALS, CONDITION, AND SELECTED
ACCOUNTS IN PAVE6 FROM PAVE3 AND PAVE2

In PAVE3, T( ) is used for processing totals of condition accounts for each period
during sample replications. The following are assignments of T( ) indexes:

1   Near-cash: cash plus accounts receivable net of uncollectible accounts
2   Total inventories
3   Total current assets
4   Total assets
5   Total current liabilities
6   Total liabilities
7   Total owners' equity

Table 14.15 (continued)

Before the computation of ratios EOP M in PAVE3, it is convenient to reassign some T( ) indexes. These reassignments apply only to the final period summary:

1   Sales achieved by firm from S and F(1)
3   Total interest expense, equal to F(17) plus F(43) (See Table 14.14)
4   Total tangible assets, equal to T(4) above less N(18) (See Table 14.12)
6   Tangible owners' equity, T(7) above less N(18)

The following arrays use index numbers K for SELECTED ACCOUNTS for all periods, an output division processed in PAVE3 and PAVE6:

E(K) for processing the first 16 accounts through sample replications in PAVE3
G(K,I) for accumulating sums of squares from E( ) (to develop standard deviations and confidence limits in PAVE6)
C(K,I) for sums and means of 17 accounts for each period I in PAVE6

NOTE: Account 17, *all fixed assets at book*, has no uncertainty, and does not require E( ) or G( )

The following are descriptions of K indexes for SELECTED ACCOUNTS:

1   Industry sales
2   Firm's industry share % of market
3   Firm net sales achieved
4   Cost of sales
5   Gross profit on sales
6   Total operating expense
7   Net operating income
8   Net income after income taxes
9   Cash and marketable securities
10   Near-cash: cash and marketable securities plus accounts receivable net of uncollectible accounts
11   Total inventories
12   Total current assets
13   Total assets
14   Total current liabilities
15   Total liabilities
16   Total owners' equity
17   Total of all fixed assets at book value

C( ) for condition values is transferred to PAVE6 from PAVE3 (See Table 14.13).

Some account reassignments for C( ) for CONDITION STATEMENTS occur on lines 2660 to 2730 of PAVE6.

Table 14.15 (continued)

Index reassignments to C( ) account indexes at this point are:

15   Near-cash (later to 10 for SELECTED ACCOUNTS)
16   Total inventories (later to 11 for SELECTED ACCOUNTS)
17   Total current assets (later to 12 for SELECTED ACCOUNTS)
18   Total assets (later to 13 for SELECTED ACCOUNTS)
19   Total current liabilities (later to 14 for SELECTED ACCOUNTS)
20   Total liabilities (later to 15 for SELECTED ACCOUNTS)
21   Total owners' equity (later to 16 for SELECTED ACCOUNTS)
22   Total liabilities and owners' equity

On lines 3480 to 3510 of PAVE6, some C( ) are reassigned again to indexes of SELECTED ACCOUNTS AS SHOWN ABOVE:

B( ) is used in PAVE2 and PAVE6 for asset accounts with no uncertainty. The plan of account indexes K over all dates I for B(K,I+1) is:

1   Indirect manufacturing supplies inventory
2   Total manufacturing fixed assets at book value
3   Total general fixed assets at book value plus unamortized intangibles (intangibles term is removed on line 2740 of PAVE6)
4   Unamortized intangibles balance
5 to 9   General fixed assets at cost, Class 1 to 5
10 to 14 General fixed assets reserve for depreciation, Class 1 to 5
15 to 19 Manufacturing fixed assets at cost, Class 1 to 5
20 to 24 Manufacturing fixed assets reserve for depreciation, Class 1 to 5

———————————— Table 14.16 ————————————
ARRAYS FOR FINANCIAL SUMMARY ACCOUNTS IN PAVE3 AND PAVE4

The following arrays use index number K for items in FINANCIAL SUMMARY FROM FINAL PERIOD output division:

U(K) for processing sums in PAVE 3
H(K,L) for developing statistics in PAVE3 and PAVE4
    L = 1 for sum in PAVE3 and process to mean in PAVE4
    L = 2 for sum of squares in PAVE3 and process to standard deviation in PAVE4

Table 14.16 (continued)

L = 3 for minimum value in PAVE3 and PAVE4
L = 4 for maximum value in PAVE3 and PAVE4

The K indexes for FINANCIAL SUMMARY

1   Firm's share of industry %
2   Net sales or revenue per year
3   Cash and marketable securities
4   Total assets
5   Total owners' equity

6   Gross margin on sales %
7   Net operating margin on sales %
8   Operating earning power %
9   Operating efficiency or operating capital turnover
10 Return on owner's equity %

11 Cash ratio %
12 Acid test on quick ratio %
13 Current ratio %
14 Debt to tangible assets %
15 Debt to tangible owners' equity %

16 Time interest earned multiple
17 Average collection period in days
18 Inventory turns per year
19 Industry sales per period—000's omitted
20 Cost of sales per year

21 Gross profit per year
22 Operating income per year
23 Net income before income taxes per year
24 Net income after income taxes per year
25 Near-cash: cash and marketable securities plus accounts receivable net of
        uncollectibles

26 Total inventories
27 Total current assets
28 Net tangible fixed assets
29 Accounts payable
30 Short-term loans and notes
31 Long-term obligations

Table 14.6 (continued)

32   Total liabilities
33   Total paid-in owners' equity

The following additional indexes are assigned in PAVE4 to obtain the mean and standard deviation in the H( ) loop. These accounts are not printed in FINANCIAL SUMMARY, but are used for VALUATION AND SCOPE.

34   Owners' equity EOP 1
35   Total assets EOP 1
36   Cash EOP 1

──────────── Table 14.17 ────────────
SYSTEM PARAMETER ASSIGNMENTS IN PAVE4

The following parameters are transferred to PAVE4 from PAVE2. The array is N( ) in PAVE4 and H( ) in PAVE2, with the same index descriptions. The percentage inputs are converted to decimals in PAVE2.

N(1)   Interpolation factor for multiple of periods to years

N(2)   Industry sales indicator from P(21) or ID 120: share % of industry=0/ direct firm sales $ per period=1

N(3)   R & D expense indicator from Q(1) or ID 330: sales %=0/$ per period=1

N(4)   All fixed assets at *book* value EOP 1 (B(2,2) + B(3,2))

N(5)   Intangible assets unamortized EOP 1 (B(4,2))

N(6)   Intangible assets unamortized EOP M end-of-run (B(4,M+1))

N(7) $ Initial tax loss carry forward, N(90) or ID 90 originally

N(8)   Number of first period owner equity units, N(91) or ID 91 originally

N(9) $ Added share cost amount—internal computation=0, N(92) or ID 92 originally

N(10)   Price-earnings multiple Year 1—internal computation=0, N(93) or ID 92 originally

N(11)   Price-earnings multiple final year—internal computation=0, N(94) or ID 94 originally

N(12)   % Assets average realized in liquidation, N(95) or ID 95 originally

N(13)   % Investor required rate of return per year—internal computation=0, N(96) or ID 96 originally

Table 14.7 (continued)

N(14)   % Long-term average growth rate—internal computation=0, N(97) or ID 97
        originally
N(15)   % Return on incremental assets—internal computation=0, N(98) or ID 98
        originally
N(16)   Real growth rate of economy *final* EOP M, D(1,M)
N(17)   Inflation rate EOP 1, D(2,1)
N(18)   Inflation rate *final* EOP M, D(2,M)
N(19)   Total growth of industry *final* EOP M, D(3,M)

Parameter transfers to G( ) in PAVE4 from M( ) in PAVE3 are listed in Table 14.12

———————— Table 14.18 ————————
ACCOUNT ARRAYS FOR STATEMENT PRINTING IN PAVE5

Scalars to PAVE5 from PAVE3

N$,   Title of run
M,   Number of periods
N,   Number of periods per year
N3,   Sample size (deterministic=1)
N5,   Frame (service=0, trade=1, manufacturing =2, environment only=3)
I1,   Industry base sales per year

Scalars to PAVE5 from PAVE4

N6,   Output division choice (0=VALUATION AND SCOPE, 1=FINANCIAL
        SUMMARY, 2=FINANCIAL STATEMENTS, 3=SELECTED ACCOUNTS)
S1,   Sales demand choice (0=firm's % share of industry, 1=direct firm sales in-
        put), from N(2) in PAVE4
R,   R & D expense choice (0=% of sales, 1=$ expense per period)

Array A(K,I) is from PAVE2 for inputs without uncertainty for each period I.
Account indexes K are determined as follows:

K=1 to 7 with revised indexes from A( ) in PAVE5 column of Table 14.11
K=8 to 22 with indexes revised from D( ) in PAVE5 column of Table 14.11

Array C(K,I+1) is from PAVE3 for condition accounts each date I which are
needed in PAVE5 statements. Accounts indexes are reassigned from those transferred to PAVE6 in Table 14.13, or reassignments in PAVE6 (Table 14.15).

Table 14.18 (continued)

Account indexes for PAVE5 are:

1,   Cash and marketable securities
2,   General supplies inventory
3,   Finished goods inventory for manufacturing or trade
4,   Goods-in-process inventory for manufacturing
5,   Direct materials inventory for manufacturing
6,   Short-term debt
7,   Indirect materials inventory for manufacturing, which is transferred in
      PAVE5 from B(1,I+1), which in turn was read from PAVE2.

Array D(K,I) is from PAVE3 for flow accounts with uncertainty each period I. Account indexes are the same as those shown in the transfers of F( ) to D( ) accounts in Table 14.14.

Array D(K,I) is reassigned for 10 flow accounts to PAVE6 on lines 1740 to 1790 of PAVE5. The revised K account indexes are:

1   Net sales achieved by firm
2   Firm's share of market
3   Industry sales
4   Cost of sales
5   Gross profit on sales
6   Total operating expense
7   Net operating income
8   Net income after income taxes
9   Owner new net investment (planned and required)
10   Dividends paid

The first 8 accounts above are used for SELECTED ACCOUNTS, and the last two for CAPITAL CHANGES statements.

Appendix

Glossary of All Inputs

Input-output system choices (applies to all PAVE simulations).

A correct set of these inputs should be available before proceeding to other input divisions. Choices in this division determine which other input sections will be presented in displays.

Values of IDs in this division are limited to nonnegative integers specified under each ID.

1 TOTAL NUMBER OF PERIODS (MAXIMUM 24) [1]

Enter from 1 to 24. Simulated values are computed for each period. Time intervals are determined by users in ID 2.

2 NUMBER OF PERIODS PER YEAR [1]

Duration of each period is the reciprocal of ID 2. Any duration works, even multiple years (fractional entry in ID 2). Run quarters (4) or months (12) for seasonal patterns. Run at least 3 years total for meaningful internal valuation under growth.

The most useful period lengths are one year (ID 2 = 1), six months (ID 2 = 2), 3 months (ID 2 = 4), and one month (ID 2 = 12).

3 SAMPLE SIZE–DETERMINISTIC=1/STATISTICAL=2 TO 30 [1]

To avoid excessive run time on slow machines, do not exceed 12. Fast machines may process samples up to size 30. Large sample sizes stabilize mean outputs within confidence intervals. An input of 1, the internal default value, eliminates generation of uncertainty for inputs, and statistical analysis of outputs. If 1 is entered, input uncertainties in any of 12 starred dynamic input sets will be disregarded. Each sample size greater than 1 offers some combination of risk level and confidence interval precision (see Table 8.2).

Deterministic mode develops all outputs from one PAVE replication. *Statistical inference* uses a Monte Carlo method of repeated sample replications. For ID 3 greater than 1, uncertainty may be introduced with triangular probability distributions for up to 12 dynamic sets. Users input the maximum percent shift in ID–1 position, which may be 0, for each of these sets. Such inputs are ignored under ID 3 = 1 *deterministic*. For *statistical* ID 3 greater than 1, outputs are approximately normally distributed.

Moving from *deterministic* to *statistical* input choice, VALUATION, FINANCIAL SUMMARY, and SELECTED ACCOUNTS shift output printing from single values to sets of four summary statistics. These summary statistics are the mean, standard deviation of the mean, and upper and lower confidence interval limits for the mean. The last three statistical measures of *spread* are inferences on the *mean* of the outputs, not on individual values of outputs. To make inferences on the latter, multiply the standard deviation and the width of the confidence interval by the square root of ID 3 sample size input. In SELECTED ACCOUNTS there is a choice of statistics to be printed. The last account, ALL FIXED ASSETS AT BOOK, has no variability in the simulation.

In VALUATION, probabilities of insolvency for *deterministic* must be either one or zero ("insolvency did not occur" message). *Going-concern value* requires risk analysis. Its amount and accompanying parameters are omitted under *deterministic*. A *statistical* choice for FINANCIAL SUMMARY prints *maximum* and *minimum* values encountered during the simulation as well as the four summary statistics listed above. FINANCIAL STATEMENTS print only *mean* values. These are equivalent to single values under *deterministic*. The figures will differ slightly, however, because statistical outputs are the means of samples.

4 SEED NUMBER–STANDARD RANDOM SERIES=0

Section 3.4 explains the Monte Carlo method of statistical sampling. Input uncertainty is developed from a series of random numbers between 0 and 1. In a computer such numbers, with approximate random properties, are usually produced by a function built in to the BASIC interpreter. Behavior of a sequence of random numbers is controlled by an *argument* supplied to the random function or *generator*. Of particular importance is the *seed number*, or argument supplied to the first call of a random *generator* during a run.

In the WANG BASIC of this book, a *seed number* of 0 always produces an identical set for a given quantity of random numbers. This feature is useful with comparative runs for sensitivity analysis. Variance among samples is reduced, thus increasing output efficiency. A seed of 0 is also useful for reproducing outputs from a prior run.

If one wishes to obtain a different sample output from the same input set, INPUT 1 in ID 4 for a *second* run. Then a different set of random numbers will be applied to the same input set. Since sample inputs will shift, so will output estimates. In general, a pooled sample of combined size in ID 3 will be more efficient than attempting to interpret separate, sequential samples.

Seed number argument rules for some computers are quite different from the system described here. There are cases where a prime number must be entered to start a duplicate random number series. Then a 0 or negative argument may call the next consecutive number. Check the rules of your particular BASIC interpreter.

RISK LEVELS AND CONFIDENCE INTERVALS FOR SAMPLE SIZE INPUT ID 3.

Confidence intervals for the mean are computed from:

confidence limit = mean ± (standard deviation of mean X t-statistic)

The smaller the t-statistic, the more precise the confidence interval.

Sample size ID 3	% risk	t-statistic	Sample size ID 3	% risk	t-statistic
2	80	3.1	16	99	3.0
3	90	2.9	17	90	1.7
4	90	2.4	18	95	2.1
5	95	2.8	19	98	2.6
			20	99	2.9
6	90	2.0			
7	95	2.4	21	90	1.6
8	98	2.9	22	95	2.0
9	90	1.9	23	98	2.5
10	95	2.3	24	99	2.8
			25	99	2.8
11	98	2.8			
12	99	3.1	26	99	2.8
13	90	1.8	27	99	2.8
14	95	2.2	28	99	2.8
15	98	2.7	29	99	2.8
			30	99	2.8

For sample size 31 to 40, the confidence level is 99% and the t-statistic is approximately 2.7.

5 FRAME: SERVICE=0/TRADE=1/MANUFACTURING=2/ENVIRONMENT ONLY=3

PAVE adjusts interactive input displays, internal logic, and output printing statements to the *frame* of a firm's operations and inventories. If inputs are entered which do not apply to a chosen frame—for example *manufacturing* expenses, inventories, or fixed asset classes under *service* frame ID 5 = 0— then such inputs are ignored during processing.

Logic changes among the first three choices are a matter of goods inventories, and scope of operations. *Services* are intangible; there are no physical product for sale accumulations. Only *general supplies* (IDs 15 and 79) inventories are maintained for *service* frame. Another inventory, *finished goods* (IDs 16 and set 152) becomes relevant for the *trade* frame. For *manufacturing* there are not only three more inventories (five total), but an additional set of inputs for expense accounts and asset classes. The additional manufacturing inventories (five total), but an additional set of inputs for expense accounts and asset classes. The additional manufacturing inventories are direct materials (IDs 18 and set 172), *goods-in-process*, (IDs 17 and set 162), and *indirect supplies*, (IDs 19 and 220). One may use the added set of manufacturing inputs to simulate production at a separate location from general administration. Since inputs are available to reduce any inventory level to zero, the *manufacturing* frame could be used for a *service* business in order to gain a richer set of expense and asset inputs. Thus *frame* choice is, in part, a matter of the desired richness of input sets. The *manufacturing* frame could more broadly have been described as *operations* or *processing*. On the other hand, *manufacturing* could be simulated under the *trade* firm in order to simplify the input set. In such cases *direct* materials and *goods-in-process* inventories must be assumed negligible.

If nonzero entries are made for inventories outside a specified frame, such inputs will be ignored. Carelessness here could create balancing problems in the *initial condition* input division.

Continuing with the first three frame choices, VALUATION outputs do not change form as the frame changes. Under *service* frame, however, a few items will be omitted from FINANCIAL SUMMARY and SELECTED ACCOUNTS. COST OF SALES and GROSS PROFIT ON SALES apply to products, and will be omitted for *service*. In FINANCIAL STATEMENTS, COST OF GOODS SOLD SCHEDULES are omitted for *service* frame, and COST OF GOODS MANUFACTURED SCHEDULES are printed only under *manufacturing* frame. COST OF SALES and GROSS PROFIT ON SALES entries are omitted from INCOME STATEMENTS under *service* frame.

The *environment only* frame prints a very limited output. Processing is restricted to the economic and industry environment; there is no internal analysis of a firm's performance. In other words, processing ends with SALES DEMAND AVAILABLE TO A FIRM. In VALUATION the only items printed under *environment only* are TOTAL SALES for the first and final years. Per share information is not printed. In FINANCIAL SUMMARY only NET SALES OR REVENUE PER YEAR will be printed if ID 120 = 1. Otherwise, FIRM'S SHARE OF INDUSTRY % and INDUSTRY SALES PER YEAR will also be printed. In FINANCIAL STATEMENTS only ENVIRONMENTAL ANALYSES OF THE FIRM statements will be printed. The maximum nonzero accounts under SELECTED ACCOUNTS are INDUSTRY SALES, FIRM'S INDUSTRY SHARE %, and FIRM NET SALES ACHIEVED.

6 OUTPUT DIVISION FOR FIRST PRINTING

VALUATION AND SCOPE for first and final years = 0
FINANCIAL SUMMARY from final period = 1
FINANCIAL STATEMENTS for all periods = 2
SELECTED ACCOUNTS for all periods = 3

An explanation of output divisions is given in sections 9.1 to 9.3. An outline of the contents of output divisions is contained in Table 9.1. An initial selection of an output division is made with ID 6. After each output has been printed, users may select another output division, return to inputs for a rerun, or END. Thus the first output division PRINT is only a passing choice. One may mix or match output divisions in any order. The amount of printing in output divisions varies with other input choices. There is extended statistical output information in VALUATION AND SCOPE, FINANCIAL SUMMARY, and SELECTED ACCOUNTS for ID 3 greater than one (see ID 3). The *frame* in ID 5 influences the number of STATEMENTS in FINANCIAL STATE-MENTS, and the number of accounts printed in all divisions. Frame choice ID 5 = 3 has very limited output printing (see ID 5).

Initial condition (applies unless ID 5 = 3 for *environment only*).

This is a record of a firm's financial position at the beginning of a simulation. It may be omitted entirely for a new firm at "ground zero," or a "skeleton" statement of condition may be entered. After inputs have been completed, the balance of ASSETS and EQUITIES (liabilities plus owners' equity) is checked internally. Imbalance information will be displayed, and processing cannot continue until such imbalance has been corrected.

Any IDs in this division may have zero or positive values. Negative inputs are allowed for ID 46.

9 $ CASH AND MARKETABLE SECURITIES

Here all cash and near-cash items should be combined. Near-cash includes certificates of deposit, time deposits, treasury bills, federal funds, commercial paper, and similar items. Shares of stock and long-term debt, such as bonds or trust certificates, may be included if readily marketable and valued conservatively. The same remarks apply to shares in subsidiaries, or other investments held by the firm. PAVE is not really designed for holding companies or firms whose principal business is investment. An excessive amount of investment ownership becomes clumsy because the program assumes that cash and near-cash is readily available to meet operational needs. If a particular firm holds surplus monetary assets, and these are not to be employed for operations, then it is suggested that initial condition be recast without these surplus assets before running PAVE. For income on near-cash see ID 531.

10 $ TRADE ACCOUNTS AND NOTES RECEIVABLE

11 $ NONTRADE CREDIT, ADVANCES, AND ACCRUED RECEIVABLES

12 $ RESERVE FOR UNCOLLECTIBLE ACCOUNTS

Collectively these accounts are intended to cover all open account and interest-bearing debt which is a short-term extension of credit by the firm in the course of doing business. There is a separate reserve for uncollectible accounts per ID 12, also known as "bad debts." In PAVE the above are collapsed into a single account for receivables with an offsetting reserve for uncollectibles. It is assumed that customer credit is the only such item of interest to the firm for future strategic planning purposes. Specifically, IDS 10 and 11 are summed into a single receivables account for processing through the periods. ID 12 is subtracted from the above during a computation of *total assets*.

13 $ PREPAID EXPENSE AND DEFERRED CHARGES

Prepaid expense arises when payables are billed before an expense has been applied. For example, one may be liable for an insurance premium now which includes protection over future periods. This intangible asset may be maintained at a fixed proportion of total payments for expenses and net asset additions over the simulation per ID 81. ID 13 establishes BOP 1 level, all other periods are computed from ID 81. Either of these IDs may be 0. Total payments are adjusted for changes in the level of *prepaid expenses* before a computation of *accounts payable*.

14 $ INTANGIBLES: ORGANIZATION EXPENSE, PATENTS, GOODWILL, LEASEHOLD IMPROVEMENTS

Here are assets without physical substance in liquidation. Included are trademarks, copyrights, franchises, patents, and legal claims. Organization expense capitalizes the start-up cost of a firm. Goodwill arises from the difference between *market* and *book* value of a firm's assets, usually recognized explicitly in the accounts at the time of purchasing a firm. Leasehold improvements are the capitalized expense and modifications to rented property. PAVE provides ID 83 for entry of incremental intangibles during Period 1 only, and ID 84 for a straight line annual amortization. Intangible accounts may be used with any frame except ID 5 = 3 for *environment only*.

15 $ INVENTORY OF GENERAL SUPPLIES, SMALL TOOLS, AND SMALL EQUIPMENT

16 $ INVENTORY OF MANUFACTURING OR TRADE FINISHED GOODS

17 $ INVENTORY OF MANUFACTURING GOODS-IN-PROCESS

18 $ INVENTORY OF MANUFACTURING INDIRECT MATERIAL AND SUPPLIES

19 $ INVENTORY OF MANUFACTURING INDIRECT SUPPLIES AND EQUIPMENT

ID 15 is used with three frames: manufacturing, trade, or service. This is the only inventory available for service frame. ID 16 is available to both *manufacturing* and *trade* frames. IDs 17 and 19 become operational only for the *manufacturing* frame. ID 18 is for *direct* or *variable* material; ID 19 for *indirect* material and supplies. Inputs to inapplicable inventories are ignored during processing. If this feature is unrecognized, initial condition imbalance could arise.

Inventories are in cost dollars, and should include freight-in or any other costs incurred in procurement. Valuation of *goods-in-process* ID 17 and *finished goods* ID 16 should be at the rate of current period cost in manufacturing class of firm. Thus PAVE uses absorption costing with first-in-first-out (FIFO) pricing.

Standard costs, direct costs, and other methods of inventory pricing are not available, but such alternatives are usually of limited interest for long-term planning.

It is not necessary to use precisely the same inventory categories as suggested by the input titles as long as user selections match the frame of firm in ID 5. PAVE logic, however, does process *direct materials* in ID 18 into *goods-in-process* ID 17, and the latter into *finished goods* in ID 16. IDs 15 and 19 are processed independently. For the *trade* frame, *finished goods* logic (ID 16) is shifted to process outside purchase of goods for sale. In this case ID 19 is not available, but ID 15 may be used for general supplies and small tools. Subject to the processing limitations mentioned above, the user may move inventory values into whatever categories fulfill his or her needs.

20 TO 24 $ CLASS 1 TO 5 MANUFACTURING FIXED ASSETS AT COST BASIS

25 TO 29 $ CLASS 1 TO 5 MANUFACTURING FIXED ASSETS RESERVE FOR DEPRECIATION

30 TO 34 $ CLASS 1 TO 5 GENERAL FIXED ASSETS AT COST BASIS

35 TO 39 $ CLASS 1 TO 5 GENERAL FIXED ASSETS RESERVE FOR DEPRE-CIATION

The *book* value of fixed assets is cost less *reserve for depreciation. Book* value is the figure used as a component of summary *total* assets.

Up to 5 classes of assets are available to accommodate up to 5 different depreciation rates (including a zero rate which may be applied to nondepreciables such as land). The entirely separate set available under ID 5 = 2 for *manufacturing* reflects PAVE capabilities for detached treatment of a processing expense center (see discussion under ID 5). The program will obtain inputs, process logic, and print outputs for only as many classes of assets as receive nonzero inputs here plus *asset net changes* nonzero inputs in IDs 280 to 329, and IDs 480 to 529. Apply nonzero values to asset classes in numerical order. Class numbers must correspond between *initial condition* here, and *net changes* in the later IDs.

40 $ TRADE ACCOUNTS AND NOTES PAYABLE

41 $ NONTRADE ACCOUNTS, DIVIDENDS, AND TAXES PAYABLE

All short-term credit, both open and interest-bearing, should be aggregated into these accounts. ID 40 is intended for trade suppliers in the regular course of business. ID 41 is for other explicit short-term debt. IDs 40, 41, and 43 are summed for further processing of payables through PAVE.

42 $ UNEARNED ADVANCES FROM CUSTOMERS

If a customer has been charged for goods or services to be delivered in the future, then a firm has acquired a liability to provide valuable goods or services. A publisher may sell a year's subscription now, but it is understood that some periodicals will not be delivered until later.

This liability may be maintained at a fixed proportion of net sales over the simulation per ID 82. ID 42 establishes BOP 1 level, all other periods are computed from ID 82. Either of these IDs may be 0. Net sales are adjusted for changes in the level of *unearned advances to customers* before computation of *accounts receivable*.

43 $ ACCRUED EXPENSE AND LIABILITIES

As compared to IDs 40 and 41, this account recognizes short-term liabilities which have not been specifically billed by creditors. Such liabilities arise from the passage of time, such as interest cost or income taxes (during certain periods).

The input of this ID is added to the values in IDs 40 and 41 before further processing of *accounts payable* through PAVE.

44 $ SHORT-TERM DEBT AND LOANS PAYABLE

Seasonal financing from bank loans and lines of credit should be entered here. Bonds and other financial obligations with less than a year to maturity should be included in this account. The ID 44 entry is repaid in full EOP 1. Further short-term borrowing is a result of need and borrowing capacity (see IDs 87 and 88).

45 $ LONG-TERM OBLIGATIONS AT FACE OF STATED VALUE

Long-term and intermediate-term capital needs are covered by this account for creditor relationships between the firm and sources of capital. This creditor relationship is from a planning (not legal) point of view. Preferred stock often is included because there is a planning obligation to meet fixed dividend payments. These are equivalent in policy effects to interest payments on long-term debt, but must be adjusted to an after-tax basis. Long-term debt is continued through the PAVE simulation, and interest or preferred dividend expense is developed periodically in accordance with average rates established by the user. There is provision in future planning to change the principal amount outstanding at the end of each period (ID set 542).

The amount entered in ID 45 should be a stated principal value on which interest or dividend payments are based, and should also equal the amount to be repaid by a firm if the securities are redeemed or called. Such amounts are often different from proceeds of bonds or preferred stock issues when the securities were first sold, which is discussed further under ID 46 below.

ID 45 may include other sources of long-term capital than bonds or preferred stock. Among these are equipment trust certificates, term loans, mortgages, conditional sales contracts, land contracts, long-term notes, convertible bonds, income bonds, etc. The user may find several categories of such sources of capital in some initial balance sheets. If so, combine them all into one value for ID 45.

46 $ BOND (AND PREFERRED STOCK) PREMIUM (DISCOUNT)

This account represents differences between the stated or maturity values of fixed-income securities, and the proceeds which a firm received when the security was originally issued. Such differences are usually charged off during the term of the security. Thus, if bonds were sold for less than the face, or maturity value, which is often the case, then the firm develops a *bond discount*, or negative offset to the face value of the bonds. This will reconcile the reduction of proceeds received in cash on the asset side with cash which eventually will have to be paid to redeem the bonds. If this discount is amortized periodically over the term of the bonds, then at maturity the amount of liability in the bond account will equal the cost of redemption. The periodic amount amortized is often treated as an additional interest expense with a corresponding liquidation of part of the negative bond discount.

The opposite changes take place if bonds are sold at a premium, or for more than face. In this case ID 46 is positive. Periodic amortization consists of a credit or reduction of interest expense with a corresponding reduction in the bond-premium account. Financial complexities such as capital premiums and discounts, are not desirable for the ongoing PAVE simulation which is primarily concerned with operations. Initial entries in ID 46 are charged off by PAVE during the first period to ID 48 retained earnings. They eventually would be amortized here through positive or negative adjustment to interest expense. If the user wishes to restore the financial influence of premiums (discounts), he or she merely needs to make appropriate adjustments to long-term interest rate inputs in ID set 572. This ID 46 is the one input of *initial condition* division which may be zero, negative, or positive.

47 $ PAID-IN OWNER EQUITY CAPITAL

Consolidate paid-in capital accounts, such as stated value of common stock and capital surplus, into this input. Initial value of investment capital accounts for partnerships or proprietorships should also be entered here.

48 $ RETAINED EARNINGS

Enter here the owners' share of undistributed earnings or profits. IDs 47 and 48 comprise initial *owners' equity* or *net worth*.

Environment of economy and industry to sales of firm—system parameters

This input division applies to all frames of ID 5. For *dynamic inputs* see IDs 102 to 139. Negative inputs here would be treated as equivalent to 0 or nonentry.

51 TO 74 SEASONAL/CYCLICAL INDEXES

The set of these IDs produces seasonal and cyclical shifts from period to period in sequential recurrence pattern. PAVE will repeat this consecutive set of factors over all periods. Each active index entered in IDs 57 through 74 must be greater than zero. The first ID in this series which carries a nonpositive or nonentry value will be taken by the program as a flag signal to terminate the set at the last preceding entry. For either a single entry or nonentry of IDs in this series, the program will supply an index of one for all periods, which eliminates seasonal/cyclical adjustment to sales.

It is not important whether these indexes be entered as decimal fractions, percentages, numbers greater than one, or numbers with a mean of one, as long as each desired index entry is greater than zero. PAVE has internal routines which rescale the set of index inputs to a mean of one. If indexes are entered in excess of the number of periods simulated, the excess will not be applied to any periods. If less indexes are entered than the number of periods, the program will recycle the entered indexes, as described above. There is often good reason to enter more indexes, or schedule more indexes in periodic repetition, than there are periods (of course 24 is the maximum number for both). This would occur when the simulation ends before the completion of an index cycle. All the ID values which make up an index cycle should be entered, even though some may not be applied to periods, because the whole set of indexes should be balanced over the cycle. This means that correct index adjustments will be made for each period, even though the number of periods for a complete index cycle exceeds the number of periods for a particular simulation run.

If the set of indexes covers one year (such as four for a quarterly simulation period or twelve for a monthly simulation period), then the index factors would normally be termed "seasonal." If the index factors were applied over a set of years (such as one per annual simulation period, or the same index over successive fractions of a year), then the index factors might be termed "cyclical." Combinations of two applications are possible for up to 24 indexes. This accounts for the combined designation of this periodic set of inputs as seasonal/cyclical. If ID 120 = 1, the *direct sales* input option, no input set of seasonal/cyclical indexes will be utilized by the program.

Manufacturing inputs—system parameters

This input division applies only to frame ID 5 = 2. For *dynamic inputs* see IDs 140 to 289. Inputs in this division must be nonnegative.

75 % OVERTIME LIMIT TO REGULAR DIRECT LABOR PAYROLL

If sales demand exceeds capacity per ID set 212, as modified by efficiency per ID set 201, then PAVE manufacturing will automatically go into overtime to the extent needed to meet the demand up to a limit established by entry of ID 75 here. The ID 75 percentage determines the extension of direct labor available, but it must be remembered that the total amount of direct labor may also be influenced by *operating efficiency* and a randomization component. Capacity is also influenced by operating efficiency and randomization. There is no upper logic limit to ID 75, but it should not be given a percentage higher than labor would be willing to work, or higher than available time when factory equipment is idle. Zero entry or nonentry in ID 75 will result in no overtime being made available if capacity is exceeded. If the program assigns overtime to *direct labor* ID set 181, then it will assign a corresponding factor of overtime to *direct supervision and support labor* ID set 192. Note that ID 75 input is an incremental percentage to direct labor available with capacity.

76 % OVERTIME PREMIUM COST

A higher wage rate is usually paid for overtime. Enter 50 for time and one-half, and 100 for double time. Zero entry or nonentry will result in no overtime premium. This would mean that labor beyond regular time would be compensated at regular rates without any premium rate for overtime. Whatever overtime premium is applied to *direct labor* ID set 181 is also assigned to *direct supervision and support labor* in ID set 192. Premium labor cost from ID 75 is applied only for the overtime portion of direct labor; regular time is charged at the original nonpremium levels.

77 % INCREASE IN PLANT CAPACITY LIMIT FROM SUBCONTRACT OPERATIONS

If an application of overtime up to the limit specified in ID 75 is still insufficient to meet sales demand, then PAVE manufacturing will automatically go into a material subcontracting or outside subassembly routine. This extends capacity further up to a limit established by entry of ID 77 here. The ID 77 percentage determines a further extension of capacity, but it must be remembered that the total amount of capacity is also influenced by operating efficiency and randomization components, both for available capacity and direct labor. The ID 77 percentage is computed in addition to capacity already extended with overtime per the maximum limit set by ID 75. Zero or nonentry of ID 77 will result in no extensions of capacity being made available from increased contracting with outside vendors. If ID 75 were zero, then capacity would not be extended with overtime labor, and inadequacies would be applied directly to the allowable extension from ID 77 here.

If both IDs 75 and 77 were zero, then manufacturing cannot be extended at all if insufficient to meet sales demand. It is not possible in PAVE to reverse the order of priorities in extending capacity. In other words one cannot go to a material subcontracting routine first, and follow this by factory overtime. At whatever levels capacity extension percentage IDs 75 and 77 are set, cases will arise when fully extended capacity is still insufficient to meet production demands. When this occurs, PAVE automatically reduces achievable sales to the highest capacity which is available. Sales lost are not backordered into future periods.

ID 77 should not be given a percentage which is higher than the extension of capacity available by subcontracting work to outside vendors. For each case determine which subassemblies or other work may be transferred from your own plant to someone else's facilities. What is the maximum percentage increase in production capacity obtainable in this manner?

78 % MATERIAL COST PREMIUM TO BE APPLIED TO SUBCONTRACT OPERATIONS

Transferring operations to outside vendors will usually result in a higher material cost component per sales dollars of product. Among other things, you usually must now pay for vendor fixed overhead as well as your own. ID 78 specifies the percentage of this material cost premium. Once capacity is expanded by changing the process to subcontract more work outside, all product will usually follow this new model. Thus the premium specified by ID 78 is applied across the board to all direct material usage once the threshold specified by the ID 77 has been passed. If subsequent period productions do not require capacity expansion from material subcontracting, then the premium cost of ID 78 is removed. If ID 78 is zero or not entered, then no material cost premium is applied. ID 78 is applied only to direct materials per ID 75 and ID set 141; it is not applied to indirect supplies per ID 222 and ID 79. The premium cost of material (if any) is used in the computation of required inventory levels per ID set 172 policy inputs.

Sales and general administrative inputs—system parameters

This input division applies to all frames except *environment only* (N5 = 3). For dynamic inputs see ID sets 352 to 522. Inputs in this division must be nonnegative.

79 GENERAL SUPPLIES INVENTORY LEVEL AS % OF ANNUAL USAGE

This ID 79 determines a normal level for general supplies, small tools, and small equipment inventories in terms of activity, in this case *annual* usage of supplies. Its analogue in manufacturing is ID set 220. ID 79 is applied to the sum of both ID set 401 direct usage series and ID set 412 indirect usage series. Purchases of general supplies are determined for the period by inventory requirements (determined here) and combined usage. If logic from policy inputs leads to negative purchases, then an automatic default routine reduces closing inventory to the point of zero purchases. All PAVE inventories are computed at cost.

80 ACCOUNTS PAYABLE LEVEL AS % OF ANNUAL ACCOUNT PAYMENTS

Credit extensions by suppliers and vendors of the enterprise arise from nonpayroll expenses and asset additions. Any credit granted to the firm from income tax payments, dividends or interest costs is not included here. These items should be entered during the periods in which they are paid. To enter ID 80 consider what percentage of *annual* credit extension to the enterprise are held on the average in *accounts payable* balances. If no credit is granted, enter 0 for immediate cash payments by the firm. Negative entries are not permitted.

An entry of 2.74 gives about 10 days credit, an entry of 4.11 gives about 15 days on the average, and an entry of 8.22 gives about 30 days. There is an assumption that credit available will vary directly with the amount of credit purchases made by the firm. The operation of this ID 80 is quite similar to ID set 391 on accounts receivable balance. A similar useful formula states that ID 80 entry equals *mean days credit to firm* times 100, divided by 365. Thus ID 80 may be considered as the number of years, on the average and multiplied by 100, over which vendors supply credit. The reciprocal of this variable, again multiplied by 100, is *accounts payable turnover* per year. To input a particular turnover policy, take its reciprocal, multiply by 100, and enter under ID 80. If application of input policy per ID 80 would result in negative payments of accounts payable during any period, then the input policy is internally modified by the program for zero payments.

81 PREPAID EXPENSE LEVEL AS % OF ANNUAL PAYMENTS

This establishes a level, which may be 0, for *unearned advances to customers*. This level is determined at the end of each period in terms of annual sales. If application of this policy would drive the input to accounts receivable and collections negative, then the policy is revised internally back to 0 input. For a discussion of the total unearned advances to customers system, consult ID 42.

82 ADVANCES BY CUSTOMERS AS % OF ANNUAL SALES

This establishes a level, which may be 0, for *unearned advances to customers*. This level is determined at the end of each period in terms of *annual* sales. If application of this policy would drive the input to accounts receivable and collections negative, then the policy is revised internally back to a 0 input. For a discussion of the total *unearned advances to customers* system, consult ID 42.

83 $ ORGANIZATION EXPENSE, GOODWILL, AND INTANGIBLES ADDED IN PERIOD [1]

Intangibles are apt to be encountered in the initial set up or reorganization of an enterprise. In PAVE, this would occur during the first simulated period. Initial intangibles may also be added to ID 14 in the *initial condition* division. Here ID 83 gives an opportunity for additions during the first period. Organization expense would arise if a new business were set up or an old one drastically reorganized. Goodwill would occur if a business were purchased at a market price different from the stated values of assets or owner equity. Goodwill might also be added if a PAVE user were interested in equating *owners' equity* with market value. Other initial intangibles are patent rights, license agreements, copyrights, contractual rights, and leasehold improvements.

84 $ AMORTIZATION OF INTANGIBLES YEARLY, NOT PER PERIOD

The amortization is straight line at a fixed dollar amount per period. The input is specified per *year*, one of only two dollar input IDs in PAVE which are not entered per period. The actual amount which is charged off each period is the *annual* base entered here divided by the number of periods per year in ID 2. If during any period the unamortized intangibles balance would be driven negative, then an internal default routine reduces the amortization during the period to a point of zero unamortized intangibles balance.

Financial and valuation control inputs–system parameters

This input division applies to all frames except environment only (ID 5 = 3). For *dynamic inputs* see ID sets 531 to 579. Inputs in this division, with the possible exception of ID 80, must be nonnegative.

87 % CASH RATIO MINIMUM, BELOW WHICH CASH DEMANDED [50]

This is a policy input ID 87 which controls the internal short-term borrowing and required additional capital routines. The cash ratio is cash and near-cash divided by total current liabilities. In PAVE this amounts to the value of cash and marketable securities account divided by total current liabilities. If the cash ratio is less than 1, then short-term borrowing will increase it towards one. If the cash ratio is more than 1, then the short-term borrowing will decrease it towards 1. In other words, the cash ratio approaches a limit of 1 as short-term borrowing is increased indefinitely. If the ID 87 entry is less than or equal to 90 (or cash ratio is 0.9), then PAVE will activate a routine which considers short-term borrowing. Such borrowing is subject to further tests based on current ratio requirements under ID 88. If ID 87 entry is more than 90, then short-term borrowing is not feasible to improve cash ratio, and the short-term routines are not activated. This does not mean that an ID 87 entry of more than 90 will not influence policy. Assuming an internal option for additional long-term capital with ID 530 equal to 1, such capital will be raised until the cash ratio given by ID 87, no matter how high, is satisfied. For ID 530 equal to 0, or no provision for internal control of long-term capital, then an ID 87 entry greater than 90 may not influence the program. Thus specified cash ratio requirements may not be reached (but see also ID 95).

A zero or nonentry for ID 87 will be overwritten by the PAVE internal value of 50, or 0.5 cash ratio. For a desired policy of negligible cash balance, enter a very small value for ID 87, such as 0.1. For an ID 87 entry of 90 or less, PAVE will attempt to borrow *short-term* funds until the ID 87 level is reached. This attempt is subject to the limitations of current ratio or liquidation value of noncash current assets as described in IDs 88 and 95 inputs below. If short-term borrowing is not sufficient to reach the ID 87 level, then PAVE may operate long-term capital additions routines under the conditions described at the end of the preceding paragraph.

88 % CURRENT RATIO MINIMUM FROM SHORT-TERM LOANS [200]

The current ratio is the ratio between total current assets and total current liabilities. Working capital, on the other hand, is current assets minus current liabilities. The general effect of short-term borrowing on the current ratio is somewhat analogous to that described for the cash ratio in ID 87 above. It is asymptotic to 1, with short-term loans increasing or decreasing the ratio toward that limit. ID 88 becomes operational only if short-term borrowing routines are instituted internally under conditions described under ID 87 above. In effect, ID 87 institutes short-term borrowing, and ID 88 acts as a check or limit against the permissible amount of short-term borrowing. Under conditions described above, PAVE will attempt short-term borrowing to reach cash ratio policy per ID 87 entry. In this process the current ratio, if greater than 1, will be driven down. Thus ID 88 specifies a lower limit of current ratio at which short-term borrowing is cut off (if reached), regardless of whether ID 87 cash ratio specification has also been reached. If ID 88 entry cuts off short-term borrowing, PAVE may still raise long-term capital under the conditions specified at the end of the first paragraph under ID 87 description. If ID 88 entry is less than 150 (1.5 current ratio), then the entry is disregarded and the program uses liquidation value of noncash current assets to limit borrowing (see ID 95 below). The 1.5 limit was incorporated because current ratios near one are insensitive to cash flows. Nonentry of zero entry results in an internal substitution of 200 (current ratio of 2). Thus current ratio values near 1, or less than 1, cannot be used for short-term borrowing potential. In summary, short-term loans must be generated from excess working capital or liquidation value of assets.

89 % COMBINED EFFECTIVE INCOME TAX RATE (LESS THAN 100) [50]

Since income tax rates are often progressive, and hence capital budgeting decisions occur at the maximum marginal rate, the selection of an appropriate entry for ID 89 may require some precalculation. ID 89 should be entered as an expected *mean* rate on net income subject to income taxes. Since there is no provision in PAVE for variable income tax rates, it is best to select a rate which is an expected average for income over a run.

Another complication in ID 89 entry is possible overlapping rates at various government levels. If there is only a federal tax, then this average rate should be entered. If there are also state or local rates, then these taxes are deductible from federal income. This lowers the effective, composite rate. It is the composite or effective rate which should be entered under ID 89. Formulas below indicate a method of computing effective rates under various conditions (all figures are percentages). A zero or nonentry in ID 89 will be reset internally to 50. Negative rates, and rates of 100 or more, are not permitted.

a. Federal and state rates

Effective rate = State rate + Federal rate x (100 – State rate)/100

b. Federal and local rates

Effective rate = Local rate + Federal rate x (100 – Local rate)/100

c. Federal, state, and local rates, if local tax is not deductible from state tax

Effective rate = Local rate + State rate + Federal rate x (100 – Local rate – State rate)/100

d. Federal, state, and local rates, if local tax is deductible from state tax

Effective rate = Local rate + State rate x (100 – Local rate)/100 + Federal rate x (100 – Local rate – State rate x (100 – Local rate)/100)/100

90 $ INITIAL TAX LOSS CREDIT FOR CARRYFORWARD

At the start of a PAVE simulation, an enterprise may have an income tax credit from previous loss operations which is available to reduce future income taxes. Such a credit may be extremely valuable due to a potential for future increases in income after taxes and net cash flow. PAVE automatically applies such initial credit (if any) against future income taxes, and carries this credit, plus any other credit generated by losses during the simulation, forward over all periods. If there is unused tax loss carryforward remaining at the end of a simulation, this information is printed in VALUATION AND SCOPE division. Zero or nonentry of ID 90 implies no initial tax loss carryforward. Negative entries are possible. These imply that a firm owes back taxes, and PAVE will deduct these taxes from first period after-tax income and net cash flow. Losses might also be carried back into past periods, but PAVE contains no direct logic for this situation.

For statistical runs, a *tax loss* may appear on statements simultaneously with *income tax* payments. This occurs because both may be encountered for different sample replications over the same periods.

91 NUMBER OF FIRST PERIOD OWNER EQUITY UNITS (1/SHARE OF FIRM) [1]

Limited per share information is supplied by PAVE (see list of per share outputs under ID 92). Per share control is supplied by IDs 91 and 92. ID 91 supplies an initial basis of number of shares EOP 1, and ID 92 the policy information to determine an incremental number of shares. These incremental shares accompany changes in owner paid-in capital.

ID 91 assumes that Period 1 is used for organization. Owner capital changes during that period do not increment number of shares from ID 91.

Usually ID 91 is simply the number of corporate common shares issued and outstanding EOP 1. For a partnership, or share of a joint venture, ID 91 may be used as a divisor. A one-third share of a business, for example, would be represented by ID 91 = 3.

Reliance on the internal default value of 1 for ID 91 is appropriate if there is no interest in per share outputs.

92 $ ADDED SHARE COST—INTERNAL COMPUTATION=0

Starting with owner shares outstanding at the end of the first simulation period, additional infusions of owner equity capital, both planned and internally determined, will usually be accompanied by the issue of additional shares. PAVE will compute the number of additional shares issued and outstanding for all periods beyond the first. The information on shares outstanding is used to compute values per share in VALUATION AND SCOPE output division. It is also used for a selected group of per share accounts for all periods in RETAINED EARNINGS AND CAPITAL CHANGES statements of FINANCIAL STATEMENTS output divisions. The latter statements PRINT the number of shares outstanding at the end of each period, and the mean *shares* outstanding per year.

After EOP 1 (see ID 91), incremental shares each period are computed from division of incremental owner equity capital for a period, both planned and internally required, by a price per share. A positive entry in ID 92 applies a fixed cost per share over all periods. A zero value in ID 91 activates an internal computation of per share price. This price is based upon *market value* of a firm (see IDs 93 and 94 below). An internal share price is established so that new shares pay proportionately to the market value of existing shares. At purchase, therefore, the value of existing shares is not diluted by an issue of new shares. Since *market values* are computed only for the first and final years of simulation, interpolation between these is used to establish values during intermediate periods.

If a value of one were entered in ID 91, useful new share information is unlikely.

93 PRICE-EARNINGS MULTIPLE YEAR 1—INTERNAL COMPUTATION=0

94 PRICE-EARNINGS MULTIPLE FINAL YEAR—INTERNAL COMPUTATION=0

These multiples are the quotient of *market value* and *earnings* (or *net income after income taxes*). Multiples are printed for the *first* year and *final* year. Information on earnings, market and other economic values of a firm, and multiples, is printed in VALUATION AND SCOPE output division.

There is a hierarchy in the determination of *market values*. For positive inputs in IDs 93 or 94, market values are simply the products of *earnings* and the input IDs 93 or 94 *multiple* values. Zero values in IDs 93 and 94 indicate internal computation of multiples. In such cases *market value* is taken as the higher of *going-concern value* or *liquidation value to owners*. For a discussion of valuation methods and a further examination of valuation parameters, see section 11.5. *Liquidation values* are always computed internally, and going-concern values, based on capitalization of earnings and earnings growth, are computed for statistical runs (ID 3 exceeds 1). For zero values in IDs 93 or 94, combined with a nonstatistical run with ID 3 = 1, internal values of 10 are supplied for IDs 93 or 94.

95 % ASSETS VALUES ON AVERAGE REALIZED IN LIQUIDATION [50]

Whereas internal valuation and IDs 96, 97, and 98 are devoted to *going-concern valuation*, ID 95 values a "dead" concern. In such case assets are to be dissembled and sold piecemeal in the market at their opportunity values in best alternate use. Even for going concerns, it is often useful to obtain liquidation value information. A comparison between going concern and liquidation values, which is printed in VALUATION AND SCOPE division of PAVE, gives the goodwill of a going concern. If negative, a firm's capital could best be deployed elsewhere.

Several classes of outputs are taken from ID 95. A PAVE user is given *liquidation value of assets* at the end of a run, and EOP 1. One is also given a *liquidation value of his ownership interest* on a total and per share basis; EOP 1 and end of run. The latter figures are equal to liquidation value of assets less total liabilities, and will often be negative if liabilities are substantial as compared to assets. This means that owners will receive nothing, and creditors only part payment, in the event of liquidation. This is a very common situation.

An amount received for assets in liquidation varies with class and particular nature. The more assets are current, the higher the liquidation percentage. For cash, the realization is 100%, and for monetary assets, including accounts receivable which may be factored at a discount in the market, something slightly less. Inventory values may vary from quite low to 100%, depending on market demand for the goods. Usually inventories of goods in process are worth little or nothing. Materials and finished goods may be worth a lot more. Fixed assets typically have low realizable values, although land and buildings are often an exception. Specialized tooling, on the other hand, may have only a scrap value. Select an average percentage for ID 95. Take into account the mix and types of assets. A zero or nonentry of ID 95 is overwritten by a value of 50 internally. Negative inputs to ID 95 are not permitted. Values above 100 are permissible, but would apply only to special cases where assets were worth more on the market in liquidation than at net book value.

As mentioned under IDs 87 and 88 descriptions, if the current ratio input specification in ID 88 is less than 150 (1.5 current ratio), it is not sufficiently sensitive to operate as a capacity limit for short-term borrowing. In this case PAVE internally substitutes the liquidation value of noncash current assets. This means that ID 95 is taken as a percentage of the sum of accounts receivable and total inventories. Short-term borrowing may not exceed this amount.

Conditions for further processing of short-term loans are described under IDs 87 and 88. If a user prefers to base short-term borrowing capacity on ID 95 logic rather than on the current ratio, enter 100 for ID 88, which in effect renders that test nonoperational.

96 % INVESTOR REQUIRED RATE OF RETURN PER YEAR—INTERNAL COMPUTATION=0

97 % LONG-TERM AVERAGE GROWTH RATE PER YEAR—INTERNAL COMPUTATION=0

98 % RETURN PER YEAR ON INCREMENTAL ASSETS—INTERNAL COMPUTATION=0

This set of inputs supplies parameters for computation of *going-concern value* under risk and inflation. The set allows user entries to selectively replace an internal determination of values for these parameters. Many simulations are atypical, erratic, involve a small span of time, or are otherwise unsuitable for internal development of long-term parameters required for valuation. Thus optional inputs allow users to substitute expectations for one or more of the key valuation parameters. The outputs affected by these parameters are *going-concern value* of a firm, for both *first* and *final* years, in VALUATION AND SCOPE output division. These inputs IDs and their outputs are operational only for a statistical simulation with ID 3 greater than 1.

A zero value for any of these IDs causes the program to develop internal values. The minimum allowable value in ID 96 is 0.001, or 0.1% input. A user must enter this value or greater in order to override internal valuation routines. Any nonzero value for ID 97, either positive or negative, will override internal computation. Thus a very small positive input in ID 97 should be used to approximate a zero long-term growth rate. ID 97 is intended to combine both real and inflationary growth.

ID 96, an *investors' required rate of return under risk and inflation*, is a market rate of return in a risk-averse and inflation-averse investment community. Under moderate inflation, a rate from 10% to 12% for stable investments might be reasonable. Rates should move toward 15% for cyclical or highly leveraged enterprises. A rate of 25% is not too high for prospective new ventures in small firms.

ID 97, a *long-term growth rate*, is a mean rate at which economic value of a firm, share price, earnings, and assets are expected to grow over the longer term. As a practical matter the long-term is between 20 and 30 years. For a particular firm or industry this rate could be positive, negative, or zero, but a reasonable range might run from -3% to +10%. The rate includes long-term inflation as well as long-term real growth. There have been some firms which have grown at high rates for many years, but it is difficult to project such rates with confidence over long spans.

ID 98, *rate of return on incremental assets*, is applied to a firm's new investment opportunities. If ID 98 exceeds ID 96, then current investors will receive a windfall gain from investment in new assets. If IDs 98 and 96 are equal, then current investors are indifferent to growth of assets. Finally, if ID 98 is less than ID 96, then current investors will lose value from new investments. Thus ID 98 deals with increments of value which accrue from a growth of capital. ID 98 is a *mean* return on capital whereas ID 96 is a mean *cost* of capital. Except as ID 96 affects the cost of capital mix after taxes, earnings on incremental capital from ID 98 are indifferent to sources of capital.

Environment of economy and industry to sales of firm—dynamic sets

This input division applies to all frames of ID 5. For *system parameters* see IDs 51 to 74.

The following is a summary of rules for dynamic input sets:

*Asterisk prefix on dynamic input set description denotes uncertainty input available in −1 position.

The following pattern applies to right-hand units digits (see sections 8.2 and 11.1 for detailed explanations):

−0 Related input parameter (if any).

−1 Input uncertainty as maximum percent change from mean value (if any).

−2 First base value of dynamic input applied in Period 1.

−3 First *annual* percent change in base value of −2 applied to the second and subsequent periods.

−4 Last period number of first input schedule from −2 and −3 (0 indicates extension to end of simulation).

−5 Second base value of dynamic input set applied in the period next to the period number of −4 (−1 indicates continuation of the schedule from −2 and −3, but with new growth rate from −6).

−6 Second *annual* percent change applied to base value of −5.

−7 Last period number of second input schedule from −5 and −6 (0 indicates extension to end of simulation).

−8 Third base value of dynamic input set applied in the period next to the period number of −7 (−1 indicates continuation of the schedule from −5 and −6, but with new *growth rate* from −9.

−9 Third annual percent change applies to base value of −8. This schedule continues until end of simulation.

102 TO 109   % ANNUAL REAL GROWTH RATE OF ECONOMY

This is the real or deflated growth of national income. Negative values are permitted.

110   INFLATE PERIOD COSTS—NO=0/YES=1

This choice works in conjunction with ID set 112 and ID 120. Inflation adjustments over periods are determined by nonzero entries in ID set 112 when ID 110 = 1 or ID 120 = 0. If ID 120 = 0 then sales demand of a firm is computed as a share of industry sales. In such case inflation adjustments are applied directly to industry sales, and indirectly to sales of the firm and all expenses *variable* with sales. If ID 110 = 1, inflation adjustments will also be applied to *period (fixed)* costs and asset changes; if ID 110 = 0 they will not. If ID 110 = 0 and ID 120 = 1, then no automatic inflation adjustments will be applied directly to sales of the firm, or to period (fixed) costs and asset changes. There is a complete range of inflation options with various combinations of IDs 110 and 120.

112 TO 119   % ANNUAL AVERAGE INFLATION RATE

Inflation rates developed for each period from these inputs are used throughout the simulation. Negative values will work in the system, but would scarcely conform to expected reality.

EOP 1 and final inflation rates are used as components of internal computations of *investors' required rates of return* (ID 96). Final inflation rate is used indirectly as a component of *long-term average growth rate* (ID 97).

120   SALES DEMAND—% INDUSTRY SHARE=0/$ PER PERIOD=1

If ID 120 = 0, industry sales over periods will be computed from *base annual industry sales* input ID 130 as compounded with three growth rates. The three rates are *real economic* ID set 102, *inflation* ID set 112, and *industry to economy comparison* ID set 132. Inputs ID 131 for uncertainty, and IDs 51 to 74 for *seasonal-cyclical indexes*, make further adjustments to industry sales. *Sales demand available to a firm* is computed as a *market share of industry* with ID set 122. There is a second uncertainty input with ID 121.

If ID 120 = 1, then dollar sales demand per period is entered directly in ID set 122. In such cases industry sales and percent of market share of industry outputs are not available. As a consequence these accounts are omitted from the FINANCIAL SUMMARY, ENVIRONMENTAL ANALYSES OF THE FIRM in FINANCIAL STATEMENTS, and SELECTED ACCOUNTS. If ID 120 = 1, all *growth* rates, *seasonal/cyclical indexes* (IDs 51 to 74), and *market share of industry* are omitted from the computation of *firm sales demand* in ID set 122.

Inflation adjustment combinations with ID 120 were discussed under ID 110 above.

121 TO 129   *NET SALES DEMAND AVAILABLE TO FIRM

Enter *percent* share of industry or *dollar* sales per period in accordance with ID 120 choice. See further explanation under ID 120 and ID set 131. Entries in ID set 121 must be nonnegative. The value in ID 120 must be checked before making entries in ID set 121. The value in ID 121 will randomize either *firm net sales demand* directly (ID 121 = 1), or else the *firm's market share* (ID 120 = 0).

130 $ INDUSTRY SALES FOR BASE (PRIOR) YEAR, NOT PERIOD

This is the figure to which growth rates over periods are applied to obtain industry sales each period (see ID set 131). ID 130 is an *annual* positive figure. ID 130 and ID 84, *amortization of intangibles*, are the only *dollar* inputs in PAVE which apply to a *year*, and not to one *period*. ID 130 may also be used for base sales of a firm (see ID set 131).

131 TO 139 *% ANNUAL INDUSTRY GROWTH COMPARED TO ECONOMY

These are inputs for the growth of an industry *compared* to the *economy*. An input of 6 in ID 132, for example, would result in an industry growing 6% per year faster than the economy. ID 131 must be nonnegative.

Total *industry sales* each period are the compound effect of three growth rates on *base industry sales* (ID 130). The rates are *real growth* (ID set 102), *inflation* (ID set 112), and *industry to economy comparison* (ID set 131). Any of these growth rates may be positive, negative, or zero. A seasonal pattern is also applied to industry sales period by period per positive indexes from IDs 51 to 74. ID 131 is in effect an uncertainty input for all *growth* components, including *inflation*, as well as for industry *sales*.

Market share percent from ID set 121 converts industry sales to demand for a firm if ID 120 = 0. There is another uncertainty input here with ID 121. To bypass industry analysis and apply growth rates and seasonal indexes directly to a *firm's sales demand*, enter base sales of a *firm* in ID 130, 100 in ID 122, and 0s in IDs 120, 121, and 123.

Manufacturing or trade inputs—dynamic sets

This input division applies to frames for ID 5 = 1 or 2. Only the first two dynamic sets, IDs 140 to 149, and 150 to 159, however, apply to both *manufacturing* and *trade*. The remaining IDs apply only to *manufacturing*. For manufacturing *system parameters*, see IDs 75 to 78.

All *payroll* accounts entries in this and the *general administration* input divisions should include *associated payroll costs*. Negative entries of *base* amounts are permitted only in ID sets 282 to 322 for fixed asset changes.

140 INITIAL GOODS INVENTORIES—COST % OF SELLING PRICE [60]

This is a special parameter which applies to the valuation of only the *initial* levels of *goods-in-process* and *finished goods* inventories. PAVE operates on the basis of establishing inventory amounts first at *sales* dollar levels for all periods. Such amounts are then revalued at actual costs encountered during a period. No such actual costs are available within the simulation for initial inventory levels of *finished goods* or *goods-in-process*. This occurs because costs encountered during the period immediately preceding *initial condition* balance are not stated. ID 140 supplies this missing information to the program. Thus the values of IDs 17 and 16 at *sales price level* are equal to the entry values (computed at cost) divided by ID 140.

For *trade* (ID 5 = 1), ID 140 is applied only to *finished goods*. In such cases compare the value of ID 140 with inputs in ID set 141. For *manufacturing* (ID = 2), ID 140 is applied to both *finished goods* and *goods-in-process* inventories.

141 TO 149   *DIRECT PURCHASED MATERIAL OR GOODS AS % OF SALES

This is the *percent* of net *sales* dollars which are absorbed into the cost of purchased direct material for manufacturing (ID 5 = 2), or the cost of goods purchased for resale in the case of trade (ID 5 = 1). IDs 141 and 142 must be nonnegative. Cost premiums for possible subcontract assembly should *not* be included (see IDs 77 and 78).

Any materials, supplies, small tools, or small equipment, which are for *direct* or *variable* use in the product, may be included in this ID set. Indirect supplies or small tools, which are planned on a period basis, and are not directly related to product volume, are handled with ID 222. Freight-in and sales taxes paid by a purchaser should be included here. Since outside purchase price and volume are often uncertain, a randomization component is available. If material cost premiums are encountered from *subcontract operations* (see IDs 72 and 78), these will be printed separately in COST OF GOODS MANU-FACTURED SCHEDULES.

For merchandising concerns (ID 5 = 1), this ID set determines on average what percentage of selling price must be allocated to the cost of purchased goods. Typical values, such as 60, indicate that on average a firm pays 60% of selling price to buy goods. It is then operating with a *discount off list* or *gross margin* of 40%. Put still another way, the *markup* over cost is 66-2/3%. Compare the inputs here with ID 140. Under *trade* there is no capacity limit and no subcontract operations.

Throughout *manufacturing* and *general* expense inputs, costs are divided into *variable* or *direct* with *production* or *sales*; and *fixed, indirect,* or *period.* The latter class are incurred on a *time* basis for a period, and are independent of sales or production volume. Inputs of *variable* cost are entered as a *percent of sales*, whereas inputs of *fixed cost* are entered as *dollars per period.* The fixed counterpart of ID set 141 is ID 222.

150   % DESEASONALIZE GOODS—PRODUCTION OR PURCHASE

The effects of this input do not appear in the environmental analysis output statements, but do relate directly to the set of *seasonal-cyclical indexes* in IDs 51 to 74.

ID 150 specifies a percent neutralization of seasonal/cyclical patterns in production scheduling with ID 5 = 2, or *finished goods* and purchases with ID 5 = 1. Specifically, ID 150 operates on the levels of *goods-in-process* and *finished goods* inventories. If no deseasonalization logic were applied, inventories would rise and fall in response to *seasonal/cyclical* sales patterns.

Then production or goods purchase would fluctuate even more than inventories because schedules must not only shift to cover sales changes, but also inventory changes. This type of combined response to sales and inventory changes is probably necessary in the long run, but is often undesirable on a period-to-period basis. An entry of -100 for ID 150 will permit full fluctuation in *both* sales and inventory to be reflected into production and goods purchases, and may be entered when this mode is desired. At -100 there is no deseasonalization. Nonentry or 0 for ID 150 will deseasonalize inventories, but production or purchase must still vary to meet sales changes. An entry of +50 will adjust inventories oppositely to sales, so that production or goods purchases are partly freed from index effects. Values between -100 and +50 produce partial compensation of the types indicated above. Values beyond 100 (either positive or negative) will overcompensate, and are not recommended. If compensation drives any inventory below zero, then the program overrides the compensation sufficiently to avoid negative inventories. It should be noted that ID 150 provides no compensation for other sources of sales variability, such as changes in growth rates of the economy or industry, changes in the firm's share of market, or randomized values. Nonpositive policies are applied to both *finished goods* and *goods-in-process* inventories for N5 = 2, but positive inputs only to *finished goods*. This occurs because an input of +100 would fully neutralize in one inventory a seasonal increment of sales. In practice there is more than one inventory level involved in determining production, hence the approximation of full neutralization with an input of +50.

152 TO 159 FINISHED GOODS INVENTORY LEVEL AS % OF ANNUAL COST OF GOODS SOLD

This ID set refers specifically to the level of *finished goods* inventories. Inventory levels in PAVE are a function of *annual* usage, in this case *cost of goods sold*. ID set 152 applies to either trade (ID 5 = 1), or *manufacturing* (ID 5 = 2).

The logic here assumes that planned levels in inventories will depend on the volume of sales. The precise relationship may vary over time according to inputs from seasonal index IDs 51 to 74. The influence of these IDs on inventory levels may be modified for ID 120 not equal to 1 by values specified for deseasonalization variable ID 150 (see discussion under ID 150). Inventory values in statements are entered at manufacturing cost. Goods into process are valued at absorbed cost over period. Thus inventories are costed on a first-in-first-out (FIFO) basis. Other methods of costing, such as direct cost or standard cost with variances, or alternative valuations methods such as LIFO or average cost, are not available within PAVE. These accounting computational variations are not particularly significant for long-term strategic planning.

Alternatively, ID set 152 may be viewed as the number of years, multiplied by 100, over which finished goods, on the average, are held in inventory. The reciprocal of this ID set 152, again multiplied by 100, is *inventory turns* per year. To input a particular turnover per year, take its reciprocal, multiply by 100, and enter the result under ID set 152. A zero entry or nonentry is completely reasonable; it simply eliminates a finished goods inventory from the manufacturing section. This elimination in no way affects the remaining logic of operations in manufacturing. If application of inventory policy per ID set 152 would result in negative process of goods, then the inventory is automatically modified for a minimum of zero production.

Values of ID set 152 are not limited to less than a year (less than 100). If a seller keeps more than a year's mean sale of goods on hand, then entries above 100 are permitted.

162 TO 169 GOODS-IN-PROCESS INVENTORY LEVEL AS % OF ANNUAL COST OF GOODS SOLD

This ID set refers specifically to the level of *goods-in-process* inventories which result from internal processing. There is no counterpart in the other input sections. Here again, the logic assumes that planned levels of inventories will depend on the volume of production.

Most of the discussion of ID set 152 above applies also to this input set. The influence of inventory policy may be modified for ID 120 equal to 0 by the deseasonalization ID 150. Statement values are entered at manufacturing cost absorbed over the period and assume first-in-first-out (FIFO) valuation basis. The preceding remarks about time span of inventory and turnover also apply here. A zero entry or nonentry eliminates goods-in-process inventories from the manufacturing processing without affecting any of the remaining logic of operations. The input inventory policy will be overridden automatically to avoid negative production. In such case the policy inventory level will be increased to reach a minimum of zero production.

172 TO 179 DIRECT MATERIAL INVENTORY LEVEL AS % OF ANNUAL USAGE

Here the ID set determines a normal level for *direct materials and supplies* according to the level of manufacturing activity, in this case *annual* usage. Purchases of direct materials and supplies for the period are determined by this inventory requirement and usage (see ID set 141). If the logic of inventory levels would lead to negative purchases, then an automatic default routine reduces closing inventory to the point of zero purchases. Note that in the *manufacturing* expense section the routines for *direct* material and supplies usage, inventory, and purchases are entirely separate from the routines for *indirect* supplies and small tools (see ID set 222). If material cost premium has been encountered from *subcontract operations* (see IDs 77 and 78), then this component will be added to the usage which determines inventories.

181 TO 189 *DIRECT LABOR PAYROLL AS % OF SALES

This is the direct labor component of processing. It is assumed that direct labor is proportional to level of production, although such proportionality may be modified over time with different inputs from ID set 181. Operating efficiency inputs from ID set 202 also affect the cost of direct labor per sales dollars of product. ID set 181 is to be entered without regard to overtime possibilities (at regular time labor cost), and at planned 100% level of efficiency. Note that this ID set is entered at a *sales* price valuation level, although goods inventory valuation in PAVE is computed at a cost level. Since the level of direct labor is often uncertain, a randomization component ID 181 is available. This component will combine with ID 201 for operating efficiency to randomize labor usage. See IDs 75 and 76 for a discussion of overtime with direct labor. Overtime premiums are printed separately in COST OF GOODS MANUFACTURED SCHEDULES.

192 TO 199 DIRECT SUPERVISION AND SUPPORT PAYROLL AS % OF SALES

A certain amount of supervision, inspection, services, and support labor varies with the level of product activity in manufacturing. It is thus *direct* or *variable*. The direct amount for regular-time labor is entered here, with the indirect component entered in ID set 232. Again, this ID set is entered as a percentage from the sales pricing level. The level of dollars spent on this payroll also varies with total direct labor (including overtime), and with operating efficiency. See IDs 75 and 76 for a discussion of overtime with direct supervision and support labor. If an *overtime premium* occurs, the output PRINT of this in COST OF GOODS MANUFACTURED schedules sums both *direct labor* and *direct supervision and support*.

202 TO 209 *% OPERATING EFFICIENCY OF PROCESSING [100 in ID 202]

This ID set is applied in two places: available plant capacity and value of labor content of product (ID sets 181 and 192). A zero entry is not permitted in ID 202 for no production. Instead, substitute a zero value in ID 212. An entry of 100 in ID 202 implies an operations level equal to regular time expectations. Values above 100 are permissible, but mean that higher than regular efficiencies are planned. Since ID set 202 is applied to overtime as well as regular time direct labor, this fact should be kept in mind in entering values for ID set 202. Also, ID set 202 applies to direct supervision and support labor because the amount of the latter is adjusted for changes in direct labor. ID set 202 may be randomized directly through ID 201. See also ID set 181 for randomization of direct labor.

212 TO 219 $ CAPACITY OF PLANT PER PERIOD IN SALES $ AT 100% EFFICIENCY

This is the normal capacity of plant production per *period* in dollar value of goods. The dollar value is set at factory *sales* level rather than at cost of goods manufactured level. If generated sales demand exceeds this capacity, then internal routines attempt to extend capacity, first with *overtime labor* and then with *subcontract operations* (see explanation under IDs 75 and 77). If capacity extensions are insufficient, then *achieved sales* will be reduced to a level which can be supported by inventory and production. A zero entry in ID 212 is acceptable to simulate strikes, facilities under construction, or changeovers.

Capacity is factored by *operating efficiency* from ID set 202. Then *capacity* may be randomized by a nonzero entry in ID 201.

220 MANUFACTURING SUPPLIES INVENTORY LEVEL AS % OF ANNUAL USAGE

Items in this inventory consist of *indirect* supplies, materials, and small equipment (not capitalized) which are used in manufacturing, but not variable with production. The *direct* counterpart is ID set 172. Sometimes items in this class are *expensed* immediately, or no inventory is maintained. In such case enter 0 in ID 220.

222 TO 229 $ INDIRECT SUPPLIES AND SMALL EQUIPMENT USED PER PERIOD—MANUFACTURING

This is the *fixed* or *indirect* component of materials, supplies, and small equipment (not capitalized) which are used up in manufacturing. The *direct* counterpart is ID set 141. The assumption for ID set 222 is that usage is based on time rather than on amount of production.

232 TO 239 $ INDIRECT MANUFACTURING PAYROLL PER PERIOD

This is the *fixed* or *period* component of manufacturing payrolls. Division of payrolls into this ID set, and ID sets 181 to 192 above, will yield a desired policy combination of fixed and variable payroll components. The salaries of general manufacturing supervision will normally be entered under this ID set 232, but that portion which is paid in accordance with production accomplishment should be included with ID set 192.

242 TO 249 $ SPACE, RENT OR OCCUPANCY PER PERIOD—MANUFACTURING

Any cost associated with the *possession* and *maintenance* of space on a continuing basis should be entered here. Rent or lease payments are the most common. For further discussion see the counterpart general expense description under ID set 442.

ID sets 242 to 322 are duplicates for *manufacturing* of ID sets 442 to 529 for *general administration*.

251 TO 259 *$ UTILITIES OR ALL INDIRECT COSTS PER PERIOD—MANUFACTURING

This is the only manufacturing *period* expense with a randomization component (ID 251). The randomization was placed here due to uncertainties about future utility costs. On the other hand, ID set 251 may be used to composite *any* or *all* period manufacturing costs in one account. For either use of ID set 251, adjustment of ID 251 may be used to approximate the total uncertainty of the set of manufacturing period costs. Utilities usually include fuels (such as gas, oil, or coal), electricity, water, and waste disposal. Telephone costs could be included in ID set 272.

262 TO 269 $ MAINTENANCE PER PERIOD—MANUFACTURING

Enter maintenance of machinery, equipment, and tools, including service contract costs. Building maintenance should be entered under ID set 242.

272 TO 279 $ TAXES, INSURANCE, LABOR RELATIONS, AND MISCEL-
LANEOUS EXPENSE PER PERIOD—MANUFACTURING

This is the account in which to enter *manufacturing period* expenses which
are not specifically listed elsewhere. Income taxes, property taxes, sales taxes
on purchases by the firm, and inventory taxes are more appropriately charged
to specific categories of costs, as mentioned elsewhere. For further discussion,
see the counterpart general expense description under ID set 472.

280, 290, 300, 310, 320 % DEPRECIATION PER YEAR ON DECLINING BAL-
ANCE FOR MANUFACTURING FIXED ASSETS CLASS 1 TO 5

A user specifies up to 5 depreciation rates in order for 0 to 5 classes of manufacturing fixed assets carried through the simulation. See IDs 20 to 39, and
ID sets 282 and 322, for a further discussion of fixed asset classes.

The depreciation method for all tangible fixed asset classes in PAVE is declining balance; straight line and sum-of-digits methods are not available. For
intangible assets, however, PAVE uses only a straight line method (see ID 84).
Returning to tangible fixed asset classes, enter 150% or 200% of depreciation
rate for 1.5 or double-declining balance, respectively.

Zero values in depreciation rates for a fixed asset class will result in no period-
by-period depreciation for that class. Such a policy is suitable for nondepreciable assets, such as land. For nonrenewable resource classes of fixed assets,
depletion allowance may be substituted for *depreciation* rates.

A negative entry in these IDs, which is always incorrect, may cause indefinite
cycling.

282 TO 289, TO 322 TO 329 $ MANUFACTURING FIXED ASSET CLASS 1 TO
5 NET CHANGES PER PERIOD

A user may specify from 1 to 5 different classes of *manufacturing* fixed assets
by nonzero values in IDs 20 to 24, or in the ID sets here. Zero values in all
these IDs will result in no classes of manufacturing fixed assets being computed
or printed. Each class is identified by number. Assets of the same general type,
particularly if they use the same depreciation rate, should be grouped in the
same class. Typical classes are land, factory buildings, production machinery
and equipment, and vehicles.

Net change entries are principally used for expanding the capital base with
new asset acquisitions. Such entries should include freight in, sales or other
taxes paid by the purchaser, and installation costs. If there is replacement or
prior assets, then entries may be made net of trade-in, resale price, or scrap
value of replaced items. These accounts may also be used for contracting the
capital base by entering negative values for sale or scrap of old assets not replaced.

The classes chosen here must correspond to the positions of nonzero (if any)
entries for initial condition values entered under the manufacturing assets at
cost in IDs 20 to 24, and to the corresponding initial reserve values in IDs
25 to 29. If net changes during any period were to drive the *book* value (cost

less reserve depreciation) *negative*, then the net change input is reset for a minimum 0 book value. Five additional classes of fixed assets are available in *general administration* input division (ID sets 482 to 522).

Research and development, sales, and general administrative inputs—dynamic sets

This input division applies to all frames except *environment only* (ID 5 = 3). For accompanying *system parameters*, see IDs 79 and 84.

All *payroll* accounts entries in this and the *manufacturing* input divisions should include *associated payroll*.

Negative entries of *base* amounts are permitted only in ID sets 482 to 522 for fixed asset changes.

330 RESEARCH AND DEVELOPMENT EXPENSES—% SALES=0/$ PERIOD=1

This choice determines the basis of inputs for ID sets 332 to 342. Be sure the value of this ID is checked before entries in the above two R&D ID sets.

332 TO 339 RESEARCH AND DEVELOPMENT PAYROLL

There are two R&D expense input sets, this ID set 332 for payrolls, and the following ID set 342 for all other R&D expenses. One has a choice per input to ID 330 to make these two sets variable with sales (*annual* percent inputs), or scheduled with dollar inputs as period expenses.

R&D functions here are intended to include any engineering or product development activities which are not specifically associated with production, service, or customer support.

342 TO 349 RESEARCH AND DEVELOPMENT MATERIAL, CONTRACTS AND MISCELLANEOUS EXPENSE PER PERIOD

This category, which is entered on the same basis as ID set 332 per ID 330, is intended to include all R&D and product engineering nonpayroll expenses. Some of these expenses are materials; supplies; contracted purchases of products or components; consulting fees; patent, licence and copyright activities; scientific and engineering travel expenses; and costs of maintaining R&D equipment.

352 TO 359 SALES SALARIES AND COMMISSIONS PAYROLL AS % OF SALES

This is the sales activity payroll component which varies directly with the level of sales. Commission, fees, bonuses, and any other employee compensation component which varies directly with sales should be assembled into this percentage. Enter period-based sales compensation in ID set 362.

362 TO 369 % INDIRECT SALES PAYROLL PER PERIOD

This is the *fixed* or *period* component of sales employee compensation payroll. Division of sales payroll into this ID set and ID set 352 above will yield the desired policy combination of fixed and variable sales employee payrolls.

372 TO 379 ADVERTISING, PROMOTION, AND MISCELLANEOUS EXPENSE AS % OF SALES

This is the sales activity nonpayroll component which varies directly with the level of sales. Any nonpayroll expense of the sales function, which is also variable with sales, should be included here. If the firm pays shipping costs for customers, then such expense should be included here. Variable sales travel should be entered here. Cooperative advertising would appear here. On the other hand, discounts off selling price should be treated as a reduction in net sales revenue. Nonpayroll period sales expense is entered in ID set 382.

382 TO 389 $ ADVERTISING, PROMOTION, AND MISCELLANEOUS SALES EXPENSE PER PERIOD

This is the *fixed* or *period* component of nonpayroll sales activity. Division of all sales expense (other than payrolls and credit to customers) into this ID set and ID set 372 above will yield the desired policy combination of *fixed* and *variable* sales expense. Sales consulting, sales training, sales convention costs, general and institutional advertising, test marketing, market research, sales travel (not variable with volume), etc., should be entered here. Promotional and display materials could be either fixed (ID set 382) or variable (ID set 372), or some combination of both.

390 % UNCOLLECTIBLE ACCOUNTS

Accounts to be collected are derived from sales and the values of accounts receivable balances. Input ID 390 gives the percentage of sales which are deemed uncollectible on a planning basis. A zero value in ID 390 is reasonable if nonpayment risk is negligible. Deductions are made at the time of collections, not at the time of sale. Uncollectibles are accumulated over the simulation in both accounts receivable balances and the reserve for uncollectible accounts. The net of accounts receivable balances less reserve for uncollectibles balance gives customer credit which is expected to be collected at a particular point in time.

391 TO 399 * ACCOUNTS RECEIVABLE LEVEL AS % OF ANNUAL SALES

On the average, what percentage of *annual* sales must be allocated to customer credit? If no credit is to be granted, enter 0 for a cash sale business. Such a policy applies to many fast-service and discount concerns which deal directly with the public. It may also apply to agribusiness or industrial sales, if payment is received immediately. An entry of 4.11 gives an average of 15 days credit for customers, an entry of 8.22 gives 30 days credit, and an entry of 24.66 gives 90 days credit. A useful formula is that ID 392 entry equals *mean days credit* times 100, divided by 365. Entries of more than 100, which result in average customer credit of more than one year, are permissible, but would be most unusual. There is an assumption for this ID set, given any particular credit policy, that customer credit will vary with the amount of business (sales or service).

Alternatively, this ID set may be viewed as the number of years, on the average and multiplied by 100, over which customers are granted credit. The reciprocal of this ID set, again multiplied by 100, is *accounts receivable turn-*

over per year. To input a particular turnover policy, take its reciprocal, multiply by 100, and enter under ID set 392. If application of this policy input would result in negative collections of receivables during a period, then the policy is automatically modified by the program for zero collections. Since there is often substantial uncertainty about demand for customer credit, randomization of this ID set is available with ID 391.

401 TO 409   * DIRECT SERVICE AND OFFICE MATERIALS AS % OF SALES

This ID set is for any service, office materials, or supplies that are *variable* with sales. Materials, supplies, small tools, or small equipment, which are purchased for service or other business activities, may be included under this ID set. Again this is the *variable* or *direct* component for such items. Small tools and small equipment are those categories of items which are normally used up in a year or less, so it would not be useful to capitalize their value as assets in *condition statements*. Office supplies, if variable with business activity, would be entered under this ID set. So would fertilizer, seed, feed, hay, and fuel (to the extent purchased) for an agribusiness. Freight-in and sales taxes paid by a purchaser should be included here. Since outside purchase price and volume are often uncertain, a randomization component is available with ID 401.

412 TO 419 $ INDIRECT SERVICE, OFFICE SUPPLIES, AND SMALL EQUIPMENT PER PERIOD

This is the fixed or indirect component of expense categories whose direct counterparts were entered under ID set 401 above. Combination of this ID set with ID set 401 will yield a desired policy combination of fixed and variable components for general supplies and small equipment.

421 TO 429   * DIRECT SERVICE AND OFFICE PAYROLL AS % OF SALES

This is the operating activity payroll which varies directly with sales, or the volume of business. It may consist of office work to process orders or the financial aspects of conducting the business. It may consist of servicing activities for customers. It may also include all operating or processing labor if the firm is not treated under manufacturing class. In this case, the manufacturing categories of expenses are not available (ID 5 equal to 0 or 1 instead of 2). Farming, fishing, forestry, conservation, or mining labor are examples of this situation, as well as professional service in the auditing, legal, brokerage, health, or consulting fields. Salesman and product engineering compensation should not be included in ID set 421 because separate ID sets 352 and 332 are available. Again, all components of this ID set must be a direct function of the level of business activity. Executive compensation bonuses, dependent on sales or profit levels, but not contractual base salaries, may be included here. Since *direct* payroll is often uncertain, a randomization component is available.

432 TO 439 $ GENERAL ADMINISTRATIVE AND INDIRECT SERVICE PAYROLL PER PERIOD

This is the fixed or period component of general, administrative, and service payroll. Division of general payrolls into this ID set series and ID set 421 above will yield a desired policy combination of *fixed* or *variable* components. ID set 432 may be used for any of the categories listed for ID set 421 above, and should exclude sales, R&D, and product engineering payrolls, since these expenses are entered under separate ID set numbers. The fixed portions of salaries of top executives of the business will normally be entered under this ID set.

442 TO 449 $ SPACE, RENT, OR OCCUPANCY PER PERIOD—GENERAL

Any cost associated with the possession and maintenance of space on a continuing basis should be entered here. Rent or lease payments are the most common. Real and business property taxes, and insurance on buildings and equipment may be entered either here (preferably) or in ID set 472 below. Routine maintenance on space (not equipment) should be entered here. If a firm owns its own space, then interest cost on purchase money mortgages may be entered here. Leasehold improvements should be entered under ID 83, and amortized with ID 84.

451 TO 459   *$ UTILITIES OR ALL INDIRECT COSTS PER PERIOD—GENERAL

This is the only general period expense with a randomization component (ID 451). The randomization was placed here due to uncertainties about future utility costs. On the other hand, ID set 451 may be used to composite any or all *period* general costs in one account. For either use of ID set 451, adjustment of ID 451 may be used to approximate the total uncertainty of the set of general period costs. Utilities usually include fuels (such as gas, oil, or coal), electricity, water, and waste disposal. Telephone cost should be included here, or allocated in full or in part to ID sets 342, 372, 382, or 472. Compare the operation of this input set with ID set 251 for manufacturing.

462 TO 469 $ MAINTENANCE PER PERIOD—GENERAL

Enter maintenance of machinery, equipment, and tools, including service contract costs. Building maintenance should be entered under ID set 442.

472 TO 479 $ TAXES, INSURANCE, TRAVEL, LABOR RELATIONS, LEGAL, AND MISCELLANEOUS EXPENSE PER PERIOD—GENERAL

This is the account in which to enter general period expenses which are not specifically listed elsewhere. Income taxes, property taxes, sales taxes on purchases by the firm, and inventory taxes are more appropriately charged to specific categories of costs, as mentioned elsewhere. On the other hand, franchises, licenses, permit costs, government inspection costs, and general business use taxes should be entered here. Travel associated specifically with sales, engineering, or manufacturing should be entered in those expense sections. Consulting fees, auditing fees, legal costs, and the cost of directors' and shareholders' meetings are appropriate components of this ID set.

480, 490, 500, 510, 520   % DEPRECIATION PER YEAR ON DECLINING BALANCE FOR GENERAL FIXED ASSET CLASS 1 TO 5

A user specifies up to 5 depreciation rates in order for 0 to 5 classes of general fixed assets carried through the simulation. See IDs 20 to 39, and ID sets 482 to 522, for a further discussion of fixed asset classes.

The depreciation method for all tangible fixed asset classes in PAVE is declining balance; straight line and sum-of-digits methods are not available. For intangible assets, however, PAVE uses only straight line method (see ID 84). Returning to tangible fixed asset classes, enter 150% or 200% of depreciation rate for 1.5 or double-declining balance, respectively.

Zero values in depreciation rates for a fixed asset class will result in no period-by-period depreciation for that class. Such a policy is suitable for nondepreciable assets, such as land. For nonrenewable resource classes of fixed assets, *depletion* allowance rates may be substituted for *depreciation* rates.

A negative entry in these IDs, which is always incorrect, may cause indefinite cycling.

482 TO 489, TO 522 TO 529 $ GENERAL FIXED ASSET CLASSES 1 TO 5 NET CHANGES PER PERIOD

A user may specify from 1 to 5 different classes of *general* fixed assets by nonzero values in IDs 30 to 34, or in the ID sets here. Zero values in all these IDs will result in no classes of general fixed assets being computed or printed. Each class is identified by number. Assets of the same general type, particularly if they use the same depreciation rate, should be grouped into the same class. Typical classes are land, buildings, machinery and equipment, and vehicles.

Net change entries are principally used for expanding the capital base with new asset acquisitions. Such entries should include freight-in, sales or other taxes paid by the purchaser, and installation costs. If there is replacement of prior assets, then entries may be made net of trade-in, resale price, or scrap value of replaced items. These accounts may also be used for contracting the capital base by entering negative values for sale or scrap of old assets not replaced.

The classes chosen here must correspond to the positions of nonzero (if any) entries for initial condition values entered under the general assets at cost in IDs 30 to 34, and to the corresponding initial reserve values in IDs 35 to 39. If net changes during any period were to drive the *book* value (cost less reserve for depreciation) negative, then the net change input is reset for a minimum 0 book value. Five more classes of fixed assets are available in *manufacturing* input division (ID sets 282 to 322).

Financial and valuation control inputs—dynamic sets

This input division applies to all frames except environment only (ID 5 = 3). For *system parameters*, see IDs 87 to 98.

Negative entries of *base* amounts are permitted only in ID sets 532 and 542.

530   INTERNAL COMPUTATION OF REQUIRED INVESTMENT—NO=0/YES=1

If ID 530 = 1, any required additional long-term capital investment will be computed internally. A portion of this investment may be placed in *long-term obligations* if ID 540 is greater than 0. Whatever portion is not in long-term obligations will be assigned to owner *paid-in capital*. An internal computation of required investment is always *incremental* to planned changes in long-term capital. These planned changes are scheduled in ID sets 532 for owner capital and 542 for debt capital. By varying the levels of planned additions, various requirements for incremental capital may be simulated.

Needs for additional capital are computed each period from analysis of cash flows. The cash decision rule is to maintain a minimum acceptable *cash ratio* (ID 87 with an internal default value of 50%). *Short-term borrowing* is initiated first up to a limit determined by working capital and inventories (IDs 88 and 95 with internal defaults of 200% and 50%, respectively). Long-term capital is added if short-term borrowing capacity is insufficient. Thus additional long-term capital is incremental to both planned capital changes and the limit of short-term borrowings.

If ID 530 = 0, a firm must depend upon planned capital changes and short-term borrowing. If these are insufficient, negative *cash*, negative *retained earnings*, and negative *owners' equity* may occur. Such negative values are permitted and the simulation will not be aborted. To examine risks of *insolvency*, input ID 530 = 0. If ID 530 = 1, *technical insolvency* cannot occur and *legal insolvency* is unlikely to occur.

531 EARN ON NEAR-CASH AS % OF SHORT-TERM INTEREST RATE

A firm may earn *interest* or *dividend* income on its liquid assets. In the case of PAVE, this applies to *cash and marketable securities (near-cash)* account. Instead of entering a mean rate of return directly, a user enters a percentage of the short-term interest rate (ID set 562) in ID 531. This percentage of the short-term interest rate is applied to the *mean* balance of *cash and marketable securities* account each period.

An input of 0 in ID 531 means that nothing will be earned on near-cash, a reasonable position if most of a firm's money is held in demand deposits. An entry of 100, on the other hand, would apply the full short-term interest rate to earnings on near-cash. In most cases a firm will earn something less than 100 because it is likely to keep some cash in nonearning accounts. Input ID 531 as an average figure over all deposits, certificates, and marketable securities.

Income on near-cash will be randomized if ID 561 is nonzero. ID 531 is the only dynamic input parameter in −1 position which is *not* a maximum change uncertainty input.

532 TO 539 $ OWNER NET CASH INVESTMENT PLANNED CHANGE PER PERIOD

These are *planned* capital changes in contrast to *required* increases. The latter are determined internally (see IDs 530 and 540). Negative entries are allowed in ID set 532 for withdrawals, but *owner paid-in capital* account is not permitted internally to become *negative*. In such cases, ID set 532 inputs will be revised for 0 *paid-in capital*. *Retained earnings* and total *owner's equity* may become negative if required additional cash is not available (see ID 530).

Note that internal action to add *required* cash (ID 530 = 1), or tests for *insolvency* (ID 530 = 0), are *incremental* to *planned* cash in ID set 532. This provides a means of testing the adequacy of various schedules of investment.

540 % LONG-TERM OBLIGATIONS IN REQUIRED ADDITIONAL INVEST-MENT

If the command option ID 530 equal to 1 is chosen, then PAVE will determine additional long-term capital needs internally. The general conditions for this are described under ID 530. *Planned* long-term capital additions of owner equity and debt (or preferred stock) are explained under ID sets 532 to 542, respectively. Internal determination of additional *required* capital (if ID 530 = 1) is over and above *short-term* determination as described under IDs 87, 88, and 95. Given ID 530 equal to 1, and given also that internal routines develop a demand for additional long-term capital, then ID 540 specifies the percentage of this capital to be placed in long-term obligations, such as bonds, trust certificates, mortgages, and preferred stock). Nonentry or zero entry for ID 540 means that all additional capital will be in owner equity, a common situation for small, cyclical, or medium to high-risk enterprises. An extreme value of 100 for ID 540 would mean all long-term capital would be raised by debt, which is usually unrealistic. Negative entries, or entries above 100, are not permitted. It is important to note that ID 540 has no influence on the *planned* mix of owner equity and long-term net additions per ID sets 532 and 542, respectively.

542 TO 549 $ LONG-TERM OBLIGATIONS PLANNED NET CHANGE PER PERIOD

This input follows the same rules as ID set 532, but applies to long-term obligations, such as bonds and preferred stock, rather than to owner paid-in common stock. Negative entries are allowed for reduction of obligations, but the *long-term obligations* account is not permitted internally to become negative. Instead, PAVE will recompute the planned change for a *long-term obligations* balance of 0.

If periodic payments are made on mortgages or term-loans, only the principal reduction should be entered here. This is a negative amount per period, which may grow at some rate (ID 543) to represent a *level* total payment. The interest cost on the *mean* loan balance will be computed automatically by PAVE from long-term interest rate inputs in ID set 572.

If the principal of a debt is to be repaid in one lump sum, then make a single negative entry for the period in ID set 542.

550 DIVIDENDS–% OF EARNINGS=0/$ PER PERIOD=1

Per this choice, inputs for *dividends* or *withdrawals* to ID set 552 will change basis between *percent* or *earnings*, and *dollar* payment per *period*. For ID 550 = 0, dividends will be computed as 0 for periods of negative earnings. For ID 550 = 1, however, the dividend stream will not be interrupted by negative earnings.

552 TO 559   DIVIDENDS OR WITHDRAWALS PER PERIOD

This has the same effect on *owners' equity* as negative inputs to ID set 532, but is processed through statement accounts as periodic withdrawals. Enter amounts at time of *payment*, not during periods containing *record* or *declaration* dates. Preferred stock dividends may be included here as "after income taxes" or be treated as a component of ID set 572. For the latter option, adjust to "before-tax" equivalent rate. ID 552 must be nonnegative.

The account title *withdrawals* or *drawings* would be used for *partnerships* or *proprietorships*, in place of *dividends*. In making entries to ID set 552, the value in ID 550 must be checked. See ID 550 for relations between *dividends* and *earnings*.

561 TO 569   *% SHORT-TERM INTEREST RATE ANNUAL

Enter a mean annual rate for short-term or seasonal borrowings by a firm. Such borrowings are determined internally to meet a minimum acceptable *cash ratio*. The source of borrowing is *current assets*, such as accounts receivable and inventories (see IDs 87, 88, and 95). Per ID 531 input, a fraction of the short-term interest rate may be earned on a firm's cash and marketable securities account. IDs 561 and 562 must be nonnegative. Nonzero values in ID 561 provide uncertainty about short-term interest rates.

Short-term borrowings are assumed to take place at the beginning of a period, and to be repaid in full immediately after the end of a period. Thus interest is charged over one full period, at the rate of ID set 562, for the amount shown EOP in CONDITION STATEMENTS. Interest is not changed on ID 44 debt under *initial condition*. It is assumed that this debt is repaid BOP 1.

571 TO 579   *% LONG-TERM INTEREST RATE ANNUAL

Long-term obligations (including preferred stock, trust certificates and mortgages, as well as bonds, for planning purposes) comes from *initial condition* ID 45, ID set 542 planned net additions, and required long-term borrowing determined internally if ID 530 equals 1 and ID 540 is greater than zero. If there are no long-term borrowings, then ID set 572 is nonoperational, and may be omitted. Zero entry or omission with long-term debt, however, will yield zero interest cost, which is usually unrealistic. Negative entries are not permitted. Since interest costs are uncertain over time, a randomization component, ID 571, is available. Long-term interest cost is computed on the beginning of period balance plus one-half of net changes during a period. This is equivalent to an interest cost on the mean between BOP and EOP long-term obligations balance each period.

Enter a *mean annual rate* for bonds, mortgages, and equipment loans. Interest cost is deducted before computing net income subject to income taxes. The long-term interest rate may be increased to cover preferred stock dividends, but such a dividend must be enlarged to its "before-tax" effect (see ID set 552). IDs 571 and 572 must be nonnegative.

Index